# M&E PROFESSIONAL STUDIES

Written by a team of practising lecturers and prepared of a leading partnership of London accountancy tutors, the M&E Professional series has been specially designed to meet the course needs of professional students in virtually all the examined subjects at appropriate professional, degree and diploma levels. The titles cover many of the subjects offered by the ACCA, ICA, ICMA, AIA, AAT, SCCA, ACEA, LCCI, RSA and numerous other bodies.

With carefully structured and thoroughly up-to-date contents, most titles include end-of-chapter progress tests based on the text, a large number of practice examination questions and suggested answers, a glossary of the more difficult key terms, and a very comprehensive index. An extensive programme of classroom testing, student surveys and independent assessment has been completed in relation to this series prior to publication.

With twenty substantial texts in the series, *M&E Professional Studies* constitutes a major contribution to business education, and will enable students throughout the English-speaking world gain the syllabus-related depth of knowledge and practice necessary to ensure a successful examination result.

## GENERAL EDITORS

**Emile Woolf**
Emile Woolf first qualified in 1961 and joined the London Office of Deloitte Haskins and Sells. Since 1964 he has played a major part in pioneering accountancy education, first at Foulks Lynch and the London School of Accountancy, and then as founder and Chairman of the Emile Woolf Colleges in London and overseas. In 1977 he also became a partner in Halpern & Woolf with special responsibility for technical auditing standards. He is an established author, and a regular contributor to numerous professional and student journals and magazines in the UK and overseas. In 1980 he received the Distinguished Services Award for Authorship at Hartford University, Connecticut, USA. Recently he was commissioned by the ACCA to produce a series of audio cassettes and workbooks for students throughout the world. Between 1973 and 1979 he was also an Examiner for the ACCA in Advanced Auditing and Investigations. Emile Woolf lectures regularly on accountancy, financial and economic matters in Ireland, the UK, USA, Trinidad, Jamaica, Singapore, Hong Kong, Malaysia, Nigeria, Ghana and elsewhere. He also conducts seminars on financial management topics for industrial and commercial clients as well as for professional accountancy firms.

**Suresh Tanna**
Suresh Tanna graduated in 1971 in chemical engineering from Edinburgh University. Following a career in business management he qualified as a chartered accountant in 1978. In 1981 he joined Karam Singh in setting up the City Accountancy Centre, which merged with the Emile Woolf Schools in March 1983, and is now Director of Studies on ACCA courses, and Financial Director of the enlarged FACT Group. He specialises in accounting, advanced accounting practice and advanced financial accounting.

**Karam Singh**
After a period of project planning with Burmah Oil as a graduate chemical engineer, Karam Singh obtained his MBA from the Liverpool Business School whilst also engaged in part-time consultancy work for clothing manufacturers and retailers and research at a P & O subsidiary. In 1971 he joined the London accountancy firm of Harmood Banner and Company which later merged with Deloittes. He qualified as a chartered accountant in 1974, and lectured for several years at the London School of Accountancy and the North East London Polytechnic. In 1981 he joined Suresh Tanna in the formation of the City Accountancy Centre, where he began to develop study material geared for in-school and home studies students. At present he is Principal Lecturer for the FACT schools for Level 2 ACCA courses, specialising in quantitative analysis. He has contributed numerous articles to the various professional and students' journals.

**Contributing authors**
The titles in this series have been prepared under the General Editorship of Emile Woolf, Suresh Tanna and Karam Singh in conjunction with the staff and tutors of the FACT Organisation, 23 Hand Court, High Holborn, London WC1V 6JF. All contributors and authors are practising lecturers with many years' experience of teaching accountancy at all levels.

M&E PROFESSIONAL STUDIES

# QUANTITATIVE ANALYSIS

General Editors

Emile Woolf FCA, FCCA, FBIM
Suresh Tanna BSc(Hons) FCA
Karam Singh BTech, MBA FCA

*M&E Professional Studies titles currently available*

Advanced Accounting Practice
Advanced Auditing and Investigations
Advanced Financial Accounting
Advanced Taxation
Auditing
Company Law
Costing
Economics
Executorship and Trust Law and Accounts
Financial Management
Foundation Accounting
Law
Management Accounting
Managerial Economics
Numerical Analysis and Data Processing
Organisation and Management
Quantitative Analysis
The Regulatory Framework of Accounting
Systems Analysis and Design
Taxation


Macdonald & Evans Ltd
Estover, Plymouth PL6 7PZ

First published 1985

© Suresh Tanna and Karam Singh 1985

British Library Cataloguing in Publication Data

    Quantitative Analysis. — (M&E Professional studies. Level 2, ISSN 0266-8475)
    1. Management – Great Britain
    I. Woolf, Emile   II. Tanna, Suresh   III. Singh, Karam   IV. Series
    657 HS5657

ISBN 0-7121-0490-9


This book is copyright
and may not be reproduced in part
or in whole (except for purposes of review)
without the express permission of the publishers in writing.


Typeset by Mathematical Composition Setters Ltd,
Ivy Street, Salisbury, UK.
Printed and bound in Great Britain by
J.W. Arrowsmith Ltd, Bristol

# Preface

This text has been specially written for the new quantitative analysis syllabus. Although we have drawn on our experience in examining and teaching the previous management mathematics and foundation statistics papers, we have taken the opportunity to structure the material in a form which we believe will best aid the learning process. We have therefore used a problem-orientated approach; that is when introducing a new topic or concept we have introduced it in the context of a particular situation, as we have found that previous generations of students have more easily achieved success with this approach.

Although for pedagogical reasons we have split the text into two parts, Statistics and Operational Research, the reader should remember that we are really concerned with the application of quantitative techniques to business problems. The problems you encounter will not necessarily require a knowledge of inventory control models drawn from operational research or the ability to handle data with a high degree of variability using standard statistical approaches.

To meet this requirement you will find in problem sections that the later problems will cover more than one technique and, perhaps even more importantly, you will be required to recognise the method of approach needed.

We have tried to write this text to give a fairly comprehensive coverage and have therefore taken some subjects to a depth or breadth beyond the current examination requirements. We have tried to anticipate the way the examination of this subject will develop over the next four or five years; this will allow the student with perhaps less time at his disposal to concentrate on the core areas and not worry about the more specialised applications.

When selecting and constructing the problems for this book we have drawn upon the various accounting bodies for up-to-date examples and have created problems based upon our own consulting and examining experience. Where possible, we have drawn material from the accounting and finance area to emphasise the relevance of our subject. It has also been necessary in areas such as linear programming, transportation, multiple regression and simulation to use computer generated problems so that we could more closely achieve our objective of creating problems which are representations of practical situations.

In the presentation of the material we have also borne in mind that some of the topics, e.g. decision analysis, learning curves and linear programming, may be examined in other papers at Level 2 and Level 3. Where appropriate, we have set the questions in the relevant management accounting or financial management context. In particular, Chapter 12 is really an introduction to the work of Markowitz and modern portfolio theory and hence should aid Financial Management studies at Level 3.

Finally when you pass the quantitative analysis examination do not have a sacrificial burning of this book, or even sell it on the black market for a fortune. Keep it—you may well find it useful at the next level!

# Contents

| | |
|---|---|
| **Preface** | v |
| **List of Abbreviations** | xiii |
| **List of Illustrations** | xv |
| **List of Tables** | xviii |

PART ONE: STATISTICS

**1 Calculation of Mean and Standard Deviation** — 3
   1. Comment — 3
   2. Example 1: ungrouped data — 3
   3. Example 2: grouped data — 4
   4. Example 3: grouped data in class intervals — 5
   5. Solution — 6
   6. Coded method for mean and standard deviation — 7
   7. Summary — 8

**2 Probability** — 9
   1. Nature of probability — 9
   2. Rules of probability — 11
   3. Multiplication rule—dependent events — 16
   4. Joint probability table — 20
   5. Summary — 23

**3 Expected Value** — 25
   1. Expected value calculation — 25
   2. Variance and standard deviation — 26
   3. Payoff table — 27
   4. Opportunity loss table — 29
   5. Expected value under perfect information — 29
   6. Decision tree — 30
   7. Summary — 33

## 4 Probability Distributions — 34
1. Permutations — 34
2. Combinations — 35
3. Binomial distribution — 36
4. Mean and standard deviation of the binomial — 37
5. Poisson distribution — 38
6. Normal distribution — 39
7. Two and three standard deviation limits — 42
8. Continuity correction — 43
9. Normal approximation to the Poisson — 44
10. Summary — 45

## 5 Large-sample Theory—Estimation — 46
1. Introduction — 46
2. Sample: Population — 46
3. Selection of sample — 46
4. Notation — 47
5. Estimators — 47
6. Sampling distribution of the mean — 48
7. Central-limit theorem — 49
8. Calculating the sample size for a given accuracy — 51
9. Finite population correction factor — 52
10. Sampling distribution of a proportion — 52
11. Confidence interval for a proportion — 53
12. Summary — 54

## 6 Large-sample Theory—Significance Tests — 55
1. The problem — 55
2. Hypothesis testing — 55
3. One-tailed and two-tailed tests — 57
4. Significance test for a proportion — 58
5. Difference between two means — 59
6. Difference between two proportions — 60
7. Type I and Type II errors — 61
8. Summary — 63

## 7 Small Samples — 65
1. Introduction — 65
2. Degrees of freedom — 66
3. Difference between two sample means — 68
4. Paired $t$-test — 70
5. Summary — 71

## 8 Chi-squared Distribution — 73
1. Goodness of fit tests — 73
2. Contingency table — 77
3. Yates correction — 79
4. Correcting for low expected values — 79
5. Summary — 79

| 9 | **Regression and Correlation** | **80** |
|---|---|---|
| | 1. Introduction | 80 |
| | 2. Linear regression | 80 |
| | 3. Scattergraph | 81 |
| | 4. Method of least squares | 81 |
| | 5. Calculation of regression line | 84 |
| | 6. Forecasting using regression line | 85 |
| | 7. Correlation | 85 |
| | 8. Explained and unexplained variation | 86 |
| | 9. Summary | 91 |
| 10 | **Sampling Theory and Regression** | **92** |
| | 1. Introduction | 92 |
| | 2. Calculation of a 95 per cent confidence interval of the estimate | 93 |
| | 3. Sources of error in the estimate | 93 |
| | 4. Recalculation of a 95 per cent confidence interval of the estimate | 95 |
| | 5. Calculations using standard error of $b$ | 96 |
| | 6. Calculations using standard error of $a$ | 97 |
| | 7. Multiple regression | 99 |
| | 8. Summary | 100 |
| 11 | **Exponential and Logarithmic Functions, Learning Curve** | **102** |
| | 1. Revision of logarithms | 102 |
| | 2. Rules for indices and logs | 102 |
| | 3. Log graphs | 103 |
| | 4. Exponential graphs | 104 |
| | 5. The learning curve | 107 |
| | 6. Equation of learning curve | 108 |
| | 7. Estimating learning rate by regression | 109 |
| | 8. Summary | 110 |
| 12 | **Variances, Covariances and $r$** | **112** |
| | 1. Variances and covariances | 112 |
| | 2. Introducing $r$ | 113 |
| | 3. Independent distributions | 114 |
| | 4. Difference of two distributions | 115 |
| | 5. Implications for portfolio theory | 115 |
| | 6. Summary | 116 |

## PART TWO: OPERATIONAL RESEARCH

| 13 | **An Introduction to Operational Research** | **119** |
|---|---|---|
| | 1. What is operational research (OR)? | 119 |
| | 2. Reasons for using OR | 120 |
| | 3. The decision-making process | 121 |
| | 4. Stages in the OR approach | 121 |
| | 5. Feedback | 123 |
| | 6. Classification of problems | 123 |

    7. Is optimisation a holy grail?   125
    8. Sensitivity analysis   125
    9. The future of OR   125

## 14 Linear Programming—Introduction and Model Construction   127
    1. Mathematical programming   127
    2. Linear programming defined   127
    3. Applications of linear programming   128
    4. Classification—linear programming methods   128
    5. Properties of linear programming   128
    6. Model construction—maximisation   130
    7. Model construction—minimisation   132
    8. General linear programming models   133
    9. Assumptions of linear programming   134

## 15 Linear Programming—Graphical Solution   136
    1. Introduction   136
    2. Graphical solution—maximisation   136
    3. Graphical solution—minimisation   143
    4. Resource utilisation and excess supply at the optimum   144

## 16 Linear Programming—Simplex Solution and Dual Values   146
    1. Introduction   146
    2. Simplex procedures—maximisation   146
    3. Simplex procedures applied to an example   147
    4. An introduction to primal and dual forms   152
    5. Primal and dual forms—the general models   152
    6. Primal and dual forms—particular examples   153
    7. Simplex maximisation—mixed inequalities   157
    8. Simplex minimisation   157

## 17 Transportation   159
    1. Introduction   159
    2. Description of the problem   159
    3. Mathematical model of the transportation situation   160
    4. Transportation procedures   162
    5. Degeneracy   167
    6. Unbalanced situations   170
    7. Prohibited routes   173
    8. Profit maximisation   174
    9. Transhipment   176

## 18 Assignment   177
    1. Introduction   177
    2. Description of the problem   178
    3. Mathematical model of the assignment problem   178
    4. Iteration procedures for an optimal assignment   180
    5. Summary of procedures for an optimal assignment   185

|     |                                                          |     |
| --- | -------------------------------------------------------- | --- |
|     | 6. Maximisation problems                                 | 185 |
|     | 7. Situations with impossible assignments                | 187 |
|     | 8. Unequal dimensions                                    | 188 |
|     | 9. Tutorial points                                       | 189 |
|     | 10. Summary                                              | 189 |
| 19  | **An Introduction to Network Analysis**                  | **190** |
|     | 1. Background                                            | 190 |
|     | 2. CPA and PERT                                          | 191 |
|     | 3. Areas of application                                  | 191 |
|     | 4. The CPA method                                        | 191 |
|     | 5. Network terminology                                   | 193 |
|     | 6. Summary                                               | 197 |
| 20  | **Network Analysis—Time and Cost**                       | **198** |
|     | 1. Introduction                                          | 198 |
|     | 2. Aim of a time analysis                                | 198 |
|     | 3. Critical path                                         | 198 |
|     | 4. Determining the critical path—simple analysis         | 199 |
|     | 5. Determining the critical path—normal analysis         | 199 |
|     | 6. Classifications of float                              | 202 |
|     | 7. Cost considerations                                   | 203 |
|     | 8. The cost analysis procedure                           | 204 |
|     | 9. Cost analysis—a worked example                        | 205 |
| 21  | **Network Analysis—Resources and Uncertainty**           | **208** |
|     | 1. Introduction—Resource analysis                        | 208 |
|     | 2. Resource analysis—an example                          | 209 |
|     | 3. An introduction to PERT                               | 211 |
|     | 4. PERT—expected time estimates                          | 211 |
|     | 5. Determining the critical path                         | 213 |
| 22  | **Inventory Control**                                    | **214** |
|     | 1. Introduction                                          | 214 |
|     | 2. Deterministic EOQ—trial-and-error solution            | 215 |
|     | 3. Derivation of the deterministic EOQ model             | 219 |
|     | 4. Quantity discounts                                    | 220 |
|     | 5. Production model                                      | 221 |
|     | 6. Lead time and reorder levels                          | 223 |
|     | 7. The effects of uncertainty—stochastic demand          | 224 |
|     | 8. Systems of stock control                              | 224 |
| 23  | **Queuing Theory**                                       | **227** |
|     | 1. The queuing situation                                 | 227 |
|     | 2. Components of the queuing system                      | 227 |
|     | 3. Measures of effectiveness                             | 228 |
|     | 4. A queuing model                                       | 229 |
|     | 5. Standard queuing formulae                             | 230 |

|   |   |   |
|---|---|---|
| | 6. Application of the formulae in a simple example | 231 |
| | 7. A more complicated problem | 232 |
| | 8. Multiple-server queue model | 234 |
| | 9. Multiple-server queue example | 235 |

## 24  Simulation — 237
1. Introduction — 237
2. Example — 238
3. Simulation and the computer — 242
4. Event-sequencing simulation — 242
5. Example — 243
6. Program flowchart — 243
7. Explanation of flowchart and simulation — 243
8. Starting events and finishing events — 246
9. Simulation language — 246
10. Summary — 246

## Appendixes
1. Index to Examination Questions and Suggested Answers — 247
2. Examination Questions — 248
3. Suggested Answers to Examination Questions — 331
4. Formulae and Extracts from Tables — 539
5. Glossary of Statistical Terms — 543

## Index — 546

# List of Abbreviations

| | |
|---|---|
| $C$ (in $^nC_r$) | = combination of $n$ and $r$ |
| $c$ (related to EOQ) | = ordering cost per batch |
| $C_c$ | = crash cost |
| $C_n$ | = direct cost |
| cov | = covariance |
| CPA | = critical path analysis |
| CPM | = critical path method |
| $d$ (related to EOQ) | = annual demand for product |
| EBQ | = economic batch quantity |
| e.e.t. | = earliest event times |
| EOQ | = economic order quantity |
| FIFO | = first in first out |
| GIGO | = garbage in garbage out |
| $i$ (related to EOQ) | = stockholding cost expressed as a percentage |
| l.e.t. | = latest event times |
| LIFO | = last in first out |
| LP | = linear programming |
| $m$ | = mean |
| $M$ | = mid-range estimates |
| $M/M/1/\infty$ | = simple queue model |
| $n!$ | = Factorial $n$ |

Network analysis diagram

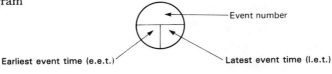

| | |
|---|---|
| OR | = operation research |
| PERT | = project evaluation and review technique |
| $Q$ (related to EOQ) | = size of order |

| | |
|---|---|
| $R$ | = rank correlation |
| $r$ | = correlation coefficient |
| $r^2$ | = coefficient of determination |
| $SE$ | = standard error |
| $SE_{est}$ | = standard error estimate |
| $T_c$ | = crash time |
| $t_e$ | = time (in PERT calculations) |
| $T_n$ | = time |
| $V$ | = degrees of freedom |
| var | = variance |
| $\bar{x}$ | = mean value of variable $x$ |
| $>$ ; $<$ | = greater than; less than |
| $\geq$ | = greater than or equal to |
| $\leq$ | = less than or equal to |
| $\therefore$ | = therefore |
| $\mu$ (Greek mu) | = population mean |
| $\hat{\mu}$ | = estimated population mean |
| $\sigma$ (Greek sigma) | = standard deviation |
| $\sigma^2$ | = statistical variance |
| $\sigma_y$ | = unbiased estimator of standard deviation of $y$ |

# List of Illustrations

| | |
|---|---:|
| 1. Probability scale | 11 |
| 2. Venn diagram | 13 |
| 3. Probability tree | 18 |
| 4. Decision tree (a) | 31 |
| 5. Decision tree (b) | 32 |
| 6. Normal distribution curve | 39 |
| 7. Normal distribution curve—computer sales (i) | 40 |
| 8. Normal distribution curve—computer sales (ii) | 40 |
| 9. Normal distribution curve—computer sales (iii) | 41 |
| 10. Normal distribution curve—computer sales target | 41 |
| 11. Normal distribution curve—area within $1.96\sigma\,(\approx 2\sigma)$ limits | 42 |
| 12. Normal distribution curve—area within $3\sigma$ limits | 42 |
| 13. Normal distribution curve—continuity correction histogram | 43 |
| 14. Normal distribution curve—continuity correction | 44 |
| 15. Normal distribution curve—demand for a special component | 45 |
| 16. Central-limit theorem: $\mu_x$ and $SE_x$ | 49 |
| 17. Central-limit theorem—confidence interval | 50 |
| 18. Calculating sample size for a given accuracy | 51 |
| 19. Confidence interval for a proportion | 53 |
| 20. Hypothesis testing—sampling distribution of $x$ | 56 |
| 21. Hypothesis testing—test limits | 57 |
| 22. One-tailed test | 58 |
| 23. Significance test for a proportion | 58 |
| 24. Test for difference between two means | 60 |
| 25. Test for difference between two proportions | 61 |
| 26. Type I and II errors | 62 |
| 27. Student's $t$-distribution | 65 |
| 28. Calculation of confidence interval | 67 |
| 29. Test for significance of sample mean | 68 |
| 30. Test for difference between two sample means | 69 |

| | | |
|---|---|---|
| 31. | Test for significant difference between typing times | 71 |
| 32. | Chi-squared distribution | 73 |
| 33. | Chi-squared test—comparison of observed and expected frequencies | 75 |
| 34. | Chi-squared test for Poisson distribution | 76 |
| 35. | Chi-squared test for association between hair colour and sex | 79 |
| 36. | Scattergraph | 80 |
| 37. | Scattergraph of labour hours against overheads | 82 |
| 38. | Determining regression line $Y$ by method of least squares | 82 |
| 39. | Variation of Pearson's product-moment correlation coefficient $r$ | 86 |
| 40. | Explained and unexplained variations of $y$ | 87 |
| 41. | Confidence limits for regression line $Y$ (variation of points about true line) | 92 |
| 42. | Calculation of confidence interval of the estimate of regression line $Y$ | 93 |
| 43. | Confidence limits for regression line $Y$ (error in estimating $a$) | 94 |
| 44. | Confidence limits for regression line $Y$ (error in estimating $b$) | 94 |
| 45. | Confidence limits for regression line $Y$ (three sources of error) | 95 |
| 46. | Recalculation of confidence interval of $Y$ | 96 |
| 47. | Calculation of 99 per cent confidence interval for slope $b$ of regression line $Y$ | 97 |
| 48. | Test for significant difference of slope $b$ from zero | 97 |
| 49. | Calculation of 99 per cent confidence interval for $a$-value | 98 |
| 50. | Test for significant difference of $a$-value from zero | 98 |
| 51. | Graph of $\log_{10} x$ | 103 |
| 52. | Graph of $\log_e x$ | 104 |
| 53. | Graph of $y = 2^x$ | 105 |
| 54. | Graph of $y = (0.5)^x$ | 105 |
| 55. | Graph of $y = e^x$ | 106 |
| 56. | Graph of $y = e^{-x}$ | 106 |
| 57. | Learning curve: average time over life of product ($y$) against number of units ($x$) | 108 |
| 58. | The decision-making process | 121 |
| 59. | Controlled and uncontrollable inputs | 123 |
| 60. | Gonda Clock Company—basic graph | 137 |
| 61. | Gonda Clock Company—component constraint | 138 |
| 62. | Gonda Clock Company—labour constraint | 139 |
| 63. | Gonda Clock Company—departmental capacity, Regular clocks | 139 |
| 64. | Gonda Clock Company—departmental capacity, Deluxe clocks | 140 |
| 65. | Gonda Clock Company—constraints combined | 141 |
| 66. | Gonda Clock Company—plotting iso-profit lines | 142 |
| 67. | Hyderabad Chemical Company | 143 |
| 68. | (a) Activity within a project | 193 |
| | (b) Events and activity within a project | 193 |
| | (c) Network | 194 |
| 69. | Network where one activity must be complete before either of two others can start | 194 |
| 70. | Network in which two activities must be complete before another can start | 194 |
| 71. | Sub-networks representing dependencies | 195 |

# LIST OF ILLUSTRATIONS

| | |
|---|---|
| 72. Single network formed by joining sub-networks | 196 |
| 73. Network whose form is unacceptable | 196 |
| 74. Network corrected by insertion of an imaginary activity or dummy | 196 |
| 75. Network with dummy inserted to maintain logical sequence of jobs | 197 |
| 76. Network for simple analysis | 199 |
| 77. How the event circle is split to show event times | 200 |
| 78. Network for normal analysis, with earliest event times | 200 |
| 79. Network as Fig. 78 with latest event times added | 201 |
| 80. Part of a network to illustrate float | 203 |
| 81. Relationship between normal time and cost and crash time and cost | 204 |
| 82. Network for cost analysis | 205 |
| 83. Network to illustrate example | 209 |
| 84. Gantt chart and labour histogram | 210 |
| 85. Skewed and symmetrical beta distributions | 212 |
| 86. Probability distribution of project duration | 213 |
| 87. General stock pattern | 215 |
| 88. Annual stock pattern | 216 |
| 89. Annual stock pattern | 217 |
| 90. Effect of order quantity on costs | 218 |
| 91. Stock pattern for economic-order-quantity model | 222 |
| 92. Lead time $L$ and reorder level $R$ | 224 |
| 93. Variation of stock level in a two-bin system | 225 |
| 94. Variation of stock level in a periodic review system | 226 |
| 95. Components of the queuing system | 228 |
| 96. Simulation of car hire business | 240 |
| 97. Queue flowchart | 243 |
| 98. Programme flowchart for simulation of shop queuing problem | 244 |
| 99–175. Illustrations for Appendixes 2 and 3 | |

# List of Tables

| | | |
|---|---|---|
| 1. | Normal distribution table | 39 |
| 2. | $t$-table | 66 |
| 3. | $\chi^2$ | 74 |
| 4. | Data used to construct graph in Fig. 37 | 81 |
| 5. | Costs, labour hours and machine hours over eight months | 99 |
| 6. | Data used in construction of learning curve | 107 |
| 7. | Evaluation of corner points (Fig. 65) | 141 |
| 8. | Evaluation of corner points (Fig. 67) | 144 |
| 9. | Comparison of gross savings with transportation costs | 165 |
| 10. | Further comparison of gross savings with transportation costs | 167 |
| 11. | Data for cost analysis example | 205 |
| 12. | Variation of costs with order quantities | 217 |
| 13–48. | Tables for Appendixes 2 and 3 | 240 |

# Part One: Statistics

CHAPTER ONE

# Calculation of Mean and Standard Deviation

## 1.0 COMMENT

This topic was covered in the Level 1 paper Numerical Analysis (Paper 1.5) and for a detailed coverage of the topic the student should refer to *Numerical Analysis and Data Processing* in the same series. For the Quantitative Analysis paper we shall cover just the essentials to enable the student to perform the necessary calculations.

## 2.0 EXAMPLE 1—UNGROUPED DATA

Fred has the following outstanding bills (£s): 58, 12, 32, 70 and 18. Calculate the mean and the standard deviation.

SOLUTION
The formulae are: mean:
$$\bar{x} = \frac{\sum x}{n};$$

standard deviation:
$$\sigma = \sqrt{\frac{\sum x^2}{n} - (\bar{x})^2}.$$

*Note: The formula for standard deviation is different from that given on p. 539 as our calculation assumes we are calculating the true standard deviation and not estimating from a sample. It will all become clear when we discuss estimating in a later section.*

It is therefore necessary for us to calculate the $\sum x$ and $\sum x^2$ terms first and then substitute the results in the formulae.

|   | $x$ | $x^2$ |
|---|---|---|
|   | 58 | 3,364 |
|   | 12 | 144 |
|   | 32 | 1,024 |
|   | 70 | 4,900 |
|   | 18 | 324 |
|   | $\sum x = 190$ | $\sum x^2 = 9,756$ |

Now $\quad n = 5;$

$$\therefore \bar{x} = \frac{190}{5} = 38$$

$$\therefore \bar{x} = \underline{\underline{£38}}.$$

$$\sigma = \sqrt{\frac{9,756}{5} - (38)^2}$$

$$= \sqrt{507.2}$$

$$= 22.5$$

$$\therefore \sigma = \underline{\underline{£22.5}}.$$

The mean amount outstanding is £38 with standard deviation £22.5.

It might also be useful at this stage to remind ourselves that the square of the standard deviation $\sigma^2$, called the variance, is also a useful statistic.

In our example $\sigma^2 = 507.2$.

This is sometimes written as $\text{var}(x) = 507.2$;

i.e. variance = 507.2.

## 3.0 EXAMPLE 2: GROUPED DATA

The demand for milk on a particular date in the village of Cowslip by fifty households is given by the following frequency distribution:

| Daily demand (pints) | 0 | 1 | 2 | 3 | 4 | 5 |
|---|---|---|---|---|---|---|
| Frequency | 3 | 10 | 18 | 13 | 4 | 2 |

Calculate the mean, variance and standard deviation.

# 1 CALCULATION OF MEAN AND STANDARD DEVIATION

**SOLUTION**

When the data is grouped we need the frequency form of the mean and standard deviation formulae:

$$\bar{x} = \frac{\sum fx}{n} \quad \text{and} \quad \sigma = \sqrt{\frac{\sum fx^2}{n} - (\bar{x})^2}.$$

*Note*: Also, $n = \sum f = 50$.

This time we need columns for $\sum fx$ and $\sum fx^2$:

| $x$ | $f$ | $fx$ | $fx^2$ |
|---|---|---|---|
| 0 | 3 | 0 | 0 |
| 1 | 10 | 10 | 10 |
| 2 | 18 | 36 | 72 |
| 3 | 13 | 39 | 117 |
| 4 | 4 | 16 | 64 |
| 5 | 2 | 10 | 50 |
|  | 50 | 111 | 313 |

$$\bar{x} = \frac{111}{50}$$

$$= \underline{\underline{2.22}} \text{ pints}.$$

$$\text{var}(x) = \frac{313}{50} - (2.22)^2$$

$$= \underline{\underline{1.33}}.$$

$$\sigma = \sqrt{1.33}$$

$$\sigma = \underline{\underline{1.15}} \text{ pints}.$$

Results are:

| | |
|---|---|
| Mean: | 2.22 pints |
| Variance: | 1.33 |
| Standard deviation: | 1.15 pints. |

## 4.0 EXAMPLE 3—GROUPED DATA IN CLASS INTERVALS

The closing prices of 150 industrial shares on the UK stock market have been recorded and grouped together in the following frequency distribution:

| Price range (pence) | Frequency |
|---|---|
| 50– | 3 |
| 60– | 8 |
| 70– | 6 |
| 80– | 15 |
| 90– | 19 |
| 100– | 25 |
| 110– | 30 |
| 120– | 24 |
| 130– | 15 |
| 140– | 5 |
| | 150 |

Calculate the mean and the standard deviation.

(*Note*: By 50– we mean the price ranges from 50p to very close to 60p. For ease we shall treat it as being the same as (50–60)).

## 5.0 SOLUTION

In this example we have not been given a set of $x$-values but have a range instead. We calculate for each class interval the mid-point of the class interval and use these mid-points as our $x$-values, and then proceed as in Example 2.

| Class interval (price) | Mid-point $x$ | $f$ | $fx$ | $fx^2$ |
|---|---|---|---|---|
| 50–60 | 55 | 3 | 165 | 9,075 |
| 60–70 | 65 | 8 | 520 | 33,800 |
| 70–80 | 75 | 6 | 450 | 33,750 |
| 80–90 | 85 | 15 | 1,275 | 108,375 |
| 90–100 | 95 | 19 | 1,805 | 171,475 |
| 100–110 | 105 | 25 | 2,625 | 275,625 |
| 110–120 | 115 | 30 | 3,450 | 395,750 |
| 120–130 | 125 | 24 | 3,000 | 375,000 |
| 130–140 | 135 | 15 | 2,025 | 273,375 |
| 140–150 | 145 | 5 | 725 | 105,125 |
| | | 150 | 16,040 | 1,782,350 |

$$\bar{x} = \frac{\Sigma fx}{n} = \frac{16,040}{150} = \underline{\underline{106.9\text{p}}}.$$

# 1 CALCULATION OF MEAN AND STANDARD DEVIATION

$$\sigma = \sqrt{\frac{\sum fx^2}{n} - (\bar{x})^2} = \sqrt{\frac{1{,}782{,}350}{150} - (106.9)^2}$$

$$= \sqrt{447{,}596} = \underline{\underline{21.2\text{p}}}.$$

The mean price of our shares is 106.9p with standard deviation $\underline{\underline{21.2\text{p}}}$

## 6.0 CODED METHOD FOR MEAN AND STANDARD DEVIATION

To simplify some of the calculations we can use a coded method to determine the mean and standard deviation.

The formula for the mean is:

$$\bar{x} = a + c\frac{\sum fd}{n}$$

and that for the standard deviation:

$$\sigma = c\sqrt{\frac{\sum fd^2}{n} - \left(\frac{\sum fd}{n}\right)^2}$$

where $a$ = the assumed or working mean,
$c$ = class interval and
$d$ = deviation of mid-point of class interval from assumed mean in class intervals.

Let us recalculate the mean and standard deviation for Example 3 using the coded method.

The mid-point of any class interval can be used as the assumed mean, but ideally it should be as close to the true mean as possible.

Let us use $a = 105$.
The class interval $c = 10$
We then need to calculate the terms $\sum fd$ and $\sum fd^2$.

| Class interval | f | d | fd | fd² |
|---|---|---|---|---|
| 50–60 | 3 | −5 | −15 | 75 |
| 60–70 | 8 | −4 | −32 | 128 |
| 70–80 | 6 | −3 | −18 | 54 |
| 80–90 | 15 | −2 | −30 | 60 |
| 90–100 | 19 | −1 | −19 | 19 |
| 100–110 | 25 | 0 | 0 | 0 |
| 110–120 | 30 | 1 | 30 | 30 |
| 120–130 | 24 | 2 | 48 | 96 |
| 130–140 | 15 | 3 | 45 | 135 |
| 140–150 | 5 | 4 | 20 | 80 |
| | 150 | | 29 | 677 |

$$\bar{x} = 105 + \frac{10 \times 29}{150} = \underline{\underline{106.9\text{p.}}}$$

$$\sigma = 10\sqrt{\frac{677}{150} - \left(\frac{29}{150}\right)^2} = 10\sqrt{4.476}$$

$$= \underline{\underline{21.2\text{p.}}}$$

This leads to identically the same result as by the uncoded method.

## 7.0  SUMMARY

The aim of this chapter has been to show how the mean, variance and standard deviation can be calculated for both grouped and ungrouped data. It is brief and to the point as it is a revision of work done at an earlier level. However, it is sufficient for the needs of the quantitative analysis paper, which is more concerned with the problems of estimation and significance testing than with the calculation of the elementary statistics. If you know all that is in this chapter you will be able to calculate any mean or standard deviation that is required as part of a more advanced question.

# CHAPTER TWO
# Probability

## 1.0 NATURE OF PROBABILITY

Consider the following statements. All three are probability comments:

(a) 50–50 chance of getting a head or a tail on one toss of a coin.

(b) Odds of 10 to 1 on a horse winning.

(c) "Haven't a hope in hell."

## 1.1 Reasoning approach

The first statement above is saying that you would expect to get on average 50 heads, and consequently also 50 tails, when you toss a coin 100 times. We say the probability of getting a head is 50 out of 100 or simplifying, 1 in 2. As a fraction this is $\frac{1}{2}$ or as a decimal 0.5.

We can also approach the same problem by the use of the following reasoning. There are two possible results, or events, that can occur when we toss a coin—a head or a tail. Out of these two *equally likely* events only one is a head.

Therefore, assuming that both events are *equally likely*, the probability of getting a head is $\frac{1}{2}$ or 0.5.

We can write this as $P(H) = 0.5$ where P stands for probability and the event is given inside the brackets, in this case H for head.

We can argue in a similar manner for the probability of getting a four on a die. There are six possible outcomes and only one is a four. Therefore probability of a four on one throw of a die is 1/6, written as $P(6) = 1/6$. This approach leads to a definition of probability that we can apply when we can use reason to determine the probability.

$$P \text{ (an event A)} = \frac{\text{Number of ways event A can occur}}{\text{Total number of events that can occur}}$$

## 1.2 Relative frequency approach

In other situations it is not possible to obtain a probability by reasoning; we have to use another approach. The one adopted in most business situations is what is called a relative frequency approach. For example if on only 10 days out of 25 trading days a shop has sales exceeding £500 we could argue that, subject to any additional information, the probability that sales on the next trading day will exceed £500 is 10/25, i.e. 0.40. We use past data to allow us to say something about the future.

This approach leads us to a slightly different worded definition of probability, but it is easy to see a similar structure.

$$P \text{ (an event A)} = \frac{\text{Number of times event A occurred}}{\text{Total number of events considered.}}$$

## 1.3 Subjective approach

The third comment at the beginning of the chapter, "Haven't a hope in hell", is really expressing a subjective probability, $P(A) = 0$, based on, presumably, the speaker's knowledge of the situation which may not be able to be clearly quantified.

In the examination you are studying for it will only be necessary to use either the reasoning or the relative frequency approach.

### Example 1
There are two bananas, one apple and two oranges in a bowl. What are the probabilities that the next fruit selected will be:

(a) a banana,
(b) an apple,
(c) an orange?

SOLUTION

(a) $P(B) = 2/5 = 0.4$,

i.e. two fruits in the bowl are bananas out of the five fruits available. Similarly:

(b) $P(A) = 1/5 = 0.2$,

(c) $P(O) = 2/5 = 0.4$.

### Example 2

| Level of weekly sales | below 100 | 100–200 | above 200 |
|---|---|---|---|
| Frequency | 18 | 27 | 15 |

What is the probability that next week's sales will be 100 or more?

SOLUTION

$$P(\text{sales} \geq 100) = \frac{27 + 15}{18 + 27 + 15} = 42/60 = \underline{\underline{0.70}}.$$

# 2 PROBABILITY

## 2.0 RULES OF PROBABILITY

### 2.1 General rules

In Example 1 we found:

$P(B) = 0.4, \qquad P(A) = 0.2, \qquad P(O) = 0.4.$

What is the value of $P(B) + P(A) + P(O)$?
  The answer is 1.
  If, in any situation, we consider the probabilities of all possible separate events that can occur then the sum of their probabilities adds up to 1. Try it for a toss of a coin or a throw of a die.
  So our first rule is that:

$$\sum P(x) = 1$$

It follows from this rule that the largest probability you can have is 1 as 1 acts as an upper limit on all the probabilities. If for example you would win a bet if you got at least two heads when three coins are tossed, if the first two coins had shown a head then your probability of winning is 1 as $P(H \text{ or } T) = 1$ when you are tossing a coin. The event is a certainty. The other extreme occurs if both the first two coins showed a tail then the probability of getting two heads out of three tosses is impossible: i.e., $P(\text{win}) = 0$.
  The second rule is then:

$$0 \leqslant P(x) \leqslant 1$$

Probabilities range from 0 (impossible) to 1 (certainty). This may be represented by a probability scale as in Fig. 1.

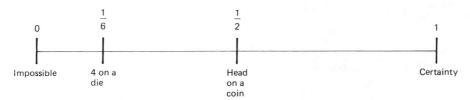

Fig. 1. *Probability scale.*

### 2.2 Addition rule—mutually exclusive events

Up to now we have been dealing with individual events and the ideas introduced should not have appeared too difficult. In more complicated probability problems it is usually possible to break the larger problem into a series of individual events which can easily be handled. The ways of combining the individual probabilities together to solve the larger problems usually fit a number of standard rules. One of these rules is the addition rule.
  Let us consider throwing a die; assume that if we get a 3 or a 4 we will win the game we are playing.

Therefore
$$P(\text{win}) = P(3 \text{ or a } 4) = 2/6$$

but note:
$$P(3) + P(4) = 1/6 + 1/6$$
$$= 2/6,$$

i.e., whether we consider the problem as a whole with two ways of winning out of six or calculate the probability of the individual winning events and then add them together we arrive at the same result.

That is, with one reservation we arrive at the *addition rule:*

$$P(A \text{ or } B) = P(A) + P(B)$$

The reservation or condition is that the events A, B have to be *mutually exclusive*. By mutually exclusive we mean that they cannot both occur simultaneously. For example, in the problem above if the die had shown a 3 it could not have shown a 4 at the same time—the events are said to be mutually exclusive.

The addition rule can be extended to deal with any number of events.

$$P(A \text{ or } B \text{ or } C \text{ or } \ldots) = P(A) + P(B) + P(C) + \ldots.$$

The important part of the rule is the <u>OR</u>.

*If you get a probability situation which uses the word "OR" (or implies it) then without fail you must* **ADD** *the probabilities together.*

We will see later that there may need to be adjustments but essentially <u>OR</u> means apply the *addition* rule.


## Example 3

In a pack of 52 cards what is the probability if one card is drawn of getting a "picture card" or a seven?

### SOLUTION

There are 12 picture cards, 4 kings, 4 queens and 4 jacks. Therefore

$$P(P) = 12/52.$$

There are 4 sevens:

$$P(7) = 4/52.$$

Therefore using the addition rule:

$$P(P \text{ or } 7) = P(P) + P(7)$$
$$= 12/52 + 4/52$$
$$= 16/52$$
$$= 4/13 \text{ or } \underline{\underline{0.308}}.$$

## 2.3 Addition rule—non-mutually exclusive events

When we are considering an OR situation but with non-mutually exclusive events we need to make an adjustment to avoid double counting.

Consider a pack of 52 cards. What is the probability, if one card is drawn, of getting a diamond or a queen? If we get a diamond the bet is won or if we get a queen the bet is won. These are not mutually exclusive events as it is possible to get a card which has the property of being a diamond and a queen, i.e. the queen of diamonds.

To analyse this situation let us draw what is called a Venn diagram (Fig. 2). The left-hand circle contains all 13 diamond cards (x), the right-hand circle contains all the 4 queen cards. Outside both circles, but inside the rectangle (the sample space) are the 36 non-diamond and non-queen cards (not all shown).

Notice in the intersection area of the circles is the card which is both a diamond and a queen.

If we total up all the cards contained anywhere within either circle we get 16, while the total number of cards in the sample space equals 52.

| | | |
|---|---|---|
| Hence | P(diamond or queen) | = 16/52. |
| Now | P(diamond) | = 13/52 |
| and | P(queen) | = 4/52. |
| Thus | P(diamond) + P(queen) | = 13/52 + 4/52 |
| | | = 17/52. |

There is a difference between the two results of 1/52. What we have done by adding the two probabilities together is to count the number in the intersection area twice, in this case 1/52 too much.

Hence our revised addition rule in this example should be:

$$P(D \text{ or } Q) = P(D) + P(Q) - P(D, Q)$$

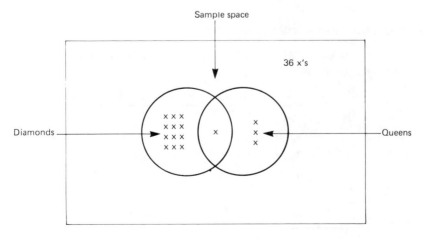

Fig. 2. *Venn diagram.*

(where P(D, Q) means being a diamond and a queen together)

$$= 13/52 + 4/52 - 1/52$$
$$= 16/52.$$

In general, for non-mutually exclusive events

$$P(A \text{ or } B) = P(A) + P(B) - P(A, B).$$

Essentially we add the probabilities and then correct for any double counting.

### Example 4
In a sample of 50 girls and 50 boys, fair and dark hair occur as follows:

|                | Girls (G) | Boys (B) |
|----------------|-----------|----------|
| Fair hair (F)  | 33        | 22       |
| Dark hair (D)  | 17        | 28       |

If a child is selected at random from the sample what is the probability of selecting a girl or a child with fair hair?

**SOLUTION**
Now
$$P(G) = 50/100, \quad P(F) = 55/100;$$
$$P(G, F) = 33/100.$$
Now
$$P(G \text{ or } F) = P(G) + P(F) - P(G, F)$$
$$= 50/100 + 55/100 - 33/100$$
$$= 72/100 \text{ or } \underline{\underline{0.72}}$$

## 2.4 Multiplication rule—independent events

Consider throwing two dice, one red and one blue; then the possible events that can occur (the sample space) are:

| R B | R B | R B | R B | R B | R B |
|-----|-----|-----|-----|-----|-----|
| 1, 1 | 1, 2 | 1, 3 | 1, 4 | 1, 5 | 1, 6 |
| 2, 1 | 2, 2 | 2, 3 | 2, 4 | 2, 5 | 2, 6 |
| 3, 1 | 3, 2 | 3, 3 | 3, 4 | 3, 5 | 3, 6 |
| 4, 1 | 4, 2 | 4, 3 | 4, 4 | 4, 5 | 4, 6 |
| 5, 1 | 5, 2 | 5, 3 | 5, 4 | 5, 5 | 5, 6 |
| 6, 1 | 6, 2 | 6, 3 | 6, 4 | 6, 5 | 6, 6 |

If we want the probability of getting a 3 on the red die and a 2 on the blue die we can see that out of the 36 possible events this only occurs once (row 3 column 2). Therefore P(3R and 2B) = 1/36.

Now let us consider the individual probabilities:

$$P(3R) = 1/6, \qquad P(2B) = 1/6.$$

But
$$1/6 \times 1/6 = 1/36,$$

i.e.
$$P(3R \text{ and } 2B) = P(3R) \times P(2B),$$

i.e. whether we consider the problem as a whole with 1 way of getting 3R and 2B out of 36 ways or calculate the probabilities of the individual event and then multiply them together we get the same result.

That is, with one reservation we arrive at the *multiplication rule:*

$$P(A \text{ and } B) = P(A) \times P(B)$$

The reservation or condition is that the events A, B have to be *independent.* By independent we mean that the result of A must not have any influence on the result or outcome of B. In our problem, obviously, getting a three on the red die does not influence what outcome will occur on the blue die.

The multiplication rule can be extended to deal with any number of events.

$$P(A \text{ and } B \text{ and } C \text{ and } \ldots) = P(A) \times P(B) \times P(C) \times \ldots .$$

The important part of the rule is the AND.
*If you get a probability situation with more than one event occurring which uses the word "AND" (or implies it) then without fail you must* MULTIPLY *the probabilities together.*

## Example 5
A double glazing salesman finds that he has a probability of making a sale of 0.3 when he calls on houses that have expressed an initial interest. What is the probability he will sell double glazing on two independent calls?

**SOLUTION**

$$P(\text{sell on both calls}) = P(\text{sell on 1st call}) \times P(\text{sell on 2nd call})$$
$$= 0.3 \times 0.3$$
$$= 0.09.$$

To illustrate the use of both the addition and multiplication rules together, let us take another problem.

## Example 6
Using the information in Example 5 what is the probability of:

(a) selling on *only* one call?
(b) selling on at least one call?

**SOLUTION**

(a) P(sell on *only* one call) = P(sell on 1st and not on 2nd call or not sell on 1st and sell on 2nd call)

$$= 0.3 \times 0.7 + 0.7 \times 0.3$$

$$= \underline{\underline{0.42}}.$$

*Note*  P(sell) = 0.3

*There are only two possible outcomes: you either sell or do not sell, and their probabilities must add to one.*

*Therefore* P(not sell) = 1 − P(sell)

$$= 1 - 0.3$$

$$= \underline{\underline{0.7}}.$$

(b) P(sell on at least one call) = P(sell on *only* one call) + P(sell on both calls).
Both of these have already been calculated, therefore

P(sell on at least one call) = 0.42 + 0.09

$$= \underline{\underline{0.51}}.$$

An alternative aproach might be:

P(sell on at least one call) = 1 − P(sell on neither call).
As you either sell at least one or you sell none,

P(sell on at least one call) = 1 − 0.7 × 0.7

$$= 1 - 0.49$$

$$= \underline{\underline{0.51}}.$$


## 3.0 MULTIPLICATION RULE—DEPENDENT EVENTS

Consider dealing two cards from a pack of 52 cards without replacing the cards. What is the probability the first card dealt is an ace *and* the second card dealt is a king?

This is an AND situation so we need to calculate the individual probabilities and multiply them together. We just have to be careful in the calculation of the second probability.

Consider the first event:

$$P(\text{ace}) = 4/52.$$

There are 4 aces in a pack of 52 cards.

Now, before calculating the probability of the second event answer the following two questions:

(a) How many cards are there left in the pack after the first card is dealt?
Answer: 51 cards.

# 2 PROBABILITY

(b) How many kings are there left in the pack after the first card is dealt, assuming the first card is an ace?
Answer: 4 kings.

Notice we can only find an answer to "How many kings are there left in the pack?" if we assume the first card was an ace. Otherwise it is possible that the first card was a king and then we cannot tell if there are 3 or 4 kings left.

Hence  P(king given the first card was an ace) = 4/51.

This is usually written as:

$$P(king/ace) = 4/51.$$

Therefore P(ace first card and king second card) = $\frac{4}{52} \times \frac{4}{51}$

$$= \underline{\underline{0.006}}$$

In general the multiplication rule becomes:

$$P(A \text{ and } B) = P(A) \times P(B/A)$$

(a) *P(B/A) is called a condition probability.*

(b) *If B is independent of A then P(B/A) becomes P(B), which brings us back to the multiplication rule for independent events. This rule can be generalised as in the following example.*

## Example 7

If three cards are dealt without replacement what is the probability they will all be queens?

### SOLUTION

P(3 queens) = P(1st Q) × P(2nd Q/1st Q) × P(3rd Q/1st and 2nd Q's)

$\qquad = 4/52 \times 3/51 \times 2/50$

$\qquad = \underline{\underline{0.00018}}.$

*Note: As each card is selected there is one less card and one less queen to be selected next time.*

Now let us consider a situation where we need both the addition and the multiplication rules for dependent events.

## Example 8

In a week a company either has good sales of 200 units or bad sales of 100 units. In the first week the probability of good sales is 0.6. In the second week the probability of good sales is 0.8 if the sales in the first week were good or 0.3 if the sales in the first week were bad. What is the probability of total sales over both weeks being:

(a) 400 units

(b) 200 units

(c) 300 units

What is the sum of your probabilities in (a), (b) and (c)?

# PART ONE: STATISTICS

**SOLUTION**
Initial working from given information:

$$P(G\ 1st) = 0.6, \qquad \therefore P(B\ 1st) = 0.4.$$
$$P(G\ 2nd/G\ 1st) = 0.8, \qquad \therefore P(B\ 2nd/G\ 1st) = 0.2.$$
$$P(G\ 2nd/B\ 1st) = 0.3, \qquad \therefore P(B\ 2nd/B\ 1st) = 0.7.$$

(a)
$$P(400\ units) = P(good\ in\ both\ weeks)$$
$$= P(G\ 1st) \times P(G\ 2nd/G\ 1st)$$
$$= 0.6 \times 0.8$$
$$= \underline{\underline{0.48}}.$$

(b)
$$P(200\ units) = P(bad\ in\ both\ weeks);$$
$$P(B\ 1st) \times P(B\ 2nd/B\ 1st) = 0.4 \times 0.7$$
$$= \underline{\underline{0.28}}.$$

(c)
$$P(300\ units) = P(good\ in\ one\ week\ only)$$
$$= P(good\ in\ 1st\ and\ bad\ in\ 2nd\ or\ bad\ in\ 1st\ and\ good\ in\ 2nd)$$
$$= P(G\ 1st) \times P(B\ 2nd/G\ 1st) + P(B\ 1st) \times P(G\ 2nd/B\ 1st)$$

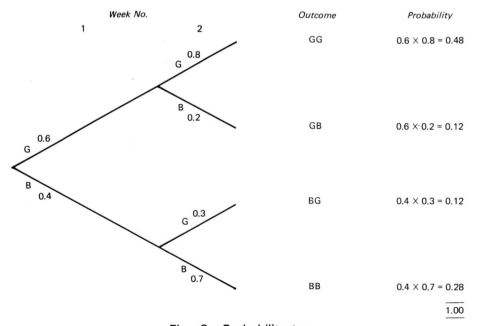

Fig. 3. *Probability tree.*

# 2 PROBABILITY

$$= 0.6 \times 0.2 + 0.4 \times 0.3$$
$$= 0.12 + 0.12$$
$$= \underline{\underline{0.24}}.$$

The sum of probabilities in (a), (b) and (c) is one, as we have considered every possible mutually exclusive event.

We could have analysed Example 8 by using a probability tree (Fig. 3).

*Notes.*
(a) *At each node the probabilities must add to one.*

(b) *The probability of an outcome can be obtained by applying the* AND *rule along the branches of the tree that lead to the outcomes.*

## 3.1 Conditional probability rule

The multiplication rule for dependent events was:

$$P(A \text{ and } B) = P(A) \times P(B/A)$$

or we can have

$$P(A \text{ and } B) = P(B) \times P(A/B).$$

If we divide both sides by $P(B)$ and interchange the left- and right-hand sides of our equation we get:

$$P(A/B) = \frac{P(A \text{ and } B)}{P(B)}$$

which is the formal definition of $P(A/B)$.

Let us examine the use of this formula in an example.

### Example 9

It is estimated that one-quarter of the drivers on the road between 11 p.m. and midnight have been drinking during the evening. If a driver had not been drinking, the probability that he will have an accident at that time of night is 0.004; if he has been drinking, the probability of an accident goes up to 0.02.

A policeman on duty sees an accident occur and jumps to the conclusion that the driver has been drinking. What is the probability that he is right?

SOLUTION
Let $D$ = drinking, $\overline{D}$ = not drinking, $\overline{A}$ = accident and $A$ = no accident.

Now
$$P(D) = 0.25$$
$$P(A/\overline{D}) = 0.004$$
$$P(A/D) = 0.02.$$

We require to know the value of $P(D/A)$.

Applying our conditional probability rule we get

$$P(D/A) = \frac{P(D \text{ and } A)}{P(A)}.$$

So we need to calculate both P(D and A) and P(A).

Now
$$P(D \text{ and } A) = P(D) \times P(A/D)$$
$$= 0.25 \times 0.02$$
$$= 0.005.$$

Also, P(A) can arise in two ways, either the driver has been drinking *and* has an accident or the driver has not been drinking *and* has an accident:

$$\therefore \quad P(A) = P(D) \times P(A/D) + P(\overline{D}) \times P(A/\overline{D})$$
$$= 0.25 \times 0.02 + 0.75 \times 0.004$$
$$= 0.005 + 0.003$$
$$= 0.008.$$

*Note:* $P(\overline{D}) = 1 - P(D) = 1 - 0.25 = 0.75.$

Therefore
$$P(D/A) = \frac{P(D \text{ and } A)}{P(A)}$$
$$= \frac{0.005}{0.008}$$
$$\therefore \quad P(D/A) = \underline{0.625}.$$

An alternative way of viewing the problem can be by use of the joint probability table, as follows.

## 4.0 JOINT PROBABILITY TABLE

|   | $A$ | $\overline{A}$ | Marginal probability |
|---|---|---|---|
| $D$ | P(D, A)<br>0.005 | P(D, $\overline{A}$)<br>0.245 | P(D)<br>0.250 |
| $\overline{D}$ | P($\overline{D}$, A)<br>0.003 | P($\overline{D}$, $\overline{A}$)<br>0.747 | P($\overline{D}$)<br>0.750 |
| Marginal probability | P(A)<br>0.008 | P($\overline{A}$)<br>0.992 | 1.000 |

# 2 PROBABILITY

$$P(D) \text{ was given as } 0.250$$
$$\therefore \quad P(\overline{D}) = 1 - 0.250 = 0.750.$$

Hence we have our marginal probabilities on the right-hand side of the table.

Now we know that

$$P(D \text{ and } A) = P(D) \times P(A/D)$$
$$= 0.25 \times 0.02$$
$$= 0.005.$$

Similarly
$$P(\overline{D} \text{ and } A) = 0.75 \times 0.004$$
$$= 0.003.$$

We can therefore fill in our first column under A and total the results. The rest of the table, which is not required for the rest of the question, can be filled in by using the marginal probabilities as row and column totals.

Hence
$$P(D/A) = \frac{P(D \text{ and } A)}{P(A)} = \frac{\text{Probability in row 1 column 1}}{\text{Probability of column total}}$$

$$= \frac{0.005}{0.008}$$

$$= \underline{\underline{0.625}}.$$

## 4.1 Bayes' Theorem

Let us reconsider the form of the conditional probability rule:

$$P(A/B) = \frac{P(A \text{ and } B)}{P(B)}.$$

Now we can write:

$$P(A \text{ and } B) = P(A) \times P(B/A)$$

and $P(B)$ can be split into its two parts containing the situation if A happens and if A does not happen.

$$P(B) = P(A \text{ and } B) + P(\overline{A} \text{ and } B)$$

then using the rule:

$$P(B) = P(A) \times P(B/A) + P(\overline{A}) \times P(B/\overline{A}).$$

This leads to a result called Bayes' theorem.

$$P(A/B) = \frac{P(A) \times P(B/A)}{P(A) \times P(B/A) + P(\overline{A}) \times P(B/\overline{A})}.$$

This formula allows us to calculate what is called a posterior probability, P(A/B), from the conditional probabilities P(B/A) and P(B/$\bar{A}$) and the prior probabilities P(A) and P($\bar{A}$).

## Example 10

A marketing manager is considering the introduction of a new product. The probability that sales of the new product exceed the break even point is estimated at 0.7. Before introducing the product on a large scale the product will be market-tested. Past market tests on similar products have produced the following probability estimates:

|                      | Actual sales         |                      |
| -------------------- | -------------------- | -------------------- |
| Result of test       | Above break even     | Below break even     |
| Above break even     | 0.8                  | 0.4                  |
| Below break even     | 0.2                  | 0.6                  |
|                      | 1.0                  | 1.0                  |

Calculate the probability that sales will be above the break even point given that the test predicts that sales will be below the break even point.

### SOLUTION

Let $A$ = actual sales above break even point
$B$ = test gives sales below break even point.

The required answer using Bayes' theorem is:

$$P(A/B) = \frac{P(A) \times P(B/A)}{P(A) \times P(B/A) + P(\bar{A}) \times P(B/\bar{A})}.$$

Now $\quad P(A) = 0.7 \quad \therefore \quad P(\bar{A}) = 0.3$

$P(B/A)$ = P(test below/Actual above)

$\quad = 0.2$

$P(B/\bar{A})$ = P(test below/Actual below)

$\quad = 0.6$

$$\therefore \quad P(A/B) = \frac{0.7 \times 0.2}{0.7 \times 0.2 + 0.3 \times 0.6}$$

$$= \frac{0.14}{0.14 + 0.18}$$

$$= \underline{\underline{0.4375}}.$$

# 2 PROBABILITY

An alternative approach using a joint probability table is:

|         | Actual |       |          |
| Test    | Above  | Below | Marginal |
| ------- | ------ | ----- | -------- |
| Above   | 0.56   | 0.12  | 0.68     |
| Below   | 0.14   | 0.18  | 0.32     |
| Marginal| 0.70   | 0.30  | 1.00     |

We know the marginal probabilities of actual-above and actual-below are 0.70 and 0.30. The joint probability of the test and the actual both being above $= 0.70 \times 0.80 = 0.56$.

Similarly, the joint probability of the test being above and the actual below $= 0.30 \times 0.40 = 0.12$.

The rest of the table can then be completed.

Therefore  P(actual sales above/test below)

$$= \text{row 2 column 1 entry over row 2 total}$$

$$= \frac{0.14}{0.32} = \underline{\underline{0.4375}}.$$

## 5.0 SUMMARY

The aim of this chapter has been to introduce you to the concept of probability and to some of the basic rules.

You should now be familiar with the following formulae and be able to apply them:

*Basic*

$$P(A) = \frac{\text{Number of times event A occurred}}{\text{Total number of events considered}}.$$

$\sum P(x) = 1.$

*Addition rule*

Mutually exclusive events:

$P(A \text{ or } B) = P(A) + P(B).$

Non-mutually exclusive events:

$P(A \text{ or } B) = P(A) + P(B) - P(A, B).$

*Multiplication rule*

Independent events:

$P(A \text{ and } B) = P(A) \times P(B).$

Dependent events

$P(A \text{ and } B) = P(A) \times P(B/A).$

*Condition probability*

$$P(A/B) = \frac{P(A \text{ and } B)}{P(B)}.$$

*Bayes' theorem*

$$P(A/B) = \frac{P(A) \times P(B/A)}{P(A) \times P(B/A) + P(\overline{A}) \times P(B/\overline{A})}.$$

# CHAPTER THREE
# Expected Value

## 1.0 EXPECTED VALUE CALCULATION

*Example 1*
A project has the following possible returns and associated probabilities:

| Possible return (£1,000) $x$ | Probability $P(x)$ |
|---|---|
| 20 | 0.3 |
| 40 | 0.5 |
| 50 | 0.2 |
|  | 1.0 |

Note that the sum of the probabilities equals one.
  This is a probability distribution.
  The expected value $E(x)$ is defined as:

$$E(x) = \sum xP(x)$$

To calculate the expected value we multiply each return $(x)$ by its associated probability $P(x)$ and add the results together:

$$\begin{array}{c} xP(x) \\ \hline 6 \\ 20 \\ 10 \\ \hline 36 \end{array} \quad \therefore \quad E(x) = 36.$$

The expected value is another name for the mean. It is the average return if the same project is repeated a large number of times.

For example if the project were repeated ten times then the outcomes would form the following frequency distribution:

| Returns $x$ | Frequency $f$ | $fx$ |
|---|---|---|
| 20 | 30 | 600 |
| 40 | 50 | 2,000 |
| 50 | 20 | 1,000 |
|  | 100 | 3,600 |

Then
$$\bar{x} = \frac{3,600}{100} = 36,$$

i.e.
$$\underline{\underline{E(x) = \bar{x}.}}$$

## 2.0 VARIANCE AND STANDARD DEVIATION

It is also possible to calculate the variance or standard deviation of a probability distribution. Now the variance of a frequency distribution is given as:

$$V(x) = \frac{\sum fx^2}{n} - \bar{x}^2$$

$$= \sum \left(\frac{f}{n}\right) x^2 - \bar{x}^2.$$

Now let
$$P(x) = \left(\frac{f}{n}\right).$$

Then
$$V(x) = \sum x^2 P(x) - \bar{x}^2.$$

Now
$$\bar{x} = E(x).$$

(Note: As we write $\sum xP(x)$ as $E(x)$, continuing the same notation we write $\sum x^2 P(x)$ as $E(x^2)$.)

$$\therefore \quad V(x) = E(x^2) - E^2(x)$$

| $x$ | $P(x)$ | $xP(x)$ | $x^2P(x)$ |
|---|---|---|---|
| 20 | 0.3 | 6 | 120 |
| 40 | 0.5 | 20 | 800 |
| 50 | 0.2 | 10 | 500 |
|  | 1.0 | 36 | 1,420 |

# 3 EXPECTED VALUE

As before,
$$E(x) = 36$$
$$\therefore V(x) = 1{,}420 - 36^2$$
$$= 1{,}420 - 1{,}296$$
$$= \underline{\underline{124}}.$$

or
$$\sigma = \sqrt{124}$$
$$= \underline{\underline{11.1}}.$$

## 3.0 PAYOFF TABLE

*Example 2*

An icecream van salesman has to decide at the beginning of each day how many "Super Blocks" to stock up with to enable him to meet the demand from his customers during the day. Each "Super Block" costs him £0.50 and he sells it for £1.20. If there are any unsold blocks at the end of the day he sells them off cheaply at 20p as he has no cold-store facilities. If he sells out of "Super Blocks" during the day and there is still a demand he has an arrangement with a local shop to purchase from them "Super Blocks" at £1. Analysis of past sales show that the demand for "Super Blocks" is as follows:

| Number | 0 | 1 | 2 | 3 | 4 |
|---|---|---|---|---|---|
| Profitability | 0.1 | 0.2 | 0.3 | 0.3 | 0.1 |

Draw up a payoff table and calculate the expected value for each possible decision. Advise the icecream van salesman on how many "Super Blocks" he should stock at the beginning of the day.

SOLUTION

We have to decide what decision alternatives the salesman should consider. From the analysis of past demand it is clear that he should only consider the decision alternative 0 to 4. We need to calculate the profit or "payoff" which results from each combination of decision alternatives and possible outcome.

There are basically three different situations:

(a) Demand = Supply.
(b) Demand > Supply.
(c) Demand < Supply.

Let us consider one example from each:

(a) Supply = 2, demand = 2.
Then Revenue = 2 × 1.20     =     £2.40
*Less:* Purchase cost = 2 × £0.50     =     1.00
Payoff     =     $\underline{\underline{1.40}}$.

(b) Supply = 2, demand = 3.
  Revenue = 3 × 1.20                   =   £3.60
  Less: Purchase cost = 2 × £0.50 = 1.00
                       1 ×  1.00 = 1.00  =   2.00
  Payoff                                =   1.60

(c) Supply = 2, demand = 1.
  Revenue = 1 × 1.20                   =   £1.20
          + 1 × 0.20                   =   0.20
                                            1.40
  Less: Purchase cost = 2 × 0.50       =   1.00
  Payoff                                =   0.40

Continuing in the same way we can generate the following payoff table:

|  |  | *Possible outcome* | | | | |
|---|---|---|---|---|---|---|
|  |  | 0 | 1 | 2 | 3 | 4 |
| Decision | 0 | 0 | 0.20 | 0.40 | 0.60 | 0.80 |
| alternative | 1 | − 0.30 | 0.70 | 0.90 | 1.10 | 1.30 |
|  | 2 | − 0.60 | 0.40 | 1.40 | 1.60 | 1.80 |
|  | 3 | − 0.90 | 0.10 | 1.10 | 2.10 | 2.30 |
|  | 4 | − 1.20 | − 0.20 | 0.80 | 1.80 | 2.80 |

A close inspection of the table reveals a number of patterns we can make use of when calculating similar tables. As the value at which demand equals supply occurs along the main diagonal the patterns all originate from the diagonal. One pattern is that the figures in the columns all *decrease* by 0.30 as we come down the column away from the diagonal. Another pattern occurs in the rows. As we move from left to right away from the main diagonal the values increase by £0.20.

To continue with the question, we now have to calculate the expected value for each decision alternative, i.e. calculate $\sum x \mathrm{P}(x)$ where the payoffs in the rows are the $x$-values. The expected value for the first row is:

$$0 \times 0.1 + 0.20 \times 0.2 + 0.40 \times 0.3 + 0.60 \times 0.3 + 0.80 \times 0.1 = £0.42.$$

Carrying out similar calculations for the remaining rows and putting all the information into our payoff table we get:

|  |  | *Possible outcome* | | | | | |
|---|---|---|---|---|---|---|---|
|  |  | 0 | 1 | 2 | 3 | 4 | *EV* |
| Decision | 0 | 0 | 0.20 | 0.40 | 0.60 | 0.80 | 0.42 |
| alternative | 1 | − 0.30 | 0.70 | 0.90 | 1.10 | 1.30 | 0.84 |
|  | 2 | − 0.60 | 0.40 | 1.40 | 1.60 | 1.80 | 1.10 |
|  | 3 | − 0.90 | 0.10 | 1.10 | 2.10 | 2.30 | 1.12 |
|  | 4 | − 1.20 | − 0.20 | 0.80 | 1.80 | 2.80 | 0.90 |
| Probability |  | 0.1 | 0.2 | 0.3 | 0.3 | 0.1 |  |

# 3 EXPECTED VALUE

The maximum expected value is £1.12 when $x = 3$, i.e. stocking three "Super Blocks" maximises the expected payoff. Therefore we recommend that the van salesman should stock three "Super blocks" each day.

## 4.0 OPPORTUNITY LOSS TABLE

Example 2 can be analysed by looking at opportunity loss rather than payoff and then calculating the minimum opportunity loss. If we look at the third column (when the possible outcome is 2) the maximum value in that column is 1.40. When the outcome is 2 we would obviously be pleased if our decision had been 2 as we would have made the most of our opportunity and got the greatest payoff for an outcome of 2. If, however, we had made a decision of 1 our payoff would have only been 0.90, an opportunity loss of $1.40 - 0.90 = 0.50$. Continuing with this concept we can calculate an opportunity loss table.

In practice as we have the payoff table we can obtain the oportunity loss table by in each column subtracting each entry in the column from the maximum value in the column:

Opportunity loss table:

|  |  | \multicolumn{5}{c}{Possible outcome} |  |
|---|---|---|---|---|---|---|---|
|  |  | 0 | 1 | 2 | 3 | 4 | EV |
| Decision | 0 | 0 | 0.50 | 1.00 | 1.50 | 2.00 | 1.05 |
| alternative | 1 | 0.30 | 0 | 0.50 | 1.00 | 1.50 | 0.63 |
|  | 2 | 0.60 | 0.30 | 0 | 0.50 | 1.00 | 0.37 |
|  | 3 | 0.90 | 0.60 | 0.30 | 0 | 0.50 | 0.35 |
|  | 4 | 1.20 | 0.90 | 0.60 | 0.30 | 0 | 0.57 |
| Probability |  | 0.1 | 0.2 | 0.3 | 0.3 | 0.1 |  |

We now calculate the expected opportunity loss in a similar manner to calculating the expected payoff. The minimum expected opportunity loss is £0.35 when $x = 3$. We make the same recommendation as before.

## 5.0 EXPECTED VALUE UNDER PERFECT INFORMATION

If we know in advance what outcome is going to occur even though we cannot control the situation we can then make the decisions that give us the highest payoff.

These highest payoffs are:

$$0 \quad 0.7 \quad 1.40 \quad 2.10 \quad 2.80.$$

If we calculate the expected value of these we get

$$0 \times 0.1 + 0.7 \times 0.2 + 1.40 \times 0.3 + 2.10 \times 0.3 + 2.8 \times 0.1 = £1.47.$$

This is the expected value of perfect information. The difference between the two expected payoffs is: £1.47 − 1.12 = £0.35, called the value of perfect information, which is equal to the expected opportunity loss. The value of perfect information tells us the maximum we should be prepared to pay for additional information as obtained, say, from market research.

## 6.0 DECISION TREE

*Example 3*

(a) Barsands Bank Ltd. has been approached by a customer for a loan of £10,000 for a year. The bank currently charges interest at 16 per cent per annum. If the loan is not granted then the £10,000 is invested in the money market paying interest of 8 per cent per annum. From past records it is estimated that 5 per cent of customers default on the loans, i.e. no interest or capital is paid. Draw a decision tree for this problem and advise Barsands Bank Ltd. whether they should grant the loan. (Ignore tax, and the time value of money.)

SOLUTION
There are three steps in constructing a decision tree:

(i) drawing the structure;
(ii) determining and then adding the cash flows to the tree;
(iii) determining the probabilities and then adding them to the tree.

The first step in drawing the decision tree is to draw a decision box and to put in a branch of the tree for each decision alternative. In our case this is just two branches: loan, and money market.

Then at the end of each branch draw in a node and from each node draw in a branch for each possible outcome. In our example there are two possible outcomes after a loan has been made: either the loan is repaid or the customer defaults.

After the money market branch there is only one outcome: capital and interest paid (we are assuming that there is no risk of losing any money on this option).

Our decision tree then becomes as shown in Fig.4.

The cash flows (£000s) have been added to the tree at the points where they occur.

After each node (not decision box) we need to allocate the probabilities. Now P(default) = 0.05, therefore P(repay) = 0.95. The P(return) = 1 as we are assuming that it is certain.

Now working backward through the network we calculate the expected value for each node (*see* value above each node). At the decision box we adjust each expected value by any cash flow on its path leaving us with 1.02 and 0.80 at D1.

We need to maximise the overall expected value; therefore at a decision box we select that pathway which has the highest expected value, i.e. 1.02, the

# 3 EXPECTED VALUE

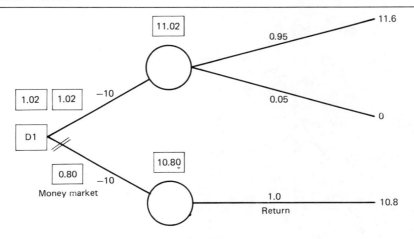

Fig. 4. *Decision tree (a)*.

loan decision. This is indicated on our tree by "pruning" the money market decision branch shown as //.

Our advice to Barsands Bank is to loan the £10,000. The expected return is £1,020.

*Example 3 continued*

(b) The bank is now *considering* carrying out a credit check on each customer before making its loan decision. You have to advise the bank:

(i) whether it should use a credit agency, and

(ii) if it does whether it should accept the credit agency recommendation or not.

To test the effectiveness of the credit check the bank has done a credit check on 100 customers and given all of them a loan. The results are as follows:

| Credit agency recommendation | Actual outcome | |
|---|---|---|
| | Repaid | Defaulted |
| Loan | 79 | 1 |
| Money market | 16 | 4 |

Each credit check cost the bank £100.

SOLUTION
*See* Fig. 5.

The first two steps of determining the structure of the tree and adding the cash flows are carried out in a manner similar to that in (a).

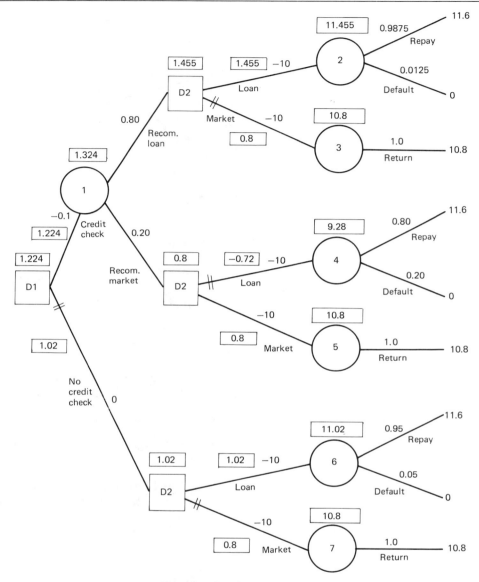

Fig. 5. *Decision tree (b)*.

We now have to calculate six new probabilities. Using the table based on 100 past customers we get:

$$P(\text{Recommend loan}) = \frac{79+1}{100} = 0.80$$

$$\therefore \quad P(\text{Recommend money market}) = \frac{16+4}{100} = \underline{0.20}$$

$$\underline{1.00}$$

# 3 EXPECTED VALUE

$$P(\text{Repay/recommend loan}) = \frac{79}{80} \qquad = 0.9875$$

$$P(\text{Default/recommend loan}) = \frac{1}{80} \qquad = \underline{0.0125}$$
$$\underline{1.0000}$$

$$P(\text{Repay/recommend money market}) = \frac{16}{20} \qquad = 0.8$$

$$P(\text{Default/recommend money market}) = \frac{4}{20} \qquad = \underline{0.2}$$
$$\underline{1.0}$$

These probabilities are added to the tree.

We now calculate the expected values as far as the decision boxes D2s. To calculate the expected value at node 1 we treat the maximum expected values of 1.455 and 0.8 at the D2 nodes as if they were cash flows and calculate their expected value,

i.e. $\qquad 0.80 \times 1.455 + 0.20 \times 0.8 = 1.324.$

Finally, at D1 we need to compare the expected values 1.224 and 1.02, the highest being 1.224. We therefore prune the "no credit check" option.

The recommendation is: Carry out the credit check and follow the loan recommendation. This results in an expected value of £1,224.

## 7.0 SUMMARY

This chapter has covered the concept of expected value of a probability distribution and applied the method to payoff tables, opportunity loss tables and decision trees.

**Definitions used:**

$$E(x) = \sum x P(x);$$
$$V(x) = E(x^2) - E^2(x).$$

# CHAPTER FOUR
# Probability Distributions

Before we can look at probability distributions it is necessary to understand permutations and combinations.

## 1.0 PERMUTATIONS

A permutation of $r$ objects from $n$ objects is the number of ways of selecting $r$ objects from $n$ objects *taking order* into account. This is denoted by $^nP_r$.

*Example 1*
In how many ways can the first two positions in a race be filled if there are four competitors?

SOLUTION
Let the competitors be A, B, C, and D.
Then the different permutations are:

$$\begin{array}{cccc} AB & BA & CA & DA \\ AC & BC & CB & DB \\ AD & BD & CD & DC \end{array}$$

Hence $^4P_2 = 12$.

This can be proved by the box method. Assume we have two boxes to fill—one for the first position and one for the second. The first box can be filled in four ways (A, B, C and D), leaving three items over. The second box can now only be filled in three ways. As any item in the first box can be associated with any item in the second box $^4P_2 = 4 \times 3 = 12$.

In general
$$^nP_r = \frac{n!}{(n-r)!}$$

# 4 PROBABILITY DISTRIBUTIONS

where $n! = n \times (n-1) \times (n-2) \ldots \times 2 \times 1$.

e.g.
$$^5P_3 = \frac{5!}{2!} = \frac{5 \times 4 \times 3 \times 2 \times 1}{2 \times 1} = 60,$$

$$^5P_5 = \frac{5!}{0!} = 5 \times 4 \times 3 \times 2 \times 1 = 120.$$

*Note: $0! = 1$.*

## 2.0 COMBINATIONS

A combination of $r$ objects from $n$ objects is the number of ways of selecting $r$ objects from $n$ objects *not taking order* into account. This is denoted by

$$^nC_r \text{ or } \binom{n}{r}.$$

## Example 2

In how many ways can a committee of two people be selected from a group of four people?

SOLUTION

This is a similar problem to Example 1 except that order is not taken into account. Therefore terms such as AB and BA are the same.

The different combinations are:

$$\begin{array}{ccc} AB & BC & CD \\ AC & BD & \\ AD & & \end{array}$$

Hence $^4C_2 = \underline{\underline{6}}$.

In general
$$^nC_r = \frac{n!}{(n-r)!r!},$$

e.g.
$$^5C_3 = \frac{5 \times 4 \times 3 \times 2 \times 1}{2 \times 1 \times 3 \times 2 \times 1} = 10.$$

Note:
$$^5C_2 = \frac{5 \times 4 \times 3 \times 2 \times 1}{3 \times 2 \times 1 \times 2 \times 1} = 10,$$

or in general
$$^nC_r = {^nC_{n-r}}.$$

*This result sometimes allows us to use a short cut in the calculation, e.g.*

$$^{100}C_{99} = {^{100}C_1} = 100.$$

## 3.0 BINOMIAL DISTRIBUTION

A binomial situation occurs when an event has only two possible outcomes, and that event is repeated a number of times. The probabilities of the two events must be constant.

Examples of binomial events are: coin tossing, winning or losing a race, gaining a contract or losing it, and being dead or alive.

The formula for the binomial distribution is:

$$P(r) = {}^nC_r p^r (1-p)^{n-r},$$

where $p$ is the probability the event will occur,
  $1-p$ is the probability the event will not occur,
  $n$ is the total number of events, and
  $r$ is number of events that is required.

### Example 3

The probability that a salesman will meet his daily sales target is 0.8.

(a) What is the probability that in a 5-day working week he will meet his sales target exactly on 3 days?

(b) What is the probability that he will meet his target on less than 2 days in a week?

(c) What is the probability that he will meet his target on 2 or more days?

**SOLUTION**

(a) $\quad n = 5,\; p = 0.8,\; 1-p = 0.2.$

$r = 3,$

$\therefore P(3) = {}^5C_3 \times (0.8)^3 \times (0.2)^2$

$= 10 \times 0.512 \times 0.04;$

$= \underline{\underline{0.2048}}.$

(b) $\quad P(\text{less than 2 days}) = P(0) + P(1).$

Now $P(0) = {}^5C_0 \times (0.8)^0 \times (0.2)^5$

$= 1 \times 1 \times 0.00032$

$= 0.00032.$

$P(1) = {}^5C_1 \times (0.8)^1 \times (0.2)^4$

$= 5 \times 0.8 \times 0.0016$

$= 0.0064.$

$\therefore P(\text{less than 2 days}) = 0.00032 + 0.0064;$

$= \underline{\underline{0.00672}}.$

(c)              P(2 or more days) = 1 − P(less than 2 days)

$$= 1 - 0.00672$$
$$= 0.99328$$
$$= \underline{\underline{0.993}}.$$

## 4.0 MEAN AND STANDARD DEVIATION OF THE BINOMIAL

For Example 3 let us calculate all the probabilities and then determine the mean and the standard deviation.

The probabilities are:

| $x$ | P($x$) | $x$P($x$) | $x^2$P($x$) |
|---|---|---|---|
| 0 | 0.00032 | 0 | 0 |
| 1 | 0.00640 | 0.0064 | 0.0064 |
| 2 | 0.05120 | 0.1024 | 0.2048 |
| 3 | 0.20480 | 0.6144 | 1.8432 |
| 4 | 0.40960 | 1.6384 | 6.5536 |
| 5 | 0.32768 | 1.6384 | 8,1920 |
|   | 1.00000 | 4,0000 | 16,800 |

$$\therefore \quad \text{Mean} = E(x) = \sum x P(x) = 4.$$
$$\text{Variance} = E(x^2) - E^2(x)$$
$$= \sum x^2 P(x) - [\sum x P(x)]^2$$
$$= 16.8 - 16$$
$$= 0.8.$$
$$\therefore \quad \sigma = \sqrt{0.8}$$
$$= \underline{\underline{0.894}}.$$

Instead of all these calculations we can use the following results for the binomial:

$$\mu = np = 5 \times 0.8 = 4,$$
$$\sigma = \sqrt{npq} = \sqrt{5 \times 0.8 \times 0.2} = \sqrt{0.8} = 0.894,$$

where              $q = 1 - p$.

## 5.0 POISSON DISTRIBUTION

The Poisson distribution is concerned with rare events and is given by the formula

$$P(r) = \frac{e^{-m} m^r}{r!} \qquad (r = 0, 1, 2, \ldots)$$

where $m$ = mean
$e = 2.718\ldots$
$r$ = number of items required.

To calculate a Poisson probability all you need to know is the mean.

### Example 4
The demand for a special component follows a Poisson distribution with an average demand of 2 a day.

(a) What is the probability that exactly 3 components will be demanded tomorrow?

(b) What is the probability that more than 4 components will be required tomorrow?

**SOLUTION**

(a) $\qquad m = 2, r = 3.$

$$P(3) = \frac{(2.718)^{-2} \times 2^3}{3!} = 0.1804.$$

*Note: A power of $-2$ just means square the term in the bracket and then take the reciprocal.*

(b) $\qquad$ P(more than 4) = $1 - P(0) - P(1) - P(2) - P(3) - P(4)$.

We need to calculate all the probabilities up to $r = 4$:

$$P(0) = \frac{(2.718)^{-2} \times 2^0}{0!} = (2.718)^{-2} \qquad = 0.1353$$

$$P(1) = \frac{(2.718)^{-2} \times 2^1}{1!} = (2.718)^{-2} \times 2 \qquad = 0.2707$$

$$P(2) = \frac{(2.718)^{-2} \times 2^2}{2!} = (2.718)^{-2} \times 2 \qquad = 0.2707$$

$$P(3) = \frac{(2.718)^{-2} \times 2^3}{3!} = (2.718)^{-2} \times 4/3 \quad = 0.1804$$

$$P(4) = \frac{(2.718)^{-2} \times 2^4}{4!} = (2.718)^{-2} \times 2/3 \quad = \underline{0.0902}$$

$$\underline{\underline{0.9473}}$$

$\therefore$ P(more than 4) = $1 - 0.9473$
$$= \underline{\underline{0.0527}}.$$

# 4 PROBABILITY DISTRIBUTIONS

## *Mean and standard deviation of the Poisson distribution*

The mean of the Poisson distribution is $m$, which is equal to the variance. Hence:

$$\text{mean} = m, \quad \text{standard deviation} = \sqrt{m}.$$

## 6.0 NORMAL DISTRIBUTION

The normal distribution, unlike the binomial and Poisson distributions, is a continuous distribution. It is important for two reasons: (a) a number of naturally occurring data fit a normal distribution and (b) it is the basis of large-sample theory.

The normal distribution has a bell-shaped curve symmetrical about the mean $\mu$ (Fig. 6). The probabilities are determined from the area under the curve. The total area under the curve is one.

Although there is a formula for the probability function $p$, represented by the shaded area in Fig. 6, it is complicated, so we will use a normal distribution table (Table 1).

To use the table we measure along the $x$-axis from the mean $\mu$ in standard deviations $\sigma$; the result is called the $Z$-statistic:

i.e.
$$Z = \frac{x - \mu}{\sigma}.$$

The table gives the value of $p$ corresponding to any given $Z$ (if $Z$ is minus, ignore sign).

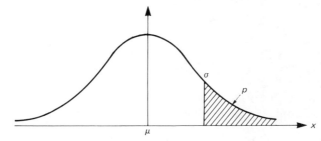

Fig. 6. *Normal distribution curve.*

Table 1. Normal distribution table.

| Z | 0.0 | 0.1 | 0.2 | 0.3 | 0.4 | 0.5 | 0.6 | 0.7 | 0.8 | 0.9 |
|---|---|---|---|---|---|---|---|---|---|---|
| p | 0.500 | 0.460 | 0.421 | 0.382 | 0.345 | 0.308 | 0.274 | 0.242 | 0.212 | 0.184 |
| Z | 1.0 | 1.1 | 1.2 | 1.3 | 1.4 | 1.5 | 1.6 | 1.7 | 1.8 | 1.9 |
| p | 0.159 | 0.136 | 0.115 | 0.097 | 0.081 | 0.067 | 0.055 | 0.045 | 0.036 | 0.029 |
| Z | 2.0 | 2.1 | 2.2 | 2.3 | 2.4 | 2.5 | 2.6 | 2.7 | 2.8 | 2.9 |
| p | 0.023 | 0.018 | 0.014 | 0.011 | 0.008 | 0.006 | 0.005 | 0.003 | 0.003 | 0.002 |
| Z | 3.0 | 3.1 | 3.2 | 3.3 | 3.4 | | | | | |
| p | 0.0013 | 0.0010 | 0.0007 | 0.0005 | 0.0003 | | | | | |

## Example 4

The average weekly sales of Freed Computers in the UK are 2,000 with a standard deviation of 80.

(a) Determine the probabilities that sales next week will
   (i)  be at least 2,160;
   (ii) not exceed 1,800;
   (iii) lie between 1,800 and 2,160.

(b) A new weekly sales target is to be set which currently represents the top 2 per cent of sales. What should the new sales target be?

SOLUTION

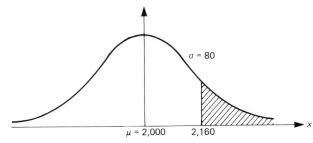

Fig. 7. *Normal distribution curve—computer sales (i).*

(a) (i) Referring to Fig. 7:

$$Z = \frac{2{,}160 - 2{,}000}{80} = 2.0.$$

Look up $Z = 2.0$ in the normal distribution table (Table 1). From this, the probability $p$ in the shaded area = 0.023.

∴ P(sales ≥ 2,160) = 0.023.

(ii) Referring to Fig. 8:

$$Z = \frac{1{,}800 - 2{,}000}{80} = -2.5.$$

As the curve is symmetrical, look up $Z = +2.5$ in Table 1.

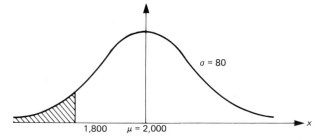

Fig. 8. *Normal distribution curve—computer sales (ii).*

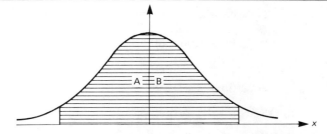

Fig. 9. *Normal distribution curve — computer sales (iii).*

Shaded area = 0.006.

∴ P(sales ⩽ 1,800) = 0.006.

(iii) Now $Z_i = 2.0$ and $Z_{ii} = -2.5$, as calculated in (i) and (ii).

Therefore, referring to Fig. 9: area $(A + B)$ can be calculated as

1 − [area in the two shaded areas ("tails") in Figs. 7 and 8, as calculated in (i) and (ii)]
= 1 − 0.023 − 0.006
= 0.971.

(b) This is the problem in reverse (Fig. 10). We need to calculate the $x$-value having been given the probability or shaded area.

Probability $p = 0.02$.

We obtain $Z$ from Table 1 by interpolation:

*Extract from Table 1*

$$\begin{bmatrix} & Z & p & \\ & 2.00 & 0.023 & \\ 0.1 & ? & 0.020 & \Bigg] 3 \\ & 2.10 & 0.018 & \end{bmatrix} 5$$

$$? = 2.00 + \frac{3}{5} \times 0.1$$
$$= 2.06.$$
$$\therefore Z = 2.06.$$

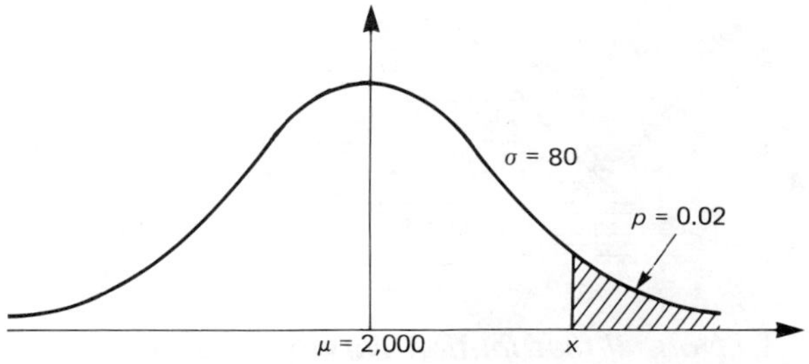

Fig. 10. *Normal distribution curve — computer sales target.*

This means that $x$ is 2.06 standard deviations above the mean.

$$\therefore \quad x = 2{,}000 + 2.06 \times 80$$
$$= 2{,}164.8$$
$$= 2{,}165.$$

$\therefore$ Weekly sales target should be set to <u>2,165</u>.

## 7.0 TWO AND THREE STANDARD DEVIATION LIMITS

A useful fact to know about the normal distribution without having to look it up in the tables every time is that 95 per cent of the area under the normal curve falls within the range: Mean $\pm 1.96$ standard deviations, i.e.

$$\mu \pm 1.96\sigma, \quad \text{(Fig. 11)},$$

or, as it is sometimes approximated,

$$\mu \pm 2\sigma.$$

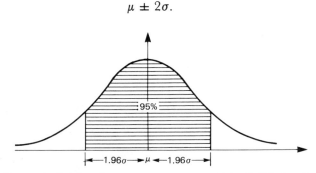

Fig. 11. *Normal distribution curve—area within $1.96\sigma\, (\approx 2\sigma)$ limits.*

Another well-used range is

$$\mu \pm 3\sigma:$$

99.8 per cent of the normal distribution falls within this range (Fig. 12).

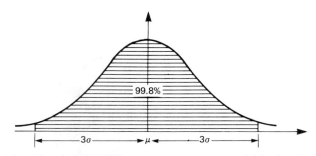

Fig. 12. *Normal distribution curve—area within $3\sigma$ limits.*

## 7.1 Normal approximation to the binomial

If in a binomial situation $n$ is large then it can become rather tedious to calculate a whole series of binomial terms which are themselves quite small.

If $0.1 \leqslant p \leqslant 0.9$ and $np > 5$, then by putting $\mu = np$ and $\sigma = \sqrt{np(1-p)}$ we can use the normal distribution as an approximation to the binomial.

### Example 5

The probability that it will rain on a day in June in Manchester is 0.2. Assuming that each day is a separate independent event, calculate the probability that Manchester will have 3 or less days of rain next June (June has 30 days).

SOLUTION
This is a binomial situation as there are only two outcomes, rain or no rain.

$$p = 0.2, \; n = 30.$$

$$P(3 \text{ or less}) = P(3) + P(2) + P(1) + P(0)$$

$$\begin{aligned}
P(0) &= {}^{30}C_0 (0.2)^0 (0.8)^{30} &&= 0.00124 \\
P(1) &= {}^{30}C_1 (0.2)^1 (0.8)^{29} &&= 0.00928 \\
P(2) &= {}^{30}C_2 (0.2)^2 (0.8)^{28} &&= 0.03366 \\
P(3) &= {}^{30}C_3 (0.2)^3 (0.8)^{27} &&= \underline{0.07853} \\
\therefore \quad P(3 \text{ or less}) & &&= \underline{0.12271}
\end{aligned}$$

But this is difficult without a good calculator. An alternative is to use the normal approximation, which is available since $p > 0.1$ and $np \; (= 0.2 \times 30 = 6) > 5$.

Now, $\mu = np = 6$, $\sigma = \sqrt{30 \times 0.2 \times 0.8} = 2.191$.

As the binomial is a discrete distribution and the normal is continuous, we need to apply the continuity correction, as explained in **8.0**.

## 8.0 CONTINUITY CORRECTION

In Fig. 13 the shaded area we require needs to include the "3" histogram centred on 3. The upper class limit of this block is 3.5, midway between 3 and 4. Therefore the equivalent normal area uses $x$ up to 3.5, i.e. $x = 3.5$.

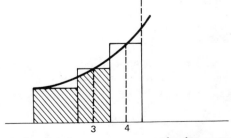

Fig. 13. *Normal distribution curve—continuity correction histogram.*

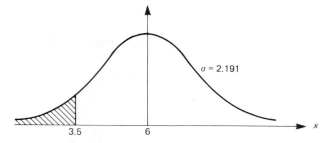

Fig. 14. *Normal distribution curve—continuity correction.*

∴ Referring to Fig. 14: $Z = \dfrac{3.5 - 6}{2.191} = -1.14$.

From normal tables,

$$0.10 \begin{bmatrix} & Z & P \\ 0.04 \begin{bmatrix} 1.10 & 0.136 \\ 1.14 & ? \end{bmatrix} & & \\ & 1.20 & 0.115 \end{bmatrix} 21$$

$$? = 0.136 - \frac{4}{10} \times 0.021$$

$$= 0.128$$

∴ $P(x \leqslant 3.5) = \underline{\underline{0.128}}$.

This represents an error of about 4 per cent over the exact solution calculated earlier. A larger sample size and a *p*-value closer to 0.5 would have made the error much smaller.

## 9.0 NORMAL APPROXIMATION TO THE POISSON

For values of *m* greater than 30 we may use the normal approximation where $\mu = m$ and $\sigma = \sqrt{m}$.

### Example 6

In Example 4 the daily demand for a special component was on average 2. What is the probability that the yearly demand (250 working days) exceeds the current stock level of 540? (You may assume that the yearly demand is still a Poisson distribution.)

$$m = 2 \times 250 = 500,$$
$$\therefore \mu = 500, \ \sigma = \sqrt{500} = 22.36.$$

# 4 PROBABILITY DISTRIBUTIONS

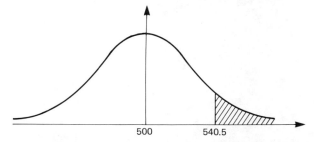

Fig. 15. *Normal distribution curve—demand for a special component.*

Now, $x = 540.5$ (Fig. 15; remember the continuity correction).

$$\therefore Z = \frac{540.5 - 500}{22.36} = 1.81.$$

From tables, probability = $\underline{\underline{0.035}}$.

## 10.0 SUMMARY

The aim of this chapter has been to cover the probability distributions—binomial, Poisson and normal.

The formulae covered were:

*Permutation*
$$^nP_r = \frac{n!}{(n-r)!}.$$

*Combination*
$$^nC_r = \frac{n!}{(n-r)!r!}.$$

*Binomial*
$$P(r) = {^nC_r}p^r(1-p)^{n-r}.$$

*Poisson*
$$P(r) = \frac{e^{-m} \cdot m^r}{r!}.$$

$$\mu = m. \quad \sigma = \sqrt{m}. \quad e = 2.718.$$

*Normal*
$$Z = \frac{x - \mu}{\sigma}.$$

95 per cent limits: $\mu \pm 1.96\sigma$.

99.8 per cent limits: $\mu \pm 3\sigma$.

# CHAPTER FIVE
# Large-sample Theory—Estimation

## 1.0 INTRODUCTION

Our work in statistics so far has been to a great extent on descriptive statistics. In this chapter we begin to study the more important area of inference statistics. We will be concerned with inferring from statistics of a sample information about the larger group the sample is drawn from—the population.

## 2.0 SAMPLE—POPULATION

It is necessary in every problem to define as clearly as possible the population. If for example we are concerned with the qualifications of accountants then we need to define what we mean by accountants before we can define our population. Do we mean only qualified accountants? Which professional qualifications are we including? Do we include only those practising accountancy at the present time? What about retired accountants—do we include them?

There are a host of questions to be answered in practice but eventually we will be able to define our population. A sample is, then, any group selected from our population: theoretically it could range from a sample of size one to a sample which includes the whole population. In this chapter we are concerned with a sample of thirty items or more.

## 3.0 SELECTION OF SAMPLE

There are numerous ways of selecting a sample, depending upon the nature of the data, how quickly the information is required and the cost of collection. Large-sample

# 5 LARGE-SAMPLE THEORY—ESTIMATION

theory assumes that the sample is a random sample. This means that each item in the population has an equal chance of being selected.

## 4.0 NOTATION

We need to distinguish between the statistics of the sample and statistics of the population. In general we use Roman letters for the sample and Greek letters for the population:

$\bar{x}$ = sample mean;  $\qquad\qquad$ $\mu$ = population mean;
$s$ = sample standard deviation;  $\qquad$ $\sigma$ = population standard deviation.

If we don't know a value and have to estimate it, say we estimate that the population mean is one hundred, then we write:

$$\hat{\mu} = 100.$$

This little hat on the $\mu$ indicates it has been estimated.

## 5.0 ESTIMATORS

When we estimate we need an *unbiased* estimator. Mathematically this means that the expected value of the estimator is equal to the statistic being estimated. For example when we estimate a population mean $\mu$ we can use the sample mean $\bar{x}$, as:

$$E(\bar{x}) = \mu.$$

In non-mathematical terms, we want an estimator which as a value is just as likely to be above the true value as below.

We can use the sample mean $\bar{x}$ to estimate the population mean $\mu$;

i.e. $\qquad\qquad\qquad\qquad \hat{\mu} = \bar{x}.$

However, the sample standard deviation $s$ is a biased estimator of the population standard deviation $\sigma$.

$$s \text{ consistently underestimates } \sigma.$$

In fact it can be shown that:

$$E(s^2) = \frac{n-1}{n}\sigma^2$$

$$\therefore \ E\left(\frac{n}{n-1}s^2\right) = \sigma^2,$$

or

$$E\left(s\sqrt{\frac{n}{n-1}}\right) = \sigma.$$

Therefore we can estimate $\sigma$ using $s\sqrt{\dfrac{n}{n-1}}$,

i.e.
$$\hat{\sigma} = s\sqrt{\dfrac{n}{n-1}} \quad \text{or} \quad \hat{\sigma} = \sqrt{\dfrac{\sum x^2 - (\sum x)^2/n}{n-1}}.$$

The term $\sqrt{\dfrac{n}{n-1}}$ is known as Bessel's correction factor.

*Note: If n is very large, say n = 500, then Bessel's correction factor equals 1.001, which will be swallowed up in any rounding error. In general it is not essential to correct s when estimating $\sigma$ in the case of large samples ($n \geqslant 30$) but it is good practice to do so.*

## 6.0 SAMPLING DISTRIBUTION OF THE MEAN

We said in the introduction to this chapter that we are interested in finding information about the population. The most useful and widely used summary statistic is the mean. Thus our basic aim is to estimate the population mean from the sample mean. It cannot be over-emphasised that whatever figure we arrive at it will be an estimate. For example, if we take a sample of size 50 and its mean $\bar{x}$ is 59 cm then this is our best estimate for the population mean $\mu$. However, if we had taken another sample still of size 50 we might have got a mean $\bar{x}$ of 61 cm. Which is the true mean? They cannot both be right. In fact they are probably both wrong, as we are not claiming that we can estimate the true mean exactly. Both of them, 59 and 61, should however be close to the true mean.

In our example we have only considered two means, yet there are a large number of different samples we can take, all of which could have been selected by random sampling. Consider the case where the population consists of 2,000 items (a relatively small number); then the number of samples of size 50 we can select is $^{2,000}C_{50}$, a value well over a million.

If we consider the means of all possible samples of size $n$ that can be selected then these means will vary and will form a distribution. This is known as the sampling distribution of the mean. To be able to determine how accurate our sample mean is as an estimate of the population mean we need to investigate the possible range of values of the sample means.

Consider throwing a single die. The values that are likely to occur vary between 1 and 6 with a mean value of 3.5 and standard deviation 1.7. (You can check this by calculating the mean and standard deviation of the numbers 1 to 6.) If a six occurred you would not be very surprised, in fact some games depend upon a 6 occurring to start the game. Now, if we throw 100 dice and calculate their mean value it is unlikely to average 6. To achieve an average of 6 all the 100 dice would have to be 6's. The probability of this occurring has 77 zeros after the decimal point before a 1 appears! A similar argument follows about the other extreme value, a 1. In fact with 100 dice the 6's tend to average out with the 1's, the 5's with the 2's etc. In practice you are unlikely to get an average on the dice outside the range 3 to 4. So we see when we move from a population (values of single items) to the sampling distribution (values of the means) the range is reduced. Consequently, the standard deviation of the sampling distribution will be reduced. The larger the sample size the smaller the standard deviation. The standard deviation of the sampling distribution is important; it is given a special name—the standard error.

## 7.0 CENTRAL-LIMIT THEOREM

One of the most important results in statistics, as it forms the basis of all our sampling theory, is the central-limit theorem. It provides us with information about the sampling distribution.

Given a population with mean $\mu$ and standard deviation $\sigma$ (which is reasonably symmetrical) and taking samples of size $n$ from that population, then for $n \geqslant 30$:

(a) the sampling distribution of the means is a normal distribution;

(b) the mean of the sampling distribution is equal to the mean of the population;

   i.e. $\mu_{\bar{x}} = \mu$

(c) the standard error of the means is equal to the population standard deviation divided by the square root of the sample size:

   i.e. $\mathrm{SE}_{\bar{x}} = \dfrac{\sigma}{\sqrt{n}}$ (Fig. 16).

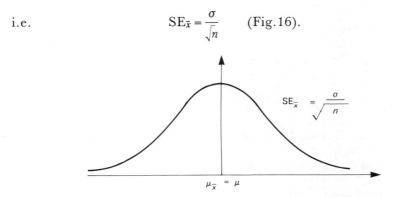

Fig. 16. *Central-limit theorem: $\mu_x$ and* $\mathrm{SE}_x$.

### 7.1 Confidence Interval

Let us use the central-limit theorem to help us estimate a population mean and give an indication of its accuracy.

*Example 1*

The average amount outstanding on a sample of 100 credit card accounts of Barsands Bank is £232 with a standard deviation of £52.

(a) Obtain a point estimate of the average amount of all Barsands credit card accounts.

(b) Estimate a 95 per cent confidence interval for the mean amount.

(c) Estimate a 95 per cent confidence interval for the total amount outstanding on all 50,000 accounts.

**SOLUTION**

(a) The best estimate of the population mean is the sample mean.

$$\therefore \hat{\mu} = \bar{x} = £232.$$

Point estimate is £232.

(b) Here we need to find the range given by the middle 95 per cent of the sampling distribution. 95 per cent of all sample means should fall within this range.

Now $\mu_{\bar{x}} = \mu$ from the central-limit theorem; but we have estimated $\mu$ to be 232,

$$\therefore \mu_{\bar{x}} = 232.$$

Now 
$$SE_{\bar{x}} = \frac{\sigma}{\sqrt{n}} = \frac{52}{\sqrt{100}}$$

$$= 5.2. \quad \text{(Fig. 17)}.$$

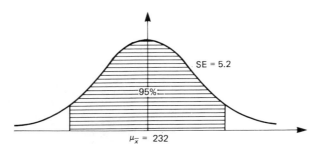

Fig. 17. *Central-limit theorem—confidence interval.*

Now $Z = 1.96$,

$$\therefore \text{95 per cent confidence interval} = 232 \pm 1.96 \times 5.2$$

$$= £232 \pm 10.19.$$

This means we are 95 per cent certain that this sample of mean £232 came from a population whose mean lies in the range of £232 ± 10.19.
Our estimate is correct to within £10.

(c) To obtain a point estimate of the total amount outstanding we should multiply our mean estimate £232 by the number of accounts.

$$\text{Estimate of total} = £232 \times 50,000$$

$$= £11.6 \text{ m}.$$

# 5 LARGE-SAMPLE THEORY—ESTIMATION

The same approach can be used for the two limits of our confidence interval. Hence

95 per cent confidence interval for the total amount = $(232 \pm 10.19) \times 50{,}000$

$$= \underline{\underline{£11.6 \pm 0.51 \text{ m.}}}$$

## 8.0 CALCULATING THE SAMPLE SIZE FOR A GIVEN ACCURACY

In Example 1 our 95 per cent confidence interval showed that we have estimated the population mean to within £10. If this is not accurate enough and it is required that we estimate to within £5 at the same confidence level then to improve the accuracy of our estimate we need to increase the sample size.

The question is—how large should the sample be so that the error is at most £5?

Figure 18 illustrates the problem. We know $\sigma = 52$, we don't know $n$, and the distance between the mean position and the confidence limits is £5.

But 95 per cent of the normal distribution lies between the mean and 1.96 standard errors.

Therefore 1.96 standard errors must be less than or equal to £5.

$$\therefore \quad 1.96 \frac{\sigma}{\sqrt{n}} \leqslant 5;$$

$$\therefore \quad 1.96 \times \frac{52}{\sqrt{n}} \leqslant 5.$$

$$\frac{1.96 \times 52}{5} \leqslant \sqrt{n};$$

$$\therefore \quad 20.384 \leqslant \sqrt{n};$$

$$\therefore \quad 415.5 \leqslant n.$$

Therefore the minimum value of $n$ should be $\underline{\underline{416}}$.

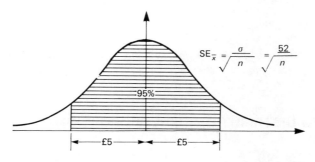

Fig. 18. *Calculating sample size for a given accuracy.*

This approach can be represented by a formula;

$$n \geq \left(\frac{z\sigma}{E}\right)^2$$

where $E$ = accuracy required

$z$ = $z$-value for level of confidence

$\sigma$ = population standard deviation.

## 9.0 FINITE POPULATION CORRECTION FACTOR

We have assumed in the previous work that we were sampling from an infinite distribution. When the sample size $n$ is greater than 5 per cent of the population size $N$ then we need to apply a correction factor to the standard error.

This is given by

$$\sqrt{\frac{N-n}{N-1}}$$

If for example $n = 50$, $N = 500$ and $\sigma = 20$ then $n$ is 10 per cent of $N$ and the finite population correction should be used.

$$\text{Now SE} = \frac{\sigma}{\sqrt{n}} = \frac{20}{\sqrt{50}} = 2.828$$

$$\text{and FPC} = \sqrt{\frac{N-n}{N-1}} = \sqrt{\frac{500-50}{499}}$$

$$= 0.9496.$$

$$\text{Corrected SE} = 2.828 \times 0.9496$$

$$= \underline{\underline{2.685}}.$$

This is a reduction of about 5 per cent.

*Note: Some text use*

$$FPC = \sqrt{1 - \frac{n}{N}}.$$

*This really requires a slight redefinition of the population standard deviation. However, if $N$ is reasonably large then dividing by $N$ rather than $N - 1$ is going to make very little difference.*

*In the above example; FPC = 0.9487, giving SE = 2.683.*

## 10.0 SAMPLING DISTRIBUTION OF A PROPORTION

In some examples we are concerned with a proportion rather than a mean. The central-limit theorem provides us with results similar to that for the mean.

## 5 LARGE-SAMPLE THEORY—ESTIMATION

(a) The sampling distribution of proportions is a normal distribution.

(b) The mean of the sampling distribution is equal to the mean of the population $\pi$, i.e.

$$P = \pi$$

(c) The standard error of the sampling distribution is given by the formula:

$$SE_p = \sqrt{\frac{P(1-P)}{n}}$$

We can use these results to calculate confidence intervals for estimates of proportions.

## 11.0 CONFIDENCE INTERVAL FOR A PROPORTION

### Example 2
Twenty people out of a hundred said they used "Brand X" washing powder. Estimate a 99 per cent confidence interval for the population proportion.

### SOLUTION

Sample proportion $P = \dfrac{20}{100} = 0.20$

Best estimate of $\pi$ is 0.20.

$$SE_p = \sqrt{\frac{0.20 \times 0.80}{100}} = 0.04.$$

Referring to Fig. 19, area in tail = 0.005; from normal table, $Z = 2.6$.

$\therefore$ 99 per cent confidence interval for $\pi = 0.20 \pm 2.6 \times 0.04$

$$= \underline{\underline{0.20 \pm 0.104}},$$

i.e., there could be between 10 and 30 per cent of the population using "Brand X" washing powder.

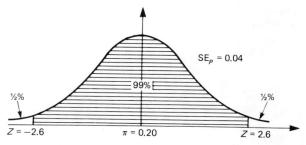

Fig. 19. *Confidence interval for a proportion.*

## 12.0 SUMMARY

The aim of this chapter has been to cover the problem of estimation using a large sample.

It has been emphasised that we are really concerned about the population and the sample is merely there to provide evidence about the population. The sample must be selected at random and used to calculate unbiased estimators of the population mean and standard deviation. For an estimation problem we calculate the mean and a confidence interval around the mean.

**Formulae**

*Estimators*

$$\hat{\mu} = \bar{x}. \quad \hat{\sigma} = s. \sqrt{\frac{n}{n-1}} = \sqrt{\frac{\sum x^2 - (\sum x)^2/n}{n-1}}.$$

*Means*

$$\mu_{\bar{x}} = \mu. \quad SE_{\bar{x}} = \frac{\sigma}{\sqrt{n}}.$$

*Proportions*

$$P = \pi. \quad SE_p = \sqrt{\frac{P(1-P)}{n}}.$$

*Finite population correction factor (applied to* SE*)*

$$\sqrt{\frac{N-n}{N-1}} \quad \text{or} \quad \sqrt{1 - \frac{n}{N}}.$$

*Sample size*

$$n \geqslant \left(\frac{Z\sigma}{E}\right)^2.$$

# CHAPTER SIX
# Large-sample Theory – Significance Tests

## 1.0 THE PROBLEM

*Example 1*
A machine is supposed to fill bottles with 125 ml of cough syrup. A sample of 200 bottles averaged 127 ml of cough syrup with a standard deviation of 4 ml. Is this evidence that the machine has been set to the wrong mean fill?

If the true setting of the machine is 125 ml then we would not expect every sample to have a mean of 125 ml. There are bound to be differences. The question is whether it is possible for a sample with mean 127 ml to have come from a population of mean 125 ml.

## 2.0 HYPOTHESIS TESTING

To examine the situation we use the scientific approach. We set up an hypothesis and test if it is true. If it is found to be false we seek an alternative hypothesis. The hypothesis we set up is called the null hypothesis; it assumes that everything is correct, that $\mu$ equals 125 ml and that the sample could have come from a population whose mean is $\mu$. We write the null hypothesis as:

$$H_0 : \mu = 125.$$

Notice that the null hypothesis always takes the form

$$H_0 : \mu = \ldots\ldots$$

We then need to set up an alternative hypothesis which we will only adopt if $H_0$ is rejected. We write the alternative hypothesis as

$$H_1 : \mu \neq 125.$$

If we assume that we are attempting to test if $\mu$ is *significantly different* from 125 then if this test fails we conclude that $\mu \neq 125$, i.e. the true value of $\mu$ is either less than or greater than 125. This is known as a two-tailed test as there are two rejection areas in our normal distribution (see Fig. 20).

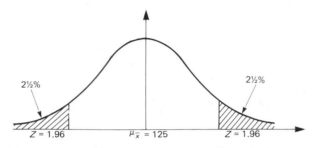

Fig. 20. *Hypothesis testing—sampling distribution of x.*

## 2.1 Test Level

We have got to decide on what range of differences we would accept as occurring purely due to chance. A commonly adopted level is the 5 per cent level.

If we look at the sampling distribution of $\bar{x}$ under the null hypothesis $\mu = 125$ and consider the region covered by the 95 per cent confidence interval, we know that 95 per cent of the sample means will fall in the range and only 5 per cent will fall outside the range. These are the limits we adopt for a 5 per cent test of significance. If the sample mean we are testing falls within the limits then we say there is no significant difference at the 5 per cent level between the sample mean and the mean given under the null hypothesis.

The argument is based on the fact that 95 per cent of all samples from the population under $H_0$ would fall within the test limits. If the sample mean falls outside the test limits then we say the difference is significant at the 5 per cent level. Here we are saying that although this difference could have occurred purely due to chance (5 per cent) the likelihood of this happening is too small so we will assume there is a difference between the sample mean and $\mu$ under the null hypothesis.

To carry out the significance test using the sampling distribution we need to know the mean and standard error. The mean we get from the null hypothesis $\mu_{\bar{x}} = 125$; the standard error is given by:

$$SE_{\bar{x}} = \frac{\sigma}{\sqrt{n}} = \frac{4}{\sqrt{200}} = 0.283.$$

To compare the differences we work in $Z$-values.

## 2.2 Test limits

Referring to Fig. 21:
Area in right-hand tail = 0.025, from tables, $Z = 1.96$.
Therefore test limits are $Z = \pm 1.96$.

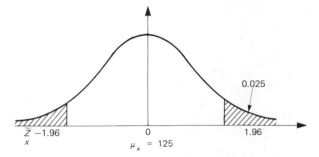

Fig. 21. *Hypothesis testing—test limits.*

To determine the $Z$-value for the sample we use:

$$Z = \frac{\bar{x} - \mu}{\text{SE}_{\bar{x}}}.$$

This calculates how far $\bar{x}$ is from $\mu$ in SEs.

$$\therefore \quad Z = \frac{127 - 125}{0.283}$$

$$= 7.07.$$

Clearly, $Z = 7.07$ lies outside the range $-1.96$ to $+1.96$ and therefore the difference is significant at the 5 per cent level. Reject $H_0 : \mu = 125$; accept $H_1 : \mu \neq 125$.

## 3.0 ONE-TAILED AND TWO-TAILED TESTS

In our example we carried out a two-tailed test as we were interested in testing if the sample mean was significantly different from the null hypothesis. However, if we want to test if the bottles have been over-filled then we will want to test if the sample mean is significantly greater than the null hypothesis; this would be a one-tailed test, as there would be only one rejection area totalling 5 per cent if we are testing at the 5 per cent level. (Notice that whatever 5 per cent test you do, either one- or two-tailed, the total rejection area equals 5 per cent).

The one-tailed test for our example becomes:

$$H_0 : \mu = 125, \ H_1 : \mu > 125.$$

Referring to Fig. 22:
Test value: area in right-hand tail $= 0.05$, from tables $Z = 1.65$.

$$\text{Sample } Z \text{ value} = \frac{127 - 125}{0.283} = 7.07 \text{ as before.}$$

This sample $Z$ value of 7.07 lies beyond the test value of $Z = 1.65$ (it is in the shaded area); therefore the difference is significant at the 5 per cent level.

Whether, in general, you use a one- or two-tailed test depends purely upon how the question is asked. If the question asks, or implies, "Is the difference significant?" then

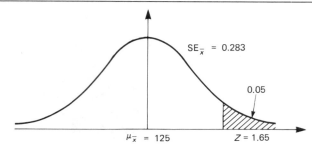

Fig. 22. *One-tailed test.*

you have a two-tailed test. If the question asks, or implies, "Is the sample mean significantly greater?" then you have a one-tailed test. Similarly, if the question is "Is the sample mean significantly less?" then we also have a one-tailed test.

## 4.0 SIGNIFICANCE TEST FOR A PROPORTION

### Example 2
It is claimed by a politician that the majority of people in the country want the reintroduction of capital punishment for certain offences. In a survey of 160 people only 35 supported the return of capital punishment. Test the claim at the 1 per cent level.

### SOLUTION
Let us test if the sample proportion is significantly less than 0.50, (the breakdown point for a majority),
i.e. $H_0: \pi = 0.50$, $H_1: \pi < 0.50$.
($\pi$ is the population proportion.)

Now
$$SE_P = \sqrt{\frac{P(1-P)}{n}}$$
$$= \sqrt{\frac{0.5(1-0.5)}{160}}$$
$$= 0.0395.$$

*Note: $P = 0.50$ follows directly from the null hypothesis; it is not derived from the sample.*

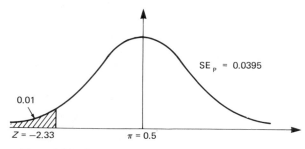

Fig. 23. *Significance test for a proportion.*

Referring to Fig. 23:
Test statistic: area in left-hand tail = 0.01, from tables $Z = 2.33$.

Now
$$P = 35/160 = 0.219.$$

$$\therefore \quad \text{sample } Z = \frac{P - \pi}{\text{SE}_P}$$

$$= \frac{0.219 - 0.5}{0.0395}$$

$$= -7.11.$$

As $Z = -7.11$ is less than the test value of $-2.33$ the difference is significant at the 1 per cent level. The claim is not supported by the evidence of the sample.

## 5.0 DIFFERENCE BETWEEN TWO MEANS

### Example 3

The Coal Board wants to compare the absentee rate on two shifts—the early shift starting at 6 a.m. and the late shift starting at 12 a.m. The average number of days lost per colliery over 50 collieries on the early shift was 72 days with a standard deviation of 6 days while on the late shift the figures were 85 days with a standard deviation of 5 days. Test at the 5 per cent level if there is any significant difference between the two shifts.

### SOLUTION

It can be shown that the sampling distribution of the difference of two means is a normal distribution (for large samples) with a mean of $\mu_1 - \mu_2$ and a standard error of

$$\sqrt{\frac{\sigma_1^2}{n_1} + \frac{\sigma_2^2}{n_2}}$$

Where $n_1$, $\mu_1$ and $\sigma_1$ are respectively the sample size, the population mean and the population standard deviation of the first sample then $n_2$, $\mu_2$ and $\sigma_2$ are similarly defined.

Assume for our null hypothesis there is no difference:

$$H_0: \mu_1 = \mu_2, \quad H_1: \mu_1 \neq \mu_2 \text{ (two-tailed test)}.$$

Now if $\mu_1 = \mu_2$ then $\mu_1 - \mu_2 = 0$, therefore the mean of the sampling distribution equals zero.

Now
$$\text{SE}_{\bar{x}_1 - \bar{x}_2} = \sqrt{\frac{\sigma_1^2}{n_1} + \frac{\sigma_2^2}{n_2}}$$

$$= \sqrt{\frac{6^2}{50} + \frac{5^2}{50}}$$

$$= 1.105.$$

*Note: we do not know $\sigma_1$ or $\sigma_2$ but we estimate them using the sample values of 6 and 5.*

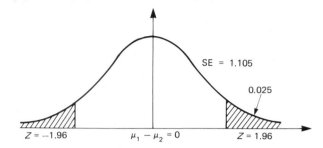

Fig. 24. *Test for difference between two means.*

Referring to Fig. 24:
Test levels ± 1.96.

$$\text{Sample } Z = \frac{(\bar{x}_1 - \bar{x}_2) - (\mu_1 - \mu_2)}{SE_{\bar{x}-\bar{x}_2}}$$

$$\therefore Z = \frac{(72 - 85) - 0}{1.105}$$

$$= -11.76.$$

The difference *is* significant at the 5 per cent level.

## 6.0 DIFFERENCE BETWEEN TWO PROPORTIONS

*Example 4*

|  | Teachers in secondary schools | |
|---|---|---|
|  | Male | Female |
| Union member | 50 | 50 |
| Non-union member | 20 | 50 |

Does the above table provide evidence that a higher percentage among male teachers are union members than among female teachers? (Test at the 2 per cent level.)

*Solution*
The sampling distribution of the difference between proportions is a normal distribution for large samples. The standard error is given by:

$$SE_{P_1 - P_2} = \sqrt{\frac{P_1(1 - P_1)}{n_1} + \frac{P_2(1 - P_2)}{n_2}}$$

## 6 LARGE-SAMPLE THEORY—SIGNIFICANCE TESTS

Therefore:
$$H_0: \pi_1 = \pi_2, \quad H_1: \pi_1 > \pi_2.$$

$$P_1 = \frac{50}{70} = 0.714, \qquad P_2 = \frac{50}{100} = 0.5.$$

Therefore pooled $P = \dfrac{50 + 50}{70 + 100} = 0.588^*$

$$SE_{P_1 - P_2} = \sqrt{\frac{0.588 \times 0.412}{70} + \frac{0.588 \times 0.412}{100}}$$

$$= 0.0767$$

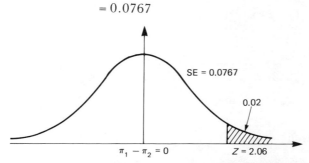

Fig. 25. *Test for difference between two proportions.*

Referring to Fig. 25:
Area of right-hand tail = 0.02, from tables $Z = 2.06$.

$$\text{Sample } Z = \frac{(P_1 - P_2) - (\pi_1 - \pi_2)}{SE_{P_1 - P_2}}$$

$$= \frac{(0.714 - 0.5) - 0}{0.0767}$$

$$= 2.79.$$

As $Z = 2.79$ is greater than the test value of 2.06 the difference is significant at the 2 per cent level. Men have a higher percentage union membership.

*Note: we had to pool the $P$'s as we assumed that $\pi_1 = \pi_2 = P$ in $H_0$.

## 7.0 TYPE I AND TYPE II ERRORS

When we carry out a significance test we have to decide between two decisions:

(a) accept $H_0$, or

(b) reject $H_0$.

In reality there are two possible states of nature either:

(a) $H_0$ is true, or

(b) $H_0$ is false.

This can be represented in the form of a table:

| Decision | State of nature | |
| --- | --- | --- |
| | $H_0$ is true | $H_0$ is false |
| Accept $H_0$ | correct decision | Type II error |
| Reject $H_0$ | Type I error | correct decision |

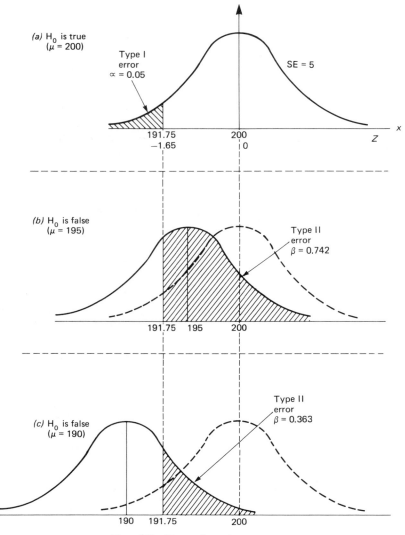

Fig. 26. *Type I and II error.*

# 6 LARGE-SAMPLE THEORY—SIGNIFICANCE TESTS

Consider an example where we assume that $\mu = 200$ and SE = 5 and we are testing using a one-tailed test at the 5 per cent level. Our test value will be $Z = -1.65$. Now if $H_0$ is true (*see* Fig. 26(a) then if $Z$ is less than $-1.65$. ($x$-value of 191.75) we will reject $H_0$ and commit a Type I error. The probability of this happening is the area of rejection region, i.e. $\alpha = 0.05$ ($\alpha$ is the probability of a Type I error). Now consider when $H_0$ is false and $\mu = 195$ (*see* Fig. 26(b)) unbeknown to us. Then we shall still be accepting $H_0$ if $Z$ is greater than $-1.65$. If, however, the true mean is 195 then the probability of accepting $H_0$ is given by the shaded area.

Now, actual $Z = \dfrac{191.75 - 195}{5} = -0.65,$

leading to an area of 0.742, i.e. $\beta = 0.742$ where $\beta$ is the probability of making a Type II error.

Similarly, if the true $\mu$ is 190 then $\beta = 0.363$ (*see* Fig. 26(c)).

Unfortunately the $\beta$-value changes as $\mu$ changes and can vary between 0 and 1.

If we decrease the chance of a Type II error in a given situation we automatically increase the chance of a Type I error and vice versa. In practice we have to decide on acceptable levels of risk in connection with these two types of errors, and design our experiments and decision rules in such a way that we satisfy both probabilities simultaneously.

## 8.0 SUMMARY

The aim of this chapter has been to introduce the concepts behind significant testing and to apply them to the large sample cases. A classical and rather formal approach has been used to avoid some of the ambiguities that seem to arise using less formal approaches.

You should understand what is meant by the following terms:

> null hypothesis
> alternative hypothesis.
> test level
> one-tailed or two-tailed test
> Type I error
> Type II error.

**Formulae**

*Mean*  $\quad SE_{\bar{x}} = \dfrac{\sigma}{\sqrt{n}}. \quad Z = \dfrac{\bar{x} - \mu}{SE_{\bar{x}}}.$

*Proportion*  $\quad SE_P = \sqrt{\dfrac{P(1-P)}{n}}. \quad Z = \dfrac{P - \pi}{SE_P}.$

*Difference between means*

$$\mathrm{SE}_{\bar{x}_1 - \bar{x}_2} = \sqrt{\frac{\sigma_1^2}{n_1} + \frac{\sigma_2^2}{n_2}}.$$

$$Z = \frac{(\bar{x}_1 - \bar{x}_2) - (\mu_1 - \mu_2)}{\mathrm{SE}_{\bar{x}_1 - \bar{x}_2}}.$$

*Difference between proportions*

$$\mathrm{SE}_{P_1 - P_2} = \sqrt{\frac{P_1(1 - P_1)}{n_1} + \frac{P_2(1 - P_2)}{n_2}}$$

$$Z = \frac{(P_1 - P_2) - (\pi_1 - \pi_2)}{\mathrm{SE}_{P_1 - P_2}}.$$

# CHAPTER SEVEN
# Small Samples

## 1.0 INTRODUCTION

In the two previous chapters we dealt with large samples, where $n \geqslant 30$. When $n$ is less than 30 we cannot use exactly the same approach. If the population is a normal distribution then the central-limit theorem still applies as long as we know the population standard deviation. If $\sigma$ is unknown, which is usually the case, then we have to estimate $\sigma$ from the sample; then the sampling distribution of $\bar{x}$ becomes Student's $t$-distribution.

$$SE_{\bar{x}} = \frac{\hat{\sigma}}{\sqrt{n}}$$

This is similar to the normal distribution in the sense that it is symmetrical and tends to the normal distribution as $n$ gets larger (Fig. 27); in general, it is flatter than the normal distribution and hence wider (remember the total area still equals one).

To apply the $t$-distribution we use $t$-tables but these are tabulated for only a few

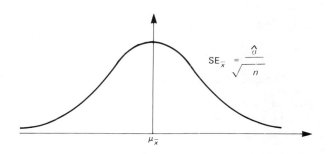

Fig. 27. *Student's t-distribution.*

Table 2. *t*-table

| Degrees of freedom, V | 1 | 2 | 3 | 4 | 5 | 6 | 7 | 8 | 9 | 10 |
|---|---|---|---|---|---|---|---|---|---|---|
| $t_{0.05}$   | 6.3   | 2.9  | 2.4  | 2.1 | 2.0 | 1.9 | 1.9 | 1.9 | 1.8 | 1.8 |
| $t_{0.025}$  | 12.7  | 4.3  | 3.2  | 2.8 | 2.6 | 2.4 | 2.4 | 2.3 | 2.3 | 2.2 |
| $t_{0.01}$   | 31.8  | 7.0  | 4.5  | 3.7 | 3.4 | 3.1 | 3.0 | 2.9 | 2.8 | 2.8 |
| $t_{0.005}$  | 63.7  | 9.9  | 5.8  | 4.6 | 4.0 | 3.7 | 3.5 | 3.4 | 3.3 | 3.2 |
| $t_{0.001}$  | 318.3 | 22.3 | 10.2 | 7.2 | 5.9 | 5.2 | 4.8 | 4.5 | 4.3 | 4.1 |
| $t_{0.0005}$ | 636.6 | 31.6 | 12.9 | 8.6 | 6.9 | 6.0 | 5.4 | 5.0 | 4.8 | 4.6 |

values of the area (*see* Table 2). As with the normal distribution, *t* is measured in standard errors:

$$t = \frac{\bar{x} - \mu}{SE_{\bar{x}}}$$

Before we can use the table for each case we also need to determine the "degrees of freedom", $V$. For the one-sample case $V = n - 1$.

## 2.0 DEGREES OF FREEDOM

To grasp the concept of degrees of freedom, imagine you have been asked to select 5 numbers whose mean is 20. Then the sum of the numbers is 100. This means the first four numbers selected can be any number you care to choose but the fifth number must be such that the total is 100. If you selected 10, 15, 18, 24, then the fifth number would have to be 33. We say you have only 4 degrees of freedom i.e. $5 - 1$ (for the mean). In general if you have $n$ numbers and the mean is specified then you have $n - 1$ degrees of freedom. If you have two samples with two means specified then you have:

$$V = n_1 + n_2 - 2 \text{ degrees of freedom.}$$

*Example 1*
The lengths in cm of 5 components are:

$$2.1, 2.4, 2.3, 2.2, 2.3.$$

(a) Estimate the population mean and calculate a 95 per cent confidence interval.

(b) Test at the 5 per cent level if the sample mean is significatly greater than 2 cm.

SOLUTION
(a) *Step 1:* Calculate $\bar{x}$, $\hat{\sigma}$ and SE.

# 7 SMALL SAMPLES

| $x$ | $x^2$ |
|---|---|
| 2.1 | 4.41 |
| 2.4 | 5.76 |
| 2.3 | 5.29 |
| 2.2 | 4.84 |
| 2.3 | 5.29 |
| 11.3 | 25.59 |

$$\therefore \quad \bar{x} = \frac{\sum x}{n} = \frac{11.3}{5} = 2.26,$$

$$\therefore \quad \hat{\mu} = \underline{\underline{2.26}}.$$

$$\hat{\sigma} = \sqrt{\frac{\sum x^2 - (\sum x)^2/n}{n-1}}$$

$$= \sqrt{\frac{25.59 - (11.3)^2/5}{4}}$$

$$= \underline{\underline{0.114}}.$$

$$\text{SE} = \frac{\hat{\sigma}}{\sqrt{n}} = \frac{0.114}{\sqrt{5}} = 0.0510.$$

Step 2: Calculate confidence interval.

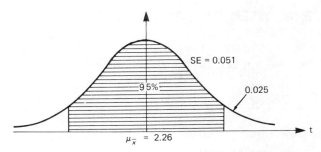

Fig. 28. *Calculation of confidence interval.*

$V = 5 - 1 = 4$ degrees of freedom.
Referring to Fig. 28:
From $t$-tables, $t_{0.025} (V = 4) = 2.8$.
$\therefore$ 95 per cent confidence interval $= 2.26 \pm 2.8 \times 0.0510$

$$= \underline{\underline{2.26 \pm 0.143}}.$$

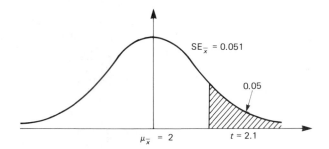

Fig. 29. *Test for significance of sample mean.*

(b) $H_0: \mu = 2$, $H_1: \mu > 2$ (one-tailed test).

$V = 5 - 1 = 4$.

Referring to Fig. 29:
From $t$-tables, $t_{0.05}\,(V=4) = 2.1$.

$$\therefore \text{Sample } t = \frac{\bar{x} - \mu}{\text{SE}_{\bar{x}}}$$

$$= \frac{2.26 - 2.0}{0.051}$$

$$= \underline{\underline{5.10}}.$$

As $t = 5.10$ is larger than the test value of 2.1 the difference is significant at the 5 per cent level. Reject $H_0: \mu = 2.0$. Accept $H_1: \mu > 2.0$.

## 3.0 DIFFERENCE BETWEEN TWO SAMPLE MEANS

The sampling distribution of the difference between two means of small samples follows a $t$-distribution with mean $\mu_1 - \mu_2$ and standard error given by:

$$\text{SE}_{\bar{x}_1 - \bar{x}_2} = \hat{\sigma}\sqrt{\frac{1}{n_1} + \frac{1}{n_2}}.$$

$\hat{\sigma}$ needs to be estimated from the two *sample* standard deviations. It is calculated as a weighted average of the variances:

$$\hat{\sigma} = \sqrt{\frac{(n_1 - 1)\sigma_1^2 + (n_2 - 1)\sigma_2^2}{n_1 + n_2 - 2}}.$$

### Example 2

Five houses in Nottingham have an average value of £40,000 with a standard deviation of £2,000, while six similar houses in Leicester have an average value of £36,000 with a standard deviation of £1,500. Is this evidence that house prices for this type of house are more expensive in Nottingham?

Test at the 1 per cent level.

# 7 SMALL SAMPLES

**SOLUTION**

We measure in £000:

$$\bar{x}_1 = 40, \quad \sigma_1 = 2, \quad n_1 = 5;$$
$$\bar{x} = 36, \quad \sigma_2 = 1.5, \quad n_2 = 6.$$

$$\hat{\sigma} = \sqrt{\frac{(5-1)2^2 + (\sigma - 1) \times 1.5^2}{5 + 6 - 2}}$$

$$= 1.74.$$

$$\therefore \quad SE_{\bar{x}_1 - \bar{x}_2} = \hat{\sigma}\sqrt{\frac{1}{n_1} + \frac{1}{n_2}}$$

$$= 1.74\sqrt{\frac{1}{5} + \frac{1}{6}}$$

$$= 1.054.$$

Assume there is no difference between house prices.

$$H_0 : \mu_1 = \mu_2, \text{ i.e. } \mu_1 - \mu_2 = 0; \quad H_1 : \mu_1 > \mu_2 \text{ (one-tailed test)}.$$

$$V = n_1 + n_2 - 2 = 5 + 6 - 2 = 9.$$

Referring to Fig.30:
Test value (from tables): $t_{0.01}$ ($V = 9$) = 2.8.

Sample:
$$t = \frac{(\bar{x}_1 - \bar{x}_2) - (\mu_1 - \mu_2)}{SE_{\bar{x}_1 - \bar{x}_2}}$$

$$= \frac{(40 - 36) - 0}{1.054}$$

$$= 3.80$$

As $t = 3.80$ is greater than the test limit of 2.8 the difference is significant at the 1 per cent level. The samples provide evidence that house prices in Nottingham for this type of house are greater than those in Leicester.

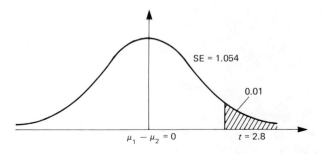

Fig. 30. *Test for difference between two sample means.*

## 4.0 PAIRED t-TEST

If we are comparing two samples which come from the same source and each item in sample 1 is comparable with an item in sample 2 then we can use the paired $t$-test.

### Example 3
Five typists were each asked to type letter A on a manual typewriter and letter B on an electric typewriter. (Both letters were previously judged to take equal times to type on manual typewriters.) The typing times for letter A and letter B for each typist were:

| Typist | A | B |
|---|---|---|
| 1 | 9.6 | 7.2 |
| 2 | 8.4 | 7.1 |
| 3 | 7.7 | 6.8 |
| 4 | 10.1 | 9.2 |
| 5 | 8.3 | 7.1 |

Test if there is any significant difference between the times taken to type the letter on manual or electric typewriters. Test at the 5 per cent level.

### SOLUTION
If we were to tackle this problem using the sampling distribution of the difference between two means we would be ignoring some of the information contained in the problem. We would be ignoring the fact that the times for each typist typing letters A and B are comparable, not just their means. A better approach to the problem is to calculate the difference of $A - B$ and then test if the mean of this difference is significantly different from zero.

Calculate the difference $x$, $\bar{x}$ and $\hat{\sigma}$ and continue as in a single-sample case.

| $x$ | $x^2$ |
|---|---|
| 2.4 | 5.76 |
| 1.3 | 1.69 |
| 0.9 | 0.81 |
| 0.9 | 0.81 |
| 1.2 | 1.44 |
| 6.7 | 10.51 |

$$\bar{x} = \frac{\sum x}{n} = \frac{6.7}{5} = 1.34.$$

$$\hat{\sigma} = \sqrt{\frac{\sum x^2 - (\sum x)^2/n}{n-1}}$$

# 7 SMALL SAMPLES

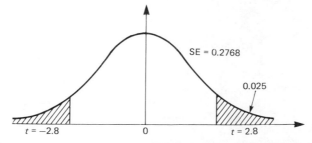

Fig. 31. *Test for significant difference between typing times.*

$$= \sqrt{\frac{10.51 - (6.7)^2/5}{4}}$$

$$= 0.6189.$$

$$\text{SE} = \frac{\hat{\sigma}}{\sqrt{n}} = \frac{0.6189}{\sqrt{5}}$$

$$= 0.2768.$$

$$H_0 : \mu = 0, \ H_1 : \mu \neq 0, \ V = 5 - 1 = 4.$$

Referring to Fig. 31:

$$t_{0.025}\ (V = 4) = 2.8.$$

$$\text{Sample } t = \frac{\bar{x} - \mu}{\text{SE}}$$

$$= \frac{1.34 - 0}{0.2768}$$

$$= 4.84.$$

The difference *is* significant.
The times taken to type letters on manual and electric typewriters are significantly different.

## 5.0 SUMMARY

This chapter has dealt with the use of *t*-distribution for small samples. Problems of estimation and significant tests were covered for both one-and two-sample cases.

### Formulae

Mean $\quad\quad\quad\quad \text{SE}_{\bar{x}} = \dfrac{\sigma}{\sqrt{n}}. \quad\quad t = \dfrac{\bar{x} - \mu}{\text{SE}_{\bar{x}}}.$

*Two means*

$$\mathrm{SE}_{\bar{x}_1-\bar{x}_2} = \hat{\sigma}\sqrt{\frac{1}{n_1}+\frac{1}{n_2}}.$$

where

$$\hat{\sigma} = \sqrt{\frac{(n_1-1)\sigma_1^2 + (n_2-1)\sigma_2^2}{n_1+n_2-2}}$$

$$t = \frac{(\bar{x}_1-\bar{x}_2)-(\mu_1-\mu_2)}{\mathrm{SE}_{\bar{x}_1-\bar{x}_2}}$$

# CHAPTER EIGHT
# Chi-squared Distribution

## 1.0 GOODNESS OF FIT TESTS

These tests are concerned with the comparison of some observed frequency distribution with a theoretical distribution, such as the rectangular, binomial, Poisson or normal distribution. We calculate the chi-squared ($\chi^2$) statistics:

$$\chi^2 = \sum \frac{(O-E)^2}{E} \qquad \text{or, using } d = O - E: \ \chi^2 = \sum d^2/E$$

where $O$ = observed frequency
$E$ = expected frequency calculated from the theoretical distribution.

Now, the sampling distribution of $\chi^2$, known as the $\chi^2$-distribution, varies as the number of degrees of freedom vary, but in general it is a positively skewed curve as in Fig. 32. Note that the lowest value of $\chi^2$ is zero, and the area under the curve is one as it is a probability distribution.

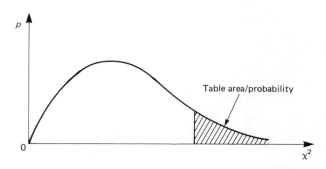

Fig. 32. *Chi-squared distribution.*

Table 3. $\chi^2$

| Degrees of freedom, $V$ | 1 | 2 | 3 | 4 | 5 | 6 | 7 | 8 | 9 | 10 |
|---|---|---|---|---|---|---|---|---|---|---|
| $\chi^2_{0.05}$ | 3.8 | 6.0 | 7.8 | 9.5 | 11.1 | 12.6 | 14.1 | 15.5 | 16.9 | 18.3 |
| $\chi^2_{0.01}$ | 6.6 | 9.2 | 11.3 | 13.3 | 15.1 | 16.8 | 18.5 | 20.1 | 21.7 | 23.2 |
| $\chi^2_{0.001}$ | 10.8 | 13.8 | 16.3 | 18.5 | 20.5 | 22.5 | 24.3 | 26.1 | 27.9 | 29.6 |

The number of degrees of freedom $V$ (Table 3) is calculated as: (The number of classes) – (The number of parameters estimated from the sample, e.g. one for the Poisson ($m$), two for the normal ($\mu$ and $\sigma$) and one for the binomial ($n$), – 1).

## Example 1
A die is thrown 120 times and the following frequencies were observed:

| Die throw | 1 | 2 | 3 | 4 | 5 | 6 | Total |
|---|---|---|---|---|---|---|---|
| Observed frequency | 9 | 22 | 17 | 21 | 21 | 30 | 120 |

Is the die biased? Test at the 5 per cent level.

SOLUTION (*see* Fig. 33)
It is clear in this problem that if there is a bias then it is the scores of 1 and 6 where the bias is occurring. Any comparison of the average of the sample with the theoretical average of 3.5 will not detect the bias as it will be cancelled out in the average. If however we use a chi-squared test then we will be comparing each observed frequency with its expected frequency and any bias should be detected.

Now if the dice is unbiased the expected frequency for each score is 1/6 of 120, i.e. 20. The following table calculates observed values of $\chi^2$ using $d = |O - E|$ (we ignore minus signs in the difference as we are going to square the difference anyway):

| $O$ | $E$ | $d$ | $d^2$ | $d^2/E$ |
|---|---|---|---|---|
| 9 | 20 | 11 | 121 | 6.05 |
| 22 | 20 | 2 | 4 | 0.20 |
| 17 | 20 | 3 | 9 | 0.45 |
| 21 | 20 | 1 | 1 | 0.05 |
| 21 | 20 | 1 | 1 | 0.05 |
| 30 | 20 | 10 | 100 | 5.00 |
|   | 120 |   |   | 11.80 = $\chi^2$ (observed). |

$V = 6 - 0 - 1 = 5$, as the number of classes is 6 and we did not have to calculate any parameters such as means or standard deviations.

# 8 CHI-SQUARED DISTRIBUTION

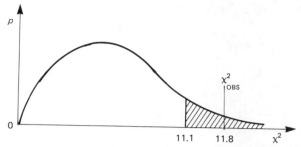

Fig. 33. *Chi-squared test—comparison of observed and expected frequencies.*

From Table 3 the test value is:

$$\chi^2_{0.05}\ (V=5) = 11.1.$$

As observed $\chi^2 = 11.8$ is greater than 11.1, the difference is significant. Therefore we conclude the die is biased. If we look at the $d^2/E$ column which gives the individual chi-squared values we see that the values contributing to the high value are the 6.05 and 5.00. These values come from the die scores of 1 and 6. Hence we conclude that as the observed frequency for the 1 throw is significantly less than expected and the observed frequency for the 6 throw is significantly higher than expected the die is biased towards the 6 and away from the 1. The other numbers are occurring as would be expected.

## Example 2

The demand for a special component over the past 200 trading days was as follows:

| Demand level | 0 | 1 | 2 | 3 | 4 | 5 or more |
|---|---|---|---|---|---|---|
| Number of days | 50 | 66 | 41 | 23 | 17 | 3 |

Test if the demand follows a Poisson distribution.

*Note:* $e^{-1.5} = 0.2231$.

**SOLUTION**

*Step 1* Calculate $m$.

| $x$ | $f$ | $fx$ |
|---|---|---|
| 0 | 50 | 0 |
| 1 | 66 | 66 |
| 2 | 41 | 82 |
| 3 | 23 | 69 |
| 4 | 17 | 68 |
| 5 + | 3 | 15 |
|  | 200 | 300 |

$$m = \frac{\sum fx}{\sum f} = \frac{300}{200} = 1.5.$$

*Step 2* Calculate Poisson probabilities and multiply them by 200 to obtain expected frequencies:

|  |  | *Expected frequency* |
|---|---|---|
| $P(0) = e^{-1.5}$ | $= 0.2231$ | 44.6 |
| $P(1) = e^{-1.5}(1.5)$ | $= 0.3347$ | 66.9 |
| $P(2) = e^{-1.5}(1.5)^2/2!$ | $= 0.2510$ | 50.2 |
| $P(3) = e^{-1.5}(1.5)^3/3!$ | $= 0.1255$ | 25.1 |
| $P(4) = e^{-1.5}(1.5)^4/4!$ | $= 0.0471$ | 9.4 |
|  | 0.9814 | 196.2 |
| ∴ Expected frequency for 5 + | = | 3.8 |
|  |  | 200.0 |

*Step 3* Calculate observed chi-squared value *(O)*:

| O | E | d | $d^2$ | $d^2/E$ |
|---|---|---|---|---|
| 50 | 44.6 | 5.4 | 29.16 | 0.65 |
| 66 | 66.9 | 0.9 | 0.81 | 0.01 |
| 41 | 50.2 | 9.2 | 84.64 | 1.69 |
| 23 | 25.1 | 2.1 | 4.41 | 0.18 |
| 17 | 9.4 | 7.6 | 57.76 | 6.14 |
| 3 | 3.8 | 0.8 | 0.64 | 0.17 |
|  |  |  | $\chi^2 =$ | 8.84 |

$V = 6 - 1$ (for $m$) $- 1 = 4$.
From Table 3, $\chi^2_{0.05}$ ($V = 4$) $= 9.5$ (*see* Fig. 34).

As the observed chi-squared of 8.84 is less than 9.5, the difference is *not* significant.

Therefore the demand distribution cannot be distinguished from a Poisson distribution, i.e. the Poisson distribution is a good fit to the demand distribution.

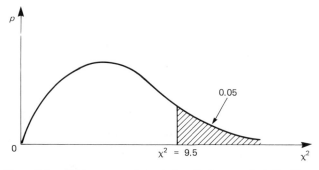

Fig. 34. *Chi-squared test for Poisson distribution.*

# 2.0 CONTINGENCY TABLE

*Example 3*
Using the data in the following table, determine if there is any association between colour of hair and the sex of the person. (Test at the 5 per cent level.)

|       | *Hair colour* |      |     |       |
|-------|------|------|-----|-------|
| *Sex* | *Dark* | *Fair* | *Red* | *Total* |
| Men   | 120  | 42   | 58  | 220   |
| Women | 60   | 78   | 42  | 180   |
| Total | 180  | 120  | 100 | 400   |

The numbers in the table are frequencies. For example there are 120 men with dark hair, and 42 men with fair hair.

### SOLUTION
All the figures in the body of the table are observed frequencies. If we take as our null hypothesis that there is no association between the sex of the person and their hair colour then we can assume that sex and hair colour are independent and use probability theory to calculate the expected frequencies; e.g. to calculate the expected frequency of men with dark hair, first calculate the probability of selecting men with dark hair:

$$P(\text{men with dark hair}) = P(\text{man}) \times P(\text{dark hair}).$$

Now $P(\text{man}) = \dfrac{220}{400}$

$\therefore$  $P(\text{man and dark hair}) = \dfrac{220}{400} \times \dfrac{180}{400}.$

Therefore the expected number of men with dark hair in a sample of 400 people is:

$$\frac{220}{400} \times \frac{180}{400} \times 400$$

$$= 99.$$

*Note: we could have got the same result by using the following formula:*

$$\text{Expected value} = \frac{\text{Row total} \times \text{Column total}}{\text{Grand total}}$$

*Men:* dark is row 1, column 1,

i.e. $$\frac{220 \times 180}{400} = 99.$$

Similarly, P (man and fair hair) $= \dfrac{220 \times 120}{400} = 66$.

The rest of the expected frequencies can be calculated using column and row totals:

|   | D | F | R | Total |
|---|---|---|---|---|
| M | 99 | 66 | 55 | 220 |
| W | 81 | 54 | 45 | 180 |
|   | 180 | 120 | 100 | 400 |

We calculate the number of degrees of freedom $V$ as follows:

$$V = (\text{Number of rows} - 1) \times (\text{Number of columns} - 1)$$
$$= (2-1) \times (3-1)$$
$$= 2.$$

In general, $V = (m-1) \times (n-1)$.

*Note: this is the number of expected values we needed to calculate using the formula.*

Now we can use the $\chi^2$-formula:

$$\chi^2 = \sum \frac{(O-E)^2}{E}$$

| O | E | d | $d^2$ | $d^2/E$ |
|---|---|---|---|---|
| 120 | 99 | 21 | 441 | 4.45 |
| 42 | 66 | 24 | 576 | 8.73 |
| 58 | 55 | 3 | 9 | 0.16 |
| 60 | 81 | 21 | 441 | 5.44 |
| 78 | 54 | 24 | 576 | 10.67 |
| 42 | 45 | 3 | 9 | 0.20 |
|   |   |   |   | 29.65 = $\chi^2_{obs}$ |

From Table 3,

$\chi^2_{0.05}\ (V=2) = 6.0$ (*see* Fig. 35).

As $\chi^2 = 29.65$ is greater than the test value of 6.0, the difference is significant at the 5 per cent level. If we look at the individual values of $\chi^2$ we have two large values 10.67 and 8.73 coming from the fair hair column, the larger of the two being in the women row. This would seem to indicate that more women have fair hair than would be expected owing purely to chance. Blonde wigs or dye must be in fashion.

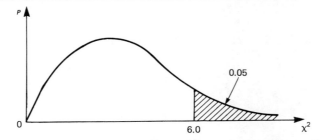

Fig. 35. *Chi-squared test for association between hair colour and sex.*

## 3.0 YATES CORRECTION

The statistic $\chi^2$ is a discrete random variable as the observed frequencies must be whole numbers. The $\chi^2$-distribution is a continuous distribution. Therefore we need to apply a continuity correction (the Yates correction). The correction is applied by subtracting $\frac{1}{2}$ from each absolute difference,

i.e. $\qquad\qquad\qquad O - E$ becomes $|O - E| - \frac{1}{2}$.

With large samples the correction makes very little difference. In practice it is usually applied when $V = 1$.

## 4.0 CORRECTING FOR LOW EXPECTED VALUES

It is recommended that when the expected frequency of a cell (or class) is less than 5 (as in the last cell of Example 2, where $E = 3.8$) the cell should be combined with an adjustment cell until the expected value is at least 5.

## 5.0 SUMMARY

The aim of this chapter was to cover the $\chi^2$-distribution applied both to goodness of fit tests and to contingency tables.

**Formulae**

$$\chi^2 = \sum \frac{(O - E)^2}{E}.$$

$$\chi^2 = \sum d^2/E.$$

$V =$ number of cells $-$ (number of parameters) $- 1$.

$$\text{Expected value } E = \frac{\text{Row total} \times \text{Column total}}{\text{Grand total}}.$$

Yates correction: replace $O - E$ by $|O - E| - \frac{1}{2}$.

# CHAPTER NINE
# Regression and Correlation

## 1.0 INTRODUCTION

If we believe there is an association between two random variables, say between demand for a product and the advertising expenditure, then trying to determine from a set of data the best functional relationship between the variables concerned is a problem of regression. This may be illustrated graphically by means of a scattergraph (*see* Fig. 36). Trying to determine how good a fit the functional relationship is to the data is a problem of correlation.

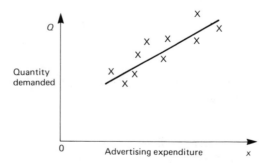

Fig. 36. *Scattergraph.*

## 2.0 LINEAR REGRESSION

Let us approach the problem of regression by trying to fit a straight line to a particular set of data.

## 9 REGRESSION AND CORRELATION

*Example 1*

Table 4. Data used to construct graph in Fig. 37.

| Month | Labour hours (000) | Overheads (£000) |
|---|---|---|
| January | 15 | 45 |
| February | 38 | 75 |
| March | 30 | 53 |
| April | 45 | 67 |
| May | 22 | 60 |
| June | 18 | 48 |
| July | 24 | 64 |
| August | 30 | 55 |
| September | 36 | 60 |
| October | 25 | 58 |
| November | 40 | 78 |
| December | 20 | 55 |

We have estimated that the number of labour hours (thousands) required next January is 40 and we want to estimate the likely overhead cost.

### 3.0 SCATTERGRAPH

To get a feel for the problem we can start with a scattergraph. We assume that the overheads depend upon the labour hours. We therefore plot the labour hours on the $x$-axis and the overheads on the $y$-axis (*see* Fig. 37).

We can see from the scattergraph that while all the points do not lie on a straight line they do appear to be scattered about a straight line. (The straight line—the line of best fit—has been drawn in by eye.) Certainly there appears to be some relationship between $x$ and $y$. For example the higher the value of $x$ the greater the value of $y$.

It is important to realise that we are dealing with a sample of data of size 12. We are trying to infer a relationship between all possible values of $x$ and $y$ from a small sample of size 12 and we know from our previous work on sampling that this will involve sampling errors.

### 4.0 METHOD OF LEAST SQUARES

The graphical method of obtaining a line of best fit by eye is clearly unsatisfactory as there are numerous different lines that might be drawn for a given set of points. In our example this would lead to a range of different overhead cost estimates from the same set of data. One approach to this problem of determining a regression line from a set of data is the method of least squares.

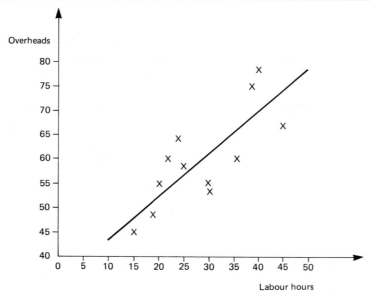

Fig. 37. *Scattergraph of labour hours against overheads.*

The general equation of a straight line is:

$$Y = a + bX \tag{1}$$

where $a$ is the intercept on the $y$-axis and $b$ the slope of the line.

Consider point P with coordinates $(x, y)$ as in Fig. 38.

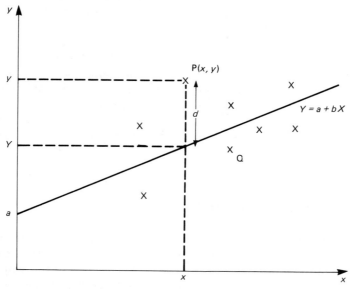

Fig. 38. *Determining regression line Y by method of least squares.*

# 9 REGRESSION AND CORRELATION

Then $d$ is defined as:

$$d = y - Y \qquad (2)$$

i.e. the distance of the point P from the regression line parallel to the $y$-axis.

*Note: The reason d is measured parallel to the y-axis is that we are trying to predict the Y-value from a given x-value, and we are interested in the difference between our predicted Y-value and an observed value y.*

In Fig. 38 the $d$-value is positive but if we take the point Q then $d$ will be negative. We are concerned with how close the observed values are to the regression line, and not whether the points are above or below the line, so to remove the sign problem we now consider the square of $d$,

i.e. 
$$d^2 = (y - Y)^2. \qquad (3)$$

Now the equation of our straight line is:

$$Y = a + bX \text{ (But } X = x.) \qquad (1)$$

Therefore replacing $Y$ in (3) by (1) we get:

$$d^2 = (y - a - bx)^2. \qquad (4)$$

If we repeat this procedure for all the points in our sample obtaining a $d^2$ value for each point and then sum all the $d^2$ values we get:

$$S = \sum (y - a - bx)^2, \qquad (5)$$

where $S$ is defined as the sum of the squares of $d$ for all points in the sample.

This expression can be used to see how well a line fits the data. If all the points actually lie on the line then all the $d$'s will be zero, making $S$ equal to zero. If the line is badly drawn then some of the $d$'s will be large, making $S$ large.

In general, all the points are unlikely to be on the regression line and the line we are seeking is the one that gives us the minimum value of $S$. Hence the expression the "least-squares regression line".

Now in general we will have $n$ points and we will know all the $x$ and $y$ values; our problem is to find $a$ and $b$ such that

$$S = \sum (y - a - bx)^2$$

is a minimum.

This problem can be solved using the calculus by partially differentiating with respect to both $a$ and $b$ and then setting the two resulting equations to zero.

Solving the two equations we get:

$$b = \frac{n \sum xy - \sum x \sum y}{n \sum x^2 - (\sum x)^2}, \qquad (6)$$

$$a = \frac{\sum y}{n} - b \frac{\sum x}{n}. \qquad (7)$$

Hence for any given set of $n$ points we can calculate $a$ and $b$ by the use of formulae (6) and (7) and then substitute in

$$Y = a + bX$$

to get our regression line.

## 5.0 CALCULATION OF REGRESSION LINE

Let us now determine the regression line for Example 1. We have the labour hours (1,000s) as our $x$-variable and overheads (£000), as our $y$-variable. To calculate $a$ and $b$ we need to determine the terms $\sum x$, $\sum y$, $\sum xy$ and $\sum x^2$. These calculations are best done in table form:

| $x$ | $y$ | $x^2$ | $xy$ | $y^2$ |
|---|---|---|---|---|
| 15 | 45 | 225 | 675 | 2,025 |
| 38 | 75 | 1,444 | 2,850 | 5,625 |
| 30 | 53 | 900 | 1,590 | 2,809 |
| 45 | 67 | 2,025 | 3,015 | 4,489 |
| 22 | 60 | 484 | 1,320 | 3,600 |
| 18 | 48 | 324 | 864 | 2,304 |
| 24 | 64 | 576 | 1,536 | 4,096 |
| 30 | 55 | 900 | 1,650 | 3,025 |
| 36 | 60 | 1,296 | 2,160 | 3,600 |
| 25 | 58 | 625 | 1,450 | 3,364 |
| 40 | 78 | 1,600 | 3,120 | 6,084 |
| 20 | 55 | 400 | 1,100 | 3,025 |
| 343 | 718 | 10,799 | 21,330 | 44,046 |

(We have also calculated $\sum y^2$, which we do not need at the moment but will require later.)

Now $$b = \frac{n \sum xy - \sum x \sum y}{n \sum x^2 - (\sum x)^2} = \frac{12 \times 21{,}330 - 343 \times 718}{12 \times 10{,}799 - (343)^2}$$

$\therefore \quad b = 0.8112.$

Now $$a = \frac{\sum y}{n} - b \frac{\sum x}{n}$$

$\therefore \quad a = \dfrac{718}{12} - 0.8112 \times \dfrac{343}{12}$

$\quad = 36.6.$

Our regression line is $\quad Y = 36.6 + 0.811x.$

# 9 REGRESSION AND CORRELATION

The slope of the regression line 0.811 (our *b*-value) gives us the variable cost, i.e. for every extra 1,000 hours of direct labour our costs will rise by £812. The fixed cost is given by the intercept on the *y*-axis (or the *a*-value) as £36,600.

## 6.0 FORECASTING USING REGRESSION LINE

Now the problem we posed in Example 1 was that we want to forecast the likely overhead cost in January, having estimated the number of labour hours (1,000s) required as 40.

We need to substitute $x = 40$ in our regression line.

$$\therefore \quad Y = 36.6 + 0.811 \times 40$$

$$= 69.04.$$

The estimate of overhead cost next January is £69,040.

## 7.0 CORRELATION

Strictly speaking, just carrying out a regression analysis does not prove that a line is a good fit or that there is a relationship between the *x*- and *y*-variables.

Given a set of any *n* points we can calculate the terms $\sum x$, $\sum y$, $\sum xy$ and $\sum x^2$ and hence calculate *a* and *b*, the coefficients of the regression line.

What we need is a measure of the fit of the data to the calculated regression line.

### 7.1 Pearson's product-moment correlation coefficient

We assumed in our regression analysis that *y* depended upon *x* and we calculated the regression line

$$Y = a + bX.$$

If now we assume that *x* depends upon *y* (merely to allow us to develop our measure) we can derive a new regression line by the least-squares method, say

$$y = a' + b'X$$

where $a'$ and $b'$ are the regression coefficients. These two lines come from the same set of data but with different assumptions about dependency. The only time that these two lines are identical is when all the points actually lie in a straight line—the perfect fit situation. If all the points lie close to a line then the angle between our two regression lines is small. If the points are all scattered then the angle between the lines approaches the extreme value of $90°$.

We can use this fact, that "the better the fit of the data to the regression line then the smaller the angle between the two regression lines," to determine a measure of correlation.

Pearson developed his product-moment correlation coefficient from this approach

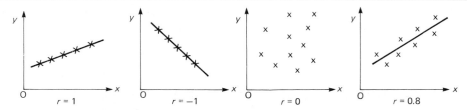

Fig. 39. *Variation of Pearson's product-moment correlation coefficient r.*

and defined the correlation coefficient $r$ as

$$r = \frac{n\sum xy - \sum x \sum y}{\sqrt{[n\sum x^2 - (\sum x)^2][n\sum y^2 - (\sum y)^2]}}$$

It can be show that r *numerically* varies from zero to one and can be positive or negative. If all the points lie on a line with a positive slope then $r = 1$; if the line has a negative slope then $r = -1$. If the points are scattered then $r$ will be close to zero (Fig. 39).

## 7.2 Calculation of correlation coefficient

Let us calculate the correlation coefficient for Example 1.

$$r = \frac{n\sum xy - \sum x \sum y}{\sqrt{[n\sum x^2 - (\sum x)^2][n\sum y^2 - (\sum y)^2]}}$$

From our previous table calculations,

$$r = \frac{12 \times 21{,}330 - 343 \times 718}{\sqrt{[12 \times 10{,}799 - (343)^2] \times [12 \times 44{,}046 - (718)^2]}}$$

$$= 0.777.$$

This is a reasonably high value of the correlation coefficient for a sample size 12; therefore we can deduce that the overhead costs are *correlated* with the number of labour hours.

Strictly speaking, we need to test if $r$ is significantly different from zero before we can comment (*see* later sections).

## 8.0 EXPLAINED AND UNEXPLAINED VARIATION

Consider the equation to determine $a$:

$$a = \frac{\sum y}{n} - b\frac{\sum x}{n}$$

Now $\quad \dfrac{\sum y}{n} = \bar{y}$ and $\dfrac{\sum x}{n} = \bar{x}$

$$\therefore \quad a = \bar{y} - b\bar{x} \quad \text{rearranged becomes}$$

# 9 REGRESSION AND CORRELATION

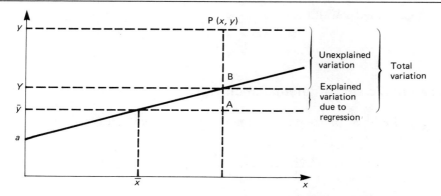

Fig. 40. *Explained and unexplained variations of y.*

$$\bar{y} = a + b\bar{x}$$

which is the regression line $Y = a + bX$ where $(X, Y)$ have been replaced by $(\bar{x}, \bar{y})$ respectively. This means that the point $(\bar{x}, \bar{y})$ lies on the regression line. The regression line passes through the means of the data. Now if $y$ is correlated with $x$ then our best estimate of $y$ is $Y$ calculated from the regression line; and if $y$ is not correlated with $x$ then our best estimate of $y$ is $\bar{y}$, the mean of the $y$'s.

We can use these results to look at correlation from another approach.

Consider the point P $(x, y)$ in Fig. 40. When a value $x$ occurred a value $y$ was observed. If there is *no regression* then the best estimate of the $y$-value is $\bar{y}$ and the difference between $y$ and $\bar{y}$, the distance PA, called the total variation, is given by the expression $(y - \bar{y})$. Now PA can be split into its two components PB and BA where PB $= (y - Y)$ and BA $= (Y - \bar{y})$.

If $y$ is correlated with $x$ then our best estimate of $y$ is $Y$, the value at B. Then the reason the estimate is B (i.e. $Y$) rather than A $(\bar{y})$ is *explained* by the fact that $y$ is correlated with $x$ and the estimate is given by the regression line $Y = a + bx$.

Hence BA (i.e., $Y - \bar{y}$) is called the explained variation, while the remaining component PB $(y - Y)$ is called the unexplained variation (*see* Fig. 40).

In practice, as each of the terms can go negative, we take the squares of the differences and repeat the same steps for all the $n$ points.

Thus the total variation becomes:

$$\sum (y - \bar{y})^2;$$

the explained variation is:

$$\sum (Y - \bar{y})^2,$$

and the unexplained variation is:

$$\sum (y - Y)^2.$$

## 8.1 The coefficient of determination

To measure the fit of the regression line to the data we can consider the ratio:

$$\frac{\text{Explained variation}}{\text{Total variation}} = \frac{\sum (Y - \bar{y})^2}{\sum (y - \bar{y})^2}.$$

If all the points lie on the line then the unexplained variation is zero and hence the explained variation equals the total variation and our ratio is one. If the unexplained variation is very large compared with the explained variation the ratio approaches zero. So we have a ratio which varies between 0 and 1. It can be shown that this ratio equals $r^2$ where $r$ is Pearson's product-moment measure of correlation.

This ratio is called the *coefficient of determination* $r^2$. $r^2$ tells us how much of the variation is explained by the regression line.

In our Example 1, $r = 0.777$, therefore

$$r^2 = (0.777)^2$$
$$= 0.604.$$

This means that 60.4 per cent of the variation is explained by the regression and conversely 39.6 per cent of the variation is unexplained.

This unexplained variation may be due to sampling errors or other factors not taken into account by the regression analysis.

## Example 2

The closing price of an electrical share and the electrical share market index have been recorded over a ten-day period:

| Market index | $(x)$ | 65 | 63 | 67 | 64 | 68 | 62 | 70 | 66 | 68 | 67 |
|---|---|---|---|---|---|---|---|---|---|---|---|
| Share price | $(y)$ | 67 | 66 | 68 | 65 | 69 | 66 | 68 | 66 | 69 | 67 |

Calculate a regression equation relating the share price to the market index. Determine the coefficient of correlation and comment on your results. Forecast the share price when the market index is 66.

# 9 REGRESSION AND CORRELATION

**SOLUTION**

| $x$ | $y$ | $x^2$ | $xy$ | $y^2$ |
|---|---|---|---|---|
| 65 | 67 | 4,225 | 4,355 | 4,489 |
| 63 | 66 | 3,969 | 4,158 | 4,356 |
| 67 | 68 | 4,489 | 4,556 | 4,624 |
| 64 | 65 | 4,096 | 4,160 | 4,225 |
| 68 | 69 | 4,624 | 4,692 | 4,761 |
| 62 | 66 | 3,844 | 4,092 | 4,356 |
| 70 | 68 | 4,900 | 4,760 | 4,624 |
| 66 | 66 | 4,356 | 4,356 | 4,356 |
| 68 | 69 | 4,624 | 4,692 | 4,761 |
| 67 | 67 | 4,489 | 4,489 | 4,489 |
| 660 | 671 | 43,616 | 44,310 | 45,041 |

$$b = \frac{n\sum xy - \sum x \sum y}{n\sum x^2 - (\sum x)^2}$$

$$= \frac{10 \times 44{,}310 - 660 \times 671}{10 \times 43{,}616 - (660)^2}$$

$$= \underline{\underline{0.429}}.$$

$$a = \frac{\sum y}{n} - \frac{b\sum x}{n}$$

$$= \frac{671}{10} - 0.429 \times \frac{660}{10} = \underline{\underline{38.79}}.$$

Regression line is:

$$y = 38.79 + 0.429x$$

$$r = \frac{n\sum xy - \sum x \sum y}{\sqrt{[n\sum x^2 - (\sum x)^2][n\sum y^2 - (\sum y)^2]}}$$

$$= \frac{10 \times 44{,}310 - 660 \times 671}{\sqrt{[10 \times 43{,}616 - (660)^2][10 \times 45{,}041 - (671)^2]}}$$

$$= \underline{\underline{0.78}}.$$

The share price and market index price are positively correlated.
Now $r^2 = (0.78)^2 = 0.608$.
Therefore 60.8 per cent of the variation is explained by the regression line $Y = 38.79 + 0.429x$.

Forecast: when $x = 66$, $y = 38.79 + 0.429 \times 66$, $Y = 67.1$.
Share price estimate is 67.1.

## 8.2 Rank correlation

Occasionally we may need to determine the correlation between two variables where suitable measures of one or both variables do not exist. If it is possible to arrange each set of data in order of increasing value then we may "rank" the data, the lowest value having the rank of 1, the next value the rank of 2 and so on up to the largest which has a rank of $n$.

It would then be possible to use the ranks of the two variables as our $x$- and $y$-values and calculate $r$ using Pearson's product-moment formula. However, Spearman showed that when the data is ranked we can simplify $r$ to become $R$ where

$$R = 1 - \frac{6 \sum d^2}{n(n^2 - 1)}$$

and where $d$ equals the difference between the corresponding ranks.

### Example 3

Eight students were ranked on the results of both a Quantitative Analysis examination (QA) and a Management Accounting examination (MA):

| Student | A | B | C | D | E | F | G | H |
|---|---|---|---|---|---|---|---|---|
| Rank QA | 1 | 3 | 5 | 2 | 8 | 7 | 6 | 4 |
| Rank MA | 2 | 1 | 6 | 3 | 7 | 8 | 5 | 4 |

Calculate Spearman's rank correlation coefficient.

### SOLUTION

|  | A | B | C | D | E | F | G | H |
|---|---|---|---|---|---|---|---|---|
| $R_1$ | 1 | 3 | 5 | 2 | 8 | 7 | 6 | 4 |
| $R_2$ | 2 | 1 | 6 | 3 | 7 | 8 | 5 | 4 |
| $|d|$ | 1 | 2 | 1 | 1 | 1 | 1 | 1 | 0 |
| $d^2$ | 1 | 4 | 1 | 1 | 1 | 1 | 1 | 0 |

$\sum d^2 = 10$.

$\therefore R = 1 - \dfrac{6 \times 10}{8(64 - 1)} = \underline{\underline{0.88}}$ positively correlated.

## 8.3 Tied ranks

If in Example 3 students B and H gained equal third position in Quantitative Analysis we would have a situation of tied ranks. The fourth position would not have been

# 9 REGRESSION AND CORRELATION

allocated. To be able to use Spearman's formula both are given a rank of 3.5, the average ranks of 3 and 4.

$R$ then becomes $\underline{\underline{0.85}}$.

## 9.0 SUMMARY

The aim of this chapter has been to introduce the ideas of regression and correlation. You should now be able to calculate a regression line from a set of data and be able to use your regression line for forecasting. You should also be able to calculate a correlation coefficient and the coefficient of determination and to interpret the results obtained.

*Regression line*

$$Y = a + bX$$

where

$$b = \frac{n\sum xy - \sum x \sum y}{n\sum x^2 - (\sum x)^2} \quad \text{and} \quad a = \frac{\sum y}{n} - b\frac{\sum x}{n}.$$

*Correlation coefficients*

$$r = \frac{n\sum xy - \sum x \sum y}{\sqrt{[n\sum x^2 - (\sum x)^2][n\sum y^2 - (\sum y)^2]}}.$$

$$R = 1 - \frac{6\sum d^2}{n(n^2 - 1)}.$$

# CHAPTER TEN

# Sampling Theory and Regression

## 1.0 INTRODUCTION

The regression line is the line that best fits the data, but it is not in general a perfect fit—all the points do not lie on the line. For a given value of $x$ we assume that the possible $y$-values will be normally distributed about the true regression line. The normal distribution has a mean and a standard deviation. Our estimate of the mean value is $Y$, the $y$-value on the regression line. We assume that the standard deviation $\sigma$ is the same for all values of $x$.

An unbiased estimator of $\sigma$ is:

$$\hat{\sigma} = \sqrt{\frac{\sum(y - Y)^2}{n - 2}}.$$

This is not a suitable form for calculation. An alternative form is:

$$\hat{\sigma} = \sigma_y \sqrt{\frac{n - 1}{n - 2} \cdot (1 - r^2)},$$

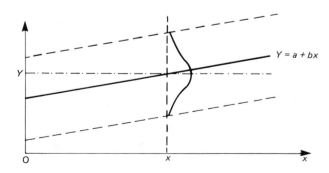

Fig. 41. *Confidence limits for regression line Y (variation of points about true line).*

# 10 SAMPLING THEORY AND REGRESSION

where $\sigma_y$ is the unbiased estimator of the standard deviation of $y$,

i.e. $$\sigma_y = \sqrt{\frac{\sum y^2 - (\sum y)^2/n}{n-1}}.$$

Using $\hat{\sigma}$ we can calculate a 95 per cent confidence interval for the $Y$-value for any value of $x$ (*see* parallel broken lines in Fig. 41).

## 1.1 Calculation of the standard deviation of the estimate for Example 1 in Chapter 9 (p.84).

Using our column totals in Chapter 9, **5.0**:

$$\sigma_y = \sqrt{\frac{44{,}046 - 718^2/12}{11}} = 9.935,$$

$$\therefore \hat{\sigma} = 9.935\sqrt{\frac{11}{10}(1 - 0.777^2)}$$

$$= \underline{\underline{6.56}}.$$

## 2.0 CALCULATION OF A 95 PER CENT CONFIDENCE INTERVAL OF THE ESTIMATE

Previously for Chapter 9 Example 1 we estimated that using the regression line $Y = 36.6 + 0.811x$, when $x = 40$, $Y = 69.04$. (*See* Chapter 9, **6.0**.) We can now calculate a 95 per cent confidence interval using the $t$-distribution (Fig. 42; $n$ is small and $\sigma$ has been estimated).

From Table 2, using $n - 2$ degrees of freedom, $t_{0.025}(V = 12 - 2) = 2.2$.

$\therefore$ 95 per cent confidence interval $= 69.04 \pm 2.2 \times 6.56$

$$= \underline{\underline{69.04 \pm 14.43}}.$$

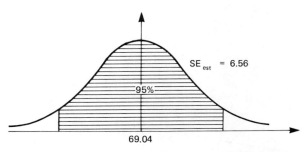

Fig. 42. *Calculation of confidence interval of the estimate of regression line Y.*

## 3.0 SOURCES OF ERROR IN THE ESTIMATE

There are three sources of error in the estimate:

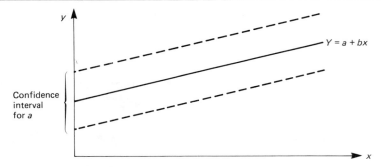

Fig. 43. *Confidence limits for regression line Y (error in estimating a).*

(a) All the points do not lie on the regression line, i.e. $r \neq 1$ or $-1$. This error was covered in **1.0** and results in parallel confidence limits (*see* Fig 41).

(b) Error in estimating $a$, the intercept on the $y$-axis. We are estimating the regression line from a sample, therefore our value of $a$ is only an estimate of the *true a* and is subject to error. This result again leads to confidence limits being parallel to the regression line (Fig. 43).

(c) Error in estimating $b$, the slope of the regression line. The regression line goes through $(\bar{x}, \bar{y})$, therefore the confidence limits due to $b$ fan out from the mean point (Fig. 44). This means that the confidence interval gets wider as $x$ deviates from $\bar{x}$.

The three sources of error combined result in curved confidence limits as in Fig. 45. The standard error is given by the expression

$$\text{SE}_{\text{est}} = \hat{\sigma}\sqrt{1 + \frac{1}{n} + \frac{(x^1 - \bar{x})^2}{(n-1)\sigma_x^2}},$$

where $x^1$ is the value for which we want to calculate the confidence interval for $y$ and $\sigma_x$; the estimated standard deviation of the $x$-values is given by

$$\sigma_x = \sqrt{\frac{\sum x^2 - (\sum x)^2/n}{n-1}}.$$

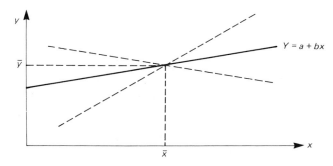

Fig. 44. *Confidence limits for regression line Y (error in estimating b).*

# 10 SAMPLING THEORY AND REGRESSION

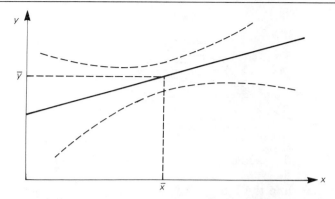

Fig. 45. *Confidence limits for regression line Y (three sources of error).*

## 4.0 RECALCULATION OF A 95 PER CENT CONFIDENCE INTERVAL OF THE ESTIMATE

Let us revisit the problem we posed in **2.0** and recalculate the 95 per cent confidence interval of the estimate using the standard error as given in **3.0**.

Using the regression line calculated in Chapter 9,

$$Y = 36.6 + 0.811x; \qquad \text{where } x = 40, \; Y = 69.04.$$

We need initially to calculate $\bar{x}$ and $\sigma_x^2$ using the totals calculated in Chapter 9:

$$\bar{x} = \frac{\sum x}{n} = \frac{343}{12} = 28.583;$$

$$\sigma_x^2 = \frac{\sum x^2 - (\sum x)^2/n}{n-1} = \frac{10{,}799 - (343)^2/12}{11}$$

$$= 90.447.$$

We have previously calculated in **2.0** that:

$$\hat{\sigma} = 6.56, \text{ giving}$$

$$\text{SE}_{\text{est}} = 6.56 \sqrt{1 + \frac{1}{12} + \frac{(40 - 28.583)^2}{11 \times 90.447}}$$

$$= \underline{\underline{7.23}}.$$

From Table 2, using $n - 2$ degrees of freedom, $t_{0.025}\;(V = 12 - 2) = 2.2$.

$$\therefore \quad \text{95 per cent confidence interval for the estimate} = 69.04 \pm 2.2 \times 7.23$$

$$= \underline{\underline{69.04 \pm 15.91}}.$$

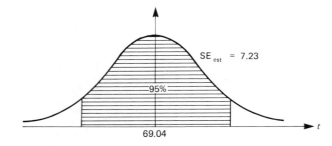

Fig. 46. *Recalculation of confidence interval of Y.*

This interval is wider than the interval calculated in **2.0** and it takes into account all three sources of error and not just one type of error.

## 5.0 CALCULATIONS USING STANDARD ERROR OF $b$

One of the three sources of error that occurs when calculating a regression line is the error in the $b$-value. The standard error of $b$ is given as:

$$SE_b = \frac{\hat{\sigma}}{\sqrt{n-1} \cdot \sigma_x}$$

$$\left(\text{An alternative form is: } SE_b = \frac{b}{r}\sqrt{\frac{1-r^2}{n-2}}.\right)$$

This allows us to calculate confidence intervals for $b$ or to carry out significance tests on the value of $b$, for example as follows.

(a) Calculate a 99 per cent confidence interval for $b$ in Chapter 9 Example 1. ($b$ was equal to 0.811.)

(b) Test if $b = 0.811$ is significantly different from zero at the 1 per cent level.

### SOLUTIONS
(a) We have calculated $\hat{\sigma}$ and $\sigma_x$ in previous sections (*see* results in **4.0**):

$$\hat{\sigma} = 6.56, \qquad \sigma_x = \sqrt{90.447} = 9.51.$$

$$\therefore \quad SE_b = \frac{6.56}{\sqrt{11} \times 9.51} = 0.208.$$

(*See* Fig. 47.)
$V = 12 - 2 = 10.$
From Table 2, $t_{0.005}(V = 10) = 3.2.$

$\therefore$ 99 per cent confidence interval for $b = 0.811 \pm 3.2 \times 0.208$

$$= \underline{\underline{0.811 \pm 0.666.}}$$

The slope varies between 0.145 and 1.477.

10 SAMPLING THEORY AND REGRESSION

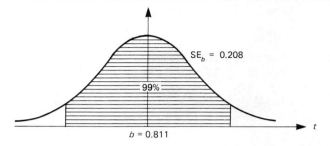

Fig. 47. *Calculation of 99 per cent confidence interval for slope b of regression line Y.*

(b) $H_0 : b = 0$, $H_1 : b \neq 0$; a two-tailed test (Fig. 48).
From Table 2, test values are: $t_{0.005} (V = 10) = \pm 3.2$;

$$t = \frac{b_{\text{sample}} - 0}{\text{SE}_b} = \frac{0.811 - 0}{0.208} = 3.90.$$

$t = 3.90$ lies outside the test limits therefore the difference is significant at the 1 per cent level.

This means that the regression line does have a slope (i.e. it is not equal to zero) and consequently the data must be correlated.

By testing that $b$ is significantly different from zero we have also indirectly tested that $r$, the correlation coefficient, is significantly different from zero. The two tests are mathematically equivalent.

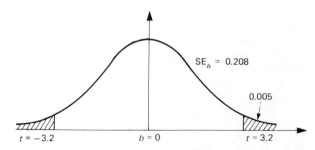

Fig. 48. *Test for significant difference of slope b from zero.*

## 6.0 CALCULATIONS USING STANDARD ERROR OF $a$

$a$, being estimated, is also a source of error. The standard error of $a$ is:

$$\text{SE}_a = \frac{\hat{\sigma}\sqrt{\sum x^2}}{\sigma_x \sqrt{n(n-1)}}.$$

We can now perform calculations for confidence intervals or significance tests, for example:

(a) Calculate a 99 per cent confidence interval for $a = 36.6$.

(b) Test at the 1 per cent level if $a = 36.6$ is significantly different from zero.

**SOLUTIONS**

(a) From previous calculations we know that
$$\hat{\sigma} = 6.56, \ \sigma_x = 9.51 \ \text{and} \ \sum x^2 = 10{,}799.$$

$$\therefore \ \text{SE}_a = \frac{6.56\sqrt{10{,}799}}{9.51\sqrt{12 \times 11}} = 6.24.$$

(*See* Fig. 49.)

Now
$$t_{0.005}\ (V = 10) = 3.2.$$

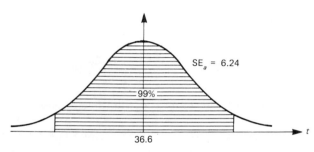

Fig. 49. *Calculation of 99 per cent confidence interval for a-value.*

$\therefore$ 99 per cent confidence interval $= 36.6 \pm 3.2 \times 6.24$
$$= \underline{\underline{36.6 \pm 20.0}}.$$

(b) $H_0 : a = 0$, $H_1 : a \neq 0$.

(*See* Fig. 50.)
Test values: $t_{0.005}(V = 10) = 3.2$.

$$t = \frac{a_{\text{sample}} - 0}{\text{SE}_a} = \frac{36.6 - 0}{6.24} = 5.87.$$

$t = 5.87$ lies outside the test limits, therefore the difference is significant at the 1 per cent level. This means there is a constant term and our best estimate of $a$ is 36.6.

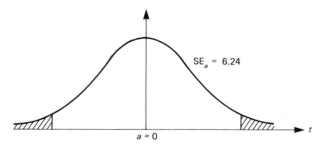

Fig. 50. *Test for significant difference of a-value from zero.*

## 7.0 MULTIPLE REGRESSION

If a variable $y$ depends upon several different variables, say $x_1$ and $x_2$, then we can obtain a linear relationship

$$Y = a + bx_1 + cx_2$$

by the least-squares method. (In practice a computer package would be used to speed up the calculations.)

To measure how well the regression line fits the data we still need to calculate the correlation coefficient and the coefficient of determination. In addition we can also calculate the partial correlation coefficients of $Y$ against $x_1$, $Y$ against $x_2$, and $x_1$ against $x_2$. These results would usually be printed out in the form of a correlation matrix.

### Example 3

The statisticians at Numerical Machines Ltd believe that the total overhead costs ($y$) depend upon the direct labour hours ($x_1$) and the machine hours ($x_2$).

The figures were recorded over an 8-month period and were as shown in Table 5.

Table 5. Costs, labour hours and machine hours over eight months.

| Month | Total overhead cost (£000) $y$ | Direct labour (100 hours) $x_1$ | Machine hours $x_2$ |
|---|---|---|---|
| 1 | 61 | 7.5 | 90 |
| 2 | 59 | 8.2 | 78 |
| 3 | 62 | 10.3 | 82 |
| 4 | 60 | 9.0 | 86 |
| 5 | 63 | 10.7 | 86 |
| 6 | 60 | 8.6 | 82 |
| 7 | 64 | 10.9 | 87 |
| 8 | 66 | 11.1 | 87 |

The computer print-out of the regression analysis gives the following information:

| Variable | Coefficient | SE | t-value |
|---|---|---|---|
| $x_1$ | 1.32 | 0.29 | 4.49 |
| $x_2$ | 0.242 | 0.10 | 2.27 |
| Constant | 28.73 | 9.03 | 3.18 |

| | |
|---|---|
| Coefficient of determination | 0.855. |
| Multiple correlation coefficient | 0.925. |
| Standard error of estimate | 1.06. |

Correlation matrix:

|     | Y    | $x_1$ | $x_2$ |
|-----|------|-------|-------|
| Y   | 1    | 0.84  | 0.52  |
| $x_1$ | 0.84 | 1     | 0.17  |
| $x_2$ | 0.52 | 0.17  | 1     |

Comment on the result.

**SOLUTION**
The regression line is:

$$Y = 28.73 + 1.32 x_1 + 0.242 x_2.$$

The coefficient of determination shows that 85.5 per cent of the variation is explained by the regression. The multiple correlation coefficient is high at 0.925. Testing at the 5 per cent level, $t_{0.025}$ ($V = 8 - 3$) = 2.6, both the constant term and the $x$-coefficient are significantly different from zero. However the coefficient of $x_2$ fails the test.

Note also that the correlation of $Y$ with $x_2$ from our correlation matrix is only 0.52. These results would indicate that the variable $x_2$ might be dropped from the analysis and some other more suitable variable considered.

## 8.0 SUMMARY

The aim of this chapter has been to relate your regression and correlation theory to your sampling theory. The major point to appreciate is that when we estimate a regression line we are estimating from a sample and therefore incur sampling errors. There are three sources of error:

(a) the variation of the points about the true regression line;

(b) error in estimating $a$;

(c) error in estimating $b$.

**Standard error formulae**

$$\text{Intercept} \quad SE_a = \frac{\hat{\sigma}\sqrt{\sum x^2}}{\sigma_x \sqrt{n(n-1)}}.$$

$$\text{Slope} \quad SE_b = \frac{\hat{\sigma}}{\sqrt{n-1}\sigma_x} \quad \text{or} \quad \frac{b}{r}\sqrt{\frac{1-r^2}{n-2}}.$$

## 10 SAMPLING THEORY AND REGRESSION

*Estimate*
$$SE_{\text{est}} = \hat{\sigma}\sqrt{1 + \frac{1}{n} + \frac{(x^1 - \bar{x})^2}{(n-1)\sigma_x^2}}$$

where $\hat{\sigma} = \sigma_y \sqrt{\dfrac{n-1}{n-2}(1-r^2)}$.

(This is the standard deviation of the individual $y$-values about the regression line.)

$$\sigma_x = \sqrt{\frac{\sum x^2 - (\sum x)^2/n}{n-1}}$$

(the standard deviation of the $x$ values)

and

$$\sigma_y = \sqrt{\frac{\sum y^2 - (\sum y)^2/n}{n-1}}$$

(the standard deviation of the $y$-values).

# CHAPTER ELEVEN

# Exponential and Logarithmic Functions, Learning curve

## 1.0 REVISION OF LOGARITHMS

$10^2 = 100$ and $\log_{10}(100) = 2$ are equivalent statements. The words "index" and "log" are interchangeable. The log of a number is merely the index of the number for a given base. Hence the log of 10,000 in the base of 10 is 4 as $10^4 = 10,000$. Also, $\log_{10} 2 = 0.3010$ may be written as $10^{0.3010} = 2$.

## 2.0 RULES FOR INDICES AND LOGS

Now $10^3 \times 10^2 = 10^{3+2} = 10^5$.

In general, $$x^a \cdot x^b = x^{a+b}.$$

When we multiply two numbers together in the same base we add the indices (or logs) together,

i.e. $$\log(AB) = \log A + \log B.$$

Now $10^3 \div 10^2 = 10^{3-2} = 10^1$.

In general, $$x^a \div x^b = x^{a-b}.$$

When we divide two numbers in the same base, we subtract the indices (or logs),

i.e. $$\log(A/B) = \log A - \log B.$$

Now $(10^3)^2 = 10^{3 \times 2} = 10^6$.

In general, $$(10^a)^b = 10^{ab}.$$

When we raise a power term to a further power we multiply the indices (or logs),

i.e. $$(\log a)^b = b \log a.$$

## 3.0 LOG GRAPHS

There are a number of log and exponential graphs you should be familiar with. The first set are the log graphs:

(a) $\qquad y = \log_{10} x,$

(b) $\qquad y = \log_e x.$

The latter is called a *natural logarithm*.
   Taking values of $x$ from 1 to 10,
   (a) $y = \log_{10} x$

| $x$ | 1 | 2 | 3 | 4 | 5 | 6 | 7 | 8 | 9 | 10 |
|---|---|---|---|---|---|---|---|---|---|---|
| $y$ | 0 | 0.30 | 0.48 | 0.60 | 0.70 | 0.78 | 0.85 | 0.90 | 0.95 | 1.0 |

*See* Fig. 51.

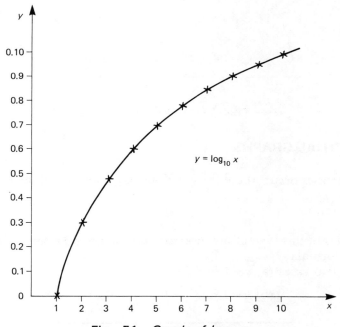

Fig. 51. *Graph of $\log_{10} x$.*

(b) $y = \log_e x$

| $x$ | 1 | 2 | 3 | 4 | 5 | 6 | 7 | 8 | 9 | 10 |
|---|---|---|---|---|---|---|---|---|---|---|
| $y$ | 0 | 0.69 | 1.10 | 1.39 | 1.61 | 1.79 | 1.95 | 2.08 | 2.20 | 2.30 |

*See* Fig. 52.

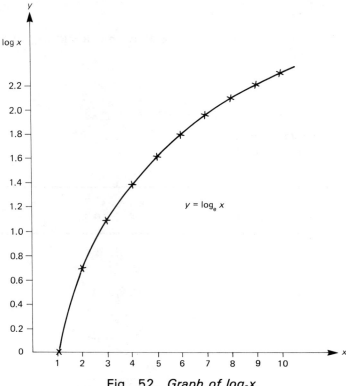

Fig. 52. *Graph of $\log_e x$.*

## 4.0 EXPONENTIAL GRAPHS

Exponential functions occur where the $x$-variable is an index and the function is of the form
$$y = ab^x.$$
Discrete examples of this type of function are the compound interest formula and the discount factor formula.

Consider the two cases (a) $a = 1$ and $b = 2$, $y = 2^x$,

(b) $a = 1$ and $b = 0.5$, $y = (0.5)^x$.

(a)

| $x$ | 0 | 1 | 2 | 3 | 4 | 5 |
|---|---|---|---|---|---|---|
| $y$ | 1 | 2 | 4 | 8 | 16 | 32 |

(b)

| $x$ | 0 | 1 | 2 | 3 | 4 | 5 |
|---|---|---|---|---|---|---|
| $y$ | 1 | 0.5 | 0.25 | 0.125 | 0.063 | 0.031 |

*See* Figs. 53 and 54.

# 11 EXPONENTIAL AND LOGARITHMIC FUNCTIONS, LEARNING CURVE

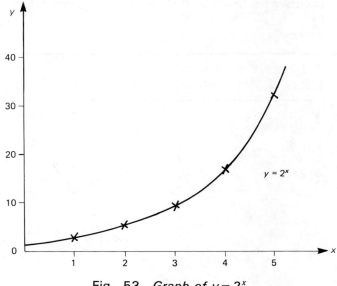

Fig. 53. *Graph of $y = 2^x$.*

In Fig. 53 as $x$ gets larger $y$ shoots off to infinity.
In Fig. 54 as $x$ gets larger $y$ gets smaller and smaller and will tend to zero.

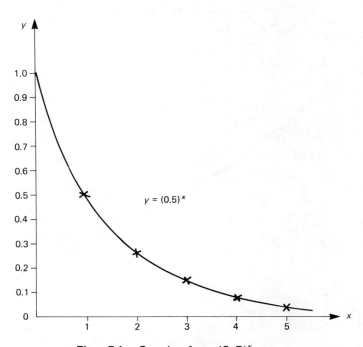

Fig. 54. *Graph of $y = (0.5)^x$.*

A special case occurs when $b = e$ and we get the exponential functions:

(c) $$y = e^x,$$

| $x$ | 0 | 0.1 | 0.2 | 0.3 | 0.4 | 0.5 | 0.6 | 0.7 | 0.8 | 0.9 | 1.0 |
|---|---|---|---|---|---|---|---|---|---|---|---|
| $y$ | 1 | 1.11 | 1.22 | 1.35 | 1.49 | 1.65 | 1.82 | 2.01 | 2.23 | 2.46 | 2.72 |

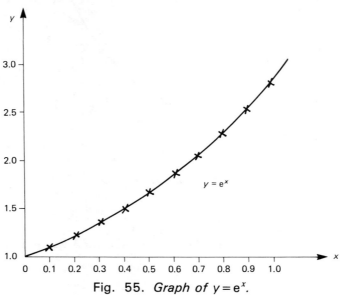

Fig. 55. *Graph of $y = e^x$.*

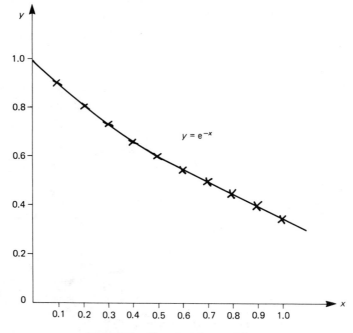

Fig. 56. *Graph of $y = e^{-x}$.*

# 11 EXPONENTIAL AND LOGARITHMIC FUNCTIONS, LEARNING CURVE

(d) $y = e^{-x}$.

| $x$ | 0 | 0.1 | 0.2 | 0.3 | 0.4 | 0.5 | 0.6 | 0.7 | 0.8 | 0.9 | 1.0 |
|---|---|---|---|---|---|---|---|---|---|---|---|
| $y$ | 1 | 0.90 | 0.82 | 0.74 | 0.67 | 0.61 | 0.55 | 0.50 | 0.45 | 0.41 | 0.37 |

*See* Figs. 55 and 56.

Figure 56 is the graph of the negative exponential function. You will meet a form of this function $y = \lambda e^{-\lambda t}$ when you consider the service time and inter-arrival distribution in the simple queue situation.

## 5.0 THE LEARNING CURVE

When new products or processes are started which have a high degree of manual skill incorporated in them then a learning situation takes place. The learning curve will allow us to predict how costs or time of the process will change as the process matures. Time or cost in relation to the curve should always be measured over the life of the product up to the time under consideration. Work in this area has shown that the time needed per unit of product should be progressively smaller at some constant percentage rate as experience is gained. The percentage rates vary between 60 and 85 per cent, 80 per cent being the most common.

Obviously, after a period of time a steady condition will arise.

A useful definition is:

"As cumulative quantities *double*, *average* time per unit (measured over the total time to date) will fall to a fixed percentage of the previous time."

Let us consider an example where the first unit has taken 100 hours of time and the 80 per cent learning curve applies. Then Table 6 can be generated.

It can be seen that the average time per extra unit is dropping, i.e. we learn from experience.

Now, if we plot the average time over the life of the product ($y$) against the number of units ($x$) we get the graph in Fig. 57.

Table 6. Data used in construction of learning curve.

| Number of units | | Average time over life of product | | Total time used | Incremental time | Average time per extra unit |
|---|---|---|---|---|---|---|
| 1 | × | 100 | = | 100 | 100 for 1 | 100 |
| × 2 | | × 80% | | | | |
| 2 | × | 80 | = | 160 | 60 for 1 | 60 |
| × 2 | | × 80% | | | | |
| 4 | × | 64 | = | 256 | 96 for 2 | 48 |
| × 2 | | × 80% | | | | |
| 8 | × | 51.2 | = | 409.6 | 153.6 for 4 | 38.4 |
| 16 | × | 41.0 | = | 656 | 246.4 for 8 | 30.8 |

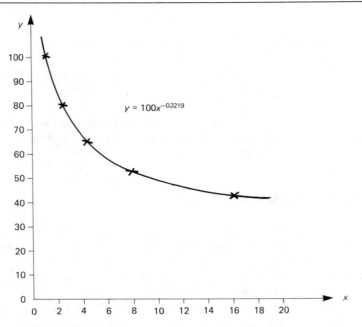

Fig. 57. *Learning curve: average time over life of product (y) against number of units (x).*

We can now use the graph for finding values of $y$ for intermediate values of $x$ other than those obtained by doubling. For example, when $x = 3$, $y = 70.2$ approximately from the graph.

## 6.0 EQUATION OF LEARNING CURVE

Alternatively, using algebra we can show that the graph in Fig.57 has the function form of

$$y = ax^{-b}.$$

Now in our example when $x = 1$, $y = 100$

$$\therefore \quad 100 = a(1)^{-b}$$
$$= \underline{\underline{a}}.$$

i.e. $a$ is the time to produce the first unit.

We now have $y = 100x^{-b}$

For our example, when $x = 2$, $y = 80$
$$\therefore \quad 80 = 100\,(2)^{-b}$$
$$\therefore \quad 0.80 = 2^{-b}$$

# 11 EXPONENTIAL AND LOGARITHMIC FUNCTIONS, LEARNING CURVE

Taking logs of both sides:

$$\log(0.80) = -b \log 2$$

$$\therefore b = -\frac{\log(0.80)}{\log 2}$$

$$= \frac{-(-0.09691)}{0.3010}$$

$$= \underline{0.3219}.$$

Therefore our learning curve is:

$$y = 100x^{-0.3219}.$$

*Note: b can be calculated from the formula*

$$b = \frac{-\log(\text{Learning curve rate expressed as a decimal})}{\log 2}$$

To show the use of the equation $y = 100x^{-0.3219}$, calculate $y$ when $x = 5$.

$$y = 100(5)^{-0.3219}$$

$$y = 59.57.$$

## 7.0 ESTIMATING LEARNING RATE BY REGRESSION

### Example 1

The following cumulative average costs have been observed for product $x$.

| Number of units ($x$) | 1 | 2 | 3 | 4 | 5 | 6 |
|---|---|---|---|---|---|---|
| Cumulative average cost ($y$) | 51 | 30 | 22 | 20 | 14 | 11 |

Using regression, estimate the learning rate.

### SOLUTION

Now the learning curve is $y = ax^{-b}$.
Take logs of both sides:

$$\log y = \log a - b \log x.$$

Now let $Y = \log y$, $A = \log a$, $B = -b$, and $X = \log x$.
Then our equation becomes:

$$Y = A + BX,$$

an equation of a straight line.

*Step 1.* Calculate $A$ and $B$ by regression.

| $x$ | $y$ | $X$ (log $x$) | $Y$ (log $y$) | $XY$ | $X^2$ |
|---|---|---|---|---|---|
| 1 | 51 | 0 | 1.7075 | 0 | 0 |
| 2 | 30 | 0.3010 | 1.4771 | 0.4446 | 0.0906 |
| 3 | 22 | 0.4771 | 1.3424 | 0.6405 | 0.2276 |
| 4 | 20 | 0.6021 | 1.3010 | 0.7833 | 0.3625 |
| 5 | 14 | 0.6990 | 1.1461 | 0.8011 | 0.4886 |
| 6 | 11 | 0.7782 | 1.0414 | 0.8104 | 0.6056 |
| | | 2.8574 | 8.0156 | 3.4799 | 1.7749 |

$$B = \frac{n\sum XY - \sum X \sum Y}{n\sum X^2 - (\sum X)^2} = \frac{6 \times 3.4799 - 2.8574 \times 8.0156}{6 \times 1.7749 - (2.8574)^2}$$

$$= \underline{-0.8147}.$$

Now $\qquad B = -b$

$\therefore \quad b = 0.8147$

but $\qquad b = \dfrac{-\log r}{\log 2}$ where $r$ is the learning rate.

$\therefore \quad \log r = -b \log 2$

$\qquad\qquad = -0.8147 \times 0.3010$

$\qquad\qquad = -0.2452$

$\therefore \quad r = 0.5686.$

Therefore learning rate is $\underline{56.9 \text{ per cent}}$.

Also:

$$A = \frac{\sum Y}{n} - B\frac{\sum X}{n} = \frac{8.0156}{6} - (-0.8147)\frac{(2.8574)}{6} = 1.7239.$$

Now $\qquad A = \log a,$

$\therefore \quad a = 52.95,$

i.e. cost of first unit = 53.

## 8.0 SUMMARY

The aim of this chapter has been to introduce logarithmic and exponential functions and to show how they appear on a graph. The major part of this chapter was concerned

# 11 EXPONENTIAL AND LOGARITHMIC FUNCTIONS, LEARNING CURVE

with the learning curve, including the important part of determining the learning rate by means of regression.

## Formulae

Log function: $y = \log_{10} x$, and $y = \log_e x$.

Exponential form: $y = ab^x$.

Exponential function: $y = e^x$.

Negative exponential function: $y = e^{-x}$.

Learning curve: $\quad\quad\quad y = ax^{-b}$

$$b = -\frac{\log(\text{learning rate})}{\log 2}.$$

# CHAPTER TWELVE
# Variances, Covariances and r

## 1.0 VARIANCES AND COVARIANCES

If we add together two distributions $x$ and $y$ then the mean of the joint distribution is the sum of the means of the separate distributions,

i.e. $$E(x+y) = E(x) + E(y).$$

Unfortunately the variances do not combine in such a simple way.

We get $$\text{var}(x+y) = \text{var}(x) + \text{var}(y) + 2\,\text{cov}(x, y)$$

Now $$\text{var}(X) = \frac{\sum x^2}{n} - \bar{x}^2$$

$$\text{var}(Y) = \frac{\sum y^2}{n} - \bar{y}^2$$

and $$\text{cov}(x, y) = \frac{\sum xy}{n} - \bar{x}\bar{y}.$$

*Example 1*

| $x$ | $y$ |
|-----|-----|
| 3   | 11  |
| 5   | 5   |
| 9   | 7   |
| 10  | 8   |
| 13  | 4   |

Calculate the mean and variance of $x+y$ by the formulae (a) and directly (b).

## SOLUTION

| $x$ | $y$ | $xy$ | $x^2$ | $y^2$ | $(x+y)$ | $(x+y)^2$ |
|---|---|---|---|---|---|---|
| 3 | 11 | 33 | 9 | 121 | 14 | 196 |
| 5 | 5 | 25 | 25 | 25 | 10 | 100 |
| 9 | 7 | 63 | 81 | 49 | 10 | 256 |
| 10 | 8 | 80 | 100 | 64 | 18 | 324 |
| 13 | 4 | 52 | 169 | 16 | 17 | 289 |
| 40 | 35 | 253 | 384 | 275 | 75 | 1,165 |

(a)
$$E(x) = \frac{40}{5} = 8, \qquad E(y) = \frac{35}{5} = 7.$$

$$\therefore \quad E(x+y) = 8 + 7 = 15,$$

$$\text{var}(x) = \frac{384}{5} - 8^2 = 12.8,$$

$$\text{var}(y) = \frac{275}{5} - 7^2 = 6,$$

$$\text{cov}(x, y) = \frac{253}{5} - 8 \times 7 = -5.4$$

$$\therefore \quad \text{var}(x+y) = 12.8 + 6 + 2 \times (-5.4).$$
$$= 8,$$

(b)
$$E(x+y) = \frac{75}{5} = \underline{\underline{15}}.$$

$$\text{var}(x+y) = \frac{1,165}{5} - 15^2 = \underline{\underline{8}}.$$

## 2.0 INTRODUCING $r$

Now
$$r = \frac{n\sum xy - \sum x \sum y}{\sqrt{\{n\sum x^2 - (\sum x)^2\} \{n\sum y^2 - (\sum y)^2\}}}.$$

Divide top and bottom by $n^2$.

$$\therefore \quad r = \frac{\frac{\sum xy}{n} - \frac{\sum x}{n} \cdot \frac{\sum y}{n}}{\sqrt{\left[\frac{\sum x^2}{n} - \left(\frac{\sum x}{n}\right)^2\right]\left[\frac{\sum y^2}{n} - \left(\frac{\sum y}{n}\right)^2\right]}}$$

$$= \frac{\text{cov}(x, y)}{\sigma_x \sigma_y}.$$

$$\therefore \quad \text{cov}(x, y) = r\sigma_x \sigma_y$$

$$\therefore \quad \text{var}(x+y) = \text{var}(x) + \text{var}(y) + 2r\sigma_x \sigma_y.$$

Let us check this for Example 1.

$$\sigma_x = \sqrt{12.8} = 3.578; \quad \sigma_y = \sqrt{6} = 2.449.$$

$$r = \frac{5 \times 253 - 40 \times 35}{\sqrt{(5 \times 284 - 40^2)(5 \times 275 - 35^2)}}$$

$$= \frac{-135}{\sqrt{320 \times 150}}$$

$$= -0.616.$$

$$\text{var}(x+y) = 12.8 + 6 + 2(-0.616)(3.578)(2.449)$$

$$= 12.8 + 6 - 10.8$$

$$= \underline{\underline{8}}.$$

## 3.0 INDEPENDENT DISTRIBUTIONS

If $X$ and $Y$ are independent then they are not correlated, i.e. $r = 0$.

$$\therefore \quad \text{var}(x+y) = \text{var}(x) + \text{var}(y).$$

### Example 2

Nuts and bolts are used together to fasten a unit together. The weight of the nuts is normally distributed with a mean of 2 g and standard deviation 0.3 g, while the weight of the bolts is normally distributed with a mean of 3 g and a standard deviation of 0.4 g. What percentage of nuts and bolts combined weigh more than 6 g?

### SOLUTION

The weights of the nuts and the bolts are obviously independent.

We have
$$E(x) = 2 \quad E(Y) = 3$$

$$\text{var}(x) = 0.3^2 = 0.09$$

$$\text{var}(y) = 0.4^2 = 0.16.$$

$$\therefore \quad E(x+y) = 2 + 3 = 5$$

$$\text{var}(x+y) = 0.09 + 0.16 = 0.25.$$

$$\therefore \quad \sigma_{x+y} = 0.5.$$

$$\therefore \quad Z = \frac{6.0 - 5}{0.5} = 2.$$

$\therefore \quad 2\tfrac{1}{2}$ per cent all nuts and bolts weigh 6 g or more.

## 4.0 DIFFERENCE OF TWO DISTRIBUTIONS

Now
$$E(x-y) = E(x) - E(y).$$

As we would expect, the variance expression is:

$$\text{var}(x-y) = \text{var}(x) + \text{var}(y) - 2\,\text{cov}(x, y).$$

*Note: There is only a minus sign in front of the covariance term, not in front of the variance y. If x and y are independent then*

$$\text{var}(x-y) = \text{var}(x) + \text{var}(y)$$

which is the same as for the sum of x and y.

## 5.0 IMPLICATIONS FOR PORTFOLIO THEORY

The risk of a portfolio of shares consists of the riskiness of the individual securities and covariance between the returns of the securities. The risk of a portfolio consisting of two shares $x$ and $y$ is given by the variance of $x$ and $y$.

$$\text{var}(P_x x + P_y y) = P_x^2\,\text{var}(x) + P_y^2\,\text{var}(y) + 2P_x P_y r \sigma_x \sigma_y$$

when $P_x$ = proportion invested in share $x$,

$P_y$ = proportion invested in share y.

For example, a sum of money is invested equally in two shares $x$ and $y$ which are expected to earn 8 and 6 per cent respectively. The variances of $x$ and $y$ are 2 per cent each and the correlation of rates of return is zero.

The expected return = $0.5 \times 0.08 + 0.5 \times 0.06 = \underline{\underline{0.7}}$.

The risk factor = $(0.5)^2(0.02) + (0.5)^2(0.02) + 2(0.5)(0.5)(0)\sqrt{0.02}\sqrt{0.02}$

$= \underline{\underline{0.01}} = 1$ per cent.

The risk of the portfolio is less than the risk in the individual shares. We have been able to diversify some of the risk away.

If $r = 1$ instead of zero then

the risk factor = $(0.5)^2(0.02) + (0.5)^2(0.02) + 2(0.5)(0.5)(1)\sqrt{0.02}\sqrt{0.02}$

$= \underline{\underline{0.02}} = 2$ per cent,

the same risk as the individual shares.

If $r = -1$ then the risk factor =

the risk factor = $(0.5)^2(0.02) + (0.5)^2(0.02) + 2(0.5)(0.5)(-1)\sqrt{0.02}\sqrt{0.02} = \underline{\underline{0}}$.

Theoretically we can reduce the risk to zero if we can find shares that are perfectly negatively correlated. In practice most shares have a correlation of less than 1 but greater than 0. Hence combining shares into a portfolio will in general reduce the risk, particularly if the shares are from different market sectors, but will not reduce it to zero.

## 6.0 SUMMARY

The aim of this chapter has been to show:

(a) that the variances, covariances and correlation are all related;

(b) what happens to variances of distribution when the distributions are mixed both in the dependent and independent cases;

(c) how the theory is relevant to modern portfolio theory which will form the basis of your later financial management studies.

### Formulae

$$\text{cov}(x, y) = \frac{\sum xy}{n} - \bar{x}\bar{y}; \quad \text{or cov}(x, y) = r\sigma_x\sigma_y.$$

$\text{var}(x+y) = \text{var}(x) + \text{var}(y) + 2\,\text{cov}(x, y);$ or $\text{var}(x+y) = \text{var}(x) + \text{var}(y) + 2r\sigma_x\sigma_y.$

If $r = 0$, $\text{var}(x+y) = \text{var}(x) + \text{var}(y),$ $\quad \text{var}(x-y) = \text{var}(x) + \text{var}(y) - 2\,\text{cov}(x, y).$

If $r = 0$, $\text{var}(x-y) = \text{var}(x) + \text{var}(y),$ $\quad \text{var}(P_x x + P_y y) = P_x^2\,\text{var}(x)$
$$+ P_y^2\,\text{var}(Y) + 2P_x P_y r\sigma_x\sigma_y.$$

# Part Two: Operational Research

CHAPTER THIRTEEN

# An Introduction to Operational Research

## 1.0 WHAT IS OPERATIONAL RESEARCH (OR)?

There are almost as many definitions of operational research as there are grains of sand on a beach.
 The following are a selection:

(a) Operational Research is quantitative commonsense.

(b) Operational Research is a multi-disciplinary scientific approach to decision making.

(c) Operational Research helps managers make decisions.

(d) Operational Research is the systematic, method-oriented study of the basic structure, characteristics, functions and relationships of an organisation. Such study is intended to provide the executive with a sound, scientific and quantitative basis for decision making.

(e) Operational Research is the application of the methods of science to complex problems arising in the direction and management of large systems of men, machines, materials and money in industry, business, government and defence. The distinctive approach is to develop a scientific model of the system, incorporating measurements of factors such as chance and risk, with which to predict and compare the outcomes of alternative decisions, strategies or controls. The purpose is to help management determine its policy and actions scientifically. (Operational Research Society definition.)

...and so on!
 The definitions vary from the very brief, e.g. (a), seeming to be clever, and inviting an almost "optimal" number of interpretations, to the long-winded, like (e), obviously agreed by a committee as it almost has "everything, but the kitchen sink".
 Attempting to find a definition of operational research is not the best way to pass

examinations. However, by looking at a few definitions we see a pattern emerging; the words "decision", "management" and "scientific" keep appearing.

The primary focus of an OR study is on decision making: it is not trying purely to describe what has happened, but to recommend a decision or group decision to meet a problem situation. This means that the main result of the analysis must directly and unambiguously have implications for managerial action.

Operational research is applied to problems concerned with the activities within an organisation. The actual nature of the organisation is irrelevant, as can be seen by the list given in the OR Society definition.

Operational research utilises the scientific method; it employs a quantitative approach requiring data which are used in the construction of a mathematical model.

In most organisations where OR is used, an inter-disciplinary team approach is adopted. The strength of OR is that it draws on the expertise, knowledge and skills of the various members of the team drawn from a wide variety of disciplines.

Most OR studies require the use of a computer owing to the volume of data and complexities of the mathematical models developed.

## 2.0 REASONS FOR USING OR

(a) The problem is so complex that it is not possible for the manager to develop a good solution without the aid of quantitative specialists.

(b) The problem is very important (it might be costly or politically important) and the manager wants a thorough analysis before he reaches a decision.

(c) It is a new problem for the company and they have no experience to draw upon.

(d) The problem is a repetitive one, and hence time would be saved by relying on a quantitative procedure to make a routine decision recommendation.

Examples of problem areas where OR has been successful are:

(a) distribution systems design

(b) inventory control

(c) resource allocation

(d) capital investment analysis

(e) portfolio selection

(f) information system design

(g) product mix and production planning

(h) marketing.

There are many more areas but these illustrate the wide variety of problem areas where OR has been useful.

## 3.0 THE DECISION-MAKING PROCESS

When a problem appears or is identified the manager has the responsibility of making a decision or selecting a course of action that will lead to the solution of the problem (see Fig.58). Before coming to his decision he will be influenced by his own experience and knowledge of the situation and similar situations as well as the recommendations arising from a quantitative analysis. To be able to compare and evaluate the qualitative and quantitative sources of decision recommendations it is necessary to be familiar with the quantitative decision making process so that he is aware of its strength and weaknesses.

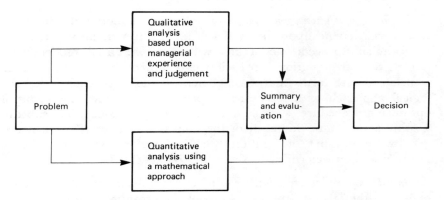

Fig. 58. *The decision-making process.*

## 4.0 STAGES IN THE OR APPROACH

The OR approach can be split into six stages:

(a) *Problem definition.* It is a common experience among OR workers to find that the problem as it is initially posed is not the problem they finally tackle and, with luck, solve. Problems are not always what they seem. The chances are that the problem is something quite different from the one originally posed; it may be something like it, but hardly ever is it the problem as originally stated. The OR man must identify the symptoms of the problem and then check back from the symptoms to dig out the underlying causes that are arousing disquiet.

Thus, if long queues are being generated in a supermarket the customers may well blame the situation on a lack of sufficient cash desks. The problem might well then be posed as "how many cash desks should there be to keep the queue lengths within reasonable bounds"? In practice, however, it might be the layout of the existing cash desks or the attitude of the staff that is producing the long queues. A common solution to this situation is sometimes to set aside certain cash desks for customers with only a few items, or to take out products like cigarettes into a kiosk outside the cash desk system.

It should be emphasised that it is important to look at the whole system and in so doing recognise the other areas that would be affected by any decisions made. A problem must not be treated in isolation.

The problem definition stage includes identifying alternative courses of action that might be taken and formulating criteria against which these alternative courses of action can be measured and a judgement made.

(b) *Construction of a model.* The first step is to obtain the quantitative data, either from existing records or by a new enquiry or survey. The second is to analyse the data by an appropriate statistical method and the third to build the mathematical model. The model might be basically of a functional nature composed of a series of inequalities (linear programming (LP)) or it might have a logical structure such as a flowchart (simulation).

(c) *Derivation of a solution from a model.* The method of deriving a solution from a model will depend upon the model used. If a functional model is used with an optimising procedure contained within it, e.g. an LP model or a calculus model, then the solution can easily be obtained and it is only necessary to translate it into terms that management would understand. If, however, a logical approach or a functional approach which does not incorporate an optimising procedure, such as queueing theory, is used, then substitution of a number of values for each of the control variables may be necessary to generate a number of solutions for comparison. The "best" or optimal solution is then determined by the criteria specified earlier.

(d) *Testing the model and its solution.* A model is only a partial representation of reality. Although we attempt to model the essential features of a problem, whether we have identified all the essential features must always remain uncertain. Therefore it is important that we test the model and its solution. If our model can adequately predict the effects of the changes in the system, however simple the model might be, then it is acceptable. The solution to the model may be evaluated by comparing the solution from the model based on the current situation to the actual result that occurred in practice from the current situation.

(e) *Establishment of controls.* The model and solution are only valid for the problem if no changes take place in our uncontrolled variables or relationships between them. This may be illustrated by Fig.59. For example, if we have changes in interest rate over which we have no control then the costs of our investment in the project under study will be affected. This could change the likely recommendation from an outcome with a relatively high investment to one with a lower investment. Therefore it is important to establish controls so that changes that make a significant difference in a solution are recognised and can be taken into account. Sensitivity analysis is useful here as a guide to which variables would, when altered, make a significant change to a solution.

(f) *Implementation.* This is an important stage in the project. A number of potentially good OR studies have faltered at this point. It was common at one stage for the OR group to make their recommendations and then to hand over the implementation to personnel already working in the application area. The danger is that these people may not be fully aware of the actual requirements

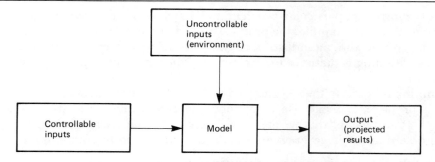

Fig. 59. *Controlled and uncontrollable inputs.*

of the implementation of the model and may, through no fault of their own, introduce errors of implementation which might undermine the basic assumptions. The other possibility is that the personnel may see the introduction of the model as a threat to their own position or ambitions and it might be in their interest for the project to fail or not to be the success it was initially judged to be.

Anyone involved with the implementation stage should be involved with the project at an early stage and be sufficiently acquainted with what is going on to be able to identify with the project, so that they regard the success of the project as one of their own aims.

The solution to the problem can sometimes be translated into a set of operating instructions, which can be operated by the area personnel. Ideally a member of the OR team should be involved in the implementation so that, if problems arise, he can give advice.

## 5.0 FEEDBACK

Although we have split the OR process into what appears to be distinct stages, in fact the edges are blurred and the steps to some extent overlap. Also, the process is cyclic at each stage, and information is produced which may conflict with earlier assumptions and decisions. This means that we need to go back to the earlier stage and modify the early work and then proceed through the stages again.

There is a continuous changing and updating of the model. The approach which seems to have been the most successful is initially to build a very simple model and test it out and then gradually complicate it until you reach a stage where further complications produce a model beyond your ability to analyse. This approach seems to be preferable to the alternative approach of developing a complex model and then simplifying it until a solution technique will fit.

## 6.0 CLASSIFICATION OF PROBLEMS

Although there is no unique classification of the set of problems that arise in operational research owing to the diverse situations in which it is applicable, it may often be seen in the many application areas that the structure of the problem is not unique and that the form of a particular problem may have been met previously in a different application area. For example, the product-mix LP model may be applied to determine the mix of products that an industrial company should produce and it can also be used in capital rationing situations to decide on which projects should be selected for investment.

Attempting to identify these forms and putting them into categories allows us when solving a problem to make use of previous analysis rather than starting from first principles. It also means that we are more likely to see the intricacies and complexities of the problem as we have previous standards with which to compare the problem.

Rivett and Ackoff suggested the following categories:

(a) inventory

(b) allocation

(c) queuing

(d) sequencing

(e) routing

(f) replacement

(g) competition

(h) search.

These classifications are largely separated from any particular technique and do not lead to a rapid solution of a problem or the rapid recognition of the important questions to be asked in approaching the problem.

Ackoff and Sasieni have suggested an alternative classification which classifies problems according to the difficulty of formulating the structure:

(a) Problems which have a simple logical structure which is transparent enough to be solved by inspection or discussion, e.g. the newsboy problem.

(b) Problems where the structure of the problem is apparent but the way in which to represent it symbolically is not clear. In many cases it is possible to solve such problems by the use of an analogy or an iconic model, e.g. finding optimal site of a warehouse.

(c) The third category is where the structure of the problem is not apparent but there is the possibility of extracting structures by data analysis, e.g. some forecasting problems where an econometric model might be used.

(d) The fourth category is the situation where it is not possible to isolate the effects of individual variables and it is necessary to experiment; e.g. such problems occur in marketing where you are trying to identify the effect of advertising upon sales where the population is not homogeneous.

(e) The fifth category is where sufficient descriptive data are not available and experimentation is precluded. In these circumstances the only approach is via a thorough understanding and formulation of basic hypotheses and by formulating experiments which we can manipulate e.g. social problems and some gaming problems. Simulation is sometimes quite a useful approach.

There have been several other attempts to produce classification systems; however, whatever system you produce it is highly likely that there will be important problems that lie outside your system. There is a further danger that using a classification system tends to make you try to fit problems into particular slots and then use particular techniques to solve them when the slots are not a good fit.

## 7.0  IS OPTIMISATION A HOLY GRAIL?

There is a tendency to always be on the lookout for the optimal solution and the textbooks with the emphasis on techniques rather than modelling encourage this approach. The ultimate objective or "holy grail" is to achieve an optimal solution when in reality all we need is a "good" solution. It should be borne in mind that our model is only an approximation to reality: the data are almost certain to be the sample data and hence subject to statistical error. There are a large number of uncontrollable variables, some of which we do not even realise exist. It is like looking for an ideal needle in a haystack; if you find one of any kind it is probably good enough to sew on a button so why spend time and money looking for an "ideal" one?

We sometimes tend to select optimising techniques to solve a problem when it might be more appropriate to use a different technique. It should also be remembered that however we define the system we are studying the system itself is bound to be a subsystem of a larger system. So, even with an optimal solution to our subsystem it may not even be a good solution to the larger system. We may have simplified purely to suit our solution technique.

## 8.0  SENSITIVITY ANALYSIS

One way of partly combating this problem of the reliability of the model structure is to see which parts of the model are critical to the recommended solution. As we implied in **7.0**, in our simple model the factors we assume to be constant may change from period to period. We need to analyse the effects of the changes. Initially we allow just one factor to change, noting the effect upon our solution. We then repeat this procedure for all the factors we feel are important in the model. By this method we should be able to identify which of the variables, when changing on their own, are having a major effect on the solution. We can then turn our attention to monitoring these variables and not waste time on those of no importance.

## 9.0  THE FUTURE OF OR

In the last three years OR has been through what some observers call a crisis. Articles have appeared such as "The future of OR is past" by R.L. Ackoff, conferences have been held with titles such as "The King is Dead". All portray the end of OR as we know it. The traditional view of OR, following a scientific approach, has been challenged, not by newcomers eager to make a name for themselves but by people who have contributed originally to the very tradition they are now challenging.

In many ways it has been a healthy discussion and one perhaps which was long overdue. The society we live in is changing and the factors that affect our models are different to some extent from what they used to be, so it is important we challenge our basic assumptions from time to time.

One of the points posed by Ackoff and others is that there is a class of problems that he called "wicked problems" where a scientific approach is unlikely to be useful. These are problems generally where there is considerable conflict of interest between powerful competing groups and the question may be posed, "Is there ever likely to be a unique solution which satisfies all parties?"

These problems really fall into the political arena.

It is not really surprising that we have found a few problems that we cannot solve; most disciplines find themselves in this predicament and our subject is multi-disciplinary.

Another problem area is the subject of fuzziness of data. We have become more aware of the errors inherent in data since the introduction of the "fuzzy set". The fact that the observer may introduce fuzziness into the data apart from the usual statistical errors is also a problem.

This surely means that OR must be concerned that its deduced advice takes proper account of the fuzziness of its data. It may well be that the fuzziness of the data only justifies the simpler mathematical models because simple models are sophisticated ones, and their justifiable deductions are usually better. This should of course in any particular instance be checked by sensitivity analysis and one should not be surprised nor despair when elaboration is shown not to be worthwhile.

A not surprising issue is the "optimising" debate. Ackoff in his paper made the following statement: "There is a greater need for decision making systems that can learn and adapt effectively than there is for optimising decision-making systems that cannot." He argues that optimal solutions have a short life and their lifetime is getting shorter and in some cases is negative. This statement, however, gives us a guide for the future. We must look to systems that are either adaptive or highly interactive. If they are highly interactive they are flexible.

In summary, there is a future for OR as long as we recognise that change is taking place in our society in fundamental ways, and therefore although our previously acquired models and methodology do not now rest in the dustbin, they may in places need to be revised to meet the challenge that society now poses. The signposts are there—we merely have to move in the direction indicated.

CHAPTER FOURTEEN

# Linear Programming – Introduction and Model Construction

## 1.0 MATHEMATICAL PROGRAMMING

The term is used to describe a group of techniques applied to problems of allocation. The allocation of limited resources among competing demands is of major interest to decision makers. Mathematical programming provides a suitable framework for tackling such problems.

Mathematical programming refers to a group of mathematical techniques which may be used to find optimal solutions to problems involving an objective function of unknown variables, subject to a number of constraints. During the formative period of operational research, the term mathematical programming was frequently used synonymously with linear programming, which is characterised by linear relationships between variables. Mathematical programming should however be viewed in a far broader sense to include techniques such as linear programming, non-linear programming and dynamic programming (to name but a few).

## 2.0 LINEAR PROGRAMMING DEFINED

Linear programming is the most widely used of mathematical programming techniques. It is a method of meeting some desired objective, such as maximising profits or minimising costs subject to limitations on available resources. Linearity implies proportionality. "Linear" means that the elements in a situation are so related that they generate straight lines when graphed. "Programming" implies that one feasible combination of resources after another is analysed till the one giving the best result is obtained. The linear programming method is applicable if the allocation problem being tackled has a linear objective function limited by a set of linear constraints (limiting factors).

## 3.0 APPLICATIONS OF LINEAR PROGRAMMING

Linear programming was developed from 1947 onwards as a tool for finding optimal solutions to military planning problems. The early applications were restricted to problems involving military operations such as logistics, transportation and procurement. Additionally it was applied to inter-industry economic problems based on Leontief's input–output analysis. Successful military applications led to business uses. These have been fostered by the rapid development and adoption of computers.

Present-day uses range from agriculture, business and industry to government, with the most extensive applications being those in industry and commerce. For example, problems involving blending of petroleum, animal-feed blending, production planning and inventory control, problems determining optimal product mix, problems dealing with training and assignment of personnel, transport of commodities and allocation of investment funds are only some of the areas of business applications of linear programming.

## 4.0 CLASSIFICATION—LINEAR PROGRAMMING METHODS

The generic nature of the term linear programming (LP) must be stressed. Within the term are encompassed a number of sub-techniques. These are divided into three main groups based on the solution method used. They are the general allocation method, the transportation method and the assignment method.

The general allocation method involves a broad class of optimisation problems dealing with the interaction of several variables subject to certain constraints. Problems with two unknowns or decision variables can be solved by a graphical method. This method may be used in situations where there are three variables and would involve the construction of a three-dimensional graph. The graphical method however has no use when the number of decision variables exceeds three (it is not recommended as a method of solution in the three-variable case). The standard solution method when there are three or more variables is termed the simplex method.

Though the simplex method can be applied in all linear programming situations, special techniques which involve less computation and are easier to use have been developed for certain situations such as transportation. The solution method is designed to provide optimum solutions to problems where goods or services are to be transported from several sources to a number of destinations. The amount available at each source is known, as is the amount required at each destination. Linearity is maintained by assuming that costs are directly proportional to the number of units moved. The objective is to minimise overall transportation costs.

The assignment method is a special case of transportation and is used when there is only one item at each of the various sources and only one item is required at each of the various destinations. Techniques available for assignment are simple in structure and easy in computation.

## 5.0 PROPERTIES OF LINEAR PROGRAMMING

The following allocation problem will be used to illustrate the properties of linear programming.

# 14 LINEAR PROGRAMMING—INTRODUCTION AND MODEL CONSTRUCTION

## Example 1

The Gonda Clock Company specialises in the manufacture of reproduction clocks. Two main types are produced, Regular and Deluxe. The electrical components necessary are supplied by another manufacturer and their supply is limited to 600 components per day. Each Regular clock requires 5 components and each Deluxe clock requires 6 components. The production of one Regular clock requires 1 man-day of labour whereas 2 man-days are required for each Deluxe clock. The production labour force has a strength of 160 employees, i.e. the supply on a daily basis is 160 man-days.

Production of the clocks takes place in two different departments (one for each type of clock). The daily departmental capacity for Regular clocks is limited to 80 and that for Deluxe clocks 60. Each Regular clock realises a profit of £50, each Deluxe clock £80.

How many Regular and Deluxe clocks should be produced on a daily basis so as to maximise profits?

### SOLUTION

The Gonda Clock Company wishes to maximise profits on a daily basis. To achieve this objective it must determine the optimal product-mix, i.e. the best combination of Regular and Deluxe clocks subject to the limitations. The numbers to be produced of each product are referred to as decision or choice variables (i.e. a decision or choice has to be made regarding the number to be produced). As there are only two decision variables it is possible to identify each one of them with one of the axes of a graph (in practice there will nearly always be more than two decision variables).

Let $x$ be the number of Regular clocks produced daily and $y$ be the number of Deluxe clocks produced daily.

The given objective is to maximise profit. This objective needs to be expressed in terms of decision variables. In Gonda's case each Regular clock yields a profit of £50 and each Deluxe clock £80. As $x$ and $y$ of these are going to be produced, the daily profit (represented by the letter $Z$) can be stated as

$$\text{Maximise } Z = 50x + 80y.$$

This is termed the objective function, i.e. the statement of the objective in the form of a mathematical expression. The stated profit function is a linear function of two decision variables $x$ and $y$. It is assumed that the profit per unit of each of the products remains the same irrespective of the level of sales. (It is assumed that all Regular and Deluxe clocks produced will be sold.)

Having identified the decision or choice variables and the objective, it is now necessary to establish the factors which limit production (limiting factors). These factors are expressed in the form of linear inequalities termed constraints. Constraints are limitations or restrictions placed on our choices. In the case of the Gonda Clock Company production will be influenced by the available resources.

Consider the electrical components. The total number used must be less than or equal to 600. This can be expressed as

$$5x + 6y \leqslant 600$$

where the sign $\leqslant$ is read "less than or equal to". Note that from the data given each Regular clock requires 5 components and each Deluxe clock requires 6 components.

As $x$ and $y$ of these are going to be produced, $5x + 6y$ components will be used. The number used cannot exceed 600 and the constraint is stated mathematically as above.

Consider now the labour. The supply on a daily basis is limited to 160 man-days. Each Regular clock requires 1 man-day and each Deluxe clock requires 2 man-days. The constraint can be expressed as

$$x + 2y \leqslant 160.$$

In a similar fashion constraints can be stated for daily departmental capacity. The clocks are assembled in two different departments. Capacity for Regular clocks is limited to 80.

$$x \leqslant 80.$$

Capacity for Deluxe clocks is limited to 60:

$$y \leqslant 60.$$

Finally, negative production is not possible. The values taken by the decision variables must be either positive or zero. If the Gonda Company does not produce any Regular clocks the value of the decision variable $x$ is zero. If they are produced, $x$ will take a positive value. However, the solution cannot be negative and thus the decision variables are expressed in the form

$$x \geqslant 0, \; y \geqslant 0$$

where the sign $\geqslant$ is read as "greater than or equal to". These statements are described as non-negativity conditions.

The problem can now be stated in full:

$$\text{Maximise } Z = 50x + 80y \text{ (objective function)},$$

subject to the following conditions:

$$5x + 6y \leqslant 600 \quad \text{(component constraint)}$$
$$x + 2y \leqslant 160 \quad \text{(labour constraint)}$$
$$x \leqslant 80 \quad \text{(capacity constraint)}$$
$$y \leqslant 60 \quad \text{(capacity constraint)}$$

and

$$x \geqslant 0, \; y \geqslant 0 \quad \text{(non-negativity conditions)}.$$

In non-mathematical terms, the problem is to choose a pair of values for $x$ and $y$ (the decision variables) which maximise the value of the objective function, subject to linear constraints. Linearity in the constraints implies that the amount of resources utilised to produce each product is constant or uniform, irrespective of production levels.

## 6.0 MODEL CONSTRUCTION—MAXIMISATION

It should be noted from the section above that the use of linear programming involves the identification and statement of the decision variables, the objective function and

# 14 LINEAR PROGRAMMING—INTRODUCTION AND MODEL CONSTRUCTION

the constraints. The application of linear programming requires, as the first step, the formulation of the appropriate model of the problem. Two further examples are given (one dealing with maximisation, the other with minimisation) to illustrate the procedure to be followed.

## Example 2—Maximisation

Aminabad Enterprises make two types of products, I and II. Three assembly lines, A, B and C, are required for the manufacture of each product. One unit of product I requires 2 hours on assembly line A, 1 hour on assembly line B and 1 hour on assembly line C. One unit of product II requires 1 hour on A, 2 hours on B and 3 hours on C. On a daily basis there are 16 hours, 11 hours and 15 hours available on assembly lines A, B and C. The contribution per unit is £30 for product I and £50 for product II. Aminabad Enterprises wish to establish daily production levels so as to maximise the overall contribution.

### MODEL CONSTRUCTION

A useful starting point is to tabulate the given data as follows:

|  | Product I | Product II | Available |
| --- | --- | --- | --- |
| Assembly line A | 2 | 1 | 16 |
| Assembly line B | 1 | 2 | 11 |
| Assembly line C | 1 | 3 | 15 |
| Contribution | £30 | £50 |  |

Note that the decision variables are the daily production figures for the two products.

Let $x$ be the number of units of product I produced,

$y$ be the number of units of product II produced.

The objective is to maximise contribution. This can be represented by the function $30x + 50y$.

Each of the $x$ units of product I requires 2 hours on assembly line A. Each of the $y$ units of product II requires 1 hour on assembly line A. Assembly line A has only 16 hours available. The constraint may be represented as

$$2x + y \leqslant 16.$$

Similar constraints can be expressed for assembly lines B and C. These are

$$x + 2y \leqslant 11$$

and

$$x + 3y \leqslant 15.$$

Finally, negative production is not allowed, so neither $x$ nor $y$ can be negative. The overall model can now be stated as follows:

Maximise contribution = $30x + 50y$  (objective function),

subject to the following conditions:

$$2x + y \leq 16 \quad \text{(assembly line A constraint)}$$
$$x + 2y \leq 11 \quad \text{(assembly line B constraint)}$$
$$x + 3y \leq 15 \quad \text{(assembly line C constraint)}$$

and $\quad x \geq 0, \quad y \geq 0 \quad$ (non-negativity conditions).

## 7.0  MODEL CONSTRUCTION—MINIMISATION

The construction of models in minimisation situations is similar to that for maximisation. This will be explained by reference to the problem below.

### Example 3—Minimisation

The Hyderabad Chemical Company specialises in the production of three different types of chemicals, A, B and C. These are used as fertilisers and have a growing demand locally. These three different chemicals are produced at the company's two different factories, I and II, with different production capacities. In a normal working day, factory I produces 5 tons of A, 4 tons of B and 1 ton of C, while factory II produces 6 tons of A, 3 tons of B and 2 tons of C. In a given period, the demand for each of these chemicals is known to be 250 tons, 150 tons and 70 tons respectively. Demand must be satisfied fully to ensure repeat orders. The daily cost of operation is £2,500 in factory I and £3,500 in factory II. Given that the objective is to minimise the total cost of operation, find the optimum number of days each factory should be operated so as to meet the demand.

MODEL CONSTRUCTION

Once again, a useful starting point is to tabulate the given data:

|  | Daily production (tons) | | Required |
|---|---|---|---|
|  | Factory I | Factory II | (tons) |
| Chemical A | 5 | 6 | 250 |
| Chemical B | 4 | 3 | 150 |
| Chemical C | 1 | 2 | 70 |
| Cost | £2,500 | £3,500 | |

The decision variables are the number of days each factory should be operated so as to minimise total cost subject to constraints. The production of each of the three different chemicals must be at least equal to or greater than the specified quantities in order to meet the demand requirements.

Let $x$ be the days factory I is operated,
  $y$ be the days factory II is operated.

# 14 LINEAR PROGRAMMING—INTRODUCTION AND MODEL CONSTRUCTION

The objective is to minimise total cost. This can be represented by the function $2,500x + 3,500y$.

The total production of each chemical cannot be less than the quantity demanded. Consider chemical A. If factory I is operated for $x$ days and factory II for $y$ days then the total production will be $5x + 6y$. This must be at least equal to 250. The constraint may be represented as

$$5x + 6y \geqslant 250.$$

Similar constraints can be expressed for chemicals B and C. These are

$$4x + 3y \geqslant 150$$

and

$$x + 2y \geqslant 70.$$

Finally, factories cannot be operated for a negative number of days, i.e. $x$ and $y$ cannot be negative. The overall problem can now be stated as follows:

Minimise cost = $2,500x + 3,500y$ (objective function),

subject to: 
$5x + 6y \geqslant 250$ (chemical A constraint)
$4x + 3y \geqslant 150$ (chemical B constraint)
$x + 2y \geqslant 70$ (chemical C constraint)

and $x \geqslant 0, y \geqslant 0$ (non-negativity conditions).

*Tutorial note: In the simple models developed above, the maximisation model had inequalities of the form "$\leqslant$", that is less than or equal to. The minimisation model above had inequalities "$\geqslant$". However, students should avoid generalisations. In any situation, whether maximisation or minimisation, the signs can operate in either direction. The simplest procedure is to treat each constraint on its own merits. For example, in the problem above there may have been a requirement that factory I could not be operated for more than 10 days. This would be represented as $x \leqslant 10$. Notice the direction of the sign.*


## 8.0 GENERAL LINEAR PROGRAMMING MODELS

If instead of a particular number of decision variables and constraints, there were $n$ decision variables and $m$ constraints, it is possible to arrive at a mathematical formulation in the general case for maximisation and minimisation situations.

In a maximisation situation:

Let 
$n$ = number of decision variables
$m$ = number of constraints
$x_j$ = decision variables
$a_{ij}, b_i, c_j$ = given constants.

Maximise $Z = c_1 x_1 + c_2 x_2 + \ldots + c_n x_n,$

subject to:
$$a_{11}x_1 + a_{12}x_2 + \ldots + a_{1n}x_n \leq b_1$$
$$a_{21}x_1 + a_{22}x_2 + \ldots + a_{2n}x_n \leq b_2$$
$$\vdots$$
$$a_{m1}x_1 + a_{m2}x_2 + \ldots + a_{mn}x_n \leq b_n$$

and
$$x_1 \geq 0, \; x_2 \geq 0, \ldots, x_n \geq 0.$$

A similar formulation exists for a minimisation situation:

Minimise $F = c_1x_1 + c_2x_2 + \ldots + c_nx_n,$

subject to:
$$a_{11}x_1 + a_{12}x_2 + \ldots + a_{1n}x_n \geq b_1$$
$$a_{21}x_1 + a_{22}x_2 + \ldots + a_{2n}x_n \geq b_2$$
$$\vdots$$
$$a_{m1}x_1 + a_{m2}x_2 + \ldots + a_{mn}x_n \geq b_m$$

and
$$x_1 \geq 0, \; x_2 \geq 0, \ldots, x_n \geq 0.$$

The basic difference between the maximisation and minimisation formulations is normally found in the signs of inequalities of the constraints. In maximisation problems, constraints are normally expressed by the "less than or equal to" signs, whereas those in minimisation are normally expressed by the "greater than or equal to" signs. Note that this is not likely to happen in all situations.

## 9.0 ASSUMPTIONS OF LINEAR PROGRAMMING

From the earlier description of properties of linear programming and model construction, it is evident that the linear programming approach is based on three assumptions, namely linearity, divisibility and certainty, as follows:

### 9.1 Linearity

The primary assumption of linear programming is the linearity in the objective function and in the side constraints. This implies that the measure of effectiveness and utilisation of each resource must be directly and precisely proportional to the level of each individual activity.

In actual business operations, a purely linear relationship may not exist. As a consequence, the objective function may be non-linear or one or more of the constraints may have non-linear relationships or both. In many instances it may be possible to represent a non-linear relationship by linear approximations. Alternatively, it may be possible in extreme cases to use the technique of non-linear programming.

### 9.2 Divisibility

Linear programming presupposes the complete divisibility of the resources utilised and the units of output produced. That is, it is assumed that the decision variables can take

# 14 LINEAR PROGRAMMING—INTRODUCTION AND MODEL CONSTRUCTION

on fractional values. Therefore, linear programming allows a production programme which uses 600 units of electrical components and $86\frac{2}{3}$ man-hours of labour time to produce 80 units of Regular clocks and $33\frac{1}{3}$ units of Deluxe clocks per day.

It is practically feasible to have fractional values in the resource utilisation and production activities in many business situations. However, there are also occasions in which fractional values are neither permissible nor practical.

Integer programming is a special technique which can be used for finding non-fractional values of resource usage and decision variables.

## 9.3 Certainty

It is assumed that the coefficients of the decision variables in linear programming are known with certainty; all the coefficients, such as unit profit contribution, prices and the amount of resources required per unit of output, are known constants. The available resources are also assumed to be known with accuracy.

In reality, the coefficients are neither known with certainty nor are they constants. Therefore, a number of special techniques such as parametric programming and sensitivity analysis are used to overcome this limitation.

CHAPTER FIFTEEN

# Linear Programming— Graphical Solution

## 1.0 INTRODUCTION

The previous chapter dealt with the formulation of a linear programming model. This one is concerned with the extraction of a graphical solution. It should be noted that there are a number of solution methods available for allocation problems falling within a linear programming framework. Problems involving two decision-variables can easily be solved by using graphical methods. A problem with three decision-variables can also be solved by a graphical approach but its presentation is not as easy as in the problem with two decision-variables because it requires three dimensions to illustrate. Larger problems use an algorithmic approach which implies step-by-step repetitive procedures that eventually yield the optimum. The most important of these iterative methods is the simplex method which forms the subject matter of Chapter 16.

## 2.0 GRAPHICAL SOLUTION—MAXIMISATION

To illustrate the graphical method, consider again the production problem facing the Gonda Clock Company. The company specialises in the production of reproduction clocks. Two main types are produced, Regular and Deluxe. The supply of components is limited to 600 per day. Each Regular clock requires 5 components and each Deluxe clock requires 6. Each Regular clock requires 1 man-day of labour and each Deluxe clock requires 2. Labour supply on a daily basis is 160 man-days. Production of the clocks takes place in two different departments.

The capacity for Regular clocks is limited to 80 and that for Deluxe clocks is 60. Each Regular clock gives a profit of £50, each Deluxe gives £80. How many of each should be produced so as to maximise profits?

# 15 LINEAR PROGRAMMING—GRAPHICAL SOLUTION

The model is restated below:

Let $x$ be number of Regular clocks to be made,

$y$ be the number of Deluxe clocks to be made.

Maximise $Z = 50x + 80y$ (objective function),

subject to:

$5x + 6y \leqslant 600$ (components constraint)

$x + 2y \leqslant 160$ (labour constraint)

$x \leqslant 80$ (capacity contraint)

$y \leqslant 60$ (capacity constraint)

$x \geqslant 0, y \geqslant 0$ (non-negativity conditions).

In the graphical method all relevant features of the problem are represented in a diagram. A two-dimensional graph needs to be constructed, with the production of Regular clocks represented on the horizontal ($x$-) axis and the production of Deluxe clocks shown on the vertical ($y$-) axis (*see* Fig. 60).

Start with the constraints. Each of these has to be plotted on the graph. Remember that each of the constraints represents a limiting factor. What is desired is some region on the graph which satisfies all the limiting factors taken together (the feasible region). The production of the clocks is limited by the availability of components.

The inequality $5x + 6y \leqslant 600$ may be represented by drawing in the line corresponding to the equation part of the constraint, i.e. $5x + 6y = 600$. The line cuts the axes at $x = 120$ and $y = 100$. The limits were established by using the following reasoning. If all components available are used for the production of Regular clocks ($x$) then 120 units can be produced. Similarly, if all the available components are used for the

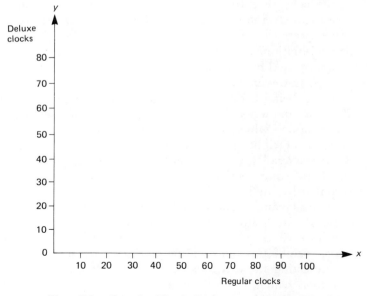

Fig. 60. *Gonda Clock Company—basic graph.*

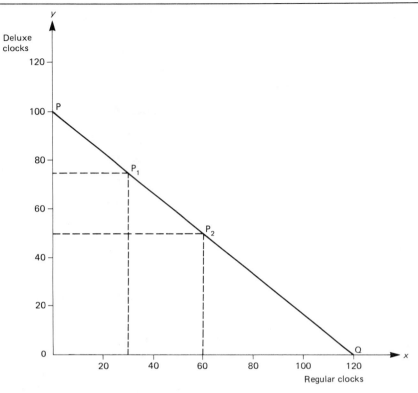

Fig. 61. *Gonda Clock Company—component constraint.*

production of Deluxe clocks, then 100 units of $y$ can be produced. The line PQ is drawn by connecting these two extreme uses and represents the equation $5x + 6y = 600$.

Points on the line PQ represent full utilisation of the available electronic components but with different combinations of products. For example, at the point $P_1$, 600 units of components are being used but the production combination is 30 units of $x$ and 75 units of $y$. At point $P_2$, however, 60 units of $x$ and 50 units of $y$ are being made but 600 components are still being used. To summarise, points on the line represent full utilisation of available components. Points to the left of the line (below the line) represent combinations of products which use less than 600 units of components and are said to be feasible. Points to the right of the line (above it) give combinations of products which use more than the available components and hence are not feasible.

The production of the components is also limited by the supply of labour. The constraint is represented by the inequality $x + 2y \leqslant 160$. The line $x + 2y = 160$ can be drawn in a similar manner and is shown in Fig. 62.

If all the available labour is fully employed for the production of Regular clocks alone, then 160 units of $x$ will be produced per day. If all labour is used for the production of Deluxe clocks, then 80 units of $y$ will be produced per day. The line RS in Fig. 62 was drawn by connecting these two extreme points. Points on the line represent combinations of products which fully utilise available labour. Points to the left of the line (below it) represent feasible combinations which use less than 160 man-days.

## 15 LINEAR PROGRAMMING—GRAPHICAL SOLUTION

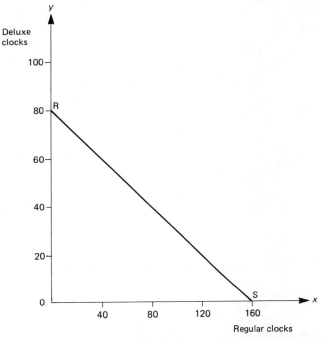

Fig. 62. *Gonda Clock Company—labour constraint.*

Points above the line represent combinations of products which cannot be made as they require more labour than is available.

We move now to the next pair of constraints which deals with departmental capacity. Because of the limited capacity in the department where Regular clocks are produced, no more than 80 clocks can be produced per day. The constraint is $x \leqslant 80$. The line $x = 80$ is drawn in Fig. 63 to represent this constraint. Note that it is a straight

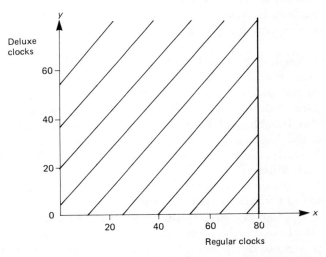

Fig. 63. *Gonda Clock Company—departmental capacity, Regular clocks.*

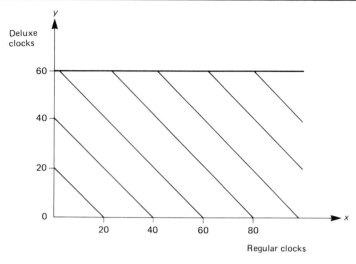

Fig. 64. *Gonda Clock Company—departmental capacity, Deluxe clocks.*

line going through $x = 80$ and parallel to the $y$-axis. Along the line $x$ is always equal to 80 irrespective of the value of $y$. To the left of the line $x$ is less than 80 and this is feasible. However, to the right of the line, $x$ will take a value greater than 80. This is not permitted because of departmental capacity. Hence points on the line and to its left are feasible. Points to the right of the line are not feasible.

A similar procedure can be adopted to show the constraint for departmental capacity affecting Deluxe clocks. The production is limited to 60 clocks on a daily basis. The constraint is $y \leqslant 60$. The line $y = 60$ is drawn in Fig. 64 to represent this constraint. Note that this is a straight line going through $y = 60$ and parallel to the $x$-axis. Along the line, $y$ is always equal to 60, irrespective of the value of $x$. Below the line $y$ is less than 60 and this is feasible. However, above the line $y$ will take a value greater than 60. This is not permitted. Hence points on the line and below it are feasible. However, points above the line represent a production programme which exceeds departmental capacity.

The procedure so far has indicated the method for plotting each constraint and the feasible region relating to it. Since all the constraints must be satisfied simultaneously (the idea behind the method is to find the feasible solution space) the constraints need to be combined. This is shown in Fig. 65. The boundary and interior of OABCDE is variously called the feasible region, feasible possibility set or opportunity set. Every point within or on the boundaries of the area OABCDE satisfies all the constraints taken together. The optimum solution is the point in OABCDE which maximises the value of the objective function.

Mathematically, it can be shown that the maximum value of the objective function always occurs at one of the corner points of the feasible region. Hence, the search for the optimum is reduced to considering only a finite number of feasible points, namely, the corner points. Mathematically, a corner point is known as an extreme point. Thus, after all extreme points are determined the optimum is the extreme point that yields the best value of the objective function. (In the next chapter it will be seen that the

# 15 LINEAR PROGRAMMING—GRAPHICAL SOLUTION

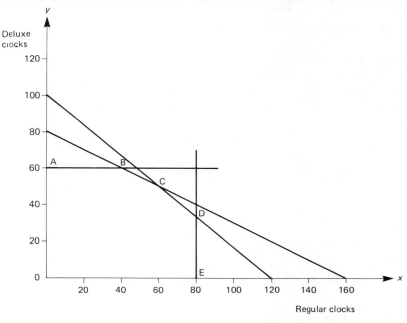

Fig. 65. *Gonda Clock Company—constraints combined.*

simplex method is based on determining only some of the extreme points in a selective manner.)

One simple way of finding the optimum solution once the feasible region is established is the evaluation of each of the corner points. Each corner point represents a combination of products which can be read off the graph. These production levels can be substituted into the objective function to find the respective values of profit at each of the corner points. The corner point that yields the maximum profit is then chosen as the optimal solution. Table 7 summarises the results:

Table 7. Evaluation of corner points (Fig.65).

| Corner point | Number of Regular clocks | Number of Deluxe clocks | Profit from Regular clocks | Profit from Deluxe clocks | Total |
|---|---|---|---|---|---|
| O | 0 | 0 | 0 | 0 | 0 |
| A | 0 | 60 | 0 | 4,800 | 4,800 |
| B | 40 | 60 | 2,000 | 4,800 | 6,800 |
| C | 60 | 50 | 3,000 | 4,000 | 7,000 |
| D | 80 | $33\frac{1}{3}$ | 4,000 | $2,666\frac{2}{3}$ | $6,666\frac{2}{3}$ |
| E | 80 | 0 | 4,000 | 0 | 4,000 |

Corner point C where $x = 60$ and $y = 50$ gives the highest daily profit of £7,000. The optimum solution then, is to produce 60 Regular clocks and 50 Deluxe clocks every day.

An alternative procedure involves plotting the objective function. As a starting point, consider an arbitrary value of daily profit, for example £2,000. For this arbitrary selection the objective function can be represented as $50x + 80y = 2,000$.

To plot this straight line find the extreme points by first setting $x$ and then $y = 0$.

$$\text{If } x = 0, \quad 80y = 2,000, \quad \therefore \quad y = 25.$$

In non-mathematical terms, production of 25 Deluxe clocks will yield a profit of £2,000.

$$\text{If } y = 0, \quad 50x = 2,000 \quad x = 40.$$

At the other extreme, production of 40 Regular clocks will yield a profit of £2,000. Line TU in Fig.66 represents a profit of £2,000. All points on the line will give a profit of £2,000, though they represent different combinations of products (iso-profit line).

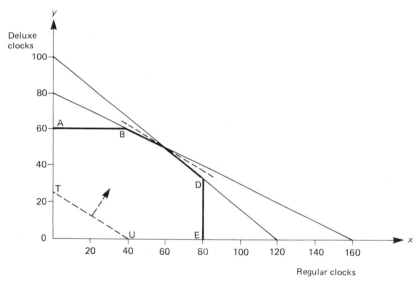

Fig. 66. *Gonda Clock Company—plotting iso-profit lines.*

If this process is repeated for different values of profit, a series of parallel lines is obtained (the slope is the same). The larger the value of profit assumed the higher the line on the diagram. Hence, for higher values of profit the original line moves upwards but remains parallel. The maximum value of the objective function is obtained by finding a point which lies on a line parallel to TU as far as possible from the origin (but part of the feasible region). Corner point C is that point. Any further movement of the iso-profit line beyond C would move the line completely outside the feasible region.

## 3.0 GRAPHICAL SOLUTION—MINIMISATION

A minimisation problem with two decision variables can be solved in a similar fashion to the maximisation situation described above. To illustrate the graphical method, consider again the production problem facing the Hyderabad Chemical Company. The company specialises in the production of three different types of chemicals, A, B and C. These three chemicals are produced at two different factories. In a normal working day, factory I produces 5 tons of A, 4 tons of B and 1 ton of C, while factory II produces 6 tons of A, 3 tons of B and 2 tons of C. In a given period, the demand for each of these chemicals is known to be 250 tons, 150 tons and 70 tons respectively. Demand must be satisfied fully to ensure repeat orders. The daily cost of operation is £2,500 in factory I and £3,500 in factory II.

Given that the objective is to minimise the total cost of operation, find the optimum number of days each factory should be operated so as to satisfy the demand.

The model is restated below:

Let $x$ be the days factory I is operated,
   $y$ be the days factory II is operated.

$$\text{Minimise } C = 2{,}500x + 3{,}500y \quad \text{(objective function)},$$

subject to:

$$5x + 6y \geqslant 250 \text{(chemical A constraint)}$$

$$4x + 3y \geqslant 150 \text{(chemical B constraint)}$$

$$x + 2y \geqslant 70 \text{(chemical C constraint)}$$

$$x \geqslant 0, y \geqslant 0 \quad \text{(non-negativity conditions)}.$$

A graphical procedure similar to that used for maximisation can now be applied to the minimisation problem above. As a starting point, the three constraints need to be

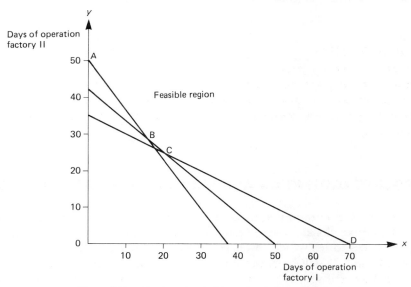

Fig. 67. *Hyderabad Chemical Company.*

depicted on a graph. This is shown in Fig.67. Note that the constraints above have inequality signs which are "greater than or equal to". Hence the feasible points are on the lines and to the right of the lines. Combinations of $x$ and $y$ that satisfy all the constraints taken together lie on the boundary ABCD or to its right. In this situation (minimisation) the minimum value of the objective function will occur once again at one of the corner points ABCD.

A similar evaluation of corner points can be done. Each corner point represents a combination of operations in days at each of the factories. These can be read off the graph. These values can then be substituted into the objective function to find the respective values of cost at each of the corner points. The corner point that yields the minimum cost is then chosen as the optimal solution. Table 8 summarises the results.

Table 8. Evaluation of corner points (Fig.67).

| Corner point | Days of operation | | Cost of operation | | |
|---|---|---|---|---|---|
| | Factory I | Factory II | Factory I | Factory II | Total cost |
| A | 0 | 50 | 0 | £175,000 | £175,000 |
| B | 16.66 | 27.78 | £41,650 | £ 97,230 | £138,880 |
| C | 20 | 25 | £50,000 | £ 87,500 | £137,500 |
| D | 70 | 0 | £175,000 | 0 | £175,000 |

Corner point C where $x = 20$ and $y = 25$ gives the lowest total cost of £137,500. The optimum solution, then, is to operate factory I for 20 days and factory II for 25 days.

*Tutorial notes*
*(a) The result can be confirmed by plotting the objective function. The series of parallel lines obtained are referred to as iso-cost lines.*
*(b) From a well-drawn graph, the values of the corner points can be read off the axes. However, the numbers may not be convenient. The values can however be obtained precisely by examining the graph to see which constraints intersect at which corner point and then solving simultaneously.*

## 4.0 RESOURCE UTILISATION AND EXCESS SUPPLY AT THE OPTIMUM

The solution obtained in the maximisation problem in **2.0** was to produce 60 Regular clocks and 50 Deluxe clocks. These values can be substituted back into the given data regarding resources to see which resources are being fully utilised and which resources are not fully utilised. It will be seen that at the optimal solution electrical components and labour are fully utilised. However, there is unused capacity in the two departments (20 Regular clocks and 10 Deluxe clocks).

# 15 LINEAR PROGRAMMING—GRAPHICAL SOLUTION

A similar exercise can be carried out on the minimisation problem. It will be seen that when the two factories are operated for 20 and 25 days respectively, this gives:

chemical A: $20 \times 5 + 25 \times 6 = 250$ tons
chemical B: $20 \times 4 + 25 \times 3 = 155$ tons
chemical C: $20 \times 1 + 25 \times 2 = 70$ tons.

Hence the two factories exactly meet the requirements for chemical A and chemical C but produce a surplus of 5 tons of chemical B.

CHAPTER SIXTEEN

# Linear Programming – Simplex Solution and Dual Values

## 1.0 INTRODUCTION

The linear programming situation with two decision-variables is easily tackled by a graphical method of solution. However, most practical linear programming problems contain more than two decision-variables. Graphic representation is difficult (three-dimensional) and requires more time for the determination of an optimal solution when there are three decision-variables. Graphical solution is impossible when more than three decision-variables are involved. The solution method in such cases is the simplex method. It is a mathematical iterative procedure and was developed by G. B. Danzig (1947).

    The routines in the method are iterative, i.e. step by step. The method starts by defining the problem in standard form and then finds an initial feasible solution (the origin) which lies on a corner of the feasible region. The computational routine gives a movement to successive corner points of the feasible region. By finding only basic feasible solutions at successive corner points, the objective function can be tested for optimality. In non-mathematical terms, the first feasible solution is amended by a series of steps, each step being chosen so as to improve the profit until a situation is reached where no further improvement can be achieved. The method is designed in such a way that it guarantees that each successive movement yields values which are closer to the optimal solution than the previous one. (The underlying mathematics is fairly complex, and hence this chapter has been kept as simple as possible.)

## 2.0 SIMPLEX PROCEDURES – MAXIMISATION

The different steps in the method have been summarised in this section. The subsequent section shows their application to a simple two-product problem.

# 16 LINEAR PROGRAMMING—SIMPLEX SOLUTION AND DUAL VALUES

*Step 1* Define the problem in standard form. This indicates the construction of a linear programming model.

*Step 2* Convert the inequalities into equations by inserting slack variables. This is necessary as matrix methods which will be used cannot be performed on inequalities.

*Step 3* Construct a matrix of the coefficients of these equations. The initial matrix is termed the initial simplex tableau. It is prepared on the assumption that there is no production. Hence available resources are totally unutilised.

*Step 4* This step amends the previous feasible solution so as to improve the profit. The implementation of the computational procedures of this step will lead to a successive simplex tableau. The detailed procedures are described below.

Examine the contribution (profit) row and select the product which gives the highest contribution. Identify the column in which this occurs. The column is termed the pivotal column.

Divide the coefficients in the solution quantity column by the appropriate coefficients in the pivotal column. Identify the row with the smallest positive value so obtained. (Obviously, the quantity of product to be made will be limited by the resources available and this step indicates the maximum production possible.) The identified row is known as the pivotal row and the coefficient at the intersection of this row and column is known as the pivot element.

Now construct a new tableau from the existing one by following the rules below:

The pivot row is reconstructed by dividing all the coefficients in it by the pivot element so that the pivot element becomes unity. Change the solution variable to the heading of the identified column.

Now use repetitive row operations using the reconstructed pivot row so that all the other elements in the pivot column are made into zero. (This implies calculating the new coefficients of the other rows of the matrix by subtracting from each row the reconstructed pivot row multiplied by the coefficient lying in the row being transformed and in the pivot column. This ensures that the pivot, which now has the value 1, is the only non-zero coefficient in the pivot column.) This step is calculating the effects of production on resources and contribution and will be clearer when applied to an example.

The procedures described in step 4 are repeated until a simplex tableau is obtained which has all elements in the contribution row zero or negative. (This implies that no positive opportunity profits exist.) At this stage the optimum has been reached.

## 3.0 SIMPLEX PROCEDURES APPLIED TO AN EXAMPLE

The procedures will be applied to the following example:

### Example 1

A manufacturer makes two types of products, I and II. Two machines, A and B, are required for the manufacture of each product. One unit of product I requires 4 hours on machine A and 3 hours on machine B. One unit of product II requires 2 hours on machine A and 6 hours on machine B. In a given period there are 24 hours available on machine A and 36 hours available on machine B.

The contribution per unit on product I is £3 and on product II is £2. How many units of each product should be made in order to maximise profit?

## SOLUTION

*Step 1* Construct a linear programming model.

Let $x$ be units of products I to be made,
$y$ be units of product II to be made.

Maximise contribution:

$$\text{Maximise } Z = 2x + 3y \text{ (objective function)},$$

subject to:
$$4x + 2y \leqslant 24 \quad \text{(machine A constraint)}$$
$$3x + 6y \leqslant 36 \quad \text{(machine B constraint)}$$
$$x, y \geqslant 0 \quad \text{(non-negativity conditions)}.$$

*Step 2* Write the constraints in the form of equations by adding a slack variable to each equation. The slack variables represent unused capacity in the constraints and can take any value from zero (when resource is fully utilised) to maximum unused capacity of a particular resource (a point of zero production). Note that each constraint will have a slack variable.

$$\text{Maximise } Z = 3x + 2y,$$

subject to:
$$4x + 2y + S_1 = 24$$
$$3x + 6y + S_2 = 36.$$

$S_1$ and $S_2$ have been used to represent slack variables.

*Step 3* Construct the initial simplex tableau. The tableau is based on zero production and hence zero contribution. The slack variables will take values of 24 and 36 respectively, as there is no resource utilisation.

Initial tableau

| Solution variables | Products | | Slack variables | | Solution quantities |
|---|---|---|---|---|---|
| | $x$ | $y$ | $S_1$ | $S_2$ | |
| $S_1$ | 4 | 2 | 1 | 0 | 24 |
| $S_2$ | 3 | 6 | 0 | 1 | 36 |
| $Z$ | 3 | 2 | 0 | 0 | 0 |

*Tutorial note:* The simplex tableau gives the following information. The tableau below has been laid out in a form consistent with the initial tableau:

# 16 LINEAR PROGRAMMING—SIMPLEX SOLUTION AND DUAL VALUES

| Solution variables | Products | Slack variables | Solution quantities |
|---|---|---|---|
| Non-zero variables | Substitution | Rates | Value of non-zero variables |
| | Opportunity profits | Dual values | |

The initial solution is $S_1 = 24$, $S_2 = 36$. This indicates that there is no production and no profit. It should be noted that the number of non-zero variables (2) does not exceed the number of constraints (2). Furthermore, these constraints (converted into equations) are satisfied. The solution is termed a basic feasible solution.

The substitution rates can be interpreted by examining the columns. Consider column headed $x$. If one unit of product I is made then it will displace 4 units of $S_1$ and 3 units of $S_2$ and increase the profit by £3.

*Step 4* This step amends the basic feasible solution above so as to improve the profit. The procedures are applied in stages for tutorial purposes.

Examine the contribution row and select the product which gives the highest contribution. Identify the column in which this occurs.

Initial tableau repeated:

| Solution variables | Products | | Slack variables | | Solution quantities |
|---|---|---|---|---|---|
| | $x$ | $y$ | $S_1$ | $S_2$ | |
| $S_1$ | [4] | 2 | 1 | 0 | 24 |
| $S_2$ | 3 | 6 | 0 | 1 | 36 |
| $Z$ | 3 | 2 | 0 | 0 | 0 |
| | ↑ | | | | |

The highest contribution in the $Z$-row is under $x$ and is £3. $x$ has been selected for production. Obviously, the amount of $x$ that can be produced must be limited by available resources.

Divide the solution quantities by the appropriate figures in the identified column and select the row giving the lowest figure:

$$24 \div 4 = 6$$
$$36 \div 3 = 12$$

The identified row is $S_1$. The identified pivot element, i.e. 4, has been placed in a square.

Reconstruct the pivot row by dividing all coefficients in it by the pivot element so that it becomes 1. Retitle the new row so obtained using the heading of the identified column.

| | | | | | | |
|---|---|---|---|---|---|---|
| Old row: | $S_1$ | [4] | 2 | 1 | 0 | 24 |

Dividing throughout by 4 and retitling,

| | | | | | | |
|---|---|---|---|---|---|---|
| new row: | $x$ | 1 | $\frac{1}{2}$ | $\frac{1}{4}$ | 0 | 6 |

Now calculate the new coefficients of the other rows of the matrix by using the reconstructed pivot row so that all the other elements in the pivot element column are made into zero. (In the previous step product $x$ gave the highest contribution and 6 units are to be produced. This step shows the effect of this production on the other rows and is adjusting the resources and contribution by an appropriate amount.)

Rows $S_2$ and $Z$ need to be altered. This is done as follows:

| | | | | | | |
|---|---|---|---|---|---|---|
| Old row: | $S_2$ | 3 | 6 | 0 | 1 | 36 |
| − 3 times row | $x$ | 3 | $1\frac{1}{2}$ | $\frac{3}{4}$ | 0 | 18 |
| = new row: | $S_2$ | 0 | $4\frac{1}{2}$ | $-\frac{3}{4}$ | 1 | 18 |

| | | | | | | |
|---|---|---|---|---|---|---|
| old row: | $Z$ | 3 | 2 | 0 | 0 | 0 |
| − 3 times row | $x$ | 3 | $1\frac{1}{2}$ | $\frac{3}{4}$ | 0 | 18 |
| = new row: | $Z$ | 0 | $\frac{1}{2}$ | $-\frac{3}{4}$ | 0 | − 18 |

The second tableau can now be set up using the altered rows:

Second tableau

| Solution variables | Products | | Slack variables | | Solution quantities |
|---|---|---|---|---|---|
| | $x$ | $y$ | $S_1$ | $S_2$ | |
| $x$ | 1 | $\frac{1}{2}$ | $\frac{1}{4}$ | 0 | 6 |
| → $S_2$ | 0 | [$4\frac{1}{2}$] | $-\frac{3}{4}$ | 1 | 18 |
| $Z$ | 0 | $\frac{1}{2}$ | $-\frac{3}{4}$ | 0 | − 18 |
| | | ↑ | | | |

The solution here is $x = 6$ and $S_2 = 18$. The contribution is 18 (ignore the negative sign as it is part of the procedure.)

Now repeat Step 4 so as to improve the contribution. Highest positive contribution is in column $y$:

$$6 \div \tfrac{1}{2} = 12$$
$$18 \div 4\tfrac{1}{2} = 4.$$

# 16 LINEAR PROGRAMMING—SIMPLEX SOLUTION AND DUAL VALUES

The pivot element is $4\frac{1}{2}$ (intersection of identified row and identified column).

Reconstruct the pivot row by dividing all coefficients in it by the pivot element so that it becomes 1. Retitle the new row so obtained using the heading of the identified column.

| Old row: | $S_2$ | 0 | $4\frac{1}{2}$ | $-\frac{3}{4}$ | 1 | 18 |
|---|---|---|---|---|---|---|

Dividing throughout by $4\frac{1}{2}$ and retitling gives

| new row: | $y$ | 0 | 1 | $-\frac{1}{6}$ | $\frac{2}{9}$ | 4 |
|---|---|---|---|---|---|---|

Now calculate the new coefficients of the other rows of the matrix by using the reconstructed pivot row so that all other elements in the pivot element column are made into zero.

Rows $x$ and $Z$ need to be altered. This is done as follows:

| Old row: | $x$ | 1 | $\frac{1}{2}$ | $\frac{1}{4}$ | 0 | 6 |
|---|---|---|---|---|---|---|
| $-\frac{1}{2}$ times row | $y$ | 0 | $\frac{1}{2}$ | $-\frac{1}{12}$ | $\frac{1}{9}$ | 2 |
| = new row: | $x$ | 1 | 0 | $\frac{1}{3}$ | $-\frac{1}{9}$ | 4 |

| old row: | $Z$ | 0 | $\frac{1}{2}$ | $-\frac{3}{4}$ | 0 | $-18$ |
|---|---|---|---|---|---|---|
| $-\frac{1}{2}$ times row | $y$ | 0 | $\frac{1}{2}$ | $-\frac{1}{12}$ | $\frac{1}{9}$ | 2 |
| = new row: | $Z$ | 0 | 0 | $-\frac{2}{3}$ | $-\frac{1}{9}$ | $-20$ |

The next tableau can now be set up using the altered rows. This represents the optimum solution as the $Z$-row does not contain any positive values:

Final tableau

| Solution variables | Products | | Slack variables | | Solution quantities |
|---|---|---|---|---|---|
| | $x$ | $y$ | $S_1$ | $S_2$ | |
| $x$ | 1 | 0 | $\frac{1}{3}$ | $-\frac{1}{9}$ | 4 |
| $y$ | 0 | 1 | $-\frac{1}{6}$ | $\frac{2}{9}$ | 4 |
| $Z$ | 0 | 0 | $-\frac{2}{3}$ | $-\frac{1}{9}$ | $-20$ |

The interpretation of the final tableau is given below. (Students will understand the complete interpretation after studying the subsequent section on primal and dual forms.)

The optimal solution is to make 4 units of $x$ (product I) and 4 units of $y$ (product

II), giving a contribution of £20. (This figure can be confirmed by substituting $x = 4$ and $y = 4$ into the objective function.) As $S_1$ and $S_2$ do not form part of the solution variable column, the resources they represent are being fully utilised. (This can once again be confirmed by substituting $x = 4$ and $y = 4$ into the resource data.)

The Z-row contains zeros under the product columns and absolute values of $\frac{2}{3}$ and $\frac{1}{9}$ in the $S_1$- and $S_2$-columns. The zeros under the product columns imply that no further substitution is possible, i.e. the optimal mix has been obtained. The values of $\frac{2}{3}$ and $\frac{1}{9}$ under the $S_1$- and $S_2$-columns are termed the shadow prices of the resources (or the dual values of the constraints). They represent the amount by which the objective function increases (or decreases) through a unit change in resource availability. The concept is only applicable for marginal changes in resource availability and only to those resources which are being fully utilised (binding constraints). If one additional hour of machine A is obtained then the contribution will increase by £$\frac{2}{3}$ and similarly for a marginal increase in machine B hours.

*Tutorial notes*
(a) *There were 24 hours available on machine A and 36 hours available on machine B. The valuation of the resources is £$\frac{2}{3}$ per hour and £$\frac{1}{9}$ per hour respectively. The total valuation is £20 which students should note is the optimal contribution.*
(b) *A graphical analysis can be carried out on the same problem. The contribution of £20 can then be confirmed at a product-mix of $x = 4$ and $y = 4$. Students should construct a graph and relate each tableau obtained to the appropriate corner point. A further exercise would involve increasing machine A hours by 1 keeping machine B constant at 36. The contribution at the new product-mix ($x = 4\frac{1}{3}$ and $y = 3\frac{5}{6}$) will be £$20\frac{2}{3}$. A similar exercise can be done for a marginal increase in machine B hours. The valuation of scarce resources can be confirmed in this way.*

## 4.0 AN INTRODUCTION TO PRIMAL AND DUAL FORMS

The simplex method described above was applied to a maximisation problem. The final tableau in the solution contained the optimal solution and useful additional information which is interpreted under the heading of the "dual problem".

The given linear programming problem, whether maximisation or minimisation, is called the primal problem because it deals with the primary relationship of the decision variables in the objective function and constraints. It is concerned with the allocation of resources so as to satisfy a desired objective.

In addition to the primal aspect, every linear programming problem has another related aspect termed the dual. If the linear programming problem being solved as the primal involves the allocation of resources then the dual involves the pricing or valuation of resources involved. The dual solution to a given primal problem is important because it contains significant economic meaning. It should be noted that although mathematical transformation is possible from primal forms to dual forms, a simple verbal interpretation cannot be found for every dual problem.

## 5.0 PRIMAL AND DUAL FORMS—THE GENERAL MODELS

Consider a linear programming problem concerned with the maximisation of an objective function $Z$ with $n$ decision variables and $m$ constraints (primal). The dual of

# 16 LINEAR PROGRAMMING—SIMPLEX SOLUTION AND DUAL VALUES

this problem is concerned with the minimisation of the value of the objective function $F$ with $m$ decision variables and $n$ constraints. Thus a maximisation problem becomes minimisation in the dual and vice versa. The number of primal decision variables determines the number of constraints in the dual and the number of primal constraints determines the number of dual decision variables.

The coefficients of the decision variables in the primal objective function become the constants of the dual constraints. The constants of the primal constraints become the coefficients of the decision variables in the dual objective function. In the dual formulation, the matrix of coefficients of the decision variables in the constraints are transformed in such a way that rows become columns and columns become rows. The direction of the inequalities in the dual problem ($\geqslant$) is exactly opposite to that in the primal problem ($\leqslant$).

In mathematical form, the primal can be stated as:

$$\text{maximise } Z = C_1 x_1 + C_2 x_2 + \ldots + C_n x_n,$$

subject to:
$$a_{11} x_1 + a_{12} x_2 + \ldots + a_{1n} x_n \leqslant b_1$$
$$a_{21} x_1 + a_{22} x_2 + \ldots + a_{2n} x_n \leqslant b_2$$
$$\vdots$$
$$a_{m1} x_1 + a_{m2} x_2 + \ldots + a_{mn} x_n \leqslant b_m$$

and
$$x_1 \geqslant 0, \; x_2 \geqslant 0, \; \ldots, \; x_n \geqslant 0.$$

The dual of this problem may be expressed in the form:

$$\text{minimise } F = b_1 y_1 + b_2 y_2 + \ldots + b_m y_m,$$

subject to:
$$a_{11} y_1 + a_{21} y_2 + \ldots + a_{m1} y_m \geqslant C_1$$
$$a_{12} y_1 + a_{22} y_2 + \ldots + a_{m2} y_m \geqslant C_2$$
$$\vdots$$
$$a_{1n} y_1 + a_{2n} y_2 + \ldots + a_{mn} y_m \geqslant C_n$$

and
$$y_1 \geqslant 0, \; y_2 \geqslant 0, \; \ldots, \; y_m \geqslant 0.$$

## 6.0 PRIMAL AND DUAL FORMS—PARTICULAR EXAMPLES

The example used to illustrate the simplex procedures is restated below.

### Example 2 (primal maximisation)

A manufacturer makes two types of products, I and II. Two machines, A and B, are required for the manufacture of each product. One unit of product I requires 4 hours on machine A and 3 hours on machine B. One unit of product II requires 2 hours on machine A and 6 hours on machine B.

The contribution per unit on product I is £3 and on product II is £2. Construct primal and dual models and interpret the dual.

SOLUTION
The primal problem may be expressed in the form:
Let $x_1$ and $x_2$ be units of product I and product II to be made.

$$\text{Maximise } Z = 3x_1 + 2x_2 \quad \text{(objective function)},$$

subject to:
$$4x_1 + 2x_2 \leqslant 24 \quad \text{(machine A constraint)}$$
$$3x_1 + 6x_2 \leqslant 36 \quad \text{(machine B constraint)}$$
$$x_1, x_2 \geqslant 0 \quad \text{(non-negativity conditions)}.$$

The primal problem has been solved by the simplex method in an earlier section. The maximum contribution of £20 is obtained by producing 4 units of product I and 4 units of product II. The resources are fully utilised at the optimal product-mix.

The dual problem may be formulated by following the transformation procedures described earlier:

Let $A$ be the hourly value of machine A,
$B$ be the hourly value of machine B.

$$\text{Minimise } F = 24A + 36B \quad \text{(objective function)},$$

subject to:
$$4A + 3B \geqslant 3 \quad \text{(product I)}$$
$$2A + 6B \geqslant 2 \quad \text{(product II)}$$
$$A, B \geqslant 0.$$

The dual problem above can be solved easily by graphical methods to give $A = \frac{2}{3}$, $B = \frac{1}{9}$ and the value of the objective function is £20.

*Tutorial notes*
*(a) It is obvious from the above problem that the optimal value of the objective function in the dual problem is simultaneously determined when the optimal solution to the primal problem is found, i.e. the values are the same.*
*(b) The values for $A = \frac{2}{3}$ and $B = \frac{1}{9}$, i.e. the shadow prices of the limited resources, should be related to the final simplex tableau obtained earlier. The final simplex tableau gives both the primal and the dual solution.*
*(c) The concept of shadow prices or dual values applies only to binding constraints, i.e. where resources are fully utilised. Non-binding constraints (resources not fully utilised) will have dual values of zero.*

## INTERPRETATION OF THE DUAL
The dual model is restated for interpretation:

$$\text{Minimise } F = 24A + 36B,$$

subject to:
$$4A + 3B \geqslant 3 \quad \text{(product I)}$$
$$2A + 6B \geqslant 2 \quad \text{(product II)}$$
$$A, B \geqslant 0.$$

In the primal problem the objective of the company is to determine the optimal output of product I and product II to realise maximum contribution with available hours on machines A and B.

# 16 LINEAR PROGRAMMING—SIMPLEX SOLUTION AND DUAL VALUES

In the dual problem, however, the objective of the company is to minimise the cost of producing these two products with 24 hours on machine A and 36 hours on machine B. The hourly costs (values) of machine A and machine B must be determined, because the total cost (value) cannot be minimised without knowing them. The dual decision variables A and B represent the hourly cost (value) of machines A and B. In the constraints, the value of the resources used to produce one unit of each of the products is related to the contribution it creates. The inequalities are in the form $\geq$, implying that if the cost of producing products is greater than the contribution obtained then it will be advisable to use the resources for other purposes.

The value of the decision variables $A = \frac{2}{3}$ and $B = \frac{1}{9}$ indicates that an hour on machine A is worth £$\frac{2}{3}$ to the company and similarly for B. These are the shadow prices of the two resources.

## Example 3 (Primal Minimisation)

Consider Example in Chapter 14. The Hyderabad Chemical Company produces three different chemicals, A, B and C. These are used as fertilisers and have a growing demand locally. These three different chemicals are produced at the company's two different factories, I and II, with different production capacities. In a normal working day, factory I produces 5 tons of A, 4 tons of B and 1 ton of C. While factory II produces 6 tons of A, 3 tons of B and 2 tons of C. In a given period the demand for each of these chemicals is known to be 250 tons, 150 tons and 70 tons respectively. Demand must be satisfied fully to ensure repeat orders. The daily cost of operation is £2,500 in factory I and £3,500 in factory II. Given that the objective is to minimise the total cost of operation, find the optimum number of days each factory should be operated so as to meet the demand.

### SOLUTION

The primal model can be stated as follows:

Let $x_1$ be the days factory I is operated,
   $x_2$ be the days factory II is operated.

Minimise $F = 2{,}500 x_1 + 3{,}500 x_2$   (objective function),

subject to:

$5x_1 + 6x_2 \geq 250$   (chemical A constraint)

$4x_1 + 3x_2 \geq 150$   (chemical B constraint)

$x_1 + 2x_2 \geq 70$   (chemical C constraint)

$x_1, x_2 \geq 0$   (non-negativity conditions).

The primal problem was solved graphically in Chapter 15. The solution is restated below.

The optimum solution is to operate factory I for 20 days and factory II for 25 days to give a minimum cost of £137,500. This operating schedule gives the following production schedule:

chemical A production = 250 tons
chemical B production = 155 tons
chemical C production =  70 tons.

Hence, Hyderabad Chemical Company exactly meets the requirements for chemical A and chemical C but produces a surplus of 5 tons of chemical B.

The dual of this problem can be set up as follows:

Let $A$ be the shadow price assigned to chemical A
$\quad\quad B$ be the shadow price assigned to chemical B
$\quad\quad C$ be the shadow price assigned to chemical C.

$$\text{Maximise } Z = 250A + 150B + 70C,$$

subject to:
$$5A + 4B + C \leqslant 2{,}500 \quad \text{(factory I)}$$
$$6A + 3B + 2C \leqslant 3{,}500 \quad \text{(factory II)}$$
$$A, B, C \geqslant 0.$$

The solution of the dual problem can be obtained by using simplex minimisation procedures (discussed later). The dual solution is $A = 375$, $B = 0$ and $C = 625$. This gives $Z = £137{,}500$.

## INTERPRETATION OF THE DUAL

In the primal problem, the objective of the company is to minimise the total cost of operations by determining the optimal number of days of operations at two different factories, while meeting the demand for three products, chemicals A, B and C.

Assume that the company is also interested in assigning a "value" to each of the three different chemicals that the company produces at its two factories. The assigned value could be taken to represent the share of the operational costs attributable to each of the chemicals produced at the two factories. The assigned value is also called a shadow price. (It is suggested by some academics that it might exert some influence on the determination of the sales price of each product.) The objective of the company in the dual is to determine the value assigned to each of the three chemicals, in such a way that the total input value is maximised.

The dual decision variables $A$, $B$ and $C$ represent the shadow prices assigned to chemicals $A$, $B$ and $C$ respectively. The values of these variables must be determined, because the total assigned value cannot be maximised without knowing them. Since the company must produce 250 tons of chemical A, 150 tons of chemical B and 70 tons of chemical C in order to meet the demand in a period, these figures are multiplied by the corresponding assigned values and added together to obtain the total assigned value denoted by $Z$.

The direction of the constraints is in the form $\leqslant$ ("less than or equal to"). The number of tons of the three different chemicals produced at each factory multiplied by the respective shadow prices gives the total shadow price assigned to each factory.

The total assigned value must not exceed the daily cost of operations, if the shadow price is to have any meaning. If the total assigned value is less than daily operational costs, the Hyderabad Company will not produce chemicals at the plants. Available resources will be used for other purposes. If the total assigned value is equal to the daily cost of operation, the facilities will be used for the production of the chemicals.

*Tutorial note: A zero shadow price will be assigned to each unit of chemical B since there is a surplus of chemical B in the company when the factories are operated 20 days and 25 days respectively.*

# 16 LINEAR PROGRAMMING—SIMPLEX SOLUTION AND DUAL VALUES

*Chemical B can be considered a by-product of the company, although it can be sold at a positive market price. The shadow prices assigned to chemicals A and B fully account for the daily cost of operation in each of the two factories. Students should appreciate the esoteric nature of the exercise.*

*In the memorable words of one writer, it "has as much significance as a group of monks debating how many angels can dance on a pin's head". However, it should be repeated that a simple verbal interpretation cannot be found for every dual problem. Further, students do need to be capable of carrying out the mathematical transformations for examination purposes.*

## 7.0 SIMPLEX MAXIMISATION—MIXED INEQUALITIES

The simplest maximising situations are normally characterised by constraints which are of the "less than or equal to" type. Occasionally however, in a maximisation situation the constraints may contain a mixture of $\leqslant$ and $\geqslant$ varieties. The usual cause of "greater than or equal to" constraints is the requirement to produce at least a certain amount of a particular product. In such situations the simplest approach is to reduce the capacity of the other limitations by the amounts of resources necessary to make just the requisite amount of the appropriate product. We can now carry out maximisation in the normal way, remembering to add back, to the solution obtained from simplex, the quantities which were required to be produced.

An alternative method of dealing with mixed limitations involves the use of artificial variables. If there were no "greater than equal to" inequalities then slack variables would be added to all the constraints and normal simplex methods applied. However, if a "greater than equal to" inequality exists then a surplus variable would be required and the normal method would lead to an infeasible solution (one of the variables would take a negative value). This difficulty can be resolved by adding an artifical variable to the constraint and setting up an additional objective function equal to the artifical variable. Initially, the normal simplex procedures will be used to minimise the new objective function. This new objective function when reduced to zero allows the artifical variable to be dropped from the problem leaving a basic feasible solution to the original problem. The normal simplex procedures can now be applied to the original objective function.

## 8.0 SIMPLEX MINIMISATION

As long as all the constraints are of the type "greater than or equal to" in a minimisation problem, the maximisation procedures can still be applied. Given such a minimisation problem, formulate the dual using the procedures outlined earlier. As the primal is minimisation, the dual will be a maximisation problem. Now use standard maximisation procedures. The only difference arises in the interpretation of the final tableau. As the dual of a dual must be the primal, the primal and dual solutions are now interchanged in the final tableau. Alternative methods for minimisation involve the use of artifical variables ("method of penalty" and the "two phase" techniques).

*Tutorial note: The primary objective of this chapter has been to provide a basic understanding of the simplex method as applied to maximisation situations and an elementary knowledge of primal and dual forms. Situations involving mixed limitations and minimisation have been briefly mentioned. This has been done deliberately. No use is served in an accounting examination by dwelling on mathematical complexities. Variation of simplex-method applications involving degeneracy, unbounded solutions, alternative optimal solutions and non-existing feasible solutions have been left out completely.*

# CHAPTER SEVENTEEN
# Transportation

## 1.0 INTRODUCTION

The simplex method outlined in the previous chapter is designed to tackle the general linear programming problem. However, for solutions to certain kinds of linear programming problems, special techniques have been developed. The transportation method is one of such special techniques. It is a method which presents a quicker method of solution than the more general simplex method. It is termed the transportation method because it deals with the transportation of products available at several sources to a number of destinations.

In its commonest form, the model seeks the minimisation of costs of transporting a commodity from a number of sources to several destinations. The amount available at each source is known as is the demand at each destination. Unit costs of transfer from each source to each destination are presumed to be known. Linearity is maintained in the costs by assuming that costs are directly proportional to the number of items moved.

## 2.0 DESCRIPTION OF THE PROBLEM

The following example will be used to give a simple description of the problem.

*Example 1*

A company has four warehouses, $W_1$, $W_2$, $W_3$ and $W_4$, which have the following amounts of a particular product in stock:

|  |  |
|---|---|
| $W_1$ | 15 units |
| $W_2$ | 20 units |
| $W_3$ | 10 units |
| $W_4$ | 25 units |
|  | 70 units. |

It is required to deliver the product from these warehouses to three retailers $R_1$, $R_2$ and $R_3$.
Their requirements are:

$$
\begin{array}{ll}
R_1 & 30 \text{ units} \\
R_2 & 28 \text{ units} \\
R_3 & \underline{12} \text{ units} \\
& \underline{70} \text{ units.}
\end{array}
$$

The unit costs of transporting one unit of the product from any warehouse to any retailer are given in the following table:

|         |       | Destinations |       |       |
|---------|-------|-------|-------|-------|
|         |       | $R_1$ | $R_2$ | $R_3$ |
|         | $W_1$ | £8    | 6     | 3     |
| Sources | $W_2$ | 9     | 12    | 8     |
|         | $W_3$ | 6     | 7     | 5     |
|         | $W_4$ | 3     | 8     | 9     |

The problem is to find a transportation schedule which minimises overall transportation costs and yet satisfies the retailers' requirements.

*Note: Although the above problem can be solved by the regular simplex method, its special properties offer a more convenient solution procedure.*

## 3.0 MATHEMATICAL MODEL OF THE TRANSPORTATION SITUATION

### 3.1 Linear programming model for a particular situation

Consider again the problem outlined above:

|         |       |    | Destinations |       |       |
|---------|-------|----|-------|-------|-------|
|         |       |    | $R_1$ | $R_2$ | $R_3$ |
|         |       |    | 30    | 28    | 12    |
|         | $W_1$ | 15 | £8    | 6     | 3     |
| Sources | $W_2$ | 20 | 9     | 12    | 8     |
|         | $W_3$ | 10 | 6     | 7     | 5     |
|         | $W_4$ | 25 | 3     | 8     | 9     |

# 17 TRANSPORTATION

For the above problem define the allocation variables as follows:

|         |       |    | $R_1$ | $R_2$ | $R_3$ |
|---------|-------|----|-------|-------|-------|
|         |       |    | 30    | 28    | 12    |
|         | $W_1$ | 15 | $x_{11}$ | $x_{12}$ | $x_{13}$ |
|         | $W_2$ | 20 | $x_{21}$ | $x_{22}$ | $x_{23}$ |
| Sources | $W_3$ | 10 | $x_{31}$ | $x_{32}$ | $x_{33}$ |
|         | $W_4$ | 25 | $x_{41}$ | $x_{42}$ | $x_{43}$ |

(Destinations across the top)

$x_{11}$ represents the amount transferred from $W_1$ to $R_1$,

$x_{21}$ represents the amount transferred from $W_2$ to $R_1$ and so on.

The problem can now be stated in linear programming form:

$$\text{Minimise } C = 8x_{11} + 6x_{12} + 3x_{13} + 9x_{21} + 12x_{22} + 8x_{23}$$
$$+ 6x_{31} + 7x_{32} + 5x_{33} + 3x_{41} + 8x_{42} + 9x_{43} \text{ (objective function)},$$

subject to:

$$\begin{aligned}
x_{11} + x_{12} + x_{13} &= 15 \quad (W_1 \text{ constraint}) \\
x_{21} + x_{22} + x_{23} &= 20 \quad (W_2 \text{ constraint}) \\
x_{31} + x_{32} + x_{33} &= 10 \quad (W_3 \text{ constraint}) \\
x_{41} + x_{42} + x_{43} &= 25 \quad (W_4 \text{ constraint}) \\
x_{11} + x_{21} + x_{31} + x_{41} &= 30 \quad (R_1 \text{ constraint}) \\
x_{12} + x_{22} + x_{32} + x_{42} &= 28 \quad (R_2 \text{ constraint}) \\
x_{13} + x_{23} + x_{33} + x_{43} &= 12 \quad (R_3 \text{ constraint})
\end{aligned}$$

and $\quad x_{11}, x_{12}, \ldots, x_{43} \geq 0 \quad$ (non-negativity conditions).

*Note. In this model, one of the constraints is redundant because it can be derived from the rest. The mathematical formulation is in linear programming form with 12 ($4 \times 3$) decision variables and six ($4 + 3 - 1$) linearly independent equations. In the general transportation situation with $m$ sources and $n$ destinations there will be ($m \times n$) decision variables and ($m + n - 1$) independent constraints. constraints.*

## 3.2 General linear programming model

The transportation situation may be described mathematically in the following general form. Assume that $a_1, a_2, \ldots, a_m$ are amounts of a particular product available at each of $m$ sources.

The amounts $b_1, b_2, \ldots, b_n$ are the requirements at each of $n$ destinations. Further, assume that the transportation cost per unit from the $i$th source to the $j$th destination is a known constant $c_{ij}$ and directly proportional to the amount shipped. The problem is then to distribute the products from $i$ sources to $j$ destinations in such a manner that total transportation costs are minimised.

The linear programming model can now be stated as:

$$\text{Minimise } Z = \sum_{i=1}^{m} \sum_{j=1}^{n} C_{ij} x_{ij},$$

subject to
$$\sum_{j=1}^{n} x_{ij} = a_i \text{ (for } i = 1, 2, \ldots, m)$$

$$\sum_{i=1}^{m} x_{ij} = b_j \text{ (for } j = 1, 2, \ldots, n)$$

and
$$x_{ij} \geqslant 0 \quad \text{(for } i = 1, 2, \ldots, m; j = 1, 2, \ldots, n).$$

## 4.0 TRANSPORTATION PROCEDURES

The procedures are iterative (i.e. step by step) and in three main stages. In the first stage a basic feasible solution is found by using one of the following methods: the northwest-corner method, the least-cost method, Russel's approximation method or Vogel's approximation method. In the second stage a test for optimality is done using a concept termed shadow costs. This will show whether there is any possibility of improvement (i.e. if the costs can be reduced any further). In the final stage, improvement is implemented and continued till no further reductions in cost are possible.

The procedures are best explained through an example and this follows:

### Example 1

The Poona Manufacturing Company has three plants which have the following amounts of a particular product in stock:

| | | |
|---|---|---|
| $P_1$ | 4 | units |
| $P_2$ | 6 | units |
| $P_3$ | 8 | units |
| | 18 | units. |

The company wishes to deliver the product from these plants to three dealers $D_1$, $D_2$ and $D_3$. Their requirements are:

| | | |
|---|---|---|
| $D_1$ | 5 | units |
| $D_2$ | 4 | units |
| $D_3$ | 9 | units |
| | 18 | units. |

# 17 TRANSPORTATION

The unit costs of transfer between the plants and the dealers are:

|        |       | Dealers |       |       |
|--------|-------|-------|-------|-------|
|        |       | $D_1$ | $D_2$ | $D_3$ |
|        | $P_1$ | 4     | 8     | 5     |
| Plants | $P_2$ | 9     | 5     | 6     |
|        | $P_3$ | 5     | 6     | 7     |

The problem is to find a transportation schedule which minimises overall transportation costs:

*Step* 1:   Find a feasible solution. The method used here is the least-cost method. The procedure allocates as many units as possible to those cells which have the lowest cost. The allocation begins with the selection of a cell with the smallest unit-transportation cost. Allocate as many units as possible to this cell; then select the subsequent cells, following the same process, and allocate accordingly. In the given problem, the cell with the lowest unit cost is $P_1D_1$. Allocate as many units as possible in this cell and repeat this procedure until the entire available quanitity is fully allocated as required.

This will yield the following allocation:

First allocation (units):

|       |   | $D_1$ | $D_2$ | $D_3$ |
|-------|---|-------|-------|-------|
|       |   | 5     | 4     | 9     |
| $P_1$ | 4 | 4     |       |       |
| $P_2$ | 6 |       | 4     | 2     |
| $P_3$ | 8 | 1     |       | 7     |

This is the first feasible solution. Note that the allocation gives 5 cells filled. In general, with $m$ sources and $n$ destinations, there should be $m + n - 1$ cells filled.

If less than $m + n - 1$ cells are filled then the solution is termed degenerate. A degenerate solution is one in which there is an insufficient number of cells filled to proceed to the next stage, i.e. to test for optimality. The next example deals with degeneracy.

On the basis of the allocation above, the total costs would be:

| Cell | | |
|------|------|------|
| $P_1D_1$ | $4 \times 4 =$ | £ 16 |
| $P_2D_2$ | $4 \times 5 =$ | 20 |
| $P_2D_3$ | $2 \times 6 =$ | 12 |
| $P_3D_1$ | $1 \times 5 =$ | 5 |
| $P_3D_3$ | $7 \times 7 =$ | 49 |
|          |                | £102 |

The solution shown above is just one of a large number of possible solutions. The minimum-cost solution could be found by a process of trial and error. However, such a method is not recommended as it becomes increasingly time-consuming as the problem becomes more complex. The following method utilising the concept of shadow costs automatically leads to the optimum solution.

*Step 2:* Test for optimality. This is done by using shadow costs. These are defined as follows:

For each occupied cell in the allocation, the actual transportation cost per unit is given by the sum of shadow costs for its row and column. By arbitrarily fixing the shadow cost of row 1 as 0 it is possible to calculate all the row and column shadow costs. Once the shadow costs are calculated (by using actual occupied cells as long as $m + n - 1$ are filled) the gross savings in unused cells can be obtained by adding appropriate row and column shadow costs. If the gross savings in an unused cell or cells exceed actual transportation costs then further minimisation is indicated (i.e. net savings are possible). If the gross savings in unused cells are less than actual transportation costs then no further minimisation is possible, i.e. the optimal solution has been reached.

These procedures are applied to the allocation obtained in Step 1. Thus:

Cell $P_1D_1$:  Actual cost per unit = Row shadow cost + Column shadow cost

i.e.  $4 = 0 +$ Column shadow cost

∴ Column shadow cost = 4.

Then for cell $P_3D_1$:  Actual cost per unit = Row shadow cost + Column shadow cost

i.e.  $5 =$ Row shadow cost $+ 4$

∴ Row shadow cost = 1.

Proceeding in this manner, using actual occupied cells, it is possible to calculate all the row and column shadow costs as below.

Calculation of shadow costs:

|  | $D_1$ | $D_2$ | $D_3$ | Row shadow costs |
|---|---|---|---|---|
| $P_1$ | 4 |  |  | 0 |
| $P_2$ |  | 5 | 6 | 0 |
| $P_3$ | 5 |  | 7 | 1 |
| Column shadow costs | 4 | 5 | 6 |  |

The gross savings in unused cells can now be obtained by adding the appropriate row and column shadow costs. For example, cell $P_1D_2$ is an unused cell. It has a row shadow cost of 0 and a column shadow cost of 5. The gross saving in this cell if it was used to transport items is given by $0 + 5 = 5$. In a similar fashion, gross savings for all unused cells can be calculated. These are shown in parentheses.

# 17 TRANSPORTATION

Gross savings in unused cells:

|       | $D_1$ | $D_2$ | $D_3$ | Row shadow costs |
|-------|-------|-------|-------|------------------|
| $P_1$ | 4     | (5)   | (6)   | 0                |
| $P_2$ | (4)   | 5     | 6     | 0                |
| $P_3$ | 5     | (6)   | 7     | 1                |
| Column shadow costs | 4 | 5 | 6 | |

The gross savings in unused cells can now be compared with actual transportation costs per unit to see if any net saving exists (Table 9).

It should be clear from the calculations in Table 9 that cell $P_1D_3$ represents further minimisation (i.e. a net saving of £1 per unit transferred into this cell). Obviously, as many units as possible should be transferred into this cell. (Note that if more than one unused cell gives a saving then the cell with the highest net saving should be selected.)

*Step* 3 Reallocate as many units as possible into cell $P_1D_3$. It should be appreciated that if items are moved into cell $P_1D_3$ then the existing allocation will have to be adjusted. The first allocation which needs adjustment is restated here:

|        |   | $D_1$ | $D_2$ | $D_3$ |
|--------|---|-------|-------|-------|
|        |   | 5     | 4     | 9     |
| $P_1$  | 4 | 4     |       |       |
| $P_2$  | 6 |       | 4     | 2     |
| $P_3$  | 8 | 1     |       | 7     |

Table 9. Comparison of gross savings with transportation costs.

| Unused cell | Gross saving per unit | Actual transportation cost per unit | Net saving per unit | Comments |
|-------------|-----------------------|-------------------------------------|---------------------|----------|
| $P_1D_2$    | 5                     | 8                                   | (3)                 | Costs will increase from £102 by £3 per unit transferred into this cell. |
| $P_1D_3$    | 6                     | 5                                   | 1                   | Costs will decrease from £102 by £1 per unit transferred into this cell. |
| $P_2D_1$    | 4                     | 9                                   | (5)                 | Costs increase by £5 per unit. |
| $P_3D_2$    | 6                     | 6                                   | 0                   | No change in costs. |

The reallocation can be achieved by using plus and minus signs. Start by putting a plus sign in the cell which represents further minimisation (cell $P_1D_3$). Now put a minus sign in the occupied cell in the same row which has an occupied cell in its column ($P_1D_1$). Continue till a plus sign occurs in the same column as the original plus. (As a simple rule, make sure that plus and minus signs are placed in such a way that only 1 unused cell, i.e. the initial plus, is moved into.)

This will give the following:

|      |   | $D_1$ | $D_2$ | $D_3$ |
|------|---|-------|-------|-------|
|      |   | 5     | 4     | 9     |
| $P_1$ | 4 | $4^-$ |       | +     |
| $P_2$ | 6 |       | 4     | 2     |
| $P_3$ | 8 | $1^+$ |       | $7^-$ |

Now examine the plus and minus signs to determine the maximum number that can be allocated into cell $P_1D_3$. The maximum number that can be transferred into $P_1D_3$ is given by the lowest number in the cells with minus signs. (Reason this out.)

The reallocation gives the second allocation below.

Second allocation:

|      |   | $D_1$ | $D_2$ | $D_3$ |
|------|---|-------|-------|-------|
|      |   | 5     | 4     | 9     |
| $P_1$ | 4 |       |       | 4     |
| $P_2$ | 6 |       | 4     | 2     |
| $P_3$ | 8 |       | 5     | 3     |

The cost of this allocation will be £98. Each unit moved into cell $P_1D_3$ gave a net saving of £1. As 4 units were moved in the original cost of £102 (first allocation) it is reduced by £4. The figure of £98 can be confirmed by reworking the total cost. (Note that $m + n - 1$ cells are filled.)

This allocation can now be tested for optimality; shadow costs need calculating again.

Second allocation – test for optimality:

|       | $D_1$ | $D_2$ | $D_3$ | Row shadow costs |
|-------|-------|-------|-------|------------------|
| $P_1$ | (3)   | (4)   | 5     | 0                |
| $P_2$ | (4)   | 5     | 6     | 1                |
| $P_3$ | 5     | (6)   | 7     | 2                |
| Column shadow costs | 3 | 4 | 5 | |

## 17 TRANSPORTATION

Table 10. Further comparison of gross savings with transportation costs.

| Unused cell | Gross saving per unit | Actual transportation cost per unit | Net saving per unit | Comments |
|---|---|---|---|---|
| $P_1D_1$ | 3 | 4 | (1) | Costs increase by 1. |
| $P_1D_2$ | 4 | 8 | (4) | Costs increase by 4. |
| $P_2D_1$ | 4 | 9 | (5) | Costs increase by 5. |
| $P_3D_2$ | 6 | 6 | 0 | No change in cost. |

The gross savings in unused cells can now again be compared with actual transportation costs per unit to see if any net saving exists (Table 10).

The table shows that this is a minimum-cost solution as no further saving exists in unused cells. Note, however, that while this solution is optimal it is not uniquely optimal. Transfer into cell $P_3D_2$ will not affect the cost structure, i.e. it will remain at £98. This means that there is an alternative solution with the same minimum total cost.

*Tutorial notes*

(a) The procedures appear to be lengthy because of the detailed explanations. Such detail is not required in the examination.
(b) The alternative optimal solution is stated below. Students should be able to arrive at it.

*Alternative optimal solution:*

|  |  | $D_1$ | $D_2$ | $D_3$ |
|---|---|---|---|---|
|  |  | 5 | 4 | 9 |
| $P_1$ | 4 |  |  | 4 |
| $P_2$ | 6 |  | 1 | 5 |
| $P_3$ | 8 | 5 | 3 |  |

(c) The example above dealt with a balanced situation, i.e. total supply = total demand. A further section (**6.0**) shows the procedure to be followed when the situation is unbalanced.

## 5.0 DEGENERACY

A degenerate allocation in transportation is one where less than $m + n - 1$ cells are filled. With less than $m + n - 1$ cells filled it is not possible to calculate all shadow costs. This implies that the test for optimality cannot proceed.

A simple computational device is used to remedy this problem. An empty cell is assigned the value $\epsilon$ (epsilon) which is defined as a very small quantity. The quantity $\epsilon$ is used to bring the number of filled cells to $m + n - 1$. It is entered in an empty cell with the lowest cost according to the least-cost criterion. Since the only purpose of entering is to carry on cell evaluations, an empty cell with the next smallest cost will be chosen if a closed path cannot be constructed with an initially chosen cell. To display its use, and that of the northwest-corner method, consider the following example.

### Example 2

The table below depicts a transportation situation where $S_1$ and $S_2$ represent sources; $D_1$, $D_2$ and $D_3$ represent destinations. The figures in the body of the matrix represent unit transportation costs. The schedule which minimises total transportation costs is required.

|  |  |  | Destinations | | |
|---|---|---|---|---|---|
|  |  |  | $D_1$ | $D_2$ | $D_3$ |
|  |  |  | 20 | 15 | 25 |
| Sources | $S_1$ | 20 | 2 | 1 | 2 |
|  | $S_2$ | 40 | 3 | 4 | 1 |

*Step 1* Find a feasible solution. Use the northwest-corner method. (This is only done for illustrative purposes. Its use is not generally recommended as it is an inefficient method compared to others.) Allocate as many units as possible into the top left-hand corner and proceed from left to right:

*First allocation*:

|  |  | $D_1$ | $D_2$ | $D_3$ |
|---|---|---|---|---|
|  |  | 20 | 15 | 25 |
| $S_1$ | 20 | 20 |  |  |
| $S_2$ | 40 |  | 15 | 25 |

The number of cells filled should be $(m + n - 1)$ or $(2 + 3 - 1) = 4$. However, the allocation only gives 3 cells filled. The test for optimality cannot proceed.

Introduce $\epsilon$ into cell $S_1D_2$. (It was chosen based on the method being used as it is an empty cell closest to the northwest corner.)

*Amended first allocation*:

|  | $D_1$ | $D_2$ | $D_3$ |
|---|---|---|---|
| $S_1$ | 20 | $\epsilon$ |  |
| $S_2$ |  | 15 | 25 |

4 cells $(m + n - 1)$ are now filled and it is now possible to proceed.

*Step 2* Test for optimality by calculating shadow costs. This gives:

# 17 TRANSPORTATION

|  | $D_1$ | $D_2$ | $D_3$ | Row shadow costs |
|---|---|---|---|---|
| $S_1$ | 2 | 1 | (−2) | 0 |
| $S_2$ | (5) | 4 | 1 | 3 |
| Column shadow costs | 2 | 1 | −2 |  |

Cell $S_2D_1$ represents further minimisation as it has a gross saving of 5 but an actual cost of 3 (net saving of 2 per unit).

*Step 3*  Reallocate by moving a plus into cell $S_2D_1$. Adjust other cells with plus and minus signs as explained previously.

This gives the following table:

|  |  | $D_1$ 20 | $D_2$ 15 | $D_3$ 25 |
|---|---|---|---|---|
| $S_1$ | 20 | $20^-$ | $\epsilon^+$ |  |
| $S_2$ | 40 | + | $15^-$ | 25 |

Inspection of the plus and minus signs shows that the maximum transfer into $S_2D_1$ is 15 units.

This gives the new arrangement:

*Second allocation*:

|  | $D_1$ | $D_2$ | $D_3$ |
|---|---|---|---|
| $S_1$ | 5 | $15 + \epsilon$ |  |
| $S_2$ | 15 |  | 25 |

4 cells are now filled properly. The $\epsilon$ has served its purpose and can be disposed of. Test the second allocation for optimality by using shadow costs:

|  | $D_1$ | $D_2$ | $D_3$ | Row shadow costs |
|---|---|---|---|---|
| $S_1$ | 2 | 1 | (0) | 0 |
| $S_2$ | 3 | (2) | 1 | 1 |
| Column shadow costs | 2 | 1 | 0 |  |

This allocation represents the optimum as no further minimisation is possible (i.e. no net saving in unused cells).

The cost of the allocation is:

$$\begin{aligned} S_1D_1 \quad & 5 \times 2 = 10 \\ S_1D_2 \quad & 15 \times 1 = 15 \\ S_2D_1 \quad & 15 \times 3 = 45 \\ S_2D_3 \quad & 25 \times 1 = \underline{25} \\ & \phantom{25 \times 1 = }\underline{£95} \end{aligned}$$

*Tutorial notes*
*(a) Students should redo the problem using the least cost method as a starting point. The optimal solution is obtained in the first allocation.*
*(b) It is possible to have a degenerate optimal solution. Remember, the purpose behind the use of $\epsilon$ is to enable the test for optimality to be carried out.*
*(c) It is possible (but not very common in examination situations) to require more than one epsilon.*
*(d) Degeneracy can arise irrespective of the method used. Avoid generalisations.*

## 6.0 UNBALANCED SITUATIONS

The problems dealt with above were balanced in that the total supply at the sources was exactly equal to the demand at the destinations. In many cases this equality does not hold. Frequently the supply may exceed the demand, or demand may exceed supply (implying either over-production or shortage). Transportation problems with unequal supply and demand are referred to as "unbalanced".

The transportation procedures explained in the previous sections work only with balanced rim conditions (supply = demand). Hence to remedy the problem, it is necessary to insert a "dummy" row or column in the table with zero transportation costs, so that there is a balance between supply and demand. Standard procedures can now be used. Two such situations are outlined below.

### 6.1 Supply exceeds demand

*Example 3*
Consider the following problem where $S_1$, $S_2$ and $S_3$ represent sources and $D_1$, $D_2$, $D_3$ and $D_4$ represent destinations. The figures within the matrix represent unit transportation costs.

|         |       |    | $D_1$ | $D_2$ | $D_3$ | $D_4$ |
|---------|-------|----|-------|-------|-------|-------|
|         |       |    | 20    | 20    | 25    | 30    |
|         | $S_1$ | 30 | £7    | £10   | £14   | £8    |
| Sources | $S_2$ | 40 | £7    | £11   | £12   | £6    |
|         | $S_3$ | 30 | £5    | £8    | £15   | £9    |

Destinations

# 17 TRANSPORTATION

The total supply is 100. The total demand is 95. The problem is unbalanced. Convert the problem into a balanced one by introducing a dummy destination which will absorb the excess supply. The dummy will have a column of zero transportation costs.

|  |  |  | Destinations | | | | |
|---|---|---|---|---|---|---|---|
|  |  |  | $D_1$ | $D_2$ | $D_3$ | $D_4$ | Dummy |
|  |  |  | 20 | 20 | 25 | 30 | 5 |
| Sources | $S_1$ | 30 | 7 | 10 | 14 | 8 | 0 |
|  | $S_2$ | 40 | 7 | 11 | 12 | 6 | 0 |
|  | $S_3$ | 30 | 5 | 8 | 15 | 9 | 0 |

Standard procedures can now be used to yield an optimal solution. One optimal solution (the solution is not unique) is presented below. Students are encouraged to use standard procedures and confirm the solution.

An optimal allocation:

|  |  |  | $D_1$ | $D_2$ | $D_3$ | $D_4$ | Dummy |
|---|---|---|---|---|---|---|---|
|  |  |  | 20 | 20 | 25 | 30 | 5 |
| Sources | $S_1$ | 30 |  | 10 | 15 |  | 5 |
|  | $S_2$ | 40 |  |  | 10 | 30 |  |
|  | $S_3$ | 30 | 20 | 10 |  |  |  |

The minimum transportation cost is £790.

## 6.2 Demand exceeds supply

### Example 4

Consider the following problem where $S_1$, $S_2$ and $S_3$ represent sources and $D_1$, $D_2$, $D_3$ and $D_4$ represent destinations. The figures within the matrix represent unit transportation costs.

|  |  |  | Destinations | | | |
|---|---|---|---|---|---|---|
|  |  |  | $D_1$ | $D_2$ | $D_3$ | $D_4$ |
|  |  |  | 20 | 20 | 30 | 40 |
| Sources | $S_1$ | 30 | 7 | 10 | 14 | 8 |
|  | $S_2$ | 40 | 7 | 11 | 12 | 6 |
|  | $S_3$ | 30 | 5 | 8 | 15 | 9 |

The total supply is 100. The total demand is 110. The problem is unbalanced. Convert the problem into a balanced one by introducing a dummy supply which provides 10 units. The dummy will have a row of zero transportation costs.

|  |  |  | Destinations |  |  |  |
|---|---|---|---|---|---|---|
|  |  |  | $D_1$ | $D_2$ | $D_3$ | $D_4$ |
|  |  |  | 20 | 20 | 30 | 40 |
| Sources | $S_1$ | 30 | 7 | 10 | 14 | 8 |
|  | $S_2$ | 40 | 7 | 11 | 12 | 6 |
|  | $S_3$ | 30 | 5 | 8 | 15 | 9 |
|  | Dummy | 10 | 0 | 0 | 0 | 0 |

Standard procedures can now be used. Postpone the allocation from the dummy source until the available quantities at other sources are exhausted because the allocation from the dummy source is a fictitious quantity.

An allocation is shown below. This allocation is degenerate and optimal. (Students should confirm this by using shadow costs.) The solution is not unique.

*An optimal allocation*:

|  |  |  | $D_1$ | $D_2$ | $D_3$ | $D_4$ |
|---|---|---|---|---|---|---|
|  |  |  | 20 | 20 | 30 | 40 |
| Sources | $S_1$ | 30 |  | 10 | 20 | $\epsilon$ |
|  | $S_2$ | 40 |  |  |  | 40 |
|  | $S_3$ | 30 | 20 | 10 |  |  |
|  | Dummy | 10 |  |  | 10 |  |

The minimum transportation cost is £800.

*Note: The degenerate optimal solution above becomes a normal optimal solution if cell $S_2D_3$ is chosen for reallocation. $\epsilon$ disappears in the process of reallocation. This new alternative optimal solution is presented below for comparison:*

*Alternative optimal solution:*

|  |  |  | Destinations |  |  |  |
|---|---|---|---|---|---|---|
|  |  |  | $D_1$ | $D_2$ | $D_3$ | $D_4$ |
|  |  |  | 20 | 20 | 30 | 40 |
|  | $S_1$ | 30 |  | 10 |  | 20 |
| Sources | $S_2$ | 40 |  |  | 20 | 20 |
|  | $S_3$ | 30 | 20 | 10 |  |  |
|  | Dummy | 10 |  |  | 10 |  |

*Students should find other alternative optimal solutions as an exercise.*

## 7.0 PROHIBITED ROUTES

In certain transportation situations it is not possible to use particular routes. The reasons for prohibited routes could be road construction, unexpected floods, weight limits on bridges etc. The simplest way of dealing with a prohibited route is to assign a very high unit transportation cost $M$ to a cell with a prohibited route. Standard transportation procedures can now be used.

### Example 5

Consider the following situation where $S_1$, $S_2$ and $S_3$ are sources, and $D_1$, $D_2$ and $D_3$ are destinations.

Unit transportation costs (£):

|  |  |  | Destinations |  |  |  |
|---|---|---|---|---|---|---|
|  |  |  | $D_1$ | $D_2$ | $D_3$ | $D_4$ |
|  |  |  | 4 | 5 | 5 | 4 |
|  | $S_1$ | 5 | 12 | 17 | 20 | – |
| Sources | $S_2$ | 5 | 18 | 20 | 12 | 15 |
|  | $S_3$ | 8 | 20 | 10 | – | 16 |

Cells $S_1D_4$ and $S_3D_3$ represent prohibited routes and hence no cost is available.

Assign a very high cost $M$ to these routes. As the procedures are based on the minimisation of cost these cells will not form part of the optimisation process. The initial cost matrix will appear as follows:

|       |   | D₁ | D₂ | D₃ | D₄ |
|-------|---|----|----|----|----|
|       |   | 4  | 5  | 5  | 4  |
| S₁    | 5 | 12 | 17 | 20 | M  |
| S₂    | 5 | 18 | 20 | 12 | 15 |
| S₃    | 8 | 20 | 10 | M  | 16 |

Standard transportation procedures can now be used based on the least cost method. An allocation is presented below:

|       |   | D₁ | D₂ | D₃ | D₄ |
|-------|---|----|----|----|----|
|       |   | 4  | 5  | 5  | 4  |
| S₁    | 5 | 4  |    | 1  |    |
| S₂    | 5 |    |    | 4  | 1  |
| S₃    | 8 |    | 5  |    | 3  |

$m + n - 1$ cells are filled.

The allocation above can be shown as being optimal, because no net savings are available in unused cells. Students should confirm this by using shadow costs. The minimum cost is £229. (The solution is not unique.)

## 8.0 PROFIT MAXIMISATION

Transportation situations involving profit maximisation are easy to follow once the procedures for minimisation are grasped. In practice, a maximisation problem in transportation is rare in comparison with minimisation problems because unit contributions do not vary significantly at different locations.

In maximisation situations the elements of the given matrix will represent revenues or profits. The method presented in earlier sections is for minimisation problems, but only a minor adjustment is required to use it on maximisation problems. As a starting point, construct a new matrix (opportunity loss matrix) by subtracting all elements in the initial matrix from the largest element. The opportunity loss is measured by the difference between the profit actually realised on a particular transfer and the largest figure of profit in the matrix.

# 17 TRANSPORTATION

Standard minimisation procedures can now be used as profit is maximised if the total opportunity loss is minimised.

## Example 6

Consider the transportation situation below. $S_1$, $S_2$ and $S_3$ are sources; $D_1$, $D_2$ and $D_3$ are destinations. The figures within the matrix are unit profits realised from particular transfers. The problem is to allocate so as to maximise total profits.

|  |  | Destinations |  |  |  |
|---|---|---|---|---|---|
|  |  | $D_1$ | $D_2$ | $D_3$ | $D_4$ |
|  |  | 40 | 30 | 50 | 30 |
| Sources | $S_1$ 50 | 5 | 4 | 5 | 7 |
|  | $S_2$ 40 | 4 | 8 | 6 | 5 |
|  | $S_3$ 60 | 6 | 3 | 4 | 5 |

*Initial step* Convert the given matrix into an opportunity loss matrix (all elements are subtracted from 8):

|  | $D_1$ | $D_2$ | $D_3$ | $D_4$ |
|---|---|---|---|---|
|  | 40 | 30 | 50 | 30 |
| $S_1$ 50 | 3 | 4 | 3 | 1 |
| $S_2$ 40 | 4 | 0 | 2 | 3 |
| $S_3$ 60 | 2 | 5 | 4 | 3 |

Standard minimisation procedures can now be applied. An optimal allocation is given below:

|  | $D_1$ | $D_2$ | $D_3$ | $D_4$ |
|---|---|---|---|---|
|  | 40 | 30 | 50 | 30 |
| $S_1$ 50 |  |  | 20 | 30 |
| $S_2$ 40 |  | 30 | 10 |  |
| $S_3$ 60 | 40 |  | 20 |  |

Students should confirm the solution as being optimal by calculating shadow costs in the usual way.

The solution yields a maximum total profit of £930.

*Tutorial note: Remember to express the optimal allocation in profit terms.*

## 9.0 TRANSHIPMENT

Situations arise where it may not be economical or practical to transport directly from sources to destinations. The commodities may pass through intermediate warehouses, for instance, before eventually reaching their ultimate destinations. The situation is described as transhipment. The transportation model cannot handle the problem directly. A slight modification, however, would allow the use of the same technique. As a starting point, work out the costs of supplying each demand centre from each supply point via all possible routes. Then select the least costly route to each destination from each source. Standard minimisation procedures can now be used.

*Tutorial note: Students are referred to question 72 in Appendix 2. This deals with transhipment and a detailed analysis is given.*

# CHAPTER EIGHTEEN
# Assignment

## 1.0 INTRODUCTION

As is evident from previous chapters on linear programming, a very broad class of allocation problems can be formulated and solved using the linear programming framework. However, in many of these problem classes the simplex method, although powerful enough to solve all these problems, is not the most efficient solution technique. One such special type of situation is transportation. A second special type of problem is the assignment problem. Just as transportation problems are special cases of linear programming problems, assignment problems are special cases of transportation problems but with a more refined structure. In reality they are transportation problems of maximal degeneracy.

The assignment problem involves the optimal allocation of various productive resources having different efficiencies to various tasks that are to be completed. Unlike the transportation problem, the techniques available for the assignment problem are relatively simple in structure and easy in computation. Their simplicity and use arise from the fact that, in most assignment problems, the number of resources is exactly equal to the number of tasks to be completed and each resource is assigned to only one task.

Examples of assignment problems are:

(a) assigning machine shop operatives to machines;

(b) assigning offices to staff members;

(c) assigning vehicles to routes;

(d) assigning salesmen to territories;

(e) assigning contracts to bidders;

(f) assigning products to factories.

## 2.0 DESCRIPTION OF THE PROBLEM

Consider the assignment of four men to do four different jobs. All four men have the necessary knowledge to perform any of the four available jobs properly. However, owing to differences in job training and experience, the cost which will be incurred by each man to complete each job is different. The cost incurred to complete the jobs by each man is known and is given in the following table. Each man is assigned to only one job and each job is to be completed by one man only. The following is a cost matrix of the assignment problem:

|     |   | Jobs |     |     |     |
|-----|---|------|-----|-----|-----|
|     |   | I    | II  | III | IV  |
|     | A | £37  | £29 | £28 | £32 |
|     | B | £61  | £82 | £92 | £15 |
| Men | C | £20  | £16 | £21 | £19 |
|     | D | £17  | £73 | £84 | £78 |

Note that the number of men (rows) equals the number of jobs (columns). If man A is assigned to job I it will cost £37 to complete the job and so on. The objective of the problem is to assign the available men to the different jobs in such a manner that the total cost required to complete the jobs is as small as possible. (If the figure in the table represented profits then the objective would be a maximisation of total profit.)

## 3.0 MATHEMATICAL MODEL OF THE ASSIGNMENT PROBLEM

### 3.1 General linear programming model

Consider the situation of assigning $n$ jobs (or workers) to $n$ machines. A job $i$ ($= 1, 2, \ldots, n$) when assigned to machine $j$ ($= 1, 2, \ldots, n$) incurs a cost $c_{ij}$. The objective is to assign the jobs to the machines (one job per machine) at the least total cost.

The formulation of this problem may be regarded as a special case of the transportation model. Here jobs represent "sources" and machines represent "destinations". The supply available to each source is 1, that is $a_i = 1$ for all $i$.

Similarly, the amount required at each destination is 1, that is $b_j = 1$ for all $j$ (using the notation as in transportation where $a_i$ indicates the amount supplied and $b_j$ the amount demanded). The cost of assigning job $i$ to machine $j$ is $c_{ij}$. If a job cannot be assigned to a particular machine, the corresponding $c_{ij}$ is taken as equal to $M$, a very high cost. (Before the model can be constructed it may be necessary to balance the problem by adding fictitious jobs or machines depending on whether $m < n$ or $m > n$. It will thus be assumed that $m = n$ without loss of generality.)

Let the variable $x_{ij}$ represent the assignment of the $i$th job to the $j$th machine. The value of $x_{ij}$ is either 1 or 0. It is 1 if the $i$th job is assigned to the $j$th machine or 0 if not assigned.

The model can now be stated as:

# 18 ASSIGNMENT

$$\text{Minimise} \quad Z = \sum_{i=1}^{n} \sum_{j=1}^{n} c_{ij} x_{ij}$$

subject to:

$$\sum_{i=1}^{n} x_{ij} = 1 \quad (\text{for } j = 1, 2, 3, \ldots, n)$$

$$\sum_{j=1}^{n} x_{ij} = 1 \quad (\text{for } i = 1, 2, \ldots, n)$$

and

$$x_{ij} \geqslant 0.$$

This last condition may also be expressed as:

$$x_{ij} = 0 \text{ or } 1.$$

## 3.2 Linear programming model for a particular situation

Consider again the problem outlined in 2.0.

|     | Jobs |     |     |     |
|-----|------|-----|-----|-----|
|     | I    | II  | III | IV  |
| A   | £37  | £29 | £28 | £32 |
| B   | £61  | £82 | £92 | £15 |
| C   | £20  | £16 | £21 | £19 |
| D   | £17  | £73 | £84 | £78 |

(Men: A, B, C, D)

For the above problem define the allocation variables as follows:

|     | Jobs     |          |          |          |
|-----|----------|----------|----------|----------|
|     | I        | II       | III      | IV       |
| A   | $x_{11}$ | $x_{12}$ | $x_{13}$ | $x_{14}$ |
| B   | $x_{21}$ | $x_{22}$ | $x_{23}$ | $x_{24}$ |
| C   | $x_{31}$ | $x_{32}$ | $x_{33}$ | $x_{34}$ |
| D   | $x_{41}$ | $x_{42}$ | $x_{43}$ | $x_{44}$ |

(Men: A, B, C, D)

$x_{11}$ represents amount transferred from A to 1,
$x_{12}$ represents amount transferred from A to 2 and so on.

The LP model can now be expressed as:

$$\begin{aligned}
\text{Minimise} \quad & 37x_{11} + 29x_{12} + 28x_{13} + 32x_{14} + 61x_{21} + 82x_{22} \\
& + 92x_{23} + 15x_{24} + 20x_{31} + 16x_{32} + 21x_{33} + 19x_{34} \\
& + 17x_{41} + 73x_{42} + 84x_{43} + 78x_{44},
\end{aligned}$$

subject to:
$$x_{11} + x_{12} + x_{13} + x_{14} = 1$$
$$x_{21} + x_{22} + x_{23} + x_{24} = 1$$
$$x_{31} + x_{32} + x_{33} + x_{34} = 1$$
$$x_{41} + x_{42} + x_{43} + x_{44} = 1$$
$$x_{11} + x_{21} + x_{31} + x_{41} = 1$$
$$x_{12} + x_{22} + x_{32} + x_{42} = 1$$
$$x_{13} + x_{23} + x_{33} + x_{43} = 1$$
$$x_{14} + x_{24} + x_{34} + x_{44} = 1$$

and
$$x_{11}, x_{12}, \ldots, x_{44} \geqslant 0.$$

## 4.0 ITERATION PROCEDURES FOR AN OPTIMAL ASSIGNMENT

In the problem outlined in **2.0** there are 4! = 24 possible assignments since there are 4 men and 4 available jobs, and each man can be assigned to 1 job only. In general, the assignment problem containing $n$ rows and $n$ columns with one-to-one pairing has $n!$ possible assignments. Solution by linear programming is not practical and direct enumeration is often impossible.

A special technique has been developed for finding the optimal solution to this problem. It is called the Hungarian method, after a Hungarian mathematician, D. König, who initially proved a theorem required for the development of this efficient solution method. To illustrate the Hungarian method consider the problem described in the following example.

### Example 1: Cost minimisation

Four men are being considered to do four different jobs. The given matrix shows the cost incurred. Assign the men to the different jobs in such a manner that the total costs are minimised.

Cost matrix of the assignment problem:

|     |   | A   | B  | C  | D  |
|-----|---|-----|----|----|----|
|     | 1 | £10 | 28 | 20 | 13 |
| Man | 2 | 16  | 30 | 7  | 28 |
|     | 3 | 33  | 22 | 21 | 17 |
|     | 4 | 21  | 29 | 27 | 12 |

The first step in the Hungarian method is to obtain the opportunity cost matrix by changing the given cost matrix. To accomplish this, the smallest element in each row is subtracted from each element in that row. There will be a zero-valued element in each row as a result. Then, select the smallest element in each column of the initially reduced matrix, and subtract this smallest element from each element in that column.

# 18 ASSIGNMENT

The reduced matrices are shown below:

Initially reduced matrix:

|  | | Job | | | |
|---|---|---|---|---|---|
|  | | A | B | C | D |
| Man | 1 | 0 | 18 | 10 | 3 |
|  | 2 | 9 | 23 | 0 | 21 |
|  | 3 | 16 | 5 | 4 | 0 |
|  | 4 | 9 | 17 | 15 | 0 |

Total opportunity cost matrix:

|  | | Job | | | |
|---|---|---|---|---|---|
|  | | A | B | C | D |
| Man | 1 | 0 | 13 | 10 | 3 |
|  | 2 | 9 | 18 | 0 | 21 |
|  | 3 | 16 | 0 | 4 | 0 |
|  | 4 | 9 | 12 | 15 | 0 |

Why subtract the smallest element from each element in that row and then in that column? Mathematically, if the original cost matrix is modified by subtracting a constant from all elements in a row or a column, the optimal solution thus obtained is exactly the same as the optimal solution to the original problem.

In addition to this mathematical theorem, the solution method is based on the economic concept of opportunity cost, which represents the hidden cost with not utilising available resources to the best possible advantage. In the above example man 1 can be assigned to any one of four different jobs. The lowest cost assignment of man 1 is to job A with a cost of £10. This assignment precludes the possibility of assigning man 1 to jobs B, C and D. However, if man 1 is assigned to job B with a cost of £28 then the opportunity to save £18 is foregone by this arbitrary assignment. This type of opportunity cost is referred to as the "job opportunity cost" because different jobs can be assigned to the same man.

There is another type of opportunity cost in this problem. Any one of four men can be assigned to job A. However, man 1 can perform job A most efficiently with a cost of £10, i.e. a zero opportunity cost. If man 2 is assigned to job A then the opportunity to save £6 is foregone. This type of opportunity cost is referred to as the "worker opportunity cost" and arises from the fact that different men (workers) can be assigned to the same job.

Either the job opportunity costs or the worker opportunity costs may be obtained for the initial reduced opportunity cost matrix. The second reduced matrix is based on the initial reduced matrix and is called the total opportunity cost matrix.

The next step is to determine whether the total opportunity cost matrix has four "independent zeros" such that the total of the opportunity costs is zero when four men are assigned to the jobs. In other words, one man should be assigned to one job only with the opportunity cost of zero.

If this type of assignment is possible, an optimal assignment exists. As a practical method of testing for optimality a minimal set of straight lines is drawn horizontally and vertically to cover all zero elements in the total opportunity cost matrix. This is shown below.

Test for optimality:

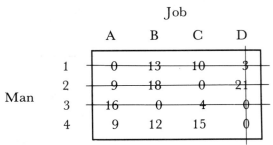

If the minimum number of lines drawn is exactly equal to the number of rows (or columns) in the matrix then an optimal assignment exists. In the above example, four lines are required and hence an optimal solution to the problem can be found.

If the minimum number of lines required to cover all the zeros is less than the number of rows (or columns) then further procedures are required (these are illustrated in Example 2).

The optimal assignment for the above example is:

| Man | Job | Cost |
| --- | --- | --- |
| 1 | A | £10 |
| 2 | C | 7 |
| 3 | B | 22 |
| 4 | D | 12 |

*Tutorial note: To assist with the assignment schedule:*
*(a) Examine rows successively until a row with only one zero is found. Make that square the assignment square (mark with a ☐ and delete all other zeros in that column). Proceed until all rows have been examined.*
*(b) Now examine columns for unmarked zeros, mark them ☐ and delete any other zeros in the same row.*
*(c) Repeat (a) and (b) until there are no single unmarked zeros in any row or column.*

### Example 2: Cost Minimisation—Advanced Procedures

Four men are to be assigned to four different machines. The following matrix shows the costs incurred. Assign the men so that total costs are kept at a minimum.

# 18 ASSIGNMENT

Cost matrix:

|  |  | Machines | | | |
|---|---|---|---|---|---|
|  |  | 1 | 2 | 3 | 4 |
| Men | A | £30 | 25 | 26 | 28 |
|  | B | 26 | 32 | 24 | 20 |
|  | C | 20 | 22 | 18 | 27 |
|  | D | 23 | 20 | 21 | 19 |

*Step 1* The smallest element in each row is subtracted from each element in that row. This gives the following initially reduced matrix:

Initially reduced matrix:

|  |  | Machines | | | |
|---|---|---|---|---|---|
|  |  | 1 | 2 | 3 | 4 |
| Men | A | 5 | 0 | 1 | 3 |
|  | B | 6 | 12 | 4 | 0 |
|  | C | 2 | 4 | 0 | 9 |
|  | D | 4 | 1 | 2 | 0 |

*Step 2* Select the smallest element in each column of the initially reduced matrix and subtract this from each element in that column. This gives the following total opportunity cost matrix:

|  |  | Machines | | | |
|---|---|---|---|---|---|
|  |  | 1 | 2 | 3 | 4 |
| Men | A | 3 | 0 | 1 | 3 |
|  | B | 4 | 12 | 4 | 0 |
|  | C | 0 | 4 | 0 | 9 |
|  | D | 2 | 1 | 2 | 0 |

*Step 3* Draw the minimum number of lines to cover all zero elements, as follows:

|  |  | Machines | | | |
|---|---|---|---|---|---|
|  |  | 1 | 2 | 3 | 4 |
| Men | A | 3 | 0 | 1 | 3 |
|  | B | 4 | 12 | 4 | 0 |
|  | C | 0 | 4 | 0 | 9 |
|  | D | 2 | 1 | 2 | 0 |

Since three lines can cover all zero elements an optimal assignment is not feasible at this stage because the number of lines drawn is less than the number of rows (or columns). Therefore, the total opportunity cost matrix must be revised.

*Step 4* This is to formulate a revised cost matrix from the last matrix above.

Select the smallest element in the matrix which was not covered by a straight line. Subtract this element from all other elements not covered by straight lines. Add this smallest element to all elements that were covered by the intersection of two lines. All other elements covered by one line remain unchanged in the revised matrix.

The revised matrix obtained is shown below:

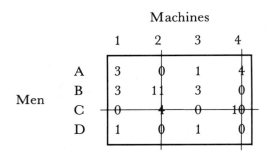

*Step 5* The test for optimality is again applied to this revised matrix by drawing straight lines as done previously. In the revised matrix just shown, three lines cover all zero elements. Thus an optimal assignment is not possible because the number of lines drawn is less than the number of rows (or columns). The revised matrix must be modified again. The procedures described in the fourth step are repeated to derive the new revised matrix. This new result is given in next; since all zero elements are covered by four lines when the test for optimality is applied, an optimal assignment can now be made.

Revised matrix 2:

|   | Machines |   |   |   |
|---|---|---|---|---|
|   | 1 | 2 | 3 | 4 |
| A | 2 | 0 | 0 | 4 |
| B | 2 | 11 | 2 | 0 |
| C | 0 | 5 | 0 | 11 |
| D | 0 | 0 | 0 | 0 |

In this revised matrix there are two or more zero elements in each column and each row except the second row. The zero appears under machine 4. Therefore the initial assignment of B to machine 4 is to be made. From the three remaining rows and columns with zero elements, the other assignments are to be made based on a one-to-one pairing. There are three possible optimal assignments in this particular problem. These are given below:

18 ASSIGNMENT

| Assignment schedule 1 | | Assignment schedule 2 | | Assignment schedule 3 | |
|---|---|---|---|---|---|
| | Cost | | Cost | | Cost |
| A to 2 | £25 | A to 3 | £26 | A to 2 | £25 |
| B to 4 | 20 | B to 4 | 20 | B to 4 | 20 |
| C to 3 | 18 | C to 1 | 20 | C to 1 | 20 |
| D to 1 | 23 | D to 2 | 20 | D to 3 | 21 |
| | £86 | | £86 | | £86 |

## 5.0 SUMMARY OF PROCEDURES FOR AN OPTIMAL ASSIGNMENT

*Step 1* Subtract the smallest element in each row from each element in that row and formulate the reduced-cost matrix.

*Step 2* Subtract the smallest element in each column of the reduced-cost matrix from each element in that column and formulate the total opportunity-cost matrix.

*Step 3* Draw a minimum number of straight lines to cover all zero elements in the total opportunity-cost matrix. An optimal assignment can be made immediately if the number of lines drawn equals the number of rows (columns). If the number of lines drawn is less than the number of rows (columns) then further procedures are required.

*Step 4* Select the smallest uncovered element. Subtract this element from all uncovered elements and add this element to all covered elements where two lines intersect. The other covered elements remain unchanged.

*Step 5* Repeat steps 3 and 4 until an optimal assignment is possible.

## 6.0 MAXIMISATION PROBLEMS

In some cases the elements of the effectiveness matrix may represent revenues or profits so that the objective will be to maximise. The method presented in the previous section is a minimisation geared approach but only a minor adjustment is necessary to use it on maximisation problems. As a starting point construct a new matrix (opportunity loss matrix) by subtracting all elements in the initial matrix from the largest element. The opportunity loss is measured by the difference between the profit actually realised from a particular job and the largest profit that would have been realised if the best assignment had been made. The standard minimisation procedures can now be used as profit is maximised if the total opportunity loss is minimised.

### Example 3: Profit Maximisation

Consider the profit matrix as shown below. The matrix gives individual profits for each man on each job. Assign men to jobs so as to maximise total profit.

                          Jobs
                   1    2    3    4

              A  | £10   14   12   13 |
              B  |  8     7    8   10 |
      Men     C  | 15    15   14   12 |
              D  |  9    11   10   11 |

*Initial Step*  Convert the given matrix into an opportunity loss matrix (all elements are subtracted from 15):

                          Jobs
                   1    2    3    4

              A  |  5    1    3    2 |
              B  |  7    8    7    5 |
      Men     C  |  0    0    1    3 |
              D  |  6    4    5    4 |

Standard minimisation procedures are now applied to the table above:

*Step 1*

                          Jobs
                   1    2    3    4

              A  |  4    0    2    1 |
              B  |  2    3    2    0 |
      Men     C  |  0    0    1    3 |
              D  |  2    0    1    0 |

*Step 2*

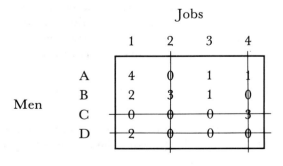

# 18 ASSIGNMENT

*Step 3* The test for optimality is also accomplished in step 2 by drawing the minimum number of straight lines to cover all zero elements.

In the total opportunity-loss matrix in step 2, all zero elements are covered by four lines. An optimal assignment can now be made, since the number of lines drawn equals the number of rows (or columns). An optimal assignment schedule and the total profits are given below:

| Assignments | Profit |
|---|---|
| A to 2 | £14 |
| B to 4 | 10 |
| C to 1 | 15 |
| D to 3 | 10 |
|  | £49 |

## 7.0 SITUATIONS WITH IMPOSSIBLE ASSIGNMENTS

In particular situations, certain workers cannot to assigned to particular jobs. The reasons for impossible assignments could be lack of required skills, insufficient or improper training, deficiency in technical know-how, physical inability and so on. The solution procedures for a problem with impossible assignments are exactly the same as the ordinary assignment problems.

Reconsider the problem given as Example 2:

Machines

| | 1 | 2 | 3 | 4 |
|---|---|---|---|---|
| A | 30 | 25 | 26 | 28 |
| B | 26 | 32 | 24 | 20 |
| C | 20 | 22 | 18 | 27 |
| D | 23 | 20 | 21 | 19 |

Men

Assume that the assignments of A to 2, B to 1 and C to 3 are impossible and all other costs remain the same. Each element of the impossible assignments is given an extremely large cost $M$, lest this assignment should be made in the optimal solution. The problem can now be presented in a cost matrix, as here:

Machines

| | 1 | 2 | 3 | 4 |
|---|---|---|---|---|
| A | £30 | $M$ | 26 | 28 |
| B | $M$ | 32 | 24 | 20 |
| C | 20 | 22 | $M$ | 27 |
| D | 23 | 20 | 21 | 19 |

Men

The two reduced-cost matrices which follow next are obtained when the iterative procedures are followed step-by-step. Note that $M$ has been defined as an extremely high cost and will be unaffected by the row and column operations.

*Step 1* Initially reduced matrix:

Men

|   | Machines |   |   |   |
|---|---|---|---|---|
|   | 1 | 2 | 3 | 4 |
| A | 4 | $M$ | 0 | 2 |
| B | $M$ | 12 | 4 | 0 |
| C | 0 | 2 | $M$ | 7 |
| D | 4 | 1 | 2 | 0 |

*Step 2* The total opportunity cost matrix:

Men

|   | Machines |   |   |   |
|---|---|---|---|---|
|   | 1 | 2 | 3 | 4 |
| A | 4 | $M$ | 0 | 2 |
| B | $M$ | 11 | 4 | 0 |
| C | 0 | 1 | $M$ | 7 |
| D | 4 | 0 | 2 | 0 |

*Step 3* An optimal assignment can be made at this stage because all zero elements in the matrix are covered by four lines as shown in step 2. An optimal assignment schedule and the total cost are given below:

| Assignment | Cost |
|---|---|
| A to 3 | £26 |
| B to 4 | 20 |
| C to 1 | 20 |
| D to 2 | 20 |
| Total cost | £86 |

## 8.0 UNEQUAL DIMENSIONS

The application of the Hungarian method requires the assignment matrix to be square, i.e. the number of rows must equal the number of columns. However, in the business world situations will arise in which this condition does not hold. The number of workers available may be greater than the number of jobs to be performed at a particular time and vice versa. For example, six men may be available but only five jobs need to be done. To apply the Hungarian method to this type of problem, a dummy column is added with costs set to 0 so that the result is expressed as a square matrix of the sixth order. The dummy column implies that one man will be idle. Similarly, a dummy row means that one job is deferred, i.e. the requirement is not met.

## 9.0 TUTORIAL POINTS

(a) Since the assignment problem is a degenerate form of the transportation problem, an optimal assignment can also be made by using the transportation method. However, it is in general impractical to cope with the problem of degeneracy (visualise the problem of degeneracy arising from a $10 \times 10$ assignment matrix).

(b) To solve an assignment problem by the Hungarian method, the problem must have the same number of rows and columns. The Hungarian method cannot be applied to a problem where there are unequal numbers of men (rows) and jobs (columns) and where several men can be assigned to one job. A special assignment technique (considered beyond the scope of this examination) is available for an optimal solution to a problem of this type. It is known as the modified index method.

## 10.0 SUMMARY

A special form of the transportation problem arises when there is only one item at each of the various sources and only one item is required at each of the various destinations. The problem is termed assignment and represents another special technique of determining an optimal allocation of resources to various tasks. The iteration procedures for an optimal assignment (Hungarian method) have been described in this chapter. The Hungarian method can be applied to determine the optimal assignments of men to jobs, jobs to machines, salesmen to territories and so on. The Hungarian method presupposes a square matrix. A one-to-one assignment of resources to tasks is desired to obtain an optimal solution.

CHAPTER NINETEEN
# An Introduction to Network Analysis

## 1.0 BACKGROUND

All organisations frequently engage in large, complex projects that require many different steps or operations to be performed in order to complete the project. The introduction of a new product is a good example of a complex project, since it requires many operations, such as research and development, product testing, market research, and package design.

Network analysis provides a methodology for planning and controlling projects such as the one mentioned above and others in the field of construction and manufacturing. The main aim of network analysis is to programme and monitor the progress of a project so that the project is completed in the minimum possible time. This is normally the main concern of managers involved with implementing the project. In doing this, the technique pinpoints the parts of the project which are "critical", i.e. those parts which, if delayed beyond the allotted time, would delay the completion of the project as a whole.

In the past, the scheduling of a project (over time) was done with little planning. Before the advent of network analysis, the best known "planning" tool then was the Gantt bar chart which specifies the start and finish times for each job on a horizontal time scale. Although this is extremely useful in many cases, it suffers from an inability to show the interrelationships between the various activities. The growing complexities of current-day projects have demanded more systematic and effective planning techniques with the objective of optimising the efficiency of executing the project. Efficiency here implies minimising the time required to complete the project while accounting for the economic feasibility of using available resources. Network analysis provides such a system.

## 2.0 CPA AND PERT

Project management evolved as a new field with the development of two analytical techniques for planning, scheduling and controlling of projects. These were the critical path method (CPM) and the project evaluation and review technique (PERT). The two techniques were developed by two different groups almost simultaneously (1956–1958). CPM was first developed by E.I. du Pont de Nemours & Company as an application to construction projects. At much the same time the US Navy Special Projects Office set up a team to devise a means of dealing with the planning and subsequent control of complex work. This investigation led to the development of PERT for scheduling the research and development activities for the Polaris missile programme.

CPM and PERT both lead to the determination of a time schedule. Although the two methods were developed independently they are strikingly similar. The most important difference is that the time estimates for the activities were assumed deterministic in CPM and probabilistic in PERT.

*Tutorial note: Since the development of CPM and PERT considerable work has been done in consolidating and improving these techniques. Unfortunately, a student now is faced with a large number of names for what is basically the same technique. The preferred term for the subject matter is critical path analysis (CPA), though a later chapter deals with uncertainty and the use of PERT.*

## 3.0 AREAS OF APPLICATION

The main incentives for using CPA are to plan and control time, the use of resources and the expenditure of capital. The following is a brief summary of some areas of application of CPA:

(a) *Marketing.* Market research, product launching and the setting up and running of advertising campaigns.
(b) *Shipbuilding.* Design and production of ships.
(c) *Product changeover.* The changing over from one product, or family of products, to another.
(d) *Construction.* Houses, flats and offices.
(e) *Civil engineering.* Motorways, bridges and road programmes.
(f) *Town planning.* Control of tendering and design procedures and subsequent building and installation of services.

Experience indicates that the use of CPA on suitable projects can reduce the completion time for a project by 10 per cent or more and increase the utilisation of resources.

## 4.0 THE CPA METHOD

The technique is applied in two main stages. The first stage is concerned with preparing the network and the second with the analysis of the network. The two stages form the basis for project control. This includes the use of the network prepared and the various analyses for making periodic progress reports. The network may thus be updated and, if necessary, a new schedule determined for the remaining portion of the project.

## 4.1 Preparing the network

This involves:

(a) defining the objective of the project;

(b) identifying the individual jobs which make up the project;

(c) determining the logical sequence of jobs;

(d) determining the estimated duration for each activity;

(e) constructing the appropriate diagram.

## 4.2 Analysing the network

Network analysis can be viewed from the following three aspects:

(a) *Time*.
Analysing a network from the aspect of time gives:

The minimum time in which the project can be completed (based on the estimated time for the various activities); comparison of this with the target completion dates will indicate whether or not the latter can be met.

A list of those activities which are critical, i.e. which must be completed on time if the target completion date is to be met.

A list of all other activities showing the amount of slack (float) available, i.e. the amount by which their start or finish can be delayed without affecting the overall completion time.

(b) *Cost*.
The object of analysing a network from the point of view of cost is to minimise the total cost of the project, i.e. the sum of the direct and indirect costs. "Direct cost" is the cost of labour, material and machines required to carry out the project. "Indirect cost" is the penalty for delaying the completion of the project, e.g. loss of profits.

(c) *Resources*.
The resources available, which are usually limited, may be required for a single project or for several projects running in parallel. The problem is to balance the requests for these resources so that the load on them is as even as possible and yet the projects are each completed in the shortest possible time. The advantage of using networks as the basis for balancing the allocation of resources is that they show clearly which activities can be delayed, and by how much, without causing delay to the whole project. These considerations apply to labour (tradesmen, semiskilled and unskilled) as well as to various types of capital equipment (cranes, bulldozers, etc.) which may be used.

# 5.0 NETWORK TERMINOLOGY

## 5.1 Activities

Once the scope of a project is defined, it is broken down into a number of jobs or "activities" which are necessary for its completion. An activity is a particular piece of work identifiable as an entity within the project. For example, if the project under consideration is the building of a house, then one of the acitivities would be "architects draw plans".

An activity within a project is represented by an arrow, with the description of the activity written above it (Fig. 68a).

Fig. 68.(a) *Activity within a project.*

*Notes*
(a) *The length of the arrow is not proportional to time.*
(b) *Activities consume time and resources.*
(c) *An activity is represented by one arrow only.*
(d) *The description of the activity may be replaced by a symbol.*

## 5.2 Events

An event is a moment in time. Events mark the moment in time when a job or jobs are complete and the next job or jobs are ready to start. Events are represented by circles (nodes) (Fig. 68b).

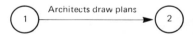

Fig. 68.(b) *Events and activity within a project.*

Event 1 is a moment in time when the architects are ready to draw the plans. Event 2 represents the moment in time when the plans are complete. It is common practice to number the circles so that subsequent nodes have higher numbers than their predecessors, though they need not be consecutive.

*Note: Activities can be described by reference to the numbers of their beginning and end events, e.g. Activity 7–8.*

## 5.3 Networks

A network is basically a series of activities and events. It can be described as a diagram showing the logical sequence of jobs within a project.

Consider a simple example of a project where there are two activities, P and Q. (P could stand for driving to a garage and Q for filling petrol.) Activity Q cannot be started until activity P is completed. The network will appear as in Fig. 68c. Event 2

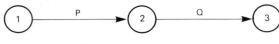

Fig. 68.(c) Network.

represents the moment in time when activity P is complete and also marks the moment in time when activity Q is ready to start.

It is possible that two or more activities may depend upon the same activity. Fig. 69 depicts a situation where neither activity Y nor Z can start until activity X is complete. Event 2 marks the moment in time when activity X is completed and also the moment in time when Y and Z can start.

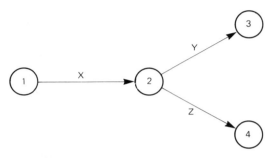

Fig. 69. *Network where one activity must be complete before either of two others can start.*

It may happen that an activity depends on more than one activity. If activity N cannot start until activities L and M are both complete, the representation will be as in Fig. 70.

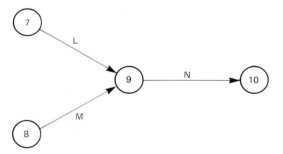

Fig. 70. *Network in which two activities must be complete before another can start.*

## 5.4 Dependency tables

The individual "activities" which make up a project having been identified, an essential feature of the network process entails determining the logical relationship between activities, i.e. sorting out the logical sequence of activities. This can be done by constructing a "dependency table". A "dependency table" is a list of all the activities in the project under consideration, with next to them a list of the activities that they

# 19 AN INTRODUCTION TO NETWORK ANALYSIS

depend upon. The following example deals with "network construction" from a dependency table.

## Example 1: Network construction
Prepare a network for a project which yields the following dependency table:

| Activity | Preceding activities |
|---|---|
| A | – |
| B, C | A |
| D | B |
| E | C |
| F | D, E |

The relationships in the dependency table can be represented by a series of "sub-networks" (Fig. 71).

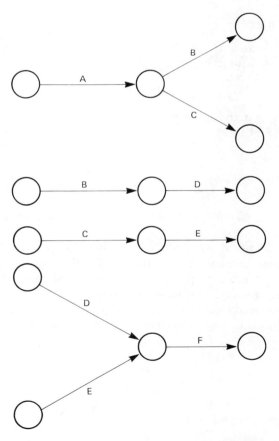

Fig. 71. *Sub-networks representing dependencies.*

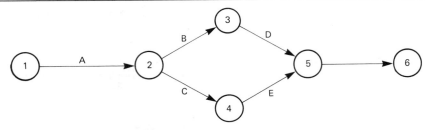

Fig. 72. *Single network formed by joining sub-networks.*

The sub-networks can now be joined together to form a single network. However, one important rule must be observed: there must be just one start event and just one end event. The completed network is shown in Fig. 72.

*Note: The sequence of activities in the network should be carefully checked against the sub-networks and dependency table. With practice it is possible to omit the sub-networks and draw the complete network directly from the dependency table.*

## 5.5 Dummy activities

A "dummy activity" is an activity which takes no time to complete, i.e. it has no duration and consumes no resources. It is represented by a broken arrow:

----->

The need for dummy activities in network analysis is best understood by considering the networks (Figs. 73 to 75).

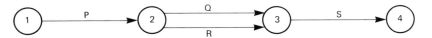

Fig. 73. *Network whose form is unacceptable.*

Figure 73 shows a logical sequence of activities but cannot be accepted, as both activities Q and R will be labelled 2–3 (in terms of linking events). To overcome this problem of identification and to preserve the sequential numbering system of events an imaginary activity termed a dummy is inserted.

The network now becomes as shown in Fig. 74. Note that the identification of activities Q and R has now been preserved as the two activities have a unique pair of linking event numbers.

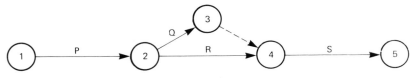

Fig. 74. *Network corrected by insertion of an imaginary activity or dummy.*

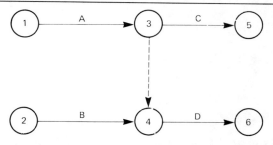

Fig. 75. *Network with dummy inserted to maintain logical sequence of jobs.*

At times it is necessary to insert a dummy not for indentification or preservation of the sequential numbering system but to maintain the logical sequence of jobs within a project. A simple example is shown in Fig. 75. Activity C depends on A. Activity D depends on B. Additionally activity D is dependent on activity A, i.e. event 4 is contingent upon event 3 being reached.

## 6.0 SUMMARY

Network analysis is a practical system for planning and controlling projects. This chapter has described the background to network analysis and the terminology appropriate to the construction of networks. A network is basically a series of activities and events. Activities are represented by arrows and consume time and resources. Events are represented by circles (nodes) and are moments in time. Networks have one starting event and one finishing event. At times dummy activities (represented by broken arrows) may be necessary to show logical relationships or preserve independence. Dummies do not consume time or resources.

CHAPTER TWENTY
# Network Analysis–Time and Cost

## 1.0 INTRODUCTION

The previous chapter explained the logic behind network drawing and dealt with network terminology and different forms of networks. It should be clear by now that network drawing is based on logic. The element of time need only be introduced once the network is drawn. This chapter introduces the concept of time or duration for individual activities and explains how a time analysis is conducted. The latter part of the chapter (7.0 to 9.0) extends a time analysis into the area of cost and explains the purpose of a cost analysis and the general procedure to be followed.

## 2.0 AIM OF A TIME ANALYSIS

A project describes a combination of interrelated activities that must be completed in a certain order before the entire project can be completed. A time analysis of a network provides the minimum time in which the overall project can be completed. The analysis is based on the estimated times for the various jobs and once the overall project time is calculated it can be compared with target completion times to see whether or not they will be met. The time analysis will indicate activities which must be completed on time to avoid extending the overall project time. These activities are said to be critical. The time analysis will also indicate which activities are not critical. These activities are termed non-critical and possess float, i.e. a measure of delay. The analysis will show the amount by which non-critical activities can be delayed without affecting the overall project time.

## 3.0 CRITICAL PATH

The critical path of a network gives the shortest time in which the overall project can be completed. The critical path is given by the longest route or routes of jobs as the

# 20 NETWORK ANALYSIS—TIME AND COST

overall project cannot be completed till the longest route is complete. Individual jobs which lie on the longest route are said to be critical, i.e. if they are delayed beyond their allotted time they delay the completion of the project as a whole. It should be noted that there may be more than one critical path in a network, i.e. there may be two or more routes which are equally the longest within the project.

## 4.0 DETERMINING THE CRITICAL PATH—SIMPLE ANALYSIS

The simplest way of finding the critical path is to examine every route of jobs through a project. The critical path is then given by the longest route. Consider the network shown in Fig. 76.

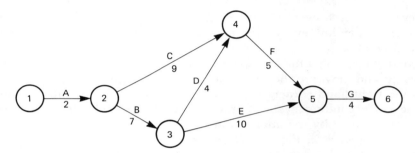

Fig. 76. *Network for simple analysis.*

The different routes of jobs are

ABEG  = 2 + 7 + 10 + 4    = 23
ABDFG = 2 + 7 +  4 + 5 + 4 = 22
ACFG  = 2 + 9 +     5 + 4 = 20.

ABEG is termed the critical path as it is the longest path in the project. The overall project will not be complete till this route is completed. Individual jobs on this route are termed critical. If delayed beyond their allotted time, the project time lengthens. This should be fairly obvious as the longest route is going to become even longer. For example, if job E is delayed by 2 units of time, i.e. it is done in 12 units rather than the allotted time of 10 units, then route ABEG becomes 25, i.e. it is delayed by a corresponding amount. This method has the disadvantage that it does not reveal the amount of delay possible on individual jobs (the float).

## 5.0 DETERMINING THE CRITICAL PATH—NORMAL ANALYSIS

The most reliable method for determining the critical path and establishing the delay on non-critical jobs is based on a calculation of float. Float is defined as a measure of delay. Jobs which are critical have no float, i.e. no measure of delay.

The critical path calculations involve two stages. The first stage is called the

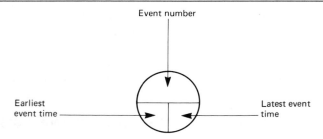

Fig. 77. *How the event circle is split to show event times.*

"forward pass" and calculations begin from the starting event and move to the finishing event. At each event a number is computed representing the earliest event time of the corresponding event. These figures are shown in Fig. 77 in the left-hand corners of the nodes.

The second stage, called the "backward pass", begins calculations from the end or finishing event and moves to the starting event. The number computed at each event (shown in the right-hand corners of the nodes in Fig. 78) represents the latest event time of the corresponding event. Earliest event times and latest event times are sometimes represented by the abbreviations e.e.t. and l.e.t.

Consider the network in Fig. 79. Durations are assumed to be in days.

Start at event 1 and assign to it a time of 0. Event 2 occurs when activity A is complete, hence its earliest event time is $0 + 2 = 2$ days. (Note that an earliest event time is the earliest time a particular moment in time can occur. An e.e.t. of 2 for event 2 can be understood by examining all that happens at event 2. It is a moment in time where job A is complete and jobs B and C are ready to start. All this can occur at the earliest time of 2.)

Similarly, it can be determined that: the e.e.t. for event 3 is $2 + 7 = 9$ days (job B complete).

Now consider event 4. This is moment in time which marks the completion of jobs

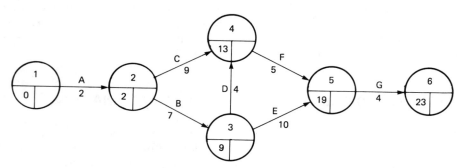

Fig. 78. *Network for normal analysis with earliest event times.*

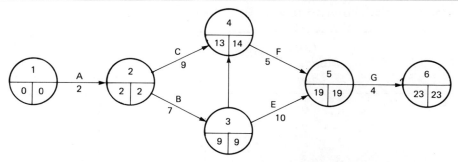

Fig. 79. *Network as Fig. 78 with latest event times added.*

C and D and the start of job F. The event cannot occur till jobs C and D are both complete.

Activity C is complete after $2 + 9 = 11$ days at the earliest. Activity D is complete after $9 + 4 = 13$ days at the earliest. Hence the earliest event time for event 4 is 13 days.

A similar analysis can be carried out for event 5. Activity E is complete after $9 + 10 = 19$ days at the earliest. Activity F is complete after $13 + 5 = 18$ days at the earliest. Hence the e.e.t. for event 5 is 19 days.

The e.e.t. for event 6 is $19 + 4 = 23$ days. Clearly, this e.e.t. for the finishing event must be the same as the total project time.

The backward pass (Fig. 79) is now commenced at event 6. The purpose is to find the latest event times, i.e. the latest time that each event can occur if the project is to be completed on time. The latest event time for event 6 must be 23 days as the project can be completed in 23 days.

The latest event time for event 5 is $23 - 4 = 19$. Similarly, the l.e.t. for event 4 is $19 - 5 = 14$.

For event 3 the calculation of the l.e.t. must consider both routes back to the event. For event 4 to occur at the latest time of 14, event 3 must occur at the latest time of $14 - 4 = 10$. For event 5 to occur at the latest time of 19, event 3 must occur at the latest time of $19 - 10 = 9$. Clearly, for the project to be completed on time, event 3 must have day 9 as its latest time. (The rule is: going backwards if there is more than one route back to a particular event, calculate the l.e.t. based on all the routes and take the smallest number obtained. Students should be able to discern the appropriate rule for the forward pass.)

Similarly, event 2 has a latest time of 2 and event 1 has an l.e.t. of 0.

It is now possible to calculate the total float on each job. This is the amount by which a job can be delayed without affecting the overall project time. Critical jobs have zero total float. The total float is easily calculated in tabular form as shown below. However, for tutorial purposes the calculation will be explained in slightly greater detail. Consider job C. It starts at event 2 and finishes at event 4. The latest time that job C can be finished is 14. The earliest time it can start is time 2. Hence the time available is $14 - 2 = 12$. However, the duration of job C is only 9. Hence there is a delay of $12 - 9 = 3$ possible on job C. Obviously job C is not critical. Similarly, it can be shown that the float on job D is 1. It can finish at the latest time of 14. It can start at the earliest time of 9. Hence the time available is $14 - 9 = 5$. The time taken is 4. Therefore the total float is $5 - 4 = 1$.

The tabulation which gives total float is shown below:

| Job | (1) Latest finish | (2) Earliest start | (3) Available time | (4) Duration | (3) – (4) Total float |
|---|---|---|---|---|---|
| A | 2  | 0  | 2  | 2  | 0 |
| B | 9  | 2  | 7  | 7  | 0 |
| C | 14 | 2  | 12 | 9  | 3 |
| D | 14 | 9  | 5  | 4  | 1 |
| E | 19 | 9  | 10 | 10 | 0 |
| F | 19 | 13 | 6  | 5  | 1 |
| G | 23 | 19 | 4  | 4  | 0 |

The critical path is that path which has zero total float, i.e. ABEG.

## 6.0 CLASSIFICATIONS OF FLOAT

Reference has been made in 2.0 to float. Float has been defined as a measure of delay. Following the determination of the critical path, the floats for the non-critical activities must be calculated. Naturally, a critical activity must have a zero float. (This is the reason it is critical.)

A distinction is drawn between three different kinds of float; total float, free float and independent float. The differences are as follows:

*Total float* is the amount of time by which an activity can be delayed without affecting the overall project time.

*Free float* is the amount of time by which an activity can be delayed without affecting the earliest start of subsequent activities.

*Independent float* is the amount of time by which an activity can be delayed if preceding activities are completed as late as possible and subsequent activities are started as early as possible.

Consider part of a network as shown in Fig. 80. The job under consideration is S.

# 20 NETWORK ANALYSIS—TIME AND COST

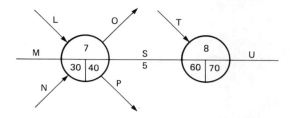

Fig. 80. *Part of a network to illustrate float.*

## 6.1 Total float for job S

| | |
|---|---|
| The latest time job S can be finished | = 70 |
| The earliest time job S can start | = 30 |
| The time available for job S | = 40 |
| The duration | = 5 |
| ∴ Total float | = 35 |

## 6.2 Free float for job S

Job U should be free to start at its earliest time which is 60. For this to happen, job S must be completed by that time.

| | |
|---|---|
| The latest time S can be finished | = 60 |
| The earliest time S can start | = 30 |
| Time available | = 30 |
| The duration | = 5 |
| ∴ Free float | = 25 |

## 6.3 Independent float for job S

Job U should be free to start at its earliest time which is 60. Jobs L, M and N should be allowed to be completed at the latest possible time which is 40.

| | |
|---|---|
| Hence, the latest time S can be finished | = 60 |
| The earliest time S can start | = 40 |
| Time available | = 20 |
| The duration | = 5 |
| ∴ Independent float | = 15 |

## 7.0 COST CONSIDERATIONS

The primary aim of analysing a network from a cost point of view is to enable the calculation of total costs at different project durations. The objective is to obtain the

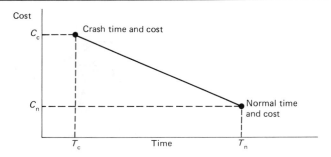

Fig. 81. *Relationship between normal time and cost and crash time and cost.*

best time and cost combination by minimising the sum total of costs. The total costs will include direct costs such as the cost of labour, materials and expenses. These tend to increase as project time is reduced as more labour, equipment and expenses will be required. Consider an activity within a project (Fig. 81). If the activity is done under normal conditions it has a time $T_n$ and a direct cost $C_n$. The time $T_n$ can be reduced by increasing the allocated resources and hence by increasing the direct costs. There is a limit, termed the crash time $T_c$, byond which no further reduction in the time will be possible. At the crash time, the associated cost is referred to as the crash cost $C_c$. Fig. 81 shows the relationship. The straight-line relationship is used mainly for convenience as a non-linear relationship will complicate the calculations.

A necessary measure for the cost analysis is the calculation of the cost slope for each activity. It is the cost of reducing an activity by a unit of time. The relationship as shown above is assumed to be linear:

$$\text{Cost slope} = \frac{\text{Crash cost} - \text{Normal cost}}{\text{Normal time} - \text{Crash time}}$$

$$= \frac{C_c - C_n}{T_n - T_c}.$$

Indirect project costs can be analysed in a similar manner. The indirect costs could include supervision or administration and in certain cases these costs could be the penalty for delaying the project duration. It is logical to assume that as the duration of the project increases the indirect costs must also increase.

The sum of these two costs (direct and indirect) gives the total cost of the project. The optimum schedule corresponds to the minimum total cost.

## 8.0 THE COST ANALYSIS PROCEDURE

The starting point is the determination of the cost–time relationships for individual jobs. This will involve a definition of normal time/normal cost and crash time/crash cost for each activity. Activities are then assigned normal times and the critical path is computed in the usual manner and the associated cost is recorded. The next step is to consider reducing the project duration. This can only be done by reducing the time on the longest route of jobs, i.e. the critical path. As the duration must be reduced at the lowest possible cost, select the critical job with the lowest cost slope. The amount

## 20 NETWORK ANALYSIS—TIME AND COST

of time by which an individual activity can be reduced is limited by its crash time. However, other factors must be taken into account. For example, the next longest route may become critical. There will then be two critical paths and any further reduction in project time must occur on both the paths for overall project time to be reduced. Continue in this manner tabulating the direct and indirect costs for each completion time. Add the direct and indirect costs and hence determine the best time and cost combination.

*Tutorial note: The procedure is best understood by example and this is done in the following section.*

### 9.0 COST ANALYSIS—A WORKED EXAMPLE

Consider a project with data as summarised in Table 11.

Table 11. Data for cost analysis example.

| Job | Preceding job | Normal time (days) | Crash time (days) | Normal cost (£) | Crash cost (£) |
|---|---|---|---|---|---|
| A | – | 5 | 3 | 200 | 400 |
| B | – | 4 | 4 | 100 | 100 |
| C | A | 2 | 1 | 500 | 800 |
| D | B | 1 | 1 | 50 | 50 |
| E | B | 5 | 3 | 150 | 300 |
| F | B | 5 | 4 | 300 | 350 |
| G | C,D | 4 | 4 | 200 | 200 |
| H | F | 3 | 2 | 300 | 500 |
|   |   |   |   | £1,800 |   |

Note that each activity which can be reduced may be reduced to the crashed duration in daily stages at pro rata cost. There is a £200 per day charge for variable overheads.

It is required to find the cost of completing the project in the shortest time. What is also required is the duration of the project if total cost is to be minimised.

The completed network is shown in Fig. 82.

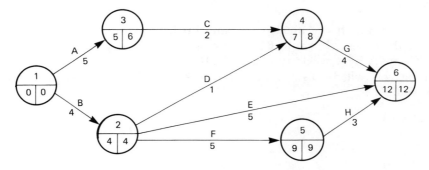

Fig. 82. *Network for cost analysis.*

The critical path is given by BFH, with a duration of 12 weeks. (This is the longest route of jobs i.e. the path with zero total float.)

The total cost of the project consists of two components, the normal (direct) cost of completing each job and the variable overhead (indirect) cost which is based on time:

| | |
|---|---:|
| Normal costs add up to | £1,800 |
| Overhead cost at £200 per week for 12 weeks | 2,400 |
| Total cost | £4,200 |

*Tutorial note: A common examination mistake is to add up the normal costs only for jobs on the critical path. Remember, for the project to be completed all jobs must be done and hence the normal costs of all jobs must be included.*

The question requires the cost of completing the project in the shortest time and the duration of the project if total cost is to be minimised. A conventional cost analysis (crashing) procedure can be adapted.

First, work out cost slopes:

| Job | A | B | C | D | E | F | G | H |
|---|---|---|---|---|---|---|---|---|
| Possible reductions | 2 | – | 1 | – | 2 | 1 | – | 1 |
| Extra cost | £200 | – | £300 | – | £150 | £50 | – | £200 |
| Cost slope | £100 | – | £300 | - | £75 | £50 | - | £200 |

Next, list all the different routes:

    BFH = 12
    ACG = 11
    BDG =  9
    BE =  9

To reduce project time, the length of the critical path must be reduced. Select that job with the lowest cost slope, i.e. F. Reduce F by 1 at a cost of £50. There will now be two critical paths, BFH and ACG. The total cost will be £4,050 (4,200 – 200 + 50). Update the times on the different routes:

    BFH = 11
    ACG = 11
    BDG =  9
    BE =  9

As there are now two critical paths, any further saving in project time must take place on both routes. On route BFH, H can be cut by 1 week at a cost of £200. On path ACG cut A by 1 week at a cost of £100.

The total cost will be £4,150 (4,050 – 200 + 200 + 100). Update the times on the different routes:

    BFH = 10
    ACG = 10
    BDG =  9
    BE =  9

# 20 NETWORK ANALYSIS—TIME AND COST

There is no further reduction in time possible on route BFH. The other critical path ACG can be cut but this is pointless as BFH would remain critical.

The required answers can now be given. The cost of completing the project in the shortest time is £4,150. The corresponding time is 10 weeks. The duration of the project if total cost is to be minimised is 11 weeks at a cost of £4,050.

*Tutorial note: The above answer was given in slightly greater detail than would be required in examinations. Updating for instance can be shown on a continuous basis, for example:*

|     |    | F by 1 | A by 1<br>H by 1 |
|-----|----|--------|------------------|
| BFH | 12 | 11     | 10               |
| ACG | 11 | 11     | 10               |
| BDG | 9  | 9      | 9                |
| BE  | 9  | 9      | 9                |

# CHAPTER TWENTY-ONE
# Network Analysis – Resources and Uncertainty

## 1.0 INTRODUCTION – RESOURCE ANALYSIS

The analysis of networks so far has ignored the requirements and the availability of resources for projects. Expressed in simple terms, a resource analysis is concerned with balancing the availability of and the requirements for resources. The resources used in a project (labour, equipment, material and finances) are subject to varying demands over the project duration. Available resources are usually limited and the problem is to balance the requirements for these resources so that the load on them is as even as possible and yet the project is completed in the minimum time possible. It is clear that a project can only be executed within the limitations of the available resources. The advantage of using networks as the basis for balancing the allocation of resources is that they clearly indicate which activities can be delayed without affecting the overall project time. By shifting non-critical activities it may be possible to lower the maximum resource requirements. Even in the absence of limited resources, a resource analysis would enable the levelling of resources over the project duration. This would imply a steady utilisation of perhaps the work force as opposed to drastic variations day by day.

In certain projects the objective may be to keep the maximum resource requirements below a predetermined limit rather than merely levelling the resources. If this cannot be done by rescheduling the non-critical activities, it may be necessary to expand the time on some of the critical activities (i.e. lengthen project duration).

Owing to mathematical complexity, there is no available technique which yields an optimum solution, i.e. minimises the maximum required resources for a project at any point in time. Instead, procedures which take advantage of the different floats for non-critical jobs are used. These are indicated in the following example.

## 2.0 RESOURCE ANALYSIS—AN EXAMPLE

Consider the project detailed in the following table. The resource required is that of labour and individual job requirements are given.

| Activity | Preceding activities | Duration (weeks) | Men required |
|---|---|---|---|
| L | – | 3 | 5 |
| M | L | 2 | 3 |
| N | L | 3 | 7 |
| O | M,N | 5 | 5 |
| P | M,N | 7 | 2 |
| Q | N | 3 | 2 |
| R | P,Q | 6 | 6 |
| S | N | 2 | 1 |

An attempt will be made to develop as smooth a schedule of manpower requirements as possible.

The starting point in the analysis is the construction of a network to determine the minimum project time (Fig. 83).

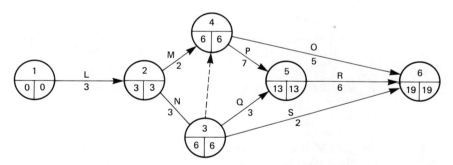

Fig. 83. *Network to illustrate example.*

The critical path is given by L–N–P–R, i.e. the path with zero total float.

The next stage involves the construction of a Gantt chart and labour histogram (Fig. 84). In the Gantt chart each job is shown by a line with a length proportional to the time taken. Each job is shown as starting at its earliest time. By examination of the chart on a daily basis it is possible to determine the daily labour requirements. These are shown in the histogram below the Gantt chart.

The histogram shows a fairly fluctuating requirement for labour on a day-to-day basis. It may be necessary to establish the constant manning force required to complete the project in the shortest possible time, i.e. 19 days. This cannot be less than 10 men. Job N is critical and requires 7 men. If the project is to be completed in time then job

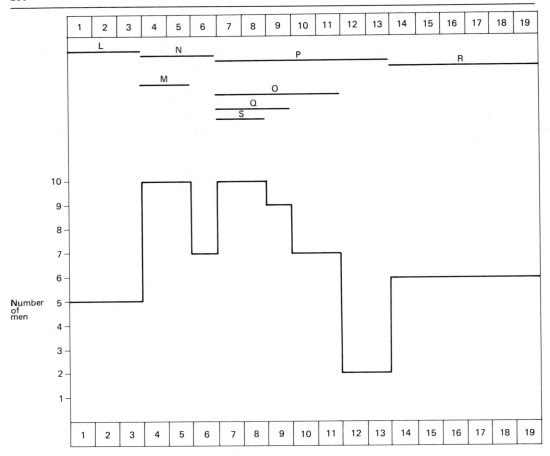

Fig. 84. *Gantt chart and labour histogram.*

N cannot be delayed. Job M is being done concurrently and has a requirement of three men. Job M is not critical, and hence can be delayed. However, it has insufficient float to be moved completely out of the range of job N. In other words, part of M will always coincide with N and hence a manning force of 10 men is necessary to ensure that the project is completed in 19 days.

*Tutorial notes*
*(a) Students are encouraged to delay all the non-critical jobs as much as possible, i.e. by their floats. They should then confirm that the constant manning force which should be available changes to 12.*
*(b) A much smoother allocation is possible by rescheduling a couple of the non-critical jobs rather than all. This should be done as the second exercise. Students should note that this is virtually a trial-and-error exercise.*
*(c) The example introduced the concept of manpower requirements and used it to work out the constant manning force which should be made available if the project is to be completed in the*

*minimum time. It may be that the availability is stipulated and falls below the requirement as determined from the Gantt chart and histogram. Using the available labour force (with no additions) will now lead to a delay in project time.*

## 3.0 AN INTRODUCTION TO PERT

The network analyses conducted so far (time/cost and resources) assume that the time for individual activities is known with complete certainty. These durations are actually only estimates. In practice, activities do not take exactly as long as estimated to complete. A more accurate model of the duration of an activity is to describe the duration by a probability distribution. This is done in PERT (project evaluation and review technique), which uses the beta distribution to model activity durations. As mentioned, PERT was introduced in 1958 by the Special Projects Office of the US Navy on its Polaris weapon systems. Since then its use has been spread widely.

In PERT time estimates are made for each activity of the network on a three-way basis, i.e. optimistic, most likely and pessimistic times are estimated by those most familiar with the activity involved. The three time estimates are required as a gauge of the measure of uncertainty of the activity. It should be noted, however, that for the purposes of computation the three time estimates are reduced to a single expected time ($t_e$) and a statistical variance ($\sigma^2$).

## 4.0 PERT—EXPECTED TIME ESTIMATES

Interpretation of the concept of optimistic, most likely and pessimistic times varies but the following definitions are the most widely used.

*Optimistic time* for an activity is an estimate of the minimum time an activity will take if everything goes right.

*Most likely time* is an estimate of the normal time an activity will take. It is a result which would occur most often if the activity could be repeated a number of times (under similar circumstances).

*Pessimistic time* is an estimate of the maximum time an activity will take. This is a result which would occur only if unusually bad luck is experienced.

In analysing the three estimates, it is clear that the optimistic and the pessimistic times should occur least often, and that the most likely time should occur most often. It is assumed that the most likely time represents the peak or modal value of a probability distribution. The beta distribution, unlike the normal distribution, is not necessarily symmetrical. There can be an optimistic estimate ($a$) very close to the most likely estimate ($m$) and the pessimistic estimate ($b$) much greater than $m$, or vice versa. This is known statistically as a skewed distribution. Figure 85 indicates skewed and symmetrical beta distributions for an activity duration; in it

$$a = \text{optimistic time}$$
$$m = \text{most likely time}$$
$$b = \text{pessimistic time.}$$

Note that
$$M = \text{mid-range} = \frac{a+b}{2},$$

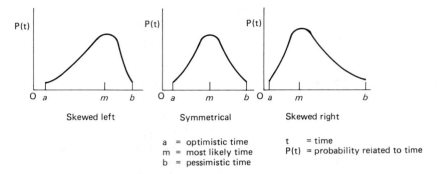

Fig. 85. *Skewed and symmetrical beta distributions.*

while $t_e$ = expected time.

The useful property of the beta distribution is that, knowing the three values $a$, $m$ and $b$ for an activity, it is possible to compute the expected time ($t_e$) and the variance of duration ($\sigma^2$).

The expected time $t_e$ is interpreted as the weighted mean of $m$ (most likely) and $M$ (mid-range) estimates, with weights of 2 and 1 respectively.

$$t_e = 1/3\ (2m + M)$$

$$= 1/3 \left(2m + \frac{a+b}{2}\right)$$

$$t_e = \frac{a + 4m + b}{\sigma}.$$

The expression for the variance of duration ($\sigma^2$) of an activity is developed as follows.

The range ($a$, $b$) is assumed to enclose about six standard deviations of the distribution since about 90 per cent or more of any probability density function lies within three standard deviations of its mean.

Thus 
$$\sigma^2 = \left(\frac{b-a}{\sigma}\right)^2$$

and 
$$\sigma = \left(\frac{b-a}{\sigma}\right).$$

*Tutorial note: The validity of the beta distribution assumption has been challenged and the expressions for $t_e$ and $\sigma^2$ for the beta distribution cannot be satisfied unless certain restrictive relationships exist between $a$, $b$ and $m$. However, the network analysis is based on the central-limit theorem which assumes normality regardless of the parent distribution of individual activities.*

## 5.0 DETERMINING THE CRITICAL PATH

Determine the expected time $t_e$ for every activity on the network in accordance with the equation

$$t_e = \frac{a + 4m + b}{6}.$$

Use the expected times for each activity in a conventional time analysis to give the expected project time (critical path).

The single most important question now concerns the variability of the project completion time, i.e. what is the probability of completing the project by a given point in time? On the basis of the central-limit theorem, it can be concluded that the probability distribution of times for completing a project consisting of a number of activities may be approximated by the normal distribution and that this approximation approaches exactness as the number of activities becomes great. (The central-limit theorem states that the distribution of sums of random variables is approximately normally distributed with mean equal to the sum of the means and variance equal to the sum of the variances.) See Fig. 86 below.

Thus, the mean project duration ($t_e$) is given by adding the expected times of activities lying on the critical path and the computation of variance of project time involves adding the variances for each activity along the critical path obtained from

$$\sigma^2 = \left(\frac{b-a}{\sigma}\right)^2.$$

Once the variance of project time is calculated, the standard deviation of project time can be obtained. The probability of meeting a scheduled date ($t_s$) is:

$$\frac{t_s - t_e}{\sigma}.$$

This will yield a value for the probability of accomplishing $t_s$ by use of the normal probability distribution table.

*Tutorial note: The assumption that the critical path is the one which determines the project duration is usually made in a PERT analysis for the sake of convenience. As individual activity times are subject to uncertainty, it should be clear that there is always some probability that a path other then the one determined as critical may actually be critical. Simulation has also been used to determine the probabilities of various paths being critical.*

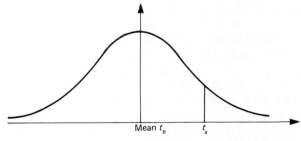

Fig. 86. *Probability distribution of project duration.*

# CHAPTER TWENTY-TWO
# Inventory Control

## 1.0 INTRODUCTION

An inventory is an idle but usable resource. The resource could be of any type; for example, equipment, materials, labour or money. Inventory is usually referred to as stock when the resource involved is material or goods in any stage of completion. Stocks can be in the form of raw materials, work in progress or finished goods. Irrespective of the form in which they are held, a fundamental reason for holding stock is to ensure that supplies are not interrupted, either to or within the transformation process, or to customers.

By holding higher levels of stock, there is a reduced likelihood of running out of stock which will carry a penalty of some kind. The penalty for stock-outs may be due to lost sales or customer dissatisfaction. Alternatively, a stock-out may incur a penalty due to delaying the necessary operations within the organisation till the goods arrive. Another benefit of holding higher levels of stocks is that they lead to fewer but larger replenishments. If goods are purchased from a supplier, each additional order will have an additional cost associated with it, such as processing the order, handling the purchases when they arrive etc. If the goods are manufactured internally, larger but less frequent production runs will lead to substantial savings.

The benefits of holding higher levels of stock are obtained at a price. This is the cost of holding stock. The total cost of stock-holding is made up of several components. The most important is termed the cost-of-capital factor. Money invested in stock often must be borrowed; thus there is an interest cost. However, if the money is on hand then by investing it in inventory it is unavailable for income-earning investments elsewhere. Some of the other components of stockholding cost are storage costs (warehousing), handling costs, insurance, obsolescence and deterioration. Many of the components of the stockholding cost are proportional to the stock value and hence it is usually assumed that the annual stockholding cost is some percentage of the average stock value.

It should be clear that there are trade-offs between ordering larger quantities, thereby maintaining higher levels of stock, and ordering smaller quantities, thereby reducing stock levels. A compromise is sought between too small an order and too large an order. The compromise attempts to ensure a balance between the benefits and costs of stockholding. This is done by finding some size of batch or order which minimises the total costs. This is termed an economic order quantity (EOQ) if items are ordered from outside or the economic batch quantity (EBQ) if they are manufactured internally.

## 2.0 DETERMINISTIC EOQ—TRIAL-AND-ERROR SOLUTION

This section develops a trial-and-error solution to a deterministic situation in which constant demand is assumed throughout the planning horizon. Consider the following example.

### Example 1

The annual demand for a company's single item of stock is 3,600 units. Each time that a replenishment order is made the company incurs a fixed cost of £10 irrespective of the size of the order. The company obtains the items from a local supplier at a cost of £4 per unit. The stockholding costs expressed as a percentage of stock value are 20 per cent. What is the economic order quantity for the company and how many replenishments per annum does this lead to?

The assumptions implicit in this solution are:

(a) a constant demand rate, known with certainty;
(b) zero lead time (i.e. instantaneous replenishment);
(c) no stock-outs permitted;
(d) constant purchase price.

Note that even if lead time is a positive value there will not be any stock-outs and hence it is unnecessary to hold safety stock or buffer stocks for contingencies. This is true because the demand rate is known and constant and therefore it is known how long any existing inventory will last. Hence a new supply of goods can always be received before the old supply runs out.

Since each additional unit of stock carried above the necessary level will cost more as a result of holding costs, all orders will be placed so that the goods will arrive just when the stock level equals zero (i.e. the reorder point $R = 0$). The stock on hand will vary between zero and the order size as shown in Fig. 87. The average stock will equal half the order size.

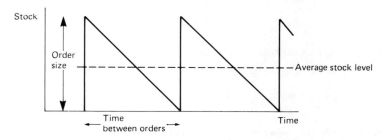

Fig. 87. *General stock pattern.*

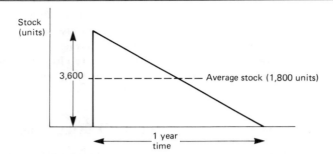

Fig. 88. *Annual stock pattern (order size 3,600 units).*

Assume an arbitrary order size of 3,600 units. Note that the annual demand is being satisfied through one order. A diagram of the resulting stock pattern due to this policy is shown in Fig. 88.

The cost of this inventory policy can be computed. Adopt as a measure of performance a time horizon of 1 year. Compute now the total cost which is affected by the choice of a value for the decision variable, the order quantity $Q$. This cost will be referred to as a total variable cost since only those costs which are affected by a choice of $Q$ will be included. For example, the cost of the goods themselves will not change over an annual cycle (3,600 units at £4 each) as $Q$ is changed.

The two components of total variable cost are the ordering cost per year and the stockholding cost per year.

Ordering cost per year = Number of orders multiplied by the cost for each order
= 1 × £10
= £10.

The stockholding cost per year is given by multiplying the cost of holding one item for a year by the average number of items held. The stockholding cost expressed as a percentage is 20 per cent. An item costs £4. Hence the cost of holding one item is 20 per cent of £4 = £0.8. If the order quantity is 3,600, the average stock held is 1,800 units.

∴ Stockholding cost per year = £0.8 × 1,800
= £1,440.

Total variable cost = ordering + stockholding
= 10 + 1,440
= £1,450.

For the next trial, select another arbitrary order size, say 1,800 units. The stock pattern for the year now is shown in Fig. 89.

Ordering cost per year = 2 × £10
= £20

Stockholding cost per year = £0.8 × 900
= £720.

## 22 INVENTORY CONTROL

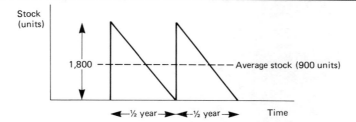

Fig. 89. *Annual stock pattern (order size 1,800 units).*

Total variable cost = ordering + stockholding
= 20 + 720
= £740.

Table 12 summarises the behaviour of ordering and stockholding costs with varying order quantities.

Table 12. Variation of costs with order quantities.

| Ordering frequency | Order quantity | Average stock | Stockholding cost per year | Ordering cost per year | Total variable cost per year |
|---|---|---|---|---|---|
| 1 per year | 3,600 | 1,800 | £1,440 | £10 | £1,450 |
| 2 per year | 1,800 | 900 | 720 | 20 | 740 |
| 4 per year | 900 | 450 | 360 | 40 | 400 |
| 6 per year | 600 | 300 | 240 | 60 | 300 |
| 9 per year | 400 | 200 | 160 | 90 | 250 |
| 12 per year | 300 | 150 | 120 | 120 | 240 |
| 18 per year | 200 | 100 | 80 | 180 | 260 |
| 36 per year | 100 | 50 | 40 | 360 | 400 |

Figure 90 shows the effect of changing the order quantity on the different components of cost. The graph helps determine that size of order which minimises total costs. The three relationships plotted are:

(a) order quantity versus stockholding cost;

(b) order quantity versus ordering cost;

(c) order quantity versus total variable cost.

From the graph it can be seen that ordering in a batch size of 300 units each time yields the lowest total variable cost of £240 per year. The total variable cost is made up of two components, i.e. stockholding and delivery. At the economic order quantity these two components are equal to one another. The number of replenishments per year = 12.

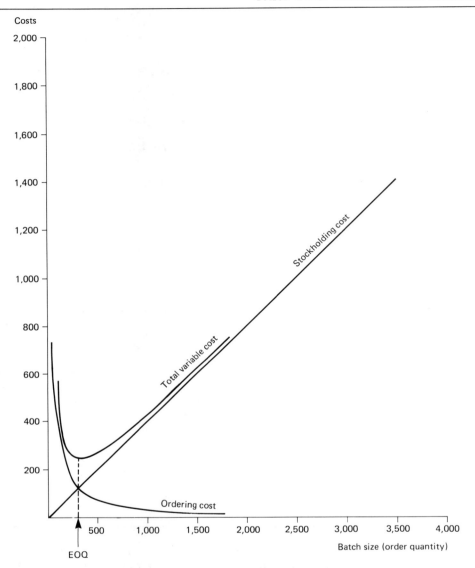

Fig. 90. *Effect of order quantity on costs.*

*Tutorial notes*
  (a) While the total variable costs are £240, the total inventory costs must include the purchase price of £14,400 i.e. 3,600 units at £4 each. Hence:

$$\text{Total inventory costs} = \text{Total variable costs} + \text{total purchase price}$$
$$= 240 + 14,400$$
$$= \underline{\underline{£14,640}}.$$

  (b) Trial and error methods are generally not used, since they are time-consuming. However, they do illustrate the method at hand.

# 22 INVENTORY CONTROL

## 3.0 DERIVATION OF THE DETERMINISTIC EOQ MODEL

The assumptions on which the derivation is based have already been stated. The symbols used in the derivation are:

$d$ = annual demand for the product
$c$ = ordering cost per batch
$p$ = cost per unit
$Q$ = size of order
$i$ = stockholding cost expressed as a percentage.

Total variable costs = Stockholding + Ordering.
Annual stockholding cost = Cost of holding one item per annum × average stock

$$= ip \times \frac{Q}{2}$$

$$= \frac{ipQ}{2}.$$

Annual ordering cost = Number of orders × Ordering cost per batch

$$= \frac{d}{Q} \times c$$

$$= \frac{cd}{Q}.$$

Total variable costs $= \frac{ipQ}{2} + \frac{cd}{Q}.$

The order quantity which makes this total variable cost a minimum is obtained by differentiating the cost curve with respect to $Q$ and equating the derivative to zero.

This gives $\quad \frac{d}{dQ}(\text{total variable cost}) = \frac{ip}{2} - \frac{cd}{Q^2}.$

The differentiation gives the slope (gradient) of the total variable cost function. At points of minimum this must equal zero.

Equating the slope to zero:

$$\frac{ip}{2} - \frac{cd}{Q^2} = 0$$

$$\frac{ip}{2} = \frac{cd}{Q^2}$$

or

$$Q^2 ip = 2cd$$

$$Q^2 = \frac{2cd}{ip}$$

$$Q = \sqrt{\frac{2cd}{ip}}.$$

This expression is termed the EOQ model.

*Tutorial notes*
(a) The example solved in the previous section by trial and error can easily be tackled using the EOQ model:

$$Q = \sqrt{\frac{2cd}{ip}}$$

$$= \sqrt{\frac{2 \times 10 \times 3{,}600}{0.2 \times 4}}$$

$$= \underline{\underline{300 \text{ units.}}}$$

(b) An alternative derivation for the EOQ model based on the trail and error solution exists. The trial and error solution showed that, at the EOQ stockholding costs = ordering costs. Using the symbols above:

$$\frac{ipQ}{2} = \frac{cd}{Q}$$

$$Q^2 ip = 2cd$$

$$Q^2 = \frac{2cd}{ip}$$

$$\therefore Q = \sqrt{\frac{2cd}{ip}}.$$

## 4.0 QUANTITY DISCOUNTS

The derivation above assumes that the purchase price per unit is constant. However, it is common to obtain discounts for volume purchases. The greater the order size, the lower the unit cost. It should be noted that in the absence of discounts the cheapest size of order quantity is the EOQ. However, a discount offers two sources of savings. The prime saving is on purchase price. The second saving is that as fewer orders are required (the order quantity is now larger) the ordering costs are reduced. On the other hand, there is a higher stockholding cost (the average stock held will be higher). A discount is only worth taking if the savings exceed the additional cost of stockholding. The simplest method for evaluating the discount is to compute total costs with and without the discount. This is shown in the following example.

### Example 2
A company has a steady demand for a product of 600 items per annum. The company buys the items from a local supplier at a cost of £6 per item. The cost of ordering and receiving delivery of an order is £10 per batch irrespective of the size of the batch. The stockholding costs expressed as a percentage of stock value are 20 per cent. The supplier is prepared to offer a 5 per cent discount on orders of 200 or more. Is the discount worth taking?

## SOLUTION

The starting point is to determine the economic order quantity. In the absence of a quantity discount this will represent the cheapest ordering quantity:

$$d = 600, \quad p = £6, \quad i = 0.2, \quad c = £10.$$

$$Q = \sqrt{\frac{2cd}{ip}}$$

$$= \sqrt{\frac{2 \times 10 \times 600}{0.2 \times 6}}$$

$$= 100 \text{ units.}$$

### AT THE EOQ

The total costs at this order quantity are made up of ordering, stockholding and purchase price.

$$\text{Total costs} = \frac{cd}{Q} + \frac{ipQ}{2} + \text{Total purchase price}$$

$$= \frac{10 \times 600}{100} + \frac{0.2 \times 6 \times 100}{2} + 600 \times 6$$

$$= 60 + 60 + 3{,}600$$

$$\therefore \text{EOQ costs} = £3{,}720.$$

### AT A BATCH SIZE OF 200 UNITS (5 PER CENT DISCOUNT)

$$\text{Total costs} = \text{Ordering} + \text{Stockholding} + \text{Purchase price}$$

$$= \frac{cd}{Q} + \frac{ipQ}{2} + \text{Total purchase price.}$$

$$= \frac{10 \times 600}{200} + \frac{0.2 \times 5.7 \times 200}{2} + 600 \times 5.7$$

$$= 30 + 114 + 3{,}420$$

$$= £3{,}564.$$

As the discount gives a total cost cheaper than the EOQ cost it is worth taking.

## 5.0 PRODUCTION MODEL

The EOQ model derived earlier can be amended for a situation where an organisation does not order items but manufactures them within the organisation, i.e. the organisation both produces and stocks the product.

As items are being produced, there is a cost of set up which replaces the ordering cost of the EOQ. In the EOQ, stock is replenished instantaneously whereas here it is replenished over a period of time. However, depending on the demand rate part of the batch will be sold while the remainder is still being produced. For the same size of batch ($Q$), the average stock held in the EOQ model ($Q/2$) is greater than the average in this situation (Fig. 91).

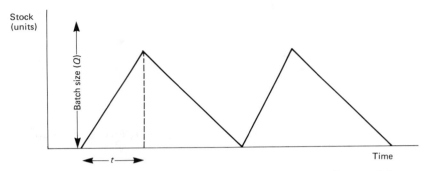

Fig. 91. *Stock pattern for economic-order-quantity model.*

Let $t$ represent the time taken to produce a batch of size $Q$ at a rate of production $r$.

The maximum stock level does not reach $Q$ as items are being sold during production.

Maximum stock level = $Q$ − Amount sold in time $t$.

The amount sold in time $t = td$.

∴  Maximum stock = $Q - td$.

Now $t = \dfrac{Q}{r}$ as it represents the time taken to produce $Q$ at a rate $r$.

Substituting this value for $t$ in the maximum stock expression:

$$\text{Maximum stock} = Q - \frac{Q}{r} d$$

$$= Q\left(1 - \frac{d}{r}\right)$$

$$\text{The average stock} = \frac{Q}{2}\left(1 - \frac{d}{r}\right).$$

The total variable costs = Annual stockholding + Annual set-up.

Using the same symbols as for the EOQ but with $c$ now representing the set-up cost per batch and $p$ the variable cost of producing one item,

$$\text{Total variable cost} = \frac{ipQ}{2}\left(1 - \frac{d}{r}\right) + \frac{cd}{Q}.$$

# 22 INVENTORY CONTROL

At the point of minimum cost, the gradient of this curve must be equal to zero. Differentiate the expression with respect to $Q$.

$$\frac{d}{dQ}(\text{Total variable cost}) = \frac{ip}{2}\left(1 - \frac{d}{r}\right) - \frac{cd}{Q^2}.$$

Equate the derivation to zero:

$$\frac{ip}{2}\left(1 - \frac{d}{r}\right) - \frac{cd}{Q^2} = 0.$$

$$\therefore Q^2 = \frac{2cd}{ip\left(1 - \frac{d}{r}\right)}$$

$$\therefore Q = \sqrt{\frac{2cd}{ip\left(1 - \frac{d}{r}\right)}}.$$

## Example 3

A manufacturer has steady demand for one of his products of 200 units per week. The product can be produced at the rate of 500 units per week (when production is in progress). The variable production cost per unit is £25 and, in addition, set-up costs of £600 are incurred for each production run. The company's cost of capital is 20 per cent (other stockholding cost components can be taken to be negligible). Calculate the economic batch quantity, assuming 50 working weeks per year.

SOLUTION

$$Q = \sqrt{\frac{2cd}{ip\left(1 - \frac{d}{r}\right)}}$$

where  $c = £600$
  $d = 10,000 \ (200 \times 50)$
  $r = 25,000 \ (500 \times 50)$
  $i = 20$ per cent
  $p = £25$.

$$\therefore Q = \sqrt{\frac{2 \times 600 \times 10,000}{0.2 \times 25 \times \left(1 - \frac{10,000}{25,000}\right)}}$$

$$= \underline{2,000 \text{ units}}.$$

## 6.0 LEAD TIME AND REORDER LEVELS

Lead time is the time lag between placing an order and receiving delivery. The preceding sections have assumed a lead time of zero. A time lag between placing an

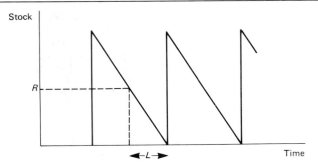

Fig. 92. *Lead time L and reorder level R.*

order and receiving delivery is of itself no problem as long as its duration is predictable and the demand rate is constant. As the demand is constant, the amount of stock that will be used up during the lead time (say $L$ weeks) is easily calculated and the replenishment order is placed when the stock falls to the lead time demand level.

This gives $R$, the reorder level (Fig. 92).

## 7.0 THE EFFECTS OF UNCERTAINTY—STOCHASTIC DEMAND

In practice, the assumptions made so far do not strictly hold true. Uncertainty enters the system so that it is no longer deterministic but essentially stochastic. Stock control problems in practice are caused by a combination of a lead time which is not zero and a demand which is not constant. This introduces the need for safety stocks (buffer stocks). These are additional stock items held to protect a firm against a fluctuating lead time demand. (Note that in the simple model safety stocks would never be required.) The level held has to cater for a variable demand in the lead time. It is assumed that the mean or average demand in the lead time is known. The larger the safety stock held, the greater the additional stockholding charges but the lower the chance of running out of stock and the lower the stock-out costs. The exercise is a balancing one and aims to find that level of buffer stock which minimises the sum total of costs (additional stockholding + stock-out).

*Tutorial note: The exercise of establishing safety or buffer stocks is best explained by example and this is done in the question and answer appendixes.*

## 8.0 SYSTEMS OF STOCK CONTROL

There are two main types of stock control systems:

(a) the reorder level (the two-bin) system;

(b) the periodic (cyclical) review system.

In a reorder level system, a replenishment order of fixed size, $Q$, is placed when the stock level falls to the fixed reorder level, $R$. Thus a fixed quantity is ordered at variable

# 22 INVENTORY CONTROL

intervals of times. On the other hand, in a periodic review system, the stock levels are reviewed at fixed points in time, when the quantity to be ordered is decided; by this method variable quantities are ordered at fixed time-intervals.

In practice, many different systems occur but they will all be found to be either variations of one or the other of the two basic types of system mentioned above, or some combination of these systems. For example, there are many different methods of determining the variable reorder quantity in a periodic review system, and each variation could be thought of as a different system.

## 7.1 Reorder level systems

Once the optimum reorder level $R$ is known, this policy requires that the amount of stock held must be reviewed continuously. This may not be feasible where paper records of the stock on hand are kept but are only updated at certain intervals of time. This situation leads to a variation of the reorder level system where reviews are done periodically. The replenishment order is placed for a fixed quantity as in the basic system but, at each review, an order is made out only if the stock lies on or below the reorder level.

The most common practical implementation of the basic reorder level system is the two-bin system (Fig. 93). Here, two bins of the stocked item are used and a replenishment order is placed when the first bin becomes empty; stock is then drawn from the second bin until the order is received. When the order arrives, the second bin is filled up to its original level and the remainder goes into the first (empty) bin. Thus the amount of stock held in the second bin gives the reorder level.

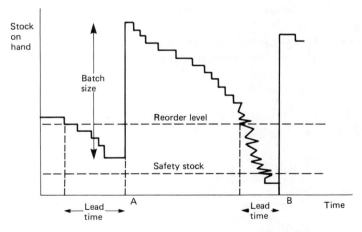

Fig. 93. *Variation of stock level in a two-bin system.*

## 7.2 Periodic review system

The review period, or cycle, used for this type of system is often chosen for administrative convenience or to fit in with production schedules. However, by considering the minimisation of the annual cost of acquiring and holding stock, it is possible to find

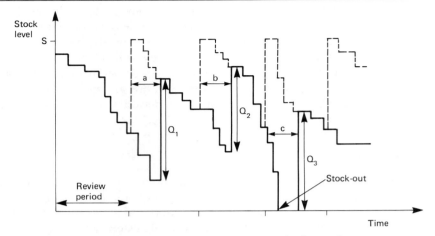

Fig. 94. *Variation of stock level in a periodic review system.*

the so-called economic review period. The only other variable in a system of this type is the replenishment order size.

In the simplest situation this is calculated as the amount of stock which, if the lead time were zero, would bring the stock on hand to some fixed level $S$. Thus the size of the order is equal to $S$ less the inventory on hand; it may therefore be different at every review. In practice, $S$ may vary (seasonally or otherwise) in accordance with the sales forecast for the period.

The diagrammatic representation of a system, where $S$ is constant, is given in Fig. 94. The dotted lines represent the stock that would be held in the ideal situation (where lead time is zero).

In the diagram $Q_1$, $Q_2$ and $Q_3$ are the reorder quantities for the first three review periods and $a$, $b$ and $c$ are the respective lead times.

# CHAPTER TWENTY-THREE
# Queuing Theory

## 1.0 THE QUEUING SITUATION

Queues arise in a number of situations. The following examples illustrate the variety of different queuing situations that can arise:

(a) people queuing at a supermarket checkout;

(b) people queuing at a bank or a post office;

(c) cars queuing at a road junction or set of traffic lights;

(d) items of stock just delivered waiting to be checked before entering a warehouse;

(e) orders for concert tickets waiting to be processed;

(f) computer terminals and other peripherals in a computer system waiting for CPU time;

(g) aeroplanes waiting to land at Heathrow;

(h) telephone users waiting to be connected.

All of these situations involve queues as in each case there is a person, or item (entity) that on some occasion has to wait or remain inactive, i.e. queue, before some service takes place.

## 2.0 COMPONENTS OF THE QUEUING SYSTEM

The queuing situation can be split for analysis into its four main elements:

(a) The input process—how do the items or people arrive?

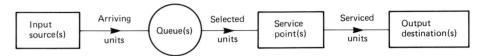

Fig. 95. *Components of the queuing system.*

(b) The queue discipline—how do the items wait for the service? Is there any priority system?

(c) The service process—how are the items served? How many service points are there?

(d) The departure process. How do items leave the system?

This may be represented diagramatically by a flowchart, as in Fig. 95.

There may be only one or several input sources, queues, service points and output destinations and for each of these we will need to know the following information:

(a) For the input process:
  (i) the number of potential customers (finite or infinite);
  (ii) the numbers arriving at one time;
  (iii) the distribution of intervals between arrivals;
  (iv) the average rate of arrivals;
  (v) any outside influences.

(b) For the queuing discipline:
  (i) how many queues;
  (ii) the rules for queuing (LIFO, FIFO, or some other discipline);
  (iii) any restrictions on length of queues;
  (iv) is queue switching permitted?
  (v) can people leave the system from a queue?

(c) For the service process:
  (i) the number of service points;
  (ii) how many items are served at a time?
  (iii) the availability of service;
  (iv) the distribution of service time;
  (v) the average rate of service.

(d) For the departure process we need to know:
  (i) the average rate of departure;
  (ii) any restrictions on departures.

## 3.0 MEASURES OF EFFECTIVENESS

It is possible in a number of cases to build simple mathematical models to analyse the queuing situation. To foresee the overall effects on the model of changes in the component parts we need to have some measure of the effectiveness of the system. Various measures have been used; the most common are:

# 23 QUEUING THEORY

(a) the average waiting time in the queue;

(b) the average time in the system;

(c) the average number in the queue;

(d) the average number in the system;

(e) the size of the queue that will be exceeded for only a small percentage of the time (say 5 per cent).

These can often be translated into costs, so that any costs incurred with the implementation of a new situation can easily be brought into the analysis.

In most practical situations only the steady-state queuing situation is considered. This is also known as a "balanced system" where service facilities are only waiting temporarily for customers and customers are only waiting temporarily for service. This should occur after a short while from the beginning of the situation if the arrival rate is less than the service rate.

## 4.0 A QUEUING MODEL

The most basic model examined is the $M/M/1/\infty$ system.

## 4.1 Arrival rate

In this system items arrive for service according to a Poisson distribution. This implies that the arrivals are occurring at random and that the probability of an arrival during a specified time interval remains constant and independent of the number of previous arrivals and the length of waiting time. All we need to know is the expected arrival rate $\lambda$ in the specified time interval, e.g. 5 arrivals per hour, $\lambda = 5$. This is the first $M$ for mean in $M/M/1/\infty$. Alternatively we could be given the average interarrival time and then deduce the arrival rate $\lambda$ from the information; e.g. average time between arrivals is 12 minutes, this implies 5 arrivals per hour, $\lambda = 5$ as before.

## 4.2 Queue discipline

We assume a first-in, first-out (FIFO) queue discipline, i.e. no queue jumping or any priorities system operating. We also assume that no item leaves the system before it receives service—no balking—and there is no limit on the queue size. (The $\infty$ in $M/M/1/\infty$.)

## 4.3 Service process

The service time is assumed to follow the negative exponential distribution. Again, all we need to know is the expected service rate $\mu$, e.g. 10 items serviced per hour $\mu = 10$ or the average time for a service is 6 minutes as this implies that 10 items can be serviced in an hour. (This is the second $M$ in $M/M/1/\infty$.) It is also assumed that there is only a single server. (The 1 in $M/M/1/\infty$.)

## 4.4 Departure

Items leave immediately they have finished being served, with no obstruction to their departure. It has been shown that under the foregoing assumptions the departure rate under a steady state, also follows a Poisson distribution with mean $\lambda$.

## 5.0 STANDARD QUEUING FORMULAE

The $M/M/1/\infty$ system has been extensively analysed as there are many situations when it may be applied.

The following standard formulae have been determined and given on the examination formulae sheet:

(a) Average number in system:
$$\overline{S} = \frac{\lambda}{\mu - \lambda}.$$

(b) Average number in queue:
$$\overline{q} = \overline{S} - \frac{\lambda}{\mu} = \frac{\lambda^2}{\mu(\mu - \lambda)}.$$

(c) Average queuing time:
$$\overline{W} = \overline{S} \times \frac{1}{\mu} = \frac{\lambda}{\mu(\mu - \lambda)}.$$

(d) Average time in system:
$$\overline{t} = \overline{W} + \frac{1}{\mu} = \frac{1}{\mu - \lambda}.$$

In addition you may find the following formulae useful:

(e) Probability of no customer in the system:
$$P(0) = 1 - \varrho$$
where
$$\varrho = \frac{\lambda}{\mu}.$$

$\varrho$ is known as the traffic intensity and measures the utilisation of the service capacity;
$\varrho$ is less than one for the steady-state situation.

(f) Probability of $n$ customers in the system:
$$P(n) = (1 - \varrho)\varrho^n.$$

(g) Average number in the queue when the queue is not empty:
$$\overline{q}(q \neq 0) = \frac{\mu}{\mu - \lambda}.$$

# 23 QUEUING THEORY

## 6.0 APPLICATION OF THE FORMULAE IN A SIMPLE EXAMPLE

### Example 1

Roger distributes manuals to students at an average rate of 20 per hour following a negative exponential distribution. Demand for the manuals follows a Poisson distribution with mean 15 per hour. Roger is asking for an assistant as he is concerned about the length of the queue waiting at the stock room door.

SOLUTION

Let us use the formulae in the previous section to analyse the queuing situation. The information obtained could form the basis of a report from which the decision to use an assistant could be made.

Now $\lambda$ = arrival rate = 15 per hour,
$\mu$ = service rate = 20 per hour.

Therefore:

Average number in system:

$$\overline{S} = \frac{\lambda}{\mu - \lambda} = \frac{15}{20 - 15} = 3 \text{ students.}$$

Average number in queue:

$$\overline{q} = \frac{\lambda^2}{\mu(\mu - \lambda)} = \frac{15^2}{20(20 - 15)} = 2.25 \text{ students.}$$

Average queuing time:

$$\overline{W} = \frac{\lambda}{\mu(\mu - \lambda)} = \frac{15}{20(20 - 15)} = 0.15 \text{ hours.}$$

$$= 9 \text{ minutes.}$$

Average time in system:

$$\overline{t} = \frac{1}{\mu - \lambda} = \frac{1}{20 - 15} = 0.2 \text{ hours}$$

$$= 12 \text{ minutes.}$$

Probability of no customers in the system:

$$P(0) = 1 - \frac{\lambda}{\mu} = 1 - \frac{15}{20} = 0.25.$$

Utilisation factor:

$$\varrho = \frac{\lambda}{\mu} = \frac{15}{20} = 0.75.$$

Probability of 2 customers in the system:

$$P(2) = (1 - \varrho)\,\varrho^n = (1 - 0.75)(0.75)^2$$
$$= \underline{\underline{0.1406}}.$$

Average number in queue when there is a queue:

$$\bar{q}\,(q \neq 0) = \frac{\mu}{\mu - \lambda} = \frac{20}{20 - 15} = 4 \text{ students.}$$

*Note: Average queuing time + Average service time = average time in system = 9 + 3 = 12 minutes.*

Average number in queue + 1 ≠ Average number in system.

i.e. $\qquad\qquad\qquad\qquad 2.25 + 1 \neq 3.$

This is because these are times when nobody is being serviced. In fact as the utilisation factor is 0.75 the average number being served is

$$0.75 \times 1 = 0.75.$$

Using 0.75 instead of 1 in the above equation would balance the equation.

Examining our results we see the average queue size is 2.25 students, but remember this is an average; the queue will, on occasions, be longer than this figure. Looking at the average times we see that the student will spend on average 12 minutes getting his manual, 9 of these minutes in à queue. This seems a bit excessive and would seem to justify an assistant. (In reality Roger is much faster and will not be getting an assistant.)

## 7.0 A MORE COMPLICATED PROBLEM

A company which operates its own fleet of ships to import a raw material is considering rebuilding the unloading berth. The following information is given about the present and new berth:

| Berth | Fixed cost per day* | Operating cost per day† | Capacity‡ |
|---|---|---|---|
| Present | £400 | £600 | 8,000 |
| New | 800 | 1,000 | 19,250 |

*The fixed costs include general maintenance and the amortisation of the original cost of the berth over the expected life (this approach has been used for simplicity).
†Operating costs are incurred only during the time intervals when the berth is in use.
‡Average tonnage unloaded per day of operation.

# 23 QUEUING THEORY

Ships to be unloaded each carry 8,000 tons of raw material, and analysis of past records shows that the number of arrivals per week approximately follows a Poisson distribution with a mean arrival rate of 4 ships per week. Unloading times are considered to be exponentially distributed. The time spent in the unloading system (queuing plus unloading time) is estimated to cost the company £800 per day.

Assuming a 7 day working week, estimate the average weekly cost of both the present and new berth systems. Do you advise the introduction of the new berth?

SOLUTION

Arrival rate $\lambda = 4$ ships per week.

$$\text{Service rate (present) } \mu_1 = \frac{7 \times 8,000}{8,000} = 7 \text{ ships a week.}$$

$$\therefore \text{ Utilisation factor } \varrho_1 = \frac{\lambda}{\mu_1} = \frac{4}{7} = 0.5714.$$

$$\text{Time in system } t_1 = \frac{1}{\mu_1 - \lambda} = \frac{1}{7 - 4} = 0.333 \text{ weeks.}$$

$$\text{Service rate (new) } \mu_2 = \frac{7 \times 19,250}{8,000} = 16.84 \text{ ships a week.}$$

$$\therefore \text{ Utilisation factor } \varrho_2 = \frac{\lambda}{\mu_2} = \frac{4}{16.84} = 0.2375.$$

$$\text{Time in system } \bar{t}_2 = \frac{1}{\mu_2 - \lambda} = \frac{1}{16.84 - 4} = 0.0779 \text{ weeks.}$$

Now

Total cost = Weekly fixed cost + Weekly operating costs + Weekly unloading costs

where:
Weekly fixed costs = 7 × Fixed cost per day,
Weekly operating costs = 7 × Daily operating costs × Utilisation factor,
Weekly unloading costs = 7 × Daily unloading costs × Average time in system
× Number of ships unloaded.

**Present system**
| | |
|---|---|
| Weekly fixed costs = 7 × 400 | = £2,800 |
| Weekly operating costs = 7 × 600 × 0.5714 | = 2,400 |
| Weekly unloading costs = 7 × 800 × 0.333 × 4 | = 7,459 |
| Total costs | = £12,659 |

**New system**

| | | |
|---|---|---|
| Weekly fixed costs = 7 × 800 | = | £5,600 |
| Weekly operating costs = 7 × 1,000 × 0.2375 | = | 1,662 |
| Weekly unloading costs = 7 × 800 × 0.0779 × 4 | = | 1,745 |
| Total costs | = | £9,007 |

Advise the introduction of the new berth as the estimated weekly costs of the new berth are less than those for the present berth.

## 8.0 MULTIPLE-SERVER QUEUE MODEL

In the $M/M/C/\infty$ system customers arrive randomly, the service time is negative exponential with $C$ servers, there is no constraint on queue size and the queue discipline is FIFO. The standard formulae are:

(a) Probability of no customers in the system:

$$P(0) = \frac{C!(1-\varrho)}{(\varrho C)^C + C!(1-\varrho)\left(\sum_{n=0}^{C-1} \frac{1}{n!}(\varrho C)^n\right)}$$

where $\varrho = \dfrac{\lambda}{c\mu}$.

(b) Average number in system

$$\overline{S} = \frac{\varrho(\varrho c)^c}{c!(1-\varrho)^2} P(0) + \varrho c.$$

(c) Average number in queue

$$\overline{q} = \overline{S} - \frac{\lambda}{\mu} \quad \text{(as in formulae sheet).}$$

(d) Average queuing time

$$\overline{W} = \frac{(\varrho c)^c}{c!(1-\varrho)^2 c\mu} P(0).$$

(e) Average time in system

$$\overline{t} = \overline{W} + \frac{1}{\mu} \quad \text{(as in formulae sheet).}$$

These formulae may look frightening but all that is needed is some elementary substitution followed by a series of multiplication and division.

It is generally best to calculate P(0) first as this expression occurs in all the other formulae.

# 23 QUEUING THEORY

## 9.0 MULTIPLE-SERVER QUEUE EXAMPLE

A main post office has three servers all of whom can handle all transactions with an average service time of 2 minutes. The customers arrive randomly at the rate of 72 per hour. There is a single queue for customers.

(a) Calculate the average number in the system and in the queue, the average queuing time and the average time in the system.
(b) What is the probability that all servers are idle?
(c) What proportion of time are the servers idle on average?

**SOLUTION**

(a) $c = 3$, $\mu = \dfrac{60}{2} = 30$ customers an hour, $\lambda = 72$ customers per hour.

Also $\varrho = \dfrac{\lambda}{c\mu} = \dfrac{72}{3 \times 30} = 0.80$.

Now, calculating P(0) first,

$$P(0) = \frac{3!(1-0.8)}{(0.8 \times 3)^3 + 3!(1-0.8) \times \sum_{n=0}^{2} \frac{1}{n!}(0.8 \times 3)^n}$$

$$= \frac{6 \times 0.2}{13.824 + 6 \times 0.2 \times (1 + 2.4 + \frac{1}{2}(2.4)^2)}$$

$$= \frac{1.2}{13.82 + 1.2 \times 6.28}$$

$$= \underline{\underline{0.05633}}.$$

Average number in system:

$$\bar{S} = \frac{0.8(0.8 \times 3)^3}{3!\,(1-0.8)^2} \times 0.05633 + 0.8 \times 3$$

$$= 2.596 + 2.4$$

$$= \underline{\underline{5.0}}.$$

∴ Average number in queue

$$\bar{q} = 5.0 - \frac{72}{30}$$

$$= \underline{\underline{2.6}}.$$

Average queuing time:

$$\overline{W} = \frac{(0.8 \times 3)^3}{3!(1-0.8)^2 \times 3 \times 30} \times 0.05633$$

$$= 0.03605 \text{ hours}$$

$$= \underline{\underline{2.16 \text{ minutes}}}.$$

∴ Average time in system

$$\overline{t} = 0.03605 + \frac{1}{30}$$

$$= 0.0694 \text{ hours}$$

$$= \underline{\underline{4.16 \text{ minutes}}}.$$

(b) The probability that all servers are idle is given by P(0), which we have already calculated as:

$$\underline{\underline{P(0) = 0.0563}}.$$

(c) As the utilisation of the servers = 0.8,

∴ the servers are idle for 1 − 0.8 = $\underline{\underline{0.2}}$ of the time.

# CHAPTER TWENTY-FOUR
# Simulation

## 1.0 INTRODUCTION

In previous chapters we looked at a number of different types of mathematical models. In the majority of cases we had to make simplifying assumptions in order to analyse the model mathematically. For example, in queuing theory we excluded situations where queue jumping could take place and we did not allow people to leave the queue once they were in the system. In inventory control we analysed only very simple demand patterns and totally ignored situations which are commonplace, where demand follows a seasonal pattern or is related to economic variables.

There is a need for a general problem-solving approach which is not restricted to an analytic and functional approach which can be made to more nearly represent a real-world situation. One such approach is simulation.

There is no clear definition of simulation, which is partly due to its strength that there are many variations of simulation, to match the many and varied areas of application. Perhaps we can say that simulation is a technique for developing a logical model of a system and using that logical model allows us to simulate experiments on that system.

We will be concerned primarily with what is called Monte Carlo simulation; this involves an element of uncertainty in the model where variables occur according to some probability distribution.

An important point that needs to be made is that as simulation involves experimentation, the results of the experimentation are sample results and hence our simulation model yields statistical estimates not optimal solutions. Consequently, when carrying out a simulation we must remember our statistical theory as the theory will be used in monitoring and controlling the simulation. It can give us some guidance in such vital questions as: How long should the simulation run? Are the results significantly different?

## 2.0 EXAMPLE

The best way to understand the technique of simulation is to carry out a simulation. Most of us at some time have carried out a simulation. For example, the game of Monopoly is essentially a simulation of the property market. Snakes and Ladders is a special simulation of a race.

Let us now consider a garage that (besides other work) hires out cars. It currently owns four cars. Cars are hired on a daily basis for a number of days. The demand pattern in the past has been as follows:

| Number of cars | 0 | 1 | 2 | 3 | 4 |
|---|---|---|---|---|---|
| Demand per day probability | 0.15 | 0.25 | 0.30 | 0.20 | 0.10 |

| Length of rental (days) | 1 | 2 | 3 |
|---|---|---|---|
| Probability | 0.6 | 0.3 | 0.1 |

The company charges £40 a day for hire. It estimates that the total fixed overheads attributed to this operation are £10 a day. If the car is hired out the extra repair and maintenance costs generated (including all extra administrative costs) are estimated at £6 a car a day. If the demand for hired cars exceeds the current number of four cars they then hire from another garage at additional cost of £24 a day.

Carry out a simulation to forecast the overall demand pattern for car hire and estimate the annual contribution to overheads and profits from the car hire business.

### SOLUTION

We need to simulate the arrival of customers and their demand for cars on a daily basis. This is an example of a time-based simulation as we will be advancing the time in the simulation at one-day intervals. It will be necessary to record for each day the number of cars available, the number of cars not rented, the number of cars rented and the number of cars rented from the other garage. This will then allow us to finally estimate the resulting contribution.

*Step 1* Simulate the customer arrivals. To do this we need to calculate the cumulative probability distribution and then allocate random numbers accordingly.

## 24 SIMULATION

| Daily demand | Probability | Cumulative probability | Random numbers |
|---|---|---|---|
| 0 | 0.15 | 0.15 | 01–15 |
| 1 | 0.25 | 0.40 | 16–40 |
| 2 | 0.30 | 0.70 | 41–70 |
| 3 | 0.20 | 0.90 | 71–80 |
| 4 | 0.10 | 1.00 | 81–00 |
|   | 1.00 |   |   |

The cumulative probabilities are calculated in the same way as we calculated cumulative frequencies previously in statistics.

As the cumulative probabilities have been calculated to *two* decimal places we use two-digit random numbers. As the cumulative probability for the zero demand is 0.15 we allocate the random numbers 01 to 15 to the zero-demand class. The cumulative probability for the 1-car demand is 0.40 so we allocate from the next random number after 15 up to the random number 40. This process is repeated until all the random numbers have been allocated.

To determine the simulated number of arrivals on any day we need to select a 2-digit random number either from a random number table or from a calculator or computer. If for example the random number selected was 48 then this lies in the range 41 to 70 associated with a car hire of 2. Hence the simulated number of cars hired on one day is two cars.

*Step 2* Simulate for each car hired the length of the rental period in days. As in step 1, we have to allocate random numbers to the probability distribution of the length of rental.

| Days | Probability | Cumulative probability | Random numbers |
|---|---|---|---|
| 1 | 0.6 | 0.60 | 01–60 |
| 2 | 0.3 | 0.90 | 61–90 |
| 3 | 0.1 | 1.00 | 91–00 |
|   | 1.00 |   |   |

To determine the length of hire for each car hired on day 1 in step 1, we need two new random numbers from a random number table. Assume these are 23 and 87. The random number 23 falls in the range 01–60, hence length of hire is 1 day. The random number 87 falls in the range 61–90, hence length of hire is 2 days.

*Step 3* Allocate the cars to the hirers. It is not necessary but it makes it easier to understand if we number the cars 1 to 4 and so on for cars hired from another garage.

The demand on day 1 was for 2 cars, car one on hire for 1 day, and car two on hire for 2 days (as determined in steps 1 and 2).

*Step 4* Move time on by one day to day 2.

*Step 5* Go back to step 1.

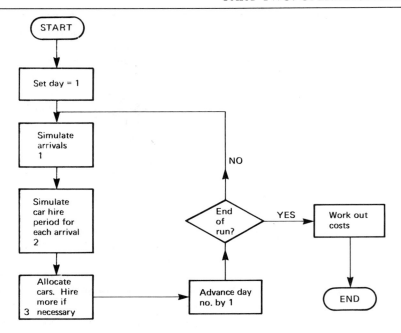

Fig. 96. *Simulation of car hire business.*

This procedure is then repeated until sufficient days have been simulated.

Let us carry out the simulation by hand for ten days to illustrate the approach, but first represent the steps in the process in the form of a flowchart (Fig. 96).

The results of the simulation are best set out in a table (Table 13).

Table 13. Results of car-hire simulation.

| Day | Demand (step 1) | Total demand | Hire car No. 1 2 3 4 | Other garage 5 6 7 8 |
|---|---|---|---|---|
| 1  | 2 | 2 | X̲ X 0 0 | |
| 2  | 3 | 4 | X X̲ X̲ X | |
| 3  | 1 | 3 | X̲ X 0 X | |
| 4  | 1 | 3 | X X̲ 0 X̲ | |
| 5  | 3 | 4 | X X X X | |
| 6  | 2 | 6 | X̲ X̲ X X | X X |
| 7  | 1 | 5 | X 0 X̲ X | X̲ X |
| 8  | 2 | 4 | X̲ X X̲ 0 | X |
| 9  | 3 | 4 | X X̲ X X | |
| 10 | 3 | 5 | X X X̲ X̲ | X̲ |
| 11 | | | X̲ X̲ | |

# 24 SIMULATION

Note the following points:

(a) The random numbers have not been included, so as to simplify the table; however all arrivals and length of hire have been determined using random numbers as in steps 1 and 2.

(b) A car hire is indicated in the table by an X. The end of the hire is indicated by underlining the X, e.g. car 2 was on hire for 2 days before the hire was terminated.

(c) A car not hired is indicated by an 0 as in day 1 when cars 3 and 4 were not hired.

(d) The cars in use each day (total demand) consist of the cars demanded on the day (as in step 1) plus the cars still out on hire from previous days.

(e) On day 6 six cars are out on hire, four from the previous days (cars 1 to 4) and the two new hires (cars 5 and 6) from another garage.

On day 7 only one extra car is demanded and this is allocated car 1, however, we cannot reallocate car 2 to hirings started the previous day so we are paying for external hire even though we have a free car.

This is what would happen in practice as cars are not returned until the end of the hire period. It is important that we model reality rather than twist the model around to the most suitable form.

Obviously a simulation of ten days is insufficient to come to any conclusion (the sample size should be at least 100 days). However, for illustration purposes we will continue and calculate the costs and revenues incurred during the *ten* days. (Ignore overflow into day 11.)

*Revenue*
Car hire 40 × £40        =        £1,600

*Costs*
Fixed overheads  10 × £10    =    £100
Repair costs etc. 34 × £6    =    £204
Garage hire cost  6 × £24    =    £144
                                  £448
                                £1,152

—an average daily contribution of £115.2.

Although it was said earlier that simulation does not provide "optimal solutions" it would be possible to investigate in this example the effect on contributions of increasing or decreasing the car hire fleet.

For example if we had five cars rather than 4 using the same simulation results (compare like with like) we get the following contribution:

*Revenue*
Car hire 40 × £40      =                £1,600

*Costs*
Fixed overheads 10 × £10    =    £100
Repair etc. cost  37 × £6    =    £222
Garage hire cost   3 × £24   =    £ 72
                                          £394
                                        ──────
                                         £1,206
                                        ══════

—an average daily contribution of £120.6.

This is greater than with a fleet of 4 cars. The question however that remains is whether £120.6 is significantly greater than £115.2; obviously on a sample of size 10 it is not worth making a judgement. However had the sample been much larger we could have used standard statistical techniques to determine the answer and hence moved towards an optimum fleet size.

## 3.0 SIMULATION AND THE COMPUTER

It has been said repeatedly in the last example that 10 days is insufficient time to make any judgement or to obtain good estimates of the profitability of the car hire business. In fact we suggested that 100 days of simulation would be more appropriate. However, doing the simulation, as we say, "by hand" over just 10 days took some time, yet the simulation was a relatively simple one compared with practical simulation problems.

Simulation is a technique designed for use with the computer; it is quite often called computer simulation. This means we can simulate for 100 days or even 1,000 days without using up a lot of computer time. This is why we need to structure the simulation in a series of repetitive steps which means that the computer program is written with a series of loops or subroutines.

In general, when designing a simulation some of it may be done by a hand simulation, as we did for the car hire problem, to test the model and to understand how it works. However, the full simulation would be done on a computer, and this should be borne in mind when designing a simulation as it influences the approach which is adopted.

## 4.0 EVENT-SEQUENCING SIMULATION

In the last example we moved through the simulation by advancing time by one day at a time. This approach is known as time-based simulation (or time slicing). In a number of applications, when events do not occur at regular intervals, it is not an appropriate approach to use; instead we use an event-sequencing approach. In this approach we move through the simulation by advancing time to the time of the next event, whether it is seconds or hours away in simulated time. To do this it is necessary to keep an "event" calendar, which contains a list in chronological order of the events that are going to occur, so that we always know the time of the next event.

# 24 SIMULATION

## 5.0 EXAMPLE

Let us consider a simple queuing problem.

People arrive at a shop with interarrival times given by the distribution in the first table below. They are served by one assistant (FIFO queue discipline) and the length of service is given by the distribution of the second table. When they are served they leave the shop immediately.

| Interarrival time (minutes) | 0 | 1 | 2 | 3 | 4 |
|---|---|---|---|---|---|
| Probability | 0.1 | 0.1 | 0.2 | 0.4 | 0.2 |

| Service time (minutes) | 1 | 2 | 3 |
|---|---|---|---|
| Probability | 0.7 | 0.2 | 0.1 |

The problem can be represented by a queue flowchart as in Fig. 97.

Let us assume that we want to measure:

(a) the average time in the system;

(b) the idle time of the assistant as a proportion of the total time.

The simulation is to be carried out for a simulated time of 8 hours.

The simulation can be represented by the simplified program flowchart shown 6.0

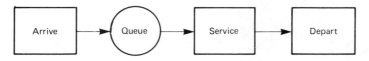

Fig. 97. *Queue flowchart.*

## 6.0 PROGRAM FLOWCHART
See Fig. 98.

## 7.0 EXPLANATION OF FLOWCHART AND SIMULATION

*Step 1* We start with initialising the variables, which is always required in any simulation program. The systems clock, the total idle item, the total time in the system, the number of customers in the queue and the service indicator are all set to zero.

244                                                    PART TWO: OPERATIONAL RESEARCH

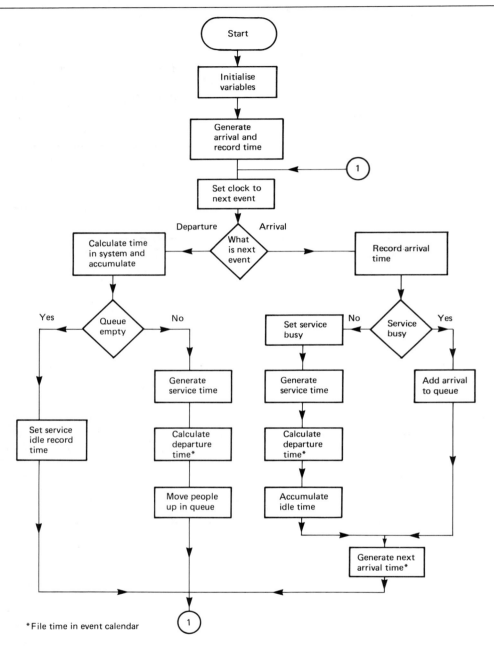

Fig. 98. *Program flowchart for simulation of shop queuing problem.*

*Step 2* Generate first customer arrival—using random number and a cumulative form of the interarrival time probability table (as we did in the car hire problem), generate an interarrival time: e.g. 2-digit random number = 46, interarrival time would be 3 minutes. Hence the first arrival would occur at 3 minutes after the start. (This is the first event on the event calendar.)

*Step 3* Set clock to next event—system clock currently at $T = 0$ goes to $T = 3$, the next event time on the event calender.

*Step 4* What is the next event? In our case it is an arrival (the arrival of the first customer at $T = 3$). We therefore move down the arrival section of the flowchart, first recording the arrival time. This will allow us later to calculate the total time in the system for customer 1.

*Step 5* Check if service is busy—if it is the customer would be added to the queue. In our case the service is idle, so set the service to busy, make the service indicator 1 instead of 0 and generate the service time using random numbers and the cumulative form of the service time probability table B, e.g. 2-digit random number 84, giving a service time of 2 minutes. Departure time is $3 + 2 = 5$. This departure event at time 5 is added to the event calendar at the correct time. Calculate service idle time; in our example this would be 3 minutes.

*Step 6* Generate next interarrival time as we did in step 2. If this is for example 4 minutes, the next arrival event will take place at $3 + 4 = 7$ minutes. This arrival event at time 7 is added to the event calendar at the correct time.

*Step 7* Go back to step 3, set clock to next event and hence continue with the simulation.

*Step 8* Later in the simulation at step 4 we are bound to come to a departure (left-hand side of flowchart). If the queue is empty we set the service indicator to zero and record the start of the idle time. (This will later allow us to calculate the amount of time the server has been idle.) If the queue is not empty we select the first one in the queue (FIFO) and generate the service time and calculate the departure time as we did in step 5. Again this departure time goes to the event calendar.

*Step 9* Go back to step 3—set the clock to next event.

Hence the simulation is continued.

To stop the simulation we need to amend our program flowchart such that after the system clock is reset to the next event (step 3) we test if the time $T$ has reached 480 (i.e. 8 hours from the start). If it has, then simulation stops and jumps to a calculation section.

The calculation section would calculate:

(a) The average time in the system. This would be done by dividing the accumulated time in the system by the number of departures.

(b) The idle time as a proportion of total time. This would be calculated as accumulated idle time divided by total time $T ( = 480)$.

In addition it would be possible to get the computer to print out various graphs such as:

(c) Cumulative idle time against simulated time

(d) Number in queue against simulated time

(e) Number in system against simulated time

(f) Service indicator against simulated time

(g) Arrivals and departures against simulated time.

## 8.0 STARTING EVENTS AND FINISHING EVENTS

In any simulation there may be problems with dealing with the starting and finishing events. For example, in the car hire problem we ignored car hires after day 10 yet they had been booked during the 10-day period. We also assumed on day 1 that there were no outstanding hires from the previous day, yet in all other days there were orders from the previous day.

There cannot be a clear unambiguous rule to deal with all possibilities but what should be borne in mind is that we are building a model to represent reality. Therefore the way we deal with these problems should lead to a situation which is likely to occur in reality. For example, if we are modelling an existing car hire firm it will have orders from previous days. Then start the simulation from the zero demand position as we did in the example and when the system has reached a steady state, say 5 days, note how many orders are to be carried over to day 6 and then record the real simulation from this point, i.e. day 6 now becomes day 1.

## 9.0 SIMULATION LANGUAGE

It is perfectly feasible to write simulation programs in languages such as BASIC or FORTRAN; however, it is easier if a special simulation language is used, such as SIMSCRIPT or GPSS.

These simulation languages contain special structures which make generating arrivals and service times from a distribution much easier to handle. Maintaining an event calendar in correct sequence is slightly difficult using BASIC or FORTRAN but is extremely easy in SIMSCRIPT or GPSS. Basically, simulation languages save time and hence money, and reduce the need for the user to have extensive programming and modelling experience. There are particular simulation packages that deal only with certain areas of application, e.g. inventory control or networks.

## 10.0 SUMMARY

Simulation is a powerful and important problem-solving tool in its own right, and is not a last resort for the feeble minded. The development of computer power and better software will increase the range of applications and the complexities that simulation will be able to deal with. Currently, most computerised stock control systems are in fact simulation models.

After reading this chapter, you should understand what simulation is about and how to build simple simulation models. You should know the difference between a time-based and an event-based simulation.

# APPENDIX 1
# Index to Examination Questions and Suggested Answers

| Question numbers | | Questions (pages) | Answers (pages) |
|---|---|---|---|
| | *Statistics* | | |
| 1–2 | Calculation of mean and standard deviation | 248–9 | 331–3 |
| 3–9 | Probability and expected value | 249–54 | 333–41 |
| 10–14 | Probability distributions | 254–6 | 341–51 |
| 15–19 | Large-sample theory | 256–8 | 351–7 |
| 20–22 | Small-sample theory | 258–9 | 357–60 |
| 23–27 | Chi-squared distribution | 259–61 | 360–6 |
| 28–32 | Regression and correlation | 261–4 | 366–74 |
| 33–35 | Exponential and logarithmic functions learning curve | 264–6 | 374–7 |
| 36–39 | Variances, covariances and $r$ | 266–8 | 377–86 |
| | *Operational Research* | | |
| 40–46 | Introduction to OR | 268–9 | 387–401 |
| 47–54 | Linear programming–model construction | 269–76 | 402–11 |
| 55–62 | –graphical method | 276–81 | 411–32 |
| 63–69 | –simplex solution and dual values | 281–9 | 432–46 |
| 70–75 | Transportation | 289–94 | 446–63 |
| 76–79 | Assignments | 294–6 | 463–8 |
| 80–81 | An introduction to network analysis | 296–7 | 468–70 |
| 82–90 | Network analysis–time and cost | 297–306 | 470–83 |
| 91–99 | –resource analysis and uncertainty | 306–13 | 483–95 |
| 100–113 | Inventory control | 313–21 | 495–516 |
| 114–122 | Queuing theory | 322–5 | 516–28 |
| 123–129 | Simulation | 325–30 | 528–42 |

# APPENDIX 2
# Examination Questions

## Acknowledgment

This Appendix includes questions from recent examinations of the:

> Association of Certified Accountants
> Institute of Chartered Accountants in England & Wales
> Institute of Cost and Management Accountants.

Permission to use these questions is gratefully acknowledged.

## STATISTICS

### Calculation of mean and standard deviation

**1.** A random sample of 80 people who owned a television set were asked to keep a record of the time they spend watching for a period of one week, with the results tabulated below. It is desired to compare these results with those obtained in another area, so determine the mean, the standard deviation and the variance of the data.

| Viewing time (hours) | No. of people |
|---|---|
| 0–4 | 5 |
| 4–8 | 25 |
| 8–12 | 30 |
| 12–16 | 11 |
| 16–20 | 4 |
| 20–24 | 2 |
| 24 or more | 3 |

# APPENDIX 2. EXAMINATION QUESTIONS

2. The table below shows a frequency distribution of the lifetimes of 500 transistors.

| Lifetime (hours) | Number of transistors |
|---|---|
| 400 and less than 500 | 10 |
| 500 and less than 600 | 16 |
| 600 and less than 700 | 38 |
| 700 and less than 800 | 56 |
| 800 and less than 900 | 63 |
| 900 and less than 1,000 | 67 |
| 1,000 and less than 1,100 | 92 |
| 1,100 and less than 1,200 | 68 |
| 1,200 and less than 1,300 | 57 |
| 1,300 and less than 1,400 | 33 |
| | 500 |

*Required:*

(a) Calculate the mean, variance and standard deviation.
(b) What percentage of transistors falls outside the range

$$\bar{x} - \sigma \text{ to } \bar{x} + \sigma?$$

## Probability and expected value

3. A woven cloth is liable to contain faults and is subjected to an inspection procedure. Any fault has a probability of 0.7 that it will be detected by the procedure, independent of whether any other fault is detected or not.

*Required:*

(a) If a piece of cloth contains three faults, A, B and C:

   (i) calculate the probability that A and C are detected, but that B is undetected;

   (ii) calculate the probability that any two of A, B and C will be detected, the other fault being undetected;

   (iii) state the relationship between your answers to parts (i) and (ii) and give the reason for this.

(b) Suppose now that, in addition to the inspection procedure given above, there is a secondary check which has the probability of 0.6 of detecting each fault missed by the first inspection procedure. This probability of 0.6 applies independently to each and every fault undetected by the first procedure.

   (i) calculate the probability that a piece of cloth with one fault has this fault undetected by both the inspection procedure and the secondary check;

(ii) calculate the probability that a piece of cloth with two faults has one of these faults detected by either the inspection procedure or the secondary check, and one fault undetected by both;

(iii) of the faults detected, what proportion are detected by the inspection procedure and what proportion by the secondary check?  *ACCA*

**4.** (a) An item produced by a company is susceptible to two types of defect, A and B. The probability that an item has defect A is 1/6. The probability that it has defect B is 1/8, independent of whether it has defect A.

*Required:*

(i) Calculate the probability that an item has:

(1) both A and B defects

(2) one defect only, A or B

(3) no defect.

(ii) What simple relationship is there between your answers to part (i)?

(b) Suppose now, in addition to the above defects, the item is susceptible to a third type of defect, C. The probability that an item contains C depends on whether it has the other defects. If it has neither A nor B then there is a probability of 1/10 that it has C. If if has one of A or B the probability of having C is 2/10 and if it has both A and B the probability of having C is 3/10.

*Required:*

(i) Show that the probability that an item has

(1) none of the three defects is $\dfrac{315}{480}$;

(2) one of the three defects is $\dfrac{131}{480}$.

(ii) If items with 1 defect can be repaired at a cost of £10 but those with 2 or more defects are scrapped at a cost of £30, determine the total cost of repair and scrapping associated with the production of 480 items.  *ACCA*

**5.** An item is made in three stages. At the first stage it is formed on one of four machines, A, B, C and D, with equal probability. At the second stage it is trimmed on one of three machines E, F and G, with equal probability. Finally it is polished on one of two polishers, H and I, and is twice as likely to be polished on the former, as this machine works twice as quickly as the other.

*Required:*

(a) What is the probability that an item is:

(i) Polished on H?

(ii) Trimmed on either F or G?

(iii) Formed on either A or B, trimmed on F and polished on H?

(iv) Either formed on A and polished on I or formed on B and polished on H?

(v) Either formed on A or trimmed on F?

(b) Suppose that items trimmed on E and F are susceptible to a particular defect. The defect rates on these machines are 10 per cent and 20 per cent respectively. What is the probability that an item found to have this defect was trimmed on F?

*ACCA*

**6.** A company employs three warehousemen, A, B and C, who select items from the warehouse to make up orders for subsequent checking and packaging. A makes a mistake in an order (gets a wrong item or the wrong quantity) one time in a hundred, B makes a mistake in an order five times in a hundred, and C makes a mistake in an order three times in a hundred. Of all the orders delivered for verification A, B and C fill respectively, 30, 40 and 30 per cent.

*Required:*

(a) What are the probabilities if an order is taken at random, that:

   (i) A selected the order and made a mistake

   (ii) a mistake was made.

(b) If a mistake is discovered in the order what is the probability it was made by A?

(c) A takes on a young assistant X who deals with a quarter of A's orders. It is found that the overall error rate is 3.87 per cent. Determine the error rate of X.

**7.** The local football club has asked for your advice on the number of programmes that should be printed for each game. The cost of printing and production of programmes for each game, as quoted by the local printer, is £1,000 plus 4 pence per copy. Advertising revenue which has been agreed for the season represents £800 for each game.

Programmes are sold for 15 pence each. A review of sales during the previous seasons indicates that the following pattern is expected to be repeated during the coming season of 50 games:

| *Number of programmes sold* | *Number of games* |
|---|---|
| 10,000 | 5 |
| 20,000 | 20 |
| 30,000 | 15 |
| 40,000 | 10 |
|  | 50 |

Programmes not sold at the game are sold as waste paper to a paper manufacturer at 1 penny per copy.

Assuming that the four quantities listed are the only possibilities you are required to:

(a) Prepare a payoff table;

(b) determine the number of programmes that would provide the largest profit, if a constant number of programmes were to be printed for each game;

(c) explain why you should buy 30,000 or 40,000 copies assuming one of these is the most profitable quantity, despite the fact that the most probable sales are 20,000 copies per game;

(d) calculate the profit which would arise from a perfect forecast of the numbers of programmes which would be sold at each game.
*ICMA*

**8.** A manufacturer of electrical components for the motor vehicle industry is faced with the problem of building a new plant for the manufacture of electronic components for vehicles. Estimates of the size of the new plant to be built have been made and two sizes selected based on forecasts of future new vehicle demands. A large plant is estimated to cost £3 million and a small plant £1.4 million. The net cash inflows per annum of each size of plant according to the demand are:

| Size of plant | Demand | |
| --- | --- | --- |
| | High (£000) | Low (£000) |
| Large | 1,200 | 300 |
| Small | 500 | 400 |

Based on a manufacturing plant life of six years, the following possible outcomes are assessed:

(a) Demand will be high for the first two years and will then fall to a low level. A probability of 20 per cent is given to this outcome.

(b) Demand will be high for the first two years and will remain at a high level for the final four years. A 40 per cent probability is assigned to this event.

(c) Demand will be low for the next two years and will remain low for the final four years. This outcome is given a 15 per cent probability.

(d) Demand will be low for the next two years, but will then recover to a high level for the final four years. This is given a 25 per cent probability of occurring.

The relevant capital costs and net cash inflows, at present values, are given in Table 14 for the two alternative plant sizes at the high and low demand levels referred to above.

APPENDIX 2. EXAMINATION QUESTIONS

Table 14. Data for new plant decision.

| Size of plant | Demand | Net cash inflow at present values | |
|---|---|---|---|
| | | Years 1 and 2 (£000) | Years 3 to 6 (£000) |
| Large | High | 2,088 | 3,132 |
| | Low | 522 | 783 |
| Small | High | 870 | 1,305 |
| | Low | 696 | 1,044 |

The net present values above have been calculated, for the two periods covered by the predictions, at the rate of 10 per cent per annum which is the expected cost of capital.

*Required:*

(a) Draw the decision tree diagram for the above information showing the probabilities assigned to each separate branch.

(b) Evaluate the decision tree and advise management which plant, if either, should be built. Your critieria should be to maximise the net present value of the project.
*ICMA*

9. Costman Limited is considering the introduction of a new product to its existing product range. It has defined two levels of sales as "high" and "low" on which to base its decision and has estimated the changes at which each market level will occur, together with their costs and consequential profits or losses. This information is summarised below:

| | | Action | |
|---|---|---|---|
| Event | Probability | Market product (£000) | Do not market product (£000) |
| Sales "high" | 0.3 | 150 net profit | 0 |
| Sales "low" | 0.7 | (40) net loss | 0 |

The company's marketing manager suggests a market research survey be undertaken to provide further information on which to base a decision. On past experience with a certain market research organisation, the marketing manager assesses its ability to give good information in the light of subsequent actual sales achievement as follows:

| Market research<br>Survey outcome | Actual | |
|---|---|---|
| | Market "high" | Market "low" |
| "High" sales forecast | 0.5 | 0.1 |
| Indecisive survey report | 0.3 | 0.4 |
| "Low" sales forecast | 0.2 | 0.5 |

*Required:*

(a) Given that to undertake the market research survey will cost £20,000, state whether or not there is a case for employing the market research organisation.
(b) Construct a decision tree for the problem with the alternatives of undertaking or not undertaking the survey and to advise the company on its best course of action.

*ICMA*

## Probability distributions

**10.** In my district 40 per cent of drivers wear seatbelts. Going to work I pass 50 drivers.

*Required:*

Find the probability that:

(a) exactly three out of the first five drivers are wearing belts;

(b) the fifth driver is the third to be wearing a belt;

(c) fewer than 17 of the 50 drivers are wearing seatbelts (approximate probability). (You may assume that the binomial distribution may be approximated by a normal distribution with

$$\mu = np \text{ and } \sigma^2 = npq.)$$

After a safety campaign it is hoped that more drivers in the district are wearing seatbelts. A random sample of 500 drivers reveals 220 wearing belts. Does this sample indicate that the campaign has had any success?

*Note: Come back to (c) after you have covered the sampling distribution of a proportion in Chapter 8.*

**11.** A tyre company tested 100 of their "Tearaway" radial steel tyres on four-wheel-drive cars in harsh conditions in Australia. They found that 9 of the tyres had a safe life of under 30,000 km, whereas 20 were still safe after 50,000 km. Assuming that it is reasonable to model the safe life of the tyres by a normal probability function, estimate the standard deviation and show the mean safe life is about 42,300 km.

A four-wheel-drive vehicle is fitted with four new "Tearaway" tyres and is to be driven under similar harsh conditions.

*Required:*

Find the probabilities:

(a) that the first tyre change will not be needed until after 35,000 km;

(b) that by the time 40,000 km have been run, exactly two of the original tyres will have needed replacement.

12. The Vulcan Van Rental Company Limited has four Type C vans which are available for hire on a daily basis at a rate of £35 per day. Experience has shown that the daily demand for vans of this type has a Poisson distribution with a mean of 2. Vulcan have also estimated that the total cost of providing each van amounts to £3,250 per year (which consists of 300 working days).

*Required:*

(a) What is the probability that, on any one day, all four vans will be out on hire?

(b) What proportion of the total demand for Type C van will be unsatisfied because all four vans have already been hired by other customers.

(c) As a result of reviewing the profitability of the business, the general manager has suggested that it might be more economical to reduce the number of Type C vans for hire. Assuming that the demand pattern does not change, what would be your advice in this regard?

13. The life of a television (TV) tube, measured in hours of use, is approximately normally distributed with a mean of 5,000 hours and a standard deviation of 1,000 hours.

*Required:*

(a) Calculate the probability that a TV tube will last for:

   (i) between 5,500 and 6,500 hours

   (ii) less than the expected life of a tube.

(b) Calculate the probability that, for someone using a TV for 1,500 hours per year the tube will last for less than five years.

(c) Suppose that the company offers a guarantee to customers, at an additional charge of £25. Under the guarantee, the TV tube will be replaced free of charge if it fails within three years of purchase and will be replaced at a cost of £40 to the customer if it fails between the end of the third year and the end of the fifth year. The cost of the tube to the company is £80.

   Assuming that a TV is used for 1,500 hours per year, calculate the expected cost to the company through offering a guarantee on a tube.

14. Manufactured items are sold in boxes which are stated to contain a weight of at least 40 ounces. The actual weight in a box varies, being approximately normally distributed with mean 41.2 ounces and standard deviation 0.8 ounces.

*Required:*

(a) Calculate the proportion of boxes whose weight is between 40 ounces and 42 ounces.

(b) Calculate the weight below which 20 per cent of boxes fall.

(c) All boxes containing less than 40 ounces are scrapped at a cost of £1 per box. Calculate the scrapping cost associated with the sale of 100 boxes.

(d) To what mean weight should the box contents be adjusted, the standard deviation remaining unchanged, if only 1 per cent of boxes are to be scrapped?

## Large-sample theory

**15.** An automatic production machine has been set up to produce aluminium rods with a length of 40 cm. The expected standard deviation is 0.20 cm and weekly output is 100,000 rods.

To check the performance of the machine, each day a random sample of 100 rods is taken. These are measured and the following data show the results for the last three days:

| Day | Sample mean ($\bar{x}$) | Sample standard deviation ($s$) |
|---|---|---|
| 1 | 39.6 | 0.19 |
| 2 | 41.5 | 0.50 |

*Required:*

(a) Explain whether or not the sample standard deviation $s$ is a sound estimate of the standard deviation of the population $\sigma$.

(b) Calculate and state the standard error of the mean for the day 1 sample.

(c) Calculate and state the 95 per cent confidence interval for the population mean based on the day 1 sample.

(d) Test and state whether or not there is a statistically significant difference between the sample means for day 1 and day 2 at the 5 per cent level of significance.

(e) State, with explanation, the level at which the difference between the sample means for day 1 and day 2 is statistically significant. *ICMA*

**16.** (a) Explain fully the meaning of the standard error of a proportion $P$, given by the formula

$$\sqrt{\frac{P(1-P)}{n}}.$$

(b) (i) Calculate the probability that, if 30 per cent of items in a batch are defective, a random sample of 100 items will contain 40 per cent or more defectives.

(ii) It is claimed that a process produces not more than 30 per cent defective. A random sample of 100 items from the process was found to contain 42 defectives. Investigate the validity of the claim.  *ACCA*

**17.** A company manufactures lengths of rope whose breaking strength varies with a mean of 3,000 lb and a standard deviation of 180 lb. It is thought that a newly developed process may change the mean breaking strength.

*Required:*

(a) It is decided to test $H_0 : \mu = 3,000$ against $H_1 : \mu \neq 3,000$ by taking a sample of 36 lengths of rope and calculating their breaking strengths. Determine the decision rule to be used if the aim is to reject $H_0$ at the 0.01 level of significance. The rule is to be "reject $H_0$ if ……, accept $H_0$ if ……".

(b) Using your decision rule obtained in (a), what conclusions would you draw if the mean breaking strength of these 36 lengths were 2,940 lb?

(c) Calculate the two critical values for the mean breaking strength of the 36 lengths, outside which $H_0$ would be rejected at the 0.01 level of significance.  *ACCA*

**18.** In order to measure a certain characteristic in a population it is decided to operate a stratified sampling scheme with two strata to be sampled, A and B. The total population within A is 4,000 and within B is 12,000 and a sample is constructed by taking 1/25 of the population of A and 1/100 of the population of B.

*Required:*

(a) 22 per cent of those sampled from A and 31 per cent of those sampled from B are found to have the characteristic. Estimate the percentage in the total population having the characteristic.

(b) Calculate 95 per cent confidence limits for the true percentage in A having the characteristic for which 22 per cent is the estimated percentage based on the sample results.

(c) Determine whether there is a significant difference between the proportions found in A and B having the characteristic.  *ACCA*

**19.** The analysis of sales for two sales managers for 1981 based on random samples from their respective areas was as given in Table 15.

*Required:*

(a) Do the average annual sales per customer differ significantly?

(b) Obtain the 95 per cent confidence limits for the two averages.

(c) What size of sample would need to be taken to estimate the average annual sales per customer in the Midland region to within £10 at the 5 per cent level?

Table 15. Analysis of sales.

| Annual sales by customer turnover | Number of customers | |
|---|---|---|
| | Midland | South-west |
| $x$ | $f$ | $f$ |
| < £10 | 1 | 1 |
| £10 and < £20 | 10 | 1 |
| £20 and < £30 | 12 | 8 |
| £30 and < £40 | 10 | 12 |
| £40 and < £50 | 6 | 17 |
| £50 and < £60 | 8 | 16 |
| £60 and < £80 | 12 | 32 |
| £80 and < £100 | 11 | 9 |
| £100 and < £300 | 30 | 2 |
| | 100 | 100 |
| Also $\sum fx$ | 9,330 | 5,770 |
| $\sum fx^2$ | 1,404,950 | 411,250 |

## Small-Sample Theory

**20.** In order to test the effectiveness of a drying agent in paint the following experiment was carried out. Each of six samples of material was cut into two halves. One half of each was covered with paint containing the agent and the other half with paint without the agent. Then all twelve halves were left to dry. The time to dry was as follows:

| | Drying time (hours) | | | | | |
|---|---|---|---|---|---|---|
| Sample number | 1 | 2 | 3 | 4 | 5 | 6 |
| Paint with agent | 3.4 | 3.8 | 4.2 | 4.1 | 3.5 | 4.7 |
| Paint without agent | 3.6 | 3.8 | 4.3 | 4.3 | 3.6 | 4.7 |

*Required:*

Carry out a $t$-test to determine whether the drying agent is effective, giving your reasons for choosing a one-tailed test. Carefully explain your conclusions.

*ACCA*

**21.** A company buys five components from a supplier who states that the expected life of a component is 1,050 hours. The five components last for 964, 1,082, 1,136, 825 and 863 hours and the company is not satisfied with the results. Before a complaint is sent to the supplier you are asked to analyse the results and give advice.

*Required:*

(a) What should be the purpose of your analysis?

(b) Carry out the appropriate analysis and say whether you should support the complaint or not.

(c) What is the minimum average life of five components which you consider to be compatible with the supplier's claim?  *ACCA*

**22.** A company selling washing machines finds that its established salesmen achieve average sales of 5.5 machines a week. Any new salesman is given a trial for 5 weeks and is not taken on permanently unless he sells an average of at least 4.8 machines a week. A new salesman sells 5, 3, 4, 6 and 5 and fails the trial. He claims that the system is unfair and that he can perform in the long run as well as the established salesman, and yet fail the trial badly.

*Required:*

(a) Carry out appropriate calculations and comment on his claim.

(b) Calculate the minimum average weekly sales that should be required on a 5-week trial if a new salesman is to be rejected only if his performance is slightly different from 5.5.  *ACCA*

## Chi-squared distribution

**23.** A garage sells three types of new car, the Tuxan, Firedash and Velotta. The following data show, for each type of car sold, the number requiring repair during the first 12 months.

|  | Number of cars sold | | |
|---|---|---|---|
|  | Requiring repair | Not requiring repair | Total |
| Tuxan | 89 | 11 | 100 |
| Firedash | 57 | 13 | 70 |
| Velotta | 118 | 12 | 130 |

*Required:*

(a) State the main feature indicated by these data.

(b) Set up an appropriate null hypothesis and test it.

(c) Explain your conclusions to the garage management.  *ACCA*

**24.** The fact that the use of an experimental drug cured 10 out of the 20 patients treated with it, a cure rate of 50 per cent compared with the cure rate of 40 per cent for the long established standard drug, cannot be considered to be statistically significant.

*Required:*

(a) Explain fully the meaning of the above statement and verify using the chi-squared test.

(b) By trying different values, calculate the minimum number of patients that would have to be cured out of the 20 treated with the experimental drug to give a significant value for $\chi^2$ at the 0.05 level.

(c) Calculate the 95 per cent confidence limits for the percentage cure rate of the experimental drug and explain the meaning of your answer. *ACCA*

**25.** A car manufacturer who produces four different models, Popular, Standard, Super and Sports, is about to raise his prices. The present and proposed prices for each model, together with the current sales of cars of each model expressed as a percentage of the total sales, are as given in Table 16.

Table 16. Car prices and sales.

|  | *Popular* | *Standard* | *Super* | *Sports* |
|---|---|---|---|---|
| Present prices (£) | 2,500 | 2,750 | 3,500 | 4,000 |
| Proposed prices (£) | 2,750 | 3,050 | 4,000 | 4,600 |
| Percentage of sales | 18 | 40 | 26 | 16 |

*Required:*

(a) Suggest three ways in which an "average" percentage price increase of its range of cars might be calculated and calculate it for each of your suggestions.

(b) Suppose that immediately after the price increase the sales of the next 200 cars are as follows:

| *Popular* | *Standard* | *Super* | *Sports* |
|---|---|---|---|
| 33 | 107 | 40 | 20 |

Determine from these figures whether there has been a statistically significant change in the distribution of sales of the company's models, compared with those under the old prices. *ACCA*

**26.** An investigation is being carried out into delays in the payment of invoices by customers of your company. Details of the present position are given in Table 17. The figures in the table represent the number of customers.

*Required:*

Prepare a statistical analysis to determine whether there is a relationship between the class of company and its status as a payer. (Test at the 5 per cent level.) *ICMA*

Table 17. Delay in invoice payments.

|  | Private limited companies | | Public limited companies |
| --- | --- | --- | --- |
| Status as a payer | Capitalised at > £1 m. | Capitalised at < £1 m. | |
| Very slow | 20 | 10 | 10 |
| Slow | 16 | 14 | 12 |
| Average | 22 | 12 | 10 |
| Prompt | 8 | 8 | 8 |

**27.** A department store has calculated that 20 per cent of telephone calls received during a day are complaints. For 100 days a random sample of 5 calls are taken and the number of these that are complaints noted giving the following results:

| Number of complaints per day | 0 | 1 | 2 | 3 | 4 | 5 |
| --- | --- | --- | --- | --- | --- | --- |
| Number of days | 36 | 36 | 17 | 9 | 2 | 0 |

*Required:*

Fit a binomial distribution and test to see whether the calculated 20 per cent is correct at the 5 per cent level of significance.

## Regression and Correlation

**28.** A geographical region is divided into areas within which engineers travel to repair machines. The data in Table 18 show for each 9 areas the size of the area, number of engineers allocated to the area, and the mean travel time from one repair job to the next.

Table 18. Areas, engineers and travel time.

| Size of area (square miles) | Number of engineers | Mean travel time (minutes) |
| --- | --- | --- |
| 900 | 3 | 36.2 |
| 1,200 | 3 | 39.5 |
| 500 | 1 | 45.1 |
| 500 | 2 | 32.2 |
| 1,500 | 5 | 31.0 |
| 800 | 4 | 28.0 |
| 1,800 | 3 | 45.5 |
| 1,000 | 3 | 32.1 |

The mean travel time, $t$ minutes, between repairs in an area of size $b$ square miles is related to the number of engineers allocated, $n$, by the approximate equation:

$$t = k\sqrt{\frac{b}{n}} \text{ where } k \text{ is constant.}$$

*Required:*

(a) Plot values of $t$ against

$$\sqrt{\frac{b}{n}}$$

on a graph; comment on the adequacy of the above relationship.

(b) Using your $x$-value

$$\sqrt{\frac{b}{n}}$$

calculate a regression line for $t$ against $x$. Comment on your "$a$" value.

(c) Estimate how many engineers would be required in an area of 2,000 square miles to give a mean travel time per repair job of 30 minutes.

(d) A machine repair takes a mean time of 30 minutes in addition to travel time. 40 repairs must be carried out in an area of 2,000 square miles. Determine whether 5 engineers could be expected to do the work in 8 hours, assuming they work continuously.

**29.** The data in Table 19 were collected from the Industrial Products Manufacturing Company Limited.

Table 19. Overheads and hours over six months.

| Month | Total overhead $y$ | Direct labour hours (DLH) $x$ | Plant hours (PH) |
|---|---|---|---|
| January | 15,000 | 736 | 184 |
| February | 14,500 | 800 | 160 |
| March | 15,750 | 1,008 | 168 |
| April | 15,250 | 880 | 176 |
| May | 16,250 | 1,056 | 176 |
| June | 15,000 | 840 | 168 |
|  | $y = 91,750$ | $x = 5,320$ |  |
|  | $\bar{y} = 15{,}291.7$ | $\bar{x} = 886.7$ |  |

*You are required to:*

(a) Compute a least-squares cost equation based on direct labour hours;

(b) compute the coefficient of determination $r^2$ for (a);

(c) compare and discuss the relationship of your solution in (a) to the equation

Total overhead = 5,758 + 4.7 DLH + 31 PH

(where DLH = direct labour hours, PH = plant hours)

obtained by a regression using DLH and PH as variables and coefficient of determination $R^2 = 0.9873$;

(d) estimate the total overhead for a month with 1,000 DLH and 168 PH, using the equation in (c).
*ICMA*

**30.** Steel bars of a rectangular cross-section are forged into bars of smaller cross-section. The time to forge a bar is found to be approximately proportional to the difference between the cross-sectional area (CSA) at the start and finish of forging, plus a fixed time which is independent of the cross-sectional areas. That is,

$$t = a + b \text{ (CSA at start} - \text{CSA at finish)}$$

The following forging times were observed for a sample of bars:

| Starting size (inches) | Finishing size (inches) | Forging time (minutes) |
|---|---|---|
| 9 × 4 | 4 × 1 | 16 |
| 8 × 6 | 4 × 2 | 24 |
| 4 × 4 | 1 × 1 | 9 |
| 8 × 2 | 2 × 2 | 12 |
| 8 × 8 | 4 × 4 | 29 |
| 7 × 7 | 5 × 2 | 21 |
| 6 × 7 | 5 × 2 | 14 |

*Required:*

(a) Find, using least squares regression, the best-fit relationship of the above type.

(b) Use your regression equation found in part (a) to:
  (i) predict how much longer it would take to forge a bar 2 inches × 3 inches from a bar 6 inches square than from a bar 5 inches square;
  (ii) estimate the CSA of the finished size of a bar if the starting CSA is 36 square inches and the forging time is 18 minutes.
*ACCA*

**31.** The Coldfield Company Ltd is analysing demand for its "Superior" chess sets and has collected the following data:

| Year | Number of chess sets purchased |
|---|---|
| 1975 | 500 |
| 1976 | 530 |
| 1977 | 510 |
| 1978 | 580 |
| 1979 | 600 |
| 1980 | 600 |
| 1981 | 630 |

*Required:*

(a) Determine a regression line relating quantity purchased in relation to time.

(b) Determine the correlation coefficient for the relationship determined in (a).

(c) Determine the coefficient of determination and comment on the result.

(d) If the regression coefficient *t*-value is 6.46, explain how you use the value to determine if the regression line is a good fit to the data.

32. Odin Chemicals Limited is aware that its power costs are a semi-variable cost and over the last six months these costs have shown the following relationship with a standard measure of output:

| Month | Output (standard units) | Total power costs (£000) |
|---|---|---|
| 1 | 12 | 6.2 |
| 2 | 18 | 8.0 |
| 3 | 19 | 8.6 |
| 4 | 20 | 10.4 |
| 5 | 24 | 10.2 |
| 6 | 30 | 12.4 |

*Required:*

(a) Using the method of least squares, determine an appropriate linear relationship between total power costs and output.

(b) If total power costs are related to both output and time (as measured by the number of the month) the following least square regression equation is obtained:

$$\text{Power costs} = 4.42 + 0.82 \times \text{Output} + 0.10 \times \text{Month}$$

where the regression coefficients i.e. 0.82 and 0.10, have t-values of 2.64 and 0.60 respectively, and the coefficient of multiple correlation amounts to 0.976.

Compare the relative merits of this fitted relationship with the one you determine in (a). Explain (without doing any further analysis) how you might use the data to forecast power costs in month 7.            *ACCA*

## Exponential and logarithmic functions learning curve

33. The monthly demand for the Cityclair new, under £50, computer for the first six months was as follows:

# APPENDIX 2. EXAMINATION QUESTIONS

| Month No. | Demand |
|---|---|
| 1 | 35 |
| 2 | 46 |
| 3 | 59 |
| 4 | 77 |
| 5 | 100 |
| 6 | 130 |

*Required:*

(a) Graph the demand against the month.

(b) Which of the following function forms might best fit the demand data?

$$y = b \log_{10} x \qquad y = b \log_e x$$
$$y = be^x \qquad y = be^{-x}$$
$$y = ab^x \text{ where } b > 1 \text{ and } a > 0$$
$$y = ab^x \text{ where } b < 1 \text{ and } a > 0$$

(c) Explain how you would fit your selected curve to the data and how you would measure the goodness of fit.

**34.** Marita produces painted beach pebbles decorated with flowers and butterflies for local craft shops in Bedfordshire. Her first batch of ten pebbles took her 30 hours to produce. Assuming a 60 per cent learning curve determine the time to produce the next batch of ten and a further batch of twenty.

Estimate the time taken to produce the first decorated pebble.

If she estimated her labour cost at £10 an hour and her material cost (for paint and pebble) at £1 per pebble, what is her breakeven price over the first 40 pebbles and how does this compare with an 80 per cent learning rate? (Assume all other costs are negligible.)

You may use the following results:

$$\log_{10}(0.6) = -0.2218$$
$$\log_{10}(0.8) = -0.0969$$
$$\log_{10}(2.0) = 0.3010$$
$$\log_{10}(5.46) = 0.7369.$$

**35.** The Heathkitty Company Limited has produced its first 10 small sailing dinghies under the name "Morning Cloud" and sold them all to a well-known musical conductor. A new client, a Mr. D. Thatcher, is enquiring about the cost of a further 30 "Morning Clouds". The total cost of the original 10 dinghies was:

|  |  |
|---|---:|
| Materials | £3,000 |
| Variable labour costs | |
| (500 hours at £10 per hour) | 5,000 |
| Variable overheads* | 1,000 |
| Other overheads† | 1,000 |
| Machine tool costs‡ | 2,000 |
| Total costs | £12,000 |

\* Directly affected by variable labour costs.
† Estimated at 20 per cent of variable labour costs.
‡ All machine tools can still be used although all costs recovered on first order.

Use an 80 per cent learning curve to estimate the total costs for a new batch of 30 "Morning Clouds".

## Variances, covariances and $r$

**36.** A university admissions officer interviews 30 candidates on Monday and then on Tuesday. On each day the mean length of all the interviews is exactly 15 minutes, but the standard deviations are 2 minutes on Monday and $2\frac{1}{2}$ minutes on Tuesday.

Determine the mean and standard deviation of the total interview time per candidate and state any assumptions you make.

**37.** In the Lazy Chance Saloon two loaded *three*-sided dice are used with the following probability distribution:

| Red die | | Blue die | |
|:---:|:---:|:---:|:---:|
| Score | Probability | Score | Probability |
| 1 | 0.4 | 1 | 0.5 |
| 2 | 0.3 | 2 | 0.4 |
| 3 | 0.3 | 3 | 0.1 |
|   | 1.0 |   | 1.0 |

*Required:*

(a) Determine the joint probability distribution.

(b) Determine the probability distribution of the sum of scores on the two dice.

(c) Determine the mean and variance for the score on each die and the mean and variance of the probability distribution of the sum of the scores on the two dice. Comment on your results.

(d) Suppose that the pair of three-sided dice is not only loaded but dependent, so that the joint probability distribution of the two scores is:

|  |  | Blue die | | |
|---|---|---|---|---|
|  |  | 1 | 2 | 3 |
| Red die | 1 | 0.2 | 0.1 | 0 |
|  | 2 | 0.1 | 0.1 | 0.2 |
|  | 3 | 0 | 0.1 | 0.2 |

(i) Calculate the *new* probability distribution of the sum of the scores on the two dice and its mean and variance.

(ii) Calculate the *new* mean and variance of both dice.

(iii) Calculate the covariance between the scores on both dice.

(iv) Comment on the relationship between your results.

(v) From the above results determine the correlation coefficient $r$ for the two dice.

**38.** Ten people in a room have the following heights and weights:

| Person | Height (inches) $h$ | Weight (pounds) $W$ |
|---|---|---|
| A | 75 | 160 |
| B | 70 | 150 |
| C | 70 | 160 |
| D | 80 | 170 |
| E | 75 | 160 |
| F | 75 | 150 |
| G | 70 | 150 |
| H | 80 | 160 |
| I | 80 | 170 |
| J | 75 | 170 |

*Required:*

(a) Find the joint probability distribution of $h$ and $W$.

(b) Find the probability distribution of $h$ and its mean and variance.

(c) Find the probability distribution of $W$ and its mean and variance.

(d) Find the covariance of $h$ and $W$.

(e) Determine the following:

$$E(W/h = 70), E(W/h = 75), E(W/h = 80).$$

(f) Are $h$ and $W$ independent?

(g) If a "size index" $I$ were defined as:

$$I = 2h + 3W$$

find the mean, variance and standard deviation of $I$.

(h) Find the probability distribution of $I$ and verify part (g) directly.

39. Over a period of time, a certain branch of the London and South Eastern Bank has analysed its daily note issue and found that the demand for one-pound, five-pound and ten-pound notes on any day of the week has an approximately normal distribution with the following parameters:

|  | Number of notes | |
| --- | --- | --- |
| Denomination | Mean | Standard deviation |
| £1 | 1,200 | 250 |
| £5 | 600 | 100 |
| £10 | 50 | 5 |

(You may ignore all other denominations.)

Furthermore, the three denominations are independent of each other in this respect.

*Required:*

(a) What is the probability that demand for cash exceeds £5,000 in any one day?

(b) At the beginning of a particular day, the branch finds that it has £1,600 in one-pound notes, £3,500 in five-pound notes and £600 in ten-pound notes. Assuming that no cash will be paid in during the day, what is the probability that the branch will be able to meet all its demands for cash during the day? (Your answer should assume that the appropriate combinations of lower denominations may not be used instead of higher denominations so that, for example, two five-pound notes cannot be issued instead of one ten-pound note.)

Which of the three denominations is most critical in respect of the bank being able to meet its demands for cash?

(c) If appropriate combinations of lower-denomination notes could be issued instead of a higher denomination, explain (but do not calculate) how your answer would have to be amended to allow for this.

*ACCA*

## OPERATIONAL RESEARCH

### Introduction to OR

40. Define the term operational research (OR) and describe its essential characteristics.

# APPENDIX 2. EXAMINATION QUESTIONS

**41.** The stages in the operational research approach to a problem may be listed as follows:

(a) Problem definition.

(b) Construction of a model.

(c) Derivation of a solution from the model.

(d) Testing the model and its solution.

(e) Establishment of controls.

(f) Implementation.

*Required:*

Explain what you understand by these various stages. *ACCA*

**42.** "Two problems seldom if ever arise which have the same content but there are relatively few forms which problems can assume".

*Required:*

Discuss the above quotation in the context of operational research problems. Your answer should include a detailed description of prototype OR problems.

**43.** Describe the term "model building" as used within an operational research framework. Outline the possible problems associated with the use of models.

**44.** Outline the features determining a successful OR approach and the role of general management in such an approach.

**45.** What do you understand by "sensitivity analysis"? Give examples of its use and discuss its value and limitations.

**46.** Explain what is meant by sub-optimisation. Illustrate your answer by giving a suitable example.

## Linear programming—model construction

**47.** A local builders' merchant has decided to venture into the field of interior decoration. In the foreseeable future the business is going to concentrate on the painting of walls within agreed structures. Estimates of total quantities of paints required based on an *ad hoc* market survey show that the business needs 400 tins of paints per month, the supply consisting of three different colours. The individual colour requirements are summarised as follows: the business requires at least 80 tins of brown paint, not more than 160 tins of blue paint and at least 40 tins of black paint.

The cost per tin is given below:

| Colour   | Blue | Brown | Black |
|----------|------|-------|-------|
| Cost/tin | £4   | £5    | £4.5  |

*Required:*

Construct a linear programming model given that the objective is to purchase tins of paint so as to minimise total costs and yet satisfy the various requirements.

**48.** The Boffin Investment Trust wishes to invest £1,000,000. There are five different investment choices, each with different growth and income potentialities. The current returns from the investment of each of these five choices are also different. The current returns on investment are as follows:

| Investment choice | Current annual yield (%) |
|---|---|
| L | 10 |
| M | 8 |
| N | 6 |
| O | 5 |
| P | 9 |

Management believes that the current yield will persist in the future and wishes to diversify the investment portfolio of the company to obtain maximum returns. Because of the risk element involved, management restricts the investment in L to not more than the combined total investment in N, O and P. Total investment in M and P combined must be at least as large as that in N. Also, management wishes to restrict its investment in M to a level not exceeding that of O.

*Required:*

Construct a linear programming model to determine the optimum allocation of investment funds amongst these five choices.

**49.** A blender of whisky imports three grades, A, B and C. He mixes them according to recipes which specify the maximum or minimum percentages of grades A and C in each blend. These are shown in Table 20.

Table 20. Specification of blends.

| Blend | Specification | Price per bottle (20 fluid ounces) |
|---|---|---|
| Blue Dot | Not less than 60% of A<br>Not more than 20% of C | £6.80 |
| Highland Fling | Not more than 60% of C<br>Not less than 15% of A | £5.70 |
| Old Frenzy | Not more than 50% of C | £4.50 |

Supplies of the three basic whiskies together with their costs are shown in Table 21.

Table 21. Availability and costs of ingredients.

| Whisky | Maximum quantity available (bottles) | Cost per bottle |
|---|---|---|
| A | 2,000 | £7.00 |
| B | 2,500 | £5.00 |
| C | 1,200 | £4.00 |

*Required:*

Formulate a linear programming model for a production policy that will maximise profits.

50. A company manufactures two types of stainless steel dish, type A and type B. The data in Table 22 refer to the material content, manufacturing process times and variable costs of each type.

Table 22. Materials, times and costs in dish manufacture.

|  | Type A | Type B |
|---|---|---|
| Material content (lb per unit) | 1 | 1 |
| Cost per lb | £0.06 | £0.10 |
| Manufacturing time (seconds per unit): | | |
|   Press shop | 20 | 20 |
|   Polishing | 20 | 10 |
| Manufacturing costs (direct labour + variable overhead): | | |
| Press shop, per press hour (£) | 3.60 | 3.60 |
| Polishing, per hour: | | |
|   machine 1 (£) | 3.60 | – |
|   machine 2 (£) | – | 5.40 |

Materials supplies each week are limited to 16,000 lb for the type A dish and 21,000 lb for the type B dish.

There are available each week 200 press hours and 120 hours each for both types of polishing machines.

Overtime working may be used to increase the hours available up to a limit of 10 per cent for each machine group. However, overtime also adds 10 per cent to the manufacturing costs of each machine group.

The type A dish sells for £0.12 each and the type B dish for £0.16 each.

The company wishes to know how many it should produce in order to maximise contribution.

*Required:*

Formulate the linear programming model.                                    *ICMA*

**51.** The management accountant of Fenton Enterprises Ltd has suggested that a linear programming model might be used for selecting the best mix of five possible products, A, B, C, D and E.

The following information is available:
(a) Table 23.

Table 23. Prices, costs and profits of Fenton Enterprises Ltd.

|  | Per unit of product | | | | |
|---|---|---|---|---|---|
|  | A | B | C | D | E |
| Selling price | £48 | £42 | £38 | £31 | £27 |
| Costs: | | | | | |
| Materials | 15 | 14 | 16 | 15 | 16 |
| Direct labour | 18 | 16 | 6 | 4 | 4 |
| Fixed overheads* | 9 | 8 | 3 | 2 | 2 |
| Total costs | 42 | 38 | 25 | 21 | 22 |
| Net profit | 6 | 4 | 13 | 10 | 5 |

*Based on 50% of direct labour cost.

(b) Expected maximum unit demand per week for each product at the prices indicated:

| A | B | C | D | E |
|---|---|---|---|---|
| 1,500 | 1,200 | 900 | 600 | 600 |

(c) Cost of materials includes a special component which is in short supply; it costs £3 a unit. Only 5,800 units will be available to the company during the week. The number of units of the special component needed for a unit of each product is:

| A | B | C | D | E |
|---|---|---|---|---|
| 1 | 1 | 3 | 4 | 5 |

(d) Labour is paid at a rate of £1.50 per hour and only 20,000 hours will be available in a week.
(e) The management of Fenton Enterprises Ltd has ruled that expenditure on materials must not exceed a sum of £30,000.
(f) All other resources are freely available in sufficient quantities for planned needs.

*Required:*

(a) Formulate a linear programming model stating clearly the criterion you use. (You are not expected to produce a numerical solution to your model.)

(b) Describe the problems likely to be encountered in the application of linear programming to determine the "best" product mix for Fenton Enterprises Ltd.

*ACCA*

**52.** Arbor Ltd is a two-division organisation and the management is considering its production plans for the forthcoming year.

The manufacturing division produces a single component MN2 which it can sell to other firms for £24 or transfer to the assembly division at an agreed price calculated as follows:

|  |  |
|---|---|
| Materials per unit | £5 |
| Labour per unit | 3 |
| Variable overheads per unit | 1 |
| Fixed overheads (100% on materials and labour) | 8 |
|  | 17 |
| Profit margin ($33\frac{1}{3}\%$ on marginal cost) | 3 |
|  | 20 |

For some years it has been the practice of the manufacturing division to supply all the requirements of the assembly division for component MN2 and to sell the remainder of its production on the open market. When working at the practical maximum capacity the manufacturing division can produce annually 2,500 units of the component MN2. Because of building restrictions the productive capacity cannot easily be increased.

It is expected that next year the demand for the finished products of the assembly division will increase substantially. Consequently, the entire output of component MN2 will be transferred to the assembly division.

The assembly division uses some components which are purchased from abroad and because of import regulations purchases of these components will be restricted to a quota of £50,000 for the coming year.

The management accountant of Arbor Ltd has prepared the statement reproduced here as Table 24 to assist the management in deciding the best plan.

The fixed overheads of the assembly division will not change irrespective of the range of products produced.

*Required:*

(a) Give your comments on the accountant's statement as a basis for decision making.

(b) Formulate the linear programme which you consider to be appropriate for determining the production plan for the assembly division. Justify this approach (a numerical solution is not required).

Table 24. Statement of demand, costs and profits for assembly division.

| Product range | F | G | H | I | J | K |
|---|---|---|---|---|---|---|
| Estimated maximum annual demand (Units) | 150 | 80 | 125 | 75 | 100 | 100 |
| MN2 components required | 4 | 5 | 8 | 6 | 7 | 2 |
| *Costs per unit* | | | | | | |
| MN2 | £80 | £100 | £160 | £120 | £140 | £40 |
| Imported components | 76 | 106 | 100 | 100 | 100 | 60 |
| Labour | 20 | 30 | 10 | 20 | 100 | 150 |
| Overheads, half of which vary with direct labour cost (200% on direct labour) | 40 | 60 | 20 | 40 | 200 | 300 |
| Total cost per unit | 216 | 296 | 290 | 280 | 540 | 550 |
| Selling price per unit | 292 | 455 | 490 | 455 | 670 | 610 |
| Total profit per unit | 76 | 159 | 200 | 175 | 130 | 60 |
| Profit per £1 of cost of imported components | £1.00 | £1.50 | £2.00 | £1.75 | £1.30 | £1.00 |
| Ranking | 5 | 3 | 1 | 2 | 4 | 5 |

(c) What are the limitations of your approach in (b) above?

**53.** Due to the introduction of new microprocessor technology, less unskilled and more skilled labour will be required by Tech Ltd over the next two years. The company wishes to determine its employment policy for this period and estimates that the manpower requirements which will have to be met are as follows:

| Year | Unskilled men | Skilled men |
|---|---|---|
| 1981 | 1,000 | 1,200 |
| 1982 | 500 | 1,500 |

The numbers currently employed are 2,000 unskilled men and 1,000 skilled men. There is a natural wastage of labour and on average 20 per cent of the unskilled men and 10 per cent of the skilled men leave each year. It is possible to recruit up to 400 extra skilled men each year at a recruitment cost of £400 for each man.

It is also possible to make an unskilled man redundant but he must be paid a lump sum of £1,000. It is company policy to employ only up to 200 men more in total than are actually needed each year. Salaries for unskilled men are £4,000 a year and for skilled men, £6,000 a year.

*Required:*

(a) By taking as your decision variables the number of men recruited and made redundant in each of the next two years, *formulate* (but do not attempt to solve) a linear programming model to determine the optimal employment policy for Tech Ltd over the next two years. Derive two objective functions to:

(i) minimise total cost;

(ii) minimise total redundancies (assume the men leave at the start of each year).

(b) It is possible to retrain up to 300 unskilled men each year to make them skilled, but this number must be limited to no more than one-quarter of the skilled labour force at the time of training. The costs of retraining are £500 a man. The training period is short, so once a man is selected for training he may be counted immediately as skilled labour as far as manpower requirements are concerned, but he is paid only £5,000 a year for his first year, rising to the normal level of £6,000 in his second year. Amend your linear programming model obtained in part (a) to accommodate this possibility of retraining unskilled men. *ACCA*

**54.** On 1st January 1982, the manager of a share portfolio finds that he has £100,000 to invest in government stocks. A preliminary analysis of his situation indicates five stocks in which he could invest. These stocks have the characteristics given in Table 25.

Table 25. Outline of government stocks.

| Stock | | Nominal yield (%) | Current Price | Redemption yield (%) |
|---|---|---|---|---|
| A | Treasury 1984 | $9\frac{1}{2}$ | £$94\frac{1}{2}$ | 13.5 |
| B | Exchequer 1988 | 12 | $91\frac{1}{8}$ | 12.2 |
| C | Treasury 1989 | $11\frac{1}{2}$ | $82\frac{3}{4}$ | 14.3 |
| D | Treasury 1998 | 14 | 92 | 14.9 |
| E | Treasury 1999 | 10 | $78\frac{1}{4}$ | 15.1 |

His objective is to maximise the overall redemption yield from his investment but conditions dictate that he must have an overall interest-only running yield of at least 13 per cent. Furthermore, at least £30,000 must be in short-term stocks (up to five years to redemption) and no more than £40,000 should be in long-term stocks (over fifteen years to redemption).

*Note: The interest-only running yield is calculated as: Nominal Yield × 100/Current Price.*

*Required:*

(a) Formulate a linear programming model for this investment problem, clearly indicating the objective function and all the relevant constraints.

(b) It may be shown that the optimum portfolio is to invest

$$£30,000 \text{ in A}$$
$$£30,000 \text{ in C}$$
$$£35,350 \text{ in D}$$
$$£4,650 \text{ in E,}$$

giving an overall redemption yield of 14.31 per cent. If there were no restriction on the proportion which could be invested in long-term stocks, determine by how much the overall redemption yield could be improved and what would be the new portfolio. (This new problem may be solved graphically if appropriate deductions and simplifications are first made).
ACCA

*Tutorial note: The second part of this question is best tackled after working through the Chapter 15.*

### Linear programming—graphical method

**55.** A company marketing fish pastes and spreads is producing a display pack for the retail trade. The pack will contain an assortment of different pastes and spreads. Pastes and spreads will have their own characteristic jars, spread jars being much taller than paste jars. Each variety of paste and spread will have a different type of label.

Each paste jar when full weighs 60 g and occupies an area of 8 cm$^2$. Each spread jar when full weighs 90 g and occupies an area of 6 cm$^2$. The cost of production per full jar is £0.15 for paste and £0.10 for spreads.

The company requires that each display pack should contain at least 30 jars and weigh a minimum of 2,000 g. (The weight of the box itself is negligible.) The space available for jars may vary between 190 and 230 cm$^2$ due to differently designed fancy partitions between the jars. (Ignore weight of partitions.)

*Required:*

(a) Formulate a linear programming model to minimise the cost per display pack and solve the problem graphically using a scale on both axes of 1 cm for 2 jars. Comment on your solution, stating any assumptions you have made when modelling.

(b) After considering your solution, the manufacturer requires a minimum number of ten paste jars to be included in the pack. Show graphically how this affects your solution and state which constraints have now become redundant. How much more does each display pack cost?
ACCA

**56.** Electropoint, a company manufacturing domestic electrical appliances, is introducing to the market its new revolutionary domestic robot.

The domestic robot, the first of its kind, is capable of doing most of the normal household chores. There are two models, called Mavis and Charles, which differ slightly in capabilities.

The only effective limits on production capacity at the present time are concerned with the specially designed positronic circuits required by both models. Only 200 can be obtained per day and there are only 80 hours of skilled labour available each day. Each Mavis model requires 3 positronic circuits and 1 hour of skilled labour, while a Charles model requires 4 positronic circuits and 2 hours of skilled labour. The contribution per model is estimated to be £60 for a Mavis and £100 for a Charles. A daily order, which must be met, has already been placed for 20 Mavis models.

*Required:*

(a) Formulate a linear programming model to maximise the company's contribution and solve graphically. Take into account the order for 20 Mavis models.

(b) If the contribution from the Charles model increases to £140, and assuming no other changes, what would be the overall percentage change in total contribution per day?

(c) By how much can the estimated £100 contribution from a Charles model change before it becomes profitable to change the production mix?  *ACCA*

57. The Superseal Company Ltd manufactures, amongst other products, two types of sealing ring (SRI and SRII) for airtight jars. These are sold to the trade in packs of 1,000. A number of processes are involved in the manufacture of both types of ring. These processes take place within three different departments and the times required in each department for each pack of rings are given in the following table:

|  | Processing time per pack (hours) | |
|---|---|---|
|  | SRI | SRII |
| Department A | 3 | 1 |
| Department B | 1 | 1 |
| Department C | 1 | 2 |

The departments have the following machine hours available for these products:

| Department | A | B | C |
|---|---|---|---|
| Machine hours | 120 | 60 | 100 |

The contribution per pack is £50 for type SRI and £80 for type SRII.

*Required:*

(a) Formulate this linear programming problem and determine graphically the optimal solution.

(b) If the number of machine hours available in department B is increased to 61 hours, how does the optimal solution change? (State any assumptions made.) How could this be determined from the optimal tableau?

(c) If the cost of increasing the machine hours available in department B is relatively small, by how many hours would you recommend that the number of hours available in department B be increased?  *ACCA*

58. Multi Ltd produces two products, Uni and Duo, at its factories in Cambridge and Oxford which are equipped with different types of machinery. At each factory, both products undergo two production processes, the machine hours available per week in each factory for both products being:

|  | Machine hours | |
|---|---|---|
|  | Oxford | Cambridge |
| Process 1 | 300 | 300 |
| Process 2 | 300 | 324 |

The process times (in hours) for a unit of each type of product in each factory are:

|  | Oxford | | Cambridge | |
|---|---|---|---|---|
|  | Uni | Duo | Uni | Duo |
| Process 1 | 10 | 30 | 10 | 15 |
| Process 2 | 30 | 10 | 18 | 9 |

In addition, each unit of Uni and Duo uses 14 units of raw material. Currently 196 units of raw material per week are allocated to the Oxford factory and 294 units per week to the Cambridge factory. At the moment the company cannot get more than 490 units of raw material. It is estimated that the contribution to fixed overheads and profit is £300 per unit for the Uni and £200 per unit for the Duo.

*Required:*

(a) Formulate a linear programming model for each factory and, assuming a profit maximisation objective, obtain by graphical means the two optimal solutions. Determine the amount of resources used at each factory.

(b) Formulate (*but do not solve*) a single linear programming model for the company as a whole so that the model will determine the optimal allocation of the 490 units of raw material between the two factories.

(c) The optimal number of units for the company to produce each week can be shown to be:

|  | Oxford | Cambridge |
|---|---|---|
| Uni | 7.5 | 16 |
| Duo | 7.5 | 4 |

Determine the optimal contribution and the resources used. Compare this with your solution to (a) above and make a recommendation to management.

*ACCA*

**59.** Annapurna Ltd is drawing up production plans for the coming year. Four products are available with the following financial characteristics:

|                          | A   | B   | C   | D   |
|--------------------------|-----|-----|-----|-----|
| Amounts per unit:        |     |     |     |     |
| Selling price            | £55 | £53 | £97 | £86 |
| Cost of materials        | £17 | £25 | £19 | £11 |
| Labour hours—grade A     | 10  | 6   | –   | –   |
| grade B                  | –   | –   | 10  | 20  |
| grade C                  | –   | –   | 12  | 6   |
| Variable overheads       | £6  | £7  | £5  | £6  |

Fixed overheads of the firm amount to £35,500 per annum. Each grade of labour is paid £1.50 per hour but skills are specific to a grade so that an employee in one grade cannot be used to undertake the work of another grade. The annual supply of each grade is limited to the following maximum: grade A, 9,000 hours; grade B, 14,500 hours; grade C, 12,000 hours. There is no effective limitation on the volume of sales of any product.

*Required:*

(a) Calculate the product mix which will maximise profit for the year and state the amount of the profit (you may use a graphical method, the simplex method or any other method which gives the optimum).

(b) Calculate the minimum price at which the sale of product A would be worthwhile.

(c) Calculate the amount by which profit could be increased if the supply of grade A labour were increased by 1 hour.

(d) Describe shortly the limitations of the technique you have used in answering (a).

*ICAEW*

**60.** Alfred Ltd is preparing its plans for the coming month. It manufactures two products, the flaktrap and the satrap. Details are as follows:

|                            | Flaktrap | Satrap | Price/wage rate |
|----------------------------|----------|--------|-----------------|
| Amounts per unit:          |          |        |                 |
| Selling price (£)          | 125      | 165    |                 |
| Materials used (kg)        | 6        | 4      | £5 per kg       |
| Labour hours—skilled       | 10       | 10     | £3 per hour     |
| semi-skilled               | 5        | 25     | £2 per hour     |

The company's overhead recovery rate is £2 per labour hour (for both skilled and semi-skilled labour) of which £1 relates to variable costs and £1 to fixed costs. The supply of skilled labour is limited to 2,000 hours per month and the supply of semi-skilled labour is limited to 2,500 per month. At the selling prices indicated, maximum demand for flaktraps is expected to be 150 units per month and maximum demand for satraps is expected to be 80 units per month. The directors of Alfred believe that demand for each product could be increased by advertising.

*Required:*

(a) Find the product mix which will maximise Alfred's profit.

(b) Find the maximum monthly expenditure on advertising which would be worthwhile if it increased the demand for flaktraps by 50 units per month.

(c) Explain the meaning of the expression "dual price" (or "shadow price") and comment briefly on the usefulness of a knowledge of dual prices.

**61.** Zaman Ltd manufactures two products, the Qa and the Mar. Details of the two products are given in Table 26. Both products require the same grade of labour (costing £3 per hour) and the same type of raw material (costing £10 per kg). Zaman Ltd expects to incur total fixed overheads of £80,000 in the coming year. Last year the company used 40,000 labour hours and has decided to allocate the expected fixed overheads between its two products on the basis of "cost per labour hour", i.e. at a rate of £2 per labour hour.

Table 26. Zaman products.

|  | Qa | Mar |
|---|---|---|
| Selling price per unit | £200 | £109 |
| Labour required per unit | 20 hours | 8 hours |
| Raw material required per week | 4 kg | 5 kg |
| Variable overheads per unit | £20 | £15 |
| Fixed overheads per unit | £40 | £16 |
| Maximum annual demand | 1,000 units | 4,000 units |

In the coming year, Zaman Ltd expects to have available a maximum of 40,000 labour hours and 20,000 kg of raw material. The company has no stocks of either the Qa or the Mar, and does not wish to have any stocks of either product at the end of the coming year.

*Required:*

(a) Prepare calculations to show the quantities of Qa and Mar that should be manufactured and sold in the coming year in order to maximise the profit of Zaman Ltd.

(b) Discuss the limitations of your calculations.

(c) Explain briefly what you understand by the dual price (or shadow price) of a resource and state, giving your reasons, which of Zaman Ltd's resources have non-zero dual prices. (NOTE: You are not required to calculate the dual prices.)

ICAEW

# APPENDIX 2. EXAMINATION QUESTIONS

**62.** Fleabane Ltd aims to maximise its profits. In one factory it manufactures two liquid products called Erigeron and Stachys. Each is a mix of readily available ingredients which passes through three successive processes of heating, blending and cooling. The finished products are transferred at open market prices to an associated company, which bears all of the related storage and transport costs.

Fleabane's management accountant has prepared an up-to-date cost statement, given here as Table 27, for the two products, expressed in pounds per gallon of final product.

Table 27. Fleabane products.

|  | Erigeron | | Stachys | |
|---|---|---|---|---|
| Selling price |  | 20 |  | 25 |
| Materials and preparation |  | 10 |  | 12 |
|  |  | 10 |  | 13 |
| Variable process costs: |  |  |  |  |
| heating process | 4 |  | 1 |  |
| blending process | 1 |  | 5 |  |
| cooling process | 2 |  | 3 |  |
|  |  | 7 |  | 9 |
| Contribution margin |  | 3 |  | 4 |

Each process is costed at £1 per hour of process time per gallon. The processing facilities have no alternative use.

Fleabane have received an enquiry for the delivery of an extra one thousand gallons of each product during the coming month.

*Required:*

(a) Draft a statement showing how Fleabane should respond to this enquiry, assuming that the remaining unused capacity available in the coming month is four thousand hours for the cooling process and six thousand hours for each of the other two processes.

(b) Draft a statement, showing how Fleabane should respond to this enquiry on the assumption instead that each process has only three thousand hours of unused capacity available in the coming month, showing the following:

  (i) Fleabane's optimal production plan, and

  (ii) the range of contribution margins per product within which the optimal production plan will not alter.

*Note: Parts (a) and (b) of this requirement are entirely independent of each other.*

## Linear programming—simplex solution and dual values

**63.** The Exbridge region of Barsands Bank is trying to determine its overall loan policy for the region for the coming month. Its customers can be classified into four groups: industrial, argicultural, personal-without solidarity, personal-with solidarity. The total amount available for loans in the coming month is estimated at £50 million.

The interest rates charged and the percentage of bad debts are given in the following table:

| Customer type | Interest rate charged per annum (%) | Risk level (% bad debts) |
|---|---|---|
| Industrial | 9 | 0.2 |
| Agricultural | 10 | 0.5 |
| Personal-without solidarity | 13 | 1.0 |
| Personal-with solidarity | 14 | 2.0 |

There are a number of restrictions on loan policy, which the region must observe, due to the regulations set by the Bank of the England and the national policy of Barsands Bank. These can be summarised as follows:

(i) Personal loans must not exceed 40 per cent of the value of total loans.

(ii) Personal-with solidarity must not exceed 20 per cent of the total personal loans.

(iii) Total agricultural loans must not exceed £10 million.

(iv) Industrial loans should not be less than £20 million.

(v) The average risk factor must not exceed 0.8 per cent.

*Required:*

(a) Formulate a linear programming model of the bank's problem. Your model should be in a form suitable for solution by a linear programming computer package. State clearly in your answer how you derive your objective function and constraints.

(b) If you were to solve this problem by the simplex method, explain (but do not solve) how you would deal with this situation where you have inequalities of both types, (i.e. "greater than" and "less than").

(c) If the bank were to reclassify the customer types to accord with the document "Classifications of advances" issued by the Bank of England, which gives a long list of groupings, then the LP model would tend to have more original variables than constraints. How would this affect the solution and what, in practice, would be the consequences for the bank? How might the bank deal with the situation?

**64.** The following details are taken from the forecasts for 1979 of XYZ Limited:

# APPENDIX 2. EXAMINATION QUESTIONS

| Sales demand | | Thousands of units per annum, maximum |
|---|---|---|
| Super de luxe model | ($x_1$) | 500 |
| De luxe model | ($x_2$) | 750 |
| Export model | ($x_3$) | 400 |

Production: two production facilities are required, machining and assembly, and these are common to each model. Capacity in each facility is limited by the number of direct labour hours available.

| | Direct labour: total hours available in millions | Direct labour: hours per unit for each model | | |
|---|---|---|---|---|
| | | $x_1$ | $x_2$ | $x_3$ |
| Machine ($x_4$) | 1.4 | 0.5 | 0.5 | 1.0 |
| Assembly ($x_5$) | 1.2 | 0.5 | 0.5 | 2.0 |

Contribution, estimated to be

| Model | Amount per thousand units |
|---|---|
| $x_1$ | £1,500 |
| $x_2$ | 1,300 |
| $x_3$ | 2,500 |

*Required:*

(a) Using the above information, set up the first tableau of a linear programme to determine the product mix which will maximise total contribution and then complete the first iteration only.

(b) Interpret the following tableau, given that it is the final solution to the above problem. The $S$ variables ($S_1$, $S_2$, $S_3$, $S_4$, $S_5$) relate to the constraints in the same sequence as presented in (a) above.

| $x_1$ | $x_2$ | $x_3$ | $S_1$ | $S_2$ | $S_3$ | $S_4$ | $S_5$ | $b_{ij}$ |
|---|---|---|---|---|---|---|---|---|
| 1 | 0 | 0 | 1 | 0 | 0 | 0 | 0 | 500 |
| 0 | 0 | 0 | 0.25 | 0.25 | 1 | 0 | $-0.5$ | 112.5 |
| 0 | 0 | 1 | $-0.25$ | $-0.25$ | 0 | 0 | 0.5 | 287.5 |
| 0 | 0 | 0 | $-0.25$ | $-0.25$ | 0 | 1 | $-0.5$ | 487.5 |
| 0 | 1 | 0 | 0 | 1 | 0 | 0 | 0 | 750 |
| 0 | 0 | 0 | $-875$ | $-675$ | 0 | 0 | $-1250$ | $-2,443,750$ |

*ICMA*

**65.** Peter Ley, who runs a small independent engineering company, has bought a job lot of 350 positronic circuits for £1,500. Naturally, he wants to put these circuits to the most profitable use so he is exploring all possible applications. First he considers using them for a small car vacuum cleaner (one circuit per cleaner). From his experience he knows that he can sell at least 350 cleaners at a price of £45 each. The other necessary components are available at £15 a set for each cleaner. The time to assemble each vacuum cleaner is one hour.

Alternatively he can use the circuits in making de luxe house vacuum cleaners (one circuit per cleaner) which will sell at £120 each, other necessary components costing £80 per set (one set per cleaner). The time to assemble each cleaner is two hours. However, the maximum estimate of sales is only ten such cleaners.

Recently several people have enquired about a slightly cheaper house vacuum cleaner. On investigation Peter finds that he can produce a standard cleaner still using one circuit for each cleaner, which he can sell at £110, extra components costing £60 per cleaner. Assembly time, however, is higher at 3 hours per cleaner and he estimates sales would be, at maximum, not more than twenty.

Assembly workers are paid £1 per hour and a fixed amount of 380 hours of assembly time will be available during the period.

*Required:*

(a) Formulate a linear programming model to help Peter decide on the best mix of products.

(b) The following is a computer print-out of the final tableau in solving Peter's problem:

|  | $X_1$ | $X_2$ | $X_3$ | $S_1$ | $S_2$ | $S_3$ | $S_4$ |  |
|---|---|---|---|---|---|---|---|---|
| $X_1$ | 1 | 0 | $\frac{1}{2}$ | $1\frac{1}{2}$ | $-\frac{1}{2}$ | 0 | 0 | 335 |
| $X_2$ | 0 | 1 | $\frac{1}{2}$ | $-\frac{1}{2}$ | $\frac{1}{2}$ | 0 | 0 | 15 |
| $S_3$ | 0 | 0 | $-\frac{1}{2}$ | $\frac{1}{2}$ | $-\frac{1}{2}$ | 1 | 0 | 5 |
| $S_4$ | 0 | 0 | 1 | 0 | 0 | 0 | 1 | 10 |
|  | 0 | 0 | 0 | $-20$ | $-10$ | 0 | 0 | 10,800 |

where $X_1$ = number of car vacuum cleaners

$X_2$ = number of standard vacuum cleaners

$X_3$ = number of de luxe vacuum cleaners

$S_1$ = number of electronic circuits not used

$S_2$ = number of assembly hours not used

$S_3$ = demand not met for standard vacuum cleaners

$S_4$ = demand not met for de luxe vacuum cleaners.

Using the tableau, explain to Peter what his production plan should be and the implications of adopting it.

(c) If assembly labour were willing to work overtime at a cost of £3 per hour, would it be worthwhile employing it and what would be the maximum additional profit obtainable?

(d) If it were possible to sell all or some of the positronic circuits at £28 each instead of using them to make vacuum cleaners, how should the linear programming model be adapted?

**66.** Electropoint manufactures three products A, B and C which use three raw materials, X, Y and Z.

The raw materials required for each unit product are:

| Raw material | Product | | |
|---|---|---|---|
| | A | B | C |
| X | 3 | 4 | 1 |
| Y | 2 | 4 | 2 |
| Z | 1 | 1 | 1 |

Currently Electropoint has 200 units of X, 300 units of Y and 200 units of Z in stock. The next delivery of raw materials will be in a week's time.

The labour requirement per item of product is:

| Product | A | B | C |
|---|---|---|---|
| Hours | 3 | 2 | 3 |

Total number of labour hours available is 400.

Current orders for the products have to be met if the company is not to run the risk of losing customers. These orders at the moment stand at 10 units of A, 10 units of B and 40 units of C. Labour is hired mainly on a weekly basis and paid at the rate of £2 per hour. Only a small proportion of the workforce is employed on a permanent basis.

Other variable costs total £2 for product A, £3 for product B and £4 for product C.

Fixed costs are estimated to be £300 a week. The products are sold at the following prices:

| Product      | A  | B  | C  |
|--------------|----|----|----|
| Unit price (£) | 13 | 14 | 17 |

*Required:*

(a) Formulate the above situation as a linear programming problem to determine production levels for the three products A, B and C.

(b) The print-out of the final tableau from a linear programming package is:

| $X_1$ | $X_2$ | $X_3$ | $S_1$ | $S_2$   | $S_3$ | $S_4$   | $S_5$ | $S_6$ | $S_7$ | $b$   |
|-------|-------|-------|-------|---------|-------|---------|-------|-------|-------|-------|
| 0     | 0     | 0     | 0     | 0.375   | 0     | $-0.25$ | 0     | 1     | 0     | 2.5   |
| 0     | 0     | 0     | 0     | $-0.25$ | 0     | 0.5     | 1     | 0     | 1     | 75    |
| 0     | 0     | 0     | 0     | $-0.125$| 1     | $-0.25$ | 0     | 0     | 0     | 62.5  |
| 0     | 0     | 0     | 1     | $-1.25$ | 0     | 0.5     | 2     | 0     | 0     | 5     |
| 1     | 0     | 0     | 0     | 0       | 0     | 0       | $-1$  | 0     | 0     | 10    |
| 0     | 1     | 0     | 0     | 0.375   | 0     | $-0.25$ | 0     | 0     | 0     | 12.5  |
| 0     | 0     | 1     | 0     | $-0.25$ | 0     | 0.5     | 10    | 0     | 0     | 115   |
| 0     | 0     | 0     | 0     | 0.875   | 0     | 1.75    | 20    | 0     | 0     | 942.5 |

where $X_1$, $X_2$ and $X_3$ are respectively the production levels of products A, B and C.
$S_1$, $S_2$ and $S_3$ are respectively the unused units of raw materials X, Y and Z.
$S_4$ is the unused number of labour hours.
$S_5$, $S_6$ and $S_7$ are respectively the amounts by which the production levels exceed the current order levels for products A, B and C.

Interpret the final tableau giving the solution to all variables used in the formulation.

(c) Briefly outline two areas, other than product selection, where the accountant could use a linear programming model.

*ACCA Pilot Paper*

**67.** Wyatt Ltd is to begin production of two new models of microcomputer during the next three months. Since these new lines necessitate an expansion of the current production facilities, the company will require working capital to finance materials, labour and selling expenses during the initial production period. Revenue from sales during the initial three-month period will not be received until after the end of the period.

The company has internal funds of £50,000 available to finance the cost of this operation. If additional funds are needed they may be borrowed from the bank on a short-term basis up to a total of £100,000 at an interest rate of 20 per cent per annum. The bank has set a condition on its lending that the total amount of internal funds made available by the company for the operation, less the actual expenditure plus the accounts receivable for the products sold, must be at least twice as great as the outstanding loan plus interest payable at the end of the initial three month period.

In addition to the financial restrictions, the company is limited to a total of 2,800 hours of assembly time and 140 hours of packaging time in the initial three-month period. Management has decided to produce at least 60 units of model A and 30 units of model B to enable market reaction to both products to be adequately tested.

Relevant costs, prices and production times for the two models are as follows:

| Model | Unit variable cost | Unit selling price | Assembly time per unit (hours) | Packaging time per unit (hours) |
|---|---|---|---|---|
| A | £500 | £750 | 12 | 1 |
| B | 1,000 | 1,600 | 25 | 2 |

Assume that all units of each model are sold as they are produced and, for simplicity, ignore the purchase of materials for use in future periods.

*Required:*

(a) Using:

$X_1$ = number of units of model A produced with company funds

$X_2$ = number of units of model A produced with borrowed funds

$X_3$ = number of units of model B produced with company funds

$X_4$ = number of units of model B produced with borrowed funds,

fomulate a linear programming model of the problem facing the company so as to maximise contribution towards fixed overheads and profit from the two products.

(b) Given that the optimum solution to the problem is

$$X_1 = 60, \; X_2 = 0, \; X_3 = 20, \; X_4 = 10,$$

indicate the form of the final simplex tableau and briefly outline how the information available in this tableau may be used for a sensitivity analysis of the solution.

*ACCA*

**68.** Balraich Ltd manufactures three products, A, B and C, which use two raw materials X and Y.

The raw materials required for each unit of product are

| | Product | | |
|---|---|---|---|
| | A | B | C |
| Raw material | | | |
| X | 2 | 1 | 5 |
| Y | 5 | 1 | 3 |

Currently, Balraich has 50 units of X and 90 units of Y available.
Variable costs total to £1 for product A, £2 for product B and £3 for product C.
The products are sold at the following prices:

| Product | A | B | C |
|---|---|---|---|
| Selling price | £11 | £6 | £18 |

*Required:*
(a) Formulate the linear programme to maximise contribution.

(b) Formulate the dual programme to your answer to (a) and explain its meaning.

(c) Solve the dual programme graphically, and hence determine the optimal product mix and optimal contributions.

(d) Solve the primal problem as per your formulation in (a) using the simplex algorithm.

(e) Interpret the output on the final tableau.

69. Jack Ltd expects to have available only a limited amount of capital during each of the next five years. It also expects restrictions on its supplies of skilled labour and raw materials type AFC during this period. The accountant of Jack Ltd has prepared a linear programme, covering the company's activities for the next five years. The objective function of the programme involves the maximisation of the present value of ordinary dividends, subject to the following constraints:

(a) that cash payments each year must not exceed cash receipts,

(b) that skilled labour hours required each year must not exceed the hours available for that year,

(c) that materials type AFC required each year must not exceed the quantity available for that year,

(d) that no project may be undertaken more than once (although fractions of projects may be accepted), and

(e) that negative quantities of projects may not be undertaken, nor may negative dividends be paid.

The solution to the linear programme reveals the following dual prices:

| Year | Cash per £ | Skilled labour per hour | Raw material AFC per unit |
|---|---|---|---|
| 1 | £2.10 | £0.90 | £9.30 |
| 2 | 1.65 | 1.30 | 8.40 |
| 3 | 1.30 | 0.00 | 6.30 |
| 4 | 1.05 | 1.10 | 4.80 |
| 5 | 0.90 | 0.00 | 1.60 |

The present total market value of the ordinary shares of Jack Ltd is £17.5 million. The directors estimate that the minimum return required by ordinary shareholders from their investment in the company is 10 per cent per annum.

Since the linear programme was formulated, the directors of Jack Ltd have learnt of a new machine which could be used on several of the projects included in the optimal plan. Purchase of the machine would result in cash savings of £30,000 in each of the years 2 to 5. Jack Ltd would also save 15,000 skilled labour hours in years 2, 3, 4 and 5. On the other hand, use of the machine would require 1,000 extra units of raw material AFC in each of the years 2 to 5.

*Required:*

(a) Explain the meaning of the dual prices given for cash, skilled labour and raw material AFC.

(b) Prepare calculations showing the maximum price Jack Ltd should be willing to pay for the new machine, if payment has to be made in year 1.

(c) Discuss the usefulness and limitations of dual prices in situations such as that described in the question.

Ignore taxation.

*ICAEW*

## Transportation

**70.** The Management Services section of Mech International Ltd is planning to expand. Two of the eleven posts currently being advertised within the section require specialised knowledge of accounting practice and carry a basic annual salary of £5,000, a further three need basic training in data processing and are worth at least £4,700, while the remainder can be filled by anyone with general experience of management services, and pay £4,400 at minimum. It has been agreed, however, that any appointee should be paid a salary equal to the greater of his current salary and the company's minimum for the job he is to do.

Of the fourteen short-listed applicants, all possess adequate general experience. Two are amply qualified in both accounting and data processing, four in accounting only and five in data processing only. The present salaries of the last three groups of applicants are respectively £4,800, £4,600 and £4,500, whereas those with no knowledge of either specialism are currently earning £4,200 or less.

*Required:*

The Head of Management Services has been asked to produce an estimate of total additional expenditure incurred in his section, for the coming year, on employee salaries.

(a) By defining suitable "sources" and "destinations", use the transportation technique to determine the lowest figure he may reasonably submit. (If your allocation is not unique, detail all other possible solutions.)

(b) Show by means of a simple algebraic example that transportation is a special case of linear programming.

*ACCA*

**71.** Newton Company Ltd specialises in the manufacture of certain electronic components for local industry. The three main demand areas for these components are Sidmouth, Liverbourne and Centapool and the company has a warehouse in each of these towns. The company's three factories are separate from its warehouses and are at East Sidmouth, West Liverbourne and Martrent. Due to the present economic climate the company is suffering from an extreme shortage of business, as indicated in the following table:

| Factory | Maximum output of factory per annum (units) | Warehouse | Expected demand in area served by warehouse for coming year (units) |
|---|---|---|---|
| East Sidmouth | 210,000 | Sidmouth | 80,000 |
| West Liverbourne | 140,000 | Liverbourne | 200,000 |
| Martrent | 290,000 | Centapool | 200,000 |

The nearest warehouse to the East Sidmouth and West Liverbourne factories are Sidmouth and Liverbourne respectively. The Centapool warehouse is roughly equidistant from all three factories.

The variable cost of distribution (£ per unit) from the factories to the warehouses are as follows:

|  | Sidmouth | Liverbourne | Centapool |
|---|---|---|---|
| East Sidmouth | 2 | 4 | 4 |
| West Liverbourne | 4 | 3 | 4 |
| Martrent | 3 | 6 | 4 |

The variable costs of production at each factory are:

|  | £ per unit |
|---|---|
| East Sidmouth | 11 |
| West Liverbourne | 14 |
| Martrent | 12 |

The present distribution policy of the company is as follows.

All Sidmouth warehouse requirements are supplied from East Sidmouth.

All West Liverbourne production is transported to the Liverbourne warehouse, the remaining demand at Liverbourne begin supplied from the East Sidmouth factory.

All Centapool requirements are supplied from Martrent.

*Required:*

(a) Evaluate the cost of applying the present distribution policy in the coming year. Why do you think the company adopted this particular policy?

(b) Determine the policy which is expected to achieve the minimum total cost of production and distribution for the coming year. What cost saving does this involve?

Is this solution unique? If not give any alternative solution you find.

(c) Assume now that the company is considering the closure of the West Liverbourne factory. What increase in the total variable cost of production and distribution will this cause assuming that the company operates in a minimum cost manner?

*ACCA*

**72.** Multel Ltd has decided to launch an addition to its product range. The new product may be distributed through any combination of the two company warehouses $W_1$ and $W_2$. The available annual production capacities for the new product are:

$$100 \text{ units at plant } P_1$$
$$200 \text{ units at plant } P_2$$
$$100 \text{ units at plant } P_3$$

The three major concentrations of customer demand are at locations $D_1$, $D_2$ and $D_3$ which are estimated to require each year:-

$$90 \text{ units at } D_1$$
$$80 \text{ units at } D_2$$
$$90 \text{ units at } D_3$$

The unit production costs amount to £3, £4 and £1, at $P_1$, $P_2$ and $P_3$ respectively. The unit handling costs at the warehouse amount to £2 and £3 at $W_1$ and $W_2$ respectively.

The unit trunking costs from plant to warehouse and unit delivery costs from warehouse to customer are as follows:

|       | $W_1$ | $W_2$ |       | $D_1$ | $D_2$ | $D_3$ |
|-------|-------|-------|-------|-------|-------|-------|
| $P_1$ | 6     | 6     | $W_1$ | 3     | 5     | 8     |
| $P_2$ | 5     | 5     | $W_2$ | 5     | 3     | 9     |
| $P_3$ | 13    | 4     |       |       |       |       |

(All costs are in £'s)

*Required:*

(a) Determine an optimum production and distribution schedule.

(Hint: first establish the least costly means of supplying each demand centre from each of the plants.)

(b) Assuming that each warehouse can handle a maximum 200 units a year explain why it would be incorrect to solve the problem using the transportation technique to obtain a solution to the flows between plant and warehouse and then apply the technique again to the flows between the warehouses and the customers.

*ACCA*

**73.** The Brown Chemical Company produces a special oil-based material which is currently in short supply. Four of Brown's customers have already placed orders which in total exceed the combined capacity of its two plants and the company needs to know how it should allocate its production capacity to maximise profits.

The following distribution costs per unit have been determined:

| Customer | $C_1$ | $C_2$ | $C_3$ | $C_4$ |
|---|---|---|---|---|
| Plant X | £16 | £15 | £14 | £18 |
| Plant Y | 15 | 15 | 14 | 15 |

The variable unit production costs are £10 for plant X and £12 for plant Y.

Since the four customers are in different industries, the pricing structure allows different prices to be charged to different customers. (The material undergoes slight variations for each customer at negligible costs.) These prices are £46 for $C_1$, £42 for $C_2$, £40 for $C_3$ and £44 for $C_4$.

The customers' orders (in units) are:

| $C_1$ | $C_2$ | $C_3$ | $C_4$ |
|---|---|---|---|
| 2,000 | 5,000 | 3,500 | 2,500 |

and the plant capacities at X and Y in the period concerned are 6,000 and 3,000 units respectively.

Due to an industrial dispute the company can only supply customer $C_3$ from plant Y.

*Required:*

(a) Formulate the problem using the transportation model explaining how you can use this model in a situation of maximising profits.

(b) Use the transportation algorithm to determine the optimum solution.

(c) If the industrial dispute were to be resolved so that customer $C_3$ could be supplied from plant X, how would this affect your solution?

*ACCA*

**74.** The following problem should be solved by the transportation method. XW Limited has four production plants and four wholesale warehouse outlets. The warehouses are situated away from the production plants. The production and transportation costs, the selling prices, production capacities, and sales quantities are given below:

## APPENDIX 2. EXAMINATION QUESTIONS

| Production plants | Warehouse | | | | Production capacity (units) | Per unit | |
|---|---|---|---|---|---|---|---|
| | 1 | 2 | 3 | 4 | | Materials | Labour and overhead |
| A | 10 | 14 | 7 | 10 | 140 | 4 | £6 |
| B | 8 | 12 | 5 | 10 | 100 | 5 | 8 |
| C | 3 | 7 | 11 | 8 | 150 | 4 | 9 |
| D | 9 | 12 | 6 | 13 | 160 | 3 | 8 |
| Warehouse requirements in units | 80 | 120 | 130 | 110 | | | |
| Selling price (ex warehouse) per unit | £26 | £32 | £30 | £25 | | | |

The cost of transporting a unit from a given plant to a warehouse is shown in the body of the matrix in pounds per unit.

*Required:*
(a) Compute a plan for production and distribution which will achieve maximum profit for the company.

(b) State the profit achieved by the plan you have given in answer to (a) above.

Your workings should be shown and the steps in the calculations described: answers not supported in this way will be regarded as inadequate.    *ICMA*

**75.** A ladies' fashion shop wishes to purchase the following quantity of summer dresses:

| Dress Size | I | II | III | IV |
|---|---|---|---|---|
| Quantity | 100 | 200 | 450 | 150 |

Three manufacturers are willing to supply dresses. The quantities given below are the maximum that they are able to supply of any given combination of orders for dresses:

| Manufacturers | A | B | C |
|---|---|---|---|
| Total Quantity | 150 | 450 | 250 |

The shop expects the profit per dress to vary with the manufacturer as given below:

|   | Sizes | | | |
|---|---|---|---|---|
|   | I | II | III | IV |
| A | £2.5 | £4.0 | £5.0 | £2.0 |
| B | 3.0 | 3.5 | 5.5 | 1.5 |
| C | 2.0 | 4.5 | 4.5 | 2.5 |

*Required:*

(a) Use the transportation technique to solve the problem of how the orders should be placed with the manufacturers by the fashion shop in order to maximise profit.

(b) Explain how you know there is no further improvement possible, showing your workings.

*ICMA*

## Assignments

76. The Weldstone Engineering Company has four plants, each of which can manufacture any one of four products. Production costs differ from one plant to another. The current rationalisation programme has as its objective one product per plant. Given the cost data below, ascertain which product each plant should produce so as to minimise overall costs.

Production costs (£000)

|   |   | Product | | | |
|---|---|---|---|---|---|
|   |   | A | B | C | D |
| Plant | 1 | 25 | 18 | 23 | 14 |
|       | 2 | 38 | 15 | 53 | 23 |
|       | 3 | 15 | 17 | 41 | 30 |
|       | 4 | 26 | 28 | 36 | 29 |

77. The Lucknow Cotton Mill have four mills, which can weave any one of four products. Capacity utilisation varies at the mills as does product quality. This had led to differing production costs and varying sales revenue from each of the products in the different mills. The production cost data and sales revenue information are summarised in the tables below:

Sales revenue (£)

|   |   | Products | | | |
|---|---|---|---|---|---|
|   |   | 1 | 2 | 3 | 4 |
| Mills | A | 50 | 68 | 49 | 62 |
|       | B | 60 | 70 | 51 | 74 |
|       | C | 55 | 67 | 53 | 70 |
|       | D | 58 | 65 | 54 | 69 |

Production costs (£)

|  | | Products | | | |
|---|---|---|---|---|---|
|  | | 1 | 2 | 3 | 4 |
| Mills | A | 49 | 60 | 45 | 61 |
|  | B | 55 | 63 | 45 | 69 |
|  | C | 52 | 62 | 49 | 68 |
|  | D | 55 | 64 | 48 | 66 |

*Required:*

Which product should each mill weave?

78. Middlesam Management Consultants have six consultants available to be assigned to do six jobs for clients. However, because of technical deficiencies in particular areas, consultant B cannot do Job 3, D cannot do Job 4 and consultant F cannot do Job 6. The costs incurred to complete the available assignments are given in the table below:

Costs (£000)

|  | | Jobs | | | | | |
|---|---|---|---|---|---|---|---|
|  | | 1 | 2 | 3 | 4 | 5 | 6 |
| Consultant | A | 7 | 7 | 3 | 6 | 10 | 11 |
|  | B | 8 | 9 | – | 5 | 8 | 10 |
|  | C | 9 | 10 | 11 | 13 | 13 | 8 |
|  | D | 6 | 6 | 8 | – | 12 | 13 |
|  | E | 5 | 5 | 9 | 10 | 10 | 12 |
|  | F | 8 | 4 | 10 | 12 | 9 | – |

*Required:*

Assign the available consultants to the different jobs in such a manner that the total costs are kept at a minimum.

79. Smitsubashi PLC within the framework of its corporate plan is considering the closure of one of its UK factories. The costs of closure will be the same for each factory. Currently, it operates five factories each of which can produce any of four products. It is envisaged that in the future individual factories will achieve production and other economies by concentrating on one product alone. The production cost data for existing operations is summarised below:

Product production cost per unit (£)

|  | | Products | | | |
|---|---|---|---|---|---|
|  | | N | I | P | O |
| Factory | 1 | 71 | 78 | 93 | 76 |
|  | 2 | 69 | 78 | 87 | 74 |
|  | 3 | 72 | 80 | 89 | 76 |
|  | 4 | 73 | 80 | 86 | 78 |
|  | 5 | 65 | 84 | 92 | 72 |

The selling price for each of the products is consistent irrespective of the factory in which it is produced.

| Product | N | I | P | O |
|---|---|---|---|---|
| SP | £80 | £90 | £100 | £85 |

*Required:*

Recommend to the board of Smitsubashi PLC which factory should be closed.

## An introduction to network analysis

80. Draw the networks for the following dependencies:

(a)

| Activity | Preceding activity |
|---|---|
| P | – |
| Q, R | P |
| S | Q |
| T | R |
| U | S, T |

(b)

| Activity | Preceding activity |
|---|---|
| A | – |
| B | A |
| C | A |
| D | A |
| E, F | B |
| G | E |
| H | F |
| I | G, H |
| J | C |
| K | D |
| L | I, J, K |

**81.** Construct the appropriate networks for the following situations:

(a)

| Activity | Linking events |
|---|---|
| A | 1–2 |
| B | 2–3 |
| C | 2–4 |
| D | 3–4 |
| E | 3–5 |
| F | 4–5 |
| G | 5–6 |

(b)

| Activity | Preceding activity |
|---|---|
| A, B, C | – |
| D | A |
| E | B |
| F | C |
| G | D |
| H | E |
| I | F |

(c)

| Activity | Preceding activity |
|---|---|
| A | – |
| B, C, D | A |
| E, F | B |
| G | E |
| H | F |
| I | G, H |
| J | G, H, C, D |
| K | D |
| L | I, J, K |

## Network analysis—time and cost

**82.** An insurance company has decided to modernise and refit one of its branch offices. Some of the existing office equipment will be disposed of but the remainder will be returned to the branch on completion of the alterations. Estimates for the alterations are to be invited from a selection of builders and the builder chosen will be responsible for all aspects of the alterations with the exception of the prior removal of the old equipment and its subsequent replacement.

The major elements of the projects have been identified as follows, along with their approximate durations and the immediately preceding elements:

|   | Element | Duration (weeks) | Preceding element |
|---|---------|------------------|-------------------|
| A | Obtain estimates from selected builders | 5 | E |
| B | Decide on builder to be used | 1 | A |
| C | Arrange details with selected builder | 2 | B |
| D | Alterations take place | 14 | K |
| E | Design new premises | 16 | – |
| F | Decide which equipment is to be retained | 1 | E |
| G | Arrange storage of equipment to be retained | 2 | F |
| H | Arrange disposal of remaining equipment | 3 | F |
| I | Order new equipment | 2 | F |
| J | Take delivery of new equipment | 3 | I, L |
| K | Remove old equipment to storage or disposal | 4 | C, G, H |
| L | Clear up after builder has finished | 2 | D |
| M | Return old equipment from storage | 2 | I, L |

*Required:*

(a) Draw a network to represent the inter-relationships between the various elements of the project.

(b) What is the minimum time that the alterations can take from commencement of the design stage?

(c) It has been suggested that if the number of builders invited to tender were reduced, the estimates could be obtained in three weeks. What effect would this have on the overall duration of the project?

(d) What is "independent float"? Do any of the activities in your network possess it and, if so, which?

*ACCA*

83. A project which is about to start comprises the activities listed in the table below.

Ignoring holiday periods, the project must be completed by the end of week 38. If the project is delayed beyond this date it is estimated that it will cost the firm £300 a week.

*Required:*

(a) Draw a critical path network to represent the project and determine the critical path. What is the earliest time at which the project can be completed and what penalty cost (if any) will be incurred?

| Activity | Immediately preceding activities | Duration (weeks) |
|---|---|---|
| A | – | 4 |
| B | A | 13 |
| C | A | 5 |
| D | C | 11 |
| E | C | 3 |
| F | D, E | 4 |
| G | – | 3 |
| H | A, G | 5 |
| I | G | 4 |
| J | H | 17 |
| K | H | 2 |
| L | J, K | 3 |
| M | F, L | 3 |
| N | B, M | 3 |
| O | I, M | 2 |
| P | O | 3 |
| Q | N, P | 4 |

(b) Activity K is a two-week course to train new salesmen. The hotel which will be used for the course has been booked for weeks 12 and 13. In the light of your analysis should this booking be changed?

(c) If activities L and E can be done in parallel, some savings can be made as they use common resources. What are the minimum savings that must be made to justify these activities being done at the same time?

(d) Briefly outline how the critical path method can be adapted to deal with projects where the activity durations involve some uncertainty. *ACCA*

84. The Computer Balance Company Ltd is developing a new minicomputer system specially designed for use in small accounting practices. The system comes complete with standard programs to deal with the routine preparation of accounts. The production of the system for a particular practice, with the necessary amendments required, can be split into the following eight activities. (The actual details are still a commercial secret.) It is possible to reduce the total time for production below the normal total time by crashing certain activities (in units of 1 week) at extra costs.

The relevant figures are given in the table below:

|  | Immediately | Normal Duration |  | Crash Duration |  |
| Activity | preceding | (weeks) | Cost | (weeks) | Cost |
| --- | --- | --- | --- | --- | --- |
| A | – | 5 | £200 | 3 | £400 |
| B | – | 4 | 100 | – | – |
| C | A | 2 | 500 | 1 | 800 |
| D | B | 1 | 50 | – | – |
| E | B | 5 | 150 | 3 | 300 |
| F | B | 5 | 300 | 4 | 350 |
| G | C, D | 4 | 200 | – | – |
| H | F | 3 | 300 | 2 | 500 |

In addition to the above cost figures, there is a £200 per week charge for variable overhead incurred during the production of the system.

*Required:*

(a) Using the normal durations and costs, determine the critical path and its length. What is the total cost of the project in this case?

(b) What is the cost of completing the project in the shortest time? What would be the duration of the project if total cost is to be minimised?  *ACCA*

85. You are given the following information concerning a project which consists of eight activities, A to H:

| Activity | Preceding activity | Duration (days) |
| --- | --- | --- |
| A | – | 4 |
| B | – | 5 |
| C | A | 2 |
| D | A | 3 |
| E | B, C | 3 |
| F | B, C | 4 |
| G | D, E | 5 |
| H | F | 2 |

*Required:*

(a) Draw a network for the project and determine the activities that lie on the critical path, and also its length.

(b) If activity F has also to precede activity G, will the critical path change?

If it does change, draw your new network and compute the length of the new critical path.

(c) Assume that it has been found that certain activities in the original network can be shortened by hiring extra resources at the following costs:

| Activity | B | D | E | F | G | H |
|---|---|---|---|---|---|---|
| Shortened duration (days) | 3 | 2 | 2 | 3 | 3 | 1 |
| Extra cost (£) | 200 | 150 | 50 | 200 | 250 | 300 |

On the assumption that the extra costs are linear, determine the possible expedited times and their associated costs.

*ACCA*

86. The following information relates to a construction project for which your company is about to sign a contract.

Seven activities are necessary and the normal duration, normal cost, crash duration and crash cost have been derived from the best available sources.

| Activity | Preceding activity | Duration in weeks | | Direct cost | |
|---|---|---|---|---|---|
| | | Normal | Crash | Normal | Crash |
| a | – | 15 | 12 | £4,500 | £5,250 |
| b | – | 19 | 14 | 4,000 | 4,500 |
| c | – | 9 | 5 | 2,500 | 4,500 |
| d | a | 6 | 5 | 1,700 | 1,940 |
| e | a | 14 | 9 | 4,300 | 5,350 |
| f | b, d | 9 | 6 | 2,600 | 3,440 |
| g | c | 8 | 3 | 1,800 | 3,400 |

Each activity may be reduced to the crash duration in weekly stages at pro rata cost. There is a fixed cost of £500 per week.

*Required:*

(a) Draw, clearly labelled, a network and indicate the notation pattern used;

(b) indicate the critical path and state the normal duration and cost;

(c) calculate the minimum total cost, showing clearly your workings, and the revised duration and cost for each activity.

*ICMA*

87 The normal cost/duration and other relevant information for a project is given below:

| Activity | Normal duration (days) | Normal total cost | Minimum duration if accelerated (days) | Cost per day accelerated |
|---|---|---|---|---|
| 1–2 | 3 | £140 | 1 | £110 |
| 2–3 | 2 | 200 | 1 | 175 |
| 2–4 | 3 | 160 | 1 | 125 |
| 2–5 | 2 | 300 | 1 | 200 |
| 3–6 | 2 | 250 | 1 | 175 |
| 4–6 | 6 | 400 | 1 | 70 |
| 5–6 | 5 | 230 | 1 | 70 |
| 6–7 | 5 | 230 | 1 | 90 |

There is a bonus of £100 per day for every day saved below the contract period of 15 days, and a penalty of £200 for each day after the 15 days.

*Required:*

(a) Calculate the normal duration and the normal cost of the project.

(b) Calculate the minimum cost of completing the project in 15 days.

(c) State the optimum plan for the company to attempt.

(d) Revert to the normal programme and normal costs and state what action you would recommend to ensure completion by the original date, if after the tenth day the actual situation was as follows:

   (i) activities completed at normal cost:
      1–2; 2–3; 3–6; 2–4; 2–5.

   (ii) activities not yet started:
      4–6; 5–6; 6–7.

What is the revised cost of the project in these circumstances?

88. Kellogs Ltd, a small construction firm have successfully tendered for a contract offered by a private oil company. The contract involves the construction of a distillation column. You have been approached in your capacity as a management accountant to advise them on this project.

The information given in Table 28 is relevant to the construction of the column.

*Required:*

(a) State the activities on the critical path.

(b) Calculate the time to complete at the normal cost.

# APPENDIX 2. EXAMINATION QUESTIONS

Table 28. Data for distillation column contract.

| Activity | Description | Preceding activity | Duration in days | Normal cost | Extra cost of saving one day | Days that could be saved |
|---|---|---|---|---|---|---|
| a | Plant definition | – | 4 | £1,000 | – | – |
| b | Mechanical design of ends and shells | a | 3 | 1,000 | £250 | 2 |
| c | Issue schedules for ends and shells | b | 2 | 1,000 | 250 | 1 |
| d | Requisition ends and shells | c | 1 | 100 | – | – |
| e | Order ends and shells | d | 1 | 100 | – | – |
| f | Procure ends and shells | e | 24 | 3,000 | 150 | 5 |
| g | Roll shells and weld ends | f, t | 3 | 450 | – | – |
| h | Complete fabrication and assembly of upper column | g, r | 5 | 750 | 350 | 2 |
| i | Test | h | 1 | 150 | – | – |
| j | Pack 1 | i | 1 | 150 | – | – |
| k* | Despatch | j | 1 | 150 | – | – |
| l | Mechanical design of remainder of upper column | b | 6 | 1,000 | 50 | 3 |
| m | Issue schedules for remainder of upper column | l | 2 | 1,000 | – | – |
| n | Material planning | m | 2 | 300 | 40 | 1 |
| p | Requisition materials | n | 1 | 100 | – | – |
| q | Order materials | p | 1 | 100 | – | – |
| r | Procure materials | q | 16 | 5,000 | 100 | 5 |
| s | Work layouts | n | 4 | 600 | 30 | 2 |
| t | Documentation | s | 1 | 150 | – | – |
| | | | | £16,100 | | |

*Activity k marks the completion of the project.

(c) Calculate the cost of completing in 40 days, indicating the activities that would be reduced.

(d) Discuss the effect of failure to complete activities $f$ and $r$ in the estimated duration.

State the advice you would offer to the management if there were two alternative suppliers of the materials involved in activity $r$:

supplier Z, for delivery in 10 days, quoted £5,000 ± £100 for every day early or late:

supplier W, for delivery in 19 days, quoted £4,000 ± £500 for every day early or late.

ICMA

89. Delco Ltd, a small engineering company, intends to produce a batch of machines to be used by a shoe manufacturer in the mass production of shoes.

The activities required in the design and manufacture of the machines are listed below, together with duration and costs.

| | Activity | Preceding Activity | Duration (weeks) | Cost (£) |
|---|---|---|---|---|
| A | Draw up estimate of costs | – | 2 | 400 |
| B | Agree estimate | A | 1 | 0 |
| C | Purchase internal machinery | B | 4 | 200 |
| D | Prepare design drawings | B | 6 | 450 |
| E | Construct main frame | D | 3 | 700 |
| F | Assemble machinery | C, E | 3 | 200 |
| G | Test machinery | F | 4 | 600 |
| H | Determine model type | D | 2 | 0 |
| I | Design outer casing | D | 3 | 250 |
| J | Construct outer casing | H, I | 8 | 600 |
| K | Final assembly | G, J | 2 | 450 |
| L | Final check | K | 2 | 200 |

In addition to the above cost figures, overheads of £250 per week will be incurred for the duration of the project.

*Required:*

(a) What is the critical path and the duration of the project?

(b) (i) What would be the effect of a strike at the factory supplying the internal machinery thereby delaying its delivery for four weeks?

(ii) What would be the effect if the test on the machinery had been done incorrectly and had to be redone, taking another four weeks?

Consider the two events above independently of each other.

(c) The times of some of the activities could be reduced, the new times and costs being as follows:

| Activity | A | B | C | D | E | F | G | H | I | J | K | L |
|---|---|---|---|---|---|---|---|---|---|---|---|---|
| Time (weeks) | 1 | 1 | 2 | 2 | 1 | 1 | 1 | 2 | 2 | 4 | 1 | 1 |
| Cost (£) | 800 | 0 | 450 | 1,150 | 1,200 | 600 | 1,000 | 0 | 450 | 950 | 700 | 350 |

If each activity can only be done in the original time or in the new time, what project time achieves minimum total cost?
*ACCA*

**90.** Labitas Ltd is a small private refinery based in a site near Ellesmere Port. It is situated just off the Manchester Ship Canal and faces the larger refineries owned by Shell and Burmah Oil. Its crude supplies arise from a small Gulf State and have been largely unaffected by recent oil crises. This is largely due to historical and personal connections cultivated over the past century. The most profitable operations at Labitas Ltd are concentrated in the sulphonation plant which produces a range of products, the most well known being a special pink tar used in prestigious sites such as the Mall in front of Buckingham Palace.

Labitas Ltd is currently planning the annual shutdown of the Sulphonation Plant for maintenance purposes. The shutdown is scheduled for August 1980. As management accountant for Labitas you are involved in working out the optimal time period for the maintenance programme so as to minimise total costs. You are working in conjunction with the works engineer who would like the shutdown period to be as short as possible.

The maintenance programme consists of six main activities and took 14 days last year. The works engineer has proposed putting more resources into the programmes and estimates that the shut-down period could be reduced to a minimum of 7 days. The use of these additional resources would increase the direct costs of the maintenance programme. However, in respect of days saved it would eliminate the opportunity cost arising from the loss of business to Labitas while the sulphonation plant is shut down. This loss has been estimated by the Sales Director as £5,000 per day.

Working in consultation with the works engineer you have prepared the following table which gives details of the order in which the maintenance jobs must occur, normal and minimum durations of individual jobs and estimates of appropriate costs. You have also established after consultation with union officials that employment agreements and practices are such that each phase will take a whole number of days.

| Activity | Preceding activities | Normal time (days) | Normal direct cost | Minimum time (days) | Extra direct cost per day saved |
|---|---|---|---|---|---|
| A | – | 8 | £8,000 | 4 | £3,000 |
| B | – | 4 | 6,000 | 3 | 1,000 |
| C | B | 2 | 10,000 | 1 | 4,000 |
| D | – | 4 | 4,000 | 2 | 1,000 |
| E | A, C, D | 3 | 1,000 | 2 | 2,000 |
| F | E | 3 | 16,000 | 1 | 6,000 |

*Required:*

Draft a formal report to the works director at Labitas stating the least cost and associated time in which the maintenance programme can be carried out. Include your detailed calculations and diagrams as an appendix to the report.

*ICAEW Adapted*

## NETWORK ANALYSIS—RESOURCE ANALYSIS AND UNCERTAINTY

91. The project leader of an operational research group has analysed a project to be tackled into eleven activities as follows:

| | Activity | Preceding activity | Duration (weeks) |
|---|---|---|---|
| A | Pilot survey | – | 2 |
| B | Investigation of computer requirements | – | 1 |
| C | Preliminary data analysis | A | 1 |
| D | Write initial report | B, C | 1 |
| E | Program design | B | 1 |
| F | Program testing and debugging | E | 2 |
| G | Main data collection | C | 4 |
| H | Data collation | G | 1 |
| I | Run program on collated data | F, D, H | 1 |
| J | Discussion and analysis of results | I | 1 |
| K | Final report | J | 2 |

*Required:*

(a) Draw a network for the project and hence determine the critical path and its duration.

(b) Activities B, E, F, H and I are all to be carried out by the computing staff but there is only sufficient staff to carry out one activity at a time. What is the latest time that activity B, investigation of computer requirements, can be carried out such that the project can be completed at the earliest possible time?

(c) If the number of staff required for each activity is as follows, what is the minimum size of the project team required to complete the project on time?

| Activity | A | B | C | D | E | F | G | H | I | J | K |
|---|---|---|---|---|---|---|---|---|---|---|---|
| Staff required | 3 | 2 | 1 | 1 | 2 | 2 | 4 | 2 | 2 | 4 | 2 |

*ACCA*

**92.** Each autumn the Quantitative Accountants' Association prepares and distributes an annual programme. The programme gives dates of meetings and a list of speakers with summaries of their talks. Also included is an up-to-date list of paid-up members. The activities to be carried out to complete the preparation of the programme are as follows:

| | Activity | Immediate predecessor | Estimated time (days) |
|---|---|---|---|
| A | Select dates for programme | – | 4 |
| B | Secure agreement from speakers and prepare summaries of their talks | A | 12 |
| C | Obtain advertising material for programme | A | 11 |
| D | Mail membership renewal notices | – | 20 |
| E | Prepare list of paid-up members | D | 6 |
| F | Send membership list to printer and read proofs | B, C, E | 7 |
| G | Print and assemble programme | F | 10 |
| H | Obtain computer-printed address labels of members | E | 5 |
| I | Send out programmes | G, H | 4 |

*Required:*

(a) Draw a network for the scheme of activities set out above. Include full information on earliest and latest event times and indicate the critical path.

(b) Draw a bar chart for the scheme and state the total float for each activity.

(c) If each activity requires one member of the office staff of the Association, so that the activities may be completed in the estimated times, what is the minimum number of staff that should be allocated to the scheme?

(d) What would be the effect on the total time if one of the allocated staff was taken ill for the duration of the scheme and not replaced?  *ACCA*

**93.** Consider the project which requires the following activities:

| Activity | | Activity time (days) | | Total cost (normal) | Resources (normal number of men per day) |
|---|---|---|---|---|---|
| Initial node | Terminal node | Normal | Crash | | |
| 0 | 9 | 6 | 3 | £480 | 4 |
| 0 | 10 | 10 | 5 | 900 | 5 |
| 10 | 7 | 7 | 4 | 490 | 5 |
| 7 | 8 | 9 | 2 | 540 | 4 |
| 9 | 2 | 8 | 4 | 560 | 6 |
| 3 | 4 | 5 | 2 | 300 | 4 |
| 7 | 3 | 6 | 3 | 500 | 4 |
| 6 | 11 | 6 | 3 | 520 | 6 |
| 1 | 6 | 7 | 4 | 510 | 5 |
| 8 | 4 | 10 | 5 | 920 | 6 |
| 4 | 5 | 8 | 4 | 580 | 6 |
| 2 | 8 | 10 | 5 | 940 | 5 |
| 0 | 1 | 9 | 6 | 560 | 4 |
| 11 | 4 | 8 | 4 | 480 | 4 |

The activities that can be "crashed" must take either the normal time or the crash time. There is no opportunity to reduce the time of an activity by one or two days. The cost of crashing any activity is £100 per day.

*Required:*

(a) Calculate the normal duration of the project, its normal cost, and the critical path.

(b) State the number of different paths from start to finish.

(c) Calculate the minimum time in which the project can be completed and state the critical activities.

(d) State the maximum number of men required to complete the project if all activities commence at the earliest start date.  *ICMA*

**94.**

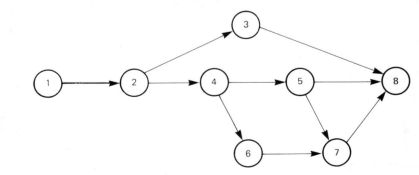

Fig. 99. *PERT estimates for project activities.*

# APPENDIX 2. EXAMINATION QUESTIONS

PERT estimates of the most optimistic, most likely and most pessimistic durations (in days) are given for the following project activities in the network shown in Fig. 99.

| Activity | Optimistic | Most likely | Pessimistic |
|---|---|---|---|
| 1-2 | 3 | 4 | 6 |
| 2-3 | 2 | 3 | 4 |
| 2-4 | 3 | 5 | 9 |
| 3-8 | 1 | 2 | 3 |
| 4-5 | 1 | 3 | 4 |
| 4-6 | 2 | 3 | 7 |
| 5-7 | 1 | 2 | 3 |
| 5-8 | 2 | 4 | 6 |
| 6-7 | 3 | 4 | 5 |
| 7-8 | 2 | 4 | 5 |

*Required:*

Determine the critical path of the network, and hence determine the probability that the project can be completed more than 3 days earlier than the mean duration.

**95.** Delta Ltd, in planning a project to introduce a new product, has listed the following necessary activities:

| Activity | Preceding activity | Expected time (weeks) |
|---|---|---|
| A | – | 6 |
| B | – | 3 |
| C | A | 5 |
| D | A | 4 |
| E | A | 3 |
| F | C | 3 |
| G | D | 5 |
| H | B, D, E | 5 |
| I | H | 2 |
| J | F, G, I | 3 |

*Required:*

(a) Draw the critical path network for the project and determine the critical path and its duration.

(b) If the start of acitivity B is delayed by 3 weeks, activity E by 2 weeks and activity G by 2 weeks, how is the total time for the project affected?

(c) Assume that the times given in the above table are the expected times of the activities, the durations of which are normally distributed with the following standard deviations:

| Activity | A | B | C | D | E | F | G | H | I | J |
|---|---|---|---|---|---|---|---|---|---|---|
| Standard deviation | 1 | 0.5 | 1 | 1 | 0.5 | 0.5 | 1 | 1 | 0.5 | 1 |

Ignoring the delays referred to in (b) and the possible effect of uncertainty in non-critical activities, determine a 95 per cent confidence interval for the expected time on the critical path.

(d) The costs of the project are estimated to be £100,000. If it is completed within 24 weeks the expected returns should be about £1,000,000 but if the deadline of 24 weeks is not met, the product will fail to penetrate the market and a revenue of only £20,000 is expected. Determine the expected profit on this project. (For simplicity, you should again ignore the delays referred to in (b) and the possible effect of uncertainty in non-critical activities.)
*ACCA*

**96.** You are in the planning department of the Finelow Construction Co. Ltd which has contracted to undertake fairly extensive motorway repairworks in the North of England. Due to problems of weather at that time of year, and as the police have asked for co-operation in stopping work from time to time if undue traffic chaos occurs, there is some doubt as to the precision of estimates for completing each phase of the work. However, Finelow are happy that the following network data is applicable to the job. To avoid candidates being confused by technicalities the activities are coded A to G as follows:

|  | Time estimates (days) | | | |
|---|---|---|---|---|
| Activity | Likely | Most pessimistic | Optimistic | Preceding activities |
| A | 7 | 13 | 4 | – |
| B | 6 | 9 | 3 | – |
| C | 4 | 6 | 2 | A |
| D | 3 | 10 | 2 | B |
| E | 3 | 11 | 1 | B |
| F | 6 | 8 | 4 | C, D |
| G | 5 | 15 | 1 | E |

*Required:*

(a) Determine the estimated length of the critical path and its standard deviation.

(b) The Finelow Company has undertaken a second project which could use equipment released from the above project if it finishes early, or it could hire up to 2 excavators at a cost of £4,000 each. For each excavator not hired when one was needed a financial penalty of £14,000 would be incurred. The situaton is summarised in the "pay-off" table (Table 29). The decision on hiring must be taken now, before the first project is started.

Table 29. Timetable to complete first project.

|  |  | Under 16 weeks | 17–18 weeks | 19 weeks and over |
|---|---|---|---|---|
| Number of extra excavators required |  | 0 | 1 | 2 |
|  |  | \multicolumn{3}{c}{Extra costs incurred} |
| Number of excavators hired | 0 | £0 | £14,000 | £28,000 |
|  | 1 | 4,000 | 4,000 | 18,000 |
|  | 2 | 8,000 | 8,000 | 8,000 |

(c) Derive the probabilities of completing the first project in the given time periods. Hence recommend to the company how many excavators should be hired using the criterion of the lowest expected cost.  *ACCA Pilot Paper*

97. Steropes Ltd undertakes special contracts. The table gives estimates of the time and cost for activities involved in completing one contract that has just been offered to the firm.

| Activity | Preceding activities | Normal time (days) | Normal cost | Minimum time (days) | Cost for minimum time |
|---|---|---|---|---|---|
| A | – | 12 | £10,000 | 8 | £14,000 |
| B | – | 10 | 5,000 | 10 | 5,000 |
| C | A | 0 | 0 | 0 | 0 |
| D | A | 6 | 4,000 | 4 | 5,000 |
| E | B, C | 16 | 9,000 | 14 | 12,000 |
| F | D | 16 | 3,200 | 8 | 8,000 |
|  |  | 60 | 31,200 | 44 | 44,000 |

Previous activities must be completed before the activity in question can be started.

The minimum time represents the shortest time in which the activity can be completed given the use of especially costly methods of operation. Assume that it is possible to reduce the normal time to the minimum time in small steps and that the extra cost incurred will be proportional to the time saved.

*Required:*

(a) Draw a network diagram for the contract and identify the critical path assuming that normal procedures are adopted.

(b) Recommend what programme should be followed if the job must be completed in 30 days, and calculate the total cost for that programme.

(c) Explain how you would modify your analysis if the estimates were subject to uncertainty. Illustrate your answer by assuming that estimates of the time required for E are uncertain. Normal time is expected to be in the range 12 to 20 days, but 2 days could still be saved by spending an extra £3,000. You remain confident about the estimates for other activities. Target time for the contract is 30 days and there would be a penalty of £5,000 for late completion. *ACCA*

98. Consider the activities required to complete the processing of a customer's order:

| | Activity | Preceding activities | Average time (days) | Normal variable cost per day |
|---|---|---|---|---|
| 1 | Receipt of order, checking credit rating etc. | – | 2 | £5 |
| 2 | Preparation of material specification, availability of material etc. | 1 | 4 | 10 |
| 3 | Inspection, packing etc. | 2 | 1 | 7 |
| 4 | Arrangement of transport facilities etc. | 1 | 5 | 5 |
| 5 | Delivery | 3, 4 | 3 | 2 |

The time for activities 1, 3 and 5 are fixed; for activity 2 there is a 0.5 probability that it will require 2 days and a 0.5 probability that it will require 6 days; for activity 4 a 0.7 probability of taking 4 days, 0.2 of taking 6 days, and 0.1 of taking 10 days.

*Required:*

(a) Draw the network (it is very simple) twice, first using an arrow diagram and secondly an activity-on-node presentation, clearly indicating the meaning of any symbols that you use;

(b) Indicate the critical path and calculate average duration and variable cost under normal conditions;

(c) Calculate the minimum and maximum times and the probabilities associated with them. *ICMA*

99. Edward Ltd is preparing plans for carrying out the work on a new contract which it has just been awarded. The following table gives estimates of the time and cost according to standard procedures for activities involved in the contract.

# APPENDIX 2. EXAMINATION QUESTIONS

| Activity | Previous activities | Time required (days) | Cost |
|---|---|---|---|
| A | – | 8–12 | £7,000– 9,000 |
| B | – | 11–13 | 6,000– 7,000 |
| C | A, B | 7–9 | 4,000– 4,500 |
| D | – | 12–16 | 12,000–15,000 |
| E | – | 13–15 | 9,000– 9,500 |
| F | E | 7–9 | 5,000– 6,000 |
| G | C, D, F | 5–7 | 6,000– 6,500 |

"Previous activities" must be completed before the activity in question can be started. Information on time required and cost for each activity is given in the form of a 95 per cent confidence interval. The probability distributions for time and cost are symmetrical about the mean values.

Alternative methods of operation could be applied to some of the activities:

(a) activity D could be completed in 11–13 days at a cost of £11,000–£13,000 (alternative (i)) or in 8–12 days at a cost of £12,000–£16,000 (alternative (ii));

(b) activity E could be completed in 9–11 days at a cost of £14,000–£15,000;

(c) activity B could be completed in 10–12 days at a cost of £8,000–£9,000.

Edward's customer is willing to increase the contract price by £2,500 for each day saved on the contract below 30 days. It is not possible to use a combination of standard procedures and alternative procedures on one activity.

*Required:*

(a) Calculate the minimum expected value of the time required to complete the contract and the expected value of the cost given the use of standard procedures.

(b) Evaluate the worthwhileness of using each of the alternative methods of operation in terms of expected values.

*ICAEW*

## Inventory control

**100.** Electropoint Ltd has expanded the production of its domestic robots and now requires, each year and at a constant rate, 200,000 positronic circuits which it obtains from an outside supplier. The cost of placing each order for the positronic circuits is £32. For any circuit in stock it is estimated that the annual holding cost is equal to 10 per cent of its cost. The circuits cost £8 each. No stock-outs are permitted.

*Required:*

(a) What is the optimal order size, and how many orders should be placed in a year?

(b) What are the ordering and holding costs and hence what is the total relevant inventory cost per annum?

(c) If the demand has been underestimated and the true demand is 242,000 circuits per annum, what would be the effect of keeping to the order quantity calculated in (a) above and still meeting demand, rather than using the new optimal order level?

(d) What does your answer to (c) tell you about the sensitivity of your model to changes in demand?
*ACCA*

101. Electropoint Ltd is concerned about the stock level of their positronic circuits which appears to be too low. They are currently ordering the circuits, which cost £4 each, in batches of 200 and demand for the circuits is fairly constant at 10 a day for each of the 250 working days in the year. The cost of ordering a batch of circuits is £25. The inventory carrying cost is estimated at $12\frac{1}{2}$ per cent of the cost of a circuit.

*Required:*

(a) Calculate the economic order quantity and the annual savings which would be made over the current policy of ordering in batches of 200.

(b) The supplier of the positronic circuits has agreed to reduce the price of the circuits for larger orders. The negotiated price structure is:

| Order level | Unit cost |
|---|---|
| 0–399 | £4.00 |
| 400–599 | 3.90 |
| 600 + | 3.80 |

How does this affect the optimal order quantity?

(c) One of the major problems in inventory control is the estimation of the inventory carrying cost. In this problem we have assumed that the carrying cost is proportional to the cost of a unit, i.e. $12\frac{1}{2}$ per cent. In practice, what approach might the accountant use when estimating the magnitude of such a cost?
*ACCA*

102. Dugetron Limited and Ainse Limited have amalgamated and now share a common head office but still have two production plants making complementary ranges of equipment in different parts of the country. Their products involve using some identical components, bought from a common sole supplier. In the case of the most important of these components they both use about 3,000 per year at a fairly consistent rate through a 50-week production year.

These components cost £4 each and are delivered by the supplier in van loads of 200 maximum. The cost of placing an order and laboratory testing an incoming delivery for acceptance into stock is about £80 at each production plant, since the laboratory testing equipment is standard throughout the industry. The current cost of capital plus storage charges is currently 30 per cent. The former Dugetron plant currently orders 5 deliveries of 600 components per year, while the former Ainse Limited plant orders monthly and has 12 deliveries of 250.

# APPENDIX 2. EXAMINATION QUESTIONS 315

*Required:*

(a) Stating clearly any assumptions that you are making, which of the two plants has the better ordering policy?

(b) Is there a better ordering policy, assuming the plants continue to order separately or combine their order?

(c) On being approached by the new joint company, the suppliers agree that they will give a 10 per cent quantity discount if a once-a-year order of 6,000 components is delivered to only one of the plants.

The cost of delivering one vanload (maximum 300 components) from one of the plants to the other, using company vans, is £40.
Is the discount worth while?

(d) What other practical considerations have to be taken into consideration other than those of pure cost?
*ACCA Pilot Paper*

**103.** The purchasing manager of Elstore Limited, an electrical components retailer, holds a regular stock of, among other things, quasitrons. Over the past year he has sold, on average, 25 a week and he anticipates that this rate of sale will continue during the next year (which you may take to be 50 weeks). He buys quasitrons from his supplier at the rate of £5 for 10, and every time he places an order it costs on average £10 bearing in mind the necessary secretarial expenses and the time involved in checking the order. As a guide to the stockholding costs involved, the company usually value their cost of capital at 20 per cent and, as the storage space required is negligible, he decides that this figure is appropriate in this case. Furthermore, the prices charged to customers are determined by taking the purchasing and stockholding costs and applying a standard mark up of 20 per cent.

*Required:*

(a) Currently the manager is reviewing his ordering and pricing policies and needs to know how many quasitrons he should order each time and what price he should charge. What would be your advice? (State any assumptions that you make.)

(b) If he now finds out that he can get a discount of 5 per cent for ordering in batches of 1,000, would you advise him to amend the ordering and pricing policy that you have suggested and, if so, to what?

(c) How large would the percentage holding cost have to be for the manager to be indifferent between taking advantage of the quantity discount and maintaining the original ordering policy that you have suggested?
Comment on the value that you have obtained.
*ACCA*

**104.** Optimum Ltd makes a single product, the Opt. Opts sell for £30 each and demand is running at 1,000 units per annum, evenly distributed over the year. Technical features in production necessitate batch production methods to supply the expected demand. Currently the company produces in batches of 200 units, although this quantity is not determined by the technology. The cost card for the production of one Opt provides the information given in Table 30.

Table 30. Costs of one Opt.

| | | | |
|---|---|---|---|
| Material cost | | | £6.00 |
| Labour costs | | | |
| machining 2 hours | @ £1.75 | £3.50 | |
| assembly 1 hour | @ £1.25 | 1.25 | |
| packing $\frac{1}{2}$ hour | @ £0.50 | 0.25 | |
| | | | 5.00 |
| Other direct costs | | | |
| 2 machine hours | @ £4.00 | | 8.00 |
| Overheads | | | 3.00 |
| | | | £22.00. |

On investigation you find that the overheads are comprised of elements for:

(a) The labour costs associated with the preparation time required for each batch of Opts of 4 hours, which is carried out by the packing staff;

(b) machine set-up costs of £40 per batch (this service is provided by an outside firm);

(c) the absorption of other fixed overheads.

Opts are stacked 3 high on pallets which require storage space 1 metre square and are stored in a warehouse. The rent of the warehouse was negotiated many years ago at the favourable price of £10 per square metre. However, as demand for Opts has been dropping the firm has been increasingly able to sub-let its surplus warehouse space for £24 per square metre. Recently Optimum Ltd's labour force has been reduced. However, there is still plenty of spare capacity in the organisation as far as all classes of its labour are concerned. Nevertheless, the management has no intention of causing further redundancies. You may assume that the opportunity cost of interest on stock holdings is negligible.

*Required:*

(a) Compute the optimum batch size of Opts to be produced, explaining the formula you have used, commenting briefly on any assumptions you have made and relevant costs you have introduced.

(b) Comment briefly on the size of the average stock of Opts held, in the light of your answer to (a) above.

*ACCA*

105. The directors of Arges Ltd are concerned at a recent increase in the company's working capital requirements. They have initiated a special study of the levels of stocks of each product in an attempt to effect economies. One of the main products is the Cyclops. It is manufactured in batches and sold at £25 per unit. At this price, sales

are expected to be 5,000 units per annum, spread evenly through the year. The Cyclops requires the following resources:

*Materials*   Cost £7 per unit.

*Labour hours*   One grade is employed for machining and assembly. Preparation and machine set-up time require 16 hours at the start of production of each batch. Subsequently each unit of output requires 2 labour hours. The wage rate is £0.99 per hour. Labour is currently subject to a substantial amount of idle time because of a recession in the industry. The directors have decided not to dismiss any employees, nor to reduce the number of hours for which employees are paid.

*Machine hours*   One standard type of machine is used. Set-up time for a batch is 9 hours and each unit of output requires 1 machine hour. Machine costs amount to £4 per hour.

Stocks are kept in a warehouse which was rented on a long lease 10 years ago for £2 per square foot per annum. Warehouse space available exceeds current requirements and spare capacity is sublet on annual contracts at £3 per square foot per annum. Each unit of Cyclops requires 3 square feet of space. Other costs of holding Cyclops in stock are estimated at £7 per unit per annum.

*Required:*

(a) Calculate the optimal batch size and the associated maximum and average stock levels.

(b) Explain briefly the rationale of the square-root formula.

(c) Explain for the benefit of the managing director (who is not familiar with accounting) the reasons for your treatment of the cost of labour and warehouse space.

*ACCA*

**106.** Vaal Ltd manufactures several products including a chemical called Zand. Stocks of the chemical have to be stored in special warehouses and the firm is now undertaking calculations of the optimal level of their stocks of Zand with a view to determining whether an additional warehouse should be purchased.

Products are manufactured in batches using common processing plant which has an output rate of 100 tons per hour. Zand is sold for £72 per ton and demand is 40,000 tons per annum, spread evenly over the year. Each time Vaal commences the processing of a "batch" of Zand, special costs of £12 for materials are incurred; 20 hours of grade E labour are also required in setting up the plant for the processing and grade E labour is paid £2 per hour; if they were not working on the setting-up of the process, however, the employees would be undertaking semi-skilled work, saving the employment of lower grade employees at £1 per hour.

The variable cost of production of a ton of Zand is £40. Warehouses suitable for Zand may be erected only in a standard size with a capacity of 500 tons. Vaal owns one such warehouse at the present time. Warehouses cost £5,000 and have indefinitely long lives; they involve annual maintenance costs of £120. Vaal's cost of capital is 10 per cent per annum.

There is to be no minimum level below which stocks are not allowed to fall.

*Required:*

(a) Calculate (i) the optimal level of maximum stocks of Zand assuming that a second warehouse is purchased; (ii) the optimal level of maximum stocks assuming that a second warehouse is not purchased; (iii) the total annual costs of the policies under (i) and (ii) and hence (iv) estimate whether purchase of the second warehouse is worthwhile.

(b) Explain, for the benefit of a director who has no familiarity with quantitative techniques, the rationale of your calculations. Ignore taxation and inflation.

*ACCA*

**107.** A small insurance company estimates that next year it will receive £5 million in premiums that will flow in a steady rate throughout the year. This income will be invested at 20 per cent per annum but the cost to the company of making an investment is £200 for each investment made and, in addition, 2 per cent of the sum invested.

*Required:*

(a) Show that this situation is an inventory problem in structure and that the "economic order quantity" model may be used to determine the optimum investment policy, i.e. the timing of making the company's investments.

(b) Explain why the optimum investment policy is independent of the variable element of the investment costs.

(c) Determine how many investments should be made during the year and the total cost of the policy as given by the "economic order quantity" model. Comment critically on this total cost from a financial point of view.

(d) A reorganisation of the company's investment department would cause investment costs to change to £450 for each investment made plus $1\frac{1}{2}$ per cent of the sum invested. How would this affect the company's optimum investment policy according to the "economic order quantity" model?

(e) Instead of reorganising the investment department the company decides to hold, as a buffer stock, cash to the value of 2 per cent of the yearly premiums. What will be the maximum holding of cash at any one time?

(f) Comment on the practical inadequacies of the "economic order quantity" model in this situation.

*ACCA*

**108.** A company has estimated its requirements for a particular component over the next twelve months to be as follows:

|                 | Jan.  | Feb.  | Mar.  | Apr.  | May   | June  |
|-----------------|-------|-------|-------|-------|-------|-------|
| Demand (units)  | 2,000 | 2,025 | 1,950 | 2,000 | 2,100 | 2,050 |

|                 | July  | Aug.  | Sept. | Oct.  | Nov.  | Dec.  |
|-----------------|-------|-------|-------|-------|-------|-------|
| Demand (units)  | 2,000 | 1,975 | 1,900 | 2,000 | 1,900 | 2,100 |

The components are purchased from an outside supplier for £2 each and the annual inventory holding costs are estimated to be 10 per cent of the cost of the component. The order cost averages £150 per order.

*Required:*

(a) As the above demand figures exhibit relatively little variability, treat the problem as one of constant demand and determine the economic order quantity (EOQ). How frequently should orders be placed and what would be the total annual inventory holding cost?

(b) It is now 1st January and you have no stock on hand. You have just received your first order of components from the suppliers. Given that the demand pattern above actually occurs and that you use an economic order quantity policy as calculated in (a), determine for each month the starting and ending stock. Hence, calculate the actual inventory holding cost assuming that all demands are to be satisfied. If, in addition, there is a shortage cost of £4 per item per year, calculate the total annual shortage cost incurred.

(c) Comment on the difference between the two inventory holding costs calculated in (a) and (b) and indicate the implications of this for the economic order quantity model.
*ACCA*

109. A manufacturer finds that he has a steady demand for product Zed of 300 units per week. He can produce Zed at the rate of 75 units per hour and his budgeted production hours are 36 hours per week for 50 weeks per year. He calculates that the production cost per unit of Zed is £2, but that in addition set-up costs of £540 are incurred for each production run. The total annual stockholding cost as a fraction of stock value is 20 per cent. The manufacturer wishes to know how many units of Zed he should produce in each production run in order to minimise his total costs.

*Required:*

(a) Derive a formula for the economic batch quantity, explaining briefly but clearly the logic of each step in your solution.

(b) Use your formula to calculate the economic batch quantity for product Zed in the situation given.
*ICMA*

110. The stock control policy of XYZ Ltd is that each item of stock is ordered twice per year, the amount of each order being one-half of the year's forecast demand.

The stock controller, however, wishes to introduce a policy in which for each item of stock, re-order levels and economic order quantities are calculated.

For item A the following information is available:

| | |
|---|---|
| Forecast annual demand | 400 units |
| Cost per unit | £10 |
| Cost of placing an order | £4 |
| Stockholding costs | 20 per cent of purchase price p.a. |
| Lead time | 1 month. |

It is estimated by the stock controller that for stock item A a safety stock of an additional 10 units should be provided to cover fluctuations in demand.

*Required:*

(a) The reorder level that should be set by the stock controller.

(b) The anticipated reduction in the value of the average stock investment.

(c) The anticipated reduction in total inventory costs in the first and subsequent years.

**111.** Zambesi Holding Co. have a 50-week working year. The demand for a particular product stocked is subject to random variability. Demand for this product during any one week of the working year is described by the probability distribution:

| Units demanded | Probability |
| --- | --- |
| 0 | 0.03 |
| 1 | 0.06 |
| 2 | 0.07 |
| 3 | 0.09 |
| 4 | 0.11 |
| 5 | 0.21 |
| 6 | 0.17 |
| 7 | 0.12 |
| 8 | 0.08 |
| 9 | 0.06 |

Demand can only be satisfied (if at all) from stocks. The stock-holding costs are £40 per unit per annum. Each time a reorder is made a cost of £50 is incurred irrespective of reorder size and the cost of the item is £180 per unit. There is a lead time of one week. The cost of being out of stock is estimated as £20 per unit short. Zambesi desires to minimise annual inventory costs.

*Required:*

(a) Determine the economic order quantity.

(b) Find the optimal reorder level and size of buffer stock.

(c) For what range of values of the shortage cost figure would the reorder level found in (b) remain optimal? (Assume all other data at their original values.) Could a similar sensitivity analysis be conducted on the holding cost figure?

**112.** Ikauna Ltd is examining its inventory policy in relation to one type of lightweight car wheel that it stores. Demand for the wheel runs at the average rate of 1,000 units per quarter. It costs £8 to hold one wheel for one year. When a reorder is necessary, there are fixed administrative costs of £40 irrespective of order size. The manufacturer charges Ikauna £12 per wheel supplied plus a charge of £120 no matter how large the order.

*Required:*

(a) (i) Determine the economic order quantity.

(ii) An alternative scheme of charges would produce total costs per annum (including the £12 per wheel) of £52,000. Should the alternative scheme be adopted?

(b) Assume a 50-week working year. Lead time is four weeks. Variance of demand in any week is 156.25 units. It can be assumed that demand in each week is normally distributed about the weekly average and is independent of demand in other weeks.

(i) Determine the reorder level that would produce a $97\frac{1}{2}$ per cent "service level".

(ii) Management, in an attempt to economise, is considering a reduction of the service level to 80 per cent. Each stock-out is estimated to cost £120. Is the planned reduction in service level advisable?

**113.** In an assembly process your company consumes annually 125,000 small screws at an even rate of 2,500 per week. The cost of the screws is £4 per 1,000. The cost of placing an order irrespective of the quantity ordered is £5. The risk of obsolescence is negligible and the cost of storage has been estimated at £1 per 1,000 screws per year. The company's minimum required rate of return on capital is 20 per cent.

*Required:*

(a) Calculate the order quantity and state the optimum ordering policy from a supplier who can guarantee immediate delivery.

(b) State the change required in the reordering policy if there were a lead time of two weeks.

(c) Calculate the optimum production policy if the company decided that it could make the screw for £2 per 1,000 plus an order cost of £5 and a set-up cost of £10, at a rate of 25,000 per week.

(d) State the considerations that should be taken into account if requirements fluctuated owing to changes in demand for the assembly.

(e) State the reordering considerations that should be taken into account if demand varies within the range of 1,000 to 4,000 screws required per week. A general stocking policy has now been agreed to ensure there is no problem if demand is 50 per cent higher than average. A stock-out owing to demand being 100 per cent higher than average will be tolerated.

*ICMA*

## Queuing theory

**114.**

(a) "Queues arise when service is not readily available."

*Required:*

(i) Give examples of queuing situations and outline their opposed economic aspects.

(ii) Describe the basic features of queuing situations.

(b) "When a simple queue has settled down some results about average characteristics can be derived from probability theory. These are known as 'simple queue formulae'."

*Required:*

(i) State the properties of simple queues and the assumptions upon which the simple queue formulae are based.

(ii) Plot a graph to show how the average time for a customer in a simple queue system varies with the traffic intensity.

Assume a mean service rate of 20 customers per hour.

**115.**

(a) Describe, with the aid of realistic examples, the basic features of a "queuing problem". Your answer should indicate what information we need for analysing:

(i) the input process;

(ii) the service mechanism;

(iii) the queue discipline.

You should also comment on the major assumptions implicit in the queuing model.

(b) Discuss in general the major limitations of queuing theory and indicate ways in which these limitations might be overcome. *ACCA*

**116.** A coin-operated telephone is installed in a canteen for the use of the staff. On average, 8 people per hour use the phone and their calls last 3 minutes. The staff association think that enough use is made of the phone to justify the installation of a second instrument, but the telephone company say that they will only do this when they are convinced that the staff would have to wait on average for at least 3 minutes to use the phone. Assuming that all calculations are based on simple queuing theory, what rate of use will have to be achieved before the need for a second telephone is justified?

**117.** On an inspection bench, items arrive for inspection on average every 5 minutes.

There is only one inspector, who takes an average of 4 minutes to inspect every item. Service times and interarrival times follow a negative exponential distribution.

# APPENDIX 2. EXAMINATION QUESTIONS

*Required:*

(a) The traffic intensity.

(b) The average number of items in the system at any moment.

(c) The average time from entering to leaving the system.

(d) The average number of items awaiting inspection.

(e) The average time an item spends awaiting inspection.

**118.** On average customers arrive at a check-out point in a supermarket every 3 minutes. The single cashier is capable of serving on average 30 customers per hour. Service times and interarrival times follow a negative exponential distribution.

*Required:*

(a) What is the probability of a customer arriving and having to wait for service?

(b) What is the probability of a customer arriving and finding at least one customer already at the check-out?

(c) What is the average number of customers at the check-out at any moment?

(d) What is the length of time that a customer would expect to spend in the system?

(e) What is the average number of customers at the check-out who are not being served?

(f) The manager feels that unless customers can expect to be served immediately on arrival 40 per cent of the time, trade will eventually drop off. With the original demand pattern, what percentage reduction in service time would be necessary to achieve this result?

**119.** Customers arrive at a service counter on average every 2 minutes. The single server takes an average of $1\frac{1}{2}$ minutes to serve a customer. The estimated cost delay per customer in the system (lost goodwill) is 5 pence per minute.

*Required:*

The serving time can be reduced to 1 minute at an extra cost of £4 per hour. Is this justified?

**120.** At a tool service centre the arrival rate is two per hour and the service potential is three per hour. Simple queue conditions exist.
  The hourly wage paid to the attendant at the service centre is £1.50 per hour and the hourly cost of a machinist away from his work is £4.

*Required:*

(a) Assumptions of simple queuing theory.

(b) Calculate the average number of machinists being served or waiting to be served at any given time.

(c) Calculate the average time a machinist spends waiting for service.

(d) The total cost of operating the system for an eight-hour day.

(e) The cost of the system if there were two attendants working together as a team, each paid £1.50 per hour and each able to service on average 2 per hour.

(f) State any assumptions you have made.

*ICMA*

121. A cost clerk in the sales office of Jupiter Metals is responsible for preparing a sales invoice, following the receipt of an order from a customer. One invoice is required for each order. Orders arrive in the office at an average rate of 5 per hour, and it takes the clerk, on average, 10 minutes to make out an invoice. The office is open for 7 hours a day: in the morning from half-past eight until midday, and in the afternoon from half-past one until five o'clock. The outgoing mail is collected from the office at 10 o'clock each morning and 3 o'clock each afternoon. In order that all sales invoices are despatched to customers as quickly as possible, the sales manager has indicated that efforts should be made to ensure that for each order received during the morning an invoice is sent out that same afternoon, and that an invoice for each order received during the afternoon should be sent the following morning.

*Required:*

(a) If this situation is to be analysed by means of the basic single-server queuing model, identify the components of the queuing system, indicate the assumptions which must be made, and comment on the appropriateness of the assumptions in this particular set of circumstances.

(b) Explain, in detail, how a simulation of the system might be carried out in order to estimate the proportion of invoices which fail to meet the despatch deadlines suggested by the sales manager.

*ACCA*

*Tutorial note: Part (b) of the question is best tackled after assimilating and understanding the chapter on simulation (Chapter 24).*

122. Cronus Ltd operates an engineering factory with a very large number of employees. Each employee has to make frequent visits to the firm's stores to obtain issues of materials for his next job. The issue of one type of material is made in section D at a counter attended by an employee of the stores section. Employees who require issues have to join a single queue and wait until the attendant is available. The average rate of arrival in the stores is 16 per hour and the average rate of service is 20 per hour.

Issues of materials are costed at the cost of materials plus 5 per cent to cover the overhead costs of storage. The overhead costs of storage in section D include £3,000 per annum for wages of the attendant at the issues counter and £600 per annum

# APPENDIX 2. EXAMINATION QUESTIONS

attributed to the attendant for fixed establishment costs—rent, rates, light and heat, and so on—of the service area. Average wages of directly productive employees who visit section D are £1.60 per hour. The length of the firm's normal working year is 2,000 hours.

The directors of Cronus are considering the desirability of employing an extra man as an attendant at the stores issue counter. His wages and efficiency would be the same as for the existing attendant. It would be necessary to spend £2,000 on capital equipment having a life of 10 years. Any savings of the waiting time of directly productive employees would make it possible to reduce the amount of labour time for which the firm pays. The cost of capital of Cronus is 15 per cent per annum.

You may assume that arrivals in and departures from the issues section are described by Poisson distributions and that the number of employees is indefinitely large. A table of standard formulae is available.

*Required:*

(a) Prepare calculations to show whether the additional attendant should be employed, and

(b) explain a technique of analysis which could be used to study the problem when Poisson distributions and simple queue discipline may not be assumed.

*ACCA*

## Simulation

**123.** Simulation has been described as "what to do when all else fails".

*Required:*

Outline the major advantages and disadvantages of the technique.

**124.** "There are two distinct approaches to problems arising from queuing situations. The more popular is simulation, but the formulae of queuing theory are equally useful. In fact, the choice of method is largely a matter of personal taste."

*Required:*

Discuss and criticise this quotation. Your answer should also include the following:

(a) an example of a problem to which queuing theory might be applied;

(b) an example of a problem for which simulation is the more appropriate method;

(c) an assessment of the relative strengths and weaknesses of each method.

*ACCA*

**125.**
(a) Aries Ltd trade in a perishable commodity. Each day Aries receive supplies of the goods from a wholesaler but the quantity supplied is a random variable, as is subsequent retail customer demand for the commodity. Both supply and demand are expressed in batches of 50 units and over the past working year (300 days) Aries have kept records of supplies and demands. The results are given in the table:

| Wholesaler supplies | No. of days occurring | Customers' demand | No. of days occurring |
|---|---|---|---|
| 50 | 60 | 50 | 60 |
| 100 | 90 | 100 | 60 |
| 150 | 90 | 150 | 150 |
| 200 | 60 | 200 | 30 |

Aries Ltd buys the commodity at £6 per unit and sells at £10 a unit. At present unsold units at the end of the day are worthless and there are no storage facilities. Aries estimates that each unit of unsatisfied demand on any day costs them £2. Using the following random numbers:

8 4 8 0 3 3 4 7 9 6 1 5,

*Required:*

(i) Simulate six days' trading and estimate annual profit.

(ii) Rerun the exercise to estimate the value of storage facilities.

(iii) Briefly, what other information could be gleaned from the exercise and what qualifications should be made in respect of the results?

(b) Kulfu Ltd produces an article which undergoes process A and thereafter process B. The pattern of production for both processes is shown below, and you are required to simulate the activity, showing in particular the interprocess stock for the first 10 hours of production. The opening interprocess stock is 5 units.

| Process A | | Process B | |
|---|---|---|---|
| Units per hour | Number of hours | Units per hour | Number of hours |
| 1 | 20 | 1 | 25 |
| 2 | 30 | 2 | 40 |
| 3 | 40 | 3 | 25 |
| 4 | 10 | 4 | 10 |

Assume that the selected random number series is:

1 7 5 4 2 7 6 1 4 8 8 9 5 7 3 1 8 0 9 0 2 8 3 4 9 9 6 0 6 4 5 4 4 3 6 9 7 6 8 1.

**126.** The number of machines arriving per day at a factory repair bench has been noted over a long period of time and found to have the following distribution:

| Arrivals | 0 | 1 | 2 | 3 | 4 | 5 | 6 | 7 | 8 | 9 |
|---|---|---|---|---|---|---|---|---|---|---|
| Percentage | 2 | 7 | 15 | 20 | 20 | 16 | 10 | 6 | 3 | 1 |

# APPENDIX 2. EXAMINATION QUESTIONS

Repair times depend on the type of fault and the number of repairs completed per day. They have been recorded and found to be represented by:

| Repairs | 1 | 2 | 3 | 4 | 5 | 6 | 7 | 8 | 9 | 10 |
|---|---|---|---|---|---|---|---|---|---|---|
| Percentage | 4 | 8 | 14 | 18 | 18 | 15 | 10 | 7 | 4 | 2 |

*Required:*

Simulate 25 days to find the maximum queue length.
  Use the following series of random numbers:

55 86 87 70 05 71 69 29 74 73 37 17 42 16 89 98 35 81
07 16 94 42 27 18 13 70 05 35 86 85 02 79 13 35 37 38
57 19 97 38 45 82 40 32 63 29 10 67 41 99.

**127.** A doctor who has introduced an appointments system for daily consultations has derived the following information regarding patient punctuality:

| | | |
|---|---|---|
| Minutes early | 3 | 6% |
| | 2 | 29% |
| | 1 | 41% |
| On time | | 12% |
| Minutes late | 1 | 7% |
| | 2 | 5% |

The doctor times his consultations over a period, and derives the following frequency distribution:

| | | |
|---|---|---|
| Minutes | 12 | 10% |
| | 13 | 15% |
| | 14 | 28% |
| | 15 | 34% |
| | 16 | 13% |

The doctor would like to issue appointments at 15-minute intervals and wishes to have an idea of his idle time, the patients' waiting time, and whether he can complete his appointments on schedule.

*Required:*

Given the following series of random numbers:

17 14 50 40 83 13 94 08 49 98 79 51 43 74 90 24 09 21 40 12 46 91 09 05 94 45 27 99 15 31 51 6,

simulate sixteen consultations and derive the required information.

## APPENDIX 2. EXAMINATION QUESTIONS

**128.** Coltel Ltd is considering the introduction of a new product and has compiled the following information:

| Variable | Expected value | Standard deviation |
|---|---|---|
| Sales quantity | 5,000 | 400 |
| Selling price per unit | £300 | £5 |
| Fixed costs | £580,000 | £10,000 |
| Variable costs per unit | £175 | £7.5 |

(For simplicity assume that all the random variables are independent and that the probability distributions are normal.)

*Required:*

(a) Calculate, using break-even analysis and expected values, the break-even volume and the expected profit for the period.

(b) Explain how you would carry out a simulation to arrive at an approximate distribution of profits. Illustrate your answer by using the cumulative normal distribution below (Table 31) and the random numbers 20 96 68 59 to obtain one simulated figure for profit.

(c) What is the value to Coltel Ltd of having carried out a simulation rather than simply estimating profit using expected values?

Table 31. Cumulative normal distribution table.

| Random number | No. of deviations from mean | Random number | No. of deviations from mean | Random number | No. of deviations from mean |
|---|---|---|---|---|---|
| 00 | −2.5 | 22−24 | −0.7 | 79−81 | 0.8 |
| 01 | −2.3 | 25−27 | −0.6 | 82−83 | 0.9 |
| 02 | −2.0 | 28−31 | −0.5 | 84−85 | 1.0 |
| 03 | −1.9 | 32−34 | −0.4 | 86−87 | 1.1 |
| 04 | −1.8 | 35−38 | −0.3 | 88−89 | 1.2 |
| 05 | −1.7 | 39−42 | −0.2 | 90−91 | 1.3 |
| 06 | −1.6 | 43−46 | −0.1 | 92 | 1.4 |
| 07 | −1.5 | 47−53 | 0.0 | 93 | 1.5 |
| 08 | −1.4 | 54−57 | 0.1 | 94 | 1.6 |
| 09−10 | −1.3 | 58−61 | 0.2 | 95 | 1.7 |
| 11−12 | −1.2 | 62−65 | 0.3 | 96 | 1.8 |
| 13−14 | −1.1 | 66−68 | 0.4 | 97 | 1.9 |
| 15−16 | −1.0 | 69−72 | 0.5 | 98 | 2.0 |
| 17−18 | −0.9 | 73−75 | 0.6 | 99 | 2.3 |
| 19−21 | −0.8 | 76−78 | 0.7 | | |

*ACCA*

**129.** The Popage Company Ltd has a contract to supply 1,000,000 cans of spinach a year for three years to a major supermarket company. This is a new venture for the company and they need to purchase three new machines, A, B and C, for the canning operation. The market situation is fluid however and the company cannot assume that the contract will be renewed after three years or that some other similar business will replace it. They are therefore reluctant to spend a substantial amount on the machines and the management has narrowed the possible choices of equipment to two manufacturers.

The less expensive equipment is built by Company X at a total cost of £60,000 and has an expected life of three years. All three types of machines are needed, and they all have to be purchased from the same company. The operating characteristics are as shown in Table 32.

Table 32. Company X.

| Machine type | A | B | C |
|---|---|---|---|
| Daily output when operating | 4,500 | 4,500 | 4,500 |
| Probability of breaking down on any particular day | 0.04 | 0.04 | 0.04 |
| If broken down, probability of down-time duration | | | |
| 1 day | 0.40 | 0.40 | 0.35 |
| 2 days | 0.35 | 0.30 | 0.40 |
| 3 days | 0.25 | 0.30 | 0.25 |

The more expensive equipment is built by Company Y at a total cost of £120,000 and also has a life expectancy of three years. The operating characteristics, which are more favourable, are as shown in Table 33.

Table 33. Company Y.

| Machine type | A | B | C |
|---|---|---|---|
| Daily output when operating | 4,500 | 4,500 | 4,500 |
| Probability of breaking down on any particular day | 0.035 | 0.035 | 0.035 |
| If broken down, probability of down-time duration | | | |
| 1 day | 0.50 | 0.50 | 0.40 |
| 2 days | 0.35 | 0.35 | 0.40 |
| 3 days | 0.15 | 0.15 | 0.20 |

At the end of the three years the scrap value of the equipment from either company is estimated to be zero.

The contract requires 1,000,000 cans of spinach a year to be produced. The yearly total can however vary slightly from that figure but if 3,000,000 cans are not delivered in three years, a substantial penalty will be imposed. The number of working days in the year for the company is 300. You may assume that the three types of machine, A, B and C, are all necessary for producing a can of spinach. Breakdown on any machine will stop all production for the duration of the breakdown.

*Required:*

Explain how you would carry out a simulation to evaluate the performance of each company's equipment in order to advise the management of Popage Company Ltd which, if either, should be purchased.
*ACCA*

# APPENDIX 3
# Suggested Answers to Examination Questions

**1.**

| Class interval | f | d | fd | fd² |
|---|---|---|---|---|
| 0–4 | 5 | −2 | −10 | 20 |
| 4–8 | 25 | −1 | −25 | 25 |
| 8–12 | 30 | 0 | 0 | 0 |
| 12–16 | 11 | 1 | 11 | 11 |
| 16–20 | 4 | 2 | 8 | 16 |
| 20–24 | 2 | 3 | 6 | 18 |
| 24 + | 3 | 4 | 12 | 48 |
|  | 80 |  | 2 | 138 |

$$\bar{x} = a + c \frac{\sum fd}{n}$$

$$\therefore \bar{x} = 10 + \frac{4 \times 2}{80}$$

$$= \underline{\underline{10.1 \text{ hours}}}.$$

$$\text{Variance} = c^2 \left[ \frac{\sum fd^2}{n} - \left( \frac{\sum fd}{n} \right)^2 \right]$$

$$= 16 \left[ \frac{138}{80} - \left( \frac{2}{80} \right)^2 \right]$$

$\therefore$ $\underline{\underline{\text{Variance} = 27.59.}}$

$\therefore$ $\underline{\underline{\sigma = 5.25 \text{ hours.}}}$

**2.**
(a)

| Class interval | f | d | fd | fd² |
|---|---|---|---|---|
| 400–500 | 10 | −5 | −50 | 250 |
| 500–600 | 16 | −4 | −64 | 256 |
| 600–700 | 38 | −3 | −114 | 342 |
| 700–800 | 56 | −2 | −112 | 224 |
| 800–900 | 63 | −1 | −63 | 63 |
| 900–1,000 | 67 | 0 | 0 | 0 |
| 1,000–1,100 | 92 | 1 | 92 | 92 |
| 1,100–1,200 | 68 | 2 | 136 | 272 |
| 1,200–1,300 | 57 | 3 | 171 | 513 |
| 1,300–1,400 | 33 | 4 | 132 | 528 |
|  | 500 |  | 128 | 2,540 |

$$\bar{x} = a + c \frac{\sum fd}{n}$$

$$= 950 + 100 \times \frac{128}{500}$$

$$= \underline{\underline{975.6 \text{ hours.}}}$$

$$\text{Variance} = c^2 \left[ \frac{\sum fd^2}{n} - \left( \frac{\sum fd}{n} \right)^2 \right]$$

$$= 100^2 \left[ \frac{2,540}{500} - \left( \frac{128}{500} \right)^2 \right]$$

$$= \underline{\underline{50,144.6.}}$$

$\therefore$ $\underline{\underline{\sigma = 223.9 \text{ hours.}}}$

(b) 
$$\bar{x} - \sigma = 975.6 - 223.9 = 751.7.$$
$$\bar{x} + \sigma = 975.6 + 223.9 = 1{,}199.5.$$

This is approximately 750 to 1,200 hours.

Adding together the frequencies in this range (using only half of the 600–700 frequency) gives:

$$\tfrac{1}{2} \times 38 + 56 + 63 + 67 + 92 + 68$$
$$= 365.$$

Hence percentage of transistors *inside* range

$$= \frac{365}{500}$$
$$= 73 \text{ per cent.}$$

Therefore percentage of transistors *outside* range

$$\bar{x} - \sigma \text{ to } \bar{x} + \sigma \text{ is 27 per cent.}$$

**3.**

(a) Let A = fault A detected, $\bar{A}$ = fault A not detected, etc.

(i) $P(A \text{ and } \bar{B} \text{ and } C) = 0.7 \times 0.3 \times 0.7$
$$= \underline{\underline{0.147}}.$$

(ii) P(any two faults detected and the third not detected)

$$P(A \text{ and } B \text{ and } \bar{C}) + P(A \text{ and } \bar{B} \text{ and } C) + P(\bar{A} \text{ and } B \text{ and } C)$$
$$= 0.7 \times 0.7 \times 0.3 + 0.7 \times 0.3 \times 0.7 + 0.3 \times 0.7 \times 0.7$$
$$= 0.147 + 0.147 + 0.147$$
$$= \underline{\underline{0.441}}.$$

(iii) Answer to (ii) = 3 × [answer to (i)].

The number 3 occurs as it is the combination term $^3C_2$. It is the number of ways of selecting two items from three items, i.e. it is the number of ways in which two faults can be selected from the three faults.

(b) Let $A_1$ = fault A detected on first inspection

$A_2$ = fault A detected on second inspection, etc.

(i) $P(\bar{A}_1 \text{ and } \bar{A}_2) = 0.3 \times 0.4$
$$= \underline{\underline{0.12}}.$$

(ii) P(only one fault out of two detected on two inspections) = ?

$P(A_1 \text{ and } \bar{B}_1 \text{ and } \bar{B}_2)$ or $P(\bar{A}_1 \text{ and } B_1 \text{ and } \bar{A}_2)$ or

$P(\bar{A}_1 \text{ and } \bar{B}_1 \text{ and } A_2 \text{ and } \bar{B}_2)$ or $P(\bar{A}_1 \text{ and } \bar{B}_1 \text{ and } \bar{A}_2 \text{ and } B_2)$

$= 0.7 \times 0.3 \times 0.4 + 0.3 \times 0.7 \times 0.4$

$\quad + 0.3 \times 0.3 \times 0.6 \times 0.4 + 0.3 \times 0.3 \times 0.3 \times 0.4 \times 0.6$

$= 0.084 + 0.084 + 0.0216 + 0.0216$

$= \underline{\underline{0.2112}}.$

(Note that in this question once a fault has been detected on the first inspection you do not look for it again at the second inspection.)

(iii) Now the probability that a fault is detected is:

$P(A_1) + P(\bar{A}_1) \times P(A_2)$

$= 0.7 + 0.3 \times 0.6$

$= 0.7 + 0.18$

$= 0.88.$

∴ Proportion detected by first inspection $= 0.7/0.88 = \underline{\underline{0.795}}$.

Hence proportion detected by second inspection $= 1 - 0.795 = \underline{\underline{0.205}}$.

If this is not clear consider 100 faults; of the 88 detected 70 would be detected on the first inspection. Hence proportion is:

$$\frac{70}{88} = 0.795.$$

**4.**

(a) Now $P(A) = 1/6$, $P(\bar{A}) = 5/6$,

$P(B) = 1/8$, $P(\bar{B}) = 7/8$.

(i) (1) $P(A \text{ and } B) = 1/6 \times 1/8$

$= 1/48.$

(2) P(one defect only) $= P(A \text{ and } \bar{B})$ or $P(\bar{A} \text{ and } B)$

$= 1/6 \times 7/8 + 5/6 \times 1/8$

$= 12/48$

$= 1/4.$

APPENDIX 3. SUGGESTED ANSWERS TO EXAMINATION QUESTIONS 335

(3) P(no defect) = P($\overline{A}$ and $\overline{B}$)

$= 5/6 \times 7/8$

$= 35/48$.

(ii) The answers sum to one.

(b) Now P(C/neither A nor B) = 1/10

P(C/one of A or B) = 2/10

P(C/A and B) = 3/10.

(i) (1) P($\overline{A}$ and $\overline{B}$ and $\overline{C}$) = P($\overline{A}$ and $\overline{B}$) × P($\overline{C}$/neither A nor B)

$= 5/6 \times 7/8 \times 9/10$

$= 315/480$.

(2) P(one of the defects) = P(one defect only A or B) × P($\overline{C}$/one of A or B) + P(no defect A or B) × P(C/neither A nor B) using the results of earlier calculations

$= 12/48 \times 8/10 + 35/48 \times 1/10$

$= 131/480$.

(ii) Out of 480 items the expected number with no defects is 315, with one defect 131 and with 2 or more defects 34. (Total adds to 480.) Hence

Expected cost = $131 \times 10 + 34 \times 30$

= £2,330.


**5.**

Now P(A) = P(B) = P(C) = P(D) = 1/4.

P(E) = P(F) = P(G) = 1/3.

P(H) = 2 × P(I).

Hence P(H) = 2/3, P(I) = 1/3.

(a) (i) P(H) = 2/3.

(ii) P(F or G) = 1/3 + 1/3 = 2/3.

(iii) P(A or B and F and H)

$= 2/4 \times 1/3 \times 2/3$

$= 1/9$.

(iv)  P(A and I or B and H)
$$= 1/4 \times 1/3 + 1/4 \times 2/3$$
$$= 1/4.$$

(v)  As A, F are not mutual exclusive events
$$P(A \text{ or } F) = P(A) + P(F) - P(A \text{ and } F)$$
$$= 1/4 + 1/3 - 1/4 \times 1/3$$
$$= 6/12$$
$$= 1/2.$$

(b) Now $P(F/\text{defective}) = \dfrac{P(F \text{ and defective})}{P(\text{defective})}.$

Now P(F and defective) = P(F) × P(defective/F)
$$= 1/3 \times 1/5$$
$$= 1/15.$$

P(defective) = P(F and defective) + P(E and defective)
$$= 1/15 + 1/3 \times 1/10$$
$$= 1/10.$$

$\therefore$  $P(F/\text{defective}) = \dfrac{1/15}{1/10} = 2/3.$

Alternatively, assume we have 300 items. Altogether then 100 would go through E and 100 through F, and of these 10 of E and 20 of F would be defective, a total of 30 defective. Hence 20 out of the 30 defectives would have come from F, i.e. 2/3.

**6.**

$P(A) = 0.3$, $P(B) = 0.4$, $P(C) = 0.3$.

Let E indicate an error.

$P(AE) = 0.01$, $P(BE) = 0.05$, $P(CE) = 0.03$.

(a) (i)  P(A and AE) = 0.3 × 0.01
$$= \underline{\underline{0.003}}.$$

(ii)  P(error) = P(A and AE) + P(B and BE) + P(C and CE)
$$= 0.003 + 0.4 \times 0.05 + 0.03 \times 0.03$$
$$= \underline{\underline{0.032}}.$$

(b) $P(A/\text{error}) = \dfrac{P(A \text{ and } AE)}{P(\text{error})}$

$= \dfrac{0.003}{0.032}$

$= \underline{\underline{0.09375}}.$

(c) Now $P(X) = 0.3 \times 0.25 \quad = \quad 0.075$

Revised $P(A) = 0.3 \times 0.75 = \quad \underline{0.225}$

Check $\quad 0.300$

Now $P(\text{error}) = P(A \text{ and } AE) + P(B \text{ and } BE) + P(C \text{ and } CE) + P(X \text{ and } XE)$

$\therefore \quad 0.0387 = 0.225 \times 0.01 + 0.4 \times 0.05 + 0.3 \times 0.03 + 0.075 \times P(XE)$

$\therefore \quad 0.0387 = 0.03125 + 0.075 \times P(XE)$

$0.00745 = 0.075 \times P(XE)$

$\therefore \quad P(XE) = 0.0993$

$\therefore \quad \underline{\underline{P(XE) \approx 0.01}}.$

## 7.

(a) Use a management accounting approach of calculating increment costs and revenues per thousand programmes:

|  |  | Increment cash flows |
|---|---|---|
| Costs per 1,000 printed | = | £40 |
| Revenue per 1,000 sold | = | 150 |
| Cost per 1,000 not sold but printed | = | 10 |

|  | Non-incremented cash flows |
|---|---|
| Advertising revenue | £800 |
| Fixed cost | 1,000 |
| Balance | – £200 |

Use these results to produce a payoff table:

|  | (000) | \multicolumn{4}{c}{Possible outcomes (000)} | EV |
|---|---|---|---|---|---|---|
|  |  | 10 | 20 | 30 | 40 |  |
| Decision variables | 10 | 1,100 | 1,100 | 1,100 | 1,100 | 1,100 |
|  | 20 | 800 | 2,200 | 2,200 | 2,200 | 2,060 |
|  | 30 | 500 | 1,900 | 3,300 | 3,300 | 2,460 |
|  | 40 | 200 | 1,600 | 3,000 | 4,400 | 2,440 |
|  | Probability | 0.1 | 0.4 | 0.3 | 0.2 |  |

(b) Highest expected value occurs when 30,000 programmes are printed. Maximum expected profit is £2,460 less £200 = £2,260.

(c) Buying 20,000 copies per game leads only to an expected value of £2,060, an opportunity loss of £400. 20,000 copies represents the model value (highest probability) which should not be confused with the mean value represented by the expected value.

(d) We need to calculate the expected value of perfect information. To do this we sum the product of each probability multiplied by the highest value in each column of our payoff table.

i.e. $0.1 \times 1{,}100 + 0.4 \times 2{,}200 + 0.3 \times 3{,}300 + 0.2 \times 4{,}400$

$$= £2{,}860$$

deduct our non-incremented flow of $\quad\quad 200$

becomes $\quad\quad\quad\quad\quad\quad\quad\quad\quad £2{,}660$

If we could make a perfect forecast of the number of programmes to be sold at each game our profit becomes £2,660, an increase of £400. This is known as the value of perfect information.

**8.**

You may find this question confusing as some of the calculations have already been done. The cash inflows as given in the first table have been discounted at 10 per cent over the six-year period and are presented in the second table. Consequently we can ignore the first table in our analysis and use the data in the second table.

(a) *See* Fig. 100. (Cash flows are in £m.)

(b) *Large plant*
Expected value:

$$-3 + 0.2 \times 2.871 + 0.4 \times 5.22 + 0.15 \times 1.305 + 0.25 \times 3.654 = 0.77145.$$

# APPENDIX 3. SUGGESTED ANSWERS TO EXAMINATION QUESTIONS

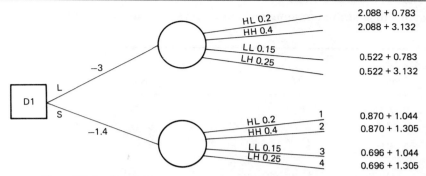

Fig. 100. *Decision tree—manufacturing plant problem.*

*Small plant*
Expected value:

$$-1.4 + 0.2 \times 1.914 + 0.4 \times 2.175 + 0.15 \times 1.74 + 0.25 \times 2.001 = 0.61405.$$

As we wish to maximise the net present value of the project we should build the large plant, giving an expected value of £771,450.

**9.**

(a) To see if the market research survey is worth considering, the value of the information from the survey must be worth more than the cost of the survey of £20,000.
   Now the expected value of the project (£1,000) is:

$$0.3 \times 150 + 0.7 \times (-40) = 17.$$

The expected value with perfect information is:

$$0.3 \times 150 + 0.7 \times 0^* = 45.$$

Hence value of perfect information is: $45 - 17 = 28$, i.e. £28,000.
   There is a case for considering a survey as the value of perfect information £28,000 is greater than the £20,000 cost of the survey.

(b) Let H  = high sales
    L  = low sales
    FH = forecast high sales
    FI = forecast indecisive
    FL = forecast low sales.

To determine the probabilities required for the decision tree first construct a joint probability table.
   Now $P(H \text{ and } FH) = P(H) \times P(FH/H)$

$$= 0.3 \times 0.5$$

$$= 0.15.$$

---

*If we have perfect information we would not invest when the return is a loss so our actual return 70 per cent of the time is zero.

Proceeding in a similar manner we can complete the joint probability table:

| Forecast | Actual H | L | Totals | |
|---|---|---|---|---|
| FH | 0.15 | 0.07 | 0.22 | = P(FH) |
| FI | 0.09 | 0.28 | 0.37 | = P(FI) |
| FL | 0.06 | 0.35 | 0.41 | = P(FL) |
| Totals | 0.30 | 0.70 | 1.00 | |
| | = P(H) | = P(L) | | |

Hence
$$P(FH) = 0.22$$
$$P(FI) = 0.37$$
$$P(FL) = 0.41$$

gives us the probabilities required at the first node on our decision tree. The remaining probabilities can be calculated as follows:

$$P(H/FH) = 0.15/0.22 = 0.682$$
$$\therefore P(L/FH) = 0.07/0.22 = \underline{0.318}$$
$$\underline{1.00} \quad \text{Check.}$$

$$P(H/FI) = 0.09/0.37 = 0.243$$
$$P(L/FI) = 0.28/0.37 = \underline{0.757}$$
$$\underline{1.00} \quad \text{Check.}$$

$$P(H/FL) = 0.06/0.41 = 0.146$$
$$P(L/FL) = 0.35/0.41 = \underline{0.854}$$
$$\underline{1.00} \quad \text{Check.}$$

Hence our decision tree becomes as shown in Fig. 101.

First calculate the expected values from the right hand side back as far as the D2 boxes. At each D2 decision box select the largest expected value and prune the other branches (// indicates branch pruned).

Now treating the expected values at the D2 boxes as cash flows calculate the expected values at the D1 box.

Remember to deduct 20 for the survey.

From the tree we see that the expected value if we do a survey is only 1.99 (£1,000) compared with 17 (£1,000) if no survey is carried out.

Hence prune the survey branch.

Recommendation: Do not carry out the market research survey but do market the product. The expected return is £17,000.

# APPENDIX 3. SUGGESTED ANSWERS TO EXAMINATION QUESTIONS

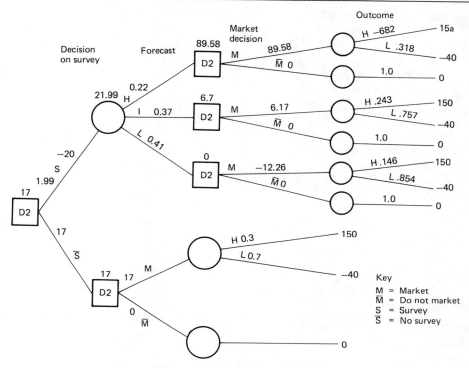

Fig. 101. *Decision tree—market research survey problem.*

**10.**

(a) Let $p = 0.4$, $N = 50$.

$r = 3$, $n = 5$.

This is a binomial distribution.

Now $P(r) = {}^nC_r P^r q^{n-r}$

$$\therefore \quad P(3) = {}^5C_3 \times (0.4)^3 \times (0.6)^2$$
$$= 10 \times (0.4)^3 \times (0.6)^2$$
$$= \underline{\underline{0.2304}}.$$

(b) If the fifth driver is the third to be wearing a seat belt that means there must be exactly two out of the first four drivers who are wearing seat belts. The probability of this is given by:

$$P(2) = {}^4C_2 \times (0.4)^2 \times (0.6)^2$$
$$= 6 \times (0.4)^2 \times (0.6)^2$$
$$= 0.3456.$$

As the probability of the fifth wearing a seat belt is 0.4 the answer is:

$$0.3456 \times 0.4 = 0.13824 = \underline{\underline{0.138}}.$$

(c)     $n = 50$, $r = 17$, $p = 0.4$,
$\mu = np = 50 \times 0.4 = 20$,
$\sigma^2 = npq = 50 \times 0.4 \times 0.6 = 12$,
$\therefore \quad \sigma = 3.464$.

Using continuity correction, fewer than 17 means $x = 16.5$.

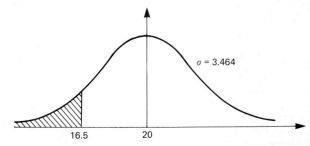

Fig. 102. *Probable numbers of drivers wearing seat belts.*

Referring to Fig. 102,

$$Z = \frac{16.5 - 20}{3.464} = -1.01.$$

From tables, area (by interpolation) = 0.157.

$$\therefore \quad P(\text{less than } 17) = 0.157.$$

Calculate the $SE_p = \sqrt{\dfrac{pq}{n}}$ assuming that $p = 0.4$

$$= \sqrt{\dfrac{0.4 \times 0.6}{500}}$$

$$= 0.0219.$$

Using a one-tailed test (Fig. 103): $H_0 : p = 0.4$, $H_1 : p > 0.4$.

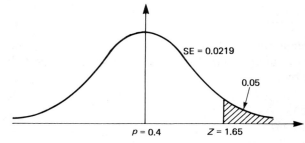

Fig. 103. *Seat belt problem — hypothesis testing.*

# APPENDIX 3. SUGGESTED ANSWERS TO EXAMINATION QUESTIONS

Test at the 5 per cent level.

Test value from tables: $Z = 1.65$.

Now sample $p = \dfrac{220}{500} = 0.44$

$\therefore$ sample $Z = \dfrac{0.44 - 0.40}{0.0219}$

$\qquad = 1.83$

As the sample $Z$-value is greater than the test value of 1.65 the difference is significant. We conclude that the safety campaign has been successful.

**11.**

Measuring $x$ in 1,000 km (see Fig. 104):

$$P(x \leqslant 30) = 0.09,$$
$$P(x \geqslant 50) = 0.20.$$

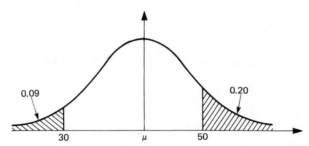

Fig. 104. *Tyre life—standard deviation and mean safe life (units: 000 km).*

Dealing with area on left-hand side first:
Z-value for area of 0.09 is $-1.34$ (interpolation of tables)

$$\therefore \quad -1.34 = \dfrac{30 - \mu}{\sigma}. \qquad (1)$$

Similarly for the right-hand side:
Z-value for area of 0.20 is $+0.84$

$$\therefore \quad 0.84 = \dfrac{50 - \mu}{\sigma} \qquad (2)$$

Multiplying both equations through by $\sigma$ gives

$$-1.34\sigma = 30 - \mu \qquad (3)$$
$$0.84\sigma = 50 - \mu \qquad (4)$$

Now (4) − (3) gives:

$$2.18\sigma = 20$$

$$\therefore \quad \underline{\underline{\sigma = 9.714.}}$$

Substitute in (3)

$$\mu = 30 + 1.34 \times 9.174$$

$$\mu = 42.29$$

Hence $\underline{\underline{\mu = 42{,}300 \text{ km}.}}$

(a) Referring to Fig. 105:

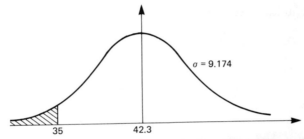

Fig. 105. *Probability of single tyre change before 35,000 km (units: 000 km).*

$$Z = \frac{35 - 42.3}{9.174}$$

$$= -0.80.$$

From tables $p = 0.212$
 Therefore the probability a single tyre will last for 35,000 km or more is 0.788. Hence the probability all four will last longer is $(0.788)^4 = \underline{\underline{0.386.}}$

(b) Referring to Fig. 106:

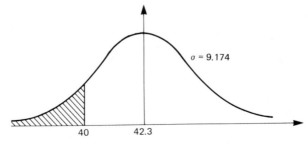

Fig. 106. *Probability of two tyre changes before 40,000 km (units: 000 km).*

$$Z = \frac{40 - 42.3}{9.174} = -0.25.$$

From tables, $p = 0.402$, i.e. the probability a single tyre will fail is 0.402. We need to calculate the probability that *exactly* two out of four will fail. This is a binomial distribution with $p = 0.402$.

$$P(2) = {}^4C_2 \times (0.402)^2 \times (0.598)^2$$
$$= 6 \times (0.402)^2 \times (0.598)^2$$
$$= 0.347.$$

**12.**

(a) All four vans will be out on hire if the demand is for four or more vans. Hence to answer this question we require the probability of 4 or more.

Now $P(4 \text{ or more}) = 1 - P(0) - P(1) - P(2) - P(3)$

From the formula sheet the Poisson distribution is given by:

$$P(r) = \frac{e^{-m} m^r}{r!}$$

and from the question $m = 2$. ($e = 2.718$.)

$$\therefore P(0) = \frac{e^{-2} \times 2^0}{0!} = 0.1353$$

$$P(1) = \frac{e^{-2} \times 2^1}{1!} = 0.2707$$

$$P(2) = \frac{e^{-2} \times 2^2}{2!} = 0.2707$$

$$P(3) = \frac{e^{-2} \times 2^3}{3!} = 0.1804$$

$$\overline{0.8571}$$

$$\therefore P(4 \text{ or more}) = 1 - 0.8571$$
$$= 0.143.$$

(b) The unsatisfied demand occurs when the demand is 5 or more, e.g. if the demand is 7 then there will be 3 unsatisfied customers.

It is slightly easier to calculate the proportion of demand that is satisfied first and then to determine the unsatisfied demand.

Let $x$ be the number of customers satisfied and $P(x)$ the probability of $x$ as given by the Poisson distribution. Then the expected demand satisfied is as follows:

| Satisfied demand $x$ | P($x$) | $x$P($x$) |
|---|---|---|
| 0 | 0.1353 | 0 |
| 1 | 0.2707 | 0.2707 |
| 2 | 0.2707 | 0.5414 |
| 3 | 0.1804 | 0.5412 |
| 4 | 0.1429* | 0.5716 |
|   | 1.0000 | 1.9249 |

(*This is the probability of 4 or more as the satisfied *demand* is only 4, even when the actual demand exceeds 4; the difference is the unsatisfied demand.)

As the average demand is 2 the satisfied proportion is:

$$\frac{1.9249}{2} = 0.9624,$$

i.e. 96.24 per cent of the demand is satisfied,

i.e. 100 − 96.24 = 3.76 per cent is unsatisfied demand.

(c) We need to calculate the expected contribution, either per year or per day, for a van fleet of 4 down to 1.

In each case we need to determine the expected satisfied demand (or average usage).

The expected satisfied demand for 4 vans was calculated in (b) as equal to 1.9249 vans. Carrying out similar calculations for 3, 2, and 1 vans:

*3 vans:*

| $x$ | P($x$) | $x$P($x$) | |
|---|---|---|---|
| 0 | 0.1353 | 0 | |
| 1 | 0.2707 | 0.2707 | |
| 2 | 0.2707 | 0.5415 | |
| 3 | 0.3233 | 0.9699 | |
|   | 1.0000 | 1.7821 | average usage = 1.7821. |

## APPENDIX 3. SUGGESTED ANSWERS TO EXAMINATION QUESTIONS

*2 vans:*

| $x$ | P($x$) | $x$P($x$) |
|---|---|---|
| 0 | 0.1353 | 0 |
| 1 | 0.2707 | 0.2707 |
| 2 | 0.5940 | 1.1880 |
|   | 1.0000 | 1.4587 |

average usage = 1.4587.

*1 van:*

| $x$ | P($x$) | $x$P($x$) |
|---|---|---|
| 0 | 0.1353 | 0 |
| 1 | 0.8647 | 0.8647 |
|   | 1.0000 | 0.8647 |

average usage = 0.8647.

### Expected daily contribution

*4 vans*  Average revenue 1.9249 × 35 = £67.37
       *Less:* Cost per day 3,250 ÷ 300 × 4 = 43.33
                                                 £24.04

*3 vans*  Average revenue 1.7821 × 35 = £62.37
       *Less:* Cost per day 3,250 ÷ 300 × 3 = 32.50
                                                 £29.87

*2 vans*  Average revenue 1.4587 × 35 = £51.05
       *Less:* Cost per day 3,250 ÷ 300 × 2 = 21.67
                                                 £29.38

*1 van*  Average revenue 0.8647 × 35 = £30.26
      *Less:* Cost per day 3,250 ÷ 300 = 10.83
                                                £19.43

The expected contribution is at its maximum when there are only 3 vans. An increase in daily contribution over the existing contribution of 29.87 − 24.04 = £5.83.

**13.**

(a) (i) Referring to Fig. 107,

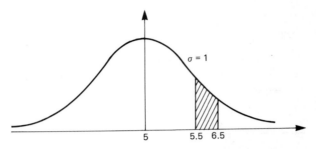

Fig. 107. *Probable TV tube life (units: 000 hours).*

$$Z = \frac{5.5 - 5}{1} = 0.5, \qquad \text{table area} = 0.308.$$

$$Z_2 = \frac{6.5 - 5}{1} = 1.5, \qquad \text{table area} = 0.067.$$

$$\text{Required area} = 0.308 - 0.067$$
$$= \underline{\underline{0.241}}.$$

(ii) Referring to Fig. 108,

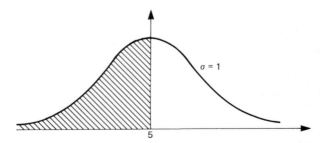

Fig. 108. *Probability of TV tube life being less than expected (units: 000 hours).*

$$Z = \frac{5 - 5}{1} = 0.$$

Probability of less than 5,000 hours is $\underline{\underline{0.5}}$.

# APPENDIX 3. SUGGESTED ANSWERS TO EXAMINATION QUESTIONS

(b) Five years' usage = 1,500 × 5

$$= 7,500 \text{ hours},$$

$$\therefore Z = \frac{7.5 - 5}{1} = 2.5, \text{ table area} = 0.006.$$

Probability of less than 5 years $= 1 - 0.006$

$$= \underline{\underline{0.994}}.$$

(c) Referring to Fig. 109,
3 year usage = 3 × 1,500 = 4,500 hours.

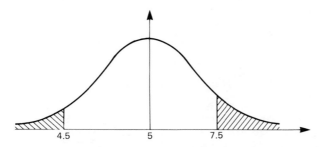

Fig. 109. *Probable TV tube failure (units: 000 hours).*

$$\therefore Z_1 = \frac{4.5 - 5}{1} = -0.5, \text{ table area} = 0.308.$$

$$\therefore Z_2 = \frac{7.5 - 5}{1} = 2.5, \text{ table area} = 0.006.$$

Hence the probability distribution is:

| Life | Probability P(x) | Cost to company (x) | xP(x) |
| --- | --- | --- | --- |
| Under 3 years | 0.308 | £80 | £24.64 |
| 3–5 years | 0.686 | 40 | 27.44 |
| Over 5 years | 0.006 | 0 | 0 |
|  | 1.000 |  | 52.08 |
|  | *Less:* Guarantee charge |  | 25.00 |
|  | Expected cost |  | £27.08 |

**14.**

(a) Referring to Fig. 110,

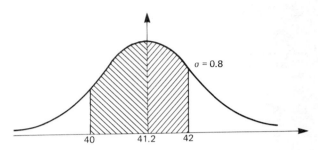

Fig. 110. *Probable weights of boxes (units: ounces).*

$$Z_1 = \frac{40 - 41.2}{0.8} = -1.5, \quad \text{table area} = 0.067.$$

$$Z_2 = \frac{42 - 41.2}{0.8} = 1.0, \quad \text{table area} = \frac{0.159}{0.226}$$

Required area = $1 - 0.226 = \underline{\underline{0.774}}$.

(b) Referring to Fig. 111,
Area = 0.20, from tables, $Z = -0.84$.

$$\therefore \quad x = 41.2 - 0.84 \times 0.8 = \underline{\underline{40.53 \text{ oz}}}.$$

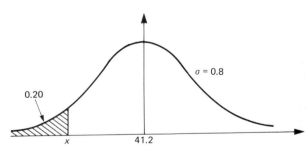

Fig. 111. *Weight (x) below which 20 per cent lightest boxes fall (units: ounces).*

(c) From (a), 6.7 per cent of boxes are scrapped, leaving 93.3 per cent of the boxes. As 100 boxes are left the number of boxes required initially is:

$$100 \times \frac{100}{93.3} = 107.2 \text{ boxes}$$

So on average 7.2 boxes would need to be scrapped at a cost of £7.2.

(d) Referring to Fig. 112,

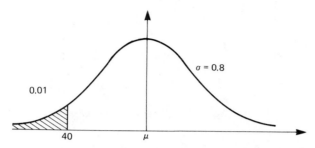

Fig. 112. *Adjusted mean weight (μ) of box contents (units: ounces).*

Table area = 0.01, $\therefore Z = 2.33$

$\therefore \mu = 40 + 2.33 \times 0.8 = \underline{41.86 \text{ oz.}}$

**15.**

(a) Note the sample standard deviation $s$ is not a sound estimate of the population standard deviation $\sigma$. It consistently underestimates the population standard deviation and is considered to be a biased estimator. An unbiased estimator of the population $\sigma$ is:

$$s\sqrt{\frac{n}{n-1}}$$

However, if $n > 30$ then the correction term

$$\sqrt{\frac{n}{n-1}}$$

is close to 1.

(b) $$\text{SE}_{\bar{x}} = \frac{\sigma}{\sqrt{n}} = \frac{0.19}{\sqrt{100}} = 0.019.$$

(c) 95 per cent confidence interval is given by:

$$\bar{x} \pm Z \times \text{SE}$$
$$39.6 \pm 1.96 \times 0.019$$
$$= \underline{39.6 \pm 0.037.}$$

(d) $H_0: \mu_1 = \mu_2,\ H_1: \mu_1 \neq \mu_2.$

$x_1 - x_2 = 39.6 - 41.5 = -1.9.$

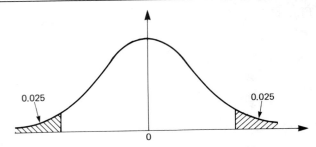

Fig. 113. *Sample mean differences significance test.*

Referring to Fig. 113:
Test value: $Z = 1.96$

Now
$$SE_{\bar{x}_1 - \bar{x}_2} = \sqrt{\frac{0.19^2}{100} + \frac{0.50^2}{100}} = 0.0535$$

$$\text{Sample } Z = \frac{-1.9 - 0}{0.0535} = -35.5.$$

As this is numerically greater than the test values of $Z = \pm 1.96$, the difference is significant.

(e) The difference is significant at any level as the probability of getting a $Z$ value of $-35.5$ is insignificantly small.

**16.**

(a) Consider a population whose mean proportion is $P$.
    Then if we take samples of size $n$ from that population the sample proportions will vary about $P$ with standard deviation

$$\sqrt{\frac{P(1-P)}{n}}.$$

This standard deviation of the sampling distribution is called a standard error.

(b) (i)  Referring to Fig. 114:

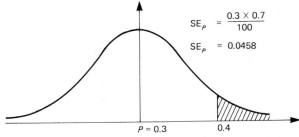

Fig. 114. *Calculation of probability of 40 per cent defective items.*

$$Z = \frac{0.4 - 0.3}{0.0458} = 2.18, \qquad \text{area from tables} = \underline{\underline{0.015}}.$$

(ii) Test whether the process is producing significantly more than 30 per cent defective.

$H_0 : P = 0.3$, $H_1 : P > 0.3$ (one-tailed test).

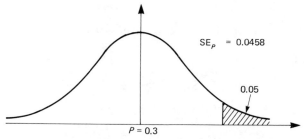

Fig. 115. *Test for significantly more than 30 per cent defective items.*

Test at 5 per cent level.

Test $Z$ from tables = 1.65.

$$\text{Sample } Z = \frac{0.42 - 0.30}{0.0458} = 2.63.$$

The difference is significant at the 5 per cent level.
Reject 30 per cent claim.

**17.**

(a) $H_0 : \mu = 3{,}000$, $H_1 : \mu \neq 3{,}000$.

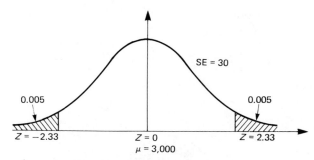

Fig. 116. *Calculation of Z-value for decision rule.*

$$\text{SE} = \frac{\sigma}{\sqrt{n}} = \frac{180}{\sqrt{36}} = 30.$$

Referring to Fig. 116:
at the 0.01 level of significance the table area = 0.005.

From normal tables, $Z = 2.33$ or $-2.33$.

The decision rule is to reject $H_0$ if $Z$ calculated for the sample is numerically greater than 2.33, accept $H_0$ if $Z$ is numerically less than 2.33.

(b) $\bar{x} = 2,940$.

Then sample
$$Z = \frac{\bar{x} - \mu}{SE} = \frac{2,940 - 3,000}{30} = -2.$$

∴ Accept $H_0$.

There is no evidence that the breaking strength has changed.

(c) The two critical values are:
$$\mu \pm Z \times SE = 3,000 \pm 2.33 \times 30$$
$$= 3,000 \pm 69.9$$
$$= 2,930 \text{ and } 3,070.$$

**18.**

(a) Number in A with characteristic $= 0.22 \times 4,000$
$$= 880.$$

Number in B with characteristic $= 0.31 \times 1,200$
$$= 3,720$$

Total $= 4,600$.

Percentage in the total population as estimated $= \dfrac{4,600}{16,000} \times 100$

$$= \underline{\underline{28.75 \text{ per cent.}}}$$

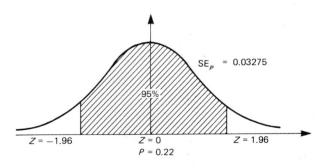

Fig. 117. *Calculation of confidence limits for possession of characteristic.*

APPENDIX 3. SUGGESTED ANSWERS TO EXAMINATION QUESTIONS 355

(b) Referring to Fig. 117:

$$SE_p = \sqrt{\frac{Pq}{n}} = \sqrt{\frac{0.22 \times 0.78}{160}} = 0.03275.$$

(Sample size $n = \frac{1}{25} \times 4,000 = 160.$)

95 per cent confidence interval for $P = 0.22 \pm 1.96 \times 0.03275$

$$= 0.22 \pm 0.064,$$

i.e.    22 per cent $\pm$ 6.4 per cent

or    16.6 per cent to 28.4 per cent.

(c) $P_A = 0.22$, $P_B = 0.31$.

$$\bar{p} = \frac{160 \times 0.22 + 120 \times 0.31}{160 + 120} = 0.259$$

$$SE = \sqrt{\frac{0.259 \times 0.741}{160} + \frac{0.259 \times 0.741}{120}} = 0.0529$$

(*Note: Size of sample B* $= \frac{1}{100} \times 12,000 = 120.$)

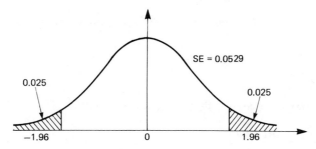

Fig. 118. *Test for significant difference between proportions.*

$H_0 : P_A = P_B$, $H_1 : P_A \neq P_B$.

Test at 5 per cent level. Test values: $Z = \pm 1.96$.

$$\text{Now sample } Z = \frac{(P_A - P_B) - 0}{SE}$$

$$= \frac{(0.22 - 0.31) - 0}{0.0529} = -1.70$$

Accept $H_0$; there is no significant difference between the sample proportions.

**19.**

(a) We need to carry out a test on the difference between the two sample means. Initially we have to calculate the means and standard deviations.

$$\bar{x} = \frac{9{,}330}{100} = 93.3, \qquad \bar{x}_2 = \frac{5{,}770}{100} = 57.7.$$

$$\sigma_1 = \sqrt{\frac{1{,}404{,}950}{100} - \left(\frac{9{,}330}{100}\right)^2}, \quad \sigma_2 = \sqrt{\frac{411{,}250}{100} - \left(\frac{5{,}770}{100}\right)^2}.$$

$$\therefore \quad \sigma_1 = 73.11, \qquad \sigma_2 = 27.99.$$

$$\text{SE} = \sqrt{\frac{\sigma_1^2}{n_1} + \frac{\sigma_2^2}{n_2}} = \sqrt{\frac{73.11^2}{100} + \frac{27.99^2}{100}}$$

$$= 7.83.$$

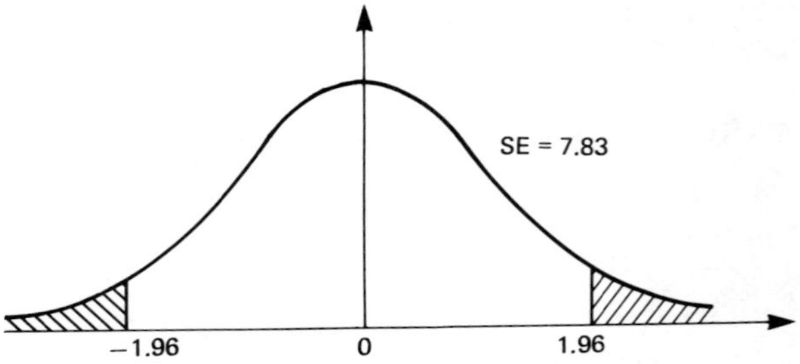

Fig. 119. *Test for significant difference between sample means.*

Referring to Fig. 119,

$$H_0 : \mu = \mu_2, \quad H_1 : \mu \neq \mu_2.$$

Test at the 5 per cent level. Test values are $\pm 1.96$.

$$Z = \frac{(\bar{x}_1 - \bar{x}_2) - (\mu_1 - \mu_2)}{\text{SE}}$$

$$= \frac{(93.3 - 57.7) - 0}{7.83}$$

$$= 4.55.$$

Reject $H_0$; the difference is significant.

(b) $\text{SE}_1 = \dfrac{\sigma}{\sqrt{n}} = \dfrac{73.11}{\sqrt{100}} = 7.331, \quad \text{SE}_2 = \dfrac{\sigma}{\sqrt{n}} = \dfrac{27.99}{\sqrt{100}} = 2.799.$

95 per cent confidence intervals are:

sample 1:  $93.3 \pm 1.96 \times 7.311$

$\phantom{\text{sample 1:}}\ \ = \underline{\underline{93.3 \pm 14.3}}.$

# APPENDIX 3. SUGGESTED ANSWERS TO EXAMINATION QUESTIONS

sample 2:     $57.7 \pm 1.96 \times 2.799$

$\underline{= 57.7 \pm 5.5}$.

(c) Currently sample 1 is estimated to within £14.3; to estimate it to within £10:

$$1.96 \text{ SE} \leqslant 10$$

as $$\text{SE} = \frac{73.11}{\sqrt{n}}.$$

$$\therefore \frac{1.96 \times 73.11}{\sqrt{n}} \leqslant 10.$$

$$\therefore \quad 14.33 \leqslant \sqrt{n},$$

$$205.3 \leqslant n$$

$\therefore$ $\underline{n \text{ must be at least } 206}$.

**20.**

Carry out a paired t-test.

A one-tailed test should be used as you are trying to test if the drying agent significantly reduces the drying time.

| $x_1$ | $x_2$ | $d = x_2 - x_1$ | $d_2$ |
|---|---|---|---|
| 3.4 | 3.6 | 0.2 | 0.04 |
| 3.8 | 3.8 | 0 | 0 |
| 4.2 | 4.3 | 0.1 | 0.01 |
| 4.1 | 4.3 | 0.2 | 0.04 |
| 3.5 | 3.6 | 0.1 | 0.01 |
| 4.7 | 4.7 | 0 | 0 |
| | | 0.6 | 0.10 |

Mean of the $d = \dfrac{0.6}{6} = 0.1$.

Standard deviation $\sigma = \sqrt{\dfrac{0.10 - (0.6)^2/6}{6-1}} = 0.0894$.

$$\therefore \text{ SE} = \frac{\sigma}{\sqrt{n}} = \frac{0.0894}{\sqrt{6}} = 0.0365.$$

Referring to Fig. 120,

$H_0 : \mu_1 = \mu_2, \ H_1 : \mu_1 \neq \mu_2$.

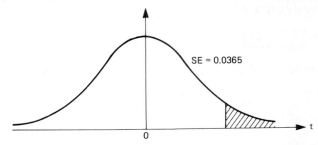

Fig. 120. *Test for significant difference between drying times.*

$$t = \frac{\bar{x} - \mu}{SE} = \frac{0.1 - 0}{0.0365} = 2.74$$

Test value: $t_{0.05}\,(V = 5) = 2.0$.

Reject $H_0$; the difference is significant. This means that the drying time of the paint with agent is significantly less than the drying time for the paint without the agent.

### 21.

(a) The purpose of the analysis would be to determine if the sample results could have come from a population whose mean life is 1,050 hours.

(b)

| $x$ | $x^2$ |
|---|---|
| 964 | 929,296 |
| 1,082 | 1,170,724 |
| 1,136 | 1,290,496 |
| 825 | 680,625 |
| 863 | 744,769 |
| 4,870 | 4,815,910 |

$$\bar{x} = \frac{4,870}{5} = 974.$$

$$\sigma = \sqrt{\frac{4,815,910 - (4,870)^2/5}{5-1}}$$

$$= 134.7.$$

$$\therefore \quad SE = \frac{134.7}{\sqrt{5}} = 60.24.$$

# APPENDIX 3. SUGGESTED ANSWERS TO EXAMINATION QUESTIONS

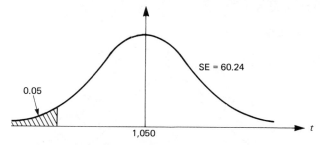

Fig. 121. *Test for significance of component failure (units: hours).*

$H_0: \mu = 1{,}050$, $H_1: \mu < 1{,}050$.

Test value: $t_{0.05}\,(V=4) = -2.1$.

One-tailed test: $t = \dfrac{974 - 1{,}050}{60.24} = -1.26$.

Accept $H_0$; the difference is not significant, no complaint should be made.

(c) Minimum average life $= \mu - t \times \text{SE}$

$$= 1{,}050 - 2.1 \times 60.24$$

$$= \underline{\underline{923.5 \text{ hours}}}.$$

**22.**

(a) We need to test if the average of the new salesman is *significantly different* from the mean of the established salesman of 5.5.

| $x$ | $x^2$ |
|---|---|
| 5 | 25 |
| 3 | 9 |
| 4 | 16 |
| 6 | 36 |
| 5 | 25 |
| 23 | 111 |

$$\bar{x} = \frac{23}{5} = 4.6$$

$$\sigma = \frac{111 - (23)^2/5}{4}$$

$$= 1.140.$$

$$\therefore \quad \text{SE} = \frac{1.140}{\sqrt{5}} = 0.510$$

(b) $H_0: \mu = 5.5$, $H_1: \mu \neq 5.5$.

Referring to Fig. 122:

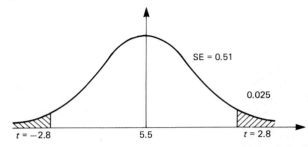

Fig. 122. *Test for significance of salesman failing trial.*

Test value $t_{0.025}$ $(V = 4) = 2.8$.

Sample $t = \dfrac{4.6 - 5.5}{0.510} = -1.76$.

Accept $H_0$; the difference is *not* significant. The new salesman's claim *is* justified.

(c) Lower test limit $= 5.5 - 2.8 \times 0.51$

$= \underline{\underline{4.07 \text{ machines}}}$.

**23.**

(a) Calculate the percentage requiring repair for each car type:

| | |
|---|---|
| Tuxan | 89 per cent |
| Firedash | 81.4 per cent |
| Velotta | 90.8 per cent |

It appears that the Velotta and Tuxan have a greater failure rate than the Firedash.

(b) Let us assume there is no difference between the failure rates of each type of car. We can therefore calculate the expected value for each cell using

$$\frac{\text{Row total} \times \text{Column total}}{\text{Grand total}}$$

and then carry out a chi-squared test.

Contingency table:

| | $R$ | $\bar{R}$ | Total |
|---|---|---|---|
| T | 89(88.0) | 11(12.0) | 100 |
| F | 57(61.6) | 13(8.4) | 70 |
| V | 118(114.4) | 12(15.6) | 130 |
| Total | 264 | 36 | 300 |

The numbers in parentheses are the calculated expected values.

| O | E | d | $d^2$ | $d^2/E$ |
|---|---|---|---|---|
| 89 | 88.0 | 1.0 | 1.00 | 0.01 |
| 11 | 12.0 | 1.0 | 1.00 | 0.08 |
| 57 | 61.6 | 4.6 | 21.16 | 0.34 |
| 13 | 8.4 | 4.6 | 21.16 | 2.52 |
| 118 | 114.4 | 3.6 | 12.96 | 0.11 |
| 12 | 15.6 | 3.6 | 12.96 | 0.83 |
| | | | $\chi^2 =$ | 3.89 |

Referring to Fig. 123:

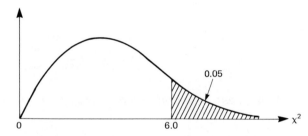

Fig. 123. *Test for significance between car model failure rates.*

Number of degrees of freedom $= (3-1)(2-1) = 2$.

Test at 5 per cent level: $\chi^2_{0.05} (V = 2) = 6.0$.

As $\chi^2$ of 3.89 is less than the test value of 6.0 the difference is not significant.

(c) There is insufficient evidence to allow us to distinguish between the proportion of cars requiring repair. The difference could have occurred owing purely to chance.

**24.**

(a) The group of twenty patients may be seen as a sample of size of 20 with the proportion cured being 0.50. Now if the true proportion cured is 0.40 then if we take samples from this population the proportion being cured in each sample will vary about 0.40. It can be shown that a cure rate of 0.50 could have come from a population whose mean is 0.40 owing purely to chance.

**VERIFICATION USING CHI-SQUARED TEST**

The observed values, are 10 cured and 10 not cured and if the true cure rate is 40 per cent ($H_0 : P = 0.4$) then the expected values will be $20 \times 0.4 = 8$ and $20 \times 0.6 = 12$ respectively.

Calculating the $\chi^2$ value:

| O | E | d | $d^2$ | $d^2/E$ |
|---|---|---|---|---|
| 10 | 8 | 2 | 4 | 0.50 |
| 10 | 12 | 2 | 4 | 0.33 |
| | | | $\chi^2 =$ | 0.83 |

Referring to Fig. 124,

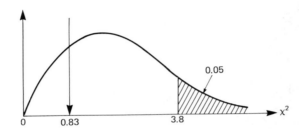

Fig. 124. *Test for significance of drug cure rates.*

from tables $\chi^2_{0.05}(V = 1) = 3.8$.

The difference is not significant.

Hence the difference in results could be due purely to chance.

(b)    Consider 11 cured

| O | E | d | $d^2$ | $d^2/E$ |
|---|---|---|---|---|
| 11 | 8 | 3 | 9 | 1.12 |
| 9 | 12 | 3 | 9 | 0.75 |
| | | | | 1.87 |

Consider 12 cured

| O | E | d | $d^2$ | $d^2/E$ |
|---|---|---|---|---|
| 12 | 8 | 4 | 16 | 2.00 |
| 8 | 12 | 4 | 16 | 1.33 |
| | | | | 3.33 |

Consider 13 cured

| O | E | d | $d^2$ | $d^2/E$ |
|---|---|---|---|---|
| 13 | 8 | 5 | 25 | 3.12 |
| 7 | 12 | 5 | 25 | 2.08 |
| | | | | 5.20 |

Test level is $\chi^2 = 3.8$ at the 5 per cent level.

# APPENDIX 3. SUGGESTED ANSWERS TO EXAMINATION QUESTIONS

Therefore the minimum number cured would have to be 13 before the difference could be taken as significant at the 5 per cent level.

(c) We require a 95 per cent confidence interval for the sample proportion of 0.5.

$$SE_P = \sqrt{\frac{0.5 \times 0.5}{20}} = 0.112.$$

Hence 95 per cent confidence interval (using normal distribution) is:

$$0.50 \pm 1.96 \times 0.112$$
$$= 0.50 \pm 0.220$$

i.e. 28 to 72 per cent cure rate.
This means that we are 95 per cent certain that the drug has a cure rate of between 28 and 72 per cent.

**25.**

(a) *Methods of obtaining average percentage price increase*

(i) $$\frac{\text{Total of proposed prices} - \text{Total of present prices}}{\text{Total of present prices}} \times 100$$

$$= \frac{14{,}400 - 12{,}750}{12{,}750} \times 100 = 12.9 \text{ per cent.}$$

This method ignores the demand pattern.

(ii) Calculate the percentage price increase for each model and average the results. Percentage price increases are 9.09, 10.9, 14.3, 15 respectively.

$$\therefore \text{ Average percentage increase} = \frac{9.09 + 10.9 + 14.3 + 15}{4}$$

$$= 12.3 \text{ per cent.}$$

Alternatively, each of these percentages could be weighted by the demand.

Average percentage
 increase $= 9.09 \times 0.18 + 10.9 \times 0.40 + 14.3 \times 0.26 + 15 \times 0.16$

$$= 12.1 \text{ per cent.}$$

(iii) Weigh all the prices by the demand and calculate the percentage increase in value.
Average new price allowing for demand:

$$2{,}750 \times 0.18 + 3{,}050 \times 0.4 + 4{,}000 \times 0.26 + 4{,}600 \times 0.16 = 3{,}491.$$

Average present price allowing for demand:

$$2{,}500 \times 0.18 + 2{,}750 \times 0.4 + 3{,}500 \times 0.26 + 4{,}000 \times 0.16 = 3{,}100.$$

$$\text{Average percentage increase} = \frac{3{,}491 - 3{,}100}{3{,}100} \times 100$$

$$= 12.6 \text{ per cent.}$$

(This gives four possible ways; there are others, but you only require three.)

(b) Let us assume there is no change in the demand pattern (null hypothesis) that the expected percentages are 18, 40, 26, 16. We can use these percentages to calculate the expected demand pattern for the 200 cars and then use the $\chi^2$ goodness of fit test at the 5 per cent level.

| O | E | d | $d^2$ | $d^2/E$ |
|---|---|---|---|---|
| 33 | 36 | 3 | 9 | 0.25 |
| 107 | 80 | 27 | 729 | 9.11 |
| 40 | 52 | 12 | 144 | 2.77 |
| 20 | 32 | 12 | 144 | 4.50 |
| 200 | 200 | | | 16.63 |

Referring to Fig. 125,

From tables, $\chi^2_{0.05}(V=3) = 7.8$.

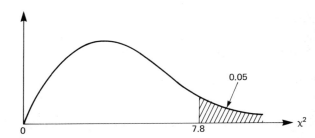

Fig. 125. *Test for significance of change in sales.*

The calculated value of 16.63 is significant. The difference in the demand pattern is unlikely to be purely due to chance. The demand pattern has changed due to the price changes. The demand for the standard model has increased significantly.

The data consist of frequencies in the form of a contingency table. We need to calculate the expected frequencies and carry out a chi-squared test.

| | | | |
|---|---|---|---|
| 20 (17.6) | 10 (11.7) | 10 (10.7) | 40 |
| 16 (18.5) | 14 (12.3) | 12 (11.2) | 42 |
| 22 (19.4) | 12 (12.9) | 10 (11.7) | 44 |
| 8 (10.5) | 8 (7.1) | 8 (6.4) | 24 |
| 66 | 44 | 40 | 150 |

# APPENDIX 3. SUGGESTED ANSWERS TO EXAMINATION QUESTIONS

The numbers in brackets are the expected values calculated by row total × column total ÷ grand total.

| O | E | d | $d^2$ | $d^2/E$ |
|---|---|---|---|---|
| 20 | 17.6 | 2.4 | 5.76 | 0.33 |
| 10 | 11.7 | 1.7 | 2.89 | 0.25 |
| 10 | 10.7 | 0.7 | 0.49 | 0.05 |
| 16 | 18.5 | 2.5 | 6.25 | 0.34 |
| 14 | 12.3 | 1.7 | 2.89 | 0.23 |
| 12 | 11.2 | 0.8 | 0.64 | 0.06 |
| 22 | 19.4 | 2.6 | 6.76 | 0.35 |
| 12 | 12.9 | 0.9 | 0.81 | 0.06 |
| 10 | 11.7 | 1.7 | 2.89 | 0.25 |
| 8 | 10.5 | 2.5 | 6.25 | 0.60 |
| 8 | 7.1 | 0.9 | 0.81 | 0.11 |
| 8 | 6.4 | 1.6 | 2.56 | 0.40 |
| | | | $\chi^2 =$ | 3.03 |

Number of degrees of freedom $= (4-1)(3-1) = 6$.

Referring to Fig. 126:

$$\chi^2_{0.05}\ (V=6) = 12.6.$$

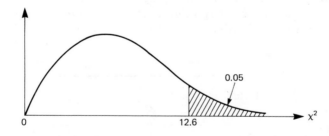

Fig. 126. *Test for significant difference between classes of payers.*

Difference is not significant.
There is no evidence of a relationship between the class of company and its status as a payer.

## 27.

To fit a binomial distribution we need first of all to calculate the binomial probabilities using:

$$n = 5,\ p = 0.20,\ q = 0.80,\ P(r) = {}^nC_r p^r q^{n-r}.$$

$$\therefore \begin{aligned} P(0) &= {}^5C_0(0.20)^0(0.8)^5 \\ P(1) &= {}^5C_1(0.20)^1(0.8)^4 \\ P(2) &= {}^5C_2(0.20)^2(0.8)^3 \\ P(3) &= {}^5C_3(0.20)^3(0.8)^2 \\ P(4) &= {}^5C_4(0.20)^4(0.8) \\ P(5) &= {}^5C_5(0.20)^5 \end{aligned}$$

| | P(x) | E(x) |
|---|---|---|
| = | 0.32768 | 32.8 |
| = | 0.40960 | 41.0 |
| = | 0.20480 | 20.5 |
| = | 0.05120 | 5.1 |
| = | 0.00640 | 0.6 |
| = | 0.00032 | 0 |
| | 1.00000 | 100 |

As the expected frequencies of the last two groups are below 1 combine the last 3 cells to give E (3 or more) = 5.7.

| Class | O | E | d | $d^2$ | $d^2/E$ |
|---|---|---|---|---|---|
| 0 | 36 | 32.8 | 3.2 | 10.24 | 0.31 |
| 1 | 36 | 41.0 | 5.0 | 25.00 | 0.61 |
| 2 | 17 | 20.5 | 3.5 | 12.25 | 0.61 |
| 3 or more | 11 | 5.7 | 5.3 | 28.09 | 4.93 |
| | 100 | 100.0 | | | $\chi^2 = 6.45$ |

$V = 4 - 2 = 2$.

Referring to Fig. 127:

$\chi^2_{0.05}(V = 2) = 6.0$.

Difference is significant at the 5 per cent level.

The group of 3 or more has occurred more often than due to chance. The distribution does not fit a binomial distribution.

**28.**

(a)

| $b$ | $n$ | $\sqrt{\dfrac{b}{n}}$ | $t$ |
|---|---|---|---|
| 900 | 3 | 17.32 | 36.2 |
| 1,200 | 3 | 20.00 | 39.5 |
| 500 | 1 | 22.36 | 45.1 |
| 500 | 2 | 15.81 | 32.2 |
| 1,500 | 5 | 17.32 | 31.0 |
| 800 | 4 | 14.14 | 28.0 |
| 1,800 | 3 | 24.49 | 45.5 |
| 1,000 | 3 | 18.26 | 32.1 |

From the graph (Fig. 128) we can see that the points lie about a straight line.

If $\qquad x = \sqrt{\dfrac{b}{n}} \qquad$ and $\qquad y = t$

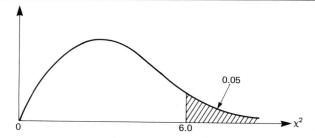

Fig. 127. *Test for correctness of estimate of percentage of complaints.*

then the equation becomes $y = kx$ which is the equation of a straight line passing through the origin.

Hence the relationship seems adequate. It will be necessary however to estimate a regression line and then to calculate the correlation coefficient to see how good a fit the data are to the regression line.

| $x$ | $y$ | $xy$ | $x^2$ | $y^2$ |
|---|---|---|---|---|
| 17.32 | 36.2 | 626.98 | 299.98 | 1,310.44 |
| 20.00 | 39.5 | 790.00 | 400.00 | 1,560.25 |
| 22.36 | 45.1 | 1,008.44 | 499.97 | 2,034.01 |
| 15.81 | 32.2 | 509.08 | 249.96 | 1,036.84 |
| 17.32 | 31.0 | 536.92 | 299.98 | 961.00 |
| 14.14 | 28.0 | 395.92 | 199.94 | 784.00 |
| 24.49 | 45.5 | 1,114.30 | 599.76 | 2,070.25 |
| 18.26 | 32.1 | 586.15 | 333.43 | 1,030.41 |
| 149.70 | 289.6 | 5,567.79 | 2,883.02 | 10,787.20 |

(b)

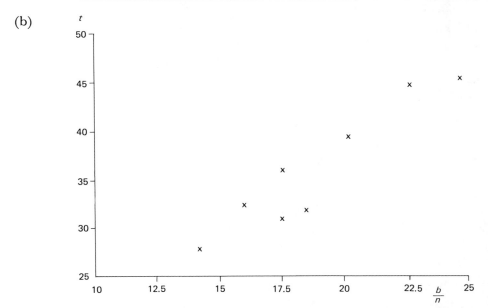

Fig. 128. *Graph of travel time against square miles per engineer.*

Now $b = \dfrac{n\sum xy - \sum x \sum y}{n\sum x^2 - (\sum x)^2}$

$= \dfrac{8 \times 5{,}567.79 - 149.7 \times 289.6}{8 \times 2{,}883.02 - (149.7)^2}$

$= \underline{\underline{1.818}}.$

$a = \dfrac{\sum y}{8} - b\dfrac{\sum x}{8}$

$= \dfrac{289.6}{n} - 1.818 \times \dfrac{149.70}{n}$

$= \underline{\underline{2.181}}.$

Regression line is $y = 2.181 + 1.818x$

Our $b$-value corresponds to the constant $k$, therefore the approximate equation is given by:

$$t = 1.818\sqrt{\dfrac{b}{n}}$$

We are assuming that the constant $a = 2.181$ is not significantly different from zero. (A test by calculating the standard error of $a$ and its corresponding $t$-value would support this assumption.)

(c) To find $n$ given $b = 2{,}000$ and $t = 30$.
Substitute equation:

$$30 = 1.818\sqrt{\dfrac{2{,}000}{n}}$$

$$\therefore \dfrac{30}{1.818} = \sqrt{\dfrac{2{,}000}{n}}$$

$$16.502 = \sqrt{\dfrac{2{,}000}{n}}$$

$$272.3 = \dfrac{2{,}000}{n}$$

$$n = 7.34.$$

Hence 8 engineers would be required to give *at least* a mean travel time of 30 minutes.

APPENDIX 3. SUGGESTED ANSWERS TO EXAMINATION QUESTIONS

(d) With 5 engineers and an area of 2,000 miles the mean travel time is:

$$t = 1.818 \sqrt{\frac{2{,}000}{5}}$$

$$= 36.36.$$

∴ Total time required per job = 36.36 + 30

= <u>66.36 minutes.</u>

∴ Total time for 40 jobs = 40 × 66.36

= <u>2,654.4 minutes.</u>

Labour time availabe = 8 × 60 × 5

= <u>2,400 minutes.</u>

Therefore more than 5 engineers are required.

**29.**

(a)

| $x$ | $y$ | $xy$ | $x^2$ | $y^2$ |
|---|---|---|---|---|
| 736 | 15.00 | 11,040 | 541,696 | 225.00 |
| 800 | 14.50 | 11,600 | 640,000 | 210.25 |
| 1,008 | 15.75 | 15,876 | 1,016,064 | 248.06 |
| 880 | 15.25 | 13,420 | 774,400 | 232.56 |
| 1,056 | 16.25 | 17,160 | 1,115,136 | 264.06 |
| 840 | 15.00 | 12,600 | 705,600 | 225.00 |
| 5,320 | 91.75 | 81,696 | 4,792,896 | 1,404.93 |

$$b = \frac{n\sum xy - \sum x \sum y}{n\sum x^2 - (\sum x)^2}$$

$$= \frac{6 \times 81{,}696 - 5{,}320 \times 91.75}{6 \times 4{,}792{,}896 - (5{,}320)^2}$$

$$= \underline{\underline{0.00454.}}$$

$$a = \frac{\sum y}{n} - b\frac{\sum x}{n}$$

$$= \frac{91.75}{6} - 0.00454 \times \frac{5{,}320}{6}$$

$$= \underline{\underline{11.265.}}$$

Least-squares cost equation is

$$y = 11.265 + 0.00454x \quad (y \text{ is measured in £000})$$

or

$$y = 11{,}265 + 4.54x.$$

(b)
$$r = \frac{n\sum xy - \sum x \sum y}{\sqrt{[n\sum x^2 - (\sum x)^2][n\sum y^2 - (\sum y)^2]}}$$

$$= \frac{6 \times 81{,}696 - 5{,}320 \times 91.75}{\sqrt{[6 \times 4{,}792{,}896 - (5{,}320)^2][6 \times 1{,}404.93 - (91.75)^2]}}$$

$$= 0.900.$$

$$\therefore \underline{\underline{r^2 = 0.81}}.$$

(c) Two equations are:

and $y = 11{,}265 + 4.54x$

and $y = 5{,}758 + 470x + 31\text{ PH}$.

(i) The multiple regression line is a better fit than the linear regression line as $r^2 = 0.9873$ compared with 0.81.

(ii) The coefficient of $x$ (DLH) is almost the same, but the fixed cost is greatly changed.

The combination of these facts means that where the linear regression line ignoring PH has attributed to fixed costs a variable cost which depends upon PH, the multiple regression equation has correctly separated out the fixed costs and the variable costs due to PH which is reflected in the improved $r^2$ value.

(d) Total OH = $5{,}758 + 4.7 \times 10{,}000 + 31 \times 168$

$= \underline{\underline{15{,}666}}.$

**30.**

(a) Let $x$ = CSA at start − CSA at finish

$y$ = forging time in minutes.

| $x$ | $y$ | $xy$ | $x^2$ | $y^2$ |
|---|---|---|---|---|
| 32 | 16 | 512 | 1,024 | 256 |
| 40 | 24 | 960 | 1,600 | 576 |
| 15 | 9 | 135 | 225 | 81 |
| 12 | 12 | 144 | 144 | 144 |
| 48 | 29 | 1,392 | 2,304 | 841 |
| 39 | 21 | 819 | 1,521 | 441 |
| 32 | 14 | 448 | 1,042 | 196 |
| 218 | 125 | 4,410 | 7,842 | 2,535 |

$$b = \frac{n\sum xy - \sum x \sum y}{n\sum x^2 - (\sum x)^2}$$

$$= \frac{7 \times 4{,}410 - 218 \times 125}{7 \times 7{,}842 - (218)^2}$$

$$= \underline{\underline{0.491}}.$$

$$a = \frac{\sum y}{n} - b\frac{\sum x}{n}$$

$$= \frac{125}{7} - 0.491 \times \frac{218}{7}$$

$$= \underline{\underline{2.566}}.$$

∴ Regression line is $t = 2.57 + 0.491$ (CSA at start − CSA at finish).

(b) (i) $x_1 = 30$, ∴ $t_1 = 2.57 + 0.491\ (30) = 17.3$.

$x_2 = 19$, ∴ $t_2 = 2.57 + 0.491\ (19) = 11.9$.

Difference = $\underline{\underline{5.4 \text{ minutes}}}$.

(ii) $t = 18$, CSA (start) = 36

Let $F$ = CSA (finish).

Then $18 = 2.57 + 0.491\ (36 - F)$

$15.43 = 0.491\ (36 - F)$

$31.426 = 36 - F$

$\underline{\underline{F = 4.57}}$.

∴ CSA at finish = 4.57 in$^2$.

**31.**

(a) Let 1975 be year 1, 1976 year 2, and so on.

Let $y$ be the number of chess sets in tens.

| $x$ | $y$ | $xy$ | $x^2$ | $y^2$ |
|---|---|---|---|---|
| 1 | 50 | 50 | 1 | 2,500 |
| 2 | 53 | 106 | 4 | 2,809 |
| 3 | 51 | 153 | 9 | 2,601 |
| 4 | 58 | 232 | 16 | 3,364 |
| 5 | 60 | 300 | 25 | 3,600 |
| 6 | 60 | 360 | 36 | 3,600 |
| 7 | 63 | 441 | 49 | 3,969 |
| 28 | 395 | 1,642 | 140 | 22,443 |

$$b = \frac{n\sum xy - \sum x \sum y}{n\sum x^2 - (\sum x)^2}$$

$$= \frac{7 \times 1{,}642 - 28 \times 395}{7 \times 140 - (28)^2}$$

$$= \underline{\underline{2.214}}.$$

$$a = \frac{\sum y}{n} - b\frac{\sum x}{n}$$

$$= \frac{395}{7} - 2.214 \times \frac{28}{7}$$

$$= \underline{\underline{47.57}}.$$

Regression line is: $y = 47.57 + 2.21x$.

(b)
$$r = \frac{n\sum xy - \sum x \sum y}{\sqrt{[n\sum x^2 - (\sum x)^2][n\sum y^2 - (\sum y)^2]}}$$

$$= \frac{7 \times 1{,}642 - 28 \times 395}{\sqrt{[7 \times 140 - (28)^2]\,[7 \times 22{,}443 - (395)^2]}}$$

$$= \underline{\underline{0.945}}.$$

(c) Coefficient of determination = $r^2 = 0.893$.
This means that 89.3 per cent of the variation is explained by the regression line. Hence the regression line is a good fit to the data.

(d) $t = 6.46$. Number of degrees of freedom = $7 - 2 = 5$.
Test if the sample value $b = 2.214$ is significantly different from zero using a 5 per cent test:

$H_0 : b = 0$, $H_1 : b \neq 0$.

Referring to Fig. 129:

From tables, $t_{0.025}\,(V = 5) = 2.6$.

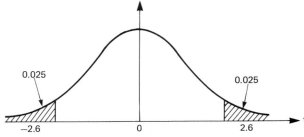

Fig. 129. *Test for whether sample value is significantly different from zero.*

As the sample $t = 6.46$ is outside the test range $-2.6$ to $+2.6$, reject $H_0 : b = 0$ and accept $H_1 : b \neq 0$, i.e. $b = 2.214$ is significantly greater than zero. Therefore the demand for chess sets is affected by the year.

This test is mathematically equivalent to testing if $r$ is significantly different from zero. As the test shows there is a significant difference, the regression line must be a good fit to the data.

**32.**

(a)

| $x$ | $y$ | $xy$ | $x^2$ | $y^2$ |
|---|---|---|---|---|
| 12 | 6.2 | 74.4 | 144 | 38.44 |
| 18 | 8.0 | 144.0 | 324 | 64.00 |
| 19 | 8.6 | 163.4 | 361 | 73.96 |
| 20 | 10.4 | 208.0 | 400 | 108.16 |
| 24 | 10.2 | 244.8 | 576 | 104.04 |
| 30 | 12.4 | 372.0 | 900 | 153.76 |
| 123 | 55.8 | 1,206.6 | 2,705 | 542.36 |

$$b = \frac{n\sum xy - \sum x \sum y}{n\sum x^2 - (\sum x)^2}$$

$$= \frac{6 \times 1{,}206.6 - 123 \times 55.8}{6 \times 2{,}705 - (123)^2}$$

$$= \underline{\underline{0.342}}.$$

$$a = \frac{\sum y}{n} - b\frac{\sum x}{n}$$

$$= \frac{55.8}{6} - 0.342 \times \frac{123}{6}$$

$$= \underline{\underline{2.289}}.$$

Regression line is: $y = 2.29 + 0.342x$.

(b) For comparison we need to calculate the correlation coefficient.

$$r = \frac{n\sum xy - \sum x \sum y}{\sqrt{[n\sum x^2 - (\sum x)^2][n\sum y^2 - (\sum y)^2]}}$$

$$= \frac{6 \times 1{,}206.6 - 123 \times 55.8}{\sqrt{[6 \times 2{,}705 - 123^2][6 \times 542.36 - 55.8^2]}}$$

$$= \underline{\underline{0.956}}.$$

We therefore have:

$$\text{power costs} = 2.29 + 0.34 \text{ (output)}, \quad r = 0.956$$

or $\quad \text{power costs} = 4.42 + 0.82 \text{ (output)} + 0.10 \text{ (month)}, \quad r = 0.976.$

The difference in the $r$-value is very small indicating that the addition of time into the regression equation makes very little difference.

This is supported by the $t$-values as the $t$-value for time is very low at $0.60$, and certainly not significant, compared with the $t$-value for output of $2.64$.

Therefore to predict total power cost we should use the simpler of the two regression equations:

$$y = 2.29 + 0.342 \text{ (output)}.$$

To forecast power costs in month seven we need first to determine the likely output. This might be already known as the output would generally be determined by the demand level and orders should have already been received. If we are forecasting from further back in time it might be necessary to forecast the output for month seven. To do this we might observe that output seems to be increasing over time and calculate a regression line relating output to time. Using our two regression lines, (i) output against time and (ii) power costs against output, we can forecast the total power costs in month seven.

**33.**

(a) *See* Fig. 130.

(b) One way of eliminating the curves is to consider the general shape of each curve.

(i) $\quad y = b \log_{10} x \quad$ decreasing positive slope

(ii) $\quad y = b \log_e x \quad$ decreasing positive slope

(iii) $\quad y = b e^x \quad$ increasing positive slope

(iv) $\quad y = b e^{-x} \quad$ decreasing negative slope

(v) $\quad y = a b^x \quad (b > 1, a > 0) \quad$ increasing positive slope

(vi) $\quad y = a b^x \quad (b < 1, a > 0) \quad$ decreasing negative slope.

From the graph it can be seen that we have a curve with an increasing positive slope.

Hence, either (c) $\quad y = b e^x$

or $\quad$ (e) $\quad y = a b^x \quad (b > 1, a > 0)$

should be considered.

Both should be fitted to the data and the curve with the best fit selected. The more general curve $y = a b^x$ is most likely to fit the data.

# APPENDIX 3. SUGGESTED ANSWERS TO EXAMINATION QUESTIONS

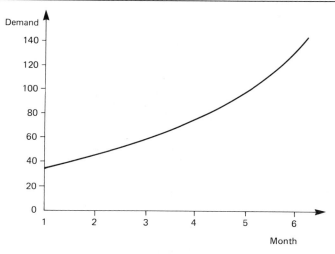

Fig. 130. *Graph of demand against month.*

(c) $y = ab^x$

Taking logs of both sides gives us:

$$\log y = a + x \log b.$$

If we now use as our $y$-variable $\log y$ we have an equation of a straight line. Therefore a linear regression approach can be adopted to determine the equation of the curve from the values of $a$ and $\log b$ and then the correlation coefficient can be calculated to measure the goodness of fit.

## 34.

(a) Using a 60 per cent learning curve:

| Total number | Average | Total | Increase |
|---|---|---|---|
| 10 | 3* | 30 | 30 |
| 20 | 1.8† | 36 | 6 |
| 40 | 1.08 | 43.2 | 7.2 |

*The *average* time to produce the first batch of ten was $30/10 = 3$ hours.

†To calculate the new average, when production is doubled, multiply old average 3 by 60 per cent = 1.8.

The total time to produce 20 pebbles at an average of 1.8 hours is $20 \times 1.8 = 36$ hours—an additional *6 hours*.

The table above can then be continued to show that the next twenty pebbles take a further 7.2 hours.

(b) General form of learning curve is: $y = ax^{-b}$
where $b$ is given by:

$$b = \frac{-\log(\text{learning rate})}{\log 2}$$

$$= \frac{-\log(0.6)}{\log 2}$$

$$= \frac{0.2218}{0.3010}$$

$$= 0.7369.$$

Now when $x = 10,\ y = 3$

$$\therefore\ 3 = a(10)^{-0.7369}$$

$$a = 3(10)^{+0.7369}$$

but in question $\log_{10}(5.46) = 0.7369$

$$\therefore\ 5.46 = 10^{0.7369}$$

$$\therefore\ a = 3 \times 5.46$$

$$= 16.38 \text{ hours.}$$

Time to produce the first pebble = 16.4 hours.

(c) Cost of first 40 pebbles:

Labour cost = 43.2 × £10   =   £432
Material cost = 40 × £1    =     40
                                                  £472

Break even price $= \dfrac{472}{40} = £11.8.$

Using an 80 per cent learning curve:

| Total number | Average | Total |
|---|---|---|
| 10 | 3.00 | 30.0 |
| 20 | 2.40 | 48.0 |
| 40 | 1.92 | 76.8 |

Hence:

Labour cost = 76.8 × £10   =   £768
Material cost = 40 × £1    =     40
                                                  £808

Break even price = $\dfrac{808}{40}$ = £20.20.

A difference of £8.4.

## 35.

The machine tool costs can be ignored, as they are recovered on the first order.

The material costs must be $3 \times £3{,}000 = £9{,}000$. The variable overheads and other overheads depend upon the variable labour-costs. The labour costs in a craft industry can be determined by use of the 80 per cent learning curve.

The original number produced was 10 and now we are considering a further 30 to make a total of 40.

Using learning curve theory we get the following table for variable labour costs:

| Total produced | Average cost | Total cost |
| --- | --- | --- |
| 10 | 500* | 5,000 |
| 20 | 400† | 8,000 |
| 40 | 320‡ | 12,800§ |

\*First average cost was calculated as total cost £5,000 over total produced 10.
†Second average cost was calculated as 80 per cent of first average cost of £500 as production had doubled.
‡80 per cent of previous average £400.
§Total cost comes from total produced 40 times average cost £320.

Therefore total variable overheads for first 40 = £12,800
but total variable overheads for first 10 = 5,000
but total variable overheads for next 30 = £7,800

Both variable and other overheads are 20 per cent of the variable labour costs, i.e. 20 per cent of £7,800 = £1,560.

Therefore an estimate for a further 30 "Morning Clouds" is:

| | |
| --- | --- |
| Materials: 30 × £300 | £9,000 |
| Variable labour costs | 7,800 |
| Variable overheads | 1,560 |
| Other overheads | 1,560 |
| Machine tool costs | – |
| Total estimate | £19,920 |

## 36.

(a) Let $\mu$ be the mean of the total interview time.

then $\mu = \dfrac{\text{Total interview time of all candidates}}{\text{Total number of candidates}}$

$= \dfrac{30 \times 15 + 30 \times 15}{30}$

$= \underline{\underline{30 \text{ minutes}}}.$

This result was rather obvious and hardly needs to be proved from first principles, but it illustrates the approach to be used in more difficult examples.

(b) The general formula for the variance of a sum is:

$$\text{var}(X + Y) = \text{var}(X) + \text{var}(Y) + 2\,\text{cov}(X, Y)$$

Now the variance of the first interview is $2^2 = 4$ and the variance of the second interview is $2.5^2 = 6.25$. We have not been given the covariance. If we assume that the length of the first interview does not affect the length of the second interview then $\text{cov}(X, Y) = 0$.

$\therefore$ Variance $= 4 + 6.25 + 0$

$= \underline{\underline{10.25}}.$

$\therefore$ Standard deviation of total interview time is

$$\sqrt{10.25} = \underline{\underline{3.20 \text{ minutes}}}.$$

## 37.

(a) Joint probability distribution:

| Possible event | | | Probability |
|---|---|---|---|
| Red | Blue | | |
| 1 | 1 | $0.4 \times 0.5 =$ | 0.20 |
| 1 | 2 | $0.4 \times 0.4 =$ | 0.16 |
| 1 | 3 | $0.4 \times 0.1 =$ | 0.04 |
| 2 | 1 | $0.3 \times 0.5 =$ | 0.15 |
| 2 | 2 | $0.3 \times 0.4 =$ | 0.12 |
| 2 | 3 | $0.3 \times 0.1 =$ | 0.03 |
| 3 | 1 | $0.3 \times 0.5 =$ | 0.15 |
| 3 | 2 | $0.3 \times 0.4 =$ | 0.12 |
| 3 | 3 | $0.3 \times 0.1 =$ | 0.03 |
| | | | 1.00 |

(b) Combining rows from above with common sums:

| Sum | | Probability |
|---|---|---|
| 2 | 0.20 = | 0.20 |
| 3 | 0.16 + 0.15 = | 0.31 |
| 4 | 0.04 + 0.12 + 0.15 = | 0.31 |
| 5 | 0.03 + 0.12 = | 0.15 |
| 6 | 0.03 = | 0.03 |
| | | 1.00 |

(c)

Red die:

| $x$ | $P(x)$ | $xP(x)$ | $x^2P(x)$ |
|---|---|---|---|
| 1 | 0.4 | 0.4 | 0.4 |
| 2 | 0.3 | 0.6 | 1.2 |
| 3 | 0.3 | 0.9 | 2.7 |
| | 1.0 | 1.9 | 4.3 |

Mean $= \sum xP(x) = \underline{\underline{1.9}}$.

Variance $= \sum x^2 P(x) - (\text{mean})^2$

$= 4.3 - (1.9)^2 = \underline{\underline{0.69}}$.

Blue die:

| $x$ | $P(x)$ | $xP(x)$ | $x^2P(x)$ |
|---|---|---|---|
| 1 | 0.5 | 0.5 | 0.5 |
| 2 | 0.4 | 0.8 | 1.6 |
| 3 | 0.1 | 0.3 | 0.9 |
| | 1.0 | 1.6 | 3.0 |

Mean $= \underline{\underline{1.6}}$.

Variance $= 3.0 - (1.6)^2 = \underline{\underline{0.44}}$.

Sum of scores:

| x | P(x) | xP(x) | $x^2P(x)$ |
|---|------|-------|-----------|
| 2 | 0.20 | 0.40 | 0.80 |
| 3 | 0.31 | 0.93 | 2.79 |
| 4 | 0.31 | 1.24 | 4.96 |
| 5 | 0.15 | 0.75 | 3.75 |
| 6 | 0.03 | 0.18 | 1.08 |
|   | 1.00 | 3.50 | 13.38 |

Mean = 3.50.

Variance = $13.38 - 3.5^2 = 1.13$.

The mean of the sum = mean of red die + mean of blue die.

Variance of sum = variance of red die + variance of blue die.

(d) (i)

| Sum | | | Probability |
|-----|---|---|------|
| 2 | 0.2 | = | 0.2 |
| 3 | 0.1 + 0.1 | = | 0.2 |
| 4 | 0 + 0.1 + 0 | = | 0.1 |
| 5 | 0.1 + 0.2 | = | 0.3 |
| 6 | 0.2 | = | 0.2 |
|   |     |   | 1.0 |

| x | P(x) | xP(x) | $x^2P(x)$ |
|---|------|-------|-----------|
| 2 | 0.2 | 0.4 | 0.8 |
| 3 | 0.2 | 0.6 | 1.8 |
| 4 | 0.1 | 0.4 | 1.6 |
| 5 | 0.3 | 1.5 | 7.5 |
| 6 | 0.2 | 1.2 | 7.2 |
|   | 1.0 | 4.1 | 18.9 |

Mean = 4.1.

Variance = $18.9 - (4.1)^2 = 2.09$.

(ii)

| Red die: | $x$ | $P(x)$ | $xP(x)$ | $x^2P(x)$ |
|---|---|---|---|---|
| | 1 | 0.3 | 0.3 | 0.3 |
| | 2 | 0.4 | 0.8 | 1.6 |
| | 3 | 0.3 | 0.9 | 2.7 |
| | | 1.0 | 2.0 | 4.6 |

Mean = $\underline{\underline{2.0}}$.

Variance = $4.6 - 2^2 = \underline{\underline{0.6}}$.

| Blue die: | $x$ | $P(x)$ | $xP(x)$ | $x^2P(x)$ |
|---|---|---|---|---|
| | 1 | 0.3 | 0.3 | 0.3 |
| | 2 | 0.3 | 0.6 | 1.2 |
| | 3 | 0.4 | 1.2 | 3.6 |
| | | 1.0 | 2.1 | 5.1 |

Mean = $\underline{\underline{2.1}}$.

Variance = $5.1 - 2.1^2 = \underline{\underline{0.69}}$.

(iii)  Covariance = $E(XY) - E(X) \cdot E(Y)$

Now  $E(XY) = 1 \times 1 \times 0.2 + 1 \times 2 \times 0.1 + 1 \times 3 \times 0 + 2 \times 1 \times 0.1$
$\qquad + 2 \times 2 \times 0.1 + 2 \times 3 \times 0.2 + 3 \times 1 \times 0 + 3 \times 2$
$\qquad \times 0.1 + 3 \times 3 \times 0.2$
$\qquad = 4.6,$

$\therefore$ covariance = $4.6 - 2.0 \times 2.1 = \underline{\underline{0.4}}$

Relationship between results:

| | Mean | Variance |
|---|---|---|
| Red | 2.0 | 0.60 |
| Blue | 2.1 | 0.69 |
| Sum | 4.1 | 2.09 |

The mean of the sum is equal to the sum of the means as the theory tells us.
The sum of the variances of the red and blue dice is less then the variance of the sum.

(iv) To find $r$, we know that covariance $= r\sigma_x\sigma_y$,

$$\therefore \quad r = \frac{\text{cov}(x, y)}{\sigma_x\sigma_y}.$$

Now $\text{cov}(x, y) = 0.4$

$$\sigma_x = \sqrt{0.60} = 0.7746$$

$$\sigma_y = \sqrt{0.69} = 0.8307$$

$$\therefore \quad r = \frac{0.4}{0.7746 \times 0.8307} = \underline{\underline{0.622}}.$$

## 38.

(a) Joint probability distribution:

|   | W |   |   |
|---|---|---|---|
| $h$ | 150 | 160 | 170 |
| 70 | 0.2 | 0.1 | 0 |
| 75 | 0.1 | 0.2 | 0.1 |
| 80 | 0 | 0.1 | 0.2 |

(b) Probability distribution of $h$:

| $x$ | P($x$) | $x$P($x$) | $x^2$P($x$) |
|---|---|---|---|
| 70 | 0.3 | 21 | 1,470 |
| 75 | 0.4 | 30 | 2,250 |
| 80 | 0.3 | 24 | 1,920 |
|   | 1.0 | 75 | 5,640 |

Mean $= \sum x\text{P}(x) = \underline{\underline{75}}$.

Variance $= \sum x^2\text{P}(x) - (\text{Mean})^2$
$= 5{,}640 - 75^2$

$= \underline{\underline{15}}.$

(c) Probability distribution of $W$:

| $x$ | P(x) | xP(x) | $x^2$P(x) |
|---|---|---|---|
| 150 | 0.3 | 45 | 6,750 |
| 160 | 0.4 | 64 | 10,240 |
| 170 | 0.3 | 51 | 8,670 |
|  | 1.0 | 160 | 25,660 |

Mean = 160.

Variance = $25{,}660 - 160^2$ = 60.

(d) Covariance = $E(XY) - E(X) \cdot E(Y)$

$E(XY) = 70 \times 150 \times 0.2 + 70 \times 160 \times 0.1 + 75 \times 150 \times 0.1$
$\qquad + 75 \times 160 \times 0.2 + 75 \times 170 \times 0.1 + 80 \times 160 \times 0.1$
$\qquad + 80 \times 170 \times 0.2$

$\qquad = 12{,}020$

$\therefore$ covariance = $12{,}020 - 75 \times 160$ = 20.

(e) $E(W/h = 70) = \dfrac{150 \times 0.2 + 160 \times 0.1}{0.3}$ = 153.3.

$E(W/h = 75) = \dfrac{150 \times 0.1 + 160 \times 0.2 + 170 \times 0.1}{0.4}$ = 160.

$E(W/h = 80) = \dfrac{160 \times 0.1 + 170 \times 0.2}{0.3}$ = 166.7.

(f) $h$ and $W$ are dependent as can be seen from the last two sections. The covariance would need to be zero for independence, and in (c) we showed that the expected value of $W$ depended upon the value of $h$.

(g) Given $I = 2h + 3W$

$\therefore E(I) = 2E(h) + 3E(W)$

$\qquad = 2 \times 75 + 3 \times 160$

$\qquad = 630.$

Also $\text{var}(I) = 2^2 \cdot \text{var}(h) + 3^2 \cdot \text{var}(W) + 2 \times 2 \times 3 \cdot \text{cov}(h, W)$

$\therefore \text{var}(I) = 4 \times 15 + 9 \times 60 + 12 \times 20$

$\qquad = 840.$

∴ SD = $\sqrt{840}$
= 28.98
= <u>29.0</u>.

(h) Probability distribution of $I$:

| $x$ | $P(x)$ | $xP(x)$ | $x^2P(x)$ |
|---|---|---|---|
| 590 | 0.2 | 118 | 69,620 |
| 600 | 0.1 | 60 | 36,000 |
| 620 | 0.1 | 62 | 38,440 |
| 630 | 0.2 | 126 | 79,380 |
| 640 | 0.1 | 64 | 40,960 |
| 660 | 0.1 | 66 | 43,560 |
| 670 | 0.2 | 134 | 89,780 |
|  | 1.0 | 630 | 397,740 |

Mean = <u>630</u>.

Variance = $397{,}740 - 630^2$ = <u>840</u>.

∴ SD = $\sqrt{840}$ = <u>29.0</u>.

These results agree with (g).

**39.**

(a) We need to calculate the mean and variance of the *amount* demanded.

Mean = $1{,}200 \times 1 + 600 \times 5 + 50 \times 10 = 4{,}700$.

Variance = $250^2 \times 1^2 + 100^2 \times 5^2 + 5^2 \times 10^2 = 315{,}000$.

∴ SD = <u>561.25</u>

As the distribution of individual notes follows a normal distribution, the amount demanded also follows a normal distribution.

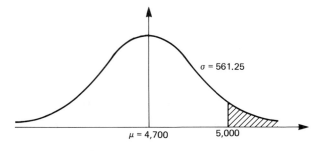

Fig. 131. *Probable daily demand for cash (£).*

Referring to Fig. 131:

$$Z = \frac{5,000 - 4,700}{561.25}$$

0.53.

From normal tables: $P(x > 5,000) = \underline{\underline{0.298}}$.

(b) £1 notes: referring to Fig. 132,

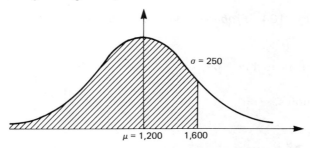

Fig. 132. *Probable daily demand for pound notes.*

$$Z = \frac{1,600 - 1,200}{250} = 1.6.$$

From tables, area = 0.055

$P(x \leq 1,600) = \underline{\underline{0.945}}$.

£5 notes: referring to Fig. 133,

$$£\frac{3,500}{5} = 700 \text{ notes.}$$

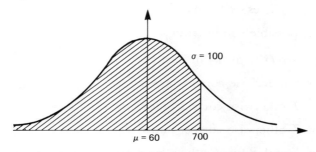

Fig. 133. *Probable daily demand for £5 notes.*

$$Z = \frac{700 - 600}{100} = 1.0.$$

From tables, area = 0.159.

$P(x \leq 700) = \underline{\underline{0.841}}$.

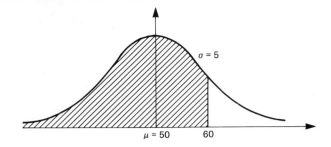

Fig. 134. *Probable daily demand for £10 notes.*

£10 notes: referring to Fig. 134,

$$£\frac{600}{10} = 60 \text{ notes.}$$

$$Z = \frac{60 - 50}{5} = 2.0$$

From tables, area = 0.023.

$$P(x \leqslant 60) = \underline{\underline{0.977}}.$$

Probability that all demands for cash will be met = $0.945 \times 0.841 \times 0.977 = \underline{\underline{0.776}}$.

Denomination most crucial is the £5 note as 0.841 is the smallest of the probabilities.

(c) Let $P$ = pounds, $F$ = fives, $T$ = tens.

There are eight possible combinations:

(i)    Use only correct notes as in part (b);

(ii)   Use $P$ for $F$ otherwise correct notes;

(iii)   Use $F$ for $T$ otherwise correct notes;

(iv)   Use $P$ for $T$ otherwise correct notes;

(v)    Use $P$ for $F$ and $P$ for $T$ otherwise correct notes;

(vi)   Use $P$ for $F$ and $F$ for $T$ otherwise correct notes;

(vii)   Use $F$ for $T$ and $P$ for $T$ otherwise correct notes;

(viii) Use $P$ for $F$, $P$ for $T$, and $F$ for $T$ otherwise correct notes.

The probabilities of all these combinations would need to be determined but we cannot assume, as we did in (b), the independence of the probabilities.

## 40.

### Definition
OR is, as the name implies, research into business operations. It may be defined as "the application of the methods of science to complex problems arising in the direction and management of large systems of men, machines, materials and money in industry, business, government and defence".

### Essential characteristics
The approach has the following characteristics:

#### (a) SYSTEMS APPROACH
A study is made of the complete system and not just separate components of it. Actions taken in one part of the organisation are likely to produce effects elsewhere. To evaluate any decision or action within an organisation, it is necessary to identify all the significant interactions and to evaluate the combined impact on the performance of the organisation as a whole, not merely on the part originally involved.

The concept of a system plays a critical role in our viewpoint of a problem. The fundamental ideal of the systems approach to problem solving is to study total systems performance rather than to concentrate on the parts. It stems from the recognition that even if each element or subsystem is optimised from a design or operational point of view the total systems performance may be suboptimal owing to interaction between the parts. Because of the increasing complexity of operational research problems the necessity for systems thinking has become more and more important.

There is a danger that newcomers to operational research may see it as a string of isolated techniques. Using a systems approach makes the practitioner more aware of the dynamic nature of most studies and the interdependencies that exist in most real-world problems.

However, a practical approach needs to be adopted. Failure in modelling complex systems often stems from being too ambitious regarding the detail and size of the system being studied. We need to be aware of the limitations of our current techniques. We need to use great care in the selection of elements to be included in our model of the systems. It may well be, as in a large number of cases, that the operational researcher is looking at less than the total system due to constraints of time and money imposed upon the study. In these situations the operational researcher should always question the validity of his work and consider whether the missing elements will jeopardise the success of his study.

It has been said that a system consists of parts, each part contributing towards achieving the objectives of the system as a whole. Attempting to optimise each part separately will not in general achieve an optimal system due to interactions between parts. However, if a part is independent of the rest of the system then changes in other parts of the system will not affect it. A part or subsystem which is independent is said to be separable.

In practice, only a few systems are truly separable, but a number have parts that have only weak interactions with other parts. In these cases, it is possible to build a series of separate models and then solve separately or, more usually, solve in a given sequence using results from the solutions to previous parts as inputs to the next part.

Thus the systems approach is not being repudiated, but adapted to give us a feasible solution procedure.

## (b) TEAM APPROACH
OR brings together personnel from a number of different disciplines. Specialisation has increased at such a rate that investigation by multi-disciplinary teams is the only feasible approach in many areas where problems can no longer be treated effectively by an individual.

## (c) THE USE OF MODELS
A model is a scaled-down version of reality which often involves considerable simplification. It can be defined as a structured quantitative statement of the dominant factors affecting a decision.

## 41.

### The phases of an operational research project
These are as follows:

### (a) PROBLEM DEFINITION
The operational researcher must analyse the objectives and the system in which the solution must operate. Further, since the purpose of formulating the problem is to determine the optimum course of action from various alternatives, measures of effectiveness as well as objectives must be clearly defined. Hence the OR man must determine alternative courses of action that might be taken and define the criteria or yardstick by which various alternative solutions are to be compared. He must take a systems approach in doing this, i.e. the problem should not be treated in isolation.

### (b) CONSTRUCTION OF A MODEL
In the second phase, some model or representation of the system has to be built. The complexity of this representation will vary enormously from problem to problem and while complexity is not in itself of any merit, it is essential to have sufficient complexity for realistic results to be achieved. The model might be of a functional nature as in LP where the essentials of the problem can be expressed in a series of equations. Alternatively, it may have a logical structure as in simulation. (Note that model construction will involve obtaining quantitative data either from existing records or by a new enquiry or survey; analysis of the data by an appropriate statistical method and then the actual construction of a mathematical representation).

We might add, expressed symbolically, the basic form of all OR models is:

$$E = f(X_1, X_2, \ldots, X_n, Y_1, Y_2 \ldots Y_n)$$

where $t$ = objective measure of the system's effectiveness

$X_1, X_2, \ldots, X_n$ = system variables subject to control

$Y_1, Y_2, \ldots, Y_n$ = system variables not subject to control.

In words, this statement says that performace depends upon significant controlled and uncontrolled aspects of the system. Now let us consider each of these components of a model.

The development of an adequate measure of the system's performace may be a very difficult—if not the most difficult—aspect of the research. It must reflect the relative importance of, and conflict between, the multiplicity of objectives involved in every executive-type decision.

In developing a measure of performance it is necessary, first, to develop a measure of the degree to which each objective is obtained. These are called measures of *efficiency*, but the scales used in these measures may not be the same. For example, the scale used to measure the degree to which the objective—to minimise cost—is obtained would be monetary; the scale used to measure the degree to which the objective—to maximise customer service—is obtained may be (delivery) time. It is necessary, therefore, to find a way of expressing units on the different scales of efficiency on some one common scale. The scale usually employed for this purpose in an industrial context is itself a monetary one. When the various measures of efficiency are transformed on to one scale and are then consolidated into a single measure, the resulting measure is one of *effectiveness*. It takes all the objectives into account.

The units on the effectiveness scale may not all be of equal value. For example, to a starving man the first dollar or pound is more valuable than is the second. Similarly the first million dollars or pounds of income may be worth more to a company than is the second. It may be necessary, therefore, to take into account the value of the units on the effectiveness scale; that is, to transform the measure of effectiveness into a measure of value. Techniques for transforming one scale into another and for evaluating the units on a scale are now highly developed but a considerable amount of research may be required to apply them appropriately.

The controlled variables may include such things as the size and frequency of production runs, the number of different products made, the price of each, departmental budgets, and the number of salesmen employed. The values of each of the controlled variables can be set by management. The problem is to determine the values at which to set them.

Among the uncontrolled variables may be such things as competitive prices, the cost of labour and raw material, the location of customers, and the amount of demand for each product. These are factors which, at least within the context of the problem, are not subject to management's control.

The basic model may have to be supplemented by a set of statements which reflect limitations or restrictions on the possible values of the controlled variables.

For example, the amounts allocated to departments in a budget cannot exceed the total amount available. Nor can the amount of product shipped to consumers be greater than the amount available. These restrictions are expressed in a set of supplementary equations or inequations (i.e. statements involving the relationship "must be less than" or "greater than").

So far we have discussed the derivation of a model by means of mathematical and statistical analysis. In some cases, however, the mathematics breaks down before the sheer complexity of the real life situation. In these cases the OR scientist behaves just as his colleague in a laboratory would behave, namely he experiments. In fact, if it were possible, all OR would involve real life experimentation. However, the problems of the industrial executive are not those in which real life experimentation can be carried out since he is faced with not trial and error but trial and disaster. Consequently, the OR worker has to find some way of experimenting in an abstract form, such that there is a close relationship between the make-up of his experiment and the real life situation in such a way that the real life situation is not affected by his experiments. These methods are called simulation.

## (c) DERIVATION OF A SOLUTION FROM THE MODEL

The method of deriving a solution will depend upon the model used. If a functional model is used, e.g. a LP model or a calculus model, it can be solved mathematically in a precise and exact way. Second, if the equations defy any unique form of solution it can be examined arithmetically by a system of trial and error. Third, even when it is not possible to put the mathematics in a formal manner, the model can be tackled by simulation techniques.

## (d) TESTING THE MODEL

Models should be tested, as by their nature they are invariably only a representation of reality. Testing may be done by using the model to solve a problem and comparing the results so obtained with what actually happens.

## (e) ESTABLISHMENT OF CONTROLS (SELECTING OPTIMUM CONDITIONS)

Whichever of the above procedures is used to examine the model, it is equivalent to applying a form of search procedure which will provide a lead to the fifth phase of the study, namely the selection of the optimum set of conditions. In carrying out this phase, it is important not only to estimate the required set of optimum conditions under the various constraints built into the model, but also to examine how sensitive this solution is to changes in these constraints. Such manipulation makes it possible to see how critically the unique solution that was originally obtained depends upon the original assumptions built into the problems. This, in turn, can be of extreme importance in helping the manager to select precisely the set of conditions under which he is going to operate. If the solution is insensitive to changes in the constraints, he has considerably more flexibility than in a situation where the optimum is poised, so to speak, on a knife-edge. (Note the use of sensitivity analysis here as a guide to which variables would, when altered, make a significant change to a solution.)

## (f) IMPLEMENTATION

The final phases of the study are connected with its implementation, first a pilot implementation test, and then the full-scale implementation. Any proposed solution should be tested as stringently as possible before it is completely accepted and put into use. Neglect to do this can lead to vital factors being overlooked whose inclusion would markedly alter the solution. The best form of pilot implementation is one where the solution is completely implemented for a portion only of the total system. Giving the proposed solution responsibility for running a complete, although small, section of the operations seems to provide a rather better form of discipline than trying to run the complete solution in parallel with the previous method of operation. It is important that, when the final implementation stage is reached, those responsible for the project would still be available. Only then can they see that the solution is being correctly implemented and also that, if there are any snags, these are ironed out and the experience gained used in tackling any future problems of this kind.

## 42.

### Form and content

Managers are generally sceptical about the possibility that a group of operational research specialists, however ingenious they may be, can come into an organisation and learn enough about it to solve problems that have given the organisation difficulty for many years. The managers already there have probably taken years to learn about the organisation and still have not solved these problems. In effect, any manager feels that his problems are different from, and more difficult than, those confronting any other manager. Even if operational research can help others, he may argue "How can it possibly help me?"

The manager is correct in thinking that his problems are different from anybody else's, but he is wrong in thinking that they are different in every respect. There is a distinction to be drawn between the so-called form and content of problems. In algebra for instance the equation $y = ax + b$ is the standard notation for a straight-line relationship. This is an algebraic formula which can be used for a wide range of problems but has no real meaning until it is applied to a particular problem, where specific numbers are put in for the constants $a$ and $b$. In exactly the same way, the content of managerial forms may be different but there are relatively few forms managerial problems can assume.

The following list accounts for virtually all the forms managerial problems can take:

(a) inventory;    (b) replacement;    (c) allocation;    (d) queuing;

(e) sequencing and coordination;    (f) routing;    (g) competition;

(h) search.

Attempting to identify these forms and putting them into categories allows us when solving a problem to make use of previous analysis rather than starting from first principles. It also means that we are more likely to see the intricacies and complexities of the problem as there will be previous guidelines with which problem comparison is possible.

However, the danger of accepting the classification above too rigidly is that we assume that each problem fits into one category only. It is difficult in practice to find a problem that fits into one category alone, most industrial/commercial problems fit into several. The problems must be analysed so that the forms can be extracted and the relationship between the forms made explicit.

*Tutorial note: The answer below is given in detail for tutorial purposes.*

### Description of prototype problems

#### INVENTORY PROBLEMS

An inventory is an idle but usable resource. The resource may be of any type; for example, men, materials, machines or money. When the resource involved is material or goods in any stage of completion, inventory is usually referred to as "stock".

Inventory problems involve idle resources which must be maintained to meet an anticipated demand. The basic problem involves determining the optimal inventory level to maintain. The subsidiary problem involves determining the best time to order, and in what quantities.

If inventories are too high, excessive costs are paid in terms of capital tied up, warehousing, insurance and obsolescence. If inventories are too low, excessive costs are incurred in terms of lost sales, quantity discounts not realised, storage space not utilised and higher ordering and delivery costs. The answer lies in determining the inventory at which the total of both kinds of costs are minimised.

Techniques available include mathematical models, economic batch quantity formulae and computer systems for materials management which permit closer matching of inventory levels to anticipated demand.

### REPLACEMENT PROBLEMS

These problems arise from the deterioration of systems with time unless some corrective action is taken. For example, men, machines and other tools and facilities wear out by virtue of age, use or obsolescence and need to be replaced.

The basic question is determining the most economical time to replace such items. Does one wait until they fail or should they be replaced before they fail? The subsidiary question involves determining whether to replace items individually or as a group.

The problem is complicated by the fact that not all items of the same make or nature fail at the same rate, and that some items fail suddenly and completely without any warning; light-bulbs for example.

Some items deteriorate gradually, leading to lower efficiency and higher costs. This is typically the case with machines that wear. By waiting until complete failure before replacing such an item, the loss in efficiency over a period of time and the loss of production when the failure occurs may be excessive.

Replacement problems can be examined using probability theory and statisical analysis and have led to the development of a branch of statistics known as replacement, failure or reliability theory. The techniques available include cost comparisons, value theory and the use of Monte Carlo simulation.

The techniques are designed to help with the timing and selection of replacements for machines, components and materials that eventually fail, either slowly (through deterioration or obsolescence) or suddenly. Taking the failure rate, or probability of failure with time into consideration, these techniques help relate the costs of failure (including loss of production and loss of sales) with preventive maintenance and replacement costs.

### ALLOCATION PROBLEMS

These problems arise when there are a number of activities to perform but there are limitations on either the amount of resources or the way in which they can be employed. This prevents the performance of each separate activity in the most effective way. In such situations it is necessary to allocate the available resources to the activities in a manner that optimises total effectiveness.

The product-mix problem is typical allocation problem. Basically the problem is: what products should the company manufacture and in what amounts in order to maximise their profit? Constraints will exist in various forms such as a limited market, availability of materials or manpower or restricted machine capacity.

The assignment of men to machines might be one of these problems. The determination of which warehouses are to serve which customers is a distribution problem of this nature. Even the best location of a plant or a warehouse in terms of customer demand is an allocation problem.

The basic question is how one can best match the sources of supply available to known or anticipated demands? The answer involves weighing a complex set of variables usually with the help of a computer.

Mathematical programming is the name given to a set of techniques developed to tackle allocation problems. These techniques include linear programming, non-linear programming and dynamic programming.

Linear programming concerns itself with problems that can be expressed by linear equations and inequations. Linearity implies proportionality, i.e. there is a straight-line relationship between the variables in a problem. There are a number of sub-techniques of linear programming which are appropriate for particular allocation problems. The most general is the simplex method, which is a technique of matrix algebra used to find the optimum value of variables connected in a system of linear inequalities. However, for particular problems, algorithms (sets of procedures) exist which are easier to use, involve less computation and should be used in preference to the simplex method. These include the transportation method (which can be used to find the cheapest way of transporting goods from a number of sources to a number of destinations) and the assignment method (used to find the best way of assigning men to machines or jobs).

In certain allocation problems, variables have non-linear relationships and non-linear programming techniques have been developed to deal with these. Among these are quadratic programming (where there is a "squared" relationship between some of the variables) and stochastic programming (where the exact relationships between some of the variables are uncertain).

Dynamic programming involves solving a series of related problems one step at a time because the solution to one problem affects the answer to the next.


## QUEUING PROBLEMS

Waiting customers or idle facilities form a waiting line or queue. Queuing problems stem from a waiting line situation that is fixed. Like inventory problems, queuing situations involve two sets of costs that must be balanced against each other: the costs of delay versus the costs of service.

A queuing problem consists of either scheduling arrivals or producing facilities, or both, so as to minimise the sum of the costs of waiting customers and idle facilities. To minimise delay, service must be maximised and vice versa.

A queuing problem is found most often in the operation of a service facility. For example, how many maintenance workers should a factory employ? By employing too few, the men may be kept busy but the costs of delay in reparing production equipment may be exceedingly high. If too many are employed, the costs of delay may go down but the men may be idle a high percentage of the time. The solution lies in determining how much idleness is most economical to build into the system.

Queuing theory (complex mathematics) and Monte Carlo simulation are the techniques available for the modelling and the solution of queuing problems. The techniques and the models involved must take into account the customer population, the service mechanism, the queue discipline and the service discipline.

## SEQUENCING AND COORDINATION PROBLEMS

Sequencing concerns the selection of a queue discipline, which, in queuing problems is taken as given or fixed. The selection of an appropriate order in which to service waiting customers is called sequencing.

Queuing models assume a rule for selecting the next job waiting for service. However, in certain situations the order in which these jobs are carried out is significant. Where this is so, it is necessary to find the sequence in which the jobs should be done so that one's objective can be reached within the shortest time possible consistent with maximum effectiveness and minimum cost.

The term sequencing is normally used where the problem concerns the order of jobs on machines. However, even in comparatively simple situations involving few jobs and machines, the number of possible sequences of jobs through the machines is so large that analytic methods have been developed only for solving very simple sequencing problems.

Coordination problems entail projects that consist of activities that must be performed in a specified sequence. The problem involves programming and monitoring the progress of projects so that the project can be completed in the minimum possible time and optimise some measure of overall project performance. The problems are frequently referred to by the names of the techniques applied to their solution: critical path analysis (CPA) and PERT.

CPA and PERT are practical systems for planning and controlling many construction projects, many systems-development and product-development projects, large maintenance and overhaul projects and the manufacture and assembly of large products (aircraft, ships etc.).

In their simplest form, these techniques are concerned with the minimum time in which these projects can be completed. They further provide a basis for allocating resources and thus help to make the total of a project a minimum by finding the optimum balance between the various costs and times involved.

## ROUTING PROBLEMS

These are problems requiring the best route or paths for the flow of work, men, vehicles and materials. While routing problems may sometimes bear a superficial resemblance to sequencing problems, the major factors are topographical rather than chronological. The basic problem involves determining the most efficient route usually expressed in cost terms.

The routing problem is normally explained in terms of the travelling salesman problem. This is formulated as follows.

A salesman has a number of cities he must visit. He knows the distances (or times or cost) of travel between every pair of cities. His problem is to select a route that starts at his home city, passes through each city once and only once and returns to his home city in the shortest possible distances (or in least time, or at the least cost).

Clearly, the problem is to find the best route without trying each one. Although there have been many efforts to solve the problem analytically, no satisfactory general method exists. However, several computational techniques for solving the problem have been suggested.

## PROBLEMS OF COMPETITION

In most business situations, the outcome of the decision taken by a given company may be affected by a decision taken by its competitors. Competitive problems are problems involved in maintaining a position *vis-à-vis* the competition. The problem may be to break into a new market, to compete effectively, to "win" a fair share of the market or to bid for a specific contract.

The theory of games has been developed to provide a conceptual framework for considering these problems. The term "games" refers to the general situation of competition in which participants are engaged in decision-making activities in anticipation of certain outcomes over time. The theory of games deals with mathematical aspects of the decision-making process and the formulation of strategies for individuals pursuing conflicting interests. Unfortunately its development has been too limited to solve any real-life problems. An extension of this theory known as statistical decision theory has been of greater value.

### SEARCH PROBLEMS

The larger the scope of problems undertaken by OR, the greater is the need for generating and collecting information. Problems that involve the determination of how much and what information to acquire, how to acquire it, and how to treat it once it has been acquired are termed "search problems".

Search is an important part of decision processes and in many instances forms a problem in itself. In its wider aspects, the problem involves the most efficient procedure for finding anything—drilling for oil, an error in a business process, the one right opportunity among many, or even the search for a ship that is lost.

The numerous factors to be considered in a search problem include cost, time, value of the "find" and the search method. The basic question is concerned with the most efficient conduct of the search. Effectiveness of the search depends upon resources that can be mobilised for the search effort, the probabilities that the target will be in a given location and recognised when seen and the ways the object sought can be concealed or stored.

Techniques available utilise mathematical models and search-and-detection theory.

The search process is important because the principle of optimal decision making rests on the assumption that all alternative courses of action possible are known to the decision maker. Unless he is aware of the decision alternatives the decision process loses any attempt at optimality. However, in practice, the number of alternative courses of action is almost limitless and the decision maker cannot possibly be expected to be aware and to evaluate all of them. This is where the search process enters into the overall decision analysis. The search process should be designed so as to inform the decision maker as to the "important" alternative courses of action. Thus the search process has got to contain some sort of selection criterion by which it can sort out the almost infinite number of alternatives in order that the decision maker is faced with a quantity of data for which he possesses an ability to evaluate rationally.

The costs involved in the search process fall into two categories. There is the cost of the search itself—the market research type of costs, and the costs of errors in the search process, that is the cost of "missing" an alternative which should have been included in the decision maker's set of alternatives or the cost of presenting the decision maker with incorrect (rather than incomplete) data.

### 43.

*OR and the model-building approach and possible problems in using models*
An essential characteristic of OR involves the use of models. "Model" in this context implies a scaled-down version of reality which often involves considerable

simplification. It can be described as a structured quantitative statement of the dominant factors affecting a decision.

An OR model is normally a mathematical representation of reality which describes the relationship between variables under study. (It could be of a logical form as in simulation exercises.) It is an abstraction that isolates those factors of a problem that are most relevant to a situation.

The model must be constructed to capture the crux of the decision-making situation, i.e. it should clarify the decision alternatives and their anticipated effects. At the same time, it must be sufficiently free of burdensome minor detail. In this situation a dichotomy occurs between the need to represent reality and the need for simplicity, i.e. the model should be simple enough to permit calculation but complex enough to bear some correspondence to reality. It is the ability to build a model consistent with the real world as characterised by the use of appropriate restrictions, meaningful variables and the securing of accurate input data to feed into the model that is the critical phase of modelling. The greater the difference between the real world problem and the problem modelled, the less satisfactory will be the solution provided by the model in relation to the real world problem. Management must discern the relevance of the model and must exercise its judgment based on experience to decide this issue.

It should be noted that business situations are not static, and management must continue to exercise its judgment well beyond initial acceptance of the model. It must monitor the system to ensure that the underlying assumptions remain valid. In short, an OR model cannot become entirely independent of judgment supplied by knowledgeable management. The model is an aid to, but never a substitute for, sound human judgment. Beware of the displacement of goals by means. Too often, data of dubious significance and validity are fed into the model. The output is of necessity equally dubious. No solution method, however refined, can overcome basic deficiencies present in the structure of the system or in the data input to that system.

The quality of the data poses an important problem. Common questions posed are:

Is the data in the right form?

Time and cost of collecting?

Staff expertise in collection?

Reliability and relevance of data?

The usual comment on the quality of data in relation to the model is neatly expressed as "garbage in, garbage out"(GIGO).

The problem-solving ingenuity of OR workers is still a limiting factor. The majority of problems do not fit into neat application packages. Tailor-made model formulations are needed, placing a substantial burden on the art of the OR worker.

Further problems may arise in the implementation stage. The system must operate in the context of managerial activity. The system needs to reflect the goals and aspirations of staff involved. Rarely is a suggested OR system in perfect harmony with existing managerial attitudes and shop-floor traditions. To ignore this fact is to invite failure.

Finally, as the model is only an approximation to reality, the "optimal" solution obtained is not necessarily the final answer to the real problem. The important issue, however, is not whether a proposed solution is optimal, but whether the solution yields

APPENDIX 3. SUGGESTED ANSWERS TO EXAMINATION QUESTIONS 397

a sufficiently significant improvement over the alternatives to make it worthy of acceptance.

Summarising, the main problems in using models are:

(a) reality versus simplicity;

(b) the need for adequate and reliable data;

(c) the need for judgment;

(d) resistance to change;

(e) the current state of the art.

**44.**

## Features determining a successful OR approach and the role of management in the use of quantitative analysis

OR has what appears to be a well-structured methodology in that the following steps can be listed in carrying out an OR study:

(a) define the problem;   (b) construct a model;   (c) derive a solution;
(d) test the model;   (e) establish controls;   (f) implement.

However, the successful application of these steps requires in addition to skill a considerable amount of flair, ingenuity and luck. This is particularly true for the first two rather critical steps. Defining the problem assumes that, to a great extent, all the personnel involved in the situation see the problem in the same way, and stress the various components in the problem with the same weight. In reality, it is unlikely that management, shop-floor workers and supervisory staff would agree with the same view of the problem, and even if they did the criteria they would want to apply to find a solution would differ.

In formulating and constructing a model it should always be noted that the problem represented by the model should be capable of solution. This forces OR workers to generate simple models that represent only the essential features of the problem. It obviously requires a considerable amount of skill to balance these two requirements of simplicity for solution purposes and complexity so that all the essential features are included.

The essential part of the OR worker's approach is not in his use of a particular mathematical technique but in his knowledge, through experience, of the power and limitations of that technique. Many a newcomer to the art of OR has produced elegant mathematical models for problems, only to find that a more straightforward and crude method yields a more realistic, more accurate and much cheaper solution.

The process of testing the model and establishing controls is an area where considerable care and judgment are necessary. The setting up of realistic controls is not always easy in a practical situation. One must make sure, for example, in a simulation problem that the input data is consistent and does not change in a way that would invalidate the model. One must also ensure that in, for example, a stock control problem that if lead times or order costs are changed due to a new supplier, then the model is adjusted accordingly.

The implementation stage is a vital part of the constraints on the modelling process. Any solution that is produced must be implemented in such a way that it does not disturb the modelling assumptions. For example, if a solution requires a reduction in the level of stock, this may also affect the staffing, warehousing and other physical resources which are not now needed. These changes may not have been considered in the model formulation.

Hence, it should be fairly apparent that the mathematical solution of a problem is a very small part of the whole approach. The success of OR will certainly be influenced by the experience, imagination and flair of the OR practitioner.

Attention should also be focused on the manager who is constantly in a decision-making situation and would like to use quantitative methods but is not himself an OR practitioner. It is an obvious statement that managers today face an environment with more intense competition than ever before. Additionally, the magnitude of capital outlay as a result of a decision in many businesses can be very high and the effect long lasting. So, what level of proficiency in quantitative analysis should a manager possess? Before answering this question it should be pointed out that most business decisions are evaluated by quantifiable measures. Profitability, revenue, and cost reduction are a few of the ways decisions are evaluated. A complex new machine is not effective if in terms of the appropriate quantifiable measure, such as production per hour, it does not achieve acceptable levels.

It is a generalisation that, for business success, managers must make decisions that minimise poor performance. This is where quantitative methods are used. They enable the manager to understand the potential consequences of each alternative outcome through more effective means of analysis. Intuition, good judgment and instinct should support the quantitative approach and not be used instead of it.

An additional factor influencing the application of quantitative analysis in decision making is the advance made in computers. The development of microcomputers, time sharing and remote access terminals are only some of the many advances made.

All that has been said does not mean that it is necessary for a manager to be a mathematician but it is essential for him to be aware of what quantitative tools are available to assist in decision making. At the minimum, future managers should be able to:

(a) identify problems that can be solved by quantitative techniques,

(b) suggest an appropriate technique,

(c) understand the solution,

(d) recognise the underlying assumptions and the solution's limitations.

Obviously it would still be necessary for the detailed analysis to be done by an experienced operational researcher, but it is the manager who makes the decisions and he must fully appreciate the consequences of his decision.

## 45.

### Sensitivity analysis

**INTRODUCTION**

Sensitivity analysis measures the effect of a variation in one or two of the key variables on profit or any other critical factors. It helps the decision maker to set the parameters of the problem and makes him more aware of the relative importance of these key variables. Such an approach has long been used in budgetary control, where the practice of indicating the impact on profits of variations in budgeted wage rates, material prices etc. is well known. Its use in recent years has been more evident in investment decisions, where it attempts to provide answers to such questions as "how will the project be affected if capital costs or operating costs are 10 per cent higher or revenues 5 per cent lower?"—in other words, how sensitive is the proposal to movements in a variable the exact value of which is doubtful?

## CATEGORISATION

Sensitivity analysis is a useful tool for setting and highlighting the boundaries of uncertainty. It facilitates the grouping of variables into categories such as:

(a) slight variation–large impact;

(b) large variation–large impact;

(c) large variation–low impact;

(d) slight variation–low impact.

Management are able to decide, on the basis of this, whether or not a further reinvestigation of some variables is required so that greater control over them can be exercised. It may be that there is little control over a factor and that because of this the particular line of action is abandoned.

## SENSITIVITY ANALYSIS AND LINEAR PROGRAMMING

Linear programming provides optimal solutions to business problems dealing with allocation of scarce resources to competing demands.

Management requires more than the optimal quantitative solution however; it should also have information on the limits within which the optimal solution is valid. What new objective function coefficients (contribution per unit of product) would be needed to alter the optimal solution? Also, what new quantity of system constraints would be needed to alter the shadow prices (contribution per unit of scarce resource)?

Answers to these questions establish limits for the objective function and the constraints which will enable management to know when changes in contributions per unit of product—or errors in their estimation—are relevant to the product-mix decision.

Objective function sensitivity analysis for linear programming deals with the question of how much the product contribution rates can change without changing the optimal solution (though the total contribution will be changed). The optimal production solution remains the same within the limits, although accompanied by a different total contribution.

Constraint sensitivity analysis for linear programming deals with the question of how much the parameters of the systems can change without changing the members in the solution set (though the quantities to be produced are changed) and without changing the shadow prices of the scarce resources.

Consider the simple product-mix problem where the linear programming formulation of the problem is as follows:

$$\text{Maximise } Z = 120x + 130y \text{ (contribution)},$$

subject to:     $14x + 15y$    (140 labour constraint)

$12x + 14y$    (150 raw-material constraint)

$x, y > 0$    (non-negativity conditions).

All these figures are normally estimates. The contribution figures of 120 and 130 are almost certainly average expected figures. They depend upon the cost of raw material which probably varies from batch to batch, and are affected by any stock losses or damage to stock. Another component of contribution is the direct labour cost, which is always difficult to determine. The constraint value of 140 hours must be made on certain assumptions about the availability of labour, its transferability between products and absenteeism. Furthermore, it tends not to be strictly variable in the short term—it is not possible to hire and fire at will. The value of 150 in the raw-material constraint assumes that the maximum availability of raw materials at the price used in calculating the contribution is a constant. In practice it usually varies from week to week.

The whole model, as we see, can be affected by changes in demand, price, cost and supply. Consequently, even ignoring the limitations of the linear programming model caused by the mathematical assumptions, any so-called optimal solution we obtain will be a crude approximation to a real solution.

Most problems we encounter are of a dynamic nature, where factors are continually changing. Most models we adopt, owing mainly to the need to formulate a simple model of the problem, tend, in most respects, to be static. Their solutions may have been right yesterday but are generally wrong today.

In our simple model the coefficients and constraint values are regarded as constant, although they may, in practice, change from one period to the next. Therefore we need to analyse the effects of these changes. Initially we allow just one coefficient or constraint value in our model to change, noting the effect upon our "solution". We then repeat this procedure for all the important variables in the model. By an important variable in this context, we mean a coefficient or constraint value that is most likely to change. In our example we might investigate the effects of changing the 120 for $x$ in our objective function. We would want to know by how much it could change before the product mix of our solution would no longer be optimal. We might also believe that the constraint value of 140 hours for labour is variable subject to change and would want to investigate again how such changes would affect our solution. We can also consider how our solution would change if we added a new variable or introduced a new constraint. This approach is known as sensitivity analysis. In this way we can determine the most critical variables and their effects upon the solution. Using these results we should be able to postulate a possible set of alternative solutions which can guide us in our formulation of possible decisions to recommend.

The major limitation of sensitivity analysis is that in itself it is a static model. We consider only one variable changing at a time. We do not consider the overall effect of several variables changing together, some of which might be linked causing some multiplier effect.

Overall, sensitivity analysis is a useful tool as it gives us a further insight into our problem. As long as we are aware of its limitations and carry out the usual testing and monitoring of our solution, we should make better decisions in the long run than those decisions we would have made without sensitivity analysis.

## CONCLUSION

Sensitivity analysis can provide some useful insights into the relationship between variables. A study in the wholesale distribution of natural gas found that investment decisions were more sensitive to variations in sales prices and sales volume than to any other factors. Further, project-life variation had a greater impact on proposals with increasing annual cash flows than on proposals with uniform cash flows.

There are, however, certain limitations with sensitivity analysis. There is a limit to the number of variations which can be handled simultaneously and yet still produce as a result a meaningful difference from the original estimate. If too many of the variables are altered then one ceases to test the sensitivity of a project but rather begins to contract two quite different projects.

In addition, while helping to gauge the effect of changes in key factors, sensitivity analysis does not help assess the likelihood of such changes occurring. Management must stipulate in advance the factors which are likely to vary and which need to be tested.

### 46.

*Sub-optimisation*

As businesses increase in size and with an increase in specialisation, organisations have tended to adopt a functional structure, i.e. separate departments such as production, marketing, finance and personnel have evolved within the organisation.

Each of these departments develops its own set of objectives against which they can measure performance. These departmental objectives lead to sub-optimisation in that conflict between departmental objectives may lead to under-optimisation for the company as a whole. Management is therefore faced with the problem of setting policies which will successfully integrate the departmental objectives in a manner which optimises overall benefits to the firm.

One of the most widely quoted examples of this problem of sub-optimisation is that of inventory policy. Manufacturing departments require long production runs to minimise costs—this implies larger inventories of few products. Marketing departments require flexibility to satisfy customers—implying large inventory but with many varied products. This leads to the marketing function pressing production for short runs and frequent changeovers.

The finance department requires low inventories because of capital tied up in stocks and will exert pressure to reduce inventories when business is slack.

The personnel department wishes to maintain production of inventory during slack periods in order to maintain morale and reduce hiring and firing costs.

The application of OR to the problem of determining an optimum inventory policy in the context of overall objectives of the firm requires consideration of the system as a whole and in particular the interaction between the various departments. The "systems approach" is adopted by OR in order to achieve optimisation. However, in large complex problems made up of sub-problems the solutions to the sub-problems may give completely opposite solutions which cannot be merged together to form a solution to the total problem. In such a situation, in an attempt to arrive at some "reasonable" solution the OR man may use a sub-optimising approach to help simplify the problem.

*Tutorial note: This is satisficing rather than optimising.*

## 47.

**LOCAL BUILDERS' MERCHANT**

To set up the given situation as a linear programming model, an objective function in cost terms is required.

Let $x_1$ represent the number of blue paint tins purchased

$x_2$ represent the number of brown paint tins purchased

$x_3$ represent the number of black paint tins purchased.

Minimise cost $C = 4x_1 + 5x_2 + 4.5x_3$ (objective function)

subject to the following conditions:

$$x_1 \leqslant 160 \text{ (blue paint constraint)}$$
$$x_2 \geqslant 80 \text{ (brown paint constraint)}$$
$$x_3 \geqslant 40 \text{ (black paint constraint).}$$
$$x_1 + x_2 + x_3 = 400 \text{ (monthly requirement in total)}$$
$$x_1, x_2, x_3 \geqslant 0 \text{ (non-negativity conditions).}$$

*Tutorial note: The direction of the inequality signs of the second and third constraints is different from that of the first, because the business does not require more than 160 tins of blue paint but at least 80 tins of brown paint and at least 40 tins of black paint.*

## 48.

**BOFFIN INVESTMENT TRUST**

The decision in the given investment problem is concerned with the allocation of available investment funds into various alternative choices.

Let the decision variables $x_1$, $x_2$, $x_3$, $x_4$ and $x_5$ represent the amounts of the total investment fund to be allocated into L, M, N, O and P respectively. The objective is to maximise the total returns from the different investment choices.

Maximise $Z = 0.1x_1 + 0.08x_2 + 0.06x_3 + 0.05x_4 + 0.09x_5$ (objective function),
subject to the following constraints:

| | |
|---|---|
| $x_1 \leqslant x_3 + x_4 + x_5$ | (limit on the investment in L), |
| $x_2 + x_5 \geqslant x_3$ | (total investment in M and P to be as large as that in N), |
| $x_2 \leqslant x_4$ | (M restricted to a level not exceeding O), |
| $x_1 + x_2 + x_3 + x_4 + x_5 = 1{,}000{,}000$ | (total investment equal to £1 million), |
| $x_1, x_2, x_3, x_4, x_5 \geqslant 0$ | (non-negativity conditions). |

APPENDIX 3. SUGGESTED ANSWERS TO EXAMINATION QUESTIONS

**49.**

It is clear that, if there were no limitations on supplies, the blender would use the maximum quantities of the cheaper of the whiskies that the specifications allow. In Old Frenzy he would use 50 per cent C and 50 per cent B. The average cost per bottle of the mixture would be £4.50, and at this price there would be no profit. Any other blend meeting the specification would result in a loss, and it may be concluded that Old Frenzy will not be made. The problem can be reduced to the blends Blue Dot and Highland Fling only.

Let $x_{11}$ = quantity of A used for Blue Dot

$x_{12}$ = quantity of B used for Blue Dot

$x_{13}$ = quantity of C used for Blue Dot

$x_{21}$ = quantity of A used for Highland Fling

$x_{22}$ = quantity of B used for Highland Fling

$x_{23}$ = quantity of C used for Highland Fling.

An amount of $x_{11} + x_{12} + x_{13}$ of Blue Dot will be produced and sold for 6.80 $(x_{11} + x_{12} + x_{13})$. An amount of $x_{21} + x_{22} + x_{23}$ of Highland Fling will be produced and sold for 5.70 $(x_{21} + x_{22} + x_{23})$. The total amounts of each ingredient used will be $(x_{11} + x_{21})$ of A, $(x_{12} + x_{22})$ of B, and $(x_{13} + x_{23})$ of C.

Hence the total profit of $Z$ is given by:

$$Z = 6.80\ (x_{11} + x_{12} + x_{13}) + 5.70(x_{21} + x_{22} + x_{23})$$
$$- 7.00(x_{11} + x_{21}) - 5.00\ (x_{12} + x_{22}) - 4.00(x_{13} + x_{23}).$$

So $Z = -0.20 x_{11} + 1.80 x_{12} + 2.80 x_{13} - 1.30 x_{21} + 0.70 x_{22} + 1.70 x_{23}$.

It is desired to maximise $Z$, subject to the limitations imposed by the specifications and the availability.

From the availability,

$$x_{11} + x_{21} \leqslant 2,000,$$
$$x_{12} + x_{22} \leqslant 2,500,$$
$$x_{13} + x_{23} \leqslant 1,200.$$

From the specification for Blue Dot

$\quad x_{11} \geqslant 0.60\ (x_{11} + x_{12} + x_{13}) \quad$ or $\quad 3 x_{12} + 3 x_{13} - 2 x_{11} \leqslant 0,$

$\quad x_{13} \leqslant 0.20\ (x_{11} + x_{12} + x_{13}) \quad$ or $\quad 4 x_{13} - x_{11} - x_{12} \quad \leqslant 0.$

From the specification for Highland Fling

$\quad x_{23} \leqslant 0.60\ (x_{21} + x_{22} + x_{23}) \quad$ or $\quad 2 x_{23} - 3 x_{21} - 3 x_{21} \leqslant 0,$

$\quad x_{21} \geqslant 0.15\ (x_{21} + x_{22} + x_{23}) \quad$ or $\quad 3 x_{22} + 3 x_{23} - 17 x_{21} \leqslant 0.$

**50.**

Let the number of units of A made be $a$,
the number of units of B made be $b$.
Also let the number of units of A made on overtime be $a_o$,
the number of units of B made on overtime be $b_o$.
Then the constraints are:

| | | |
|---|---|---|
| Amount of raw material available | $a + a_o$ | $\leqslant 16{,}000$ |
| | $b + b_o$ | $\leqslant 21{,}000$ |
| Normal time spent in press shop | $20a + 20b$ | $\leqslant 720{,}000$ |
| Overtime spent in press shop | $20a_o + 20b_o$ | $\leqslant 72{,}000$ |
| Normal time spent on machine 1 | $20a$ | $\leqslant 432{,}000$ |
| Overtime spent on machine 1 | $20a_o$ | $\leqslant 43{,}200$ |
| Normal time spent on machine 2 | $10b$ | $\leqslant 432{,}000$ |
| Overtime spent on machine 2 | $10b_o$ | $\leqslant 43{,}200$ |

Manufacturing costs $= 0.06a + 0.06a_o + 0.10b + 0.10b_o$ (raw materials)

$$+ \frac{20 \times 3.6}{3{,}600} a + \frac{20 \times 3.6}{3{,}600} b.$$

$$\left(\text{normal time in press shop: cost per second} = \frac{3.6}{3{,}600}\right)$$

$$+ \frac{20 \times 3.6 \times 1.1}{3{,}600} a_o + \frac{20 \times 3.6 \times 1.1}{3{,}600} b_o$$

(overtime in press shop: 10 per cent dearer than normal)

$$+ \frac{20 \times 3.6}{3{,}600} a \qquad \text{(normal time on machine 1)}$$

$$+ \frac{20 \times 3.6 \times 1.1}{3{,}600} a_o \qquad \text{(overtime on machine 1)}$$

$$+ \frac{10 \times 5.4}{3{,}600} b \qquad \text{(normal time on machine 2)}$$

$$+ \frac{10 \times 5.4 \times 1.1}{3{,}600} b_o \qquad \text{(overtime on machine 2)}$$

$= 0.06a + 0.06a_o + 0.10b + 0.10b_o + 0.02a + 0.02b + 0.022a_o + 0.022b_o + 0.02a$
$\quad + 0.022a_o + 0.015b + 0.0165b_o$

$(0.06 + 0.02 + 0.02)a + (0.06 + 0.002 + 0.022)a_o + (0.10 + 0.02 + 0.015)b$
$\quad + (0.10 + 0.22 + 0.0165)b_o$

$= 0.10a + 0.104a_o + 0.135b + 0.1385b_o.$

Return $= 0.12a + 0.16b + 0.12a_o + 0.16b_o.$

Contribution = $0.12a + 0.16b + 0.12a_o + 0.16b_o - (0.10a + 0.104a_o + 0.135b + 0.1385b_o)$

$= 0.02a + 0.016a_o + 0.025b + 0.0215b_o$.

Problem is to:

Maximise $0.02a + 0.016a_o + 0.025b + 0.0215b_o$,

subject to:

$$\begin{aligned}
a + a_o &\leq 16{,}000 \\
b + b_o &\leq 21{,}000 \\
20a + 20b &\leq 720{,}000 \\
20a_o + 20b_o &\leq 72{,}000 \\
20a &\leq 432{,}000 \\
20a_o &\leq 43{,}200 \\
10b &\leq 432{,}000 \\
10b_o &\leq 43{,}200 \\
a, a_o, b, b_o &\geq 0.
\end{aligned}$$

**51.**

**FENTON ENTERPRISES LTD**
(a) To set up the given situation as a linear programming model, an objective function in contribution terms is required. (The "net profit" figures per unit of product include an arbitrary absorption of overheads. This will lead to a distortion of the appropriate product mix.)

Let the decision variables $x_1$, $x_2$, $x_3$, $x_4$, and $x_5$ represent the amounts of product A, B, C, D and E to be produced.

Maximise contribution $C = 15A + 12B + 16C + 12D + 7E$ (objective function),

subject to the following conditions:

$$\left.\begin{aligned}
x_1 &\leq 1{,}500 \\
x_2 &\leq 1{,}200 \\
x_3 &\leq \phantom{0}900 \\
x_4 &\leq \phantom{0}600 \\
x_5 &\leq \phantom{0}600
\end{aligned}\right\} \text{expected maximum demand}$$

$x_1 + x_2 + 3x_3 + 4x_4 + 5x_5 \leq 5{,}800$ (special component constraint)

$12x_1 + 10\tfrac{2}{3}x_2 + 4x_3 + 2\tfrac{2}{3}x_4 + 2\tfrac{2}{3}x_5 \leq 20{,}000$ (labour constraint)

$15x_1 + 14x_2 + 16x_3 + 15x_4 + 16x_5 \leq 30{,}000$ (material expenditure constraint)

$x_1, x_2, x_3, x_4, x_5 \geq 0$ (non-negativity conditions).

(b) The purposes which needed mentioning here are those associated with linear programming in general.

(i) Linearity—is the assumption of linear relationships realistic?

(ii) Non-integer solutions—LP may produce fractional solutions. This may be avoided by the use of integer programming but is expensive.

(iii) LP assumes certainty but cannot fully model the on-going nature of business. The situation is dynamic but is depicted through a static model.

(iv) Accuracy of estimates. The solution will obviously be only as good as the accuracy of the input data.

(v) Problems of implementation. Traditional patterns of working may have to be changed.

**52.**

**ARBOR LTD**

(a) The following are some of the points which should be included in comments on the accountant's statement as a basis for decision making. The statement:

has an arbitrary absorption of fixed overheads;

ignores differential cash flow;

should have used a contribution approach;

ignored the opportunity cost of MN2.

The given statement can be redrafted as given in Table 34.

(b) There are two scarce resources. A linear programming approach is needed. Formulation would be:

Maximise $C = 80x_1 + 169x_2 + 178x_3 + 171x_4 + 202x_5 + 202x_6$ (objective function),

subject to the following conditions:

$4x_1 + 5x_2 + 8x_3 + 6x_4 + 7x_5 + 2x_6 \leq 2{,}500$ (MN2 constraint)

$76x_1 + 106x_2 + 100x_3 + 100x_4 + 100x_5 + 60x_6 \leq 50{,}000$ (import quota)

$$
\left.
\begin{array}{l}
x_1 \leq 150 \\
x_2 \leq 80 \\
x_3 \leq 125 \\
x_4 \leq 75 \\
x_5 \leq 100 \\
x_6 \leq 100
\end{array}
\right\} \text{demand conditions}
$$

$x_1, x_2, x_3, x_4, x_5, x_6 \geq 0$ (non-negativity conditions).

(c) Other factors:

(i) Effect on demand if full range of products is not offered.

(ii) Linear relationships.

Table 34. Redrafted statement of demand, costs and profits.

|  | F | G | H | I | J | K |
|---|---|---|---|---|---|---|
| Selling price per unit | 292 | 455 | 490 | 455 | 670 | 610 |
| Component MN2 | 96 | 120 | 192 | 144 | 168 | 48 |
| Other components | 76 | 106 | 100 | 100 | 100 | 60 |
| Variable overheads | 20 | 30 | 10 | 20 | 100 | 150 |
| Labour | 20 | 30 | 10 | 20 | 100 | 150 |
|  | 212 | 286 | 312 | 284 | 468 | 408 |
| Contribution per unit | 80 | 169 | 178 | 171 | 202 | 202 |

(iii) Efficiency levels in all situations.

(iv) Interest costs.

(v) Are demand functions independent of each other?

(vi) Non-quantifiables.

(vii) Are there better opportunities outside this plan?

**53.**

(a) What is required is a linear programming model to determine the optimal employment policy for Tech Ltd over the next two years.
The given data are summarised below:

|  | Unskilled | Skilled |
|---|---|---|
| Current year | 2,000 | 1,000 |
| 1981 requirement | 1,000 | 1,200 |
| 1982 requirement | 500 | 1,500 |
| Natural wastage | 20% | 10% |
| Recruitment possibility |  | 400 max. at £400 each |
| Redundancy | £1,000 each |  |
| Salaries | £4,000/year | £6,000/year |

Company policy is to only employ up to 200 men more in total than are actually needed each year.

Linear programming model:

Let $S_1$ = number of skilled men recruited in 1981
$S_2$ = number of skilled men recruited in 1982
$U_1$ = number of unskilled men made redundant in 1981
$U_2$ = number of unskilled men made redundant in 1982.

Requirements constraints:

1981: Unskilled amount $\geqslant 1{,}000$
$\qquad 2{,}000 \times 0.8 - U_1 \geqslant 1{,}000$
$\qquad$ (Amount after wastage $-$ Redundant $\geqslant 1{,}000$)
$\qquad 1{,}600 - U_1 \geqslant 1{,}000$
$\qquad 1{,}600 - 1{,}000 \geqslant U_1$
$\qquad \therefore \quad U_1 \leqslant \underline{\underline{600}}.$

1981: Skilled amount $\geqslant 1{,}200$
$\qquad$ (Amount after wastage $+$ Recruited $\geqslant 1{,}200$)
$\qquad 1{,}000 \times 0.9 + S_1 \geqslant 1{,}200$
$\qquad 900 + S_1 \geqslant 1{,}200$
$\qquad \therefore \quad S_1 \geqslant \underline{\underline{300}}.$

1982: Unskilled amount
$\qquad (1{,}600 - U_1) \times 0.8 - U_2 \geqslant 500$
$\qquad 1{,}280 - 0.8\,U_1 - U_2 \geqslant 500$
$\qquad 1{,}280 - 500 \geqslant 0.8 U_1 + U_2$
$\qquad \therefore \quad 0.80\,U_1 + U_2 \geqslant \underline{\underline{780}}.$

1982: Skilled amount
$\qquad (900 + S_1) \times 0.9 + S_2 \geqslant 1{,}500$
$\qquad 810 + 0.9\,S_1 + S_2 \geqslant 1{,}500$
$\qquad \therefore \quad 0.9\,S_1 + S_2 \geqslant \underline{\underline{690}}.$

Constraints for recruitment restriction for skilled men:

1981: $S_1 \leqslant 400$,

1982: $S_2 \leqslant 400$.

Total manpower constraint (Company policy: up to 200 more men.)

$\quad$ 1981: $1{,}600 - U_1 + 900 + S_1 \leqslant 1{,}000 + 1{,}200 + 200$
$\qquad$ (i.e. Unskilled $+$ Skilled $\leqslant 1{,}000 + 1{,}200 + 200$)
$\qquad \therefore \quad 2{,}500 + S_1 - U_1 \leqslant 2{,}400$
$\qquad \therefore \qquad 100 \leqslant U_1 - S_1$
$\qquad \therefore \qquad U_1 - S_1 \geqslant \underline{\underline{100}}.$

$\quad$ 1982: Unskilled $+$ Skilled $\leqslant 500 + 1{,}500 + 200$
$\qquad 1{,}280 - 0.8\,U_1 - U_2 + 810 + 0.9\,S_1 \leqslant 2{,}200$
$\qquad 2{,}090 - 0.8\,U_1 - U_2 + 0.9\,S_1 + S_2 \leqslant 2{,}200$
$\qquad \therefore \quad 0.9\,S_1 + S_2 - 0.8\,U_1 - U_2 \leqslant \underline{\underline{110}}.$

1st objective function—minimise total cost:
Three components of cost must be accounted for:

$\qquad$ Recruitment $+$ Redundancy $+$ Salary (unskilled and skilled)

# APPENDIX 3. SUGGESTED ANSWERS TO EXAMINATION QUESTIONS

i.e. $400\ S_1 + 400\ S_2 + 1{,}000 U_1 + 1{,}000\ U_2 + 4{,}000\ (1{,}600 - U_1 + 1{,}280 - 0.8 U_1 - U_2) + 6{,}000\ (900 + S_1 + 810 + 0.9\ S_1 + S_2)$.

Summing, $C = 21{,}780{,}000 + 11{,}800\ S_1 + 6{,}400 S_2 - 6{,}200 U_1 - 3{,}000 U_2$.

2nd objective function—minimise redundancies:

$$\text{Minimise } Z = U_1 + U_2.$$

(b) The linear programming model obtained above must be amended to accommodate the possibility of retraining unskilled men.

Let $R_1$ = number of unskilled retrained in 1981.

$R_2$ = number of unskilled retrained in 1982.

Requirements constraint:

1981: Unskilled amount $\quad 1{,}600 - U_1 - R_1 \geqslant 1{,}000$
$\therefore \quad U_1 + R_1 \leqslant \underline{\underline{600}}$.

Skilled amount $\quad 900 + S_1 + R_1 \geqslant 1{,}200$
$\therefore \quad S_1 + R_1 \geqslant \underline{\underline{300}}$.

1982: Unskilled $\quad 1{,}280 - 0.8 U_1 - 0.8 R_1 - U_2 - R_2 \geqslant 500$
$\therefore \quad 0.8 U_1 + U_2 + 0.8 R_1 + R_2 \leqslant \underline{\underline{780}}$.

Skilled $\quad 810 + 0.9 S_1 + 0.9 R_1 + S_2 + R_2 \geqslant 1{,}500$
$\therefore \quad 0.9 S_1 + S_2 + 0.9 R_1 + R_2 \geqslant \underline{\underline{690}}$.

$\therefore$ Recruitment and total manpower remains unchanged.

Additional constraints:

Limits on numbers to be trained:

$$R_1 \leqslant 300,\ R_2 \leqslant 300.$$

Also $\quad R_1 \leqslant 1/4\ (900 + S_1)$

$\therefore \quad 4 R_1 - S_1 \leqslant 900$.

And $\quad R_2 \leqslant 1/4\ (810 + 0.9\ S_1 + 0.9 R_1 + S_2)$.

Costs:
Recruitment and redundancy remain the same.
The salary changes to:

$4{,}000\ (1{,}600 - U_1 - R_1 + 1{,}280 - 0.8 U_1 - 0.8 R_1 - U_2 - R_2)$
$+ 5{,}000\ (R_1 + R_2)$
$+ 6{,}000\ (900 + S_1 + 810 + 0.9\ S_1 + 0.9\ R_1 + S_2)$.

Training costs are $500\ R_1 + 500\ R_2$.

## 54.

(a) The question requires a linear programming model for the given investment problem.

Let $x_1$ be the amount invested in stock A
$x_2$ be the amount invested in stock B
$x_3$ be the amount invested in stock C
$x_4$ be the amount invested in stock D
$x_5$ be the amount invested in stock E.

The manager wishes to maximise overall redemption yield.

$$\therefore \text{ Maximise } Z = 0.135x_1 + 0.122x_2 + 0.143x_3 + 0.149x_4 + 0.151x_5$$

(objective functions),

subject to the following conditions:

$$x_1 + x_2 + x_3 + x_4 + x_5 \leq 100{,}000 \text{ (limit on investment)}$$
$$x_1 \geq 30{,}000 \text{ (short-term stocks constraint)}$$
$$x_4 + x_5 \leq 40{,}000 \text{ (long-term stocks constraint)}.$$

The final condition dictates that the overall interest-only running yield must be at least 13 per cent. This is calculated as

$$\frac{\text{Nominal yield}}{\text{Current price}} \times 100$$

| $x_1$ | $x_2$ | $x_3$ | $x_4$ | $x_5$ |
|---|---|---|---|---|
| $\dfrac{9}{94.5}$ | $\dfrac{12}{91.125}$ | $\dfrac{11.5}{82.75}$ | $\dfrac{14}{92}$ | $\dfrac{10}{78.25}$ |
| = 0.0952 | = 0.1317 | = 0.1390 | = 0.1522 | = 0.1278 |

The constraint can now be set up as follows:

$$0.0952x_1 + 0.1317x_2 + 0.1390x_3 + 0.1522x_4 + 0.1278x_5$$
$$\geq 0.13 \times (x_1 + x_2 + x_3 + x_4 + x_5)$$

Rearranging:

$$0.13 \times (x_1 + x_2 + x_3 + x_4 + x_5)$$
$$\leq 0.0952x_1 + 0.1317x_2 + 0.1390x_3 + 0.1522x_4 + 0.1278x_5$$

$$\therefore \quad 0.13x_1 + 0.13x_2 + 0.13x_3 + 0.13x_4 + 0.13x_5 - 0.0952x_1 - 0.1317x_2 -$$
$$0.1390x_3 - 0.1522x_4 - 0.1278x_5 \leq 0.$$

$$\therefore \quad 0.348x_1 - 0.0017x_2 - 0.0090x_3 - 0.0222x_4 + 0.0022x_5 \leq 0.$$

This can be expressed as:

$$3.48x_1 - 0.17x_2 - 0.9x_3 - 2.22x_4 + 0.22x_5 \leq 0.$$

# APPENDIX 3. SUGGESTED ANSWERS TO EXAMINATION QUESTIONS

(b) The restrictions on the proportion of the long-term stocks have been removed. Examination of the running yields and redemption yields shows that stocks B and C are both inferior to D. So is A, but the short-term constraint indicates that A must take a value of at least £30,000.

The model now becomes:

$$\text{Maximise } Z = 0.135x_1 + 0.149x_4 + 0.151x_5,$$

subject to:
$$x_1 + x_4 + x_5 \leqslant 100{,}000 \text{ (total investment)},$$

i.e.
$$30{,}000 + x_4 + x_5 \leqslant 100{,}000,$$

$$\therefore \quad x_4 + x_5 \leqslant 70{,}000;$$

and
$$3.48x_1 - 2.22x_4 + 0.22x_5 \leqslant 0 \quad \text{(running yield)},$$

$$3.48 \times 30{,}000 - 2.22x_4 + 0.22x_5 \leqslant 0,$$

$$\therefore \quad 2.22x_4 - 0.22x_5 \geqslant 104{,}400.$$

These two constraints can be depicted graphically to obtain an optimum solution.
(Confirmation of the optimal solution can be obtained by solving the two equations simultaneously.)

The values obtained will be $x_4 = £49{,}100$
$x_5 = £20{,}900$

The portfolio is:

 £30,000 invested in stock A
 £49,100 invested in stock D
 £20,900 invested in stock E.

This gives an overall redemption yield of 14.52 per cent

$$(0.135 \times 30{,}000 + 0.149 \times 49{,}100 + 0.151 \times 20{,}900 = 14{,}522).$$

## 55.

### DISPLAY PACKS

(a) The question requires the formulation of a linear programming model to minimise the cost per display pack and a graphical solution. The display packs are to contain an assortment of different pastes and spreads.

 Let $x$ be the number of paste jars in the display pack,
  $y$ be the number of spread jars in the display pack.

The objective is to minimise the cost per display pack.

$$\text{Minimise } C = 0.15x + 0.10y \text{ (objective function)},$$

subject to the following conditions:

Each display pack should contain at least 30 jars:

$$x + y \geqslant 30;$$

the minimum weight of the display pack must be 2,000 g. As each paste jar weighs 60 g and each spread jar 90 g:

$$60x + 90y \geqslant 2,000;$$

the space available for jars may vary between 190 and 230 cm$^2$ (pastes occupy 8 cm$^2$ and spreads occupy 6 cm$^2$):

$$8x + 6y \geqslant 190$$
$$8x + 6y \leqslant 230;$$

and $\quad x, y \geqslant 0$ (non-negativity conditions).

The given conditions have been displayed in the graph in Fig. 135. The iso-cost line shows that the minimum cost occurs at a point where $x = 0$ and $y = 31\frac{2}{3}$. The corresponding cost figure is £3.17.

The display pack will have no paste jars and $31\frac{2}{3}$ spread jars. (In practice this would be rounded off to 32.)

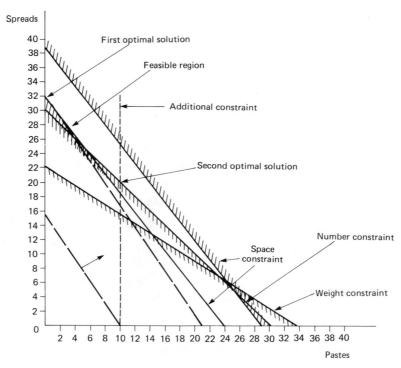

Fig. 135. *Conditions for optimal mix of paste and spread jars.*

# APPENDIX 3. SUGGESTED ANSWERS TO EXAMINATION QUESTIONS

(b) The manufacturer now requires a minimum of 10 paste jars in the pack. An additional constraint will be required to reflect this condition. The model now becomes:

$$\text{Minimise } C = 0.15x + 0.10y \text{ (objective function)},$$

subject to:

$$x + y \geqslant 30 \quad \text{(number constraint)}$$
$$60x + 90y \geqslant 2{,}000 \quad \text{(weight constraint)}$$
$$8x + 6y \geqslant 190 \quad \text{(space constraint)}$$
$$8x + 6y \leqslant 230$$
$$x \geqslant 10 \quad \text{(paste jar minimum)}$$
$$x, y \geqslant 0 \quad \text{(non-negativity conditions)}.$$

The new constraint is shown as a vertical line on the graph. There is now a new optimal solution where $x = 10$ and $y = 20$. This implies that the display packs should contain 10 paste jars and 20 spread jars, with a total cost of £3.50.

The imposition of the additional constraint $x \geqslant 10$ makes the constraint $8x + 6y \geqslant 190$ redundant. This can be confirmed by checking the graph.

## 56.

### ELECTROPOINT LTD

(a) The given data are tabulated below:

|  | Model | | |
|---|---|---|---|
|  | Mavis | Charles | Available |
| Positronic circuits | 3 | 4 | 200 |
| Skilled labour | 1 | 2 | 80 |
| Daily order | 20 |  |  |
| Contribution per unit | £60 | £100 |  |

Let $x$ be the number of Mavis models to be made,
$y$ be the number of Charles models to be made.

The objective is to maximise total contribution:

$$\text{Maximise } Z = 60x + 100y \quad \text{(objective function)},$$

subject to:
$$3x + 4y \leqslant 200 \quad \text{(circuits constraint)}$$
$$x + 2y \leqslant 80 \quad \text{(labour constraint)}$$
$$x \geqslant 20 \quad \text{(daily order)}$$
$$x, y \geqslant 0 \quad \text{(non-negativity conditions)}.$$

The conditions are displayed in the graph in Fig. 136.

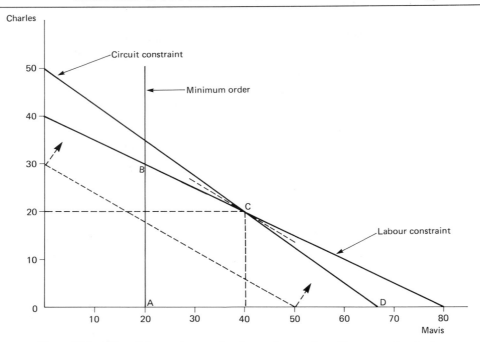

Fig. 136. *Conditions for optimal product mix—Electropoint Ltd.*

From the graph it will be seen that the feasible region is the area bounded by ABCD. Using iso-contribution lines, corner point C can be confirmed as being the optimal solution. At corner point C, $x = 40$ and $y = 20$. (The exact values can be confirmed by solving appropriate simultaneous equations.)

The optimal product-mix is 40 units of Mavis, 20 units of Charles and a contribution of £4,400.

(b) The contribution from the Charles model increases to £140 but no other changes occur. The only change in the model is in the objective function to $Z = 60x + 140y$. The feasible region remains the same as before and the optimal solution can now be obtained either by replotting the new objective function or by evaluating the corner points. Use corner-point evaluation (Table 35).

Table 35. Evaluation of corner points (Fig. 136).

| Corner point | Units of Mavis | Units of Charles | Contribution Mavis | Contribution Charles | Total contribution |
|---|---|---|---|---|---|
| A | 20 | – | £1,200 | – | £1,200 |
| B | 20 | 30 | 1,200 | £4,200 | 5,400 |
| C | 40 | 20 | 2,400 | 2,800 | 5,200 |
| D | $66\frac{2}{3}$ | – | 4,000 | – | 4,000 |

# APPENDIX 3. SUGGESTED ANSWERS TO EXAMINATION QUESTIONS

The new optimal solution is to produce 20 units of Mavis and 30 units of Charles with a total contribution of £5,400. This represents an increase in contribution of £5,400 − £4,400 = £1,000 and expressed as a percentage of the original contribution, gives an increase of:

$$\frac{1{,}000}{4{,}400} \times 100 = 22.73 \text{ per cent.}$$

(c) This part asks by how much the estimated £100 contribution from a Charles model can change before it becomes profitable to change the production mix.

The binding constraints at the optimal product mix are the labour and the circuit constraints. The optimal production mix will change if the slope of the objective function lies outside the range established by the gradients of the binding constraints.

The existing objective function is $Z = 60x + 100y$.

The slope of the objective function is $\frac{-60}{100}$, i.e. $-0.6$.

If the contribution from a Charles model changes, then the slope of the objective function will change as well. Let the contribution from a Charles model be C instead of £100.

The new objective function will be $Z = 60x + Cy$.

The slope of the objective function now is $\frac{-60}{C}$

The labour constraint is $x + 2y \leq 80$.

The slope of the labour constraint is $-\frac{1}{2}$.

The circuit constraint is $3x + 4y \leq 200$.

The slope of the circuit constraint is $-\frac{3}{4}$.

The optimal mix changes if the slope of the objective function lies outside the range

$$-\frac{3}{4} \text{ to } -\frac{1}{2}.$$

The production mix will not change as long as

$$\frac{3}{4} \geq \frac{60}{C} \geq \frac{1}{2},$$

that is, $\qquad C \geq 80 \quad$ or $\quad \leq 120.$

The contribution for a unit of Charles should not drop below £80 or exceed £120. If the contribution per unit changes beyond these levels then the optimal mix will change.

## 57.

**SUPERSEAL COMPANY LTD**

(a) The given data are tabulated below:

|  | Products | | Available |
|---|---|---|---|
|  | SRI | SRII |  |
| Department A | 3 | 1 | 120 |
| Department B | 1 | 1 | 60 |
| Department C | 1 | 2 | 100 |
| Contribution per unit | £50 | £80 |  |

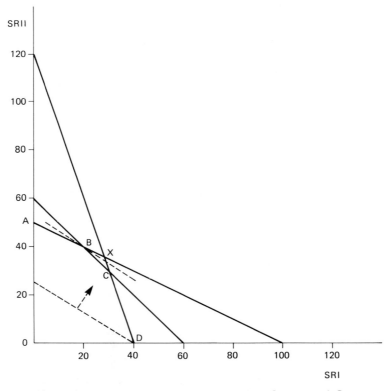

Fig. 137. *Conditions for optimal product mix—Superseal Company Ltd.*

Let $x$ be the number of type SRI packs to be made,
$y$ be the number of type SRII packs to be made.
The objective is to maximise contribution:

$$\text{Maximise } Z = 50x + 80y,$$

subject to:
- $3x + y \leq 120$ (department A constraint)
- $x + y \leq 60$ (department B constraint)
- $x + 2y \leq 100$ (department C constraint)
- $x, y \geq 0$ (non-negativity conditions).

The conditions are displayed in the graph in Fig. 137. The feasible region is bounded by OABCD.

Table 36. Evaluation of corner points (Fig. 137).

| Corner point | Units SRI | Units SRII | Contribution SRI | Contribution SRII | Total contribution |
|---|---|---|---|---|---|
| 0 | – | – | – | – | – |
| A | – | 50 | – | 4,000 | 4,000 |
| B | 20 | 40 | 1,000 | 3,200 | 4,200 |
| C | 30 | 30 | 1,500 | 2,400 | 3,900 |
| D | 40 | – | 2,000 | – | 2,000 |

From Table 36, corner point B with 20 units of SRI and 40 units of SRII represents the optimal solution. The contribution is £4,200. The optimal solution can be confirmed by drawing iso-contribution lines.

(b) If the number of hours in department B increases, the model becomes:

$$\text{Maximise } Z = 50x + 80y,$$

subject to:
- $3x + y \leq 120$ (department A)
- $x + y \leq 60$ (department B)
- $x + 2y \leq 100$ (department C)
- $x, y \geq 0$.

The increase in contribution can be evaluated in two ways:

(i) The graph can be redrawn (only one constraint alters) and the corner points re-evaluated. If this is done, it will be seen that the new solution would be $x = 22$, $y = 39$ and contribution increases to £4,220. (This could be confirmed by solving $x + y = 61$ and $x + 2y = 100$ to locate the new optimum.)

(ii) From the final simplex tableau.

(c) This part required establishing the increase in department B hours (assuming the cost of increasing machine hours was relatively small).

Inspection of the graph shows that department B constraint ($x + y \leqslant 60$) could be moved up to point X which represents the intersection of department A and C constraints. At point X, SRI = 28, SRII = 36 and department B constraint would be $x + y \leqslant 64$. However, if the value exceeded 64, department B constraint would move beyond and out of the feasible region.

Hence department B hours should be increased by 4.

## 58.

**MULTI LTD**

(a) This part requires a linear programming model for each factory and graphical solutions. The data are tabulated below:

| Oxford | Uni | Duo | Available |
|---|---|---|---|
| Process 1 | 10 | 30 | 300 |
| Process 2 | 30 | 10 | 300 |
| Raw material | 14 | 14 | 196 |
| Contribution | £300 | £200 | |

| Cambridge | Uni | Duo | Available |
|---|---|---|---|
| Process 1 | 10 | 15 | 300 |
| Process 2 | 18 | 9 | 324 |
| Raw material | 14 | 14 | 294 |
| Contribution | £300 | £200 | |

Let $x_1$ = units of Uni made at Oxford,
$y_1$ = units of Duo made at Oxford.

Maximise $300x_1 + 200y_1$ (objective function),

subject to:

$10x_1 + 30y_1 \leqslant 300$ (Oxford process 1)

$30x_1 + 10y_1 \leqslant 300$ (Oxford process 2)

$14x_1 + 14y_1 \leqslant 196$ (material)

$x_1, y_1 \geqslant 0$.

Let $x_2$ = units of Uni made at Cambridge,
$y_2$ = units of Duo made at Cambridge.

Maximise $300x_2 + 200y_2$ (objective function),

subject to:

$10x_2 + 15y_2 \leqslant 300$ (Cambridge process 1)

$18x_2 + 9y_2 \leqslant 324$ (Cambridge process 2)

$14x_2 + 14y_2 \leqslant 294$ (material)

$x_2, y_2 \geqslant 0$.

The two separate factory conditions have been graphed (separately) in Figs. 138 and 139.

*Optimal solutions:*

| | Oxford | Cambridge |
|---|---|---|
| | Uni = 8 | Uni = 15 |
| | Duo = 6 | Duo = 6 |
| | Contribution = £3,600 | Contribution = £5,700 |

Substituting the appropriate mixes into the two separate sets of conditions, unused resources can be calculated. 40 hours on the Oxford process 1 are unused.

# APPENDIX 3. SUGGESTED ANSWERS TO EXAMINATION QUESTIONS

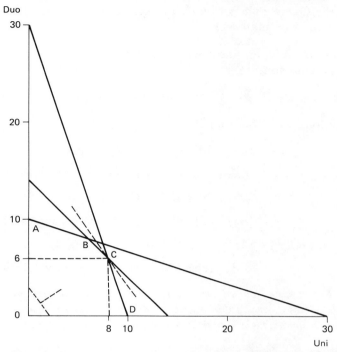

Fig. 138. *Conditions for optimal Oxford product mix—Multi Ltd.*

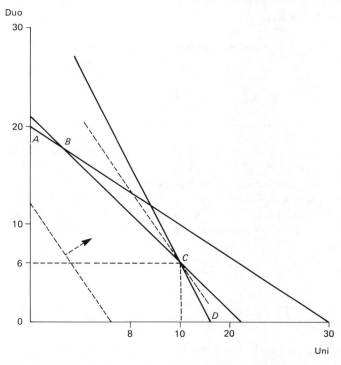

Fig. 139. *Conditions for optimal Cambridge product mix—Multi Ltd.*

60 hours on the Cambridge process 1 are unused. Process 2 at both sites is fully utilised as are the raw materials.

(b) The model for the company as a whole is stated below:
Maximise total contribution:

$$\text{Maximise } Z = 300x_1 + 200y_1 + 300x_2 + 200y_2 \text{ (objective function)},$$

subject to the following conditions:

$$10x_1 + 30y_1 \leqslant 300 \text{ (Oxford process 1)}$$
$$10x_2 + 15y_2 \leqslant 300 \text{ (Cambridge process 1)}$$
$$30x_1 + 10y_1 \leqslant 300 \text{ (Oxford process 2)}$$
$$18x_2 + 9y_2 \leqslant 324 \text{ (Cambridge process 2)}$$
$$14x_1 + 14y_1 + 14x_2 + 14y_2 \leqslant 490 \text{ (raw material)}$$
$$x_1, x_2, y_1, y_2 \geqslant 0 \text{ (non-negativity conditions)}.$$

*Tutorial note: The question required the formulation of a linear programming model for the company as a whole so that the model will determine the optimal allocation of the 490 units of raw material. In other words the solution to the above model will optimise the raw-material utilisation.*

(c) The optimal number of units for the company to produce each week is given to be:

|     | Oxford | Cambridge |
| --- | --- | --- |
| Uni | 7.5 | 16 |
| Duo | 7.5 | 4 |

The given solution can be substituted into the model constructed in (b) to arrive at the resource allocation. This will give a total contribution of £9,350 as compared with £9,300 (part (a) solution). The allocation of raw materials based on this solution will be 210 units to Oxford and 280 units to Cambridge. There are now no unused resources at Oxford but 60 unused hours on process 1 at Cambridge. The new solution should be implemented if possible as it represents an improvement in company profits.

59.

ANNAPURNA LTD
(a) The data are summarised in Table 37.

# APPENDIX 3. SUGGESTED ANSWERS TO EXAMINATION QUESTIONS

Table 37. Given data for Annapurna Ltd.

|  | Product | | | | Availability |
|---|---|---|---|---|---|
|  | A | B | C | D | |
| Selling price | £55 | £53 | £97 | £86 | |
| Cost of materials | £17 | £25 | £19 | £11 | |
| Variable overheads | £6 | £7 | £5 | £6 | |
| Labour hours: | | | | | |
| grade A | 10 | 6 | – | – | 9,000 |
| grade B | – | – | 10 | 20 | 14,500 |
| grade C | – | – | 12 | 6 | 12,000 |

Fixed overheads amount to £35,500 per annum.
Labour is paid £1.50 per hour.

The starting point in the solution method is to establish a contribution figure for each product (Table 38).

Table 38. Contribution figures for Annapurna products.

|  | Contribution | | | | | | | |
|---|---|---|---|---|---|---|---|---|
|  | A | | B | | C | | D | |
| Selling price |  | 55 |  | 53 |  | 97 |  | 86 |
| Less: | | | | | | | | |
| Materials | 17 | | 25 | | 19 | | 11 | |
| Variable overheads | 6 | | 7 | | 5 | | 6 | |
| Labour (grade A) | 15 | | 9 | | – | | – | |
| (grade B) | – | | – | | 15 | | 30 | |
| (grade C) | – | 38 | – | 41 | 18 | 57 | 9 | 56 |
| Contribution/unit |  | £17 |  | £12 |  | £40 |  | £30 |

The linear programming model can now be constructed.
Let $x_1$ be the number of units of A produced,
   $x_2$ be the number of units of B produced,
   $x_3$ be the number of units of C produced,
   $x_4$ be the number of units of D produced.

The objective is to maximise contribution:

$$\text{Maximise } C = 17x_1 + 12x_2 + 40x_3 + 30x_4 \text{ (objective function)},$$

subject to the following conditions:

$$10x_1 + 6x_2 \leq 9{,}000 \text{ (grade A labour)}$$
$$10x_3 + 20x_4 \leq 14{,}500 \text{ (grade B labour)}$$
$$12x_3 + 6x_4 \leq 12{,}000 \text{ (grade C labour)}$$
$$x_1, x_2, x_3, \text{ and } x_4 \geq 0 \quad \text{(non-negativity conditions)}.$$

*Tutorial notes*

(a) *The fixed overheads will be subtracted in total from the contribution to give the profit.*

(b) *Examination of the constraints above shows that $x_1$ and $x_2$ are only affected by grade A labour. $x_3$ and $x_4$ are affected by grade B and grade C labour. Rather than using the simplex method it is possible to break the total problem into two self-contained problems. Simpler methods of solution can then be used.*

The two separate models and their solutions are stated below:

*Model 1*

Maximise $\quad\quad 17x_1 + 12x_2 \quad\quad$ (objective function)

subject to: $\quad\quad 10x_1 + 6x_2 \leq 9{,}000$ (grade A labour)

$\quad\quad\quad\quad\quad\quad x_1, x_2 \geq 0 \quad$ (non-negativity conditions).

The above model only has one constraint and hence only one of the variables will be non-zero. Using simple management accounting rules it is possible to use a ranking mechanism based on contribution per unit of limiting factor.

| Product | Contribution/unit of limiting factor | Ranking |
|---|---|---|
| $x_1$ | £ $\frac{17}{10}$ = £1.7 | 2 |
| $x_2$ | £ $\frac{12}{6}$ = £2.0 | 1 |

Product $x_2$(B) should be made in preference to product $x_1$(A). The number of units that can be manufactured is $9{,}000/6 = 1{,}500$. This gives a contribution of $12 \times 1{,}500 = £18{,}000$.

*Model 2*

Maximise $\quad\quad 40x_3 + 30x_4 \leq 12{,}000$ (objective function),

subject to: $\quad\quad 10x_3 + 20x_4 \leq 14{,}500$ (grade B labour)

$\quad\quad\quad\quad\quad 12x_3 + 6x_4 \leq 12{,}000$ (grade C labour)

$\quad\quad\quad\quad\quad\quad x_3, x_4 \geq 0 \quad$ (Non-negativity conditions).

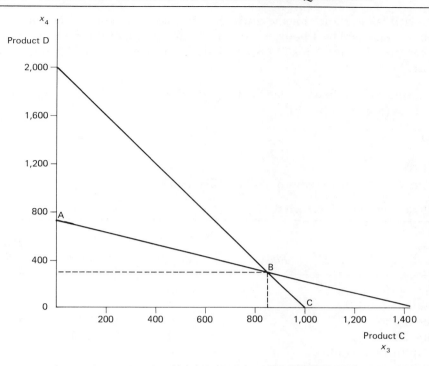

Fig. 140. *Conditions for optimal product mix—Annapurna Ltd.*

This can be solved graphically. The conditions are shown in Fig. 140. The feasible region is given by OABC. It can be shown that the optimal solution is at point B where $x_3 = 850$ units, $x_4 = 300$ units. (This can be confirmed by plotting iso-contribution lines.) The contribution is $850 \times 40 + 300 \times 30 = £43,000$.

The overall solution is:

Make 1,500 units of product B.
Make 850 units of product C.
Make 300 units of product D.

Total contribution is £61,000.

Profit = Contribution − Overheads (fixed)
= £61,000 − £35,500
= £25,500.

(b) This part required a calculation of the maximum price at which the sale of A would be worth while. The present contribution of product A is £17 per unit. To give the same benefit per unit of limiting factor as product B the contribution would have to increase by £3 to £20 per unit (B gives £2 per hour of grade A labour). Assuming the costs remain unchanged, the price would have to be increased by £3 per unit from £55 to £58.

(c) Product B is the choice for the utilisation of grade A labour. If the supply of grade A labour increases by 1 hour, 1/6 of an additional unit of B can be made increasing the contribution by $1/6 \times £12 = £2$. This is in effect the dual value of grade A labour.

(d) The limitations of linear programming are described in detail in answers to other questions (e.g. number 61).

60.

**ALFRED LTD**

(a) The given details are summarised in Table 39.

Table 39. Given data for Alfred Ltd.

|  | Products | | Availability | Price/wage rate |
|---|---|---|---|---|
|  | Flaktrap | Satrap | | |
| Selling price | £125 | £165 | | |
| Materials used (kg) | 6 | 4 | | £5 per kg |
| Skilled labour (h) | 10 | 10 | 2,000 | £3 per hour |
| Semi-skilled (h) | 5 | 25 | 2,500 | £2 per hour |
| Maximum demand | 150 | 80 | | |

The company's overhead recovery rate is £2 per labour hour (for both skilled and semi-skilled labour) of which £1 relates to variable costs and £1 to fixed costs.

The starting-point in determining the optimal mix is the calculation of contribution per unit of flaktraps and satraps (Table 40).

Table 40. Contribution figures for Alfred products.

|  | Contribution | |
|---|---|---|
|  | Flaktrap | Satrap |
| Selling price | £125 | £165 |
| Materials | 30 | 20 |
| Skilled labour | 30 | 30 |
| Semi-skilled labour | 10 | 50 |
| Variable overheads | 15 | 35 |
|  | 85 | 135 |
| Contribution per unit | £40 | £30 |

Let $x$ be units of flaktraps to be made,
$y$ be units of satraps to be made.

# APPENDIX 3. SUGGESTED ANSWERS TO EXAMINATION QUESTIONS

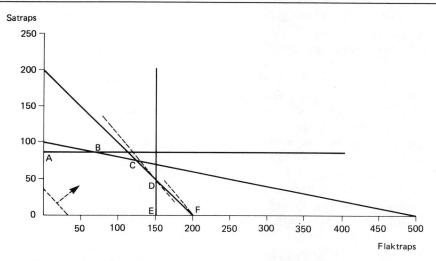

Fig. 141. *Conditions for optimal product mix—Alfred Ltd.*

The objective is to maximise contribution:

$$\text{Maximise } Z = 40x + 30y \text{ (objective function)},$$

subject to:   $10x + 10y \leqslant 2{,}000$   (skilled labour)

$5x + 25y \leqslant 2{,}500$   (semi-skilled labour)

$x \leqslant 150$   (demand)

$y \leqslant 80$   (demand)

$x, y \leqslant 0$   (non-negativity conditions).

The conditions above are shown in Fig. 141. The feasible region is given by the convex set OABCDE. Plotting iso-contribution lines shows the optimal solution as lying at corner point D. This represents a product mix of 150 flaktraps and 50 satraps and an optimal contribution of £40 × 150 + £30 × 50 = £7,500.

(b) This part requires the maximum monthly expenditure on advertising which would be worthwhile if it increased the demand for flaktraps by 50 units per month. Currently $x \leqslant 150$. This would be relaxed to $x \leqslant 200$. The new condition is shown on the graph. The feasible region is now given by the convex set OABCF. The optimal solution can now be seen as lying at corner point F where $x = 200$ and $y = 0$. This represents a production of 200 flaktraps and no satraps with a new contribution of 200 × £40 = £8,000. This is an increase of £500 over the previous contribution. Hence, the maximum the firm should spend is £500.

(c) The dual value of a scarce resource measures the increase possible in the value of the linear programming objective function if one additional unit of the scarce resource becomes available—or the decrease if one of the available units is lost.

Alternatively, it may be defined as the maximum amount to be paid for an additional unit of a scarce or limited resource.

As dual prices are the product of a linear programming framework they suffer the same limitations and are based on the same assumptions as are relevant to linear programming (e.g. selling price and variable cost per unit are assumed constant for all output levels, fractional output levels are assumed to be possible, non-financial benefits and costs are excluded, demand and supply inter-dependencies are ignored and no explicit account is taken of uncertainty). Within these limits they provide a useful measure of the opportunity cost involved in using scarce resources.

However, there is a further reason for caution when dual prices are being used. They measure contribution changes resulting from marginal increases or decreases in resource availability. A large increase in the availability of a particular resource may mean that it is no longer an effective constraint on production and its shadow price becomes zero. Hence dual prices are of limited use in assessing the impact of non-marginal changes; in such cases the linear programme usually needs to be reformulated and resolved.

Provided the limitations mentioned above are borne in mind, dual values discriminately applied have a number of possible uses.

First, they provide an indication of which constraints are the most severe. A zero dual price attached to a resource indicates that it is not an effective constraint on production. Hence, it will not be worth while devoting any time finding additional units of such a resource. However, a company might usefully seek ways of relieving other constraints as a relaxation of them will lead to an increase in total contribution (as long as they have dual prices).

A second application of dual prices may arise when new opportunities, not in the original plan, are presented for consideration. Dual prices reflect the best marginal use of resources within the framework of the optimal plan, and, to be acceptable, a new opportunity should use the resources at least as profitably as this marginal use; in a situation of scarce resources the new opportunity, if accepted, will displace one or more of the opportunities included in the optimal plan.

However, dual prices alone will not reveal precisely how the production levels of opportunities within the optimal plan should be adjusted. The dual values act merely as a screening device for new opportunities.

A third use arises when all decisions are not taken by a central decision-making body with access to the linear programme (i.e. decentralised decision-making). To reduce the chance that resources are used sub-optimally they should be charged to those responsible for decisions at their total opportunity cost. As this includes the dual price value of scarce resources, only projects at least as efficient as those included in the optimal plan should be accepted.

A fourth use of dual prices is in the area of pricing and this is related to the second and third uses mentioned above.

## 61.

ZAMAN LTD
(a) The product mix which optimises contribution (and hence profit) may be found using linear programming. See Table 41 for contribution figures.

Table 41. Contribution figures for Zaman products.

|  | Contribution Qa | Mar |
|---|---|---|
| Selling price | £200 | £109 |
| Labour 20 × £3 = | (60) | 8 × £3 = (24) |
| Raw materials 4 × £10 = | (40) | 5 × £10 = (50) |
| Variable overhead (per unit) | (20) | (15) |
| Contribution per unit | £80 | £20 |

Let $x$ = number of units of Qa to be produced,
$y$ = number of units of Mar to be produced.

$$\text{Maximise contribution } C = 80x + 20y \quad \text{(objective function)},$$

subject to the following conditions:

(i) demand $\quad x \leq 1{,}000$
$\quad y \leq 4{,}000 \quad$ (there are no stocks)

(ii) labour $\quad 20x + 8y \leq 40{,}000$

(iii) raw materials $\quad 4x + 5y \leq 20{,}000$

(iv) non-negativity conditions $\quad x \geq 0; y \geq 0.$

The graph (Fig. 142) shows the feasible region as being OABCD. The optimal solution lies at corner point C. Optimal product mix is

<u>1,000 units of Qa</u> and <u>2,500 of Mar</u>

with a contribution of $C = 80(1{,}000) + 20(2{,}500) = £130{,}000$.

Optimal profit (i.e. less expected fixed overheads) is £50,000.

(b) Limitations of the linear programming approach:

(i) Linearity: costs, revenues or any physical properties which form the basis of the problem vary in direct proportion (i.e. linearly) with the quantities or number of components produced.

(ii) Divisibility: quantities, revenues and costs are infinitely divisible—i.e. any fraction or decimal answer is valid. (If required, integer constraints (Gemory constraints) can be introduced to give whole-number answers).

(iii) Certainty: the technique makes no allowance for uncertainty in the estimates made (although the evaluation of dual values indicates the sensitivity of the solution to marginal uncertainty in constraint values).

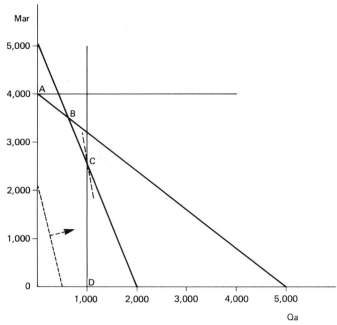

Fig. 142. *Conditions for optimal product mix—Zaman Ltd.*

(iv) The usefulness of linear programming models for decision making depends on how well they simulate the conditions under which the firm actually operates. The solution is only optimal for the available input data.

(v) Interdependence between demand for products is ignored: products may be complementary or a substitute for one another.

(vi) The model relies on costs being split into fixed and variable elements. This may be difficult to achieve in practice, furthermore it is difficult to make allowance for fixed costs in determining the solution—any attempt to absorb them on a unit basis (i.e. treating them as variable costs) is likely to result in non-linear relationships.

This could result in a situation where the solution (based on variable costs) suggests a small quantity of a component should be produced, but consideration of the fixed set-up costs makes this unattractive.

(vii) Time factors are ignored. All production is assumed to be instantaneous.

(viii) Costs and benefits which cannot be quantified easily, such as liquidity, goodwill and labour stability, are ignored. This limitation is not specific to linear programming; it is a problem that obviously affects other areas. However, in practice, consideration of liquidity is often almost as important as the results obtained from whatever optimisation technique is being employed.

(c) (i) The dual price of a resource is the amount by which the optimal contribution may be increased or decreased when a unit charge in resource availability occurs.

# APPENDIX 3. SUGGESTED ANSWERS TO EXAMINATION QUESTIONS

(ii) The dual prices of the resources are the solutions to the dual linear programme (this models the problem of an investor wishing to purchase resources of the programme).

(iii) If the dual price is zero then not all the resource is used in the optimal product mix.

The resource limitations which give rise to the binding constraints in the optimal product mix for Zaman Ltd are:

(1) labour; (2) demand for Qa.

These are the only resources having non-zero dual values.

## 62.

### FLEABANE LTD.

*Comment:* At first sight this is an easy question until you try to make some sense of the process costs. These are referred to as *variable* costs and as such would be incremental (i.e. are dependent on output). Then the question says that processing *facilities* have no alternative use. The problem is this: do the process costs simply represent a notional cost allocation, in which case they can be ignored; or do they represent variable (i.e. incremental) costs as indicated in the table? Much hinges on your interpretation of the words "variable" and "facilities".

It will be assumed that the "variable process costs" are notional cost allocations. The incremental contribution margins are therefore £10 per gallon for Erigeron and £13 per gallon for Stachys.

(a) Unused scarce resources:

| | |
|---|---|
| Cooling process | 4,000 hours |
| Heating process | 6,000 hours |
| Blending process | 6,000 hours |

If the output of both products were increased by 1,000 gallons, the extra resource requirements would be:

| | | | Total |
|---|---|---|---|
| Cooling hours: | E | 2 × 1,000 | |
| | S | 3 × 1,000 | 5,000 |
| Heating hours: | E | 4 × 1,000 | |
| | S | 1 × 1,000 | 5,000 |
| Blending hours: | E | 1 × 1,000 | |
| | S | 5 × 1,000 | 6,000 |

Unfortunately, the cooling hour constraint has been violated. It is necessary to restrict output of one of the products. Which one gives the lower contribution per cooling hour?

E : contribution per cooling hour £10/2 = £5

S : contribution per cooling hour £13/3 = £4⅓

Thus output of S should be restricted to 1,000 gallons less

$$\frac{1000}{3}$$

(since the availability is exceeded by 1,000 units and each gallon requires three hours).

Fleabane should respond as follows:

|   | *Extra gallons produced* |   |   | *Extra contribution* |
|---|---|---|---|---|
| E | 1,000 | @ £10 = | | £10,000 |
| S | 666⅔ | @ £13 = | | £ 8,666⅔ |
|   |   |   |   | £18,666⅔ |

(b) If each process has only 3,000 hours of unused capacity per month, the linear programming is required to find the optimal solution.

(i) Let E be the number of gallons of Erigeron produced,
S be the number of gallons of Stachys produced.

$$\text{maximum } 10E + 13S$$

subject to
$$4E + S \leqslant 3{,}000 \quad \text{(Heating hours)}$$
$$E + 5S \leqslant 3{,}000 \quad \text{(Blending hours)}$$
$$2E + 3S \leqslant 3{,}000 \quad \text{(Cooling hours)}$$
$$E, S \geqslant 0 \quad \text{(non-negativity)}.$$

The graph in Fig. 143 shows the optimal solution to be at point B, i.e. at the intersection of:
$$E + 5S = 3000$$
$$4E + S = 3000$$

Solving simultaneously gives E = 631.6 gallons,
S = 473.7 gallons.

(ii) Let $e$ be the contribution of E,
$s$ be the contribution of S.

The objective function is $P = eE + sS$ where P = total contribution.
The gradient of the objective function is found as follows:

$$eE = P - sS$$

$$\therefore E = -\frac{s}{e}S + \frac{P}{e}$$

i.e. the gradient is $-\frac{s}{e}$.

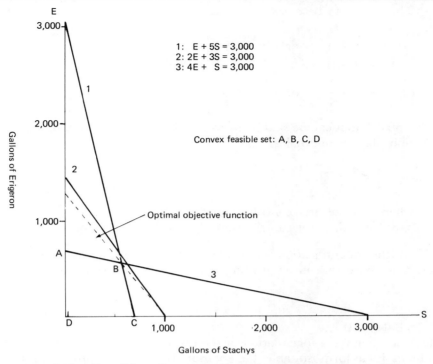

Fig. 143. *Conditions for optimal product mix—Fleabane Ltd.*

If $s$ increases relative to $e$, the gradient will become more negative, i.e. the objective function rotates clockwise. Point B on the graph will be optimal until the objective function is parallel to:

$$E + 5S = 3{,}000$$

The gradient of this is found from:

$$E = -5S + 3{,}000$$

i.e. the gradient is $-5$.

Similarly, if $s$ decreases relative to $e$, the gradient of the objective function will become less negative. Point B is optimal until the objective function is parallel to:

$$4E + S = 3{,}000$$

i.e.

$$E = -\frac{1}{4}S + \frac{3{,}000}{4}$$

i.e. the gradient is $-\frac{1}{4}$.

Thus for B to be optimal, we have:

(1) $-\dfrac{s}{e} > -5$ or $\dfrac{s}{e} < 5$

(2) $-\dfrac{s}{e} < -\dfrac{1}{4}$ or $\dfrac{s}{e} > \dfrac{1}{4}$

Thus all that can be said in answer to this question is that the present production plant is optimal given

$$\dfrac{1}{4} < \dfrac{s}{e} < 5$$

where $s$ is the unit contribution of Stachys per gallon
and $e$ is the unit contribution of Erigeron per gallon.

No further quantification is possible. All in all, this is a pretty loose question and with a bit more care in its drafting, it could have been much better.

### 63.

**BARSANDS BANK LTD**

(a) This part requires a formulation of the linear programming model of the bank's problem in a form suitable for solution by a linear programming computer package.

The bank is trying to determine its overall loan policy for the region for the coming month. The customers have been classified into four groups: industrial, agricultural, personal without solidarity, personal with solidarity. The total amount available for loans is £50 million.

Let $x_1$ be the amount of industrial loan (£ million),
$x_2$ be the amount of agricultural loan (£ million),
$x_3$ be the amount of personal without solidarity loan (£ million),
$x_4$ be the amount of personal with solidarity loan (£ million).

The objective is to maximise return. This is given by:

$$x_1(0.998 \times 0.09 - 0.002) + x_2(0.995 \times 0.1 - 0.005)$$
$$+ x_3(0.990 \times 0.13 - 0.010) + x_4(0.980 \times 0.14 - 0.020).$$

The formulation above has taken into account the appropriate interest rates and risk levels.

This can be simplified to:

$$Z = 0.0878 x_1 + 0.0945 x_2 + 0.1187 x_3 + 0.1172 x_4 \text{ (objective function)}.$$

This objective must be maximised subject to a number of conditions:
The amount available is limited to £50 million,

$$\therefore \quad x_1 + x_2 + x_3 + x_4 \leqslant 50.$$

The personal loans must not exceed 40 per cent of the value of total loans,

$$\therefore \quad x_3 + x_4 \leqslant 0.4(x_1 + x_2 + x_3 + x_4).$$

Rearranging,

$$-0.4x_1 - 0.4x_2 + 0.6x_3 + 0.6x_4 \leqslant 0.$$

Personal with solidarity loans must not exceed 20 per cent of the total personal loans:

$$x_4 \leqslant 0.2(x_3 + x_4), \quad -0.2x_3 + 0.8x_4 \leqslant 0.$$

The total agricultural loans must not exceed £10 million:

$$x_2 \leqslant 10.$$

The industrial loans should not be less than £20 million:

$$x_1 \geqslant 20.$$

The average risk factor (i.e. the percentage of bad debts) must not exceed 0.8 per cent:

$$\frac{0.002x_1 + 0.005x_2 + 0.01x_3 + 0.02x_4}{x_1 + x_2 + x_3 + x_4} \leqslant 0.008;$$

this can be simplified by multiplying both sides by 100 and rearranging:

$$-0.6x_1 - 0.3x_2 + 0.2x_3 + 1.2x_4 \leqslant 0.$$

And finally, $x_1, x_2, x_3, x_4 \geqslant 0$ (non-negativity conditions).

(b) The simplest maximising situations are normally characterised by constraints which are of the "less than or equal to" type. Occasionally however, in a maximisation situation the constraints may contain a mixture of $\leqslant$ and $\geqslant$ varieties. The usual cause of "greater than or equal to" constraints is the requirement to produce at least a certain amount of a particular product. In such situations the simplest approach is to reduce the capacity of the other limitations by the amounts of resources necessary to make just the requisite amount of the appropriate product. Maximisation can now be carried out in the normal way, remembering to add back the quantities which were required to be produced, to the optimum solution obtained from simplex.

An alternative method involves the use of artificial variables. In the Barsands Bank problem the industrial loans should not be less than £20 million, i.e. there is one "greater than equal to" inequality. If this was not the case, slack variables would be added to all the constraints and normal simplex methods applied. However, in the above constraint a surplus variable would be required and the normal method would lead to an infeasible solution (one of the variables would take a negative value). This difficulty can be resolved by adding an artificial variable to the constraint and setting up an additional objective function equal to the artificial variable.

Initially, the normal simplex procedures will be used to minimise the new objective function. This new objective function when reduced to zero allows the artificial variable to be dropped from the problem leaving a basic feasible solution to the original problem. The normal simplex procedures can now be applied to the original objective function.

(c) In a linear programming model, the number of constraints determines the maximum number of non-zero solutions. In a situation where there are more variables than constraints, the optimal solution must contain some original variables with a value of zero. In the Barsands Bank example this would imply the bank refusing loans to some categories. The difficulty can be resolved by increasing the number of constraints. These for instance could impose lower limits on loans.

## 64.

### XYZ Ltd

(a) Using the given information, the question requires the setting up of the first tableau and the first iteration.

Let $x_1$ be the units (in thousands) of the super deluxe model
$x_2$ be the units (in thousands) of the deluxe model
$x_3$ be the units (in thousands) of the export model.

The objective is to maximise contribution:

$$\text{Maximise } C = 1{,}500x_1 + 1{,}300x_2 + 2{,}500x_3 \text{ (objective function)},$$

subject to:
$$x_1 \leqslant 500 \text{ (maximum demand)}$$
$$x_2 \leqslant 750 \text{ (maximum demand)}$$
$$x_3 \leqslant 400 \text{ (maximum demand)}$$
$$0.5x_1 + 0.5x_2 + x_3 \leqslant 1{,}400 \text{ (direct labour hours—machining)}$$
$$0.5x_1 + 0.5x_2 + 2x_3 \leqslant 1{,}200 \text{ (direct labour hours—assembly)}$$
$$x_1, x_2, x_3 \geqslant 0 \text{ (non-negativity conditions).}$$

Introducing slack variables:

$$C = 1{,}500x_1 + 1{,}300x_2 + 2{,}500x_3,$$

subject to:
$$x_1 + S_1 = 500$$
$$x_2 + S_2 = 750$$
$$x_3 + S_3 = 400$$
$$0.5x_1 + 0.5x_2 + x_3 + S_4 = 1{,}400$$
$$0.5x_1 + 0.5x_2 + 2x_3 + S_4 = 1{,}200.$$

# APPENDIX 3. SUGGESTED ANSWERS TO EXAMINATION QUESTIONS

The initial simplex tableau can now be set up:

| Solution variable | Product | | | Slack variable | | | | | Solution quantity |
|---|---|---|---|---|---|---|---|---|---|
| | $x_1$ | $x_2$ | $x_3$ | $S_1$ | $S_2$ | $S_3$ | $S_4$ | $S_5$ | |
| $S_1$ | 1 | 0 | 0 | 1 | 0 | 0 | 0 | 0 | 500 |
| $S_2$ | 0 | 1 | 0 | 0 | 1 | 0 | 0 | 0 | 750 |
| $S_3$ | 0 | 0 | 1 | 0 | 0 | 1 | 0 | 0 | 400 |
| $S_4$ | 0.5 | 0.5 | 1 | 0 | 0 | 0 | 1 | 0 | 1,400 |
| $S_5$ | 0.5 | 0.5 | 2 | 0 | 0 | 0 | 0 | 1 | 1,200 |
| $C$ | 1,500 | 1,300 | 2,500 | 0 | 0 | 0 | 0 | 0 | 0 |

The normal simplex procedures can be applied to give the second tableau shown below:

| Solution variable | Product | | | Slack variable | | | | | Solution quantity |
|---|---|---|---|---|---|---|---|---|---|
| | $x_1$ | $x_2$ | $x_3$ | $S_1$ | $S_2$ | $S_3$ | $S_4$ | $S_5$ | |
| $S_1$ | 1 | 0 | 0 | 1 | 0 | 0 | 0 | 0 | 500 |
| $S_2$ | 0 | 1 | 0 | 0 | 1 | 0 | 0 | 0 | 750 |
| $x_3$ | 0 | 0 | 1 | 0 | 0 | 1 | 0 | 0 | 400 |
| $S_4$ | 0.5 | 0.5 | 0 | 0 | 0 | $-1$ | 1 | 0 | 1,000 |
| $S_5$ | 0.5 | 0.5 | 0 | 0 | 0 | $-2$ | 0 | 1 | 400 |
| $C$ | 1,500 | 1,300 | 0 | 0 | 0 | $-2,500$ | 0 | 0 | 1,000,000 |

(b) The given tableau does not have a column labelling the solution variables. However, the variables concerned can be found by reading across the rows until a unit entry is found in a column which otherwise contains zeros. Thus the first entry in the column headed $b_{ij}$ refers to $x_1$, the second entry refers to $S_3$ and so on. The complete table is restated below.

| Solution variable | Product | | | Slack variable | | | | | Solution quantity |
|---|---|---|---|---|---|---|---|---|---|
| | $x_1$ | $x_2$ | $x_3$ | $S_1$ | $S_2$ | $S_3$ | $S_4$ | $S_5$ | |
| $x_1$ | 1 | 0 | 0 | 1 | 0 | 0 | 0 | 0 | 500 |
| $S_3$ | 0 | 0 | 0 | 0.25 | 0.25 | 1 | 0 | $-0.5$ | 112.5 |
| $x_3$ | 0 | 0 | 1 | $-0.25$ | $-0.25$ | 0 | 0 | 0.5 | 287.5 |
| $S_4$ | 0 | 0 | 0 | $-0.25$ | $-0.25$ | 0 | 1 | $-0.5$ | 487.5 |
| $x_2$ | 0 | 1 | 0 | 0 | 1 | 0 | 0 | 0 | 750 |
| $C$ | 0 | 0 | 0 | $-875$ | $-675$ | 0 | 0 | $-1,250$ | $-2,433,750$ |

The solution in units of 1,000 is:

$$x_1 = 500 \quad S_1 = 0$$
$$x_2 = 750 \quad S_2 = 0$$
$$x_3 = 287.5 \quad S_3 = 112.5$$
$$S_4 = 487.5$$
$$S_5 = 0.$$

The total contribution made is £2,443,750. $S_3$ is part of the solution, implying that the upper limit on $x_3$ has not been reached. $S_4$ is in the solution, representing unused machine hours.

The dual values can be interpreted as follows. If the upper limit on $x_1$ was relaxed by 1,000 units then an extra £875 contribution could be made. Similarly, if the upper limit on $x_2$ could be relaxed by 1,000 units an extra £675 contribution could be made. Finally, if an additional 1,000 hours of assembly time were available at the existing price then £1,250 would be added to contribution. (Confirm that the dual solution is equivalent to the primal solution.)

## 65.

**PETER LEY**

(a) This part requires a linear programming model to help Peter Ley decide on the best product mix. As the final tableau is given, it is essential that the model constructed is consistent with the final tableau. In other words, the LP model formulated, if operated on by standard simplex procedures, should lead to the examiner's final tableau.

The first step is to determine an objective function.

|  | Product | | |
|---|---|---|---|
|  | Car cleaner | Standard cleaner | Deluxe cleaner |
| Selling price | 45 | 110 | 120 |
| Variable costs | 15 | 60 | 80 |
| Contribution per unit | £30 | £50 | £40 |

The notation adopted has already been defined as:

$x_1$ = number of car cleaners,

$x_2$ = number of standard cleaners,

$x_3$ = number of deluxe cleaners.

The objective is to maximise contribution:

$$\text{Maximise } C = 30x_1 + 50x_2 + 40x_3 \text{ (objective function)},$$

subject to the following conditions:

$$x_1 + x_2 + x_3 \leqslant 350$$

(the circuits available are limited to 350);

$$x_1 + 3x_2 + 2x_3 \leqslant 380$$

(assembly time is limited to 380 hours);

$$x_2 \leqslant 20$$

(upper sales limit on standard cleaners);

$$x_3 \leqslant 10$$

(upper sales limit on deluxe cleaners); and

$$x_1,\ x_2,\ x_3 \geqslant 0 \quad \text{(non-negativity conditions)}.$$

*Tutorial notes*

(a) The £1,500 paid initially for the circuits is a sunk cost.
(b) The assumption made is that the labour payment of £1 is not a relevant cost as it occurs whether labour is used or not.
(c) On the basis of the model above, the initial tableau can now be set up. Though it was not required it is stated below. The model with slack variables is:

$$\text{Maximise } C = 30x_1 + 50x_2 + 40x_3,$$

subject to:
$$x_1 + x_2 + x_3 + S_1 = 350$$
$$x_1 + 3x_2 + 2x_3 + S_4 = 380$$
$$x_2 + S_3 = 20$$
$$x_3 + S_4 = 10.$$

| Solution variable | Product | | | Slack variable | | | | Solution quantity |
|---|---|---|---|---|---|---|---|---|
| | $x_1$ | $x_2$ | $x_3$ | $S_1$ | $S_2$ | $S_3$ | $S_4$ | |
| $S_1$ | 1 | 1 | 1 | 1 | 0 | 0 | 0 | 350 |
| $S_2$ | 1 | 3 | 2 | 0 | 1 | 0 | 0 | 380 |
| $S_3$ | 0 | 1 | 0 | 0 | 0 | 1 | 0 | 20 |
| $S_4$ | 0 | 0 | 1 | 0 | 0 | 0 | 1 | 10 |
| $C$ | 30 | 50 | 40 | 0 | 0 | 0 | 0 | 0 |

(b) The final simplex tableau indicates that Peter Ley's optimal production plan is to make 335 units of car cleaners and 15 units of standard cleaners to give a contribution of £10,800. Note that, using the given tableau, deluxe cleaners do not form part of the optimal solution. (However, the index row number under $x_3$ is zero. This means that there is another solution, in which $x_3$ is included which is just as good. One further iteration produces the alternative best plan involving $x_3$. This can be shown to be 300 car vacuum cleaners, 10 standard cleaners and 10 deluxe cleaners giving the same contribution of £10,800.)

In the given tableau, $S_3$ and $S_4$ feature as solution variables with values of 5 and 10 respectively. These represent the demand not met for standard and deluxe cleaners (i.e. upper bound is not reached). $S_1$ and $S_2$ do not form part of the solution variables as they represent the number of circuits not used and assembly hours not used. With the given plan circuits and assembly hours are fully utilised. As they are fully utilised they have dual values and these are 20 and 10 respectively. The valuation of scarce resources can be confirmed as being £10,800 (i.e. the primal solution is equal to the dual solution).

(c) The dual value for assembly time labour is given in the index row under slack variables $S_2$ as £10. Increasing the hours available by 1 the objective function will increase by £10, i.e. the contribution will increase by £10 which is £7 greater than the overtime cost of £3. Hence, it is worth employing. If the given final table is examined only 10 hours overtime is desirable as above this, the variable $S_3$ would go negative leading to an infeasible solution. (Note however that while the above interpretation would have been suitable for the examination answer, it is possible to improve on it by starting from the alternative optimal production schedule involving $x_3$. If this were done, it can be shown that 20 hours overtime would be optimal with a production schedule of 320 car vacuum cleaners, 20 standard vacuum cleaners and 10 deluxe cleaners. This gives a total contribution of £10,940.)

(d) The linear programming model needs to be adapted to include the possibility of selling all or some of the circuits at £28 each.

$x_1$ is the number of car cleaners,

$x_2$ is the number of standard cleaners,

$x_3$ is the number of deluxe cleaners.

Let $x_4$ be the number of circuits sold.

Maximise $C = 30x_1 + 50x_2 + 40x_3 + 28x_4$   (objective function),

subject to the following conditions:

$$x_1 + x_2 + x_3 + x_4 \leqslant 350 \quad \text{(circuits constraint)}$$
$$x_1 + 3x_2 + 2x_3 \leqslant 380 \quad \text{(assembly labour)}$$
$$x_2 \leqslant 20 \quad \text{(maximum demand)}$$
$$x_3 \leqslant 10 \quad \text{(maximum demand)}$$
$$x_1, x_2, x_3, x_4 \geqslant 0 \quad \text{(non-negativity conditions)}.$$

APPENDIX 3. SUGGESTED ANSWERS TO EXAMINATION QUESTIONS

**66.**

**ELECTROPOINT LTD**

(a) The three products manufactured by Electropoint are A, B and C. The final tableau indicates the symbols that should be used in setting up the model.

Let $x_1$ be the production level of product A,
$x_2$ be the production level of product B,
$x_3$ be the production level of product C.

|  | $x_1$ | $x_2$ | $x_3$ |
|---|---|---|---|
| Selling price per unit | £13 | £14 | £17 |
| *Less:* Labour costs | £6 | £4 | £6 |
| Other variable costs | £2 | £3 | £4 |
| Contribution per unit | £5 | £7 | £7 |

The objective is to maximise contribution:

$$\text{Maximise } Z = 5x_1 + 7x_2 + 7x_3 \text{ (objective function)},$$

subject to the following conditions:

$$3x_1 + 4x_2 + x_3 \leqslant 200 \quad \text{(raw material X)}$$
$$2x_1 + 4x_2 + 2x_3 \leqslant 300 \quad \text{(raw material Y)}$$
$$x_1 + x_2 + x_3 \leqslant 200 \quad \text{(raw material Z)}$$
$$3x_1 + 2x_2 + 3x_3 \leqslant 400 \quad \text{(labour limitation)}$$
$$x_1 \geqslant 10 \quad \text{(current orders)}$$
$$x_2 \geqslant 10 \quad \text{(current orders)}$$
$$x_3 \geqslant 40 \quad \text{(current orders)}$$
$$x_1, x_2, x_3 \geqslant 0 \quad \text{(non-negativity)}.$$

(b) The given tableau does not have a column labelling the variables. However, the variables concerned can be found by reading across the rows until a unit entry is found in a column which otherwise contains zeros. The complete final table is restated below:

| Solution variable | Product | | | Slack variable | | | | | | | Solution quantity |
|---|---|---|---|---|---|---|---|---|---|---|---|
| | $x_1$ | $x_2$ | $x_3$ | $S_1$ | $S_2$ | $S_3$ | $S_4$ | $S_5$ | $S_6$ | $S_7$ | |
| $S_6$ | 0 | 0 | 0 | 0 | 0.375 | 0 | −0.25 | 0 | 1 | 0 | 2.5 |
| $S_7$ | 0 | 0 | 0 | 0 | −0.25 | 0 | 0.5 | 1 | 0 | 1 | 75 |
| $S_3$ | 0 | 0 | 0 | 0 | −0.125 | 1 | −0.25 | 0 | 0 | 0 | 62.5 |
| $S_1$ | 0 | 0 | 0 | 1 | −1.25 | 0 | 0.5 | 2 | 0 | 0 | 5 |
| $x_1$ | 1 | 0 | 0 | 0 | 0 | 0 | 0 | −1 | 0 | 0 | 10 |
| $x_2$ | 0 | 1 | 0 | 0 | 0.375 | 0 | −0.25 | 0 | 0 | 0 | 12.5 |
| $x_3$ | 0 | 0 | 1 | 0 | −0.25 | 0 | 0.5 | 10 | 0 | 0 | 115 |
| | 0 | 0 | 0 | 0 | 0.875 | 0 | 1.75 | 20 | 0 | 0 | 942.5 |

$x_1$, $x_2$ and $x_3$ are production levels.
$S_1$, $S_2$ and $S_3$ represent unused raw material X, Y and Z.
$S_4$ is unused number of labour hours.
$S_5$, $S_6$ and $S_7$ are amounts by which the production levels exceed current order levels for A, B and C.

The optimum production schedule is to make 10 units of product A, $12\frac{1}{2}$ units of product B and 115 units of product C to give a contribution of £942.5. (The weekly profit can now be calculated as £642.5.) Raw material Y is completely used but 5 units of X and 62.5 units of Z will be left in stock. Labour is fully used. The resources fully used, i.e. material Y and labour have dual values of 0.875 and 1.75 respectively.

(c) The uses of linear programming range from the government sector to agricultural, business and industrial sectors. Its uses can also be found in economic theory, dietetics, industrial engineering and applied mathematics. However, business and industrial applications have been most extensive. For example, problems involving blending of petroleum, animal feed blending, production planning and inventory control; problems dealing with personnel assignment and training, transportation of commodities, problems concerned with allocation of investment funds are some of the areas of business applications of linear programming where the accountant may be involved.

## 67.

**WYATT LTD**

(a) The relevant data are summarised below:

| | Model A | Model B | Availability |
|---|---|---|---|
| Assembly time per unit | 12 h | 25 h | 2,800 h |
| Packaging time per unit | 1 h | 2 h | 140 h |
| Unit variable cost | £500 | £1,000 | |
| Unit selling price | £750 | £1,600 | |

# APPENDIX 3. SUGGESTED ANSWERS TO EXAMINATION QUESTIONS

Let $x_1$ = number of units of model A produced with company funds,
$x_2$ = number of units of model A produced with borrowed funds,
$x_3$ = number of units of model B produced with company funds,
$x_4$ = number of units of model B produced with borrowed funds.

The objective is to maximise contribution:

$$\text{Maximise } Z = (750 - 500)x_1 + (750 - 500 \times 1.05)x_2 + (1{,}600 - 1{,}000)x_3 + (1{,}600 - 1{,}000 \times 1.05)x_4.$$

Simplifying: $Z = 250x_1 + 225x_2 + 600x_3 + 550x_4$.

(Note that the interest rate is 20 per cent per annum, which is 5 per cent for a three-month period.)

This objective function must be maximised subject to the following conditions: the internal funds are limited to £50,000;

$$500x_1 + 1{,}000x_3 \leq 50{,}000;$$

the borrowed funds are limited to £100,000,

$$500x_2 + 1{,}000x_4 \leq 100{,}000.$$

The bank has imposed a condition on its lending that the total amount of internal funds made available by the company for the operation, less the actual expenditure plus the accounts receivable for the products sold, must be at least twice as great as the outstanding loan plus interest payable at the end of the initial three-month period:

$$50{,}000 - (500x_1 + 1{,}000x_3) + 750(x_1 + x_2) + 1{,}600(x_3 + x_4) \geq 2(500x_2 + 1{,}000x_4)1.05.$$

Simplifying: $-250x_1 + 300x_2 - 600x_3 + 500x_4 \leq 50{,}000$.

The assembly time is limited to 2,800 hours,

$$12x_1 + 12x_2 + 25x_3 + 25x_4 \leq 2{,}800;$$

the packaging time is limited to 140 hours,

$$x_1 + x_2 + 2x_3 + 2x_4 \leq 140.$$

Market test constraints:

$$x_1 + x_2 \geq 60, \qquad x_3 + x_4 \geq 30.$$

$$x_1, x_2, x_3, x_4 \geq 0 \quad \text{(non-negativity conditions).}$$

(b) The optimal solution to the problem is given as $x_1 = 60$, $x_2 = 0$, $x_3 = 20$, $x_4 = 10$.
There are seven slack variables (one for each constraint) and these can be determined by substituting the given solution into the constraints. Assuming $S_1$, $S_2$, $S_3$,

$S_4$, $S_5$, $S_6$, $S_7$ are used to define the constraints in the order the model was constructed then:

$$x_1 = 60 \qquad S_3 = 72,000$$
$$x_2 = 0 \qquad S_4 = 1,330$$
$$x_3 = 20 \qquad S_5 = 20$$
$$x_4 = 10 \qquad S_6 = 0$$
$$S_1 = 0$$
$$S_2 = 90,000 \qquad S_7 = 0.$$

Contribution = $250 \times 60 + 600 \times 20 + 550 \times 10 = £32,500$.

The form of the final tableau can now be indicated. It should be borne in mind that the final tableau reflects the optimal production plan and gives the following information:

(i) the optimal product mix, i.e. the quantities of products to be made so as to maximise contribution;

(ii) the amount of the contribution realised through the optimal mix;

(iii) the slack on resources not fully utilised and an indication of those resources which are fully utilised;

(iv) the dual values of scarce or limited resources.

The final tableau would take the following form:

| Solution variable | Product | | | | Slack variable | | | | | | | Solution quantity |
| --- | --- | --- | --- | --- | --- | --- | --- | --- | --- | --- | --- | --- |
| | $x_1$ | $x_2$ | $x_3$ | $x_4$ | $S_1$ | $S_2$ | $S_3$ | $S_4$ | $S_5$ | $S_6$ | $S_7$ | |
| $x_1$ | 1 | | 0 | 0 | | 0 | 0 | 0 | 0 | | | 60 |
| $x_3$ | 0 | | 1 | 0 | | 0 | 0 | 0 | 0 | | | 20 |
| $x_4$ | 0 | | 0 | 1 | | 0 | 0 | 0 | 0 | | | 10 |
| $S_2$ | 0 | | 0 | 0 | | 1 | 0 | 0 | 0 | | | 90,000 |
| $S_3$ | 0 | | 0 | 0 | | 0 | 1 | 0 | 0 | | | 72,000 |
| $S_4$ | 0 | | 0 | 0 | | 0 | 0 | 1 | 0 | | | 1,330 |
| $S_5$ | 0 | | 0 | 0 | | 0 | 0 | 0 | 1 | | | 20 |
| | 0 | | 0 | 0 | | 0 | 0 | 0 | 0 | | | 32,500 |

The unit matrix for the solution variables is indicated above. Substitution rates for columns $x_2$, $S_1$, $S_6$ and $S_7$ would arise in their appropriate columns. The shadow prices for $S_1$, $S_6$ and $S_7$ (fully utilised resources) would be given under the appropriate columns in the objective function row. As $x_2$ does not form part of the optimal solution the figure in the objective function row under the appropriate column, i.e. $x_2$, would represent a loss of contribution through its production. This would indicate a diversion of resources from a more profitable to a less profitable use.

The dual values available in the tableau may be used for a sensitivity analysis of the solution—a study of the effect on the optimal plan of changes in assumptions in the specification of the problem, designed to evaluate the implications of uncertainty in those assumptions. The conditions assumed in formulating a linear programming problem are rarely entirely fixed. The quantities of products which can be sold at various prices are subject to uncertainty; moreover, it may be possible, by special effort, to increase the supply of some resources beyond the assumed limit.

Dual prices represent estimates of the effect of small changes in conditions assumed in the formulation of a problem. They indicate the amount by which the objective function increases if the supply of a resource is increased by one unit. Organisations would therefore be well advised to put a good deal of effort into increasing the supply of resources which have the highest dual prices.

Dual prices also provide a basis for estimating how much the cash surplus of a firm could be increased if the sales potential of a product could be increased.

## 68.
**BAHRAICH LTD**

(a) The given data are summarised below:

|  | *Products* | | | *Availability* |
|---|---|---|---|---|
|  | A | B | C |  |
| Material X | 2 | 1 | 5 | 50 |
| Material Y | 5 | 1 | 3 | 90 |
| Contribution/unit | £10 | £4 | £15 |  |

Let $a$ be units of product A produced
$b$ be units of product B produced
$c$ be units of product C produced.

The objective is to maximise contribution:

$$\text{Maximise } Z = 10a + 4b + 15c \text{ (objective function),}$$

subject to:
$$2a + b + 5c \leqslant 50 \quad \text{(material X)}$$
$$5a + b + 3c \leqslant 90 \quad \text{(material Y)}$$
$$a, b, c \geqslant 0 \quad \text{(non-negativity conditions).}$$

*Tutorial note: The solution of the problem above can be shown as being:*

$a = 13\frac{1}{3}$ units

$b = 23\frac{1}{3}$ units

$c = 0$

*with a total contribution of* £$226\frac{2}{3}$.

(b) Dual model:
The dual problem may be formulated by following standard transformation procedures.

Let $x$ be the dual value for material X,
$y$ be the dual value for material Y.

$$\text{Minimise } C = 50x + 90y \quad \text{(objective function)},$$

subject to:
$$2x + 5y \geqslant 10 \quad \text{(product A)}$$
$$x + y \geqslant 4 \quad \text{(product B)}$$
$$5x + 3y \geqslant 15 \quad \text{(product C)}$$
$$x, y \geqslant 0 \quad \text{(non-negativity conditions)}.$$

*Tutorial note:* The solution of the dual programme can be shown to be:

$$x = 3\tfrac{1}{3}$$
$$y = \tfrac{2}{3}$$

The value of the objective function is $226\tfrac{2}{3}$.

## INTERPRETATION OF THE DUAL

In the primal problem, the objective of the company is to determine the optimal output of products A, B and C to realise the maximum contribution with the available amounts of raw material. In the dual problem, however, the objective of the company is to minimise the cost of producing these products with the available capacity.

### 69.

**JACK LTD**

(a) The dual (or shadow) price of a *resource* is the amount by which total net revenue is increased when an additional unit of a resource becomes available and is incorporated into a *new* optimal production plan (the same adjustment takes place for marginal decrease), e.g.

   (i) If £1.00 extra cash is available to Jack Ltd in year 3 an additional revenue of £1.30 will be attainable.

   (ii) If 1 hour extra labour is available in year 5 no extra contribution will be attainable.

   (iii) If 1 less unit of raw material is available in year 4 the reduction in attainable contribution will be £4.80.

These adjustments are only applicable for marginal charges in resource availability.

# APPENDIX 3. SUGGESTED ANSWERS TO EXAMINATION QUESTIONS

(b) Let the price to be paid be £x.

| Year | Cash savings | Labour savings | Raw material AFC | Total (£000) |
|------|--------------|----------------|------------------|--------------|
| 2 | 30 × 1.65 | 15 × 1.30 | (1 × 8.4) | 60.6 |
| 3 | 30 × 1.30 | – | (1 × 6.5) | 32.5 |
| 4 | 30 × 1.05 | 15 × 1.10 | (1 × 4.8) | 43.2 |
| 5 | 30 × 0.90 | – | (1 × 1.6) | 25.4 |

Net increase = 161.7

Each £ spent in year 1 decreases the present value of dividends by £2.1. Therefore the maximum price that Jack would pay is:

$$\frac{161.700}{2.1} = \underline{\underline{£77,000}}.$$

Since in the primal problem the objective function was the *net present value* of ordinary dividends the dual prices obtained are in net present value terms, i.e. they have already been discounted.

The calculation of maximum price is possible without using the 10 per cent p.a. dividend figure because this is included in the primal objective function. The £17.5 present total market value serves only to suggest that the analysis is marginal in relation to the total capital.

(c) *Limitations and usefulness of dual values*

The dual value of a scarce resource measures the increase possible in the value of the linear programming objective function if one additional unit of the scarce resource becomes available—or the decrease if one of the available units is lost. Alternatively, it may be defined as the maximum amount to be paid for an additional unit of a scarce or limited resource.

As dual prices are the product of a linear programming framework they suffer the same limitations and are based on the same assumptions as are relevant to linear programming (e.g. selling price and variable cost per unit are assumed constant for all output levels, fractional output levels are assumed to be possible, non-financial benefits and costs are excluded, demand and supply interdependencies are ignored and no explicit account is taken of uncertainty). Within these limits they provide a useful measure of the opportunity cost involved in using scarce resources.

However, there is a further reason for caution when dual prices are being used. They measure contribution changes resulting from marginal increases or decreases in resource availability. A large increase in the availability of a particular resource may mean that it is no longer an effective constraint on production and its shadow price becomes zero. Hence dual prices are of limited use in assessing the impact of non-marginal changes; in such cases the linear programme usually needs to be reformulated and resolved.

Provided the limiations mentioned in the previous section are borne in mind dual values discriminately applied have a number of possible uses.

First they provide an indication of which constraints are the most severe. A zero dual price attached to a resource indicates that it is not an effective constraint on production. Hence, it will not be worth while devoting any time finding additional units of such a resource. However, a company might usefully seek ways of relieving other constraints as a relaxation of them will lead to an increase in total contribution (as long as they have dual prices).

A second application of dual prices may arise when new opportunities not in the original plan are presented for consideration. Dual prices reflect the best marginal use of resources within the framework of the optimal plan, and, to be acceptable, a new opportunity should use the resources at least as profitably as this marginal use; in a situation of scarce resources the new opportunity, if accepted, will displace one or more of the opportunities included in the optimal plan.

However, dual prices alone will not reveal precisely how the production levels of opportunities within the optimal plan should be adjusted. The dual values act merely as a screening device for new opportunities.

A third use arises when all decisions are not taken by a central decision-making body with access to the linear programme (i.e. decentralised decision-making). To reduce the chance that resources are used sub-optimally they should be charged to those responsible for decisions at their total opportunity cost. As this includes the dual price value of scarce resources, only projects at least as efficient as those included in the optimal plan should be accepted.

A fourth use of dual prices is in the area of pricing and this is related to the second and third uses mentioned above.

## 70.

**MECH INTERNATIONAL LTD**

(a) The question requires the use of the transportation technique to tackle a recruitment problem. The fourteen applicants who have been short-listed represent the sources and the eleven jobs available the destinations. As the supply is greater than the demand, a dummy destination needs to be set up to absorb the excess supply.

Table 42. Given data for Mech International Ltd.

| | Available | | | Required | |
|---|---|---|---|---|---|
| Number | Category | Current salary | Number | Category | Salary offered |
| 2 | Accounts and DP | £4,800 | 2 | Accounts | £5,000 |
| 4 | Accounts | 4,600 | 3 | DP | 4,700 |
| 5 | DP | 4,500 | 6 | General | 4,400 |
| 3 | General | 4,200 | | | |
| 14 | | | 11 | | |

# APPENDIX 3. SUGGESTED ANSWERS TO EXAMINATION QUESTIONS

The three applicants who end up in the dummy will be those not offered posts. The costs of transportation are the salaries being offered, bearing in mind that an appointee will be paid a salary equal to the greater of his current salary and the company's minimum for the job.

The given data are summarised in Table 42.

The initial transportation tableau can be set up on basis of the data above. If an applicant cannot do a particular job then a very-high-cost $M$ is put into that cell to prevent an allocation being made.

Initial transportation matrix:

|  |  | Destinations | | | |
|---|---|---|---|---|---|
|  |  | Accounts 2 | DP 3 | General 6 | Dummy 3 |
| Accounts and DP | 2 | £5,000 | £4,800 | £4,800 | 0 |
| Accounts | 4 | £5,000 | $M$ | £4,600 | 0 |
| DP | 5 | $M$ | £4,700 | £4,500 | 0 |
| General | 3 | $M$ | $M$ | £4,400 | 0 |

First allocation; based on least cost:

|  |  | Accounts 3 | DP 3 | General 6 | Dummy 3 |
|---|---|---|---|---|---|
| Accounts and DP | 2 |  | 1 |  | 1 |
| Accounts | 4 | 2 |  |  | 2 |
| DP | 5 |  | 2 | 3 |  |
| General | 3 |  |  | 3 |  |

A check shows $m + n - 1$ cells are filled.

The cost of the above allocation is:

$$
\begin{aligned}
2 \times £5,000 &= £10,000 \\
1 \times £4,800 &= 4,800 \\
2 \times £4,700 &= 9,400 \\
3 \times £4,500 &= 13,500 \\
3 \times £4,400 &= 13,200 \\
&\phantom{=} \overline{£50,900}
\end{aligned}
$$

Test the first allocation for optimality by using shadow costs:

|  | $D_1$ | $D_2$ | $D_3$ | $D_4$ | Row shadow costs |
|---|---|---|---|---|---|
| $S_1$ | (50) | 48 | (46) | 0 | 0 |
| $S_2$ | 50 | (48) | (46) | 0 | 0 |
| $S_3$ | (49) | 47 | 45 | (−1) | −1 |
| $S_4$ | (48) | (46) | 44 | (−2) | −2 |
| Column shadow costs | 50 | 48 | 46 | 0 | |

*Tutorial notes*

(a) References $S_1, S_2, \ldots$ and $D_1, D_2, \ldots$ have been used for convenience.
(b) Shadow costs have been calculated using the equation $A = R + C$.
(c) Gross savings in cells not occupied have been shown in parentheses.

Comparing the gross savings with actual transportation costs shows that no further minimisation is possible. Hence the cheapest allocation is £50,900.

However, there are a number of alternative optimal solutions as the above solution is not unique. These alternatives can be obtained by reallocating into those cells where gross savings are equal to transportation costs. For example, cell $S_1D_1$ has a gross saving of 50 and an actual cost of 50. Similarly, cell $S_2D_3$ has gross savings equal to actual cost.

The reallocation process is indicated below considering cell $S_1D_1$. The existing solution is:

|  |  | Accounts 2 | DP 3 | General 6 | Dummy 3 |
|---|---|---|---|---|---|
| Accounts and DP | 2 | + | 1 |  | 1 − |
| Accounts | 4 | 2 − |  |  | 2 + |
| DP | 5 |  | 2 | 3 |  |
| General | 3 |  |  | 3 |  |

The reallocation gives:

|  | Accounts 2 | DP 3 | General 6 | Dummy 3 |
|---|---|---|---|---|
| Accounts and DP 2 | 1 | 1 |  |  |
| Accounts 4 | 1 |  |  | 3 |
| DP 5 |  | 2 | 3 |  |
| General 3 |  |  | 3 |  |

Cost: £50,900.

Other alternative solutions can be found in a similar fashion. They are listed below:

|  | Accounts 2 | DP 3 | General 6 | Dummy 3 |
|---|---|---|---|---|
| Accounts and DP 2 |  |  |  | 2 |
| Accounts 4 | 2 |  | 1 | 1 |
| DP 5 |  | 3 | 2 |  |
| General 3 |  |  | 3 |  |

|  | Accounts 2 | DP 3 | General 6 | Dummy 3 |
|---|---|---|---|---|
| Accounts and DP 2 | 2 |  |  |  |
| Accounts 4 |  |  | 1 | 3 |
| DP 5 |  | 3 | 2 |  |
| General 3 |  |  | 3 |  |

|  | Accounts<br>2 | DP<br>3 | General<br>6 | Dummy<br>3 |
|---|---|---|---|---|
| Accounts and DP   2 | 1 |  |  | 1 |
| Accounts   4 | 1 |  | 1 | 2 |
| DP   5 |  | 3 | 2 |  |
| General   3 |  |  | 3 |  |

(b) This part requires students to show by means of a simple algebraic example that transportation is a special case of linear programming.

Consider the following matrix:

|  | 20<br>$D_1$ | 20<br>$D_2$ | 25<br>$D_3$ | 35<br>$D_4$ |
|---|---|---|---|---|
| $S_1$   30 | £7 | £10 | £14 | £8 |
| $S_2$   40 | £7 | £11 | £12 | £6 |
| $S_3$   30 | £5 | £8 | £15 | £9 |

$S_1$, $S_2$ and $S_3$ represent sources with amounts of 30, 40 and 30 units of a particular product.

$D_1$, $D_2$, $D_3$ and $D_4$ represent destinations with requirements of 20, 20, 25 and 35 units. The unit costs of transportation are shown in the matrix.

The construction of a linear programming model for the situation above will adequately demonstrate that transportation is a special case of linear programming.

Let $x_{11}$, $x_{12}$, ... be the quantities to be transported from each source to each destination. The transportation matrix is restated with amounts transported shown in the appropriate cells and unit costs of transfer in the appropriate cell corner.

|  | $D_1$<br>20 | $D_2$<br>20 | $D_3$<br>25 | $D_4$<br>35 |
|---|---|---|---|---|
| $S_1$   30 | 7 / $x_{11}$ | 10 / $x_{12}$ | 14 / $x_{13}$ | 8 / $x_{14}$ |
| $S_2$   40 | 7 / $x_{21}$ | 11 / $x_{22}$ | 12 / $x_{23}$ | 6 / $x_{24}$ |
| $S_3$   30 | 5 / $x_{31}$ | 8 / $x_{32}$ | 15 / $x_{33}$ | 9 / $x_{34}$ |

# APPENDIX 3. SUGGESTED ANSWERS TO EXAMINATION QUESTIONS

This problem can be stated mathematically in the form:

Minimise $C = 7x_{11} + 10x_{12} + 14x_{13} + 8x_{14} + 7x_{21} + 11x_{22} + 12x_{23} + 6x_{24}$
$+ 5x_{31} + 8x_{32} + 15x_{33} + 9x_{34}$ (objective function),

subject to the following conditions:

$$x_{11} + x_{12} + x_{13} + x_{14} = 30 \quad (S_1 \text{ constraint})$$
$$x_{21} + x_{22} + x_{23} + x_{24} = 40 \quad (S_2 \text{ constraint})$$
$$x_{31} + x_{32} + x_{33} + x_{34} = 30 \quad (S_3 \text{ constraint})$$
$$x_{11} + x_{21} + x_{31} = 20 \quad (D_1 \text{ constraint})$$
$$x_{12} + x_{22} + x_{32} = 20 \quad (D_2 \text{ constraint})$$
$$x_{13} + x_{23} + x_{33} = 25 \quad (D_3 \text{ constraint})$$
$$x_{14} + x_{24} + x_{34} = 35 \quad (D_4 \text{ constraint})$$
$$x_{11}, x_{12}, \ldots, x_{34} \geqslant 0 \quad \text{(non-negativity conditions)}.$$

**71.**

**NEWTON COMPANY LTD**

(a) The given data are summarised below:

| Factory | Maximum output | Warehouse | Expected demand |
|---|---|---|---|
| ES | 210,000 | S | 80,000 |
| WL | 140,000 | L | 200,000 |
| M | 290,000 | C | 200,000 |
| | 640,000 | | 480,000 |

Variable distribution costs per unit:

| | S | L | C |
|---|---|---|---|
| ES | £2 | £4 | £4 |
| WL | 4 | 3 | 4 |
| M | 3 | 6 | 4 |

Variable costs of production at each factory per unit:

| | |
|---|---|
| ES | £11 |
| WL | £14 |
| M | £12 |

452   APPENDIX 3. SUGGESTED ANSWERS TO EXAMINATION QUESTIONS

The initial transportation matrix (bearing in mind that maximum supply exceeds demand) can be summarised as follows:

|  |  | Destination | | | |
|---|---|---|---|---|---|
|  |  | S<br>80,000 | L<br>200,000 | C<br>200,000 | Dummy<br>160,000 |
| Sources: | ES 210,000 | 13 | 15 | 15 | 0 |
|  | WL 140,000 | 18 | 17 | 18 | 0 |
|  | M 290,000 | 15 | 18 | 16 | 0 |

The present distribution schedule is:

All S requirements are from ES
L gets 140,000 from WL and 60,000 from E
C requirements are from M.

The costs of the present schedule (including transportation and production costs) are:

| S | 80,000 × £13 | = | £1,040,000 |
|---|---|---|---|
| L | 140,000 × £17 | = | 2,380,000 |
|  | 60,000 × £15 | = | 900,000 |
| C | 200,000 × £16 | = | 3,200,000 |
|  | Total cost |  | £7,520,000 |

The present distribution policy is based on distance, i.e. supplying warehouses from those factories which are closest to them.

(b) This part required students to determine the policy which achieved the minimum total cost. The transportation matrix is restated below:

|  |  | S<br>80,000 | L<br>200,000 | C<br>200,000 | Dummy<br>160,000 |
|---|---|---|---|---|---|
| Sources: | ES 210,000 | 13 | 15 | 15 | 0 |
|  | WL 140,000 | 18 | 17 | 18 | 0 |
|  | M 290,000 | 15 | 18 | 16 | 0 |

First allocation, based on least cost:

|  |  | Destination | | | |
|---|---|---|---|---|---|
|  |  | S<br>80 | L<br>200 | C<br>200 | my<br>0 |
| ES | 210 | 80 | 130 |  |  |
| WL | 140 |  | 70 |  |  |
| M | 290 |  |  | 20 |  |

$m = 3$
$n = 4$
$m + n - 1 = 6$.

The above solution is feasible as $m + n - 1$ cells are occupied. The cost of the above solution is £7,380,000.

Test for optimality:

|     | S    | L    | C    | Dummy | Row shadow costs |
|-----|------|------|------|-------|------------------|
| ES  | 13   | 15   | (14) | (−2)  | 0                |
| WL  | (15) | 17   | (16) | 0     | 2                |
| M   | (15) | (17) | 16   | 0     | 2                |
| Column shadow costs | 13 | 15 | 14 | −2 | |

The allocation above is optimal as no unoccupied cells represent further minimisation. However, in cell MS the gross savings are equivalent to actual transportation costs. This represents an alternative optimal solution. The reallocation to arrive at this is shown below:

|        |     | S 80 | L 200 | C 200 | Dummy 160 |
|--------|-----|------|-------|-------|-----------|
| ES     | 210 | 80⁻  | 130⁺  |       |           |
| WL     | 140 |      | 70⁻   |       | 70⁺       |
| M      | 290 | +    |       | 200   | 90⁻       |

Reallocation:

|        |     | S 80 | L 200 | C 200 | Dummy 160 |
|--------|-----|------|-------|-------|-----------|
| ES     | 210 | 10   | 200   |       |           |
| WL     | 140 |      |       |       | 140       |
| M      | 290 | 70   | 200   | 200   | 20        |

Cost: £7,380,000.

Note that in relation to 'normal procedures' the optimal solutions represent savings of £140,000.

(c) The company is considering the closure of the WL factory. The question enquires as to the increase in the total variable cost of production and distribution this will cause. Inspection of the alternative optimal solution above shows that factory WL does not make any supplies. Hence in production and distribution terms there is no change or effect if factory WL is closed.

## 72.

**MULTEL LTD**

(a) Situations arise where it may not be economical or practical to ship directly from sources to destinations. The commodities may pass through intermediate warehouses, for instance, before eventually reaching their ultimate destination. This case is referred to as the transhipment problem. The transportation model cannot handle this problem directly. A slight modification, however, would allow the use of the same technique.

In Multel Ltd. the question gave the hint that the starting point is to establish the least costly means of supplying each demand centre from each of the plants. Figure 144 should help clarify the various routes which can be taken.

Figure 144 shows that plant 1 can supply $D_1$, $D_2$ and $D_3$ either through $W_1$ or through $W_2$. Similar routes could be shown from plants 2 and 3.

A useful starting point in the solution is to extract the mass of data given:

|       | *Production capacity* |       | *Demand*   |
|-------|----------------------|-------|------------|
| $P_1$ | 100 units            | $D_1$ | 90 units   |
| $P_2$ | 200 units            | $D_2$ | 80 units   |
| $P_3$ | 100 units            | $D_3$ | 90 units   |
|       | 400 units            |       | 260 units  |

Costs are:

|       | *Production* |       | *Handling* |
|-------|--------------|-------|------------|
| $P_1$ | £3/unit      |       |            |
| $P_2$ | £4/unit      | $W_1$ | £2/unit    |
| $P_3$ | £1/unit      | $W_2$ | £3/unit    |

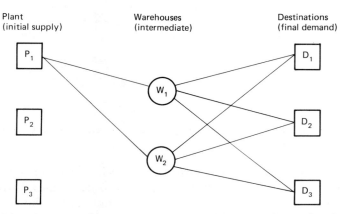

Fig. 144. *Choice of routes from one of three plants to three destinations via two warehouses.*

|  | Transport (Plants to warehouses) | | | Transport (Warehouses to destinations) | | |
|---|---|---|---|---|---|---|
|  | $W_1$ | $W_2$ |  | $D_1$ | $D_2$ | $D_3$ |
| $P_1$ | 6 | 6 | $W_1$ | 3 | 5 | 8 |
| $P_2$ | 5 | 5 | $W_2$ | 5 | 3 | 9 |
| $P_3$ | 13 | 4 |  |  |  |  |

A total cost matrix can now be built up showing the costs of each route. Remember that each demand centre can be supplied by each plant in two different ways. The route to be selected will be the one that is cheaper.

A convenient format for summarising the problem is shown in Fig. 145.

Destinations

|  |  | $D_1$ | | $D_2$ | | $D_3$ | |
|---|---|---|---|---|---|---|---|
|  |  | $W_1$ | $W_2$ | $W_1$ | $W_2$ | $W_1$ | $W_2$ |
| Plants | $P_1$ | **14** | 17 | 16 | **15** | **19** | 21 |
|  | $P_2$ | **14** | 17 | 16 | **15** | **19** | 21 |
|  | $P_3$ | 19 | **13** | 21 | **11** | 24 | **17** |

Fig. 145. *Total cost matrix for three plants, two warehouses and three destinations.*

The figures in squares represent the cheapest way of supplying each destination from each plant.

For example, it is cheaper to supply $D_1$ from $P_1$ through $W_1$ (14) rather than through $W_2$ (17).

The initial matrix can now be reduced to transportation format:

|  |  |  | Destinations | | | |
|---|---|---|---|---|---|---|
|  |  |  | $D_1$ 90 | $D_2$ 80 | $D_3$ 90 | Dummy 140 |
| | $P_1$ | 100 | 14 | 15 | 19 | 0 |
| Plants: | $P_2$ | 200 | 14 | 15 | 19 | 0 |
| | $P_3$ | 100 | 13 | 11 | 17 | 0 |

Standard transportation procedures can now be applied to arrive at an optimal solution.

First allocation, based on least cost:

|     |     | D₁ 90 | D₂ 80 | D₃ 90 | Dummy 140 |
|-----|-----|-------|-------|-------|-----------|
| P₁  | 100 |       |       |       | 100       |
| P₂  | 200 | 70    |       | 90    | 40        |
| P₃  | 100 | 20    | 80    |       |           |

$m + n - 1$ cells are filled.

First allocation, tested for optimality:

|     |     | D₁ 90 | D₂ 80 | D₃ 90 | Dummy 140 |     |
|-----|-----|-------|-------|-------|-----------|-----|
| P₁  | 100 | (14)  | (12)  | (19)  | 0         | 0   |
| P₂  | 200 | 14    | (12)  | 19    | 0         | 0   |
| P₃  | 100 | 13    | 11    | (18)  | (−1)      | −1  |
|     |     | 14    | 12    | 19    | 0         |     |

Cell P₃D₃ represents further minimisation as actual costs are 17 but gross saving is 18. Hence there will be a net saving of 1 for every item moved into this cell. Reallocate as many items as possible into this cell.

First allocation, reallocated:

|     |     | D₁ 90 | D₂ 80 | D₃ 90 | Dummy 140 |
|-----|-----|-------|-------|-------|-----------|
| P₁  | 100 |       |       |       | 100       |
| P₂  | 200 | 70⁺   |       | 90⁻   | 40        |
| P₃  | 100 | 20⁻   | 80    | +     |           |

The maximum units that can be moved into P₃D₃ are 20.

# APPENDIX 3. SUGGESTED ANSWERS TO EXAMINATION QUESTIONS

Second allocation:

|  |  | D₁ 90 | D₂ 80 | D₃ 90 | Dummy 140 |
|---|---|---|---|---|---|
| P₁ | 100 |  |  |  | 100 |
| P₂ | 200 | 90 |  | 70 | 40 |
| P₃ | 100 |  | 80 | 20 |  |

$m + n - 1$ cells are filled.

Second allocation, tested for optimality:

|  |  | D₁ 90 | D₂ 80 | D₃ 90 | Dummy 140 |  |
|---|---|---|---|---|---|---|
| P₁ | 100 | (14) | (13) | (19) | 0 | 0 |
| P₂ | 200 | 14 | (13) | 19 | 0 | 0 |
| P₃ | 100 | (12) | 11 | 17 | (−2) | −2 |
|  |  | 14 | 13 | 19 | 0 |  |

Comparison of gross savings in unused cells with actual costs shows that no further minimisation exists. However, the solution is not unique as alternative solutions with the same costs exist. (For example cell P₁D₃).

The costs of the solution are:

$$£90 \times 14 + £80 \times 11 + £70 \times 19 + £20 \times 17 = \underline{\underline{£3,810}}.$$

*Tutorial note: Alternative optimal solutions are listed below:*

|  | D₁ | D₂ | D₃ | Dummy |
|---|---|---|---|---|
| P₁ |  |  | 70 | 30 |
| P₂ | 90 |  |  | 110 |
| P₃ |  | 80 | 20 |  |

|    | $D_1$ | $D_2$ | $D_3$ | Dummy |
|----|-------|-------|-------|-------|
| $P_1$ | 90 |   |    | 10  |
| $P_2$ |    |   | 70 | 130 |
| $P_3$ |    | 80| 20 |     |

|    | $D_1$ | $D_2$ | $D_3$ | Dummy |
|----|-------|-------|-------|-------|
| $P_1$ | 90 |   | 10 |     |
| $P_2$ |    |   | 60 | 140 |
| $P_3$ |    | 80| 20 |     |

(b) This part of the question deals with the concept of sub-optimisation. Splitting the problem into two and solving the two parts separately does not necessarily lead to the best solution for the total problem.

## 73.

**BROWN CHEMICAL COMPANY**
(a) and (b)
   The given problem has to be formulated using the transportation model and solved. The situation is concerned with profit maximisation.
   The given data are summarised below:

|   | Plant capacities |       | Customers' orders |
|---|------------------|-------|-------------------|
| X | 6,000            | $C_1$ | 2,000             |
| Y | 3,000            | $C_2$ | 5,000             |
|   |                  | $C_3$ | 3,500             |
|   |                  | $C_4$ | 2,500             |
|   | 9,000            |       | 13,000            |

Costs:

|   | Distribution |       |       |       | Variable production/unit |     |
|---|--------------|-------|-------|-------|--------------------------|-----|
|   | $C_1$ | $C_2$ | $C_3$ | $C_4$ |   |     |
| X | £16   | £15   | £14   | £18   | X | £10 |
| Y | £15   | £15   | £14   | £15   | Y | £12 |

# APPENDIX 3. SUGGESTED ANSWERS TO EXAMINATION QUESTIONS

Selling price per unit:  To $C_1$  £46
 To $C_2$  £42
 To $C_3$  £40
 To $C_4$  £44

The starting point is to calculate the contribution per unit of supplying $C_1$, $C_2$, $C_3$ and $C_4$ both from plant X and plant Y.

*From plant X:*

|  | Contribution/unit | | | |
| --- | --- | --- | --- | --- |
|  | $C_1$ | $C_2$ | $C_3$ | $C_4$ |
| Distribution | £16 | £15 | £14 | £18 |
| Variable production | 10 | 10 | 10 | 10 |
|  | 26 | 25 | 24 | 28 |
| Selling price | 46 | 42 | 40 | 44 |
| Contribution | 20 | 17 | 16 | 16 |

*From plant Y:*

|  | Contribution/unit | | | |
| --- | --- | --- | --- | --- |
|  | $C_1$ | $C_2$ | $C_3$ | $C_4$ |
| Distribution | £15 | £15 | £14 | £15 |
| Variable production | 12 | 12 | 12 | 12 |
|  | 27 | 27 | 26 | 27 |
| Selling price | 46 | 42 | 40 | 44 |
| Contribution | 19 | 15 | 14 | 17 |

The initial transportation matrix can now be formulated in contribution terms.

|  |  | $C_1$ 2,000 | $C_2$ 5,000 | $C_3$ 3,500 | $C_4$ 2,500 |
| --- | --- | --- | --- | --- | --- |
| X | 6,000 | 20 | 17 | — | 16 |
| Y | 3,000 | 19 | 15 | 14 | 17 |
| Dummy | 4,000 | 0 | 0 | 0 | 0 |

Customer $C_3$ can only be supplied from plant Y.

The contribution matrix above can be converted into an opportunity loss matrix to facilitate application of standard minimisation procedures. The underlying theme here is that, by minimising opportunity losses, profits (contributions) will automatically be maximised. The conversion process is straightforward. Subtract all elements in the table from the highest contribution figure. This gives:

|       |       | $C_1$ 2,000 | $C_2$ 5,000 | $C_3$ 3,500 | $C_4$ 2,500 |
|-------|-------|-------------|-------------|-------------|-------------|
| 6,000 | X     | 0           | 3           | —           | 4           |
| 3,000 | Y     | 1           | 5           | 6           | 3           |
| 4,000 | Dummy | 20          | 20          | 20          | 20          |

First allocation, based on least cost:

|       |       | $C_1$ 2,000 | $C_2$ 5,000 | $C_3$ 3,500 | $C_4$ 2,500 |
|-------|-------|-------------|-------------|-------------|-------------|
| X     | 6,000 | 2,000       | 4,000       |             |             |
| Y     | 3,000 |             | 500         |             | 2,500       |
| Dummy | 4,000 |             | 500         | 3,500       |             |

$m + n - 1$ cells are filled.

The solution can be tested for optimality.

First allocation, tested for optimality:

|       | $C_1$ | $C_2$ | $C_3$ | $C_4$ |     |
|-------|-------|-------|-------|-------|-----|
| X     | 0     | 3     | (3)   | (1)   | 0   |
| Y     | (2)   | 5     | (5)   | 3     | 2   |
| Dummy | (17)  | 20    | 20    | (18)  | 17  |
|       | 0     | 3     | 3     | 1     |     |

Comparing gross savings in unused cells with actual transportation costs it will be seen that further minimisation is possible. Cell $YC_1$ for instance which at present is unused represents further reductions in cost.

# APPENDIX 3. SUGGESTED ANSWERS TO EXAMINATION QUESTIONS

First allocation, reallocated:

|   |   | $C_1$ 2,000 | $C_2$ 5,000 | $C_3$ 3,500 | $C_4$ 2,500 |
|---|---|---|---|---|---|
| X | 6,000 | 2,000⁻ | 4,000⁺ |   |   |
| Y | 3,000 | + | 500⁻ |   | 2,500 |
| Dummy | 4,000 |   | 500 | 3,500 |   |

Reallocate as many units as possible into cell $YC_1$. The maximum amount possible is 500.

Second allocation:

|   |   | $C_1$ 2,000 | $C_2$ 5,000 | $C_3$ 3,500 | $C_4$ 2,500 |
|---|---|---|---|---|---|
| X | 6,000 | 1,500 | 4,500 |   |   |
| Y | 3,000 | 500 |   |   | 2,500 |
| Dummy | 4,000 |   | 500 | 3,500 |   |

Second allocation, tested for optimality:

|   | $C_1$ | $C_2$ | $C_3$ | $C_4$ |   |
|---|---|---|---|---|---|
| X | 0 | 3 | (3) | (2) | 0 |
| Y | 1 | (4) | (4) | 3 | 1 |
| Dummy | (17) | 20 | 20 | (19) | 17 |
|   | 0 | 3 | 3 | 2 |   |

The allocation above is optimal as no further saving arises.

>    Plant X supplies $C_1$ with 1,500 units
>    Plant X supplies $C_2$ with 4,500 units
>    Plant Y supplies $C_1$ with   500 units
>    Plant Y supplies $C_4$ with 2,500 units
>         Total profit = £158,500.

*Tutorial note: On the basis of the allocation above $C_3$ receives no items and $C_2$ receives only 4,500 units (i.e. he is 500 short).*

(c) Even if the industrial dispute were resolved and customer $C_3$ could be supplied from plant X the solution remains unchanged. Examination of cell $XC_3$ in the second optimality test shows that no improvement is possible through this cell.

## 74.

### XW LIMITED

The given problem is one of maximisation. The answer given below is abbreviated as previous answers were given in great detail.

The first step would be to find unit profits. These are given by selling price, minus transportation material and labour costs.

The profit table is:

|        |   |     | Warehouse 1 — 80 | Warehouse 2 — 120 | Warehouse 3 — 130 | Warehouse 4 — 110 | Dummy — 110 |
|--------|---|-----|----|-----|-----|-----|-----|
| Plants | A | 140 | 6  | 8   | 13  | 5   | 0   |
|        | B | 100 | 5  | 7   | 12  | 2   | 0   |
|        | C | 150 | 10 | 12  | 6   | 4   | 0   |
|        | D | 160 | 6  | 9   | 13  | 1   | 0   |

The table above can be converted into an opportunity loss table and standard minimisation procedures applied. The solution obtained will not be unique and will give a total profit of £4,330. One possible solution will be for:

A to supply 30 to 3 and 110 to 4,

B to supply 100 to dummy,

C to supply 80 to 1 and 70 to 2,

D to supply 50 to 2, 100 to 3 and 10 to dummy.

## 75.

Once again an abbreviated answer is given so as to encourage students to work through the various stages rather than merely auditing answers.

The total requirements of the shop are 900 dresses but the total availability is only 850 dresses. A dummy supply capable of providing 50 dresses must be included so that the table balances. The dummy will be given zero profit per dress.

# APPENDIX 3. SUGGESTED ANSWERS TO EXAMINATION QUESTIONS

The allocation which yields maximum profit is listed below:

|  |  | Profit |
|---|---|---|
| Manufacturer A | 100 size I dresses | £250 |
|  | 50 size IV dresses | 100 |
| Manufacturer B | 450 size III dresses | 2,475 |
| Manufacturer C | 200 size II dresses | 900 |
|  | 50 size IV dresses | 125 |
|  | Total profit | £3,850 |

Students can easily confirm that the solution is not uniquely optimal (some dresses can be ordered from manufacturer A in sizes II and III and from manufacturer B in size I).

**76.**

**WELDSTONE ENGINEERING COMPANY**
The given table is restated below:

|  |  | Product |  |  |  |
|---|---|---|---|---|---|
|  |  | A | B | C | D |
| Plant | 1 | 25 | 18 | 23 | 14 |
|  | 2 | 38 | 15 | 53 | 23 |
|  | 3 | 15 | 17 | 41 | 30 |
|  | 4 | 26 | 28 | 36 | 29 |

*Step 1* Subtract the smallest element in each column from all elements in that column:

|  |  | Product |  |  |  |
|---|---|---|---|---|---|
|  |  | A | B | C | D |
| Plant | 1 | 10 | 3 | 0 | 0 |
|  | 2 | 23 | 0 | 30 | 9 |
|  | 3 | 0 | 2 | 18 | 16 |
|  | 4 | 11 | 13 | 13 | 15 |

*Step 2* Subtract the smallest element in each row from all elements in that row:

|  |  | Product |  |  |  |
|---|---|---|---|---|---|
|  |  | A | B | C | D |
| Plant | 1 | 10 | 3 | 0 | 0 |
|  | 2 | 23 | 0 | 30 | 9 |
|  | 3 | 0 | 2 | 18 | 16 |
|  | 4 | 0 | 2 | 2 | 4 |

*Tutorial note: The order of steps 1 and 2 does not influence the optimal solution.*

*Step 3* Draw the minimum number of lines (horizontal and/or vertical to cover all the zero):

Product

|  | | A | B | C | D |
|---|---|---|---|---|---|
| Plant | 1 | ~~10~~ | ~~3~~ | ~~0~~ | ~~0~~ |
|  | 2 | ~~23~~ | ~~0~~ | ~~30~~ | ~~9~~ |
|  | 3 | 0 | 2 | 18 | 16 |
|  | 4 | 0 | 2 | 2 | 4 |

As the number of lines (3) is less than the number of assignments to be made further procedures are required.

*Step 4* This is to formulate a revised cost matrix from the matrix of the table in step 3.

Select the smallest element in the matrix which was not covered by a straight line (in the step 3 table this value is 2).

Subtract this element from all other elements not covered by straight lines.

Add this smallest element to all elements that are covered by the intersection of two lines.

All other covered elements not at an intersection remain unchanged.

The revised matrix obtained is shown next:

Product

|  | | A | B | C | D |
|---|---|---|---|---|---|
| Plant | 1 | 12 | 3 | 0 | 0 |
|  | 2 | 25 | 0 | 30 | 9 |
|  | 3 | 0 | 0 | 16 | 14 |
|  | 4 | 0 | 0 | 0 | 2 |

*Step 5* Repeat step 3. The minimum number of lines now equals the number of assignments to be made. This is shown below:

Product

|  | | A | B | C | D |
|---|---|---|---|---|---|
| Plant | 1 | ~~12~~ | ~~3~~ | ~~0~~ | ~~0~~ |
|  | 2 | 25 | 0 | 30 | 9 |
|  | 3 | 0 | 0 | 16 | 14 |
|  | 4 | ~~0~~ | ~~0~~ | ~~0~~ | ~~2~~ |

# APPENDIX 3. SUGGESTED ANSWERS TO EXAMINATION QUESTIONS

An optimal assignment can now be made. This is:

| Plant | Product | Cost |
|---|---|---|
| 1 | D | £14,000 |
| 2 | B | 15,000 |
| 3 | A | 15,000 |
| 4 | C | 36,000 |
| | | £80,000 |

## 77.

### LUCKNOW COTTON MILLS

This question is concerned with profit maximisation. The first step is to arrive at a profit matrix by subtracting production costs from appropriate sales revenue. The resulting profit matrix is given below:

|  | | Products | | | |
|---|---|---|---|---|---|
| | | 1 | 2 | 3 | 4 |
| Mills | A | 1 | 8 | 4 | 1 |
| | B | 5 | 7 | 6 | 5 |
| | C | 3 | 5 | 4 | 2 |
| | D | 3 | 1 | 6 | 3 |

*Preliminary step* Convert the matrix into a form suitable for minimisation. Subtract each element in the table from the largest figure (8) to produce the matrix for minimisation:

|  | | Products | | | |
|---|---|---|---|---|---|
| | | 1 | 2 | 3 | 4 |
| Mills | A | 7 | 0 | 4 | 7 |
| | B | 3 | 1 | 2 | 3 |
| | C | 5 | 3 | 4 | 6 |
| | D | 5 | 7 | 2 | 5 |

Standard minimisation procedures can now be applied.

*Step 1* Subtract the smallest element in each row from all elements in that row:

|  | | Products | | | |
|---|---|---|---|---|---|
| | | 1 | 2 | 3 | 4 |
| Mills | A | 7 | 0 | 4 | 7 |
| | B | 2 | 0 | 1 | 2 |
| | C | 2 | 0 | 1 | 3 |
| | D | 3 | 5 | 0 | 3 |

*Step 2* Subtract the smallest element in each column from all elements in that column:

Products

|  | | 1 | 2 | 3 | 4 |
|---|---|---|---|---|---|
| Mills | A | 5 | 0 | 4 | 5 |
|  | B | 0 | 0 | 1 | 0 |
|  | C | 0 | 0 | 1 | 1 |
|  | D | 1 | 5 | 0 | 1 |

*Step 3* Draw the minimum number of lines to cover all the zeros:

Products

|  | | 1 | 2 | 3 | 4 |
|---|---|---|---|---|---|
| Mills | A | 5 | 0 | 4 | 5 |
|  | B | 0 | 0 | 1 | 0 |
|  | C | 0 | 0 | 1 | 1 |
|  | D | 1 | 5 | 0 | 1 |

As the minimum number of lines is equal to the number of assignments to be made an optimal assignment can now be made:

| *Mill* | *Product* | *Profit* |
|---|---|---|
| A | 2 | £8 |
| B | 4 | 5 |
| C | 1 | 3 |
| D | 3 | 6 |
|  |  | £22 |

The overall profit is found to be £22.

## 78.

**MIDDLESAM MANAGEMENT CONSULTANTS**

The given situation is concerned with cost minimisation and the table is restated below:

Jobs

|  |  | 1 | 2 | 3 | 4 | 5 | 6 |
|---|---|---|---|---|---|---|---|
| Consultants | A | 7 | 7 | 3 | 6 | 10 | 11 |
|  | B | 8 | 9 | – | 5 | 8 | 10 |
|  | C | 9 | 10 | 11 | 13 | 13 | 8 |
|  | D | 6 | 6 | 8 | – | 12 | 13 |
|  | E | 5 | 5 | 9 | 10 | 10 | 12 |
|  | F | 8 | 4 | 10 | 12 | 9 | – |

Because of technical deficiencies particular jobs cannot be done by particular consultants. These cells are assigned a very high cost $M$ and standard minimisation procedures are used.

It can be shown that there is no unique solution and one optimal arrangement is shown below:

|  | | Jobs | | | | | |
|---|---|---|---|---|---|---|---|
|  | | 1 | 2 | 3 | 4 | 5 | 6 |
| Consultants | A | 6 | 6 | 0 | 3 | 4 | 8 |
|  | B | 5 | 6 | $M$ | 0 | 0 | 5 |
|  | C | 3 | 4 | 3 | 5 | 2 | 0 |
|  | D | 0 | 0 | 0 | $M$ | 1 | 5 |
|  | E | 0 | 0 | 2 | 3 | 0 | 5 |
|  | F | 4 | 0 | 4 | 6 | 0 | $M$ |

The optimal assignment based on the above table:

| Consultant | Job | Cost |
|---|---|---|
| A | 3 | £3 |
| B | 4 | 5 |
| C | 6 | 8 |
| D | 1 | 6 |
| E | 5 | 10 |
| F | 2 | 4 |
|  |  | £36 |

## 79.

**SMITSUBASHI PLC**

The given problem has unequal rows and columns and is concerned with the closure of a particular factory.

The given data is restated below:

Product production cost per unit (£)

|  |  | Products | | | |
|---|---|---|---|---|---|
|  |  | N | I | P | O |
| Factory | 1 | 71 | 78 | 93 | 76 |
|  | 2 | 69 | 78 | 87 | 74 |
|  | 3 | 72 | 80 | 89 | 76 |
|  | 4 | 73 | 80 | 86 | 78 |
|  | 5 | 65 | 84 | 92 | 72 |

Selling prices for products are:

|    | N   | I   | P    | O   |
|----|-----|-----|------|-----|
| SP | £80 | £90 | £100 | £85 |

The first stage in the solution is to convert the given data into profit format. In addition, to use standard procedures a balanced matrix is needed. This is done by introducing a fifth column as a dummy with zero profits.

The profit matrix is shown below:

|         |   | \multicolumn{5}{c}{Profits (£) Products} |
|---------|---|----|----|----|----|-------|
|         |   | N  | I  | P  | O  | Dummy |
|         | 1 | 9  | 12 | 7  | 9  | 0     |
|         | 2 | 11 | 12 | 13 | 11 | 0     |
| Factory | 3 | 8  | 10 | 11 | 9  | 0     |
|         | 4 | 7  | 10 | 14 | 7  | 0     |
|         | 5 | 15 | 6  | 8  | 13 | 0     |

The next stage would involve transforming the above matrix into an opportunity loss matrix. Standard minimisation procedures can then be applied.

It will be easily confirmed that factory 3 should be closed.

**80.**

(a) *See* Fig. 146.

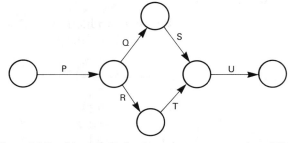

Fig. 146. *Network for answer to question 80(a).*

(b) *See* Fig. 147.

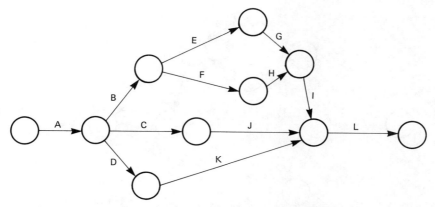

Fig. 147. *Network for answer to question 80(b).*

*Tutorial note: A useful drawing method is to construct a rough diagram first, check the logic of the diagram constructed against the given logic and then make the diagram presentable.*

**81.**

(a) *See* Fig. 148.

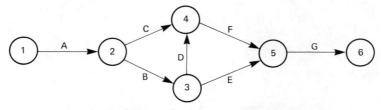

Fig. 148. *Network for answer to question 81(a).*

(b) *See* Fig. 149.

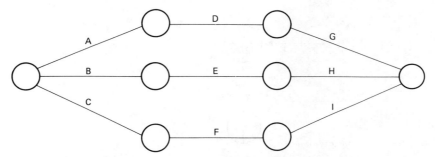

Fig. 149. *Network for answer to question 81(b).*

(c) *See* Fig. 150.

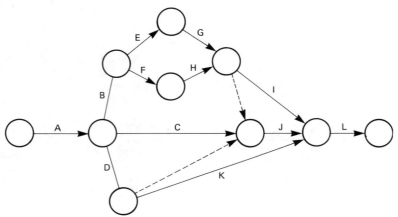

Fig. 150. *Network for answer to question 81(c).*

**82.**

(a) Network for insurance company: *See* Fig. 151.

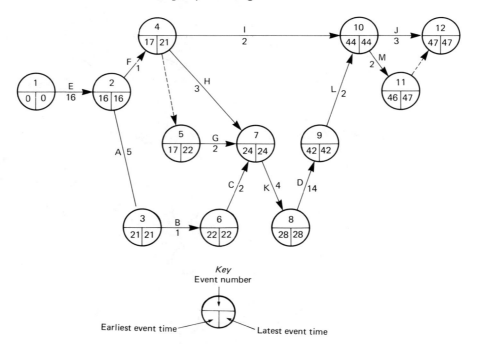

Fig. 151. *Network for answer to question 82(a).*

# APPENDIX 3. SUGGESTED ANSWERS TO EXAMINATION QUESTIONS

(b) The minimum time that the alterations can take from commencement of the design stage is taken to represent the minimum project time. This is given by the critical path E–A–B–C–K–D–L–J with a duration of 47 weeks. (This is the longest route of jobs, i.e. the path with zero total float.)

(c) It is suggested that by reducing the number of builders invited to tender, the estimates could be obtained in three weeks. The original time given for this was five weeks (job A). As job A lies on the critical path, this will reduce the duration of the critical path to 45 weeks. As there is sufficient float on the non-critical routes (this can be confirmed by examining all the routes) the project duration can be reduced to 45 weeks.

(d) Independent float is the amount of time an activity can be delayed when all preceding activities are completed as late as possible and all succeeding activities are started as early as possible (Fig. 152).

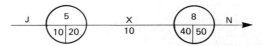

Fig. 152. *Network for answer to question 82(d).*

| | |
|---|---|
| The earliest start for N is time (hence *x* must be completed by this time) | 40 |
| The latest finish for J is time (hence *x* cannot start before this time) | 20 |
| The time available for *x* | 20 |
| Time taken by *x* | 10 |
| ∴ Independent float for *x* | 10 |

## 83.

*See* critical path network in Fig. 153.

(a) The critical path is given by A–H–J–L–M–O–P–Q with a duration of 41 weeks. The project had to be completed by the end of week 38. Hence the deadline has been extended by three weeks costing an extra 3 × £300 = £900.

(b) Activity K has an earliest start of 9 weeks and a latest finish of 26 weeks. The booking can remain as it is as K has a total float of 13 weeks.

(c) Doing L and E in parallel can be shown to extend the project duration by 4 weeks. This would increase the cost by £1,200 and hence the minimum savings would have to be £1,200.

# 472 APPENDIX 3. SUGGESTED ANSWERS TO EXAMINATION QUESTIONS

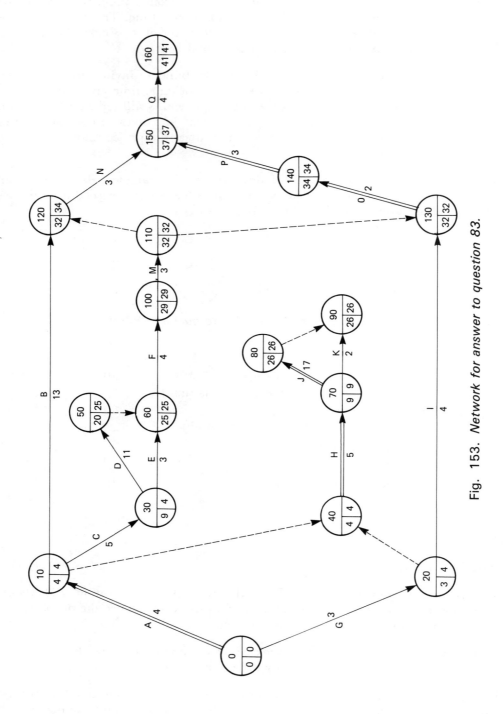

Fig. 153. Network for answer to question 83.

APPENDIX 3. SUGGESTED ANSWERS TO EXAMINATION QUESTIONS 473

(d) A possible approach where activity durations involve some uncertainty is to use PERT (project evaluation and review technique). PERT allows for uncertainty by assigning 3 times to each job (optimistic, most likely and pessimistic). The critical path calculation is similar to that for CPA, but it has the advantage of calculating variances for each activity and hence probabilities associated with different project times.

### 84.

COMPUTER BALANCE COMPANY LTD

(a) The completed network is shown in Fig. 154. The critical path is given by B–F–H with a duration of 12 weeks. (This is the longest route of jobs, i.e. the path with zero total float.)

The total cost of the project consists of two components: the normal (direct) cost of completing each job and the variable overhead (indirect) cost which is based on time.

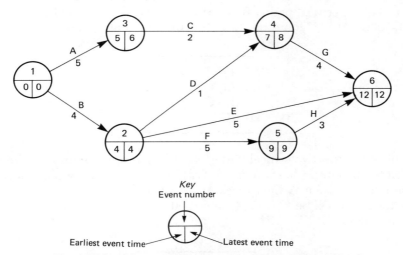

Fig. 154. *Network for answer to question 84.*

| | |
|---|---:|
| Normal costs add up to | £1,800 |
| Overhead cost at £200/week for 12 weeks | 2,400 |
| Total cost | £4,200 |

*Tutorial note: A common examination mistake is to add up the normal costs only for jobs on the critical path. Remember, for the project to be completed all jobs must be done and hence the normal costs of all jobs must be included.*

(b) This part requires the cost of completing the project in the shortest time and the duration of the project if total cost is to be minimised. A conventional cost analysis (crashing) procedure can be adapted. First, work out cost slopes.

| Job | A | B | C | D | E | F | G | H |
|---|---|---|---|---|---|---|---|---|
| Possible reductions | 2 | – | 1 | – | 2 | 1 | – | 1 |
| Extra cost | £200 | – | £300 | – | £150 | £50 | – | £200 |
| Cost slope | £100 | – | £300 | – | £75 | £50 | – | £200 |

Next, list all the different routes.

$$\begin{aligned} B-F-H &= 12 \\ A-C-G &= 11 \\ B-D-G &= 9 \\ B-E &= 9 \end{aligned}$$

To reduce project time, the length of the critical path must be reduced. Select the job with the lowest cost slope, i.e. F. Reduce F by 1 at a cost of £50. There will now be two critical paths, B–F–H and A–C–G. The total cost will be £4,050 (4,200 − 200 + 50). Update the times on the different routes:

$$\begin{aligned} B-F-H &= 11 \\ A-C-G &= 11 \\ B-D-G &= 9 \\ B-E &= 9 \end{aligned}$$

As there are now two critical paths, any further saving in project time must take place on both routes. On route B–F–H, H can be cut by 1 week at a cost of £200. On path A–C–G cut A by 1 week at a cost of £100.

The total cost will be £4,150 (4,050 − 200 + 200 + 100). Update the times on the different routes.

$$\begin{aligned} B-F-H &= 10 \\ A-C-G &= 10 \\ B-D-G &= 9 \\ B-E &= 9 \end{aligned}$$

There is no further reduction in time possible on route B–F–H. The other critical path A–C–G can be cut but this is pointless as B–F–H would remain critical.

The required answers can now be given. The cost of completing the project in the shortest time is £4,150. The corresponding time is 10 weeks. The duration of the project if total cost is to be minimised is 11 weeks at a cost of £4,050.

*Tutorial note: The above answer was given in slightly greater detail than would be required in examinations. Updating for instance can be shown on a continuous basis, for example:*

|  | F by 1 | A by 1<br>H by 1 |
|---|---|---|
| B–F–H | 12 | 11 | 10 |
| A–C–G | 11 | 11 | 10 |
| B–D–G | 9 | 9 | 9 |
| B–E | 9 | 9 | 9 |

**85.**

(a) The network is shown in Fig. 155. The minimum time in which the project can be completed is given by the critical path A–C–E–G, which has a length of 14 days.

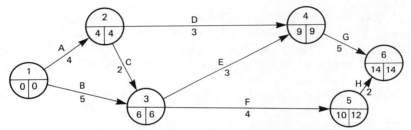

Fig. 155. *Network for answer to question 85(a)*.

(b) The given conditions are changed so that activity F has also to precede activity G. The network will have to be adapted and is shown in Fig. 156. The minimum time in which the project can now be completed is given by the new critical path ACFG, which has a length of 15 days.

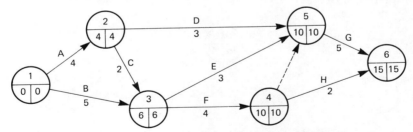

Fig. 156. *Network for answer to question 85(b)*.

(c) This part requires a crashing exercise based on the following data:

| Activity | A | B | C | D | E | F | G | H |
|---|---|---|---|---|---|---|---|---|
| Normal time | 4 | 5 | 2 | 3 | 3 | 4 | 5 | 2 |
| Crash time | 4 | 3 | 2 | 2 | 2 | 3 | 3 | 1 |
| Extra cost | – | 200 | – | 150 | 50 | 200 | 250 | 300 |
| Cost slope | – | 100 | – | 150 | 50 | 200 | 125 | 300 |

(The crashing exercise is to be carried out on the original network.)

|         |    | E by 1 | G by 1 | G and F by 1 |
|---------|----|--------|--------|--------------|
| A–C–E–G | 14 | 13     | 12     | 11           |
| B–E–G   | 13 | 12     | 11     | 10           |
| A–D–G   | 12 | 12     | 11     | 10           |
| A–C–F–H | 12 | 12     | 12     | 11           |
| B–F–H   | 11 | 11     | 10     | 10           |

*Crashing*

*Step 1*  Reduce E by 1. The critical path will reduce to 13 days and the extra cost will be £50.

*Step 2*  Reduce G by 1. There will now be two critical paths, both with a length of 12 days. The total extra cost is £175 (50 + 125).

*Step 3*  Reduce G by 1 and F by 1. A–C–E–G and A–C–F–H will remain critical with a length of 11. The total extra cost is now £500 (175 + 125 + 200).

No further crashing is possible as the longest routes cannot be reduced any further.

**86.**

**CONSTRUCTION PROJECT**

(a) The completed network is shown in Fig. 157.

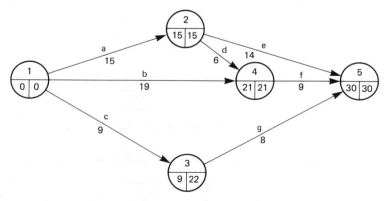

Fig. 157. *Network for answer to question 86(a).*

(b) The critical path is a–d–f, with a duration of 30 weeks and a total cost of £36,400 (£21,400 is the total normal cost and £15,000 represents the fixed cost of £500 per week for 30 weeks).

# APPENDIX 3. SUGGESTED ANSWERS TO EXAMINATION QUESTIONS

(c) This part requires the calculation of the minimum total cost. The different routes which will be used for updating are:

|       |        | d by 1 | a by 1 | a by 2<br>b by 2 | e by 3<br>f by 3 |
|-------|--------|--------|--------|------------------|------------------|
| a–d–f | 30     | 29     | 28     | 26               | 23               |
| a–e   | 29     | 29     | 28     | 26               | 23               |
| b–f   | 28     | 28     | 28     | 26               | 23               |
| c–g   | 17     | 17     | 17     | 17               | 17               |

Each activity can be crashed at a cost lower than the fixed cost of £500 per week, with the exception of activity c, so that crashing can be worthwhile if the total crash costs of the activities crashed are less than the £500 per week, since by so doing the total cost of the project will be reduced.

Inspection of the cost data indicates that activity d can be crashed by one week, thereby reducing the overall cost to £36,140 (i.e. £36,400 + 240 − 500) and the duration to 29 weeks. There will then be two critical paths, namely, a–d–f and a–e.

Crashing activity a by one week would reduce the overall cost to £35,890 (£36,140 + 250 − 500) and the duration to 28 weeks.

There will be three critical paths, a–d–f, a–e and b–f.

By crashing a and b at the same time a further saving can be made to reduce the time to 26 weeks and the cost to £35,590 (i.e. £35,890 + 2(250 + 100) − 2(500)).

Crashing activities e and f for three weeks would reduce the overall cost finally to £35,560 (i.e. £35,890 + 3(210 + 280) − 3(500)). The duration of the project would be 23 weeks and the final network would be as shown in Fig. 158.

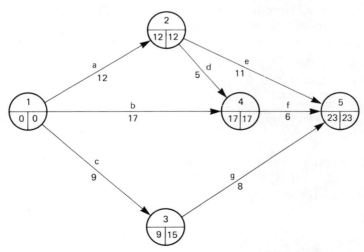

Fig. 158. *Network for answer to question 86(c).*

**87.**

(a) The complete network is shown in Fig. 159. The normal duration of the project is given by the longest route of jobs i.e. the critical path and has a time of 17 days.

The normal cost of the project is given by the total of the normal cost of each job plus the penalty as the project has been extended beyond 15 days. This gives £1,910 + £400 penalty = £2,310.

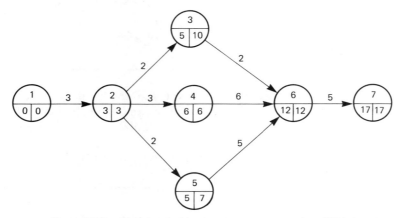

Fig. 159. *Network for answer to question 87(a).*

(b) This part required the minimum cost of completing the project in 15 days. The longest route of jobs must be reduced by 2 days. The job with the lowest cost slope on the critical path is 4–6 and a saving of two days can be made here. This gives an additional cost of £140 and a total cost of £1,910 + £140 = £2,050. (Note that at this stage there will be two critical paths.)

(c) The optimum plan for the company to attempt is based on the trade-off that must be made between the bonus payments on one hand and the costs of time saving on the other. Overall time reductions that can be achieved for less than £100 per day will be worthwhile.

The optimal plan is:

job 4–6 in 4 days
job 6–7 in 1 day
other jobs at normal time.

This gives an overall project duration of 11 days. The total cost is £2,410 – £400 (bonus) = £2,010.

(d) The action recommended is to save 4 days on job 6–7 (cost £360), 2 days on job 4–6 (cost £140) and 1 day on job 5–6 (cost £70), giving a total cost of £1,910 + £570 = £2,480.

**88.**

*See* Fig. 160.

# APPENDIX 3. SUGGESTED ANSWERS TO EXAMINATION QUESTIONS

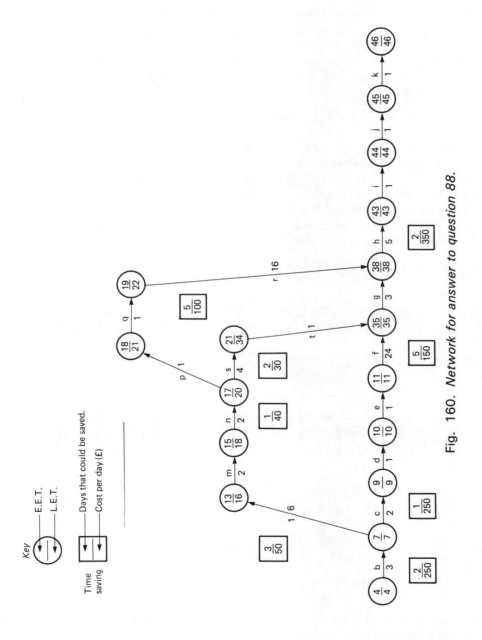

Fig. 160. Network for answer to question 88.

(a) The critical path is a–b–c–d–e–f–g–h–i–j–k i.e. the path with zero total float.

(b) The duration is 46 days and the cost is as shown in the question, i.e. £16,000.

(e) To complete in 40 days the necessary 6 days can be saved as follows:

   (i)   3 days at f at a cost of £450, there are then two critical paths;

   (ii)  2 days can be saved on this second path at l and n for a cost of £90 and on the first critical path at f for a cost of £300, and another day at b for a cost of £250.

   (iii) A total additional cost of £1,090.

(d) Activity f is critical and delay here could delay the project completion date, but activity r is not, there being a float of 3 days so that a delay of up to 3 days on this activity would not be likely to prejudice the completion date and supplier W should be used since 16 days is allowed and while delivery in 19 days would be satisfactory each day's delay beyond 19 days will involve W in a penalty of £500 per day. Two days could be saved on the next activity H at a cost of only a difference of £1,000 between the basic prices quoted by Z and W.

**89.**

**DELCO LTD**

(a) The network for the project is shown in Fig. 161. The critical path is the path with zero total float and is given by A–B–D–I–J–K–L, which has a duration of 24 weeks.

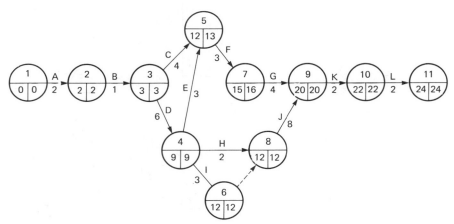

Fig. 161. *Network for answer to question 89(a).*

(b) (i) A strike at the factory supplying the internal machinery thereby delaying its delivery for four weeks has no effect on the total project time. The purchase of internal machinery is represented by job C. This has a total float of 6 weeks, i.e. it can be delayed by six weeks without affecting the total project time.

# APPENDIX 3. SUGGESTED ANSWERS TO EXAMINATION QUESTIONS

(ii) Test on machinery is represented by job G. The job has a total float of 1 week. If G is extended by 4 weeks the total project time will be extended by 3 weeks (duration 27 weeks).

(c) This part requires the calculation of project time which achieves minimum total cost. However, unlike standard reduction analyses, activities which can be reduced can only be done in the original time or in the new time.

| Activity | A | B | C | D | E | F | G | H | I | J | K | L |
|---|---|---|---|---|---|---|---|---|---|---|---|---|
| Normal duration (weeks) | 2 | 1 | 4 | 6 | 3 | 3 | 4 | 2 | 3 | 8 | 2 | 2 |
| Normal cost (£) | 400 | 0 | 200 | 450 | 700 | 200 | 600 | 0 | 250 | 600 | 450 | 200 |
| New time (weeks) | 1 | 1 | 2 | 2 | 1 | 1 | 1 | 2 | 2 | 4 | 1 | 1 |
| New cost (£) | 800 | 0 | 450 | 1,150 | 1,200 | 600 | 1,000 | 0 | 450 | 950 | 700 | 350 |
| Time saved (weeks) | 1 | – | 2 | 4 | 2 | 2 | 3 | – | 1 | 4 | 1 | 1 |
| Cost slope* (£s) | 400 | – | 125 | 175 | 250 | 200 | 133 | – | 200 | $87\frac{1}{2}$ | 250 | 150 |

*The concept of cost slope is not strictly applicable as the jobs cannot be reduced in stages. However, it does give an indication of the order of reduction.

The various routes and updating are shown below:

|  |  | L by 1 | D by 1 | I by 1 | K by 1 | J by 4<br>G by 3 |
|---|---|---|---|---|---|---|
| A–B–D–I–J–K–L | 24 | 23 | 19 | 18 | 17 | 13 |
| A–B–D–H–J–K–L | 23 | 22 | 18 | 18 | 17 | 13 |
| A–B–D–E–F–G–K–L | 23 | 22 | 18 | 18 | 17 | 14 |
| A–B–D–F–G–K–L | 18 | 17 | 17 | 17 | 16 | 13 |

The various steps and associated costs are given below:

| Reduction | Project time | Additional cost | Saving in overheads | Net saving | Cumulative saving |
|---|---|---|---|---|---|
| L by 1 | 23 | £150 | £250 | £100 | £100 |
| D by 4 | 19 | £700 | £1,000 | £300 | £400 |
| I by 1 | 18 | £200 | £250 | £50 | £450 |
| K by 1 | 17 | £250 | £250 | – | £450 |
| J by 4 | 14 | £350 | £750 | – | £450 |
| G by 3 |  | £400 |  |  |  |

*Tutorial Notes*
(a) Note that certain jobs are not reduced. Job A as the additional cost exceeds the overhead saving. Jobs B and H because they cannot be reduced.
(b) Project durations of 18 weeks, 17 weeks and 14 weeks all give the same total cost.

## 90.

### Labitas Ltd

TO: Works Director  FROM: Management Accountant

RE: Annual Furnace Shutdown

The following duration for individual activities is suggested bearing in mind the estimated opportunity cost of £5,000 per day. The optimal time period is 10 days.

| Activity | Duration (days) | Estimated direct cost |
|---|---|---|
| A | 5 | £17,000 |
| B | 3 | 7,000 |
| C | 2 | 10,000 |
| D | 4 | 4,000 |
| E | 2 | 3,000 |
| F | 3 | 16,000 |
|   |   | 57,000 |
| Ten days' opportunity cost | | 50,000 |
|   |   | £107,000 |

The calculations are detailed in the Appendix.

*Appendix*

Network: *See* Fig. 162.

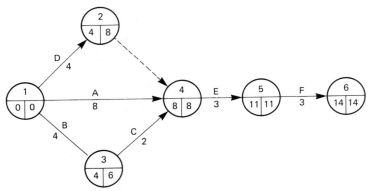

Fig. 162. *Network for answer to question 90.*

The critical path is A–E–F, i.e. the path with zero total float. Normal duration 14 days.

*Paths*

| A–E–F | = | 14 | 13 | 11 | 10 |
| B–C–E–F | = | 12 | 11 | 11 | 10 |
| D–E–F | = | 10 | 9 | 9 | 9 |

APPENDIX 3. SUGGESTED ANSWERS TO EXAMINATION QUESTIONS    483

(a) Reduce E by 1    Project time 13    Cost £1,000    Critical path A–E–F.

(b) Reduce A by 2    Project time 11    Cost £6,000    2 critical paths—A–E–F and B–C–E–F.

(c) Reduce A by 1,    Project time 10    Cost £4,000.
    B by 1

Further reductions cost more than £5,000 per day and so are not worth while.

**91.**

(a) The network for the project is given in Fig. 163. The critical path is A–C–G–H–I–J–K, i.e. the path with zero total float. The length of this path is 12 weeks.

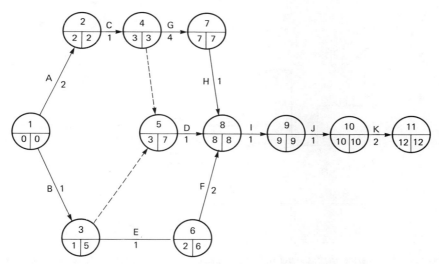

Fig. 163. *Network for answer to question 91(a).*

(b) Activities B, E, F, H and I are to be performed by the computing staff but there is only sufficient staff to carry out one activity at a time. The question asks for the latest time that B can be carried out.

The Gantt chart (Fig. 164) shows the scheduling of the various jobs. The chart is drawn on the assumption that each job starts at the earliest possible time. (Ignore the numbers below each job. These are the number of men required for the calculation in (c).) If the given restrictions did not apply job F could be done on days 7 and 8, i.e. job I could still start on time. However, this would have F overlapping with H. This is not permitted. The latest time F can be done is days 6 and 7. The latest time E can be done is day 5. Hence the latest time B can be done is day 4.

*Note:* Students should confirm this answer by constructing the chart and shifting the jobs.

(b)

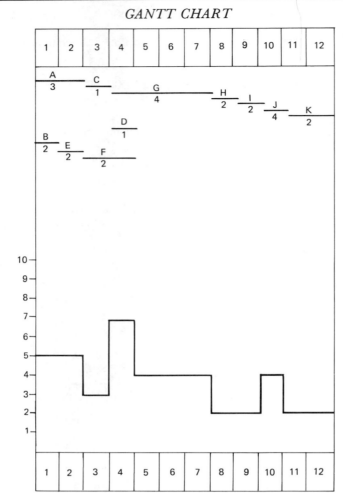

Fig. 164. *Gantt chart and labour histogram for answer to question 91(b).*

(c) Given the number of staff required for each job it is possible to construct a labour histogram as shown in Fig. 164. The highest requirement is on day 4 where jobs G, D and F are being done. Job D can be shifted as it has sufficient float. However jobs G and F will always overlap at some time. This implies that the constant manning force must be 6 men.

**92.**

(a) Network: *See* Fig. 165. Critical path: D–E–F–G–I. Length 47 days.

# APPENDIX 3. SUGGESTED ANSWERS TO EXAMINATION QUESTIONS

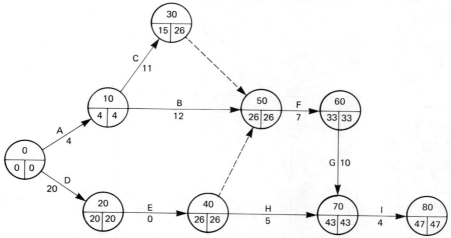

Fig. 165. *Network for answer to question 92(a).*

(b) Bar chart: *See* Fig. 166. This shows each job starting at its earliest possible time. The floats have been indicated by dotted lines. The total float on each job is:

| | |
|---|---|
| A | 10 |
| B | 10 |
| C | 11 |
| D | 0 |
| E | 0 |
| F | 0 |
| G | 0 |
| H | 12 |
| I | 0 |

(c) Each activity requires one member. The question requires the calculation of the minimum number of staff that should be allocated to the scheme. From the chart it will be seen that the number is three (there is no need to construct a histogram). At no time do more than three activities overlap.

(d) If one of the allocated staff were taken ill for the duration of the scheme and not replaced then the total project time will be delayed by one day. Job B can be worked on after C or C after B. This would delay the start of F by only one day.

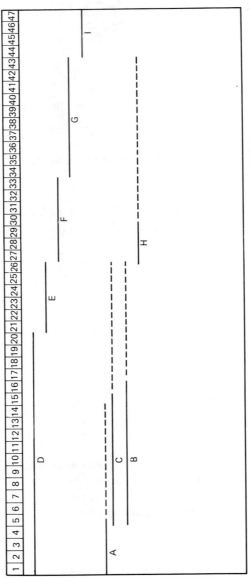

Fig. 166. *Bar chart for answer to question 92(b)*.

# APPENDIX 3. SUGGESTED ANSWERS TO EXAMINATION QUESTIONS

**93.**

(a) The given network is shown in Fig. 167. The normal duration is given by the longest route of jobs, which is 0–10–7–8–4–5. The length of this route is 44 days. The normal cost of the project is given by adding all the normal costs to give £8,280.

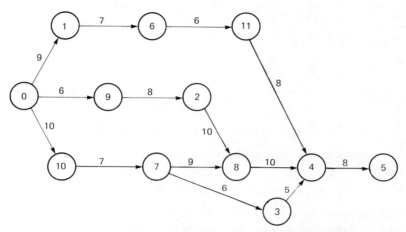

Fig. 167. *Network for answer to question 93.*

(b) There are four different paths from start to finish. These are listed below:

$$0\text{–}10\text{–}7\text{–}8\text{–}4\text{–}5 = 44 \text{ days}$$
$$0\text{–}9\text{–}2\text{–}8\text{–}4\text{–}5 = 42 \text{ days}$$
$$0\text{–}1\text{–}6\text{–}11\text{–}4\text{–}5 = 38 \text{ days}$$
$$0\text{–}10\text{–}7\text{–}3\text{–}4\text{–}5 = 36 \text{ days}.$$

(c) The question requires the minimum time in which the project can be completed and a statement of the critical activities. As there is no cost constraint, crash times can be used on all jobs giving a minimum completion time of 21 days. There will be two equally long routes, i.e. two critical paths 0–9–2–8–4–5 and 0–1–6–11–4–5.

(d) This part required a statement of the maximum number of men required to complete the project if all activities start at the earliest time. The maximum number is 19 and this can be easily confirmed by constructing a Gantt chart.

**94.**

The expected duration of each activity is calculated by using the formula:

$$\tfrac{1}{6} \times (\text{Optimistic} + 4 \times \text{Most likely} + \text{Pessimistic}).$$

The durations are shown in Fig. 168 (to the nearest half-day). The variance is also

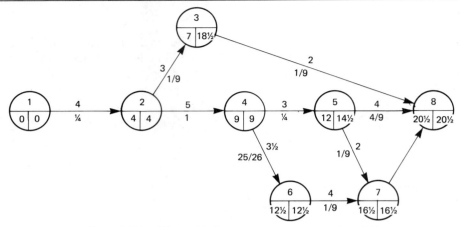

Fig. 168. *Network for answer to question 94.*

shown. By determining the path with zero total float it will be found that the critical path lies along:

$$1-2-4-6-7-8.$$

The expected duration on this path is $20\frac{1}{2}$ days.

The variance of this duration is the sum of the individual variances, assuming the combined estimates follow a normal distribution.

This sum is: $\frac{1}{4} + 1 + \frac{25}{36} + \frac{1}{9} + \frac{1}{4} = \frac{83}{36} = 2.3$.

Standard deviation = variance = 1.5.

Thus, to complete more than three days earlier than expected, the duration would have to be more than two standard deviations less than the expected duration. Hence, the required probability is 0.025, since $2\frac{1}{2}$ per cent of the normal distribution lies less than two standard deviations under the mean.

## 95.

(a) Network: *See* Fig. 169. Critical path: A–D–H–I–J.

(b) E only has a float of 1; project delayed by 1 (B has a float of 7, G a float of 2).

(c) Variance of the total time on the critical path equals sum of individual variance

$$= V(A) + V(D) + V(H) + V(I) + V(J)$$
$$= 1^2 + 1^2 + 1^2 + 0.5^2 + 1^2$$

∴  Variance = 4.25.
∴  Standard deviation of project time = $\sqrt{4.25}$ = 2.06 weeks,

i.e.        1 standard deviation accounts for 2.06 weeks.

95 per cent confidence is 1.96 standard deviation.

∴ $20 \pm 1.96 \times 2.06 = 20 \pm 4 = 16$ to 24 weeks.

APPENDIX 3. SUGGESTED ANSWERS TO EXAMINATION QUESTIONS     489

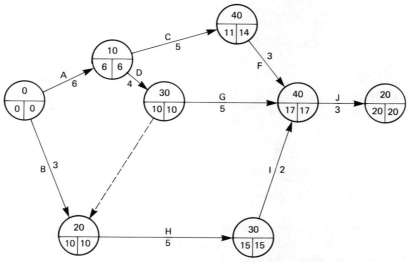

Fig. 169. *Network for answer to question 95.*

(d) Probability of exceeding 24 weeks = 0.025 (i.e. $2\frac{1}{2}$ per cent each side).

∴  Expected return = 1,000 × 0.975 + 20 × 0.025

   = 975.5

   Cost           = 100
∴  Profit expected = £875,500.

*Note: The standard deviation of project time is not given by adding standard deviations of individual jobs. First find the variance of project time, then the standard deviation.*

## 96.

**FINELOW CONSTRUCTION CO. LTD**
(a) The first step in finding the critical path would involve converting given times (optimistic, most likely and pessimistic) into expected times for each job. This is shown in the table below:

| Activity | Optimistic<br>a | Most likely<br>m | Pessimistic<br>b | Expected time<br>$\frac{a + 4m + b}{6}$ |
|---|---|---|---|---|
| A | 4 | 7 | 13 | $7\frac{1}{2}$ |
| B | 3 | 6 | 9 | 6 |
| C | 2 | 4 | 6 | 4 |
| D | 2 | 3 | 10 | 4 |
| E | 1 | 3 | 11 | 4 |
| F | 4 | 6 | 8 | 6 |
| G | 1 | 5 | 15 | 6 |

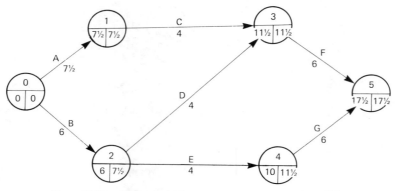

Fig. 170. *Network for answer to question 96.*

The network can now be drawn using the given dependency table and using expected times for individual jobs as calculated above.
The network is shown in Fig. 170.
The critical path is given by A–C–F with an expected time of $17\frac{1}{2}$ weeks.
The variance of project time is given by adding the variances of jobs that lie on the critical path. The variance of individual jobs is given by using the expression:

$$\left(\frac{b-a}{6}\right)^2.$$

$$\text{Variance (A)} = \left(\frac{13-4}{6}\right)^2 = \frac{81}{36}$$

$$\text{Variance (C)} = \left(\frac{6-2}{6}\right)^2 = \frac{16}{36}$$

$$\text{Variance (F)} = \left(\frac{8-4}{6}\right)^2 = \frac{16}{36}$$

$$\therefore \text{ Variance of project time} = \frac{81}{36} + \frac{16}{36} + \frac{16}{36} = \frac{113}{36}.$$

$$\therefore \text{ Standard deviation} = \sqrt{\frac{113}{36}}$$

$$= \underline{\underline{1.77 \text{ weeks.}}}$$

(b) The expected project time is $17\frac{1}{2}$ weeks. The standard deviation is 1.77 weeks.
The probability of completing the project in 16 weeks is given by:

$$P\left(Z \leqslant \frac{16-17.5}{1.77}\right) = P(Z \leqslant 0.85) = 0.1977 \approx 0.20.$$

The probability of being completed in 19 weeks or over is given by:

$$P\left(Z \geqslant \frac{19-17.5}{1.77}\right) = P(Z \geqslant 0.85) = 0.1977 \approx 0.20.$$

∴ Probability of being completed in 17–18 weeks = 1 − 0.3954 = 0.6046 ≈ 0.6.

The probabilities calculated above could now be used with the extra cost table to show that 1 extra excavator should be hired as it has the least expected cost of £6,800 as compared with an expected cost of £8,000 for 2 excavators and £14,000 for no excavators.

## 97.

**STEREOPES LTD**

(a) The network is shown in Fig. 171. The critical path is A–D–F with a duration of 34 days.

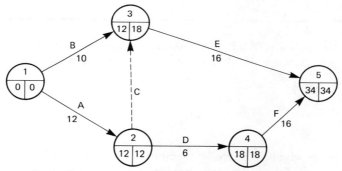

Fig. 171. *Network for answer to question 97.*

(b) The project must be completed in 30 days, i.e. the longest route must be reduced by 4 days. The reduction must be carried out in the cheapest manner.

On the critical path, activity A has a cost slope of £1,000, D has a cost slope of £500 and F has a cost slope of £600. Therefore activity D is cheapest to reduce and a maximum of 2 days can be saved at a cost of £1,000. This will reduce the longest route to 32 days and the cost will be £32,200 (i.e. original £31,200 + £1,000).

The next cheapest job to reduce is F and this will be reduced by 2 days to give the required 30 days' duration. The cost will be £33,400 (£32,200 + £1,200).

The reduction is summarised below:

|       |    | D by 2 | F by 2 |
|-------|----|--------|--------|
| A–D–F | 34 | 32     | 30     |
| A–C–E | 28 | 28     | 28     |
| B–E   | 26 | 26     | 26     |

It will be seen that A–D–F remains critical.

(c) PERT provides a system for dealing with situations where the estimates are subject to uncertainty. As the distribution for job E is not given it is not strictly possible to give a solution to the stated problem.

However, as only job E is assumed to vary, a simple tabulation can list all possibilities. In the calculations above, to complete the project in 30 days:

A takes 12 days
D takes  4 days
F takes 14 days.

As long as activity E takes 17 days or under, the critical route remains A–D–F. However, when E takes 18 days or more, other possibilities exist.

| Duration of E | Critical path(s) | Project duration |
| --- | --- | --- |
| 18 days | A–D–F and A–C–E | 30 days |
| 19 days | A–C–E | 31 days |
| 20 days | A–C–E | 32 days |

Because of the penalty of £5,000 it would clearly be worth spending £3,000 to reduce E to a maximum of 18 days, when there would be two paths, A–D–F and A–C–E.

## 98.

(a) The activities are given in terms of numbers. The network has to be drawn twice, first using an arrow diagram and then an activity-on-node presentation.

The arrow diagram is shown in Fig. 172.
The activity on node diagram is shown in Fig. 173.

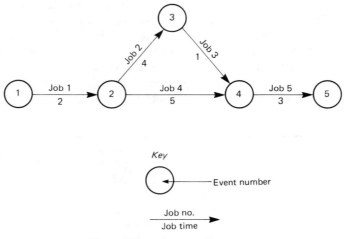

Fig. 172. *Arrow diagram.*

# APPENDIX 3. SUGGESTED ANSWERS TO EXAMINATION QUESTIONS

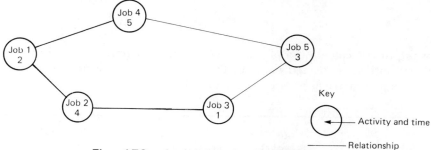

Fig. 173. *Activity on node diagram.*

(b) There are two equally long routes:

   Jobs 1–2–3–5

   Jobs 1–4–5.

On the basis of average durations both these routes will have average durations of 10 days.

$$\text{Average variable cost} = £(2 \times 5) + (4 \times 10) + (1 \times 7) + (5 \times 5) + (3 \times 2)$$

$$= £88.$$

(c) This part requires a calculation of minimum and maximum times and associated probabilities. It is possible to show the full range of possibilities as:

|      | Route   | Time | Probability |
|------|---------|------|-------------|
| Jobs | 1–2–3–5 | 8    | 0.5         |
|      | 1–2–3–5 | 12   | 0.5         |
|      | 1–4–5   | 9    | 0.7         |
|      | 1–4–5   | 11   | 0.2         |
|      | 1–4–5   | 15   | 0.1         |

All the interactions between the two routes and their associated probabilities are shown below:

| Jobs 1–2–3–5 time | Probability | Jobs 1–4–5 time | Probability | Maximum time | Probability |
|---|---|---|---|---|---|
| 8  | 0.5 | 9  | 0.7 | 9  | 0.35 |
| 8  | 0.5 | 11 | 0.2 | 11 | 0.10 |
| 8  | 0.5 | 15 | 0.1 | 15 | 0.05 |
| 12 | 0.5 | 9  | 0.7 | 12 | 0.35 |
| 12 | 0.5 | 11 | 0.2 | 12 | 0.10 |
| 12 | 0.5 | 15 | 0.1 | 15 | 0.05 |

From the above, it can be seen that the maximum project time is 15 days with a probability of 0.10 and the minimum time is 9 days with a probability of 0.35.

## 99.

**EDWARD LTD**

(a) This requires a calculation of the expected value of time required to complete the contract and the expected value of the cost. The distributions for time and cost given are symmetrical about the mean value.

| Activity | Time range (days) | Mean time (days) | Cost range (£) | Mean cost (£) |
|---|---|---|---|---|
| A | 8–12 | 10 | 7,000–9,000 | 8,000 |
| B | 11–13 | 12 | 6,000–7,000 | 6,500 |
| C | 7–9 | 8 | 4,000–4,500 | 4,250 |
| D | 12–16 | 14 | 12,000–15,000 | 13,500 |
| E | 13–15 | 14 | 9,000–9,500 | 9,250 |
| F | 7–9 | 8 | 5,000–6,000 | 5,500 |
| G | 5–7 | 6 | 6,000–6,500 | 6,250 |

The network in Fig. 174 is based on mean times. The critical path, i.e. the path with zero total float, is E–F–G, with an expected time of 28 days. The expected value of the cost, on the basis of the figures given, is £53,250.

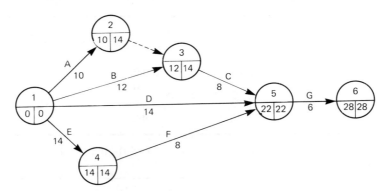

Fig. 174. *Network for answer to question 99.*

(b) This part requires an evaluation of each of the alternative methods of operation.

   (i) (1) D can be completed in 11–13 days at a cost of £11,000–£13,000. This gives a mean time of 12 days and a mean cost of £12,000. While D is not critical this new schedule is cheaper than the normal.

   (2) Alternatively, D can be done in a mean time of 10 days at a mean cost of £14,000. This is more expensive and will not change the total project time.

(ii) E can be completed in 9–11 days at a cost of £14,000–£15,000. The mean time and cost are 10 days and £14,500 respectively. If E is done in 10 days then B–C–G will become critical and the project time will reduce to 26 days. This reduction will cost £5,250, which exceeds the savings of £5,000. It is not a worthwhile alternative.

(iii) B can be completed in a mean time of 11 days with a mean cost of £8,500. This is not worth while as B is not critical and the costs are higher than with standard procedures.

*Note: If B is completed in 11 days and E in 10 days together, then B–C–G will be critical with a length of 25 days. This represents a saving of £7,500 and a total cost of £7,250, hence it is worthwhile.*

## 100.

(a) As the demand is at a constant rate and no stock-outs are allowed, the EBQ model can be used.

The optimal order size $= \sqrt{\dfrac{2cd}{ip}}$,

where $c$ = order cost

$d$ = annual demand

$p$ = price per item

$i$ = stock holding cost expressed as a percentage.

$\therefore$ Optimal order size $= \sqrt{\dfrac{2 \times 200{,}000 \times 32}{8 \times 0.1}} = \underline{\underline{4{,}000}}$.

$\therefore$ Order frequency $= 200{,}000/4{,}000$

$= \underline{\underline{50 \text{ times a year.}}}$

(b) Order cost = Order frequency × Order cost

$= £50 \times 32$

$= \underline{\underline{£1{,}600}}$.

Holding cost $= \frac{1}{2} \times$ Order quantity $\times i \times p$

$= \frac{1}{2} \times 4{,}000 \times 0.1 \times 8$

$= \underline{\underline{£1{,}600}}$.

Therefore total relevant inventory cost per annum $= £1{,}600 + £1{,}600$

$= \underline{\underline{£3{,}200}}$.

(c) If same order level of 4,000 is maintained, the new order frequency

$$= 242{,}000/4{,}000$$
$$= \underline{60.5 \text{ times a year.}}$$

New order cost per annum $= £60.5 \times 32$
$$= \underline{£1{,}936.}$$

Holding cost per annum as before $= \underline{£1{,}600.}$

Therefore total relevant inventory costs per annum $= £1{,}936 + 1{,}600$
$$= \underline{£3{,}536.}$$

If the optimal level is used the new order quantity needs to be calculated:

$$\text{Order level} = \sqrt{\frac{2 \times 242{,}000 \times 32}{8 \times 0.1}}$$

$$= \underline{4{,}400.}$$

Therefore new order frequency $= 242{,}000/4{,}400 = \underline{55}$.

Order cost $= £55 \times 32 = \underline{£1{,}760.}$

and holding cost $= £\tfrac{1}{2} \times 4{,}400 \times 0.1 \times 8 \quad = \underline{£1{,}760.}$

Therefore total relevant cost per annum $= £1{,}760 + 1{,}760$
$$= \underline{£3{,}520.}$$

Difference $= £(3{,}536 - 3{,}520) = \underline{£16.}$

(d) From the example we can see that if we use an estimate of 200,000 units of demand instead of 242,000 units, an underestimate of 17.4 per cent, we get a difference of only £16 per annum, i.e. 0.45 per cent of £3,520 (minimum cost) above the optimal level of costing.

So an error of about 17 per cent in the forecast for demand leads to operations at less than ½ per cent above the optimal level. Hence the EBQ model is insensitive to changes in demand. (This is true in general and not only in this particular case.)

**101.**

(a) The given current data are as follows:

$p$ = purchase price per unit = £4

batch size = 200

# APPENDIX 3. SUGGESTED ANSWERS TO EXAMINATION QUESTIONS

$d$ = demand = 10 per day = 2,500 per year

$c$ = delivery cost per batch = £25

$i$ = stockholding cost as a percentage = $12\frac{1}{2}$ per cent.

The economic order quantity $Q$ can be calculated as follows:

$$Q = \sqrt{\frac{2cd}{ip}} = \sqrt{\frac{2 \times 25 \times 2{,}500}{0.125 \times 4}} = \underline{\underline{500 \text{ units}}}.$$

Total annual cost using $Q = 500$ = Stockholding + Delivery + Purchase price

$$= \tfrac{1}{2} \times 0.125 \times 4 \times 500 + \frac{2{,}500}{500} \times 25 + 2{,}500 \times 4 = \underline{\underline{£10{,}250}}.$$

Total annual cost using $Q = 200$

$$= \tfrac{1}{2} \times 0.125 \times 4 \times 200 + \frac{2{,}500}{200} \times 25 + 2{,}500 \times 4 = \underline{\underline{£10{,}362.5}}.$$

$\therefore$ Saving = $\underline{\underline{£112.5}}$ if the optimal order quantity is used.

(b) In the range 0–399 the purchase price per unit is £4. This is not worth considering as at a price of £4 the cheapest size of batch has already been shown as being 500.

The range 400–599 is now available at £3.90. The question asks how this affects the optimal order quantity.

This could be argued in two ways:

*Either:* EBQ at £4 is 500. If we order in 500s new items are at £3.90. This must be cheaper and can be confirmed.

Total cost = $\tfrac{1}{2} \times 0.125 \times 3.90$

$\times 500 + \dfrac{2{,}500}{500} \times 25 + 2{,}500$

$\times 3.90$

$= 121.875 + 125 + 9{,}750$

$= \underline{\underline{£9{,}996.88}}.$

*Or:* As the price structure around the EBQ has changed let us modify the EBQ:

$$Q = \sqrt{\frac{2 \times 25 \times 2{,}500}{3.90 \times 0.125}} = 506.$$

Total cost = $\tfrac{1}{2} \times 506 \times 3.9$

$\times 0.125 + \dfrac{2{,}500}{506} \times 25 + 2{,}500$

$\times 3.9$

$= \underline{\underline{£9{,}996.84}}.$

Regardless of what strategy has been adopted, the cost must be compared with the cost of ordering in a batch size of 600.

Total cost = Stockholding + Delivery + Purchase price

$$= \tfrac{1}{2} \times 0.125 \times 3.8 \times 600 + \frac{2{,}500}{600} \times 25 + 2{,}500 \times 3.8$$

$$= \underline{\underline{£9{,}747}}. \text{ This is the cheapest.}$$

(c) This part should have contained a mention of the opportunity cost of stockholding, i.e. the interest which has been lost through investing in stock.

**102.**

(a) The assumptions made include the following:

Demand is constant during the year. Purchase price is constant. No stockouts are allowed. The lead time is assumed to be zero.

Total variable cost for Dugetron = $5 \times 80 + 300 \times 1.2 = £760$.

Total variable cost for Aisne = $12 \times 80 + 125 \times 1.2 = £1{,}110$.

Hence Dugetron has the better ordering policy in that the total variable costs are lower.

(b) If the orders are placed separately the economic-order quantity (EOQ) can be calculated as:

$$Q = \sqrt{\frac{2 \times 80 \times 3{,}000}{1.2}} = 632 \text{ or } 633.$$

= 4.7 orders per year on average for each plant.

This can be rounded to 5 orders of 600.

Total variable cost = $2 \times 760 = £1{,}520$ (when rounded).

Ordering together, the annual demand in total will be 6,000 and the EOQ can once again be calculated:

$$Q = \sqrt{\frac{2 \times 80 \times 6{,}000}{1.2}} = 894.$$

This gives 6.4 orders. In practice the orders would probably be 6 of 1,000 each.

Total variable cost = $6 \times 80 + 1.2 \times 500 = £1{,}080$.

Hence the optimum policy is to combine the orders and have 6 in total of 1,000 each. Three deliveries of 1,000 can be made to each plant.

APPENDIX 3. SUGGESTED ANSWERS TO EXAMINATION QUESTIONS    499

(c) 10 per cent discount saves  $0.1 \times 6{,}000 \times 4 = £2{,}400$
    One delivery saves           $5 \times 80 \qquad\qquad = \quad 400$
                                 Total saving $= £2{,}800$

Increased stockholding cost $= \dfrac{6{,}000 \times (4 - 0.4) \times 0.3}{2} - \dfrac{1{,}000 \times 4 \times 0.3}{2}$

$\qquad\qquad\qquad\qquad\qquad = £3{,}240 - 600 \qquad\qquad - £2{,}640$

Increased within company delivery charge £10 × 40    $\underline{\quad 400\quad}$
Total extra charges                                  $= \underline{\underline{£3{,}040}}$

Hence on cost grounds alone the discount is not worthwhile.

(d) Other factors that should be taken into account should include:
   (i)   market conditions;
   (ii)  deterioration and obsolescence of the stock;
   (iii) possible reduction in sales with competition from new and/or better components coming onto the market;
   (iv)  the possibility that the higher numbers stored may impose storage problems and so increase the current cost of storage; and
   (v)   possible changes in other costs during the year.

## 103.

**ELSTORE LIMITED**

(a) The data given in the question are as follows:

    Annual demand $\qquad\qquad = d = 25 \times 50 = 1{,}250.$

    Cost of ordering $\qquad\qquad = c = £10$ per batch.

    Purchase price $\qquad\qquad\quad = p = 50$ pence per unit.

    Stockholding cost as a percentage $= i = 20$ per cent.

The quasitrons which the purchasing manager should order each time are given by the economic order quantity model:

$$Q = \sqrt{\dfrac{2cd}{ip}} = \sqrt{\dfrac{2 \times 10 \times 1{,}250}{0.2 \times 0.5}} = \underline{\underline{500}}.$$

The prices charged to customers are determined by taking the purchasing and stockholding costs and applying a standard mark-up of 20 per cent. The first step in the calculation is to find the annual total cost.

This is given by:

Total annual cost = Stockholding + Delivery + Purchase Price

$$= \frac{ipQ}{2} + \frac{cd}{Q} + 1{,}250 \times 0.5.$$

$$= \frac{0.2 \times 0.5 \times 500}{2} + \frac{10 \times 1{,}250}{500} + 1{,}250 \times 0.5$$

$$= £25 + £25 + £625$$

$$= £675.$$

$$\therefore \quad \text{Total cost per unit} = \frac{\text{Total cost}}{\text{Total number of units}}$$

$$= \frac{675}{1{,}250} = \underline{£0.54}.$$

The price charged will be 0.54 + 20 per cent = <u>65 pence per quasitron</u>.

(b) Ordering in batches of 1,000 gives a discount of 5 per cent.
Total annual costs can be recalculated and if they are lower than at the EOQ then the discount is worth taking:

Total annual cost = Stockholding + Delivery + Purchase Price

$$= \frac{ipQ}{2} + \frac{cd}{Q} + 1{,}250 \times 0.5 \times 0.95$$

$$= \frac{0.2 \times 0.5 \times 0.95 \times 1{,}000}{2} + \frac{10 \times 1{,}250}{1{,}000} + 1{,}250 \times 0.5 \times 0.95$$

$$= 47.5 + 12.5 + 593.75$$

$$= £653.75.$$

This gives a saving of £21.25 and hence is worth taking.
If he maintains a mark-up of 20 per cent on cost the price will be:

$$\frac{£653.75}{1{,}250} + 20 \text{ per cent} = \underline{63\text{p}}.$$

(c) The question asks how large would the percentage holding cost have to be for the manager to be indifferent between taking advantage of the discount and maintaining the original ordering policy. This really implies calculating a value of $i$ at which the total costs are the same under both systems:

# APPENDIX 3. SUGGESTED ANSWERS TO EXAMINATION QUESTIONS 501

*Batch size 500*

$$\text{Total annual costs} = \text{Stockholding} + \text{Delivery} + \text{Purchase Price}$$
$$= 125i + 25 + 625$$
$$= \underline{\underline{125i + 650}}.$$

*Batch size 1,000*

$$\text{Total annual costs} = \text{Stockholding} + \text{Delivery} + \text{Purchase Price}$$
$$= 237.5i + 12.5 + 593.75$$
$$= \underline{\underline{237.5i + 606.25}}.$$

To find the appropriate value of $i$ equate the two equations of cost.

$$125i + 650 = 237.5i + 606.25$$
$$112.5i = 43.75$$
$$i = 0.389 \text{ (approximately 39 per cent)}.$$

It should be noted that at this level of stockholding cost the manager will be indifferent between the two systems. In practice it is unlikely that a stockholding cost would be this high.

## 104.

**OPTIMUM LTD**

(a) The optimum batch size to be produced can be obtained from the following model:

$$Q = \sqrt{\frac{2cd}{ip}}$$

where $Q$ = the optimum batch size to produce (in the case of ordering the optimum order quantity);

$d$ = the annual demand for the product;

$c$ = the initial fixed costs associated with each batch (in the case of manufactured products the set-up costs, and in the case of purchased goods the cost of placing an order);

$ip$ = the annual cost of holding one unit of stock; this is obtained from the annual cost of holding stock expressed as a percentage of the value of the stock concerned, multiplied by the cost of a unit of production of stock.

The assumptions made in the application of this formula are:

(i) the costs of production are assumed to be constant (there are no economies or diseconomies of scale);

(ii) in the substitution of figures for notation the costs used are the relevant costs.

In this case the following data are used in the formula:

$$d = 1{,}000; \quad c = £40; \quad ip = £8.$$

In obtaining $c$ it is only the relevant costs of setting up to produce a batch that are included, which are the costs of the specialist firm. The preparation time of the packing staff is not relevant because of the spare capacity as far as labour is concerned and because no redundancies are envisaged. Thus labour costs will be the same whatever the number of batches produced, so labour costs can be considered fixed and be omitted from the analysis on the assumption that it has no opportunity cost. The holding costs of one unit of the produce per annum cannot be obtained in this case by the method stated above.

In fact, from the data provided it is impossible to work out holding costs as a percentage of product cost. $ip$ is the opportunity cost of one square metre of warehouse space which is £24 divided by the 3 Opts stacked on it (not the original contract price of renting the warehouse which is historic and not relevant in this decision analysis).

Substituting these values in the formula:

$$Q = \sqrt{\frac{2 \times 1{,}000 \times 40}{8}}$$

$$= \sqrt{10{,}000}$$

$$= \underline{\underline{100}} \text{ as the optimum batch size.}$$

The validity of the approach used derives from the fact that two costs, the set-up and holding costs, have to be balanced. When an organisation produces larger and fewer batches, although the set-up costs are reduced the holding costs are increased. The converse applies when fewer and smaller batches are produced; this reduces holding costs and causes an increase in set-up costs associated with the production of more batches. The optimum number in a production batch is found where the aggregate of set-up and holding costs for a period is minimised. It is interesting to note that as a general principle, when either the set-up or the holding costs are high then these will have a great influence on whether it is better to produce large batch sizes or not. High set-up costs have the effect of making it beneficial to reduce the number of batches produced, whereas high stockholding costs weigh against the production of large batches.

The batch-size optimising model used is based on the assumption that demand patterns are fairly stable throughout the period concerned.

There is also the fact that the formula provides a quantitative model which appears to produce a deterministic decision, whereas results from the model should be weighed against any qualitative factors not included in it, for example, possible frequency of stock-outs, i.e. the number of times that stock is likely to run out and the cost of any stock-outs in terms of bad will engendered amongst customers. The figures produced have not allowed for a safety margin.

# APPENDIX 3. SUGGESTED ANSWERS TO EXAMINATION QUESTIONS

*Note: It would have been acceptable to have computed the optimum batch size working from first principles.*

(b) Currently, Opts are being produced in batches of 200. Assuming a 50-week year this means that with demand at 1,000 per annum a batch of Opts will cover demand for:

$$\frac{200}{1,000} \times 50 = \underline{\underline{10 \text{ weeks}}}.$$

The average stock held during this period will be $\underline{100 \text{ units}}$. If Opts are produced in the optimum batch size then a batch will last for:

$$\frac{100}{1,000} \times 50 = \underline{\underline{5 \text{ weeks}}},$$

and the average stockholding will be reduced to $\underline{50 \text{ units}}$.

Currently, Opts are being produced in batch sizes of 200. Using the optimum model it is found that the EBQ is 100.

Thus when a batch of 200 is produced it will cover 100 weeks' sales and show an average stockholding of 100 units.

A reduction of batch size to 100 will cover only 5 weeks' demand but will show a reduction in the average stockholding of 50.

## 105.

**ARGES LTD**

(a) The optimal batch size can be calculated from the EBQ model:

$$Q = \sqrt{\frac{2cd}{ip}}$$

where $Q$ = economic batch size

$c$ = set-up costs per batch

$d$ = annual demand

$ip$ = cost of holding one unit of stock for a year.

Clearly $d = 5,000$. The fixed costs per batch are the set-up costs, 9 hours at £4 per hour. Thus $c = 36$. The holding costs are properly viewed on an opportunity cost basis. Each unit stored reduces sub-letting revenue by £3 × 3 = £9. Other holding costs are £7. Thus $ip = 16$.

$$\therefore \quad Q = \sqrt{\frac{2cd}{ip}} = \sqrt{\frac{2 \times 36 \times 5,000}{16}} = 150.$$

(b) The rationale of the basic square-root formula is explained in Chapter 22 on inventory control.

(c) The labour costs are invariant with respect to $Q$. In fact they are totally fixed. Thus they cannot affect the EBS decision. In terms of warehouse space, although the "over the counter" payment is only £2 per square foot the company would lose money over the year if it employed this figure. Each square foot used to store the Cyclops reduces rental revenues by £3. People who have difficulty accepting the reality and relevance of opportunity costs might imagine that the full rental moneys are actually received and a refund (of £3) has to then be paid for every square foot occupied by Cyclops.

*Tutorial notes*

(a) *The wealth of redundant information characterises real-life situations.*

(b) *The production formula could not be used as the rate of production was not given.*

## 106.

**VAAL LTD**

(a) Annual demand $d = 40{,}000$. Fixed costs per replenishment are £32. This is made up of the £12 materials cost plus £20 labour costs. In the labour costs 20 hours are required, and although the wages are £2 per hour the true cost is only £1. This arises from the fact that the £2 per hour is paid no matter what, but if they are not employed on Zand then costs of £1 per hour can be saved. Thus the opportunity cost is £2 − £1 = £1. Annual holding costs come in two forms. With the existing single warehouse there are the inescapable maintenance costs of £120 per annum. This figure has nothing to do with $H$.

The best estimate we can make of the holding cost per unit per annum is from the cost of capital. It costs £40 to make a unit of Zand. If this £40 was not spent on Zand it could be invested elsewhere or used to retire debt or reduce overdraft and save interest charges at 10 per cent. Thus the holding cost is again an opportunity cost figure, and is $0.1 \times £40 = £4$. Now, we are given a figure for hourly production but unless we assume a number for hours worked per day, and days worked per year, we cannot find $r$ for the formula:

$$\text{EBQ} = \sqrt{\frac{2cd}{h\left(i - \dfrac{d}{r}\right)}}.$$

So, with the reservation that the production rate formula would have been used if data had been available, we shall proceed with the basic square-root expression. This gives the result:

$$\text{EBQ} = \sqrt{\frac{2 \times 32 \times 40{,}000}{4}} = 800.$$

However, there is a limit on storage of 500 with only one warehouse. The shape of the cost function gives no alternative to setting the batch size at 500. Total annual costs will then be:

$$C = \tfrac{1}{2} \times 500 \times 4 + \frac{32 \times 40{,}000}{500} + 40 \times 40{,}000 + 120$$

$$= 1{,}000 + 2{,}560 + 1{,}600{,}000 + 120$$

in which the 1,600,000 figure swamps virtually everything else. Clearly, in this case inventory is a minor contributor to costs overall. However, the costs of £1,600,000 are incurred regardless of inventory, so, leaving these out and calling the remainder $C^*$, we have:

$$C^* = 1{,}000 + 2{,}560 + 120 = 3{,}680.$$

Now, if the second warehouse is obtained the EOQ of 800 can now be stored, but the maintenance costs total £240 so $C^*$ here is:

$$C^* = \frac{1}{2} \times 800 \times 4 + \frac{32 \times 40{,}000}{800} + 240 = 1{,}600 + 1{,}600 + 240 = 3{,}440.$$

So in operating terms there would be a saving of £3,680 – £3,440 = £240 per annum. However, in order to secure this saving, capital of £5,000 must be invested. This represents the initial outlay on an investment for which the returns are cost savings. Due to the indefinite life of the warehouse the investment is a perpetuity having a net present value of:

$$\text{NPV} = \frac{240}{0.1} - 5{,}000 = -2{,}600.$$

So the second warehouse is not worth while.

(b) The rationale of the method employed is explained fully in Chapter 22 on inventory control.

## 107.

(a) The application of the EOQ model can be considered by classifying the costs incurred by the insurance company and comparing them with the equivalent costs in an inventory situation:

| | Given situation costs | EOQ model costs |
|---|---|---|
| (i) | Fixed cost of £200 for each investment. | The costs of ordering and delivery. |
| (ii) | The loss of interest for premiums not invested at the rate of 20 per cent per annum. | The cost of holding stock. |
| (iii) | The variable cost of 2 per cent of the sum invested at any one time. | The cost of items being stocked. |

Further, as the annual premium inflow is at a steady rate (corresponding to a constant demand in the EOQ model) the economic order quantity model can be used.

(b) The optimum investment policy is independent of the variable element of the investment costs as the charge of 2 per cent of the sum invested will over a year be applied to the whole of the £5m. This will give a total annual charge of £100,000.

(c) The EOQ model is:

$$Q = \sqrt{\frac{2cd}{ip}}$$

Where $c$ = £200

$d$ = £5,000,000

$ip$ = cost of holding £1 in cash for one year (This is £1 × 0.2 = £0.20 and represents the foregone interest.),

$$Q = \sqrt{\frac{2 \times 5,000,000 \times 200}{0.2}}$$

$$= £100,000.$$

Number of investments = 50 times a year.

Total costs of policy, as given by EOQ model:

| | | |
|---|---|---:|
| Fixed cost (£200 per investment) | = 50 × £200 | £10,000 |
| Interest lost | = ½ × 100,000 × 0.2 | 10,000 |
| Variable cost: 2 per cent of sum invested at any time | = £5m × 0.02 | 100,000 |
| | | £120,000 |

A major criticism of the above representation is that it ignores the reduction of the weekly investment of £100,000 to take account of the costs of investment.

(d) The investment costs have changed to £450 for each investment made plus $1\frac{1}{2}$ per cent of sum invested. This changes the value of $Q$ from £100,000 to:

$$Q = \frac{2 \times 5,000,000 \times 450}{0.2}$$

$$= £150,000$$

Number of investments = approximately 33 times a year.

# APPENDIX 3. SUGGESTED ANSWERS TO EXAMINATION QUESTIONS

New total costs as given by EOQ model:

| | | |
|---|---|---:|
| Fixed cost (£450 per investment) | $= 33\frac{1}{2} \times £450$ | £15,000 |
| Interest lost | $= \frac{1}{2} \times 150{,}000 \times 0.2$ | 15,000 |
| Variable cost $1\frac{1}{2}$ per cent | $= £5\text{m} \times 0.015$ | 75,000 |
| | | £105,000 |

This gives a reduction in costs of £15,000 per year.

(e) The company has decided to hold, as a buffer stock, cash to the value of 2 per cent of the yearly premium. This does not affect the economic order quantity but will increase the maximum stock level from £100,000 to £100,000 + 2 per cent of £5m, which is £200,000.

## 108.

(a) Annual demand $D = 24{,}000$

  Price $p = £2$

  $i = 10$ per cent

  $c = £150$.

  $$\therefore Q = \frac{2 \times 24{,}000 \times 150}{0.1 \times 2}$$

  EO $Q = \underline{\underline{6{,}000}}$.

Order 6,000 items every three months.
Annual holding cost

$$\frac{1}{2} \times 6{,}000 \times 2 \times 0.1 + 4 \times 150$$

$$= \underline{\underline{£1{,}200}}.$$

(b) *See* Table 43.

| | | | |
|---|---|---:|---:|
| Proportion of time in stock | | $= \dfrac{1{,}925}{1{,}925 + 125}$ | $= 0.939$ |
| $\therefore$ Average monthly stock in June | $= \frac{1}{2} \times 1{,}925 \times 0.939$ | | $= 903.8$ |
| Proportion of time out of stock | $= 1 - 0.939$ | | $= 0.061$ |
| $\therefore$ Average monthly stock-out in June | $= \frac{1}{2} \times 125 \times 0.061$ | | $= 3.8$. |

Stock-out only occurs at end of June.

Stockholding cost $= \dfrac{35{,}703.8}{12} \times 0.1 \times 2 = £595.06$.

Shortage cost $= \frac{1}{12} \times 3.8 \times 4 \quad = £1.27$.

Table 43. Monthly stock position.

| Month | Stock at beginning | Demand | Stock at end | Average stock | Average shortage |
|---|---|---|---|---|---|
| January | 6,000 | 2,000 | 4,000 | 5,000 | – |
| February | 4,000 | 2,025 | 1,975 | 2,987.5 | – |
| March | 1,975 | 1,950 | 25 | 1,000 | – |
| April | 6,025 | 2,000 | 4,025 | 5,025 | – |
| May | 4,025 | 2,100 | 1,925 | 2,975 | – |
| June | 1,925 | 2,050 | (125) | 903.8 | 3.8 |
| July | 5,875 | 2,000 | 3,875 | 4,875 | – |
| August | 3,875 | 1,975 | 1,900 | 2,887.5 | – |
| Septembr | 1,900 | 1,900 | 0 | 950 | – |
| October | 6,000 | 2,000 | 4,000 | 5,000 | – |
| November | 4,000 | 1,900 | 2,100 | 3,050 | – |
| December | 2,100 | 2,100 | 0 | 1,050 | |
| | | | | 35,703.8 | |

∴ EOQ estimate of holding cost is £600 while holding cost + shortage cost under (b) is;

$$595.06 + 1.27 = £596.33.$$

(c) The difference is negligible, showing that the EOQ model is not very sensitive to small changes in demand.

**109.**

(a) Derivation of economic batch quantity.
Let order quantity be $Q$ units:

$d$ = annual demand for the product

$t_1$ = time interval stock is actually being produced.

For the above, maximum stock, which occurs the instant production ceases, is the amount produced, $Q$, minus the amount used up in time interval $t_1$.

Maximum stock is therefore $Q - t_1 d$.

Let $r$ = production rate.
As $t_1$ is the time to produce a quantity $Q$, $T_1 = \dfrac{Q}{r}$.

Substituting this value of $t_1$ in the expression for maximum stock above,

$$\text{Maximum stock} = Q - \frac{dQ}{r}$$

$$= Q\left(1 - \frac{d}{r}\right).$$

# APPENDIX 3. SUGGESTED ANSWERS TO EXAMINATION QUESTIONS

$$\text{Average stock} = \frac{Q}{2}\left(1 - \frac{d}{r}\right).$$

Let $p$ = cost price per item,

$i$ = stockholding cost p.a. (expressed as a fraction of stock value).

Stockholding cost per annum = $ip$

and Total annual stockholding cost = $\frac{ipQ}{2}\left(1 - \frac{d}{r}\right)$

$$\text{Number of runs per annum} = \frac{d}{Q}$$

If $C$ = set-up cost per batch, the annual set-up cost = $\frac{cd}{Q}$.

Therefore the total variable cost (stockholding and set-up) is

$$\frac{ipQ}{2}\left(1 - \frac{d}{r}\right) + \frac{cd}{Q^2}.$$

Minimize by differentiation and equate derivative to zero:

$$\frac{d}{dQ}(\text{total cost}) = \frac{ip}{2}\left(1 - \frac{d}{r}\right) - \frac{cd}{Q^2} = 0.$$

$$\therefore \quad \frac{ip}{2}\left(1 - \frac{d}{r}\right) = \frac{cd}{Q^2}.$$

$$\therefore \quad Q = \sqrt{\frac{2cd}{ip\left(1 - \frac{d}{r}\right)}}.$$

(b) Economic batch quantity $Q = \sqrt{\dfrac{2cd}{ip\left(1 - \dfrac{d}{r}\right)}}$ as above

$$= \sqrt{\frac{2 \times 540 \times 15{,}000}{0.2 \times 2\left(1 - \dfrac{15{,}000}{135{,}000}\right)}}$$

*Note:* $d = 300 \text{ units} \times 50$, $r = 75 \text{ units} \times 36 \times 50$.

$$= \sqrt{\frac{1{,}080 \times 15{,}000}{\frac{4}{10}\left(1 - \frac{1}{9}\right)}}$$

$$= \sqrt{\frac{1{,}080 \times 15{,}000}{\frac{16}{45}}}$$

$$= \sqrt{\frac{1{,}080 \times 15{,}000 \times 45}{16}}$$

$$= \sqrt{67.5 \times 15{,}000 \times 45}$$

$$= \sqrt{45{,}562{,}500}$$

$$= \underline{\underline{6{,}750 \text{ units.}}}$$

**110.**

Annual demand $d = 400$ units
Cost per unit $p = £10$
Cost of ordering $c = £4$
Stockholding costs $i = 20$ per cent
Lead time $= 1$ month
Safety stock $= 10$ units

(a) *Reorder level*

The reorder level is the sum of safety stock and the expected demand in the lead time. So, reorder level

$$= 10 + \frac{400}{12} = 43 \text{ units.}$$

(b) *Reduction in stock investment*

*New system.* The economic order quantity $Q$ is given by:

$$Q = \sqrt{\frac{2cd}{ip}}.$$

Substituting, 

$$Q = \sqrt{\frac{2 \times 4 \times 400}{0.2 \times 10}}$$

$$= 40 \text{ units.}$$

Thus on average the total stock held under the new system

$$= \text{safety stock} + \frac{Q}{2} = 10 + 20 = 30 \text{ units.}$$

APPENDIX 3. SUGGESTED ANSWERS TO EXAMINATION QUESTIONS 511

The average stock investment is then the product of this average number of units held and the cost per unit = £(10 × 30).
New stock investment = £300.

*Old system.* Previously, 200 units were ordered at a time and so the number held was 100 giving stock investment of £1,000.
Thus the reduction in stock investment is £700.

(c) *Reduction in inventory costs*
Inventory costs comprise the ordering costs and holding costs.

*New system:* Annual ordering costs $= \dfrac{cd}{Q}$ $= £\left(\dfrac{4 \times 400}{40}\right)$

$\phantom{New system: Annual ordering costs = cd/Q} = £40$

Stockholding costs = 20 per cent of £300 = £60
∴ Total inventory costs = £100

*Old system:* Annual ordering costs with 2 orders p.a. = £8
Stockholding cost = £200
∴ Total inventory cost = £208

Thus total annual inventory costs can be anticipated to fall by £108. However, in the first year the safety stock has to be purchased at a cost of 10 × £10 = £100. Therefore, while the savings in the first year would be £108 the cost reduction of the system would be only £8. In subsequent years the cost reduction would be £108 since the cost of holding the safety stock has been included in the calculation.

## 111.

(a) First find the expected weekly demand. This is $\sum PX$ where:

$$
\begin{array}{r}
PX \\
0.00 \\
0.06 \\
0.14 \\
0.27 \\
0.44 \\
1.05 \\
1.02 \\
0.84 \\
0.64 \\
\underline{0.54} \\
\sum PX = \underline{5.00}
\end{array}
$$

We have therefore: $d = 50 \times 5 = 250$; $H = 40$; $c = 50$, so that

$$EOQ = \sqrt{\frac{2 \times 50 \times 250}{40}} = 25.$$

∴ 10 orders are placed per annum.

(b) Now find expected shortages for the different levels of buffer stock.

With buffer stock = 0, reorder level = 5.

In this case:

| Demand | Stock-out in units | Probability | Probability stock-out in units |
|---|---|---|---|
| 6 | 1 | 0.17 | 0.17 |
| 7 | 2 | 0.12 | 0.24 |
| 8 | 3 | 0.08 | 0.24 |
| 9 | 4 | 0.06 | 0.24 |
| | | | $\Sigma = 0.89$ |

With buffer stock = 1 we have reorder level = 6 and in this case:

| Demand | Stock-out in units | Probability | Probability stock-out in units |
|---|---|---|---|
| 7 | 1 | 0.12 | 0.12 |
| 8 | 2 | 0.08 | 0.16 |
| 9 | 3 | 0.06 | 0.18 |
| | | | $\Sigma = 0.46$ |

With buffer stock = 2 and reorder level = 7:

| Demand | Stock-out in units | Probability | Probability stock-out in units |
|---|---|---|---|
| 8 | 1 | 0.08 | 0.08 |
| 9 | 2 | 0.06 | 0.12 |
| | | | $\Sigma = 0.20$ |

# APPENDIX 3. SUGGESTED ANSWERS TO EXAMINATION QUESTIONS

and with buffer stock = 3 and reorder level = 8:

| Demand | Stock-out in units | Probability | Probability stock-out in units |
|---|---|---|---|
| 9 | 1 | 0.06 | 0.06 |
| | | | $\Sigma = 0.06$ |

Of course, with buffer stock = 4 the expected shortage is zero. Now produce the table of costs. Recall that there are 10 cycles per annum and that each unit of shortage costs £20. The table is:

| Buffer stock | Expected stock-outs per cycle | Expected stock-outs per annum | Stock-out cost | Buffer stock holding stock | Total |
|---|---|---|---|---|---|
| 0 | 0.89 | 8.9 | 178 | 0 | 178 |
| 1 | 0.46 | 4.6 | 92 | 40 | 132 |
| 2 | 0.20 | 2.0 | 40 | 80 | 120* |
| 3 | 0.06 | 0.6 | 12 | 120 | 132 |
| 4 | 0.00 | 0.0 | 0 | 160 | 160 |

Hence the optimum size of buffer stock is two units. This gives a recorder level of 7.

(c) Now, if the shortage cost was stock-out in units the total column would read:

| Buffer stock | Total |
|---|---|
| 0 | 8.9 stock-out in units |
| 1 | 4.6 stock-out in units + 40 |
| 2 | 2.0 stock-out in units + 80 |
| 3 | 0.6 stock-out in units + 80 |
| 4 | 160 |

For buffer stock = 2 optimal we must have 2 stock-out in units + 80 $\leqslant$ 4.6 stock-out in units + 40,

$\therefore$ stock-out in units $\geqslant$ 15.38 (greatest lower bound).

2 stock-out in units + 80 $\leqslant$ 8.9 stock-out in units,

$\therefore$ stock-out in units $\geqslant$ 11.59.

2 stockout in units + 80 ⩽ 0.6 stock-out in units + 120,

∴ stock-out in units ⩽ 28.57 (least upper bound).

2 stock-out in units + 80 ⩽ 160,

∴ stock-out in units ⩽ 40.

So, the solution is optimal for 15.38 ⩽ stock-out in units ⩽ 28.57.

A sensitivity analysis can be conducted on $H$ but it is rather more complicated than the above analysis on stock-out in units because the EOQ depends on $H$.

## 112.

### IKAUNA LTD

(a) (i) Let $d$ = annual demand = 4,000 units,

$ip$ = cost of holding one item for a year = £8,

$c$ = ordering costs per batch = £40 + £120 = £160.

The economic order quantity is given by:

$$Q = \sqrt{\frac{2cd}{ip}}$$

$$= \sqrt{\frac{2 \times 160 \times 4,000}{8}}$$

= 400 wheels.

(ii) On the basis of an order quantity of 400 wheels, there will be 10 orders per annum.

Total annual costs = Stockholding + Delivery + Purchase Price

$$= \frac{ipQ}{2} + \frac{cd}{Q} + £4,000 \times 12$$

$$= \frac{8 \times 400}{2} + \frac{160 \times 4,000}{400} + £48,000$$

= £1,600 + £1,600 + £48,000

= £51,200.

The alternative scheme produces total costs of £52,000. As this is greater than the total annual costs it should be rejected.

(b) (i) The data given are as follows:

Fifty-week working year.

APPENDIX 3. SUGGESTED ANSWERS TO EXAMINATION QUESTIONS        515

Lead time 4 weeks.

Variance of demand in any week 156.25 units.

Annual demand is 4,000.

$\therefore$ Weekly demand is $\dfrac{4{,}000}{50} = 80$.

The standard deviation $= \sqrt{156.25}$

$\qquad\qquad\qquad\qquad\quad = 12.5$.

$\therefore$ For a $97\tfrac{1}{2}$ per cent service level:

Reorder level $= 4 \times 80 + 1.96 \times 12.5 \times \sqrt{4} = \underline{\underline{369}}$.

(This implies that the buffer stock $= \underline{\underline{49}}$.)

(ii) At a $97\tfrac{1}{2}$ per cent service level, the buffer stock $= 49$ units.

| | | |
|---|---|---|
| Hence additional stockholding charges | $= 49 \times 8$ | $= £392$ |
| The probability of a stock-out | $= 0.025$ | |
| $\therefore$ With ten orders the number of stock-outs | $= 0.025 \times 10$ | |
| $\therefore$ The cost of a stock-out | $= 0.025 \times 10 \times 120$ | $= \underline{£30}$ |
| Total additional costs | | $\underline{\underline{£422}}$ |

At an 80 per cent service level the buffer stock is:

| | | |
|---|---|---|
| $0.84 \times 12.5 \times 2$ | $= 21$. | |
| Hence additional stockholding charges | $= 21 \times 8$ | $= £168$ |
| The probability of a stock-out | $= 0.2$. | |
| $\therefore$ Expected stock-outs per annum | $= 0.2 \times 10 = 2$ | |
| $\therefore$ Stock-out costs | $= 2 \times 120$ | $= \underline{£240}$ |
| Total additional costs | | $= \underline{\underline{£408}}$ |

On the basis of costs, the reduction in service level is advisable.

## 113.

(a) The given data are summarised below:

| | |
|---|---|
| Annual consumption | 125,000 screws |
| Cost of screws | £4 per 1,000 |
| Cost of storage | £1 per 1,000 screws per year |
| Minimum return required | 20 per cent |
| Cost of order | £5. |

The total annual holding cost is made up of two components here—the cost of storage and the opportunity cost of capital.

Hence $ip = 0.001 + 0.0008 = 0.0018$.

The economic order quantity is given by:

$$Q = \sqrt{\frac{2cd}{ip}}$$

$$= \sqrt{\frac{2 \times 5 \times 125{,}000}{0.0018}}$$

$$Q = \underline{\underline{26{,}352}}.$$

(b) There is no change in the reordering policy if there is a lead time of two weeks. Instead of ordering when the stock level is zero an order will be placed when two weeks' supply (i.e. 5,000 units) remain. Hence the EOQ is unchanged.

(c) Instead of buying from outside, the company has decided to produce the screws. Hence the production model will apply.

Variable production costs are £2 per 1,000.
Holding costs are now £1.4 per 1,000.
Set-up costs per batch are £15.

$$\therefore \quad Q = \sqrt{\frac{2cd}{ip\left(1 - \dfrac{d}{r}\right)}}$$

$$= \sqrt{\frac{2 \times 15 \times 125{,}000}{0.0014\left(1 - \dfrac{125{,}000}{1{,}250{,}000}\right)}}$$

$$= \underline{\underline{54{,}554}}.$$

(d) Here a decision has to be taken as to which system to utilise to deal with fluctuating demand. The company has to decide either on an optimum level of buffer stock or an appropriate service level.

(e) This part of the question is not expressed very clearly. Presumably a buffer stock of 2,500 is required. This will give a reorder level of 7,500.

## 114.

(a) (i) Queues form when the service required by a customer is not immediately available. Queues are usually composed of people but objects too can form queues, e.g. broken-down machines awaiting maintenance attention.

### Queuing situations
Examples of queuing situations are:

> customers queuing for service in a shop;
> passengers queuing for a bus;
> ships queuing for berths or locks;
> people on a council waiting list;
> semi-processed parts queuing for the next process.

As the above list indicates, queues differ. Some form rapidly and disperse slowly (e.g. at a ticket barrier after a train has pulled in), some form slowly and disperse rapidly (e.g. a bus queue) and some form and disperse erratically (e.g. queues at a Post Office counter).

### The economics of queues
Queues involve two opposing economic aspects.

Having idle items in a queue costs money, e.g. production lost while a machine is out of order. The smaller the service facility the longer the queues and the higher the costs.

Conversely, it costs money to increase the service facility. Moreover, the larger the service facility the quicker it will disperse queues and, therefore, the more often it will stand idle.

Queues are studied so as to enable the optimum service facility to be selected so that the overall cost of a service is minimised.

### Basic queue features
Queuing situations reveal certain basic features:

> the arrival pattern
> the service pattern
> the service mechanism
> the queue discipline.

#### ARRIVAL PATTERN
A variety of patterns can exist. Components can arrive in large groups, regularly or irregularly (e.g. passengers disembarking from trains) or at random (e.g. customers at a supermarket). Random arrival is both the commonest and the most complex to analyse.

#### SERVICE PATTERN
Servicing similarly takes a variety of patterns. Servicing can be regular (e.g. machining identical parts) or virtually instant with periods of no service at all (e.g. passengers boarding a bus at a bus stop), or again random.

#### SERVICE MECHANISM
The service mechanism at which customers arrive may be the most controllable feature of a queueing system.

The simplest form of service mechanism is a single facility through which all customers must pass if they are to be served. More complicated systems arise when there are several channels, which may or may not have the same characteristics.

Multiple service channels may be arranged in parallel so that a customer is served by any one channel. A single queue may form, from which a customer is drawn when the next channel becomes available; or a queue may form in front of each channel; or the number of queues may be greater than one but less than the number of channels.

Banks, supermarkets and toll-booths are often arranged in this way.

### QUEUE DISCIPLINE

The simplest discipline is for all arrivals to form a simple queue and wait until they receive service.

Queue discipline appertains to the different ways in which customers are transferred from the queue to the service channel when one becomes available.

The classical discipline (FIFO) is for the customer who has been queueing the longest to be served next.

However, it may be possible to have a priority system of customer selection (e.g. aircraft landing). Sometimes a LIFO system may exist (papers from an in-tray) and sometimes components are served at random (getting through to an engaged telephone number).

None of the disciplines for transferring customers from the queue to the service channel affects the rate at which the channel operates, but the way in which waiting time is suffered by different customers is affected, and hence probably the overall economics of the system.

(b) (i) SIMPLE QUEUES

A simple queue is defined as one that has the following features:

> variable arrivals
> single service channel
> single queue, infinite capacity
> first come first served queue discipline
> single, follow-on service discipline
> variable service times
> discrete customers
> infinite population of potential customers
> no simultaneous arrivals
> traffic intensity less than one (*see* below).

### TRAFFIC INTENSITY

An important measure of a simple queue is its traffic intensity, where traffic intensity is defined as the average service time divided by the average interval between successive arrivals at the service point. It can be expressed as:

$$\text{Traffic intensity } (e) = \frac{\text{Average rate of arrival}}{\text{Average rate of service}} = \frac{\lambda}{\mu}.$$

A necessary condition for the system to have settled down is that the traffic intensity is less than 1, i.e. that the average rate of arrival is less than the average rate of service. If this is not so then the size of the queue gets longer and longer as time goes on.

*Tutorial note*
Using symbols  e = *traffic intensity*
$\mu$ = *rate of service*
$\lambda$ = *rate of arrival*

*the following formulae have been derived for a simple queue with traffic intensity less than 1:*

$$\text{Average time in system } \bar{t} = \frac{1}{\mu - \lambda}.$$

$$\text{Average time in queue } \bar{w} = \frac{\lambda}{\mu(\mu - \lambda)}.$$

$$\text{Average number in system } \bar{s} = \frac{\lambda}{\mu - \lambda}.$$

$$\text{Average number in queue } \bar{q} = \frac{\lambda^2}{\mu(\mu - \lambda)}.$$

(ii) Mean service rate = 20 customers per hour

As $\bar{t} = \frac{1}{\mu - \lambda}$ divide top and bottom of the fraction by $\mu$. This gives

$$\bar{t} = \frac{1}{\mu(1 - e)}$$

Assuming various traffic intensities, Table 44 can be drawn up.

Table 44. Traffic intensity and time in system.

| $e$ | $1 - e$ | $\dfrac{e}{1 - e}$ | Time in system $\dfrac{1}{\mu(1 - e)}$ (*minutes*) |
|---|---|---|---|
| 0.1 | 0.9 | 1/9 | 3.33 |
| 0.2 | 0.8 | 2/8 | 3.75 |
| 0.3 | 0.7 | 3/7 | 4.29 |
| 0.4 | 0.6 | 4/6 | 5 |
| 0.5 | 0.5 | 5/5 | 6 |
| 0.6 | 0.4 | 6/4 | 7.5 |
| 0.7 | 0.3 | 7/3 | 10 |
| 0.8 | 0.2 | 8/2 | 15 |
| 0.9 | 0.1 | 9/1 | 30 |

The graph in Fig. 175 can be now be drawn.

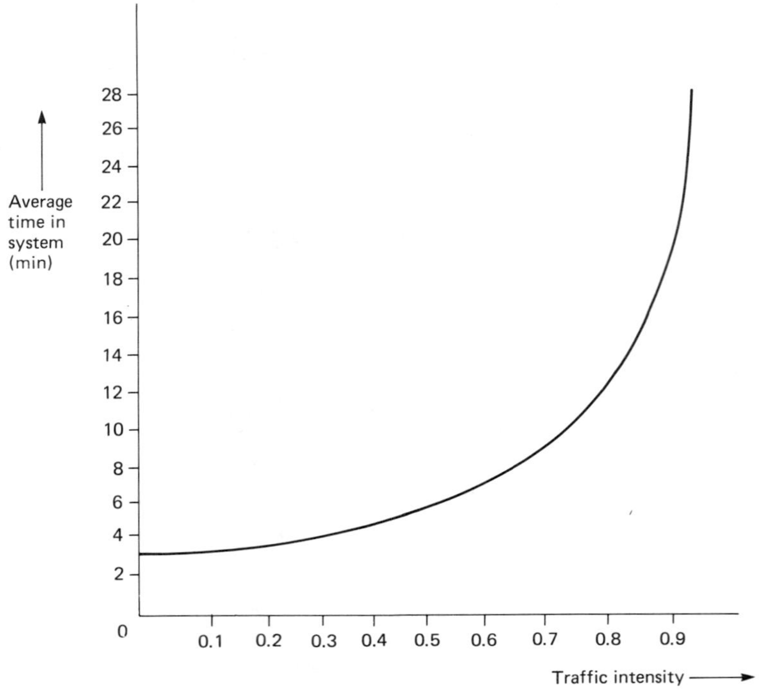

Fig. 175. *Graph of traffic intensity against average time in system (simple queue).*

**115.**

(a) This part of the question has been answered in great detail in the previous question.

(b) **MAJOR LIMITATIONS OF QUEUING THEORY**
Queuing theory, and the standard models developed as part of its framework, have limited application. Simple queuing situations may be capable of explicit mathematical analysis. Some systems, however, are so complicated that they defy straightforward mathematical form. For example, the distribution of service times may not follow any well-known statistical distribution that can be written down in straightforward mathematical form. Similarly, current queuing theory cannot deal with a situation which has two types of arrivals with different arrival patterns (both using the same service point) where one type of arrival has priority. In such situations an alternative approach is the use of simulation. Simulation is simply a means of creating a typical life history of the system under given conditions, working out step-by-step what happens to each customer as he arrives and passes through the different parts of the system.

# APPENDIX 3. SUGGESTED ANSWERS TO EXAMINATION QUESTIONS

**116.**

Average service rate $\mu = \dfrac{60}{3} = 20$ per hour.

Average arrival rate $\lambda = 8$ per hour.

$\therefore$ Traffic intensity $e = \dfrac{\lambda}{\mu} = \dfrac{8}{20} = 0.4$.

Present waiting time (i.e. time in queue) $= \dfrac{\lambda}{\mu(\mu - \lambda)} = \dfrac{8}{20(20 - 8)} = 2$ minutes.

The current waiting time is only 2 minutes which (as far as the telephone company are concerned) does not justify installation of a second telephone.

To achieve the minimum of 3 minutes waiting time (the company's requirements), the traffic intensity would need to satisfy:

$$\overline{w} = \dfrac{\lambda}{\mu(\mu - \lambda)} = \dfrac{3}{60}$$ (where it is given that average queueing time is 3 minutes).

*Note: the above is the formula for waiting time (i.e. time in queue).*

With $\mu = 20$ this gives:

$$\dfrac{\lambda}{20(20 - \lambda)} = \dfrac{1}{20}$$

$$20\lambda = 20(20 - \lambda)$$

$$\therefore \lambda = 20 - \lambda$$

$$\therefore 2\lambda = 20$$

$$\therefore \lambda = 10,$$

i.e. an arrival rate of 10 per hour; the inter-arrival time is 6 minutes. Thus the usage must increase to at least 10 callers per hour before the telephone company will install another telephone.

**117.**

(a) Average rate of arrival $\lambda = 12$ per hour.

Average service rate $\mu = 15$ per hour.

Traffic intensity $= \dfrac{\text{Average arrival rate}}{\text{Average service rate}}$

$= \dfrac{12}{15}$

$= \underline{\underline{0.8}}$.

(b) Average number in the system

$$\bar{s} = \frac{\lambda}{\mu - \lambda} = \frac{12}{15 - 12}$$

∴ Number in the system = 4.

(c) The average time from entering to leaving the system represents "time in the system".

$$\text{Average time in system } t = \frac{1}{\mu - \lambda} = \frac{1}{15 - 12} = \tfrac{1}{3} \text{ hour} = \underline{20 \text{ minutes}}.$$

(d) The average number of items awaiting inspection is the number in the queue.

$$\text{Average number in the queue } \bar{q} = \frac{\lambda^2}{\mu(\mu - \lambda)} = \frac{12^2}{15(15 - 12)} = 3.2.$$

On average there are 3.2 items in the queue.

(e) The average time an item spends awaiting inspection is the average time in the queue.

$$\text{Average time in the queue } \bar{w} = \frac{\lambda}{\mu(\mu - \lambda)} = \frac{12}{15(15 - 12)} = 0.267 \text{ hour}$$

$$= \underline{16 \text{ minutes}}.$$

(This could have been obtained by subtracting from the time in the system the average service time.)

**118.**

$$\text{Average arrival rate} = \frac{60}{3} = 20 \text{ per hour}.$$

Average service rate = 30 per hour.

$$\text{Traffic intensity } (e) = \frac{20}{30} = 0.667.$$

(a) The probability of a customer arriving and having to wait for service is given by the traffic intensity. The traffic intensity is a measure of use of the system and hence is also the probability of an arrival having to wait. In other words, it is the probability that there are one or more customers already in the system,

  i.e.  $e = \tfrac{2}{3}$

(b) This is also $e = \tfrac{2}{3}$.

# APPENDIX 3. SUGGESTED ANSWERS TO EXAMINATION QUESTIONS

(c) This is the average number in the system

$$\bar{s} = \frac{\lambda}{\mu - \lambda} = \frac{20}{30 - 20} = 2.$$

(d) Average time in system $\bar{t} = \frac{\lambda^2}{\mu - \lambda} = \frac{20^2}{30 - 20} = \frac{1}{10}$ hour = 6 minutes.

(f) $e$ is the probability that there are one or more customers already in the system.
$1 - e = p_0$ is the probability that there are no customers in the system at any time.
In the given situation, the manager wants customers to be served immediately on arrival 40 per cent of the time. A person will be served immediately only if there is no one there already.

Thus $\qquad p_0 = 1 - e = 0.4,$

$\qquad \therefore \quad e \quad = 0.6.$

The existing arrival rate $\lambda = 20$ per hour,

$$\therefore \quad e = 0.6 = \frac{20}{\mu},$$

$$\therefore \quad \mu = 3.33 \text{ per hour,}$$

an average service time of 1.8 minutes.

Original service time was 2 minutes. This new time is a 10 per cent reduction based on original time.

(*Note:* The calculations above were designed to reduce service time so as to produce $p_0 = 0.4$.)

**119.**

Average arrival rate $\lambda = 30$ per hour.

Average service rate $\mu = 40$ per hour.

$\therefore \quad$ Traffic intensity $e = \frac{30}{40} = \frac{3}{4}.$

Average time in system $\bar{t} = \frac{1}{\mu - \lambda} = \frac{1}{40 - 30} = \frac{1}{10} = 6$ minutes.

Under the new system the serving time can be reduced to 1 minute, i.e. 60 an hour.

$\therefore \qquad$ Traffic intensity $= \frac{30}{60} = 0.5.$

The new average time in system $t = \frac{1}{\mu - \lambda} = \frac{1}{60 - 30} = \frac{1}{30}$ hour = 2 minutes.

The saving in system time per customer is $6 - 2 = 4$ minutes.

A customer arrives every 2 minutes. Therefore 30 customers arrive every hour.

Hence the total time saved by all the customers in one hour = 4 × 30 = 120 minutes. This gives a benefit of 120 × £0.05 = £6. As the cost of achieving this is £4 the reduction in service time is justified.

**120.**

(a) Assumptions of simple queuing theory:

  (i)   variable arrivals
  (ii)  single service channel
  (iii) single queue, infinite capacity
  (iv)  first come first served queue discipline
  (v)   single, follow-on service discipline
  (vi)  variable service time
  (vii) discrete customers
  (viii) infinite population of potential customers
  (ix)  no simultaneous arrivals
  (x)   traffic intensity less than one.

(b) The average number being served or waiting to be served is the number in the system.

$$\text{Average number in the system } \bar{s} = \frac{\lambda}{\mu - \lambda}$$

Now, $\lambda = 2$, $\mu = 3$,

$$\therefore \quad \text{Average number in system } \bar{s} = \frac{2}{3-2} = 2.$$

(c) The average time a machinist spends waiting for service is the time in the queue.

$$\text{Average time in the queue } \bar{q} = \frac{\lambda}{\mu(\mu - \lambda)} = \frac{2}{3(3-2)} = 0.667 \text{ hour} = 40 \text{ minutes}.$$

(d) The average number of machinists in the system = 2.

$$\text{Average time in system } \bar{t} = \frac{1}{\mu - \lambda} = \frac{1}{3-2} = 1 \text{ hour}.$$

The cost of machinists away from work = £4 per hour.

$\therefore$ Two machinists every hour at £4 = £8 per hour
Attendant cost = £1.5 per hour
$\therefore$ Total cost per hour = £9.5 per hour
$\therefore$ Cost per 8 hour day = £9.5 × 8 = £76.

(e) It is assumed that there is still a single service point but the average service rate is now 4 per hour,

i.e. $\mu = 4$, $\lambda = 2$.

$$\text{Average number in system } \bar{s} = \frac{\lambda}{\mu - \lambda} = \frac{2}{4-2} = 1.$$

$$\text{Average time in system } \bar{t} = \frac{1}{\mu - \lambda} = \frac{1}{4-2} = \frac{1}{2} \text{ hour.}$$

The costs can be calculated:

Machinist costs per hour are £4 but on average there is 1 in the system who spends $\frac{1}{2}$ hour. This costs £2 and attendant cost per hour is now £3. Total hourly cost now is £5 and the cost for an eight hour day = £40.

(f) The question did not give full definitions and assumptions were made in the solution that "arrival rate" represented "average arrival rate", that "service potential" is "average service rate" and that two attendants working as a team implied a single service point operating at twice the speed.

## 121.

(a) The basic data are summarised below:

The cost clerk is responsible for preparing an invoice following the receipt of an order from a customer. One invoice is required for each order. For each order received during the morning, an invoice should be sent out the same afternoon. For each order received during the afternoon an invoice should be sent the following morning.

The situation is to be analysed by means of the simple queuing model, identifying the components of the queuing system and indicating the assumptions which must be made.

To analyse a queuing system it needs to be broken down into three parts:

(i) input process;

(ii) queuing discipline;

(iii) service mechanism.

In the given situation the orders coming in form the input to the system. The pile of orders that builds up represents the queue and the preparation of the invoice for each order represents the service.

The assumptions which have to be made are those of the basic model ($M/M/1$ system). These are: customers arrive randomly for service and are described by a Poisson distribution. The customers form a single queue (FIFO) and there is a single follow-on service discipline. The service time distribution is negative exponential with a single server and no constraint on queue size.

In the given situation, these assumptions may or may not hold true. How for instance does the cost clerk receive the orders? Is their arrival truly random? Does he actually deal with them on a FIFO basis? Does the time taken to create the invoice follow a negative exponential distribution, i.e. is it a random event?

Certainly a reasonable sample would need to be analysed before giving suitable answers to the above questions.

(b) Simulation has a part to play in the above situation because exact mathematical solution of queuing situations is very involved and usually not possible. So the best approach to the design of a service facility to meet a particular demand (and this is the purpose of the given situation) is to collect data on arrival rates and service times together with likely variations in these factors and build a model which simulates arrivals and service in a way that represents real life.

In the given situation an arrival time distribution and a service time distribution are required for the simulation to proceed (a model must be set up based on the factors affecting the outcome, taking into account the interrelationship).

Each factor (here the arrival time and service time, i.e. creation of invoice) must be represented by the range of possible values it can take together with the probability of each value actually occurring.

The Monte Carlo method approximates the required result (the probability distribution of the outcome) by taking a *controlled* random sample of combinations of the variables in the model in such a way that the probability distributions of the variable values are reflected in the result obtained.

Random numbers are allotted pro rata to the relative probability of occurrence of each value in the data and the interaction of the elements is developed by taking each number (or combination of numbers) in turn from a chosen series in a random-number table, each number indicating the occurrence of a certain value.

In a given situation, a pair of random numbers would be applied to the arrival time distribution to give the actual arrival time of a particular order. A pair of random numbers would then be applied to the service time distribution to give the time taken to create an invoice. The order would obviously be dealt with immediately if there was no queue or otherwise join the queue of waiting orders. A number of simulation runs will be performed to give a statistically representative set of possible outcomes. (This would represent a long sequence of mornings and afternoons.) The simulation would indicate which orders did not get dealt with by the stated deadline. The total number not dealt with in time expressed as a percentage of total arrivals gives the required proportion.

## 122.

**CRONUS LTD**

(a) In the original situation the average rate of arrival in the stores is 16 per hour and the average rate of service is 20 per hour.

$$\text{Traffic intensity } e = \frac{\lambda}{\mu} = \frac{16}{20} = 0.8.$$

$$\therefore \text{ Average time in queue } \bar{w} = \frac{\lambda}{\mu(\mu - \lambda)} = \frac{16}{20(20 - 16)} = \underline{\underline{0.2 \text{ hours}}}.$$

If the second attendant is employed there is a single-queue, multi-server case. The models used here were given in the examination:

$$e = \frac{\lambda}{c\mu}$$

$$\text{Average time in queue } = \frac{(eC)^c}{c!(1-e)^2 c\mu} p_0$$

and

$$p_0 = \frac{c!(1-e)}{(eC)^c + c!(1-e)\left(\sum_{n=0}^{c-1} \frac{1}{n!}(eC)^n\right)}$$

where $e$ = traffic intensity
$\lambda$ = mean rate of arrivals
$\mu$ = mean rate of service
$c$ = number of service points
$p_0$ = probability that there are no customers in the system.

On substituting,

$$e = \frac{16}{2 \times 20} = 0.4$$

$$p_0 = \frac{1.2}{2.8},$$

and the average time in queue is:

$$\frac{0.64}{2 \times 0.36 \times 2 \times 20} \times \frac{1.2}{2.8} = 0.009524 \text{ hour}.$$

Employing the second attendant gives a reduction in waiting time of $0.2 - 0.009524$ hours per arrival. As there are 16 arrivals every hour and the length of the normal working year is 2,000 hours the annual saving can be worked out. The wages of employees visiting section D are £1.60 per hour.

$$\therefore \text{ Annual saving} = 1.6 \times (0.2 - 0.009524) \times 16 \times 2,000$$

$$= \underline{\underline{£9,750}} \text{ approximately}.$$

The initial cost is £2,000 on capital equipment and the cost of capital is 15 per cent.

```
              0     1     2     3     4     5     6     7     8     9    10
              |     |     |     |     |     |     |     |     |     |     |
Investment  2,000
Saving            9,750 9,750 9,750 9,750 9,750 9,750 9,750 9,750 9,750 9,750
Wages            (3,000)(3,000)(3,000)(3,000)(3,000)(3,000)(3,000)(3,000)(3,000)(3,000)
```

| Year | Flow  | Discount factor |       | Present value |
|------|-------|-----------------|-------|---------------|
| 0    | 2,000 | 1               |       | 2,000         |
| 1–10 | 6,750 | 5.0188          |       | 33,876.9      |
|      |       |                 | NPV = | + 31,876.9    |

This implies that the second attendant should be employed.

(b) Students are required to give a brief description of simulation and its application to queuing situations.

## 123.

*Advantages and disadvantages of simulation*

Simulation is at times described as indirect experimentation. An essential phase of operational research is representation of the system under study through the construction of a model. Simulation is the process of experimenting on the model rather than on the operation which the model represents.

The following are some of the commonly described advantages of simulation.

(a) It makes the study of very complicated systems and subsystems possible.

(b) By use of simulation, the consequences for a system of possible changes in parameters or structural alterations can be investigated in terms of the model.

(c) The knowledge of a system obtained in designing and conducting the simulation is often very valuable.

(d) It can be a useful teaching aid (e.g. business games, case studies etc.).

(e) The simulation of complicated systems can identify which variables have the most important influences on system performance.

(f) It can be used to experiment with novel and unfamiliar systems so as to prepare for both routine and extreme eventualities.

(g) It can provide a "pre-service test" for possible new policies before the risk of actually implementing these policies is taken.

However, there are a number of disadvantages:

(a) Simulation does not guarantee optimal solutions.

(b) The simulation exercise can be time-consuming.

(c) Important variables may be left out of the model.

(d) Unnecessary constraints may have been included.

(e) Over-simplification is possible.

(f) Business games (a form of simulation) may be viewed as artificial and seen only as games and not as learning experiences.

## 124.

The simple queuing theory formulae deal with extremely simple queuing situations. Further, they represent only a small fraction of the formulae that have been derived. Multichannel queuing situations involve complex mathematics.

Further, some systems are so complicated that they defy straightforward mathematical form. For example, the distribution of service time may not follow any well-known statistical distribution that can be written down in straightforward mathematical form. In such a situation an alternative approach is the use of simulation.

Simulation is simply a means of creating a typical life history of the system under given conditions, working out step by step what happens to each customer as he arrives and passes through the different parts of the system. In order to do this, one needs to know the detailed characteristics and rules of operation of the system, and to have the relevant measures of the system.

For a queuing situation where units arrive (input), are then serviced and finally leave (output), data are needed about:

(a) the distribution of intervals between arrivals;

(b) the distribution of service times (e.g. how long the cashier takes to add up and take the money);

(c) the processing or service facilities available (e.g. the number of counters and whether these are all general or have some restriction on the type of service offered);

(d) the priority system, if any, operated in the queue or waiting line, i.e. the queue discipline which determines whether there is a common queue or a separate one for each facility.

Given these quantities, a schedule could be written up of the appropriate times for service and exit for a set of arrivals under the various alternatives which it was desired to investigate, say changes in the service facilities available. Using the data ((a) to (d) above), the actual situation is replaced by a model in the form of a flow diagram. For example, original intractable mathematical problems of the effects of alternative methods of operation are now tackled by simulation techniques.

The effect of variability on a queuing situation as a whole is reproduced by sampling from the relevant distributions. For example, sampling from a distribution of the time interval between successive arrivals produces a typical sequence of moments when a customer arrives. Similarly, sampling from a service time distribution gives a typical sequency of the time taken by each customer to be served. The interaction between these can be worked out and hence the time of arrival and departure is determined for each customer. From this sample the average time in the system, for example, is calculated.

When the simulation is carried out for existing conditions, a check is made to see that the correspondence between actual results and the simulation results is sufficiently close.

The simulation can be used again, for different conditions that might arise in the future, in order to predict the likely effects of new conditions. Thus it is possible to experiment with the simulation in a very different way that is impossible with the system itself.

It should be noted that because of the complexity of some situations it has become standard practice to combine two approaches. The first is to use simple queuing models as rough approximations to the real system. Then, with these results, it is possible to develop a computer simulation model to take account of those facets that are important but hard to deal with by mathematical analysis.

In general, queuing theory is quicker to apply and cheaper than simulation and gives firm results. However, it can only be applied to very simplified situations. Simulation is more useful in such situations but more expensive.

## 125.

### ARIES LTD

(a) (i) The given supply and demand distributions are converted to probability distributions and random numbers allotted for each level of supply and demand in accordance with the relevant relative probabilities.

Supply

| Number supplied | Number of days | Probability | Numbers allocated |
|---|---|---|---|
| 50 | 60 | 0.2 | 0–1 |
| 100 | 90 | 0.3 | 2–4 |
| 150 | 90 | 0.3 | 5–7 |
| 200 | 60 | 0.2 | 8–9 |

# APPENDIX 3. SUGGESTED ANSWERS TO EXAMINATION QUESTIONS

Demand

| Number demanded | Number of days | Probability | Numbers allocated |
|---|---|---|---|
| 50 | 60 | 0.2 | 0–1 |
| 100 | 60 | 0.2 | 2–3 |
| 150 | 150 | 0.5 | 4–8 |
| 200 | 30 | 0.1 | 9 |

*Tutorial note: It is possible to use single-digit numbers here.*

The figures for six days trading can be given (Table 45).

Table 45. Six days trading, Aries Ltd.

| Day | Random number | Supply | Random number | Demand | Sales in units | Cost | Revenue | Loss through shortage | Profit (Loss) |
|---|---|---|---|---|---|---|---|---|---|
| 1 | 8 | 200 | 4 | 150 | 150 | £1,200 | £1,500 | – | £300 |
| 2 | 8 | 200 | 0 | 50 | 50 | 1,200 | 500 | – | (700) |
| 3 | 3 | 100 | 3 | 100 | 100 | 600 | 1,000 | – | 400 |
| 4 | 4 | 100 | 7 | 150 | 100 | 600 | 1,000 | £100 | 300 |
| 5 | 9 | 200 | 6 | 150 | 150 | 1,200 | 1,500 | – | 300 |
| 6 | 1 | 50 | 5 | 150 | 50 | 300 | 500 | 200 | 0 |
| | | | | | | | | | £600 |

The estimated daily profit is £100.

∴ Annual profit is £100 × 30 = £30,000.

(ii) The exercise has to be rerun to estimate the value of storage facilities (Table 46).

Table 46. Rerun of Table 45.

| Day | Random number | Supply | Random number | Demand | Sales in units | Cost | Revenue | Shortage loss | $\Sigma$ Store | Profit (Loss) |
|---|---|---|---|---|---|---|---|---|---|---|
| 1 | 8 | 200 | 4 | 150 | 150 | £1,200 | £1,500 | – | 50 | £300 |
| 2 | 8 | 200 | 0 | 50 | 50 | 1,200 | 500 | – | 200 | (700) |
| 3 | 3 | 100 | 3 | 100 | 100 | 600 | 1,000 | – | 200 | 400 |
| 4 | 4 | 100 | 7 | 150 | 150 | 600 | 1,500 | – | 150 | 900 |
| 5 | 9 | 200 | 6 | 150 | 150 | 1,200 | 1,500 | – | 200 | 300 |
| 6 | 1 | 50 | 5 | 150 | 150 | 300 | 1,500 | – | 100 | 1,200 |
| | | | | | | | | | | £2,400 |

The provision of a storage facility increased the 6-day profit by £1,800. (This is £90,000 in a year.)

(iii) Rather than using the single-point estimate obtained above, it would be possible to establish a confidence interval for annual profit. The number of runs needs to be increased to further the value of the exercise.

**KULFU LTD**

(b) The given distributions are converted to probability distributions and numbers allotted for each level in accordance with probabilities (Table 47).

Table 47. Kulfu Ltd.

|  | Process A | | | Process B | | |
|---|---|---|---|---|---|---|
| Units produced | Hours | Allotted random numbers | Units produced | Hours | Allotted random numbers |
| 1 | 20 | 00–19 | 1 | 25 | 00–24 |
| 2 | 30 | 20–49 | 2 | 40 | 25–64 |
| 3 | 40 | 50–89 | 3 | 25 | 65–89 |
| 4 | 10 | 90–99 | 4 | 10 | 90–99 |
|  | 100 |  |  | 100 |  |

The first 10 hours simulation is shown in Table 48. (Opening inter-process stock was 5 units.)

Table 48. First 10 hours' simulation.

| | Process A | | Process B | | |
|---|---|---|---|---|---|
| Completed hours | Random number | Output | Random number | Output | Inter-process stock |
| – | – | – | – | – | 5 |
| 1 | 17 | 1 | 54 | 2 | 4 |
| 2 | 27 | 2 | 61 | 2 | 4 |
| 3 | 48 | 2 | 89 | 3 | 3 |
| 4 | 57 | 3 | 31 | 2 | 4 |
| 5 | 80 | 3 | 90 | 4 | 3 |
| 6 | 28 | 2 | 34 | 2 | 3 |
| 7 | 99 | 4 | 60 | 2 | 5 |
| 8 | 64 | 3 | 54 | 2 | 6 |
| 9 | 43 | 2 | 69 | 3 | 5 |
| 10 | 76 | 3 | 81 | 3 | 5 |

**126.**

Sampling numbers for the two distributions can be obtained by considering the cumulative percentages as shown below:

# APPENDIX 3. SUGGESTED ANSWERS TO EXAMINATION QUESTIONS

| Arrivals | % | Cumulative % | Sampling numbers | Repairs | % | Cumulative % | Sampling numbers |
|---|---|---|---|---|---|---|---|
| 0 | 2 | 2 | 00–01 | 1 | 4 | 4 | 00–03 |
| 1 | 7 | 9 | 02–08 | 2 | 8 | 12 | 04–11 |
| 2 | 15 | 24 | 09–23 | 3 | 14 | 26 | 12–25 |
| 3 | 20 | 44 | 24–43 | 4 | 18 | 44 | 26–43 |
| 4 | 20 | 64 | 44–63 | 5 | 18 | 62 | 44–61 |
| 5 | 16 | 80 | 64–79 | 6 | 15 | 77 | 62–76 |
| 6 | 10 | 90 | 80–89 | 7 | 10 | 87 | 77–86 |
| 7 | 6 | 96 | 90–95 | 8 | 7 | 94 | 87–93 |
| 8 | 3 | 99 | 96–98 | 9 | 4 | 98 | 94–97 |
| 9 | 1 | 100 | 99 | 10 | 2 | 100 | 98–99 |

By reading two series of random numbers from tables the arrivals and repairs can be simulated over 25 days to find the queue lengths:

| Day | Random number (1) | Arrivals | Random number (2) | Repairs | Queue length* |
|---|---|---|---|---|---|
| 1 | 55 | 4 | 86 | 7 | 0 |
| 2 | 87 | 6 | 70 | 6 | 0 |
| 3 | 05 | 1 | 71 | 6 | 0 |
| 4 | 69 | 5 | 29 | 4 | 1 |
| 5 | 74 | 5 | 73 | 6 | 0 |
| 6 | 37 | 3 | 17 | 3 | 0 |
| 7 | 42 | 3 | 16 | 3 | 0 |
| 8 | 89 | 6 | 98 | 10 | 0 |
| 9 | 35 | 3 | 81 | 7 | 0 |
| 10 | 07 | 1 | 16 | 3 | 0 |
| 11 | 94 | 7 | 42 | 4 | 3 |
| 12 | 27 | 3 | 18 | 3 | 3 |
| 13 | 13 | 2 | 70 | 6 | 0 |
| 14 | 05 | 1 | 35 | 4 | 0 |
| 15 | 86 | 6 | 85 | 7 | 0 |
| 16 | 02 | 1 | 79 | 7 | 0 |
| 17 | 13 | 2 | 35 | 4 | 0 |
| 18 | 37 | 3 | 38 | 4 | 0 |
| 19 | 57 | 4 | 19 | 3 | 1 |
| 20 | 97 | 8 | 38 | 4 | 5 |
| 21 | 45 | 4 | 82 | 7 | 2 |
| 22 | 40 | 3 | 32 | 4 | 1 |
| 23 | 63 | 4 | 29 | 4 | 1 |
| 24 | 10 | 2 | 67 | 6 | 0 |
| 25 | 41 | 3 | 99 | 10 | 0 |

*Maximum queue length = 5.

**127.**

The given patient punctuality and consultation time frequency distributions are converted to probability distributions and random numbers are allotted to each level of punctuality and consultation time (in accordance with the relevant relative probabilities).

| Patient punctuality | | Probability % | Random numbers allocated |
|---|---|---|---|
| Minutes early: | 6 | 6 | 00–05 |
|  | 2 | 29 | 06–34 |
|  | 1 | 41 | 35–75 |
| On time: | | 12 | 76–87 |
| Minutes late: | 1 | 7 | 88–94 |
|  | 2 | 5 | 95–99 |

| Consultation time (minutes) | Probability % | Random numbers allocated |
|---|---|---|
| 12 | 10 | 00–09 |
| 13 | 15 | 10–24 |
| 14 | 28 | 25–52 |
| 15 | 34 | 53–86 |
| 16 | 13 | 87–99 |

The given series of random numbers is:

1714504083139408499879514374902409214012469109059544527991531516.

These are read as pairs and used to determine the patient punctuality and consultation time for each patient in turn in a simulated period of activity.

| Consultation number | Random number | Arrival time | Start | Random number | Consultation time | End | Idle time | Waiting time |
|---|---|---|---|---|---|---|---|---|
| 1 | 17 | −2 | 0 | 14 | 13 | 13 | 0 | 2 |
| 2 | 50 | 14 | 14 | 40 | 14 | 28 | 1 | 0 |
| 3 | 83 | 30 | 30 | 13 | 13 | 43 | 2 | 0 |
| 4 | 94 | 46 | 46 | 08 | 12 | 58 | 3 | 0 |
| 5 | 49 | 59 | 59 | 98 | 16 | 75 | 3 | 0 |
| 6 | 79 | 75 | 75 | 51 | 14 | 89 | 1 | 0 |
| 7 | 43 | 89 | 89 | 74 | 15 | 104 | 0 | 0 |

| Consultation number | Random number | Arrival time | Start | Random number | Consultation time | End | Idle time | Waiting time |
|---|---|---|---|---|---|---|---|---|
| 8 | 90 | 106 | 106 | 24 | 13 | 119 | 2 | 0 |
| 9 | 09 | 118 | 119 | 21 | 13 | 132 | 0 | 1 |
| 10 | 40 | 134 | 134 | 12 | 13 | 147 | 2 | 0 |
| 11 | 46 | 149 | 149 | 91 | 16 | 165 | 2 | 0 |
| 12 | 09 | 163 | 165 | 05 | 12 | 177 | 0 | 2 |
| 13 | 95 | 182 | 182 | 44 | 14 | 196 | 5 | 0 |
| 14 | 52 | 194 | 196 | 79 | 15 | 211 | 0 | 2 |
| 15 | 91 | 211 | 211 | 53 | 15 | 226 | 0 | 0 |
| 16 | 15 | 223 | 226 | 16 | 13 | 239 | 0 | 3 |

*Note: It has been assumed that a base of 0 marks the start of the first consultation.*
*Alternatively, it could be assumed that the first patient is waiting and hence the first pair of random numbers would be applied to consultation. A different table would then result.*

## 128.

**COLTEL LTD**

(a) The company is considering the introduction of a new product and has compiled data on sales quantity, selling price, variable costs and fixed costs. The data are summarised below:

|  | Sales quantity | Selling price per unit | Variable cost per unit | Fixed cost |
|---|---|---|---|---|
| Expected value | 5,000 | £300 | £175 | £580,000 |
| Standard deviation | 400 | 5 | 7.5 | 10,000 |

Using break-even analysis and expected values it is possible to calculate the break-even volume and expected profit for the period.

$$\text{Break-even volume} = \frac{\text{Fixed costs}}{\text{Contribution per unit}}$$

$$= \frac{580,000}{300 - 175}$$

$$= \underline{\underline{4,640 \text{ units.}}}$$

$$\text{Expected profit} = \text{Expected sales} \times \text{Contribution per unit} - \text{Fixed costs}$$
$$= £5,000 \times 125 - £580,000$$
$$= \underline{\underline{£45,000}}.$$

(b) This part requires an explanation of how a simulation would be carried out to arrive at an approximate distribution of profits. The following random numbers 2 0 9 6 6 8 5 9 were given to obtain one simulated figure for profit.

The relationships between the critical variables can be shown as a simple formula:

$$\text{Profit} = \text{Quantity} \times (\text{Sales Price} - \text{Variable Cost}) - \text{Fixed Cost}.$$

The simulation needs to be done a large number of times to arrive at a distribution of profits. It would be carried out by randomly selecting a value for each of the four variables using a random number series. The resulting value of profit can be calculated by using the model above.

In establishing a value for each variable, select a random number and apply it to the cumulative normal distribution table to obtain the number of deviations from the mean. The value of the variable can then be calculated using the expected value, the standard deviation and the number of deviations from the mean.

| Variable | Expected value | Standard deviation | Random number | Deviation from mean | Simulated value of variable |
|---|---|---|---|---|---|
| Sales (units) | 5,000 | 400 | 20 | − 0.8 | 4,680 |
| Price (£) | 300 | 5 | 96 | 1.8 | 309 |
| Fixed costs (£) | 580,000 | 10,000 | 68 | 0.4 | 584,000 |
| Variable costs (£) | 175 | 7.5 | 59 | 0.2 | 176.5 |

The simulated values of the variables are combined in the formula to arrive at a simulated profit figure:

$$\text{Profit} = 4,680 \; (309 - 176.5) - 584,000$$
$$= \underline{\underline{£36,100}}.$$

*Tutorial notes:*
  (a) *The simulated value of sales is calculated as* $5,000 - 0.8 \times 400 = 4,680$. *The other variables can be calculated in a similar fashion.*

  (b) *The experiment needs to be repeated a large number of times to obtain an approximate distribution of profit.*

(c) The value to Coltel Ltd of having carried out a simulation is that it will indicate the range or variability of the profit figure rather than relying on a single point estimate.

# APPENDIX 3. SUGGESTED ANSWERS TO EXAMINATION QUESTIONS

**129.**

The Popage Company is deciding on its choice of equipment from two manufacturers, Company X and Company Y. The equipment (3 machines are necessary) is needed so that Popage can satisfy a contract to supply 1 million cans of spinach a year for three years to a local supermarket group.

The question requires an explanation of how a simulation would be carried out to evaluate the performance of each company's equipment in order to advise the management which, if either, should be purchased.

The given data in the question do not really provid a suitable base for a useful comparison. There are vague phrases such as "the yearly total can however vary slightly from the figure" and a "substantial penalty" will be imposed. There are no data regarding operating and maintenance costs, the labour components or the material usage. The only financial figures given are the initial costs. If the penalty figures were given then it would be possible to calculate the different probabilities of achieving output figures using alternative equipment (this could be in the form of an expected value calculation involving initial costs).

Within the context of given data, the most useful comparisons are those of output. The simulation should give the probabilities of achieving annual requirements (1 million cans) and the respective probabilities of producing three million cans during the three-year period.

The time span under consideration is 900 days. To obtain the appropriate probability distributions it will be necessary to repeat the simulation of a three-year period a large number of times. Within each three-year period annual outputs should be recorded.

The day-by-day simulation is relatively straightforward. The critical variables are breakdown of machines and down time if breakdown does occur.

Consider Company X. For each machine there is a 96 per cent probability of no breakdown. For example:

| *Machine A* | | *Numbers allotted* |
|---|---|---|
| Breakdown | 0.96 | 00–95 |
| No breakdown | 0.04 | 96–99 |

Similar allocations would be necessary for Machines B and C. Separate tables would be required for the downtime of each machine to reflect the appropriate probabilities for each level.

| | *Machine A* | | *Machine B* | | *Machine C* | |
|---|---|---|---|---|---|---|
| *Down time* | *Probability* | *Numbers* | *Probability* | *Numbers* | *Probability* | *Numbers* |
| 1 day | 0.40 | 00–39 | 0.40 | 00–39 | 0.35 | 00–34 |
| 2 days | 0.35 | 40–74 | 0.30 | 40–69 | 0.40 | 35–74 |
| 3 days | 0.25 | 75–99 | 0.30 | 70–99 | 0.25 | 75–99 |

The output of Company X's machines can now be evaluated. On days when there is no breakdown the output will be 4,500 units. If breakdowns do occur output will be zero for the period of the longest downtime (assuming more than one machine breakdown). Output would then be summed on an annual basis. The sum for the three years would give one observation and this procedure would be repeated.

Similar procedures would be applied to Company Y's machines so that comparisons could then be made between the machines.

# APPENDIX 4
# Formulae and Extracts from Tables

The main formulae used in Chapters 2–14 are listed in summaries at the end of each chapter.

(a) *Sample statistics:*

  (i) Arithmetic mean $= \dfrac{\sum x}{n}$.

  (ii) Standard deviation $= \sqrt{\dfrac{\sum(x-\bar{x})^2}{n-1}} = \sqrt{\dfrac{\sum x^2 - (\sum x)^2/n}{n-1}}$.

(b) *Probability distributions:*

  (i) Binomial: $P(r) = {}^nC_r p^r (1-p)^{n-r}$.

  (ii) Poisson: $P(r) = \dfrac{e^{-m} m^r}{r!}$.

(c) *Standard errors:*

  (i) Mean: $\dfrac{\sigma}{\sqrt{n}}$.

  (ii) Proportion: $\sqrt{\dfrac{P(1-P)}{n}}$.

  (iii) Difference between means: $\sqrt{\dfrac{\sigma_1^2}{n_1} + \dfrac{\sigma_2^2}{n_2}}$.

  (iv) Difference between proportions: $\sqrt{\dfrac{P_1(1-P_1)}{n_1} + \dfrac{P_2(1-P_2)}{n_2}}$.

(d) *Test statistics:*

(i) $Z = \dfrac{\bar{x} - \mu}{\sigma/\sqrt{n}}$ (one sample); $Z = \dfrac{(\bar{x}_1 - \bar{x}_2) - (\mu_1 - \mu_2)}{\sqrt{\dfrac{\sigma_1^2}{n_1} + \dfrac{\sigma_2^2}{n_2}}}$ (two samples).

(ii) $t = \dfrac{\bar{x} - \mu}{\hat{\sigma}/\sqrt{n}}$ (one sample); $t = \dfrac{(\bar{x}_1 - \bar{x}_2) - (\mu_1 - \mu_2)}{\hat{\sigma}\sqrt{\dfrac{1}{n_1} + \dfrac{1}{n_2}}}$ (two samples).

(iii) $\chi^2 = \sum \dfrac{(O - E)^2}{E}$.

(e) *Correlation and regression:*

(i) Product moment correlation coefficient:
$$r = \dfrac{n\sum xy - \sum x \sum y}{\sqrt{[n\sum x^2 - (\sum x)^2][n\sum y^2 - (\sum y)^2]}}.$$

(ii) Spearman's rank correlation coefficient:
$$R = 1 - \dfrac{6\sum d^2}{n(n^2 - 1)}.$$

(iii) Least-squares regression line $y = a + bx$:
$$b = \dfrac{n\sum xy - \sum x \sum y}{n\sum x^2 - (\sum x)^2}, \qquad a = \dfrac{\sum y}{n} - \dfrac{b\sum x}{n}.$$

(f) *Single-server queues* $(M/M/1)$:

(i) Average number in system:
$$\bar{s} = \dfrac{\lambda}{\mu - \lambda}.$$

(ii) Average number in queue:
$$\bar{q} = \bar{s} - \dfrac{\lambda}{\mu} = \dfrac{\lambda^2}{\mu(\mu - \lambda)}.$$

(iii) Average queuing time:
$$\bar{w} = \bar{s} \times \dfrac{1}{\mu} = \dfrac{\lambda}{\mu(\mu - \lambda)}.$$

(iv) Average time in system:
$$\bar{t} = \bar{w} + \dfrac{1}{\mu} = \dfrac{1}{\mu - \lambda}.$$

# APPENDIX 4. FORMULAE AND EXTRACTS FROM TABLES

(g) *Extracts from tables:*

(i) Normal distribution (shaded area = $p$)

| $Z$ | 0.0 | 0.1 | 0.2 | 0.3 | 0.4 | 0.5 | 0.6 | 0.7 | 0.8 | 0.9 |
|---|---|---|---|---|---|---|---|---|---|---|
| $p$ | 0.500 | 0.460 | 0.421 | 0.382 | 0.345 | 0.308 | 0.274 | 0.242 | 0.212 | 0.184 |

| $Z$ | 1.0 | 1.1 | 1.2 | 1.3 | 1.4 | 1.5 | 1.6 | 1.7 | 1.8 | 1.9 |
|---|---|---|---|---|---|---|---|---|---|---|
| $p$ | 0.159 | 0.136 | 0.115 | 0.097 | 0.081 | 0.067 | 0.055 | 0.045 | 0.036 | 0.029 |

| $Z$ | 2.0 | 2.1 | 2.2 | 2.3 | 2.4 | 2.5 | 2.6 | 2.7 | 2.8 | 2.9 |
|---|---|---|---|---|---|---|---|---|---|---|
| $p$ | 0.023 | 0.018 | 0.014 | 0.011 | 0.008 | 0.006 | 0.005 | 0.003 | 0.003 | 0.002 |

| $Z$ | 3.0 | 3.1 | 3.2 | 3.3 | 3.4 |
|---|---|---|---|---|---|
| $p$ | 0.0013 | 0.0010 | 0.0007 | 0.0005 | 0.0003 |

Student's *t*-distribution (shaded area = $p$)

| Degrees of freedom | 1 | 2 | 3 | 4 | 5 | 6 | 7 | 8 | 9 | 10 |
|---|---|---|---|---|---|---|---|---|---|---|
| $t_{0.05}$ | 6.3 | 2.9 | 2.4 | 2.1 | 2.0 | 1.9 | 1.9 | 1.9 | 1.8 | 1.8 |
| $t_{0.025}$ | 12.7 | 4.3 | 3.2 | 2.8 | 2.6 | 2.4 | 2.4 | 2.3 | 2.3 | 2.2 |
| $t_{0.01}$ | 31.8 | 7.0 | 4.5 | 3.7 | 3.4 | 3.1 | 3.0 | 2.9 | 2.8 | 2.8 |
| $t_{0.005}$ | 63.7 | 9.9 | 5.8 | 4.6 | 4.0 | 3.7 | 3.5 | 3.4 | 3.3 | 3.2 |
| $t_{0.001}$ | 318.3 | 22.3 | 10.2 | 7.2 | 5.9 | 5.2 | 4.8 | 4.5 | 4.3 | 4.1 |
| $t_{0.0005}$ | 636.6 | 31.6 | 12.9 | 8.6 | 6.9 | 6.0 | 5.4 | 5.0 | 4.8 | 4.6 |

(iii) Chi-squared distribution (shaded area = $p$)

| Degrees of freedom | 1 | 2 | 3 | 4 | 5 | 6 | 7 | 8 | 9 | 10 |
|---|---|---|---|---|---|---|---|---|---|---|
| $\chi^2_{0.05}$ | 3.8 | 6.0 | 7.8 | 9.5 | 11.1 | 12.6 | 14.1 | 15.5 | 16.9 | 18.3 |
| $\chi^2_{0.01}$ | 6.6 | 9.2 | 11.3 | 13.3 | 15.1 | 16.8 | 18.5 | 20.1 | 21.7 | 23.2 |
| $\chi^2_{0.001}$ | 10.8 | 13.8 | 16.3 | 18.5 | 20.5 | 22.5 | 24.3 | 26.1 | 27.9 | 29.6 |

$H$ = Basic form of OR models is:

$$E = f(X_1, X_2, \ldots, X_n, Y_1, Y_2, \ldots, Y_n)$$

where:

$E$ = objective measure of systems effectiveness

$X_1, X_2, \ldots, X_n$ = system variables subject to control

$Y_1, Y_2, \ldots, Y_n$ = system variables not subject to control.

# APPENDIX FIVE
# Glossary of Statistical Terms

*Note: The chapter and paragraph numbers indicated in brackets show where a full explanation is given in the text.*

**Artificial variables.** A method for dealing with mixed inequalities. An artificial variable is added to the constraint associated with a normal simplex maximisation problem. The resulting objective function for the variable can be reduced to zero. The variable is then dropped and a feasible solution to the problem is left. (16, 7.0)

**Bayes' theorem.**

$$P(A/B) = \frac{P(A) \times P(B/A)}{P(A) \times P(B/A) + P(A) \times P(B/A)}.$$

(2, 4.1, 5.0)

**Bessel's correction factor.**

$$\sqrt{\frac{n}{n-1}}. \quad (5, 5.0)$$

**Binomial distribution.**

$$P(r) = {}^nC_r p^r (1-p)^{n-r}. \quad (4, 3.0)$$

**Central limit theorem.** The basis of all sampling theory. It provides us with information about the sampling distributions. (5, 7.0)

**Chi-squared distribution.**

$$\chi^2 = \sum \frac{(O-E)^2}{E}$$

when: O = observed frequency;
E = expected frequency. (8, 1.0)

**Computer simulation.** The practice of simulating events over periods of time using repetitive steps (either subroutines or loops) which save computer time. (24, 3.0)

**Conditional probability rule.**

$$P(A/B) = \frac{P(A \text{ and } B)}{P(B)}. \quad (2, 3.1)$$

**Continuity correction (Yates correction).** The $\chi^2$ distribution is a continuous distribution. We can apply a Yates correction to it by subtracting $\frac{1}{2}$ from each absolute difference, e.g. $O - E$ becomes $|O - E| - \frac{1}{2}$. (8, 3.0)

**Degenerate solution.** This is a solution where there is insufficient number of cells filled to proceed to the next stage of transportation analysis. (17, 4.0)

**Dual prices.** The product of linear programming frameworks based on the same assumptions as linear programming and providing a useful method of calculating the opportunity cost involved in using scarce resources. (Appendix 3, 60(c), 61(c)(i), 69(c))

**Dual problem.** The transposed problem and the primal problem in linear programming. (16, 4.0)

**Effectiveness measures (queuing methods).** Once various mathematical models have been built to analyse queuing situations it is possible to evaluate their overall likely metamorphosis when component parts of the model are altered. These tests check the effectiveness of the model. (23, 3.0)

**Hungarian method..** Of use in assignment problems. The Hungarian method requires the assignment matrix to be square. A dummy column is added so that the result is expressed as a square matrix of the sixth order. (18, 8.0)

**Initial simplex tableau.** The standard layout of coefficients and constraint values in a linear programming problem. (16, 2.0, Step 3)

**Integer programming.** A special technique which can be used for finding non-fractional values of resource usage and decision variables in linear programming. (14, 9.0)

**Iso-profit line.** (From "iso" meaning "the same".) The line on which the profit is constant. (15, 2.0)

**Leontief's input–output analysis.** The method whereby linear programming was applied to inter-industry economic problems. (14, 3.0)

**Monte Carlo simulation.** That form of simulation which involves an element of uncertainty in the model where variables occur according to some probability distribution. (24, 1.0)

**Most likely time (PERT analysis).** The estimated time of an activity which is taken as the most likely duration; could be called the modal time or most popular time. (21, 4.0)

**Negative exponential function** $(y = e^{-x})$. A form of this function represented as $y = \lambda e^{-\lambda t}$ occurs in work on service time and inter-arrival distribution in simple queuing theory. (11, 4.0 and 5.0)

**Normal approximation to the Poisson.** In a Poisson problem this is where the mean has become so large that the normal distribution can be used as an approximation method for speed and ease of calculation. (4, 6.0)

**Null hypothesis.** An hypothesis which is proven to be false after initial testing. It may be written as: $H_0: = \ldots$ . (6, 2.0)

**Pearson's product-moment correlation coefficient.**

$$r = \frac{n\sum xy - \sum x \sum y}{\sqrt{[n\sum x^2 - (\sum x)^2][n\sum y^2 - (\sum y)^2]}}$$

(9, 7.0)

**Portfolio theory.** A theory used to describe the performance of a group of shares in terms of both the expected return and the risk factor. (12, 5.0)

**Rank correlation.** When we need to determine the correlation between two ranked variables where suitable measures of one or other do not exist:

$$R = 1 - \frac{6\sum d^2}{n(n^2 - 1)} \qquad (9, 8.0)$$

**Sensitivity analysis.** A method of combatting the problem of model reliability by seeing which of the parts of the model are critical to the recommended solution. (13, 8.0)

**Shadow costs (or price).** The opportunity cost associated with a contract. (17, 4.0)

**Skewed distribution.** Non-symmetrical distributions with a long tail to the right. (21, 4.0)

**Standard error.** The standard deviation of a sampling distribution. (5, 6.0)

# APPENDIX 5 GLOSSARY OF STATISTICAL TERMS

**Sub-optimisation.** Where optimal solutions are found only to the parts of the total problem rather than to the problem as a whole. (Appendix 3, 46)

***t* distribution.**

$$t = \frac{\bar{x} - \mu}{SE_{\bar{x}}} \qquad (7, 1.0)$$

**Value of perfect information.** The difference between two expected payoffs. It is equal to the expected opportunity loss. (3, 5.0)

***Z*-statistic.**

$$Z = \frac{x - \mu}{\sigma}. \qquad (4, 6.0)$$

# Index

Ackoff, R.L. and Rivett, B.H.P., 124–6
activities in network analysis, 193
addition rule in probability, 11–14, 23
allocation problems, 128, 392–3
allocation variables in transportation problem, 161
alternative hypothesis, 55–6
answers to examination questions, 331–542
arrival rate in queuing model, 229
artificial variables used in simplex maximisation, 157
assignment problem, 177–89
association for contingency table, test for, 77

"backward pass" in critical path analysis, 200–1
balanced rim conditions, 170
BASIC computer language, 246
Bayes' theorem, 21–4
Bessel's correction factor for the estimate of the standard deviation, 48
beta distribution in PERT, 211–12
biased estimators, 47–8
binomial distribution, 37–8
    normal approximation to, 43–4
box method in permutations, 34–5
buffer stocks in inventory control, 224

capital rationing, 124
car hire business, example of a simulation problem, 238–42
cells, combining, in $\chi^2$ test, 79
central-limit theorem, 49–51
certainty assumption in linear programming, 135
chi-squared ($\chi^2$) distribution and goodness of fit tests, 73–9

coded method for calculating mean and standard deviation, 7–8
combinations and permutations, 34–5
competition problems, 394–5
computers and simulation, 242, 246
conditional probability, 17, 19–20, 24
confidence interval
    for estimate of the regression line, 93–8
    for intercept $a$ of regression line, 97–8
    for population mean in large samples, 49–51
    for population mean in small samples, using $t$-distribution, 67–8
    for proportion, 53–4
    for slope $b$ of regression line, 96–7
constraints in linear programming, 129–30, 137–40
contingency table, test for association, 77
continuity correction for normal approximation to the binomial distribution, 43–4
coordination problems, 394
corner points in linear programming, 140–2
correlation, 85–91
    calculation of, coefficient, 85–6
    coefficient of determination, 88
    rank, 90–1
    of two distributions, 113–16
cost analysis in networks, 203–7
cost of capital factor in inventory control, 214
cost minimisation, assignment problem, 180–5
    in CPA, 192
covariances, 112–16
CPA—*see* critical path analysis
CPM—*see* critical path method
crash cost and time in cost analysis, 204
critical path analysis (CPA)
    areas of application and method, 191–2, 394

# INDEX

float, 199, 202–3
normal, 199–203
project evaluation and review technique (PERT), 191, 211–13
simple, 199
critical path defined, 198–9
critical path method (CPM)—*see* critical path analysis
cumulative probability distribution in simulation, 238–9
cyclical review system for stock control, 225–6

Danzig, G.B., 146
decision making process, 121
decision tree, 30–3
decision variables, 129–30
degeneracy in transportation problems, 167–70
degrees of freedom
in chi-squared ($\chi^2$) distribution and tests, 73–9
in Students's $t$-test, 66–7
demand exceeds supply in transportation problem, 171–2
departmental capacity constraints in linear programming, 139–40
departure in queuing model, 228, 230
dependency tables in network analysis, 194–6
dependent and independent events in probability, 14–19
determination, coefficient of, 88
deterministic economic order quantity (EOQ)
derivation of, model, 219–20
trial and error solution, 215–18
difference of two distributions, variance of, 115–16
discounts, quantity, in inventory control, 220–1
divisibility in linear programming, 134–5
dual forms in linear programming, 152–8
dual prices, 426, 445
dummy activities in network analysis, 196–7
dummy column or row in transportation problem, 171–3
dynamic programming, 393

earliest event time (e.e.t.) in critical path analysis, 200–1
economic batch quantity (EBQ) in inventory control, 215
economic order quantity (EOQ)
deterministic model, derivation of, 219–20
trial and error solution, 215–18
e.e.t.—*see* earliest event time
effectiveness measures in queuing theory, 228–9
E.I. du Pont de Nemours & Company, 191
EOQ model—*see* economic order quantity
estimation, large-sample theory, 46–54
estimators, unbiased and biased, 47–8

event calendar in simulation, 242
event-sequencing simulation, 242–3
events in network analysis, 193
examination questions, 247–330
answers, 331–542
operational research, 268–330
statistics, 248–68
expected value, 25–33
explained variation, 86–7
exponential distribution, negative, in queuing theory, 229, 231–2, 234–6
exponential functions and graphs, 104–7

feasible region in linear programming, 137–42
feedback in operational research, 123
finite population correction factor (FPC) for standard error, 52
float in critical path analysis, 199, 202–3
flowchart in queuing problem, 243–6
forecasting using regression line, 85
FORTRAN, 246
"forward pass" in critical path analysis, 200–1
FPC, finite population correction factor, 52
free float in CPA, 202–3
fuzzy set, 126

Gantt bar chart, 190, 209–10
general allocation method in linear programming, 128
problems, 392–3
goodness of fit test, 73–9
GPSS, 246
graphical solution in linear programming, 136–45
grouped and ungrouped data, mean, standard deviation and variance, 3–8

Hungarian method for assignment problem, 180–2
hypothesis testing, 55–72
difference between two means in large samples, 59–60
difference between two means in small samples, 68–72
difference between two proportions, 60–1
one-tailed and two-tailed tests, 57–8
paired $t$-tests, 70–2
significance test for a proportion, 58–9
Student's $t$-test, 65–72
test level and limits, 56–7
Type I and Type II errors, 61–3

impossible assignments, 187–8
independent and dependent events in probability, 14–19
independent distributions, 114–16
independent float in CPA, 202–3

index to examination questions, 247
indices and logs, rules for, 102
initial simplex tableau, 147
input process in queuing theory, 227–8
integer programming, 135
inventory control, 214–26
    problems, 391–2
iso-cost line, 144
iso-profit line, 142
iteration procedure for an optimal assignment, 180–5

job opportunity cost, 181
joint probability table, 20–1

König, D., 180

labour constraint in linear programming, 137
large-sample theory
    estimation, 46–54
    significance tests, 55–64
latest event time (l.e.t.) in critical path analysis, 200–1
lead time and reorder levels in inventory control, 223–4
learning curve, 107–11
least cost method in transportation, 162–7
least squares method for regression line, 81–5
Leontief's input-output analysis in linear programming, 128
l.e.t.—*see* latest event time
linear programming, 127–80
    assignment problem, 177–80
    assumptions of, 134–5
    graphical solution, 136–45
    introduction and model construction, 127–35
    simplex solution and dual values, 146–58
    transportation method, 159–76
linear regression, (*see also* regression), 80–101
linearity assumption in linear programming, 134
log graphs, 103
logarithms, 102–3

mathematical model—*see* model, mathematical
mathematical programming, 127
maximisation in linear programming
    graphical solution, 136–42
    model construction, 127–32
maximisation problems in assignment problem, 185–7
mean
    central-limit theorem, 49–51
    sampling distribution of, 48–9
    significance tests for, 55–60, 68–72
    standard error of, 49
mean and standard deviation
    of binomial distribution, 37

    calculation of, 3–8
    of normal distribution, 39–42
    of Poisson distribution, 38–9
minimisation
    cost, in assignment problem, 180–5
    graphical solution in linear programming, 143–4
    in linear programming, model construction, 132–3
$M/M/1/\infty$ system, queuing model, 229–34
$M/M/C/\infty$ system, queuing model, 234–6
model, mathematical
    assignment problem, 178–85
    construction in linear programming, 127–35, 160–2
    construction in operational research, 122–3, 388–90
    economic order quantity (EOQ) model, 215, 219–20
    general linear programming models, 133–5
    multiple-server queue model, 234–6
    of the transportation situation, 160–2
    queuing system, 229–30
modified index method for assignment problem, 189
Monte Carlo simulation, 237, 392
most likely time in PERT, 211
multiple regression, 99–100
multiple-server queue model, 234–6
multiplication rule in probability, 14–19, 24
mutually exclusive events in probability, 11–14

natural logarithms, 103
negative exponential distribution in queuing theory, 229, 231–2, 234–6
negative production, 130
net present value, 445
network analysis
    critical path analysis, 191–2, 198–203
    introduction, 190–7
    resources and uncertainty, 208–13
    terminology, 193–7
    time and cost, 198–207
normal approximation to the binomial and Poisson distribution, 43–5
normal distribution, 39–45
    percentage limits, 42–4
    table, 39
northwest corner method in transportation, 162–7
null hypothesis, 55

objective function in linear programming, 129
one-tailed and two-tailed tests, 57–8
operational research *see also particular subjects*
    classification of problems, 123–5, 388–98
    introduction to, 119–26

opportunity loss matrix in transportation, 174–5
opportunity loss table, 29
optimal allocation, 162–7, 177–89
optimal assignment
 iteration procedures, 180–5
 summary of procedures, 185
optimal product mix in linear programming, 129, 154
optimisation in operational research, 125
optimistic time in PERT, 211

paired $t$-test, 70–2
pay-off table, 27–9
Pearson's product-moment correlation coefficient, 85–6
percentage limits, normal distribution, 42–4
periodic (cyclical) review system for stock control, 225–6
permutations, 34–5
PERT—see project evaluation and review technique
pessimistic time in PERT, 211
pivot column, element or row in simplex procedures, 147
Poisson distribution, 38–9
 chi-squared ($\chi^2$) test, 75–6
 normal approximation, 44–5
 in queuing theory, 229–32
population defined, 46
portfolio theory, 15–16
posterior probability, 22
primal and dual forms in linear programming, 152–8
prior probability, 22
probability, 9–24
 conditional, 17, 19–20, 24
 relative frequency approach, 10
 rules, 11–20, 23–4
 subjective approach, 10
 tree, 18
probability distribution
 binomial, 37–8, 43–4
 expected value, 25–6
 normal, 39–45
 Poisson, 38–9, 44–5
 standard deviation and variance, 26–7
probability rules, 11–20, 23–4
product mix model, 124, 392
production model in inventory control, 221–3
profit maximisation
 in assignment problem, 185–7
 in transportation problem, 174–5
prohibited routes in transportation problem, 173–4
project evaluation and review technique (PERT), 191, 211–13

projects, network analysis for planning new, 190–7
proportion
 confidence interval, 53–4
 sampling distribution, 52–4
 significance tests, 58–61
"pruning" a decision tree, 31

quadratic programming, 393
quantity discounts in inventory control, 220–1
queuing problem in simulation, 243–6
queuing theory, 227–36, 393, 516–20

random numbers in simulation, 238–42
rank correlation, 90–1
regression line, 80–101
 calculation of, 84–5
 confidence intervals for estimates, 92–8
 estimating learning rate by, 109–111
 explained and unexplained variation about the, 86–7
 forecasting using the, 85
 sampling theory, 92–101
relative frequency in probability, 10
reorder level (the two-bin) system for stock control, 224–5
replacement problems, 392
resource analysis of networks, 208–11
Rivett, B.H.P. and R.L. Ackoff, 124
routing problems, 394
rules in probability, 11–20, 23–4
Russel's approximation method in transportation, 162–7

sample selection, 46–7
sample size, calculation, 51–2
sampling distribution
 of mean, 48–9
 of proportion, 52–4
sampling theory
 large samples, 46–64
 regression, 92–101
 small samples, 65–72
Sasieni, 124
scattergraph, 80–1
sensitivity analysis in operational research, 125, 398–401
service process in queuing model, 229
shadow
 costs, 162–7
 prices, 154, 444–5
ships and queuing theory, 232–4
significance tests—see hypothesis testing
simplex method in linear programming, 146–58
SIMSCRIPT, 246
simulation, 237–46
 computers, 242, 246

simulation, *continued*
   event-sequencing, 242–3
   program flowchart, 243–6
   queuing problem, 243–6
skew distribution, 211–12
slack variables in linear programming, 148–56
small samples, 65–72
Spearman's rank correlation coefficient, 90–1
standard deviation
   of binomial distribution, 37
   calculation, 3–8
   of normal distribution, 39–42
   of Poisson distribution, 38–9
   of probability distribution, 26–7
   of $y$ about the regression line, 93
standard error
   of the intercept of the regression line, 97–8
   of means, 49
   of the slope of the regression line, 96–8
steady-state situation in queuing model, 230
stochastic demand in inventory control, 224
stock control, systems of, 224–6
stock pattern for EOQ model, 222
stockholding costs, components, 214
Student's $t$-distribution, 65–72, 93–8
sub-networks, in network analysis, 195–6
sub-optimisation, 401
supply exceeds demands in transportation problem, 170–1
systems approach to operational research problems, 387–8

$t$-distribution, Student's 65–72, 93–8
tableau, simplex, 147
tables
   of chi-squared ($\chi^2$) distribution, 74
   extracts, 541–2
   normal distribution, 39
   Student's $t$-distribution, 66
team approach to operational research problems, 388
test level in significance tests, 56
theory of games, 395
tied ranks, 90–1
time analysis, 192, 198
time based simulation (time slicing), 242

total float in CPA, 202–3
traffic intensity in queuing model, 230
transshipment in transportation, 176
transportation, 159–76
   assignment problem, 177–89
   degenerate allocation, 167–70
   linear programming models, 160–2
   optimal allocation, 162–7
   profit maximisation, 174–5
   transshipment, 176
   unbalanced situations, 170–3
travelling salesman problem, 394
tree
   decision, 30–3
   probability, 18
two-bin system for stock control, 224–5
two-tailed significance test, 57–8
Type I and Type II errors in significance tests, 61–3

unbalanced situations in transportation, 170–3
unbiased estimator of the standard deviation of $y$ about the regression line, 93
unbiased estimators, 47–8
unequal dimensions in assignment problems, 188–9
unexplained variation, 86–7
unloading ships and queuing theory, 232–4
US Navy Special Projects Office, 191

value of perfect information, 29–30
variance, calculation, 3–8
variance and standard deviation of a probability distribution, 26–7
variances and covariances, 112–16
Venn diagram, 13
Vogel's approximation method in transportation, 162–7

"wicked problems", 126
worker opportunity cost, 181

Yates correction for continuity, 79

$Z$-statistic, 39